La Fenice, Venice

Epidaurus, Greece

Paris Opéra

Bellas Artes, Mexico City

Maria Callas

MARIA CALLAS
Sacred Monster

Stelios Galatopoulos

FOURTH ESTATE · *London*

To my father
Yiannis Galatopoulos
and my mother
Maria Galatopoulou (née Stylianaki)

First published in Great Britain in 1998 by
Fourth Estate Limited
6 Salem Road
London W2 4BU

10 9 8 7 6 5 4 3 2 1

A catalogue record for this book is available from the British Library.

ISBN 1-85702-826-0

Designed by Robert Updegraff
Typeset by Rowland Phototypesetting Limited, Bury St Edmunds, Suffolk
Printed in Great Britain by Butler and Tanner Ltd, Frome, Somerset

Frontispiece: Maria Callas preparing for Violetta in *La traviata*

CONTENTS

· ACKNOWLEDGEMENTS AND CREDITS ·

The people who have helped with the long preparation of *Maria Callas: Sacred Monster* are many. Several (including famous singers and musicians) do not want to be mentioned, I know, because they feel their help was minute. I disagree. All help is important and they should know how grateful I will always be.

Nevertheless, my debt to some people is so huge that without their help, encouragement and friendship, I might have never completed the book that became so great a part of my life.

I can never forget the eminent conductor Tullio Serafin (Callas's mentor), whose words spoke volumes. He allowed me to attend rehearsals and answered numerous questions. Elvira de Hidalgo (Callas's teacher), of equal pre-eminence, shed illuminating light on the artistry and mentality of her most illustrious pupil. The brief encounter I had with Luchino Visconti had such profound influence on me that my horizons, particularly about Callas's artistry, were greatly widened. It was like discovering another dimension of the meaning of art.

Nicola Zaccaria, longtime friend, helped with photographs and the chronology of Callas's Greek career and was a valued link with La Scala. The late Harold Rosenthal, founder editor of *Opera* and an outstanding chronicler, put me on course a few times.

Special thanks to Lorenzo Siliotto of Museo Teatrale alla Scala and Biblioteca Livia Simoni; Antonio Bussetto of the Archivio, La Fenice, Venice; Giovanni Altavilla of San Carlo, Naples; Walter Talevi of Rome; Francis Robinson of the Metropolitan, New York; Katherine Wilkinson and colleagues of Covent Garden. Alas, most of them are no longer with us. Among librarians, that special breed of people, so necessary to a writer, thanks to A. Sopher, former Head of Music Services, Westminster City Libraries, Dr M. A. Baird, music librarian of London University and particularly R. Howard Wright, former Borough Music Librarian, Richmond-upon-Thames, who has been helpful not only in obtaining useful information but also in criticising constructively the entire manuscript.

Dottore Pierluigi Pizzocaro of Milan belongs to a different category. A lifelong friend, he — together with his family — helped with the Italian language, did endless and useful errands for me in Italy and offered proverbial hospitality.

Finally, my gratitude is perforce directed towards my publisher Fourth Estate — to my editor Christopher Potter who, with perception, guided me to do my best. In this I was also aided by the fastidious copy-editing of Ilsa Yardley, which enables her to find needles in haystacks.

Conversations with Callas

I first met Maria Callas on 14 August 1947 in Verona, where I was spending a few days before coming to England to study. Among the first things I noticed in Verona were numerous placards announcing the programme of the famous opera festival in the Arena, which was reinaugurated the previous summer, following the war years.

Of the operas advertised, Ponchielli's *La Gioconda* was completely unknown to me, as was the protagonist, Maria Kallas. She spelled her name then with a 'K' and that made me imagine she was possibly Greek. I promptly obtained a ticket for the 14 August performance.

Even though at the time my knowledge of opera was limited, the timbre of Callas's voice, the quality of her singing with its many inflexions and colorations, had the most extraordinary effect on me. For a time I did not know whether the feeling was terrible or wonderful. It was certainly a new sensation. But I was captivated, at least deep down in my heart, even if I was unable to explain the magic. Her voice remained in my ears and I knew then that I would never forget it, nor mistake it for any other.

At the end of the performance, I wandered around by the stage and found the artists' dressing-rooms. There was a lot of commotion and noise as I stood by the entrance to Callas's, which was full of people. I could see she was sitting down – apparently she had had an accident during rehearsals and was resting her leg.

After a while, when the commotion subsided, I went straight to her and my first words were, 'Are you a "little bit" Greek?'

She put her glasses on and looked at me closely. A warm smile followed and, greeting me with both hands on my wrist, she said, in Greek, 'I am not a "little bit" Greek, I am completely Greek.' And, pointing to her figure (the twenty-three-year-old Callas was at that time overweight), she added, 'Shall we say a "huge bit"?'

We spoke for several minutes, largely about the reason for my presence in Verona, the length of my stay and so forth. It was time for her to leave. 'Do you realize that it is practically dawn?' she remarked. 'And it is also my "name day" [an important occasion for Greeks]. Come to my hotel after 6 p.m. today and tell me all about yourself and what you plan to do in England. Tell me about *Gioconda* too.'

At the hotel our conversation still centred on me, especially about my forthcoming studies in England and about my parents. Of *La Gioconda* we spoke little and she laughed when I clumsily told her that when she began to sing I was at first 'confused and rather frightened'. She said practically nothing about herself and I was too shy to ask. I left for England the following day happy, bemused and dazzled by this extraordinary young Greek singer.

For the next six years I saw Callas only in the theatre. My holidays were mainly spent in Italy and I never missed an opportunity to go to the opera, particularly to hear Callas. I was there at her début at Covent Garden in 1952, when she sang the title role in Bellini's *Norma*, and it was there that I first began to appreciate that opera as drama can be one of the highest forms of art, perhaps *the* highest. The following year, I met Callas again in London when she was appearing at Covent Garden in *Aida*. She was with her husband, Giovanni (Gian) Battista Meneghini, and she greeted me as if I were an old friend. Subsequently, whenever I went to Italy I visited her in her theatre dressing-room and once, together with a mutual friend, at her villa in Sirmione on Lake Garda.

However, my friendship – as distinct from an acquaintanceship – with Callas dates from 1957, during the time she was singing with the La Scala company at the Edinburgh Festival. From then on I saw more of her, on and off the stage. Our conversations at this time were mostly confined to her art. There was one other subject that seemed to gain her interest: Maria was over-eager to get people to marry. 'I am not a successful matchmaker, am I?' she sometimes remarked.

Callas certainly seemed happy with her own marriage, but since her work was the main purpose of her existence she had little to say about personal matters. There were of course problems from time to time, but these also related to her career. The adverse publicity she was receiving over her quarrels with several theatres and the way some people tried to exploit her distressed her deeply. As the criticism increased and she was often misquoted, she became very cautious. When a close friend let her down by writing a personal, inaccurate and unflattering article about her, Maria felt bitter about it and, although she later forgave her, the friendship was not resumed. 'How can I trust anybody,' she said to me, 'when even a close friend as well as my own family sold me for money?'[1]

Worse was to come. She suffered mental and physical exhaustion in the summer of 1957 and, less than a year later, fell out with her husband over his fraudulent administration of her earnings. And then the first signs of her vocal deterioration appeared, albeit mildly, and before long she began to cut the number of her performance. Her marriage broke down in the autumn of 1959 and her liaison with Aristotle Onassis, the Greek shipping magnate, began. She continued to sing – though her performances were few and far between – until July 1965, when she retired from the operatic stage.

As she then had more free time, and as I was able to see more of her, my friendship with her grew. After the legal separation from her husband Maria became a warmer person, her hitherto rather limited sense of humour developed and the strain that was particularly noticeable towards the end of 1958 and during 1959 all but disappeared. She was more fun and even a little outspoken about herself, but not about Onassis. Even though it was common knowledge that her 'new life' was largely tied up with his, she had little of consequence to say about him.

In the summer of 1960, Maria introduced me to Onassis[2] when we met accidentally on the island of Tinos. She was there between her performances in *Norma* at Epidaurus, in order to make a pilgrimage to the miraculous icon of the Virgin Mary. (Tinos, in the Aegean, is the Lourdes of Greece.) Afterwards I met them together in Greece, at Monte Carlo and on board Onassis's yacht, the *Christina*. I also saw him on his own in Paris. He was generally friendly and amusing in his teasing way. Yet in his absence Maria would avoid mentioning him. I had learned by then that the best I could do was stick to the English policy, 'Don't ask personal questions if you want straight answers.' This principle applied to many things as far as Maria was concerned. The moment one asked an irrelevantly intimate question or inadvertently referred to Onassis, even after 1968, when he had married Jacqueline, the widow of President Kennedy, she would almost always change the subject. There were of course exceptions, though very few before 1976 and even then she said little of a personal nature — at least in public. Her references to Onassis in an interview with David Frost revealed hardly more than that they had been the best of friends.

Concerning her first husband, Meneghini, she reacted somewhat differently. On the very few occasions, after their separation in 1959 and before 1976, that Callas referred to him, she was brief and impersonal. Only once, to my knowledge, about two years after their separation, did she allow herself to be provoked into discussing him. A woman said to her, in a rather patronizing manner, that she had heard, apparently from 'good sources', that Maria was returning to her husband. 'Not me,' Maria snubbed. 'That stingy old man does not need a wife.' Callas, a very private person, particularly with acquaintances, was visibly ruffled — not because of what she had said but because she had been made to lose her composure. Regaining her self-control, and with a slightly forced smile, she concluded this conversation in no uncertain terms. 'My dear "knowledgeable" lady, life is too short to worry about other people's matrimonial problems.' Except for the oblique remark about her mother's book, only on one other occasion in my presence did she talk publicly about her family. A tiresome Greek woman was professing that Iakinthy, Maria's sister, had been a failure as a singer. 'My sister', Maria replied, putting the woman in her place, 'is a good artist, and could have been a great pianist if she had wanted.'

During the year that followed the publication of my semi-biographical book, *Callas, Prima Donna Assoluta*,[3] in 1976, my friendship with Callas became much closer. In January 1977 she began to telephone me often. One afternoon she came to lunch at my home in Richmond. She was in excellent spirits and she led me to believe that after a period of artistic inactivity,[4] which she attributed to insomnia and blood pressure (throughout her adult life she suffered from low blood pressure), she was again interested in singing. Before she left I played an excellent tape of her 1957 Athens concert. Her joy was great (she had not known it existed and praised the 'pirates' for preserving it) and at certain passages in the 'Liebestod' (from *Tristan und Isolde*) she sang along with the recording.

Afterwards her telephone calls from her home in Paris became ever more frequent. I also visited her there several times and to my surprise Maria began, on her own initiative, to speak more about herself, her family, Meneghini and even Onassis. A year before, this would have been unthinkable. I listened with interest but at first refrained from passing any searching remarks, especially about Onassis. Even so, she would sometimes become aloof or moody and drop the matter quite abruptly, leaving me somewhat puzzled.

Our conversations began to take on the nature of discussions — sometimes quite philosophical discussions: we were after all both Greeks. But what encouraged me eventually to ask personal questions was Maria's increasing interest in my own private life. I sensed that she needed to tell me about her feelings, particularly what her true relationship with Onassis had been, and how she felt about him — he had died in March 1975. She also now wanted to talk about the break-up of her marriage to Meneghini. My first question was to ask why she did not refute the many untruths that had been written about her in the past. Her answer was that there was no point in giving people who make a living out of the personal affairs of others more rope with which to hang her.

The true facts about her relationship with her family, Meneghini and Onassis — and, more importantly, what led this highly disciplined, intelligent and rather puritanical woman to break her own rules — are recorded for the first time in this book. Meneghini's account in *My wife Maria Callas — Maria Callas mia Moglie —* (1981) rightly stops in 1959, after which time she had (contrary to what he says) absolutely no contact with him. By and large he tells the truth, though not the whole truth. Callas's own point of view is missing.

For some time after her death I often wondered why she spoke to me about the very personal side of her life and particularly about Onassis, a subject which had in the past been more or less 'forbidden' because of the exaggerated and scandalous publicity. Subsequently I thought I had found an answer. Ingrid Bergman, who knew and liked Callas, had for many years refused to write her autobiography, until her children pointed out that the moment she died there would be many who would profit from scandalmongering about her private life. Her children would be powerless to protect her reputation. Consequently, Bergman wrote her life story. I believe Callas wanted me to know the truth because, having known her for so many years, she knew that I would never misquote her nor exploit her for cheap sensationalism.

In a review of my *Callas, Prima Donna Assoluta* one critic tried to provoke an argument with me in the hope that Callas herself would also be brought into it. Contrary to his expectations, in my answer I merely corrected him without involving her. Someone sent her this review and my answer. Almost certainly, this finally made Maria put her trust in me. Referring to this book, she asked whether I had kept the letter she wrote to me at the time I was preparing it. 'Well,' she commented, 'you can use it. Of course it is late now but it can still be useful against these opportunists.' I then reminded her that she herself had learned to live with the lies and irresponsible accusations of publicity-seeking people, believing that in the long run she would be vindicated. 'Yes, you are absolutely right,' she replied, 'but it has been far too long a run.'

Unlike her other letters, usually written in Greek – the language we often conversed in – this one is in English. (The book itself was written in English.) The letter is formal and concise. As was the custom for many Greeks of the previous generation, Callas affectionately addressed Greek friends by their surnames. Onassis called her Callas.

Dear Galatopoulos – Another book about me . . . Goodness gracious! I feel terribly embarrassed and like I'm dead and buried already. All this is wonderful, I confess, and I suppose. And it is too much, I think. It gives the impression of extreme exaggeration and I am only an interpreter of great music, actually thinking very modestly of myself and eating my heart out because I have set myself a standard that is almost impossible to keep, for in each performance I find I could have done much better and yet the public is enthusiastic.

Best of luck to you. Hope you get things straight at least. I know you are a sincere and devoted admirer of art but you are undertaking a hell of a responsibility, don't you think?

Most sincerely,

Maria Callas

PS Teresa can give you some information – Herman also.[5]

Since her death in 1977 several books have been written about her. Some have even proclaimed authorization from Callas herself. As late as July 1977 I let slip in conversation, 'Would it not be wonderful if you wrote your biography, Maria? You will find this form of self-expression rewarding.'

The response was an immediate 'No!' in a tone in which fleetingly the voice of Norma was echoed. After a brief pause, Maria added, 'My memoirs are in the music I interpret – the only way I can write about my art or about myself – and my recordings, for what they are worth, have preserved my story. In any case, you have already written about me.' And then, deliberately changing the subject, rather frivolously but with captivating charm, she said conclusively, 'Listen Stelio,[6] don't you think I am too young to write my memoirs? I am not eighty yet, you know.'[7]

Her reaction gave me the cue to announce to her that I was planning another book about her – a documentary picture book. Even though she said nothing, I sensed that she found the idea interesting, so I elaborated on it, telling her that my intention was to include photographs from all her roles – a visual record of her career with accompanying text. After a pensive moment her first comment was that obviously photographs of her when she was 'big' (meaning fat) would be included. 'Well, yes,' I added, 'Don't you think they should?'

Without looking at me, she exclaimed, 'No!' but followed it up with a mischievous wink, saying, 'Of course you will, my dear, but you will use those in which I look slim and elegant as well, won't you? I am really only teasing you just to see how you react.' She then left the room, but within a few minutes returned. 'I am quite sure you will like these pictures for your documentary,' she said. 'For heaven's sake do not lose them.' When I looked at them I was so moved that the only thing I could think to say was that they were of historical importance.[8]

Presently, Maria stood in front of me, holding a score in her arms as if it were a baby. Smiling, she announced that she was going to record the role of Charlotte in Massenet's *Werther*. Alfredo Kraus would sing the title role and Georges Prêtre was to conduct. 'I am still a little down', she continued, 'because of my recent bout of influenza and can't take antibiotics but, God willing, I will be all right in the autumn. You know how the dryness of the summer affects my voice.' She also said that she would be having a holiday in Cyprus in September before the recording and, knowing that members of my family lived there, wondered whether I would by any chance be there too. I said that since she was going I most certainly would be there. However, I added, in the interim I was going to lecture in the United States and Mexico, where-upon she gave me names of friends who might be of help to me.

Waving her hand, she diverted the conversation by asking me rather coyly whether I preferred ice-cream for my dessert rather than a song from her. I pretended that the matter required my most serious consideration. She was so amused when I opted for the ice-cream (her fondness for ice-cream was legendary) that she said, with an exaggerated gesture of her hands, that as I had as usual exercised sound judgement ('You are so clever!'), I would be rewarded with both 'desserts'. Accompanying herself on the piano, she sang 'Pleurez, mes yeux' from *Le Cid*. Her voice was in fairly good condition and I asked for an encore, which was granted, but not before she had made a joke to the effect that she had never learned any songs about ice-cream (*arie di sorbetto*[9]). She then sang 'Ah! Non credea mirarti' from *La sonnambula* and reduced me to tears.

It was time for me to leave. Maria stood barefoot at the door. 'When will they learn to make shoes that are both elegant and comfortable?' she muttered. Eventually realizing that we had been standing talking for a good twenty minutes (an incorrigible habit with Greeks), she burst out laughing and began to push me out of the house while singing an improvised recitative (using the first bars of Gilda's aria 'Caro nome' from *Rigoletto*), 'Get out my house, write to me.' 'See you on Aphrodite's island [Cyprus],' we both said. I glanced at her as I left. She looked like a figure from an unknown painting by El Greco. I never saw her again.

On the afternoon of 16 September 1977 I lectured on Maria Callas on board the *QE2*. Within minutes of the lecture ending, information reached me that she had died in Paris a few hours before. My first reaction was to dispute the terrible news – she was, after all, not yet fifty-four years old. I wandered about the ship for a long time before I began to comprehend what had happened.

At the time of Callas's death I had already begun preliminary work for a book on Bellini. Also, I had to undertake extensive research for photographs of Callas to complete my collection. It took me some time before I abandoned the preparation of the documentary picture book I had mentioned to her. I began to think on different lines and in due course I embarked on writing another type of book, *Maria Callas – Aspects of Artist and Woman*. Before completion, the publication of other books about her made it necessary to adopt a different approach in an attempt to set the record straight and establish an authoritative work: *Maria Callas – Sacred Monster* has therefore been long in gestation and maturation.

But to go back to the beginning. Soon after my meetings and frequent telephone conversa-tions with Callas began I realized their special significance and so started to make notes in Greek. I must, however, explain that I have not 'ghosted' her autobiography. A significant part of the present book is, in effect, autobiographical and it will become apparent to the reader that Callas had an honest and intelligent understanding of herself and of her art.

If I eventually felt compelled to write as a result of my unique situation, it was not always so. After Callas's death my relationship with her, or more correctly her memory, itself developed.[10] Distance brought with it a more accurate and realistic perspective and I began to feel liberated.

Before 1976–7, without being aware of it at the time, I did not always find it easy really to see both woman and artist objectively. Later, when my friendship with her became closer (though not too close to become a dangerous privilege), and after going through the stages a serious biographer does, my affection for the woman grew. At other times, when I had difficulty in understanding her motives she became somewhat antipathetic to me. Certainly, there were flaws in her character. Although material gain was of secondary importance to Callas she was governed to a degree by ambition, obstinacy, single-mindedness and a touch of selfishness. These idiosyncracies which, in the right circumstances, lent her strength in the development of her artistic career – and she did put her career above everything else – did not always make her very endearing. Nevertheless, at the same time I discovered that her shortcomings were substantially redeemed by a warm and kind heart, sincerity, modesty and, with time, tolerance and compassion.

'I am a very simple woman and I am a very moral woman,' she said in an interview with Kenneth Harris (*Observer*, 1970). 'I do not mean that I claim to be a "good" woman, as the word is: that is for others to judge; but I am a moral woman in that I see clearly what is right and wrong for me, and I do not confuse them or evade them.'

Speaking from personal experience over the years I knew her, I found this statement to be true. Her character was not diminished in my eyes by those flaws, but enhanced by a knowledge of her profound moral awareness. I began to see her in sharper focus; my feelings and opinion of her consolidated into enormous respect for her mission in life. Henceforth my appreciation was directed not towards a demi-goddess to whom the fluctuating response lies polarized between eulogy and apologia, but to a sensitive, vulnerable and down-to-earth human being with whom one could identify. But I still did not believe that I was in a position to write a balanced biography. On the contrary.

Perhaps Callas would have made a better-balanced fictional character, but life very rarely, if ever, works like that. It is the contradictions and the imbalances that make human beings, particularly highly creative artists.

As my conversations with her were not in the form of conventional interviews her beliefs, though obviously less calculated than this, may have been somewhat based on her reactions and motivation at the time. This is not meant to imply that Callas may have had wildly changing opinions about her code of practice in life, but there is some calculation, often unconscious, in most people which may not be of special importance in everyday life but cannot be entirely

ignored when one evaluates, as one has to, a human being's character. One must remember that even in Callas's case, where the human being was so much a part of the artist, her stagecraft alone will never be sufficient to illuminate her motivation as a woman. Naturally, I was not able to test absolutely the claims she made for herself. Judgements of people, perhaps particularly judgements of oneself, are never absolute or final. None the less, her own views were disclosed to me at a period when it was reasonable to assume that her recollections of past events were intended by her to be objective. Even so, in my role as her confidant and biographer I have struggled to present the subject in a perspective detached from her own so that my assessment of both woman and artist will be based on fact and constructive imagination, not fantasy.

After Callas's death, certain writers repainted her picture – artistic and personal – distorting beyond recognition the Callas I knew. Not that she was perfect, but her reputation has been impaired by those who weigh unduly on a few operatic excerpts recorded when she was in rather poor voice and at the end of her career – recordings which were issued without her permission and after her death.

Some writers have also been easy prey, sometimes wittingly, of people who had social or business contacts with either Callas or Onassis, or who worked in the Onassis household even after his marriage to another woman. Their determination to link their own name to that of a famous woman has led them to invent, or simply quote out of context. They seized on Callas's relationship with her mother or some other person and built it up into sensational exposure. Such stories, some amounting to character assassination, have described her variously as suffering from a massive inferiority complex, as ruthlessly ambitious, as a virginally chaste and desperately lonely woman and, being a prima donna, unreasonably temperamental – all totally misinformed views when considered in their extreme form. One bizarre theory maintained that Callas, with her superhuman demands on her voice, destroyed herself out of masochism, and another deliberately and wrongly turned her liaison with Onassis into the most important event of her life. In an effort to cast her as a 'soap-opera queen' it was declared, with assumed authority, that she sacrificed everything, including her career, for Onassis without return and with tragic consequences. Onassis was of necessity unfairly presented as a confirmed philistine and male chauvinist pig who, after ruining her career and forcing her to abort their child, abandoned her. Hence Callas became a recluse in Paris, where she died from a broken heart . . . or so this story would have it.

Callas never sacrificed anything that would have harmed her art or curtailed her career. She would unhesitatingly have sacrificed all for the sake of her art. Moreover, it will suffice to say that I saw more of this so-called recluse in the last two years of her life than I had in the previous ten years.

The 'soap-opera' biographers cast Meneghini as the obligatory third party of the proverbial triangle, a secondary villain. More recently, another villain has been invented: recording director Walter Legge, who supervised Callas's recordings for EMI. He stands accused of making her record operas which were unsuitable for her voice and talent, thus shortening, if not ruining, her career. (In fact, for many years since 1947 Callas exclusively sought the advice on all artistic matters of her mentor, the celebrated conductor Tullio Serafin, with whom she studied her roles. Serafin also conducted nearly all her recordings and, with few exceptions, Callas sang her roles on the stage, before making the records. Even though this fabricated scenario doesn't stand up to scrutiny, it is from time to time expanded by new writers who derive their embroidery from 'dead villains' corner' and pretentiously present their account as a new, authentic version. Their pseudo-psychological analysis is based on 'What I tell you three times is true'.

I felt strongly that the record, warts and all, must be set straight, especially for the sake of new generations. The Callas fresco needs not merely cleaning but major restoration. Of course, many opinions about her, particularly with regard to her artistic achievement, are sound and enlightening. A strong element of my motivation is to keep these accounts alive and to augment them.

Since the 1950s, when my interest in opera and music in general took a serious turn — I became a writer, music critic and lecturer — I have heard most of the important singers. I have been enchanted by their lyric beauty, their warmth and ardency, captivated by their humane characterizations and by this or that other outstanding quality to varying degrees. But for me, it was Callas's artistry that for two decades defined the age.

Stelios Galatopoulos
Richmond, Surrey

1   In 1957 Callas's mother gave malicious interviews against her famous daughter and later wrote a denigrating book, *My daughter Maria Callas* (1960).
2   I had met Onassis a year before, when Callas was singing Medea in London, but he could not recall that meeting.
3   An expanded and updated version of *Callas, La Divina* (1963).
4   In July 1965 she gave her last performance in an opera. Seven years later, she embarked on a recital tour with the tenor Giuseppe di Stefano.
5   Teresa D'Addato had been Callas's secretary for several years and was very helpful to all my queries. By the time I located two Hermans — one Robert Herman and another Herman Krawitz, both on the staff of the Metropolitan Opera, New York — it was too late. They would have been helpful with annals of Callas's performances at the Met — information I already had.
6   When Callas was mildly 'cross', she addressed me by my first name.
7   Unexpectedly, Callas died in September of that year.
8   One is of Callas as Santuzza in *Cavalleria rusticana*, the very first time she sang in an opera. Still a student, she was not quite fifteen and a half years old. Another shows the eighteen-and-a-half-year-old Callas in the assassination scene in *Tosca*, her first professional performance of a major role.
9   Aria sung by a minor character, providing some of the audience with the opportunity to leave the auditorium and have ice-cream. A practice fortunately abandoned a long time ago.
10   Numerous audio and some video tapes of her 'live' performances refreshed my memories of her — I had seen her 123 times in twenty-eight of her forty-three stage roles.

PART ONE

Beginnings

CHAPTER ONE

ROOTS

M Y MOTHER WAS the first person who made me realize that I had an extraordinary musical appreciation. It was always put into my head that I had it – and that I'd better have it.

I am sorry for any children who grew up in that period [the late 1920s and early 1930s] of infant prodigies, when parents were getting such wonderful ideas about becoming rich and famous. Although my mother was right about me, the majority of others are not and they ruin their children. As for myself, I did have this voice and I was pushed into a career. I, too, was considered a sort of infant prodigy. You know, as a child I won various radio contests in America and sang in school at graduations. Then in 1937, at the age of thirteen, I was taken back to Athens by my mother (there was considerable discord between my parents) and began my musical studies seriously ...

As things turned out, of course, I can't complain. But to load a child so early with responsibility is something there should be a law against. Infant prodigies are always deprived of genuine childhoods. It's not a special toy – a doll or a favourite game – that I remember but the songs that I was made to rehearse time and time again, sometimes to the point of exhaustion, so that I would shine at the end of a school year. A child should not be taken away from its youth for any reason – it becomes exhausted before its time!

These were Maria Callas's reflections in 1961 at a time when her remarkable operatic career was having its final glow, and again in 1977, the last year of her life, by which time it can reasonably be assumed that youth's sentimentality and superficiality are not significantly distorting the real picture.

Callas's upbringing and her relationship with her parents, especially her mother, influenced her greatly both as a person and as an artist. Although she inherited from her father such character traits as dignity, a considerable puritanical streak and an almost stubborn though usually constructive belief in her own convictions, it was from her mother, or to be precise from that side of the family, that her artistic talent probably came; her mother always maintained that music was highly esteemed in her family inasmuch as they all sang well, her own father having a particularly fine voice and one of her brothers being a promising poet who killed himself at the age of twenty-one. Maria largely inherited her looks from her maternal grandmother and her poet uncle. Her mother's contribution was different. Until the age of twenty-one Callas was brought up in an almost completely matriarchal environment, her father having had little influence on the careers chosen for his two daughters. Judging from her mother's later behaviour – Callas was a triumphant success but her sister was not – her ruthless ambition was motivated by an effort not only to find fulfilment through her daughters, but also to profit materially. There is no denying that her mother's ambition, however misguided, contributed in a fundamental way towards the discovery of Callas's extraordinary talent. Once aware of it, however, she herself – with her teachers' guidance (at first Maria Trivella and later Elvira de Hidalgo and Tullio Serafin) – took over completely.

For Callas the human being the picture was different. Throughout her life her actions, as well as her unhappiness, had some basic connection with the frustrations and loneliness that resulted from lack of genuine maternal love in her youth. The character of Callas the woman, which was basically integrated with that of the artist, can better be understood by examining her parents' backgrounds and relationship.

Her mother, Evangelia Dimitroadou, was one of eleven children of an army officer whose father came from a well-to-do Greek family, the Fanari of Istanbul (at that time a large part of present-day Greece belonged to Turkey). They later moved to Stylis, a town across the Gulf of Lamia from Thermopylae, where Evangelia was born. Much later, the family settled in Athens and there she fell in love with the dashing Georges Kalogeropoulos, from the Peloponnese, a student of pharmacy at Athens University. Her father, however, was initially unimpressed with his daughter's choice. Kalogeropoulos was much older than Evangelia and the Dimitroadises considered his family, who were farmers, inferior to theirs. Nevertheless, after Kalogeropoulos had graduated Evangelia's father was persuaded, both by her and by his wife, to give his blessing, albeit reluctantly, to his daughter's wedding, although he died of a stroke a fortnight before the event.

Evangelia and Georges were married in August 1916 (she was seventeen, he thirty) and settled at Meligala, a town in the Peloponnese, where he opened his own pharmacy. A year later their daughter Iakinthy was born and three years after that they had a son, Vasily, who died at the age of three from meningitis. This was an unforgettable blow to the family.

Unfortunately husband and wife did not turn to each other for comfort in their grief. According to Evangelia their happiness only lasted about six months; possibly their initial passion for one another was infatuation, all too soon extinguished, rather than love. The birth of their daughter created a new interest, if not quite a bond, between them and Evangelia resigned herself to being an efficient though rather dictatorial housewife. Vasily, during his brief life, had brought a much more promising turn to his parents' relationship, which was shattered by his untimely death.

Within the year the Kalogeropouloses emigrated to New York. Afterwards Evangelia said that this was her husband's unilateral decision, only revealed at the last minute. It was a strange step to take, as Kalogeropoulos was doing extremely well as a chemist at Meligala and was able to afford a big and comfortable house with servants.

Undoubtedly Vasily's tragic death seriously upset the balance of their lives and it was natural that both husband and wife would want to make a new start in a different environment. Happily Evangelia was pregnant again and they felt confident they would have another son, another Vasily. With good reason, therefore, she was set to move to Athens, where one of her cousins whose family was linked to the medical profession offered to help Kalogeropoulos to open a pharmacy in a most desirable part of the city centre. But Kalogeropoulos would not even consider it. He had suffered enough from his wife's chronic nagging and her attitude to almost everything. She hardly ever lost an opportunity to boast about the superiority of her family: allegedly her father and grandfather were generals, her cousin physician to the king – 'and I married a mere pharmacist'.

The most plausible reason for Kalogeropoulos's desire to emigrate to America was his longing for a more exciting life, where credit for achievement would be his alone and certainly not attributable to his wife's 'fantastic' family; the dreadful loss of his son provided ample justification to start afresh in a completely different, preferably foreign, environment where, he hoped, his wife's constant nagging would be curtailed.

In spite of his rather over-confident and adventurous spirit, Kalogeropoulos did not find life in New York as easy and exciting as he had hoped; it took him five years to master sufficient English to pass the pharmaceutical examination required for a licence to practise on his own. Nevertheless in the meantime, being a hard-working man, he obtained employment with another pharmacist at Astoria in the Queens area of New York – a neighbourhood favoured by Greek immigrants. There, his family also set up home and he taught Greek in the evenings at a local school.

Four months after their arrival in America, on 2 December 1923, Evangelia gave birth to another daughter in the Fifth Avenue Hospital (then called the Flower Hospital), New York. The child was a disappointment to the mother, who had desperately hoped for a son to take Vasily's place. So great, in fact, was her frustration that although she nursed the baby it took her four days to bring herself to take her first look at her daughter. Even before that she had opposed her husband's wish to call the child Cecilia. Her daughter's name would be Sophia, she decreed. Later a compromise was reached, though surprisingly for a Greek family the child was almost three years old (rather than the customary six months) before she was christened in the Greek Orthodox Cathedral in Manhattan, New York, as Maria Anna Sophia Cecilia, to be known to

Maria celebrating her first birthday (1924) with her parents and sister.

the family as Mary or sometimes Maryanne and, later on, to the world as Maria Callas. (For practical reasons Kalogeropoulos had shortened his surname legally to Callas.) Her godfather was another Greek emigrant, Dr Leonidas Lantzounis, an orthopaedic surgeon and Kalogeropoulos's best friend who was in all probability the referee in the dispute over the child's name and remained a lifelong friend and dutiful godfather.

Gradually Evangelia got over her disappointment and developed considerable affection, if not real love, for both her daughters. Her idea of maternal love was how much discipline, as she knew it, she could impose upon them to meet her own misguidedly snobbish standards — a treatment she also applied to her husband.

Maria, short-sighted and therefore bespectacled from the age of five, grew up a rather shy, quiet girl, well behaved and religious. She did well at school, her marks being consistently above average. But it was a lonely life for a child who, apart from her much older sister whom she adored, had practically no opportunities to make friends. Every change of apartment also meant a new school. This need not have been a problem, had not her mother discouraged her daughters from mixing with other children. Evangelia, who always felt far superior to the Greek community of the neighbourhood — just as she had at Meligala — had few friends herself. As she was not keen to have other youngsters in the house her daughters were seldom invited to their school-friends' homes.

Even so, when their mother was not arguing with her husband or being stern with them, the family were reasonably happy during the first New York years. Used to a comfortable life at Meligala, both parents were at first extravagant, even though Kalogeropoulos was earning only a modest salary. Consequently, before long he had spent all the capital brought from Greece and in order to open his own drugstore five years later had to borrow money from Dr. Lantzounis.

From the beginning, Kalogeropoulos's venture met with considerable success, despite the fact that the shop was in the rather rough neighbourhood known as Hell's Kitchen. Their situation improved, at least financially, and for a time Evangelia was less disgruntled, though she would often moan about the location of their business. At the start of 1929 Evangelia was overjoyed when, unexpectedly, one of her cousins, married to a Greek-American, invited the family to Tarpon Springs in Florida. As Kalogeropoulos could not leave his shop Evangelia and the girls travelled without him. Once there, she became almost a different person. Assuming the grand manner which was second nature to her, she constantly praised her daughters, making the girls feel as though they were in heaven. Not only could they enjoy the sea but more important, for the first time in their lives they found marvellous playmates: three boys and a girl, their second cousins.

Neither Iakinthy nor the five-year-old Maria was ever to forget this holiday, especially because, soon after returning to New York, things changed dramatically for the worse. Kalogeropoulos had known success for barely six months when the 1929 Wall Street crash, and the Depression that followed, caught up with him; he lost his business but a few weeks later managed to get a job as a travelling salesman for a wholesale pharmaceutical company specializing in women's cosmetics.

The years following the Depression brought a great deal of unhappiness to the Kalogeropoulos family, who were forced for a time to move to cheaper apartments, finally in 1932 settling at 157 Street West, Washington Heights, then a pleasant middle-class residential district of northern Manhattan. This was made possible through Kalogeropoulos's ingenuity when in the desperation and exhaustion of trying to make ends meet for his family he found time to perfect his own ointment for the treatment of gingivitis. Trying to sell it on his own travelling round many states was an almost impossible task, but he succeeded and the small amount of extra money he earned made all the difference.

Evangelia considered Kalogeropoulos's loss of his drugstore the last straw: the status of a chemist was in those times, and particularly in certain neighbourhoods, only a little below that of a doctor. She refused to accept the situation or set aside delusions of grandeur and began to attack her husband at the slightest provocation as if the Depression were his fault. Kalogeropoulos was all too often accused of incompetence and he was also embarrassed by his wife's continual reminiscences about the comfortable and civilized life to which she had been accustomed with her parents.

Writing about her life in *Sisters* (1989) Iakinthy revealed that even before the Depression, by the time she was nine years old, she was 'a little American girl, happy at school, desperately unhappy at home. Mary and I were serious children. . . . How could we [be happy] when the only example of motherhood we knew was a woman forever bemoaning the fact that she married our father.'

Georges Kalogeropoulos, who genuinely tried his best to support his family, eventually lost much of his confidence, feeling in his heart that his wife had no love for, or appreciation of, him. He never again had his own business, later working as a chemist with the municipality. His decision to treat Evangelia with indifference, in order to keep the peace at any price, misfired and she reacted ever more violently. Their rows became so intense that she suffered a real, or imaginary, mental breakdown and attempted suicide. After a month in the Belleview psychiatric institution in New York State she recovered and returned home. Although suicide attempts were illegal and could carry a term of imprisonment, Kalogeropoulos used his connections with doctors at the institution and Evangelia's grave action – almost certainly a *coup de théâtre* – was declared a mishap that could happen to anybody. Her relationship with her husband was never to improve although they remained married for many years, living under the same roof as irritable strangers.

Henceforth Evangelia turned her full energies towards her daughters' musical talents – Iakinthy was twelve and Maria five. Their only source of music was the family radio from which they, especially Maria, picked out songs. This delighted Evangelia whose fascination for music and the theatre went back to her girlhood in Greece. Much more important, her dormant ambition for an operatic career of her own was now fired again with the prospect of finding a musical future for her daughters. By the time Maria was almost eight a gramophone and records – mostly of operatic arias – and a pianola, were bought and an Italian teacher, Signorina Santrina, was engaged to give the girls piano lessons. When she was ten Maria could sing, either to her own piano accompaniment or Iakinthy's (who was by far the more proficient pianist), her favourite childhood songs: 'La paloma' and 'The heart that's free'. Evangelia enjoyed developing this talent in her children, particularly Maria (Iakinthy had found a female friend of her own age and was spending a lot of her free time with her). There was, however, nothing special in little Maria's singing; her sweet, light mezzo-soprano was no more than agreeable. Even Evangelia, always ready to exaggerate and dramatize everything, did not see anything special in her voice until a Swedish neighbour offered to give the young singer free lessons. He was a professional singing coach and had overheard her practising.

After some rudimentary work on Maria's repertoire of two songs her voice opened up, the higher notes as well as the timbre suggesting strongly that she was a soprano. Within a month, when she had learned from recordings Gounod's 'Ave Maria', the 'Habanera' from *Carmen* and 'Je suis Titania' from *Mignon*, her vocal range extended appreciably; the first piece developed the middle register and its lyricism, the second the lower notes and the third the upper, as well as an all-important flexibility. With these qualities Maria's soprano singing began to acquire some distinctive colours, which her ever-vigilant mother immediately decided to exploit: one daughter would be a great singer, the other a concert pianist, though Evangelia involved herself more with Maria's craft, believing it to be rooted in her own unfulfilled passion.

For a time Maria enjoyed all this. At school concerts she was popular, her first part being a small role in Gilbert and Sullivan's *Mikado*. It was a new interest in an otherwise relatively drab life at home. Before long, however, even her music became something of a chore. Her mother would constantly urge her on, while her father objected, accusing his wife of seeking to bask in her daughters' possible future glory. He felt that it was wrong to push both girls into hard work, instead of allowing them to play and act their age. Be that as it may, Maria, as she reminisced many years later, learned more or less to put up with her parents' bickering. She was beginning to

Maria, at the age of eleven (top left), her sister Iakinthy (top right), her father Georges (standing right), her mother Evangelia (seated by her husband) and Greek friends in New York, 1934.

discover that singing was a foolproof way of attracting attention – the best substitute for affection. Her desire to prove her worth was not only directed at her forceful and ambitious mother but also at her father, who held the opposite view. He had little time for the theatre and did not consider it a sufficiently respectable profession for his daughter. His love for both girls was great, but he would have preferred that one day Maria would work with him in his own pharmacy. Even so, his attitude helped to relieve some of Evangelia's pressure and Maria translated this as love. Besides, contrary to her mother's efforts to alienate her and her sister from their father, they found him very congenial on the rare occasions they were alone with him, for he made clear to them that he did not think there was anything wrong either with their appearance or behaviour, as their mother constantly insisted and above all he treated them as grown-ups.

In any event, neither her husband's opposition nor the lack of money to pay for proper lessons dampened Evangelia's determination to seek musical careers for her daughters. She was convinced that Maria was endowed with an exceptional voice – that she was indeed an infant prodigy – and losing no time, she entered her for various radio competitions. Thus, in 1934 Maria sang, to Iakinthy's piano accompaniment, 'La paloma' and 'The heart that's free' in the *Major Bowes Amateur Hour,* for which she won second prize (the first went to an accordion player).

As 1936 drew to a close, Maria's graduation was approaching and Evangelia had already made plans. They might have weathered their worst financial storms but the strain was still considerable. Above all, few prospects were visible for Maria and Iakinthy even on the remotest edge of the American musical horizon and in the circumstances Evangelia turned to the only possible solution: her large and presumably comfortably off family in Greece. Once there, she would seek their help for Maria to study singing and Iakinthy the piano. In the early part of December 1936 Iakinthy, now nineteen, sailed alone for Greece, where she would stay with her grandmother, awaiting her mother and sister who were to follow in a few months when Maria's schooling was at an end. Georges would remain in New York.

Many years later Evangelia insisted that when she told her husband she was taking her daughters to Greece, where they would receive musical instruction, he agreed to pay their fares and to send them $125 per month. Iakinthy said her mother also told her he was so pleased to hear his wife was leaving that he knelt down, crossed himself and thanked God for taking pity on him.

On 28 January 1937, Maria's graduation day, she was understandably excited. Her marks were very good and she was participating, naturally, in the musical programme for the ceremony. She sang in excerpts from Gilbert and Sullivan's *HMS Pinafore* and was warmly applauded by an audience consisting mostly of parents. No one could possibly have imagined that next time this thirteen-year-old graduate was to sing in the United States, seventeen years later on the stage of the Lyric Theater in Chicago, she would cause a sensation.

Maria (bespectacled) at her school graduation.

Six weeks after her graduation Maria and her mother sailed on board the *Saturnia* for Greece, the country of their ancestors. It did not take very long, with Evangelia around, for fellow passengers to discover that the young girl could sing. One evening in the tourist lounge, after many requests, she sang 'La paloma' and Gounod's 'Ave Maria', accompanying herself at the piano. A couple of days later the captain asked her to perform at a party he was giving for the officers and crew. Maria liked the idea, especially as she was formally invited, and agreed immediately. After singing a few of her favourite songs she chose the 'Habanera' from *Carmen* as her finale. She had sung in public before, but now, maybe because she was no longer a schoolgirl, her approach was different: at the end of her song she pulled a red carnation from a vase on the piano and threw it to the captain, who was sitting immediately in front of her. He returned the compliment by kissing it, after which he presented the young singer with a bouquet of flowers and a doll.

The *Saturnia* anchored at the beautiful port of Patras in the northern Peloponnese, this being Maria's first glimpse of Greece. Mother and daughter then travelled by train to Athens and were soon at her grandmother's house where, together with Iakinthy, they were to stay until they found a home of their own.

Neither Maria nor the formidable Evangelia was aware, as yet, of the magnitude of the adventure on which they were embarking.

CHAPTER TWO

FIRST FLIGHTS

E VANGELIA SPENT THE first few weeks in Athens seeing old and new relatives, friends and acquaintances, not so much settling in as finding out who could be useful to her. Undoubtedly her strategy, practically from the moment of arrival, was to commence her campaign for her daughters' careers – the paramount reason, after all, for coming to Greece.

To her horror, Iakinthy, on her grandmother's advice, had already enrolled at a secretarial school, so for the moment music was suspended. For young Maria it was different. Wasting no time, Evangelia made her reluctant daughter sing for anyone with the patience to listen, but nobody expressed an interest at all comparable to her own enthusiasm. Even her brother, Efthemios, who knew several singers and people connected with the theatre, in whom Evangelia placed her greatest hope, conceded only vaguely that while his niece had an agreeable voice it was nothing out of the ordinary. So did many girls and, more to the point, there was nothing he could do to further Maria's career. Perhaps her relations deliberately appeared uninterested because they were not prepared, or able, to help financially. Evangelia's claims of family fortunes were exaggerated: her brothers, sisters and mother were now dependent on pensions and none offered help. Instead, most of them, including Efthemios, offered unsolicited advice that she cease pushing Maria as she was still a little girl. Moreover, the more courageous members of her family, delighted though they were to see Evangelia back in her motherland, hinted in no uncertain terms that following the holiday in Greece she could do worse than return to her husband in America.

Undaunted, Evangelia determined to press on with her endeavours regardless of problems, financial or otherwise. With the money that her husband was sending them they could live fairly comfortably, but that was all. American dollars went some way in Greece, but not far enough to finance a career of any kind. With help from her family, Evangelia and her daughters moved from her mother's very small home into a furnished house in Terma Pattission, while she continued, relentlessly but in vain, to press and sometimes pester her brothers to do something for their niece.

She was at the end of her tether when her brother Dukas told her of a taverna on the coast not far from Athens where the customers sang operatic arias, some of them young professional singers. It was not the sort of venue where Evangelia wished to be seen but, having no other door to knock on, without further thought she took her daughters to the taverna with Dukas in attendance. Maria did not like the place and was very upset and embarrassed when her mother ordered her to go up on to the platform and sing. But with Iakinthy accompanying her on the piano, she sang 'La paloma' and 'The heart that's free', and was given an ovation. Furthermore, as soon as she sat down Zannis (Yannis) Cambanis, a young tenor who was then embarking on a promising career with the Athens Opera (Lyric Stage), came to congratulate her. Evangelia was delighted and, hearing that Cambanis's teacher was the illustrious Maria Trivella at the National Conservatory, immediately planned her next move. Efthemios, a friend of Trivella's brother-in-law, had so far evaded using this connection, but now, surely, with Cambanis's favourable opinion of Maria's voice Evangelia could persuade him to do something.

This, however, proved easier said than done and in addition Georges had apparently been taken ill with pneumonia and had stopped the allowance, at least for the time being, in order to meet his hospital bills. Evangelia could not afford the rent on the house and, as the landlord wished to reclaim the property for his own use, mother and daughters moved to a much cheaper unfurnished and, as they soon discovered, very cold house. What little money they had came mostly from Evangelia's family. 'They gave us as much as they could spare,' she reminisced later. Iakinthy, who was attending secretarial school, also took a part-time job translating film titles and thus was able to pay her own way.

When the National Conservatory reopened at the beginning of September, Efthemios at last made the necessary introduction and arranged for Maria to audition for Maria Trivella, a Greek and in all probability of Italian descent, a good coach, if not a great singer. Accompanied by her mother, sister, grandmother, two aunts and her uncle Efthemios, Maria arrived apparently in rather a phlegmatic mood. (Thirty-five years later Callas remembered that she was very nervous until she met Trivella who, contrary to expectation, was sympathetic and put her at ease.) Maria sang the 'Habanera' and was instantly accepted, Trivella being so impressed by the significant expression in her singing that she exclaimed, 'But this is talent!' Many years later, recalling this audition, she said, 'I accepted little Maria as my pupil with great pleasure, for I felt, there and then, enthusiastic over the possibilities of her voice.'

Aware of the family's financial difficulties, Trivella also recommended Maria for a scholarship which covered all tuition fees. A problem, however, arose as the conservatory could not grant a scholarship to any student under sixteen. Without the slightest hesitation Evangelia, with the full knowledge of the teacher, settled the matter by forging her daughter's birth certificate (adding two years). Since Maria was tall, Evangelia reasoned, acted older than her years and was conveniently born in New York, who would have the audacity to dispute her mother's word?

Maria studied technique with Trivella and vocal expression and operatic history with Georges Karakantas. A little later she also attended the piano classes of Evie Bana. She was studious and

*The National Conservatory in Athens where Maria became a student in
September 1937.*

very quickly established a good relationship with Trivella, who took a special interest in her 'young' student, very often giving Maria supper in her studio when she stayed behind for extra coaching. Her progress was constant and considerable, so much so that at the end of her second term in April 1938 she was allowed to take part in the annual student concert of the conservatory. Her turn came at the end of a long programme, when she sang Agathe's aria 'Leise, leise' (*Der Freischütz*), Balkis's 'Plus grand dans son obscurité' from Gounod's *La Reine de Saba* and 'Two nights', a Greek song by Yiannis Psaroudas. The concert ended with Maria and Cambanis performing the duet 'Quale occhio al mondo' from *Tosca*. It was difficult and rather varied music for the fourteen-year-old pupil who was singing in an organized concert for the first time only six months after she had entered the conservatory. She won first prize and thus proved worthy of Cambanis's expectations who, as a professional singer, was taking a gamble by agreeing to sing with her, as well as justifying Trivella's decision to let her take part in the concert.

A few months after Iakinthy arrived in Athens she had struck up a friendship with Milton Embiricos, eldest son of a very wealthy shipping family. Although he was in love with her from the beginning and a little later she reciprocated his love, his father never allowed them to marry; he wanted his own girls to find husbands, after which his son should wed the daughter of a shipowner. Iakinthy remained Milton's mistress-fiancée until his death in the 1950s. Practically from the beginning of this liaison Milton considered Iakinthy's family as his own, or so he professed. When he learned of their financial difficulties he furnished their cold house, employed a maid for them and, as he objected to Iakinthy getting a job even after she had obtained her secretarial diploma, provided for her upkeep, in effect also helping her mother and sister. At her mother's insistence Iakinthy then resumed her piano lessons.

It is not clear whether Evangelia began again to receive money from her husband after he recovered from his illness. If she did she never told her daughters because she did not want them to think well of their father. She certainly got nothing after the Italian occupation of Greece in 1940. Nor did she have any help from her family, with whom she had quarrelled shortly after Maria's enrolment at the conservatory.

At the end of the summer in 1938 they moved to a comfortable and spacious apartment at 61 Patission, provided by Milton for his secret fiancée. He lived elsewhere in the vicinity. As they had six rooms, Evangelia sublet one, which was separate from their apartment, to a woman for much-needed income.

Maria dedicated her portrait to her first teacher, Maria Trivella, at the National Conservatory in 1938. She inscribed it, 'To my darling teacher to whom I owe all'.

Maria at fifteen with her mother and sister in their apartment at Patission 61, Athens (top floor at the back).

Some time after the concert in 1938 Maria experienced her first artistic contretemps. Even though she was exceptionally promising in her studies, Manolis Kalomiris (1883–1949), one of the most illustrious Greek composers and the autocratic artistic director of the conservatory, took a dislike to her mainly because of her inelegant appearance: Maria had become fat and suffered from a form of acne. Kalomiris had a reputation as a chaser of attractive girls still in their middle teens. When one day he completely ignored Maria's accomplished singing and offensively remarked on her size, the fourteen-and-a-half-year-old pupil, who was by nature reserved and polite, lost patience and put him in his place, pointing out the responsibility of the teacher, let alone the director, towards his students. He reacted to such impertinence by instantly expelling her and Maria departed in tears. As soon as she got home her mother rushed her to Karakantas, who lived in the same block, and on his advice the three of them went to see Kalomiris. After Karakantas put in a good word for her and Maria, kneeling, tearfully begged for forgiveness pledging never to be impertinent again, Kalomiris relented, allowing her to return to her classes.

No other incident followed during her time at the conservatory and she continued to make well above average progress, leading to a prize at the end of her first year.

At the beginning of the new year the conservatory announced that Mascagni's *Cavalleria rusti-*

Maria was sixteen when she was photographed with Menis Fotopoulos, a friend.

cana and Leoncavallo's *Pagliacci* would be staged as a double bill in the forthcoming March. The leading roles for both operas were given to the most experienced and best students who, in fact, were about to graduate: Nedda in *Pagliacci* went to Zozo Remoundou, Santuzza in *Cavalleria* to Hilda Woodley. However Karakantas, the producer and translator of both works, insisted that Maria should also sing Santuzza. So strongly did he believe that she would be successful in this relatively short but technically very difficult role that he managed to persuade a rather reluctant Trivella to allow her star pupil to sing and two performances were scheduled. Maria then studied Santuzza in Greek with Trivella, the conductor Michales Bourtsis and Karakantas. Woodley sang creditably in the first performance on 19 March. On 2 April 1939, when actually only fifteen years and four months old, Maria made her operatic début as Santuzza, scoring a stupendous success and winning first prize for opera. Many years later Karakantas told me that

> Maria sustained the role of Santuzza like a true professional, paying full attention to the minutest details. She was determined to win the prize and she did. At rehearsals she would listen as if in a trance and sometimes she would walk nervously up and down the room repeating passionately to herself, 'I'll get there one day.' Even then her concern about the composer's markings and the importance of words were great. She may not have had full control of her voice, but I remember she made such a dramatic impact on 'Voi lo sapete' and the 'Easter Hymn' that one did not notice any vocal imperfections. One could not forget how this young débutante conveyed so memorably the conflict in the forsaken peasant girl who still loves but resents her betrayer.

Writing in *Eleftheron Vima* (20 April 1939) Yiannis Psaroudas praised both Santuzzas, 'they sang the difficult role with beautiful voices and considerable insight'. The difference, however, was that Maria's exciting interpretation of the role had created a public demand which extended far beyond parents, students and officials, and two more performances were given, one attended by Greek President Metaxas and Costas Kotzias, the Minister of Culture.

Following her daughter's exceptional success, Evangelia asked Trivella to give Maria a graduating diploma at the end of her second year in the forthcoming June. The teacher declined, saying 'We must wait one more year. There is in Maria excellent material but it needs more work.' There was more to Evangelia's request than met the eye. Pleased though she and Maria were with the teachers at the National Conservatory, it had not escaped their attention that at the highly prestigious Athens Conservatory Elvira de Hidalgo could open new horizons for the precocious singer. Evangelia had attended one of Hidalgo's master classes and was so taken by the way she taught her students that she decided there and then to transfer her daughter to her.

Hidalgo (1892–1980), a Spaniard, had until the early 1930s been a famous coloratura soprano in the opera houses of the world, where she had sung with some of the greatest artists including Feodor Chaliapin, Titta Ruffo, Beniamino Gigli, Tito Schipa. Born at Val de Robles, Aragón, she was considered a musical prodigy. She had studied the piano, then singing in Barcelona and Milan with Melchior Vidal, a brilliant lyric tenor and renowned teacher of the *bel canto* method. In 1908, her opera début at the age of sixteen as Rosina in *Il barbiere di Siviglia* at the San Carlo in Naples was such a success that she soon repeated the role in Paris. Her triumph there brought engagements in Monte Carlo, Prague, Cairo and at the Metropolitan in New York. Engagements followed throughout Italy, in Buenos Aires, Chicago and a return to the Met. Her repertoire included Amina (*La sonnambula*), Gilda (*Rigoletto*), Elvira (*I Puritani*), Adina (*L'elisir d'amore*), Violetta (*La traviata*), Marie (*La fille du régiment*), Zerlina (*Don Giovanni*), Mimi (*La bohème*) and the title roles in *Lucia di Lammermoor, Lakmé, Linda di Chamonix* and *Mireille*.

Hidalgo's voice was distinguished by its brilliance and flexibility, and above all by her expressive qualities which enabled her to sing coloratura dramatically. One believed in the character she was portraying and her inborn charm, vivacity and physical beauty were contributing assets. Today she is primarily remembered as Callas's teacher – she continued to teach at the Athens Conservatory until 1948[1] – her own considerable success as an opera singer most unfairly all but forgotten.

After *Cavalleria* Maria continued her studies with Trivella until the close of the school year, participating with creditable success in three student concerts, the last being on 25 June, when she sang excerpts from Verdi's *Un ballo in maschera* and in the second scene of *Cavalleria*. When she

The Athens Conservatory.

Elvira de Hidalgo.

Hidalgo as Rosina (Il barbiere), *her greatest role.*

presented herself at the Athens Conservatory for her audition, fat, pimpled and nervously biting her fingernails, Hidalgo could not believe her eyes. 'I did notice this girl sitting, waiting her turn,' Hidalgo told me over twenty years later.

> The idea of her wanting to be an opera singer seemed ridiculous to me. It was even more ridiculous when her turn came and she produced the music of 'Ocean'! [*Oberon*]Until she began to sing. Of course her vocal technique was by no means perfect but there was innate drama, musicianship and a certain individuality in her voice that moved me deeply. In fact, I shed a tear or two and turned away so that she could not see me. I immediately decided that I would be her teacher and when I looked into her most expressive eyes I also knew that, in spite of everything else, she was a beautiful girl. After I had expressed my pleasure, I immediately assumed my teaching persona and said to her, 'Now that you have sung so well my dear, you must put this music away immediately. This is no music for a young girl like you.'

Hidalgo promptly arranged that Maria's admission to the conservatory be free of tuition fees. The young, eager pupil was thrilled and after the summer holidays joined full time. Now that

Hidalgo had accepted her the whole idea of her singing assumed a wider perspective and at once she decided that no interest was going to find room in her heart, other than to become a great singer. Moreover, her increasing confidence was beginning to help her cope better with the problems of puberty, which manifested themselves at around this time.

Concurrently with this upheaval in her life her older sister, now a beautiful and elegant woman of twenty-one, was in some ways detached from Maria and their mother. It was all very well living in the spacious apartment that Milton Embiricos had provided for them, and for which they were naturally grateful, but when it dawned on Maria that her beloved sister, on whom she had always doted, was actually sleeping with a man who was not her husband she was devastated. This was perhaps naïve, but understandable as in 1939, especially for a Greek from a middle-class family, the situation was scandalous. There was a further factor, equally important, adding to Maria's distress: although she liked Milton and all he had done for her family, his disinclination to marry Iakinthy while in effect taking her away from Maria, by nature a rather solitary girl, was unacceptable. Worse still, Maria could not turn to her mother for comfort and advice as Evangelia had little patience with such mundane details. Nor could she turn to her sister, who was now preoccupied with her own life and rapidly growing away from her.

Writing about this period in *Sisters*, Iakinthy said that Maria seemed to be forever with Marina Papageorgopoulou, the woman who rented a room from them, asking her how she could make herself attractive and so forth: 'I would give up everything if I could find true love,' Maria declared, 'Why is only Iakinthy always loved?' and when Marina tried to comfort the fifteen-year-old, telling her that she was endowed with a marvellous voice, Maria replied cheekily, 'What is a voice? I am a woman, that's what matters!'

The young singer was keen to work hard not only because she felt that she had found her true vocation, but also because singing was in her eyes the only means of gaining her mother's love. In this she succeeded only partially and was forced to look elsewhere: Maria saw in her teacher a kind of mother substitute and was always anxious to do as much housework for her as she could. The perceptive Hidalgo, however, did not encourage this. As late as 1977, after Callas's death, the octogenarian teacher fondly remembered her beloved pupil:

She was an extraordinarily gifted girl, but she was more than that to me. I was aware of the child's loneliness, but even though I loved her – and I always will – as a daughter, it would have been wrong for me to take over from her mother. In any case I would not allow her to do housework but instead encouraged her to look after her hands, her fingernails and so forth. The future prima donna was expected to have elegance both in her singing and appearance. Nevertheless I gave her all the love I could in my way and in her way she could not have been a better pupil or a better daughter, and surely this is a great thing in life. Maria never forgot me, never lost her love and affection and gratitude for her old teacher. She always kept in touch with me. Not only when she had problems but also when she had triumphs. This gave me the greatest satisfaction in life.

So far the programme for Maria's career had been set primarily by her mother. Of course Trivella was her teacher but it was Evangelia who made the policy decisions. Hidalgo, however, took over completely the shaping of her pupil into an opera singer; Maria's natural instinct for dramatic expression began to develop and music was in no way a chore, as it had been at times in America with her forceful mother.

Ever since I can remember [Callas said, many years later] my mother demanded of me to become a singer – something that she herself wanted to be but could not. I was not really unhappy about it, especially after I graduated from school in America. As my interest, perhaps my only interest, in life was music, I was before long so fascinated listening to all Hidalgo's pupils, not only the sopranos but also the mezzos and even the tenors, singing both light and heavy operas, that I used to go to the conservatory at ten in the morning and leave with the last pupil in the evening. Hidalgo was quite amazed and often asked me why I stayed there so long. My answer was that I felt that even the least talented pupil could teach me something. Studying at the conservatory was not hard work for me. It was really an amusement.

On 16 June 1940 Hidalgo produced Puccini's *Suor Angelica* at the conservatory. It was a major success for a student effort and the sixteen-and-a-half-year-old Callas as Angelica, her second complete leading role, made an even greater impact than as Santuzza the previous year. Nevertheless, while Hidalgo wisely treated the whole affair with sufficient praise necessary for the development of her students, she did not encourage them to believe that they had become stars overnight.[2]

It was during rehearsals for *Suor Angelica* that the ever-thoughtful teacher (who also designed the costumes) began in earnest her campaign to try to make Maria more conscious of her looks and movements. Reminiscing in 1957 Maria, who had by then acquired great elegance, related to me how her teacher

deplored my incredible clothes. Once, when I presented myself to her in ridiculously clashing shades of red and with a ghastly hat, she nearly hit the roof. Not only did she tear off my absurd hat but she threatened to stop giving me lessons if I did not make a serious effort to improve my appearance. I did try but to be frank, then I never paid much attention to clothes or how I looked. My mother simply decided what I should wear and would not allow me to look in the mirror very often. Besides, I had more important things

A day by the sea with fellow students from the Athens Conservatory. Standing: Vassilakis, Hadjioannou, Salingaros. Top: Andreadou, Mandikian. Sitting: Callas, Vlachopoulos.

to think about. I had to study and could not waste my time with nonsense.

Although my mother's strict discipline helped me to acquire extensive artistic experience for my age, it deprived me entirely of the joys of adolescence and of its innocent pleasures, which are fresh, naïve and irreplaceable. And there was another thing: a diet (based on fats!) wrongly prescribed to cure acne caused me to put on a lot of weight. It became a vicious circle as by way of compensation for the discipline my mother put me through I began to over-eat and of course I became fat.

It was some twelve years later when I really changed my attitude, lost all the fat and generated positive interest in clothes and how I looked generally off-stage. The first time I appreciated the importance of my stage appearance was in 1947, before I slimmed, during my preparation of Isolde [*Tristan and Isolde*] with my mentor, the conductor Tullio Serafin, who insisted that I should have appropriately beautiful costumes, especially in this role which is static. His argument was that for a relatively long period the audience has nothing to do but look at me. Therefore, if I do not completely fascinate them with my voice and the role (but even if I do) they have all the time in the world to cut me to pieces. It is vital that my appearance should be as harmonious as the music.

33

Following Maria's personal success as Angelica, Hidalgo proceeded to lay the foundation for her pupil's career. With the help of Costis Bastias, the director of the Royal Theatre for drama, of which the Athens Opera was a part, Callas was engaged on 1 July 1940 as a member of the chorus of the opera company at a monthly salary of 1500 drachmas. The purpose of this contract was to help her financially and give her the opportunity, at first, to sing in small roles in order to gain stage experience. She was neither intended for, nor did she ever sing in, the chorus. The contract as such was a formality, a pretext to make her engagement possible.

After singing in the wings for a production of Shakespeare's *The Merchant of Venice* at the Royal Theatre and for other plays which were given with songs (members of the opera often sang in the wings for the actors) Callas undertook the small role of Beatrice in Suppé's *Boccaccio*. This event, which marked her professional début — albeit in operetta — most probably took place in February 1941. She shared the part with Nausica Ghalanou, then a more established singer. Even though the role is of limited scope, the seventeen-year-old débutante must have made a good impression as later, in July, when the work was revived she sang Beatrice in all fifteen performances. No official reviews have survived but Callas's success was recorded (published in *Nike*, Athens, 9 August 1962) by Ghalatia Amaxopoulou, a fellow student and then a member of the Athens Opera. She reminisced how 'from the rehearsal it was evident that Maria as Beatrice was to be stunning . . . her actual performance was a real triumph — the public gave her an ovation'.

Despite Callas's success it was, surprisingly, to be a whole year before she sang at the Athens Opera again. It seems that machinations by jealous colleagues may have been a reason for her relatively long absence from the stage. Amaxopoulou continued,

> From that first day [rehearsals of *Boccaccio*] several of Maria's colleagues reacted against her. They alleged that as her voice was neither suitable for nor capable of this role, she should be dismissed from the cast but the theatre adminstration would not hear of it . . . After her triumph, her detractors began to sabotage her. As Maria was born and brought up in America, she pronounced Greek with a slightly foreign accent [generally this did not affect her singing in Greek, but *Boccaccio* contains spoken dialogue] and this was used as a pretext against her being given another role. Maria was dismayed by her colleagues' appalling behaviour and vowed never to forgive them. She never did . . .

It has also been noted that during the revival of *Boccaccio* Callas developed a slight wobble in her upper register, which may have prompted Hidalgo to withdraw her from the professional stage until she had corrected this vocal defect. Recalling the period, Hidalgo told me that as she felt her student should follow Beatrice with an impressive leading role, they had to wait for the right opportunity:

Remember it was wartime and Athens an occupied city. Maria, to be sure, did have vocal problems. Even then her striving for dramatic expression was considerable and at that time her vocal technique was not sufficient to meet this challenge all the time. Naturally we constantly endeavoured to improve the technique without narrowing, but rather widening, the scope of expression. As for the machinations of jealous colleagues, they only made Maria work even harder. I believe that it was after Boccaccio that Maria learned to be a fighter and a survivor, not a victim.

Although battles had been raging in most of Europe since 1939, it was not until 28 October 1940 that Mussolini declared war on Greece. The Greek army, small but brave, proved more than a match for the large invading forces. Soon the Italians were repelled and driven into Albania for the whole of the winter. Then Hitler's army came. On 6 April 1941 Salonika was extensively bombed and after sixteen days of bloodshed the Greek army was obliterated. The German occupation of Athens began on 27 April 1941, lasting until 12 October 1944. The Italian troops arrived in late 1941 and left in September 1943. For a time Greece was in a chaotic state, and starvation was soon killing the old and the weak. Quite often people had to walk to far-away farms in the hope of getting vegetables. For the Callas family any communication with Kalogeropoulos in New York was impossible and his dollars, however few, no longer arrived. 'Only those', Maria often recalled (*Oggi*, 1957, and on other occasions to me),

who have experienced the miseries of occupation and starvation can know what liberty and a normal existence mean. The occupation of Athens was the most painful period of my life and even now I find it difficult to talk about it for fear of opening old wounds. I remember the winter of 1941 only too well. It was the coldest in Athens within living memory, and it snowed for the first time in twenty years. For the whole summer I ate only tomatoes and cabbage, which I managed to get after walking miles and begging farmers in the country to spare a few vegetables. It was extremely dangerous for the farmers to let anybody have even a little bit of their produce; if the implacable Germans had found out the farmers would have faced the firing squad. Nevertheless, I always managed to get something from the poor farmers.

Then, I think in March 1941, my sister's wealthy fiancé brought us a small cask of oil, some cornflour and potatoes. I will never forget the incredulous stupefaction with which my mother, Jackie [Iakinthy] and myself looked at those most precious goods. We feared at the same time that they might vanish through some kind of witchcraft.

Later on, when the Italians came, conditions generally improved a little. It was, however, a miracle when a butcher, who admired my singing in the theatre, probably took pity on my increasing emaciation. As his shop had been requisitioned by the army of occupation he introduced me to the Italian official in charge of distributing provisions to the troops. The Italian was willing to sell me ten kilos of meat once a month for a meagre sum of money. So I gladly strapped the rather heavy package to my shoulders and walked for an hour under the hottest sun, as if I were happily carrying flowers. That meat, which we could not store as we did not have a refrigerator, became our only capital; we resold most of it to our neighbours and friends, and with the proceeds we were able to buy other indispensable things and, with God's help, we survived. Since the occupation I have not been able to bear the thought of wasted food.

During these years the Callases met several Italian officers, who very often brought them food, and Maria was able to practise her Italian with them. Hidalgo had often urged her to learn the language. 'It will be very useful for you,' she kept on telling her pupil, 'because sooner or later you will have to go to Italy. Only there will it be possible to pursue your career and if you are to interpret your music well it is imperative to know the exact meaning of every word.'

Although Maria was very keen on her teacher's idea she did not know how to go about it:

I couldn't pay for private lessons and I most certainly wasn't going to ask help from the Fascists' headquarters as some people suggested, because my compatriots would rightly have considered me a traitor. Nevertheless, I bet my teacher that in three months I would be conversing in Italian with her. At that time, luckily, I had met four young Greek doctors who had studied in Italy and promised to help me and perhaps because I liked the language so much and the opportunity came my way to practise conversation with Italians, I won the bet with my teacher.

But to return to the early days of the occupation: when a few months later life somehow eased a little and the Germans allowed schools, theatres and public places to reopen, the Athens Opera also resumed its activities, albeit on a somewhat restricted scale. Even so, Hidalgo's plan (she was a great artistic influence at the Athens Opera) for Maria materialized: Callas returned to the stage in the title role in *Tosca* in the summer of 1942. Writing (*Vradhyni*, Athens, 28 August 1942) about Callas's first Tosca, Alexandra Lalaouni showed extraordinary perception:

Tosca is a difficult opera to produce and especially on the small stage of the theatre at Klathmonos Square. But everything, the scenic mistakes of the first act and so forth were forgotten from the moment Maria Kalogeropoulou [Callas], a young girl, a child seventeen years old, who is still a student of the famous singer Elvira de Hidalgo, appeared on the stage. Not only does she sustain the role comfortably, and sing it correctly but at the same time she is able to live it with insight and convey it to the audience who were often moved. A true miracle. Her voice is rich all through its long register and she knows how to produce it and give meaning to the words. But, however good her training is, it seems to me that there is something else about her; the deep natural musicianship, instinct and understanding of theatre are qualities that she could not have learnt at school, not at her age anyway; she was born with them. It was not at all surprising that she electrified her audience.

Sophia Spanoudi (*Athenaika Nea*, 28 August 1942) also praised the young singer but felt that 'her magnificent, dramatic soprano voice had not yet fully formed'. Hamoudopoulos (*Proia*, 29 August 1942) detected a slight hardness that once or twice crept into her voice, but was stunned by the way 'Kalogeropoulou acted her role with her voice as well as with her body – such accomplishment one rarely finds even among the most experienced artists'.

Callas's extraordinary success in a major role established her as one of the most important singers in Greece. Her detractors were unable to criticize her artistic achievement but these performances provided the *mise-en-scène* of a fabricated incident which effectively presented to the world a distorted picture of Callas's personality and which was widely publicized in 1956 in the United States, at a time when she was about to make her Metropolitan Opera début. The alleged incident referred to an occasion in 1941 when the seventeen-and-a-half-year-old Callas successfully substituted, at twenty-four hours' notice, for an indisposed soprano as Tosca at the Athens Opera. The story held that the indisposed soprano sent her husband to stop this upstart taking her role and that Maria scratched his face, but apparently received a black eye in return. Another version alleged that Maria collected her black eye when she attacked someone backstage who had used abusive language against her to the effect that 'this fat bitch will never last the performance out'.

None of the people who were present and closely associated with the performance remembered such an incident. Nikos Zographos, who made her dress for the performance, her first stage dress, did not recall anything of the kind, nor did Antonis Dhellentas, the leading tenor. To me, Callas merely said that it had never happened. Nor did she ever substitute for another singer in *Tosca*. Furthermore, in Greece she never sang in *Tosca* at short notice: on the contrary, her performances were meticulously rehearsed.

An examination of the theatre's archives vindicates Callas completely. *Tosca* was first performed at the Athens Opera on 27 August 1942 (not in 1941 when the incident is supposed to have occurred) with Callas as the eponymous heroine in all the performances. She was chosen for the role from the beginning and as it was a new production (the first in this theatre) it was fully rehearsed over the unusually long period of three months, and rehearsals photographs have survived.

The commander of the Italian army of occupation was so impressed with *Tosca* that he arranged for Callas, Dhellentas, Petros Epitropakis, Fanny Papanastassiou, Spiros Kalogheras and other singers from the Athens Opera to give a concert of Rossini's music in Salonika for the

Callas rehearsing Tosca *with Kourousopoulos*
(Cavaradossi) in Athens, 1942.

Salonika, 1942: Standing: Epitropakis, Papanastasiou, Evangelia (Callas's mother), Kalogheras, Flery, Paridis. Kneeling: Callas.

150th anniversary of the composer's birth. Maria, accompanied by her mother and her colleagues, arrived there in mid-October and at their own request they were paid in food supplies, which they took back to Athens.

After *Tosca* Maria Kalogeropoulou, as she was known in Greece, became one of the Athens Opera's leading sopranos. Her salary – doubled to 3000 drachmas (about £2.50) per month – though not high, did amount to something in those difficult times. However, for the next year her appearances were few, possibly because the situation restricted the authorities' abilities to offer her a new role. Her next engagement was in February 1943, when she sang in the intermezzo of Kalomiris's *Ho Protomastoras*, and in April at the Italian Institute of Culture for Greece in Pergolesi's oratorio *Stabat Mater*, a performance which was also broadcast live.

During the following July she embarked on a series of revivals of *Tosca* and gave her first concert in Athens at the Mousouri Theatre. Her long programme, which included arias by Handel, Rossini, Cilea and Verdi, formed the first part of the concert (the second comprised orchestral music) as Callas was also appearing as Tosca later the same evening.

Encouraged by her success, she returned to Salonika with her mother, the instigator of the project, who quickly arranged for them to stay with relations so that Maria could give two recitals for the people, rather than Italian soldiers. When Callas, looking fat, appeared on the stage of the White Tower theatre the audience at first chuckled, but once she began to sing (Rossini arias and *Lieder* by Schubert and Brahms), they were immediately captivated. Her second recital was sold out.

Italy's surrender to the Allied forces in September 1943 greatly strengthened Greek resistance fighters, who increasingly began to drive the Germans out of the countryside. Within a year only Athens and the larger cities were still occupied. Maria's contributions to the rejoicing were concerts in Athens on 26 September in aid of Greek–Egyptian students and in December in aid of consumptives. She was in excellent voice and her dramatic interpretations and versatility (the programmes included arias from *Fidelio, Aida, Thaïs, Il trovatore, Semiramide,* and Spanish and Greek songs) were very impressive. 'Bel raggio lusinghier' (*Semiramide*) persuaded the critic Psaroudas that this dramatic soprano was capable of singing coloratura brilliantly and he recommended that she be offered a lyric-coloratura part. Her success paved the way to her being entrusted with the leading role of Marta in the Greek première of D'Albert's *Tiefland,* which the Athens Opera was mounting in April 1944.

Iakinthy wrote in *Sisters* that several singers refused to sing in this very German opera but that Maria seized the opportunity with alacrity. This is an odd comment as the artists engaged were the most accomplished of their time and would not have been anyone's second choice. Dhellentas was cast as Pedro and the baritone Evangelios Mangliveras as Sebastiano. Mangliveras was one of Greece's most famous singers who had also sung with success abroad. Although he was now over forty and vocally somewhat past his prime, his amazing acting ability and stage

Maria in the spring of 1944.

experience still commanded attention. His friendship with the twenty-year-old Maria was immediate and he taught his young friend important points of stagecraft. *Tiefland* was an all-round artistic success.

Herzog, a German musicologist, recorded (*Deutche Nachrichten in Griechenland*, 23 April 1944) that 'There was earthy naturalness in Kalogeropoulou's portrayal of Marta. Whereas most singers have to learn their art, she is naturally endowed with dramatic instinct, great intensity and freedom in her acting. There is a powerful metallic quality in her upper register and the quiet passages exhibit the great variety of precious colours that her youthful and innately musical soprano voice possesses'.

Two weeks later, before the *Tiefland* performances were completed, Callas followed with Santuzza in *Cavalleria rusticana* – the first role she had sung as a student. She restudied the part with her teacher and, with the new assurance she had acquired, confirmed that her achievements were by no means happy accidents. The critic of the *Deutsche Nachrichten in Griechenland* (9 May 1944) gave his unqualified praise: 'Kalogeropoulou made a Santuzza of impulsive temperament. She is a dramatic soprano who produces her voice effortlessly and most sensitively; the "tears in the voice" are very much in evidence'.

Nevertheless Spanoudi (*Athenaika Nea*, 7 June 1944) had her reservations. She wrote: 'Kalogeropoulou's Santuzza is very interesting, passionate and never dull. However, I must mention that although her vocalization is generally accomplished, she does on occasion tend to shout. If she learns to exercise more control over her voice she will be even more moving'.

Callas further proved her worth on 21 May, when she sang 'Casta Diva' (*Norma*), one of the loveliest and most difficult of arias, in a concert given in aid of the artists' benevolent fund. Her success as Marta and Santuzza, and no less her 'Casta Diva', played a significant part in Kalomiris's decision to offer her – his ex-student at the conservatory who had once been so arrogant – the lead, Smaragda, in his opera *Ho Protomastoras*, composed in 1915. The role was to be shared by three prima donnas, each giving two performances. Callas mastered the difficulties and proved worthy of the composer's expectations (he also conducted) even though at her first performance she was far from well. Lalaouni (*Vradhyni*, 9 August 1944) wrote that with 'Kalogeropoulou as Smaragda I have once more enjoyed the innate theatrical talent that this very young artist possesses, even though on this occasion vocally she was not up to her role because of serious indisposition'.

The bass, Nicola Zaccaria, who sang in the chorus on these occasions, told me that Callas did recover from her indisposition and gave her best, both vocally and dramatically, at her second performance.

A few days later Callas was faced with an exciting prospect: the Athens Opera found itself without a Leonore in Beethoven's *Fidelio*. She recalled the circumstances in which she was given

The cast of Ho Protomastoras. *Standing: Doumanis (Old Man), Callas (Smaragda), Dhellentas (Protomastoras), Mangliveras (Rich Man), Remoundou (Smaragda). Front: Kalomiris (sitting, the composer), Zoras (conductor), Ghalanou (Singer).*

this most demanding role in an article in *Oggi* (10 January 1957): 'When the Athens Opera decided to produce *Fidelio* another soprano was determined to get the role and succeeded. However, she did not bother to learn it and as rehearsals had to begin without delay they asked me to substitute as I was the next in line. I accepted the offer without hesitation because I already knew the role perfectly'.

Lalaouni (*Vradhyni* 17 August 1944) declared that as Leonore 'Kalogeropoulou gave all her rich theatrical talent, her beautiful voice, her musical perception and was genuinely moving. Of course vocally she has a lot to correct and learn. However, if we consider her youth and inexperience we can only applaud the first Greek Leonore'.

The critic of *Kathimerini* (18 August 1944) thought 'Kalogeropoulou interpreted the role of Leonore with disciplined ardour, warmth and complete understanding. Hers is a big talent and if she corrects some unevenness in her voice and diction, she will go very far'.

Elvira de Hidalgo interestingly told me that 'Maria sang this role like an opera singer of the front rank. I say opera singer because her portrayal was not merely an accomplished exercise in

42

A break from rehearsals of Fidelio: *Dhellentas (Florestan), Hörner (conductor), Callas (Leonore).*

Cast of Fidelio. *Left: Moulas, Vlachopoulos, Hörner, Callas, Mangliveras, Dhellentas, Generalis. Kneeling: Bardi-Kokolios.*

vocalization but already the expression was convincing and moving. Although she was young and relatively without much experience, she succeeded in a role that other established singers take years to do'.

Nicola Zaccaria, who sang in the chorus, was deeply moved by Callas's Leonore. Years later, after he had sung the role of Don Fernando with other famous Leonores in Salzburg and elsewhere, he could never forget these performances: 'Even though Leonore is a very difficult role,' he commented, 'there have always been good singers with creditable performances to their name. But I have never heard anyone who excelled both vocally and dramatically and had, at the same time, the freshness, the spontaneity of the twenty-year-old Callas'.

Callas's imaginative characterization turned out to be her most noteworthy success so far. It went beyond artistic achievement. But first we must examine the circumstances and the state of affairs that prevailed in occupied Athens at the time when *Fidelio* was to have its first ever performance in Greece, on 14 August 1944. It was also the last year of the occupation, which turned out to have been the most difficult, the most tragic.

While the allied troops were victoriously advancing in North Africa and Southern Italy, the National Greek Resistance pushing the occupational forces out of the countryside, the Gestapo and the SS adopted the tactic of attack as the best defence; thousands of Greeks were executed for unspecified revolutionary activities. In this precarious atmosphere, the Greeks, united, endeavoured to keep their spirits high, giving special attention to the performances of *Fidelio* at Herodes Atticus theatre on the Acropolis.

Beethoven's *Fidelio*, the most profound hymn of freedom, is depicted allegorically through Leonore's selfless love and devotion for her imprisoned husband, whom she eventually succeeds in freeing. It was, therefore, courageous of the artist, especially for Callas as Leonore, to impress upon their German conquerors (who, together with the Greeks, crowded the vast theatre), the triumph of liberty.

The nineteen-year-old Callas, whose prodigious artistry had already made its mark with the Greeks, the Germans and the Italians, surpassed herself in the crucial scene, 'Abscheulicher' ('Accursed monster ... Doesn't the voice of humanity touch your Tiger-mind?'), which precedes the scene when the prisoners are allowed out of their cells for a breath of fresh air. The enthusiasm of the Greeks, who readily understood the message, knew no bounds, their deafening applause giving Callas and the 'temporarily' liberated prisoners, a standing ovation.

There was more to come. The final scene, after the prisoners are freed, and Leonore, united with her husband ('Oh, indescribable joy'), proceeds to unlock his fetters, moved the oppressed audience first to tears and then to an incredible demonstration of jubilation, which culminated in the apotheosis of Leonore, their own Maria Kalogeropoulou, and all the cast of this historic performance.

Word of these patriotic demonstrations spread like lightning outside the theatre to the whole of Athens. The news seemed to be assuring the people that the hour of their liberation was imminent, and as it happened, a few weeks later on 12 October 1944, Athens was indeed liberated by Greek resistance troops.

The rejoicing, however, was short-lived. Greece was facing a new major crisis. On 3 December civil war broke out over the issue of Communist domination. Many died in the street fighting that followed and life came to a standstill, which was more terrifying than the occupation. For a time food was impossible to find and as the fighting continued most people remained shut in their homes for several days.

Maria's life also changed course. Following the performance of *Fidelio* the Athens Opera granted her three months' leave, whereupon her mother promptly found a job for her at the British headquarters.

> I was assigned to the department for the distribution of confidential mail [Maria later recalled]. We started work at eight, but I had to get up at six thirty because in order to save money I always walked all the way to the office which was very far from my house. The British offered us a plentiful midday meal, which I did not eat at the headquarters but had put in a pot which I then carried home to share with my mother. (My sister was not living with us at the time.) My lunch break was one and a half hours but it took me over an hour to walk home and back. I did this until the winter.

The intervention of the British troops ended the civil war, which had lasted forty bloody days. Maria Kalogeropoulou, the new star of the Athens Opera, however, was beginning her own battle. Some of her less successful colleagues tried to justify their inactivity by accusing her of having been too friendly with, and too anxious to sing for, the armies of occupation.

Both the Germans and the Italians had kept a sharp eye on the Greek theatres, particularly the opera. Callas sang during those years, as did many other artists. No Greek singer is known to have turned down any engagement offered by the company at this time. Those who were not asked to sing became pseudo-patriots through misfortune rather than choice and if they directed their accusations more fiercely against Callas it was because she was young, bright, exciting and above all successful. 'For her part,' Amaxopoulou confirmed,

> Maria was natural, quiet and kind. A good and loyal friend with a straight character . . . she always had the courage of her own sincere convictions. She could not tolerate insincere, deceitful people . . . never pried into other people's business, neither when she was a student nor when she joined the Athens Opera, but would only comment favourably on their achievements. Her studies and art were her only interest . . . Everybody really

admired her, but many, deep down, hated her for her success, for her great talent . . . and by undermining her they strove to destroy her artistic career, hoping to banish her from the theatre world of her country.

This hatred and condemnation is vividly expressed in an article by Margarita Dalmati, published in the magazine *New Thought* (no. 176/7, 1977), who wrote: 'During the occupation we were all united . . . in our hatred for the traitors, the black marketeers, and those who were friendly with the Germans and Italians. In such a silent conspiratorial atmosphere it was inevitable for Kalogeropoulou not to be liked . . . We were deprived of all those things that can transform even the ugliest side of life into something beautiful. She had plenty to eat and she could "scream", as we said about her. This was her whole life'. Neither Dalmati's credibility nor her sincerity can stand up to scrutiny, for she does not name, obviously purposely, those united in their resentment of Callas. Because she sang during the occupation Dalmati declared her, by implication, to have been a traitor. It is amazing that Dalmati chose not to remember the grand concert on 21 May 1944, organized and paid for fully by the German Broadcasting Corporation in occupied Athens, when all the most accomplished Greek actors, singers, conductors (as well as the German Hans Hörner), dancers, instrumentalists and others (Dalmati not included) connected with the theatre world participated in a very long programme of thirty-four items. Callas sang 'Casta Diva'. What the pseudo-patriots did not want to understand was that during the occupation Greek artists had to do their public relations work with the enemy. In the absence of military strength it is only through the arts that an occupied people can fight with honour and those who help the people to survive are the true patriots.

Pierre-Jean Remy says (*Callas – Une Vie*, Paris 1978) that *Tiefland* 'was clearly put on to please the Germans and this may have been one of the reasons for the accusations levelled against Maria once the war was over'. However, the facts are different. After the liberation (12 October 1944), the Athens Opera resumed its activities on 4 November. *Manon* and *Lucia di Lammermoor* were the first works performed, both being revivals without Callas but with singers who had originally sung in these productions. With the outbreak of the civil war on 3 December all the theatres in Athens closed down until the end of January 1945. On 14 March Callas began a series of performances as Marta in a revival of *Tiefland*, certainly not to please the Germans or any other enemy of Greece. Her own enemies, to be sure, continued their attack, pressurizing the administration of the opera not to renew her contract. Maria found out through her uncle, Constantine Louros, that several of her colleagues had protested passionately to Prime Minister Rallis that if he allowed the superintendent of the Athens Opera to renew her contract they would resort to an all-out strike. 'It was downright disgraceful', they argued vociferously, 'that a girl of twenty-one be considered on the same level with artists of their calibre and seniority'.

The whole episode, in its evident unfairness, was hurtful to Callas. It was clear to her that her colleagues were motivated by personal jealousy – artistic talent and the ability to apply it constructively never has anything to do with seniority based on age. Consequently Callas faced the superintendent with full confidence and not a little defiance. She listened attentively to his lame excuses for not re-engaging her and retaliated: 'Let's hope that you will not regret this one day! I can only tell you that I have, in fact, already decided to go to America.'

With the ending of the war the American Embassy in Athens strongly urged Callas to return to the United States without delay, so that she could retain her American citizenship. In fact, they lent her money for her passage to New York. Furthermore Athens, irrespective of her dismissal from the opera, could hardly offer much more for such an ambitious artist. America was another matter entirely.

There was a dissenting voice. Although Hidalgo agreed that Maria should leave Greece, she insisted that her pupil's future lay most definitely in Italy and not in America or anywhere else. 'Once you are established in Italy', Hidalgo maintained, 'the whole world will come to you.' But Maria's mind was made up, chiefly because she had a father there to go to and not out of any disrespect for her teacher and friend. Apparently Hidalgo was insistent up to the last minute and, as she was bidding her a final tearful farewell at Piraeus, raised her parasol and her voice, and declared, 'I still think you should to go Italy'.

There was yet another dissenting voice. Mangliveras's friendship, which began with their performances in *Tiefland*, soon grew into love and he declared himself willing to leave his wife and children in order to marry her. Even though Maria admired the artist and was fond of the man, at that time she felt that there was only room for music in her heart. But he would not accept this answer and continued in vain to woo her, writing her passionate love letters. She returned them and told him firmly but affectionately, 'You must not ask of me my life. You are the finest of men but you are not free. Even if you were, my answer would have been the same. I can only be married to my art for the moment. You will always be a wonderful friend and that is really more important.'

Although Callas's relationship with Mangliveras was rather closer than ordinary friendship, it is difficult to determine the degree of intimacy involved. When in 1977 she spoke to me about her personal life she remembered Mangliveras fondly, but only as a very good artist, and a marvellous colleague and friend. Evangelia, a very shrewd woman who was until 1947 Maria's constant chaperone, said in her book *My Daughter Maria Callas* (1960) that she grew up with a sound moral sense and without conscious prudery. 'She had her flirts with whom she laughed and innocently enjoyed herself. But I am positive that she had no lover or wanted one . . . even then she cared more for her career than for love.'

In the meantime the Athens Opera was producing Millöcker's operetta, *Der Bettelstudent*. As her contract had not yet officially expired, Callas was very keen to sing the leading part of Laura: 'Before departing I wanted to give them a last sample of my art to remember me more vividly; they were obliged to entrust the difficult role to me because no one else could sing it.' Callas dazzled the Athenians with her versatility, prompting Sophia Spanoudi (*Ta Nea*, 7 September 1945) to declare her performance an unqualified success: 'Kalogeropoulou is a dramatic artist of high calibre both vocally and musically – as Cornélie Falcon was – who has the difficult-to-attain ability to unravel the fascinations of a lyric soprano in a light role and after she has already given us her memorably dramatic portrayal in *Tiefland*.'

The critic of *Ethnos* described Callas as 'a unique artist. The Athens Opera must try, with every possible means, to keep her here.'

After completing eight performances, the last on 13 September, Callas prepared to leave Greece the next day. Following her mother's advice, she did not inform her father, whom she had not seen for almost eight years, of her imminent arrival in New York. She had written to him nine months before, when she proudly sent him a stage picture of herself as Leonore (*Fidelio*) with a note: 'I send you a souvenir of what the newspapers here described as a historical event.' She signed it, 'Your younger daughter, Maria'. It is not known how Kalogeropoulos reacted to his daughter's early success. His answer did not reach Athens. Even so, Evangelia's advice to her daughter was obviously based on ulterior motives; she was hoping that Maria might well be disillusioned with him if she caught him living with some loose woman. This was all the more surprising as Evangelia and Iakinthy did not see Maria off at Piraeus. According to her, her mother and sister simply refused to come because they thought they wouldn't have been able to stand the commotion. Evangelia's version, given many years later and after she broke with her younger daughter, was entirely different. She alleged – or invented – that her famous daughter was not dismissed by the Athens Opera and that the mayor of Piraeus gave her a farewell luncheon to which neither she nor Iakinthy was invited, because Maria did not want them there. This story does not hold water. It was Dr Papatesta and his wife, family friends and neighbours of the Kalogeropouloses, who gave Maria a farewell luncheon at Piraeus and both Evangelia and Iakinthy declined the invitation to join the party, which included Elvira de Hidalgo. Maria bade farewell to her family at home.

Her personal feelings at the time, which she could remember vividly many years later, were those of a penniless young woman whose courage in meeting the unknown, alone but with a purpose, overcame her many fears:

> It is only now, after so many years, that I realize what dangerous risks I was taking and
> what grave consequences I could have encountered in returning to America at twenty-one,
> alone and without a cent and so soon after the end of a world war, and with the terrible

prospect of failing to track down either my father or any of my old friends. I do not mean to imply that I was brave but the naïve innocence of youth gave me the courage and ambition to accomplish something with my singing. There was something deeper behind what we normally call courage; an instinct, unlimited faith in God that would not fail me.

Maria Kalogeropoulou sailed on the SS *Stockholm* for the New World to pursue her mission in life.

1   Hidalgo taught singing in Ankara from 1949 to 1959, later moving to Milan, where she was engaged as a voice coach at La Scala for two seasons. Afterwards she taught singing privately. She died in Milan on 21 January 1980.
2   In due course Callas's growing repertoire included, apart from opera, other vocal music: the soprano parts in Handel's *Messiah*, Pizzetti's *I tre canti Greci*, Bach's *St Matthew Passion*, Mozart's *Requiem*, Haydn's *Requiem*, Pergolesi's *Stabat Mater*, Purcell's opera *Dido and Aeneas* and *Lieder* by Schubert and Brahms.

CHAPTER THREE

AMERICA REVISITED

GEORGES KALOGEROPOULOS HAD learned by chance of his daughter's arrival in New York from the passenger list published in one of the American Greek-language newspapers, but with good reason could not recognize her when she disembarked in the autumn of 1945. He had not seen her for eight years and the slim thirteen-year-old girl he knew was now a tall, attractive, if rather fat, woman. Maria, however, knew him from photographs they had in Athens. 'I really could not find words', she later recalled, 'to describe my boundless happiness and relief when I recognized my father, the person I least expected to see on my arrival in New York.' For a while time stood still. It was as if neither the Depression in America nor the terrible occupation and civil war in Greece had ever happened, and father and daughter were moved to tears of joy.

At the time Kalogeropoulos was working in a Greek drugstore and had an apartment on West 157th Street. Maria was happy to stay with him until she realized that the Greek woman, Alexandra Papajohn, an old family friend who now lived upstairs in their block, was her father's mistress. The situation soon became tense and after an argument with her father, who was reluctant to change the situation, Maria moved to the Astor Hotel. Eventually she returned home, when Georges paid her hotel bill and agreed to her condition that Miss Papajohn would no longer run their home.

Maria adored her father and during the long years she was away from him she never stopped hoping that one day she would enjoy his affection. She was not prepared, now, to let 'that woman' take him away from his family, but with Miss Papajohn more or less out of the way Maria resumed her relationship with Georges. She also missed her mother, from whom she was separated for the first time in her life, and wanted her to come to New York. Above all, she wanted her parents together again. Evangelia was also eager to return to New York, if she could find the fare. As her husband could not afford to send it, Maria herself eventually borrowed the money from her godfather and made it possible for her mother to join them in America by Christmas 1946. Iakinthy remained in Athens with her fiancé. Maria was happy to see her parents under the same roof and if there was not much conjugal love between them they were at least friendly enough towards one another. Furthermore, the presence of her mother would be the most effective deterrent to her father's association with Miss Papajohn.

Maria with her father, New York, 1945.

In other ways, and this was of paramount importance to Maria, America soon proved to be a great disappointment, for hardly anybody seemed interested in the twenty-one-year-old star of the Athens Opera with several roles to her credit; she realized all too clearly, with bitterness, that she would have to start all over again. At first, she tried to get help from the Greek singer Nicola Moscona, whom she had met in Greece and who had predicted a great future for her. Moscona, now a permanent member of the Metropolitan Opera, forgot all about his prediction and refused even to see her. He let it be understood later that he was wary of young, unknown sopranos who wanted him to arrange auditions for them with Arturo Toscanini, the celebrated conductor, for whom Moscona had already sung in concerts. Whether this was a genuine reason or a mere pretext on his part will never be known. He could have put in a good word for Maria with Edward

Johnson, the general manager of the Metropolitan Opera. When she got no response from Moscona she persisted independently and eventually was given an audition with Johnson.

The result was an offer to sing Leonore (*Fidelio*) in English and the title role in *Madama Butterfly* in Italian in the Metropolitan's forthcoming 1946–7 season. Strong-willed and determined to get ahead, but only in the way she considered right, Maria, in spite of great hardship, turned down the offer. She would not sing a German opera in English, nor would she, weighing over 90 kilos at the time, appear as the fragile Butterfly. It is almost certain that language was not the main reason for her refusal to sing in *Fidelio*. After all, in 1944 she had sung the opera with great success in Greek in occupied Athens. As her subsequent career demonstrated and from what we later learned about her own views on operatic repertory it is my belief that Callas, even then, wanted to make her début, especially in such an important theatre as the Metropolitan, in a role, preferably Italian, which dominates the opera and thus would have provided her with the opportunity to appear at her most impressive and to be accepted as a singer of the front rank. Had she not been fat and been offered Butterfly for her début, she might well have accepted. According to her she suggested Aida or Tosca instead, even without pay, but Johnson would not hear of it. He had made his offer and that was that. Maria had given her answer, perhaps too rashly, but it seems that she knew what she wanted.

Many years later Johnson, recalling this audition said, 'We were very much impressed and recognized her as a talented young woman. We did offer Callas the contract but she did not like it. She was right in turning it down. It was frankly a beginner's contract; she was without experience, without repertory. She was quite overweight, but that did not come into our thinking at all – the young ones are usually too fat.'

Johnson's rather ambiguous statement vaguely implies that Callas refused the contract because of its bad terms, not the roles on offer, which is hard to believe. He would not, or possibly could not, be flexible, for the repertoire of a major opera house cannot readily be altered to suit an individual singer, let alone an unknown. It is his dictatorial dismissal of Maria on the grounds that she was without experience that is debatable: subsequently Johnson gave the role in *Fidelio* to Regina Resnik, as untried then as the Callas of the Athens Opera. Furthermore, whoever was going to sing the part would have been following in the footsteps of the great Kirsten Flagstad and Lotte Lehmann, which makes it distinctly odd that a beginner should have been considered in the first place.

'One day,' the rebuffed Callas told Johnson in parting, 'the Metropolitan will go down on its knees to me, begging me to sing. Not only shall I then sing a suitable role but I shall not do it for nothing either.'

Another audition followed, this time with the San Francisco Opera, but nothing came of it. Gaetano Merola found her quite good, but as she was unknown and so young he offered her unsolicited advice: 'First make a name for yourself in Italy and then I'll sign you up.' Feeling rejected and furious, Maria retaliated, 'Thank you very much, but when I make my career in Italy I will most certainly no longer need you.'

Even though Richard Eddie Bagarozy's project for establishing an opera company in Chicago in 1947 with Callas as his star prima donna proved abortive, the event undoubtedly, though inadvertently, played a crucial part in the direction of her career. Bagarozy was a lawyer in New York, who, because opera was his main interest in life, before long gave up his profession to become an impresario, with the intention not only of managing the affairs of singers but one day to have his own opera company. His wife, Louise Caselotti, was a mezzo-soprano who had only found limited success dubbing voices in Hollywood musicals and had also gained a certain reputation as a singing teacher in New York.

Maria met the Bagarozys through Louise Taylor, an ex-singer, in January 1946 when she was desperately looking for work in New York. They liked her and her singing very much (Maria sang 'Casta Diva' for them) and soon became close friends. Louise began to coach Maria, who visited them practically every day. By the autumn of that year Eddie's enthusiasm for her singing and his association with Ottavio Scotto, an Italian agent for singers who had also worked for many years at the Teatro Colón in Buenos Aires, encouraged him to embark on his life's ambition – to create his own company, the United States Opera Company, with the policy of presenting the best European singers, as well as his wife, in America. For his venture Bagarozy chose Chicago, a city with memories still fresh of great operatic performances in the past, but without any current opera. Puccini's *Turandot*, then rarely performed, with Callas (billed as Marie Calas) in the title role, was to launch the company in January 1947. Since many European opera houses were not functioning in 1946 as a result of the war, Bagarozy and Scotto easily engaged quite a number of young and accomplished European singers – Cloe Elmo, Mafalda Favero, Galliano Masini, Luigi Infantino and Nicola Rossi-Lemeni came from Italy, the sisters Hilde and Anny Konetzni and Max Lorenz from Vienna and various singers came from the Paris Opéra. Sergio Failoni from Italy was to conduct. This was quite an achievement, for Bagarozy had no money, relying on his wits and flair to drum up enthusiasm and a sense of participation in something excitingly creative with artists, the press and of course would-be financiers. He succeeded in overcoming all problems – rehearsals took place in his apartment – except one. At practically the eleventh hour the promised financial support failed to appear and the American Guild of Musical Artists demanded a considerable deposit that would safeguard the salaries of the members of the chorus. Bagarozy and Scotto, failing to raise the money within three weeks, had no alternative but to declare themselves bankrupt and consequently there was no *Turandot* with 'Marie Calas', or anything else. A benefit concert helped the stranded artists to return home.

Callas on board the SS Rossia *to Italy, June 1947.*

One of them, the bass Nicola Rossi-Lemeni, was engaged to sing for the forthcoming Opera Festival season at the Arena di Verona in Italy.[1] The famous septuagenarian ex-tenor, Giovanni Zenatello (Puccini's original Pinkerton in *Madama Butterfly*), the artistic director of the festival, was at the time in New York looking for a soprano for the title role in Ponchielli's *La Gioconda* to open the season at the Arena. As his first choice, Herva Nelli, who was highly recommended by Toscanini, was too expensive, Zenatello was considering Zinka Milanov when Rossi-Lemeni suggested to him that he also hear Callas. He agreed and a delighted Maria auditioned for him at his apartment. With Louise at the piano she sang 'Suicidio', the aria from *La Gioconda*, and so impressed Zenatello that without fuss, he offered her a contract for at least four performances of *La Gioconda* at twenty pounds each. (Strangely Zenatello's evaluation of Callas in his letter to Gaetano Pomari, a Veronese restaurateur and one of the administrators of the Arena, said no more than 'She is rather interesting'. To the distinguished Maestro Tullio Serafin, who was to conduct the performances, however, Zenatello wrote that he thought very highly of Callas, although she had only sung in Greece so far, and that with her remarkable voice she should make an excellent Gioconda.)

Callas accepted the offer at once – certainly not for the money, which was shamefully little (no expenses were provided even though she was expected to be in Verona a month in advance for rehearsals), but because she wanted to sing the opera in Italy, if only for the future prospects it held out. However, she needed cash for her journey to Verona. With difficulty her father gave her some but it was the loan from her godfather that enabled her to go to Italy. Louise, who hoped to sing in opera but after the breakdown of her husband's company had no visible prospects in America, was also going to Italy to look for work. Four days before they sailed on the SS *Rossia* on 17 June 1947 Maria signed a contract appointing Bagarozy her general agent.

The journey was, for most of the time, rough, conditions on the Russian ship appalling. In my conversations with Maria in early 1977 she remembered this awful crossing:

> The ship was filthy, the attitude of the crew was just as filthy. It was like a troop-ship, and they had the audacity to expect the passengers, at the end of it all, to thank them in writing for the wonderful way they looked after us. Well, I needn't tell you what I did. Let us say I threw their document, which was filthy too, right into their faces. But really throughout the journey I had other more important things on my mind.
>
> I was reasonably well prepared with the score of *Gioconda* which I had studied in Greece and also with Louise and on my own as fastidiously as I could, for three months before I left America for Verona. Nevertheless, I was very tense and at times my worst fears were not so much for my work (I was fairly confident about it even then) but for

*Callas with **Louise** Caselotti and Nicola Rossi-Lemeni on the SS* Rossia.

life itself. Even though I was then twenty-three years old, it was the first time that I was alone, away from home, from my family and going to a foreign country. What gave me courage was my teacher, Hidalgo, whom I often felt to be with me (I still do sometimes) even when she was thousands of miles away. Her 'screaming' at me in Greece that for my career I should go to Italy and not America was the greatest incentive and strength that enabled me to pull myself together and get on with my life.

The *Rossia* arrived in Naples on 29 June and Maria, accompanied by Louise and Rossi-Lemeni, continued her journey to Verona by train. At that time this city meant nothing to her other than that she was going to sing Gioconda there. Not even in her most extravagant day-dreams would she have been able to envisage that precisely in Verona the most important events in her life would come to fruition.

1   The Verona Festival was inaugurated in 1913 with performances of *Aida*. Zenatello and his wife Maria Gay were the protagonists, Serafin the conductor. Except for the years of the World Wars, the Festival has been running regularly to the present day.

CAVALLERIA RUSTICANA

Opera in one act by Mascagni; libretto by Menasci and Targioni-Tozzetti. First performed at the Teatro Costanzi (Rome Opera) on 17 May 1890.

Under the name Maria Kalogeropoulou, Callas successfully made her operatic début in the principal role of Santuzza in *Cavalleria* (three performances) on 2 April 1939 at the National Conservatory in Athens where she was still a student and only fifteen years and four months old. In May 1944 she sang Santuzza (three performances) as a member of the Athens Opera.

Callas as Santuzza (front left, kneeling) in the scene of the 'Easter Hymn'.

BOCCACCIO

Operetta in three acts by Suppé; libretto by F. Zell (pseudonym of Camillo Walzell) and R. Genée. First performed at the Carl Theater, Vienna, on 1 February 1879.

Callas sang Beatrice in *Boccaccio* (her professional début) in Athens in February and July 1941, a total of about eighteen performances.

Left Scalza, the barber (Kaloyannis), accompanied by Lotteringhi, a cooper (Ksirellis) and Lambertuccio, a grocer (Stylianopoulos), surprises his young wife Beatrice (Callas), who is entertaining her lover at home. Cleverly she creates a diversion by appearing frightened, though relieved that her husband has come, in the nick of time, to protect her from an 'intruder'.

Below left Having been mistaken for Boccaccio, Prince Pietro receives a beating from those Florentines who want to banish the poet from the city. Scalza, however, recognises the Prince, who eventually pardons his floggers. From right: Prince Pietro (Horn), Checco (Generalis), Lambertuccio, Fiametta (Vlachopoulos), Peronella (Moustaka), Isabella (Kourahani) and Beatrice.

Below Callas's first professional curtain-call.

TOSCA

Opera in three acts by Puccini; libretto by Giacosa and Illica. First performed at the Teatro Costanzi (Rome Opera) on 14 January 1900.

Callas first sang Tosca (her first professional major role) in Athens on 27 August 1942, with considerable success. Afterwards she sang the role very rarely until 1964 when her characterization became supreme.

Above Act 1: The entrance of Tosca (Callas). Dhellentas as Mario.

Above right Act 2: Tosca comforts the tortured Mario.

Right Tosca curses the dying Scarpia (Ksirellis): 'Muori dannato! Muori!' ('Die damned!') Athens Opera, 1942.

HO PROTOMASTORAS

Opera in two parts by Manolis Kalomiris; libretto arranged from Nicos Kazantzakis's tragedy of the same title which in turn was based on the *Legend of Arta*. First performed at the Municipal Theatre, Athens on 11 March 1916. Callas sang the role of Smaragda twice at the Athens Opera (Herodes Atticus Theatre) in July/August 1944.

Above The Old Woman (Bourdakou, centre) decrees to Protomastoras, the Master Builder (Dhellentas, left) that further disorders can only be averted if he names the woman who has given herself to him. Right: Smaragda (Callas), The Rich Man (Mangliveras) and the Old Peasant (Doumanis).

Left The Rich Man (Athenaios) curses Smaragda, his daughter, who has to go through with her sacrifice.

TIEFLAND

Opera in a prologue and two acts by d'Albert; libretto by Lothar. First performed at the Neues Deutsches Theater, Prague, on 15 November 1903.

Callas sang Marta in *Tiefland* at the Athens Opera eight times in April 1944 and three in March 1945.

Right *Act 1: The interior of the mill.* Marta (Callas) despairs ... She had not been brave enough to kill herself to be free of Sebastiano (Mangliveras), her employer, and now she is forced to marry Pedro, a mountain lout. Nevertheless when she repulses Sebastiano's amoral advances, he makes it clear that Marta is still his property – even after her marriage.

Below left and right Sebastiano stops the newly weds from returning to the mountains and orders Marta to dance for him. When Pedro forbids her to do so Sebastiano's men throw him out and Marta faints. Revived, Sebastiano tries to rape her, but after a desperate struggle she frees herself and her cries bring Pedro back. The two men fight and Pedro strangles him.

FIDELIO

Opera in two acts by Beethoven; libretto (final version as revised in 1814) by Treitschke. First performed (final version) at the Kärnthnerthor Theater, Vienna, on 23 May 1814.

Callas sang Leonore (in Greek) ten or twelve times in Athens during August and September 1944.

Left *Act 1: The courtyard of the State Prison.* Rocco, naïvely believing that Fidelio returns the love of his daughter Marzelline, hints that the young man will be rewarded. While Marzelline is very happy, 'Mir ist so wunderbar' ('It is so wonderful'), Fidelio (Leonore in disguise) is upset by the situation. Left to right: Fidelio (Callas), Rocco (Moulas), Marzelline (Vlachopoulos).

Below Fidelio has overheard Pizarro, the Governor of the Prison, bribing Rocco to murder the special prisoner kept isolated in the dark dungeon. Suspecting that this prisoner is Florestan, her husband, she is horrified: 'Abscheulicher!' ('Accursed monster!') . . . Her courage returning, Fidelio determines to rescue her husband.

Right *Act 2: A dark subterranean dungeon.* As Pizarro (Mangliveras) is about to stab Florestan, Fidelio springs between them: 'Töt' erst sein Weib!' ('First you must kill his wife!'). When Pizarro attempts to kill them both, Leonore draws a pistol. A trumpet announcing Don Fernando, the Minister of State, forces Pizarro to leave the dungeon and Florestan is saved.

Below Leonore and Florestan (Dhellentas) are reunited: 'O namenlose Freude' ('O indescribable joy').

Above *The Parade Ground outside the Prison.* Don Fernando (Generalis) asks Leonore to remove her husband's fetters: 'Euch, edle Frau, allein, euch ziemt es ganz ihn zu befrein.' ('You, noble lady, alone have the right to set him free').

LA GIOCONDA

Opera in four acts by Ponchielli; libretto by Arrigo Boito (pen-name 'Tobia Gorrio'). First performed at La Scala on 8 April 1876.

Callas first sang Gioconda at the Arena di Verona (her Italian début) on 3 August 1947 and last at La Scala in February 1953, a total of thirteen performances.

Above Act I: Callas as Gioconda (Verona, 3 August 1947).

Right *The courtyard of the Doges' Palace, Venice.* Gioconda, a ballad singer, leads her blind mother, La Cieca (Danieli) to church. Barnaba (Tagliabue), a minstrel and spy of the Inquisition who lusts after Gioconda, watches unseen.

At her first utterance 'Madre adorata' ('Beloved mother'), Callas confirmed her loving relationship with her mother, and when Barnaba appeared revealed Gioconda's fiery side: 'Mi fai ribrezzo!' ('You disgust me!'). Confiding in her mother that Enzo, the man she loves, is to elope with Laura, Callas's deeply felt sorrow, her loneliness, carried the hint of fatalism that often precedes a tragedy in life: 'Il mio destino e questo: O morte o amor!' ('My destiny is either love or death!') (La Scala, 1952).

Above Gioconda promises to give herself to Barnaba if he will save Enzo.

Callas infused 'Il mio corpo t'abbandono, o terribile cantor' ('I will surrender my body to you, gruesome minstrel') with desperate yet dignified pathos – self-sacrifice remains her only weapon.

Right Act 4: *The hall of a dilapidated palace on the Orfano Canal, Giudecca, Venice.* Gioconda, seized by despair – Enzo is lost to her, her mother has disappeared – is contemplating suicide: 'Suicidio!' ('Suicide!')

Callas rose magnificently to the climax of the drama. She poured forth vast molten and lyrical sounds with fine musicianship – projected from dramatic soprano to opulent contralto. Through masterly inflexion and fusion of the music and words, Callas went through the gamut of emotion: introspective fatalism in 'Ultima croce del mio cammin' ('The final cross of my life'), almost ethereal beauty in 'E un dì leggiadre volavan l'ore' ('Once time flew gaily by'), complete resignation in 'Or piombo esausta fra le tenebre' ('I now sink exhausted in the darkness').

When Barnaba arrives to claim Gioconda, she stabs herself. Callas declaimed 'Demon maledetto! E il corpo ti do!' ('You cursed demon! You now have my corpse!') with stark realism, devoid of any sentimentality.

TRISTAN UND ISOLDE

Opera in three acts by Wagner; libretto by the composer. First performed at the Munich Hoftheater on 10 June 1865.

Callas first sang Isolde at La Fenice in December 1947 and last at the Rome Opera in February 1950, a total of twelve performances.

Act 2: *The garden in King Marke's castle in Cornwall. A summer night.* Tristan (Tasso), a Cornish knight, falls in love with the Irish Princess Isolde (Callas) whom he has brought as bride to King Marke, his beloved uncle. Eventually the King, led by Melot, surprises the lovers. When Isolde confirms that she will follow her lover anywhere and he kisses her, Melot wounds Tristan, who does not defend himself (La Fenice, 1947).

Act 3: *The garden of Tristan's Castle of Kareol on the coast of Brittany.* Gravely wounded by Melot, Tristan dies in Isolde's arms. Meanwhile King Marke (Christoff), having learned from Brangaene (Barbieri) that it was her potion that made Tristan fall in love with Isolde, arrives too late to pardon the lovers. Absorbed in her vision that she will find bliss in the profound depths of the spiritual world, Isolde sinks dead upon Tristan's body.

Callas's sensuous tone combined with sad tenderness created the illusion that Isolde's soliloquy, the 'Liebestod', is a long sigh constantly gaining in haunting ecstasy: her moving portrayal captured the essence, which is the reconciliation of love and death.

DIE WALKÜRE

Opera (Part 2 of *Der Ring des Nibelungen*) in three acts by Wagner; libretto by the composer. First performed in Munich on 26 June 1870.

Callas first sang Brünnhilde in *Die Walküre* at La Fenice in January 1949 and last at the Teatro Massimo, Palermo, in February 1949, a total of six performances.

Above Act 2: *A wild, craggy mountain pass.* Wotan (Torres) tells Brünnhilde to harness her horse and be ready to defend Siegmund in his fight with Hunding, who is of no use to them. Brünnhilde joyously leaps from rock to rock: 'Ho-jo-to-ho! Hei-a-ha!' (La Fenice, 1949).

Left Sadly Wotan tells Brünnhilde of the reversal of his decision to defend Siegmund: Wotan must yield to Fricka's demand that Siegmund shall die.

Left Act 3: *The summit of a rocky mountain.* Brünnhilde brings the pregnant Sieglinde to her sisters, the Valkyries, for their help; she is being furiously pursued by Wotan for having disobeyed his command to let Siegmund die. (During the fight Wotan interposed his spear, shattering Siegmund's sword. Hunding then killed Siegmund.) As Wotan approaches, Brünnhilde gives Sieglinde the pieces of the broken sword and makes her flee to safety.

Right Wotan disowns Brünnhilde; she will now be put to sleep on the rock until the first human awakens her with a kiss and claims her for his own. Brünnhilde protests: she defied her father's command because it had been imposed on him by Fricka. Wotan understands her, but cannot forgive her for giving way to emotion — their paths must part for ever. He will, however, encircle the sleeping Brünnhilde with fire so that only a hero will possess her. A long embrace follows, Wotan kisses her and she sinks, unconscious, to the ground.

Parsifal

Opera in three acts by Wagner; libretto by the composer. First performed at the Festspielhaus, Bayreuth, on 26 July 1882.

Callas sang Kundry at the Rome Opera in January 1949 (four performances) and in a concert performance for Italian Radio in November 1950.

Right and below Act 2: *Klingsor's Magic Garden.* Under Klingsor's command Kundry (Callas), transformed into a beautiful Flower Maiden, seeks to seduce the pure and unsophisticated youth. He pays attention when Kundry calls him: 'Parsifal! Weile!' ('Parsifal! Stay!'). She explains that his noble father, while dying on the battlefield in Arabia, called his son fal-par-si (Arabic for unsophisticated) and that his mother died from a broken heart when her son left. Parsifal (Beirer) blames himself for his mother's death, thus knowing grief for the first time. When Kundry gives him the first 'love kiss' he realises the strength of sensuality. Kundry then desperately confesses her sin – she mocked the Saviour – and implores Parsifal to redeem her with his love.

I PURITANI

Opera in three parts by Bellini; libretto by Count Carlo Pepoli. First performed at the Théâtre-Italien, Paris, on 24 January 1835.

Callas first sang Elvira in *I Puritani* at La Fenice in January 1949 and last in Chicago in November 1955, a total of sixteen performances.

Part I: *Elvira's apartment in the castle.* Elvira (Callas) is jubilant to learn from her beloved Uncle Giorgio (Christoff) that her father at last will allow her to marry her true love, Arturo.

Primarily through vocal means, Callas readily established Elvira as an innocent, hypersensitive and passionate young woman: 'Ah! quest'alma al duolo avezza, è si vinta dal gioia' ('Ah, my grief-stricken soul is now overcome with joy') (Teatro Communale, Florence, 1951).

Right Part 2: *A large salon in the castle.* Believing that Arturo has abandoned her at the altar steps for another woman, Elvira has lost her reason.

Through wide-ranging melody Callas evoked Elvira's blurred recollections and refocusings of mind. Her melting tone in the prayer-like 'O rendetemi la speme o lasciatemi morir!' ('Ah, give me back my faith or let me die!'), sung most affectingly offstage, created a suspension of disbelief. She then appeared to be in a private world of fantasy and infinite pathos; the meditative melancholy, the appealing sensuousness in her voice on the word 'morir', as if she were choking, and the deceptive simplicity filled her portrayal with eloquent significance.

'Vien diletto, è in ciel la luna' ('Come beneath the moon and sky') was breath-takingly brilliant and yet, incomparably, Callas integrated the numerous descending scales into the drama, now with ecstasy, now with exuberance, now with abandon, to signify subtly the fragility of Elvira's mental state – the dislocation of a suffering soul.

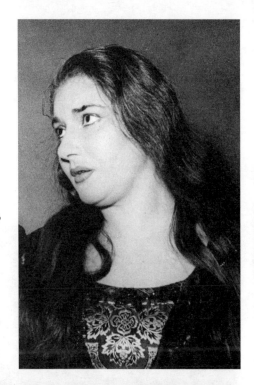

Below Part 3: *A terrace in the castle grounds near Elvira's apartment.* The exiled Arturo (Conley) returns secretly and brings Elvira out with his song. The sudden joy of seeing her beloved restores her sanity and they express their love for each other ecstatically: 'Vieni fra queste braccia' ('Come let me embrace you').

AIDA

Opera in four acts by Verdi; libretto by Ghislanzoni. First performed at the Teatro Khediviale, Cairo, on 24 December 1871.

Callas first sang Aida in Turin in September 1948 and last at the Arena di Verona in August 1953, a total of thirty performances.

Act 2: *A room in Amneris's apartments at Thebes.* Determined to find out if Aida (Callas), her Ethiopian slave, is her rival in love, Amneris (Stignani), the Pharaoh's daughter, tells her that Radames has been killed in battle and then that he is alive. Aida's distress and subsequent jubilation practically betray her love for Radames (San Carlo, Naples, 1950).

Left During her verbal fencing with Amneris, Callas's agitation increased until her resistance was all but broken and, forgetting herself, she exclaimed boldly, 'Mia rivale! . . . Anch'io son tal!' ('My rival! . . . I also am such'). But it was her resignation that so poignantly conveyed her hopelessness: 'Numi, pietà del mio soffrir' ('Gods, have mercy on my suffering').

Below *A great square near the main gate of Thebes.* Among the Ethiopian prisoners of war that Radames (Picchi) has captured, Aida recognises her father, King Amonasro (Savarese), but she does not reveal his true identity.

Callas charged 'Che veggo? Egli? Mio padre!' ('What do I see? Him? My father!') with startling intensity, her soliloquy then becoming a heart-rending cry: 'A lui la gloria, il trono, a me l'oblio, le lacrime d'un disperato amor' ('For him, glory and the throne. For me, oblivion and the tears of a desperate love'), as Radames and Amneris leave together amidst the jubilation of the crowds.

PART TWO

Prima Donna

• CHAPTER FOUR •

THE TWO GENTLEMEN OF VERONA

ON HER FIRST evening (30 June 1947) in Verona, at a dinner party for the singers appearing at the Arena, Maria met one of the two men who were to play crucial parts in her life and career.

Giovanni Battista Meneghini, a Veronese industrialist, then fifty-two, short, plump, with a dynamic personality, had wanted to become a journalist after he had graduated from school in Verona, but had entered the Commercial High School in Venice so that he could be suitably trained to work for the family business of manufacturing building materials. Eighteen months later his studies were interrupted by the First World War. Afterwards he returned to the school in Venice, but a year later his father died and Meneghini took charge before he had completed his studies. A very hard-working man, he did extremely well with the business, which by 1945 had grown to include twelve factories. Meneghini was so fully occupied both at work and looking after his family — he adored his mother and took care of his many brothers like a father — that he reached the age of fifty-two without having found the time to get married. Such an act on his part would have been seen by the family as a betrayal and he tried to live with his loneliness. Nevertheless, he was quite a ladies' man, with a particular predilection for young opera singers.

It was therefore not too much of a coincidence that he was present at a dinner given for the singers who were opening the season; Gaetano Pomari, who represented the management of the Arena, introduced Meneghini to Callas with a view to his being an escort for the new prima donna. As it happened, Meneghini was immediately very much taken with Maria's unusual personality. She was at that time a rather quiet, almost melancholy person without the exaggerated enthusiasm of the young, yet she had a youthful vitality all her own that he found infectious. That Maria was fat and inelegant did not bother Meneghini in the slightest; he liked large women and for this reason never befriended the ballerinas who appeared at the Arena, but stuck to the prima donnas. The day after they met — Meneghini took Maria, Louise and Rossi-Lemeni on an excursion to nearby Venice — he saw Maria in daylight for the first time and was further impressed with the dignity with which she conducted herself. She was completely different in this respect from all the other woman he had known.

In one of my meetings with Meneghini in 1978 he elaborated on his first impressions of Callas (though he did not include what he told me in his book, *Maria Callas mia moglie*, in 1981): 'I felt that Maria liked me for myself and not because I might be useful to her. This made me happy as I had never been before in my "long" fifty-two years. You see, it was such a mutual feeling. I, too, felt affection (I dare not say love) for her before I heard her sing a single note. That is why I was willing, anxious, to help her with her career, not in any artistic way (I am not a musician though I do appreciate music) but in every other way possible.'

Maria gave her portrait to Meneghini to celebrate their first meeting and their falling in love with one another, Verona, July/August, 1947. She inscribed it 'To Battista, With all of me, Your Maria'.

Maria Callas. Verona, 1949.

Maria's recollection of her first meeting with Meneghini and her subsequent friendship with him was equally romantic:

At that time in Verona Battista shared a flat with Pomari, because his own had been requisitioned during the war; and since he enjoyed opera, he took part in all the discussions that normally precede the opening of the Verona season at the Arena. On that occasion his main duty was to look after the American prima donna (that is, me) at the dinner. However, when he returned from his office, late that evening, he felt so tired (Battista was working very hard at that period) that he decided to skip the dinner and rest in his flat which was above the Pedavena, the restaurant where we were eating. But as he was going up the stairs a waiter told him that if he did not go to the restaurant Mr Pomari will be furious with him. . . . My first impressions of him when Pomari introduced us were that he was an honest and sincere person. I liked him. Then I forgot him, because he wasn't seated next to me at the table and without my glasses I could not see him very well. At a certain moment Louise, who was beside me, passed on to me a message from Meneghini that he wanted to take her, Rossi-Lemeni and me to Venice the next morning. I accepted the invitation at once, but changed my mind the next day because my trunk hadn't yet arrived from Naples and consequently I had no other dress to wear. Rossi-Lemeni, however, persuaded me to go in what I had on. I went to Venice with Battista and during that trip our love was born – and if it wasn't at first sight, it was undoubtedly at the second.

Concurrently with preparations for *Gioconda* Meneghini sent Maria, at his own expense, to Ferruccio Cusinati, an excellent coach and chorus master at the Arena, so that she could continue to study her role. On 20 July Tullio Serafin, the conductor, arrived to start rehearsals.

Serafin (1878–1968) was born in the small village of Rottanova di Cavazere near Venice on 8 December. He studied the violin at the Milan Conservatorio under de Angelis, and composition under Saladino. While still a student he played the violin on a La Scala tour and later, after further studies, he appeared at the age of twenty-two at the Teatro Comunale in Ferrara, conducting *L'elisir d'amore*. After working in several provincial theatres he appeared successfully at the Teatro Augusteo in Rome in 1907, making his Covent Garden début in the same year. Three years later he was engaged as principal conductor at La Scala.

With Toscanini's death in 1957 Serafin became the last link with Verdi. Although he was only twenty-one years old at Verdi's death, he had known the great composer personally. Serafin was fourteen when he was taken to La Scala to hear Verdi conduct for the last time: 'It was the Prayer from Rossini's *Mosè* that made such an impact on me and which I have never forgotten,' Serafin recalled more than seventy years later. Verdi became his idol and the occasion played a great part in his decision to take up conducting professionally.

More than any other, Serafin could claim the mantle of Toscanini, inasmuch as he became the grand master of Italian operatic conducting. Apart from the Italian repertory, among the novelties he brought to La Scala during his long association with the theatre were the Italian premières of Richard Strauss's *Der Rosenkavalier* (1911) and *Feuersnot* (1912), Dukas's *Ariadne et Barbe-bleue* (1911), Weber's *Oberon* and others. At the Metropolitan (1924–33) he further demonstrated that he possessed a universally versatile style. A very progressive conductor, Serafin was always eager to introduce new works of merit. In addition to the American premières of several operas, he gave the world premières of Falla's *La vida breve* (1926), Deems Taylor's *The King's Henchman* (1927) and *Peter Ibbetson* (1931).

In 1934 he returned to Italy as artistic director and chief conductor of the Rome Opera, where he stayed for ten years. It was one of the most enterprising and glorious periods of this theatre, with Serafin conducting several world premières including Pizzetti's *L'Orseolo* and Alfano's *Cyrano de Bergerac*, and in 1942 he introduced Berg's *Wozzeck* to Italy.

It is no exaggeration to say that Serafin influenced and even shaped the best singers of his long reign. He was often described a 'singer's conductor', a well-deserved compliment, for his understanding of the human voice and its artistic application was profound and uncompromising. Moreover, his extraordinary feeling for style and good taste, together with his unfailing consideration for the singer while at the same time maintaining full control, raised him, at least as an opera conductor, to the highest level of the art. Notwithstanding his unique talent, he approached music with respect and a humility that was, and remains, all too rare. He was the other man who was to play a crucial part in Callas's career.

Her first feelings about him were a combination of affection and respect. 'It was a marvellous experience to rehearse with such a considerate and artistic conductor who would be always ready to help you – direct you is perhaps a better description – correct your faults and allow you to find out the hidden possibilities in a score by yourself.' For the whole of the fortnight before opening night Maria worked hard, trying to absorb as much as she could from this wonderful man. A lifelong friendship began and she was to follow his advice, guidance and teaching for the rest of her professional life.

July passed all too quickly, without any interest shown in the new prima donna either by the press or the Veronese public, which normally follows avidly what is going on at the Arena. At the dress rehearsal, however, the way Callas's personality dominated everything around her stunned those present. On-stage she assumed an incredible aura and her well-chosen movements an elegance that amounted to nobility, until disaster nearly struck in the second act: Maria fell through an open chute on the stage. The fall, which could have been fatal had her head hit the rocks, resulted in bruises and a painfully sprained ankle. Recalling the accident years later, she said, 'At the end of the third act my ankle was so swollen that I couldn't even touch the ground with my foot. A doctor was called, but by then it was too late to do anything drastic about it and, because of the excruciating pain, I was unable to sleep that night. I remember well the gratitude and affection I felt for Battista whom I had only known for a month, and who sat by my bed until dawn to help me and comfort me.' With medical attention Callas was just able to walk, two days later, at the first performance of *Gioconda*.

Callas's Italian début took place on 3 August 1947, and when the little candles that customarily burn in thousands during the overture of an opera performance at the vast Arena were extinguished nobody guessed how triumphantly Hidalgo's words 'I still think you should go to Italy' were to be proved correct. Callas had a considerable success with the twenty-five-thousand-strong audience. Although her first Italian critics noticed some technical faults, specifically the unevenness of her vocal registers, they generally liked her as Gioconda, appreciating 'her expressive singing as well as the vibrant and effortless quality of her high notes'. A more revealing comment, however, came from Lord Harewood, who had been present at Callas's first Gioconda and wrote about it in *Opera* (November, 1952). He thought her a remarkable Gioconda 'whose then rather metallic timbre of voice seemed to me already to have a most moving and individual quality, and whose phrasing was unusually musical'.

According to Serafin, who recalled the occasion for me some twenty years later, he liked her singing from the first rehearsals:

> I was most impressed by her professionalism and approach to art generally. One felt that whatever difficulties would occur (and problems always do in the preparation of opera performances if your standards are high) she would try to overcome them. This in itself is not usual, even among very good singers.

> What struck me first was the way she would sing recitatives. This young singer (she was twenty-three in 1947, when I first heard her), who was not Italian, had never been to Italy before and who obviously was in no way brought up in the Italian tradition, was able to bring so much meaning to Italian recitative. I believe that she achieved this entirely through music. She had of course a sound vocal training but the way she spoke through music was something inborn. Were it possible for her to be musically trained when an infant, she would have had this gift then. If I hesitate to call Callas a musical phenomenon it is because usually the meaning of this word is misconstrued. Nor was I her 'Svengali' as somebody from the press called me. Naturally I gave her all the guidance I could but she really did it herself. She would listen to advice and everything to her was important.

> Although I felt from the beginning that there was in her a future great singer, she was not perfect. She had some difficulties with her diction and intonation, but looking back on it now, I believe that she began to progress and improve from the very first moment she sang in Italy. Can you imagine another singer who would come to orchestral rehearsals? At first she did this secretly but afterwards whenever I commented about it she always used to say, 'Maestro, am I not expected to be the first instrument of the orchestra?' We studied together a great deal. Maria also had a great friend, admirer and staunch supporter in my late wife [Elena Rakowska] who, as you know, was also a singer.

Our conversation then turned to other great artists he had worked with. I had hardly mentioned Rosa Ponselle when he immediately said: 'I remember them all – their faces, their mannerisms, their names but not their voices, except Callas's voice. Sometimes when I play the piano (I no longer conduct), I feel she is standing beside me. It was very satisfying to work with her. One role we did not study together from the beginning was Cherubini's *Medea*. Callas, as you know, sang it first in Florence in 1953 with another conductor [Vittorio Gui]. A few years later I was the conductor for her recording of *Medea*. Not a single idea clashed and I am talking about an opera that had been all but buried for a century before Callas resurrected it.'

'And yet, Maestro,' I interrupted, 'a statement you made not so long ago is not quite in keeping with these most enlightening comments about Callas. You said, "In my long lifetime there have been three miracles – Caruso, Titta Ruffo and Ponselle."'

With a smile the octogenarian conductor was delighted to explain:

These singers had voices which were naturally endowed with beauty, power and considerable technique – they were indeed nothing short of a miracle. Of course they perfected their vocal technique but they started with exceptional vocal material, perhaps unprecedented. They did not have Callas's genius, nor did they really throw new light on their art. Callas was no miracle. She too was naturally highly gifted but all God's gifts were given in the raw-material state. Everything had to be achieved by sheer hard work, determination and complete dedication.

Returning to Verona in 1947, Callas really came into her own by the third performance and confirmed to me that here was exceptional potential. I suggested that she continue to study with a good coach to smooth out some rough edges in her voice. She could do it because she had the right approach to music and she was eager to learn.

When the *Gioconda* performances were over and everyone associated with them had gone, Maria found herself alone with Meneghini and with no further engagement. Ten days later she was asked to sing Gioconda at Vigevano, a small place near Milan but, following Serafin's advice, she decided against it and remained free in case something better turned up. But nothing did during the next two months and she had no contact with Serafin, who was away working in other theatres. Her attention was really turned towards La Scala, Milan, but as she soon found out, the gates of the great theatre do not open easily, however eager singers may be and Meneghini with all his good intentions could not help. Their relationship was proceeding smoothly and they were very happy with one another – their only problem was Maria's career.

Meneghini was almost at his wits' end when he decided on impulse in mid-October to take Maria to an opera agency run by Liduino Bonardi in Milan. Bonardi had nothing to offer Maria. What was more, he added, the opera houses in Italy were closed at that time of the year. Coming out of the agency Meneghini and Maria, feeling rather perturbed, bumped into Nino Catozzo, then director of La Fenice in Venice. He recognized Meneghini and said that he was there to find a suitable singer who knew the role of Isolde in *Tristan and Isolde*, the opera with which he wanted to open his inaugural season at the end of December. Promptly Meneghini suggested Maria, lying that she knew the role. Catozzo was very pleased, but most surprised, to hear this.

Apparently he had heard her in *Gioconda* at the Arena and when he decided to produce *Tristan* had thought she would be suitable for Isolde provided she knew this difficult role, as there would not be sufficient time to learn it. In fact on the previous day he had left an urgent message with Angelina Pomari, a singer and sister of Pomari in Verona, to ask Callas if she would be ready to sing Isolde at La Fenice. When he did not hear from her he took it for granted that she was not interested. It did not occur to him that Pomari would not pass on the message. The next step now was to have the approval of Serafin, who would be conducting the opera, before drawing up a contract.

On that afternoon Serafin was delighted to see Maria in Milan. Sight-reading the score, she sang several scenes to his accompaniment. Not only did he find her voice much improved but he also thought she knew the opera and believed that she would make a very interesting Isolde. He arranged for her to go to Rome, where he would coach her himself. Deliriously happy, Meneghini and Maria returned to Verona. For two weeks she worked with Cusinati on Isolde and then, on 28 October, went to Rome to study with Serafin for twelve days.

The maestro was gratified to discover a mature artist in this twenty-three-year-old singer, who combined musical intelligence and style with a capacity for hard work, all essential for a success-ful Isolde. His wife, Elena Rakowska, the former Polish soprano who had had a distinguished career excelling in Wagnerian roles, was before long also taken by the young Callas. At first Rakowska was apprehensive about Maria tackling this role with only a two-month study period. All the Isoldes she had known, including herself, had required two years to master it. Nevertheless, by Callas's second session with Serafin, Rakowska, who sat in on the lessons, was not only surprised by how quickly this young woman was grasping the intricacies of the music but even more amazed that she was acquiring the *physique du rôle*, a rare attribute indeed. After the performances of *Tristan* Rakowska became Callas's greatest champion.

For Maria her Roman sojourn was a marvellous experience; she was actually studying with the great maestro and she threw herself passionately into the hard work. Before long, she con-fessed that she had not known the role on that afternoon in Milan when she sight-read the music. 'Well, you had two months to learn it,' Serafin commented in his usual friendly but rather phlegmatic way.

While in Rome Maria missed Battista a great deal. It was their first separation and she spent her free time writing loving letters to him, at least twice a day:

> You cannot imagine how much I miss you. I cannot wait to be in your arms again. . . . The more I sing Isolde the better she develops. It is rather an impetuous role but I like it. . . . Even at the end of my stay here I shall only know what Serafin expects of me with the score in front of me. Afterwards I shall have to memorize it all on my own . . .

Yesterday I heard Serafin speaking on the telephone so glowingly of me to Catozzo that I was moved to tears. . . . How I would like you Battista, to be near me. . . . If I express all my feelings for you, through Isolde, I will be marvellous . . .

Maria returned to Verona to continue her studies on her own and with Cusinati.

The première of *Tristan und Isolde* at La Fenice on 30 December was a major success. The opera, sung in Italian as was the custom in Italy at the time, was meticulously prepared by Serafin and included Fiorenzo Tasso (Tristan), Fedora Barbieri (Brangaene) and Boris Christoff (King Marke). Callas as Isolde achieved an undisputed triumph both with the public and the critics, who immediately appreciated the way she used the dramatic accents in her voice to enhance the musical interpretation of the complex role.

The critic of *Il Gazzettino* said, 'Isolde was the young soprano Maria Callas. An artist endowed with unusual musical sensibility and sure stage presence, she expressed the amorous passion of the heroine more with feminine sweet abandon than with druidic virility. Her beautiful, very warm voice, especially in the higher register, was resounding and full of appropriate lyricism.'

Before the *Tristan* performances were over Catozzo, who was proud of Callas, offered her Turandot which she sang on 29 January 1948. She had, as stated, first studied the role in America on her own and with Louise Caselotti. At La Fenice the opera was conducted by Nino Sanzogno and Callas's success was in many ways even more resounding than her Isolde. *Tristan* was, after all, for Wagnerians, while *Turandot*, despite the fact that at that time it was not performed as frequently as other Puccini works, was an Italian opera with which the audience could identify.

The critic of *Il Gazzettino* wrote that 'Callas made an admirable Turandot; her voice was precise and resounding, especially in the highest register. There is, to be sure, some unevenness in her voice but she easily makes one forget it. An artist endowed with unusual finesse, sensibility and intelligence, as well as with a most impressive stage presence, Callas tackled the arduous tessitura of the role with energy and confidence. There was in her singing a plastic neatness and even a profound sweetness when the role demanded it.'

Almost immediately after the success of her Turandot other engagements followed in rapid succession. But first Serafin had to be consulted – Callas would not undertake anything without his sanction. By August she had sung Turandot in Udine, Terme di Caracalla in Rome, the Arena di Verona and Genoa. Between these performances she repeated her Isolde in Genoa and sang Leonora (*La forza del destino*) in Trieste and the title role in *Aida* in Turin and Rovigo. She did well and her fame as a new dramatic soprano was spreading. Nevertheless, for Callas all this, wonderful though it was, was not enough. Apart from La Fenice, no major opera house, not to mention La Scala, had yet paid her any attention.

What was to become, however, an artistic turning-point in her career began when Francesco Siciliani, then the director of the Teatro San Carlo in Naples, heard the live broadcast of *Tristan* from La Fenice. He was so impressed with Isolde's voice that he immediately made it his business to find out that the singer was a young Greek-American, a protégée of Tullio Serafin. He did not however, pursue the matter because he was very busy and about to be appointed director of the Teatro Comunale in Florence. Serafin conducted Callas in *Aida* in September of that year and, in an effort to obtain further engagements for her, telephoned his enterprising friend Siciliani, who had just taken over in Florence. 'Serafin called me in October 1948,' Siciliani reminisced years later, 'and asked me to go to Rome without delay. "I have a girl here whom you must hear. Unfortunately she is so discouraged that she wants to return to America. Maybe you can help me to persuade her to stay. I cannot lose a singer like her."' (Undoubtedly Serafin was creating an urgency so that Siciliani would take action promptly. Maria may not yet have made La Scala but she was not exactly living an idle life, however high her aspirations. At that period she was certainly not contemplating a return to America, but Serafin obviously knew the ropes.) Remembering the Isolde he had heard on the radio, Siciliani went to Rome to hear her in the flesh:

> So, at Serafin's home I met Maria Callas. She was tall and fat but with good presence. Her face was expressive and interesting and I thought her intelligent. Accompanied by Serafin on the piano she sang 'Suicidio' (*La Gioconda*), 'O patria mia' (*Aida*), 'In questa reggia' (*Turandot*) and the 'Liebestod' (*Tristan und Isolde*). I thought that her voice and singing were by and large very beautiful; only certain sections of the voice were perhaps relatively rather empty and her portamenti a little unusual. When presently I found out that she had been the pupil in Greece of the coloratura soprano Elvira de Hidalgo, Callas said that she could sing coloratura music too. Without much more talking she embarked on 'Qui la voce', the mad scene from Bellini's *I Puritani*. Hearing this music sung, at last, in the correct style, I was overwhelmed and when I looked at Serafin there were tears streaming down his face. I took action immediately, first telling her that she was not going to America or anywhere else and then I telephoned Pariso Votto, the general manager of the Comunale. 'Look,' I said to him, 'forget *Butterfly*. I have found an extraordinary soprano and we shall open the season with *Norma*.'

With *Norma*, Bellini created a work of profound lyrical and dramatic beauty. Norma's predicament concerns her love for a man of hostile race, for whom she has sacrificed everything, including her duty to her country. Her characterization constitutes one of the most powerful portraits in the history of opera. It is also generally considered to be the most difficult role in the operatic repertoire. *Norma* disintegrates if its protagonist cannot meet fully the extraordinary demands of the role: essentially, she must be a dramatic soprano with prodigious agility, command a vocal technique of the highest order and sing cantilena without distorting Bellini's very personal melodic line. Moreover, she must have enough in reserve for sheer dramatic impact through both the medium of her voice and her phyriscal presence.[1]

At that time Callas's knowledge of the score of *Norma* was limited to 'Casta Diva' and the duet 'Mira o Norma' which she had studied with Hidalgo in Athens in the early 1940s. But to master the role is a mammoth undertaking for any singer. Immediately after her encounter with Siciliani Callas began to study it with Serafin, working closely with him almost in seclusion. During seven weeks of hard labour she learned the part that, more than any other, was destined to become so much her own.

On 30 November 1948, under Serafin's direction, Callas sang *Norma* at the Comunale; Mirto Picchi was Pollione, Fedora Barbieri Adalgisa and Cesare Siepi Oroveso. The most constructive evaluation of Callas's first Norma came from Serafin himself, who told me in 1960 that her portrayal was from the beginning both musically and dramatically accomplished.

> There were, to be sure, vocal inequalities, mainly in the recitatives and the audience at those performances in Florence (only two in that season) were so puzzled by the uneven but dramatic delivery of the opening recitative 'Sediziose voci' that they did not really appreciate the ensuing 'Casta Diva' as much as they should. You see at that time, in the late forties, most people unfortunately only had ears for pure lyricism and what they considered to be beauty of sound irrespective of the dramatic situation. However, I believe that by the end of her first Norma Callas's impact was so great that henceforth the audience, at least in their subconscious, were changing their approach to opera. Although there were no special ovations at the end of the first performance, it was significant that, and I had this from good authority at the theatre, half the same audience attended again the second, and last, performance.

The critics, on the other hand, received the new Norma without any significant reservations. Gualtiero Frangini (*La Nazione*, December 1948) wrote:

> Maria Callas, a soprano new to us, immediately impressed us as Norma. An artist of truly noteworthy ability, she has a powerful, steady voice with an appealing timbre which can be penetrating and carry well in loud passages but also acquire appropriate sweetness in delicate moments. Although her technique is secure and perfectly controlled, her schooling is rather different from what we are accustomed to hearing, as indeed her vocal colour is unusual. Nevertheless her merits are undeniable; her highly accomplished portrayal of Norma is rich in subtle and moving accents of femininity – she is the woman

in love, the woman betrayed, the mother, the friend and in the end the implacable priestess.

More important, Callas's first Norma re-introduced a vocal dimension to the approach of opera that had hitherto been practically absent from theatres for many years. Both Serafin and Siciliani were convinced that in Callas they had found a dramatic soprano *d'agilità*, an artist who could sing coloratura dramatically and integrate it in her portrayal of a character – the voice of legendary singers such as Giuditta Pasta and Maria Malibran. She could serve now to revive some of the great but neglected operas: through Siciliani's initiative, Cherubini's *Medea*, Haydn's *Orfeo ed Euridice* and Rossini's *Armida* were subsequently unearthed specifically for Callas, who triumphed in them. But before these materialized, other surprises lay in store both for the singer and the operatic world.

Hardly had *Norma* in Florence ended when Callas was hard at work with Serafin on another formidable role: Brünnhilde in *Die Walküre*, with which La Fenice was opening its new season on 8 January 1949. Apart from some minor vocal reservations almost always made in the evaluation of the great Wagnerian roles, Callas was able to express primarily through her voice both the heroic and humanly vulnerable aspects of Brünnhilde's character.

Giuseppe Pugliese (*Il Gazzettino*, Venice, January 1949) wrote that Callas was 'imbued with a typical Wagnerian soul – proud and full of emotions yet simple and precise, with a splendid and powerful voice in the higher passages and in the declamation. Only very occasionally during the long evening would a somewhat unpleasant tone momentarily creep into her middle register.'

Serafin told me that Callas as Brünnhilde brought tears to his eyes, especially in the closing scenes. Dr Molinari, an old Italian professor of music and a Wagner specialist, also described her Brünnhilde as unforgettable. He had heard all the notable interpreters of his day and, in his opinion, Callas could have become the leading Wagnerian soprano had she chosen this path. 'I was equally moved by the brilliance of the "Ho-jo-hos" in her first scene and in the last scene by the eloquence of her pleading to Wotan.'

The second opera of the season at La Fenice, also to be conducted by Serafin, was Bellini's *I Puritani* with Margherita Carosio as Elvira. Because of the enormous difficulty in casting the opera – the demands for the role of Elvira are far greater than those with which the ordinary coloratura soprano can cope – *I Puritani* was then rarely performed even in Italy. Carosio, though not quite the perfect interpreter, was competent and at the time possibly the best available soprano. But nine days before the performance she suddenly fell ill with influenza and had to withdraw. As a substitute was extremely difficult to find, especially at such short notice, the management were seriously considering cancellation of the performances when Serafin came up with a solution. Apparently his daughter Vittoria had heard Callas sing an aria from *I Puritani* in her room (Callas was staying in the same hotel as the Serafins) as an exercise to warm up for her Brünnhilde. Vittoria was so moved by the lyric beauty of Maria's voice that she immediately called her mother to listen. Later in the evening mother and daughter informed Serafin that a singer for the role of Elvira did exist. Rakowska, who naturally took the lead in this conversation, told her husband that his conservative short-sightedness prevented him from seeing the obvious. 'Our Elvira', she proclaimed, 'is right here, now sleeping under this roof.'

Of course Serafin knew all about Maria's superb singing of 'Qui la voce', the only aria from *I Puritani* that she knew. Now he needed the right singer who knew the whole part and this person had to be found without delay. Pushed by his wife, Serafin finally decided to take a chance with his sleeping Brünnhilde and telephoned Catozzo in the middle of the night to tell him that he had found their Elvira. Because Serafin was going to ask Callas to take this great responsibility, he also telephoned Meneghini (with whom she was living and who was managing her affairs) in Verona to put him in the picture. Meneghini was flabbergasted and after getting over the shock of being telephoned so late at night exclaimed, without knowing what he was talking about, 'Of course Maria will sing! She's not ill, is she? Tell her I shall come to Venice the day after tomorrow.'

With what must have been considerable trepidation the theatre management, on Serafin's advice, gave Callas an impromptu audition. It was quite early the following morning and she was asleep when she was summoned downstairs and commanded to sing, still in her dressing-gown, the aria from *I Puritani* to Serafin's piano accompaniment. On being offered the role she at first protested that her voice was too heavy. But if Serafin was confident that she could do it, who was she to contradict? She therefore accepted the challenge of having only six days to learn it, during which time she was also to sing two performances of *Die Walküre*. No two roles could be less similar, but Callas, coached by Serafin, did learn the *Puritani* Elvira for the dress rehearsal, which took place on the same day as her last Brünnhilde. Three days later she scored a stupendous success. Musical Italy enthused about the event and Maria Callas's versatility was heralded as nothing less than phenomenal.

Mario Nordio (*Il Gazzettino*, Venice, February 1949) described everybody's astonishment that the magnificent Isolde, Turandot and Brünnhilde could portray Elvira. 'However and despite the fact that her first notes in this role were not those of the expected traditional light soprano, even the most sceptical readily acknowledged the miracle that Callas performed. For this, credit must be given to her exceptional teacher Elvira de Hidalgo and to the flexibility of her limpid, beautifully suave voice and splendid high notes. The warmth and expressiveness of her interpretation cannot be found in the fragile, transparent coldness of all other Elviras.'

Elvira – who practically dominates the drama – loses and regains her reason several times, not always with sufficient justification. But as Elvira is extremely vulnerable and lives on the precipice between fantasy and reality, insanity and reason, it is unnecessary to justify each change in her mental balance provided an accomplished singing actress can convey these subtle changes. It was Callas's ability to convey convincingly the way Elvira's mind teeters on the brink of sanity (achievable only through dramatic coloratura) that made the character credible, assuming Pirandellian stature; a parallel can, in fact, be drawn between Elvira and Zara in Pirandello's play *As you desire me.*

When I referred to this event later – of utmost significance in the renaissance of early nineteenth-century Italian opera – Callas commented that 'It was by a miracle that I managed. The great urgency of the matter left me without much time to get scared out of my wits.' On another occasion I implied to Serafin that in the circumstances he was asking Callas for the impossible. He smiled mischievously and replied: 'Yes, I was. But I knew she could do it because Callas had the voice, the technique, the intelligence and everything else. To me she was the kind of artist whom, until then, one had only read about in operatic history books. It was not even then really so clever or so daring to entrust her with the Bellini role as one might naturally imagine. You see, she had already studied and sung Norma for me. After that I would have entrusted her with any role. She had proved herself. There was no miracle.'

After her three performances of *I Puritani* Callas rushed to Palermo for more Brünnhildes, with Francesco Molinari-Pradelli as conductor. Interestingly, in a letter to Meneghini she wrote that a critic in Palermo said that '"although Callas, the Brünnhilde, sang with intensity – she has a beautiful voice with the most attractive timbre – [she] failed to be a barbaric Valkyrie …" How stupid. Here they seem to expect people on the stage to pull their hair out. I feel quite angry about this.'

Callas then made her San Carlo début as Turandot. She was so impressive that she whetted further the appetite of the public and the theatre's management to hear her in a coloratura role. For the moment, however, a challenging engagement awaited her at the Rome Opera, where she was to sing Kundry in *Parsifal.* She had been studying it on her own for the last twenty-five days and now she had five days to rehearse it with Serafin, who was to conduct. Hans Beirer was Parsifal, Cesare Siepi Gurnemanz and Marcello Cortis Amfortas. Her success on 26 February was proclaimed unanimously and confirmed that she was becoming a major singer.

Adriano Bellin (*Il Quotidiano*, February 1942) described Callas as 'a magnificent Kundry who, with her secure vocal technique, marvellous equalization of registers – the upper one possessing a fine extension – overcame all difficulties with flying colours. She also portrayed most convincingly the fascinating and tormented character of Kundry, the sinner who longs for redemption.'

Again Serafin's perceptive evaluation of Callas is most interesting. As he told me several years later, in her he was able to hear Kundry's true voice:

Her physical acting, too, especially in the garden scene with Parsifal, had all the right seductiveness because it had its source primarily in the music. She was in good voice and with the simplest of means she was convincing in every respect. It was amazing how this young girl, working on her own, understood and mastered both the text and the music in such a short time. I taught her very little at the rehearsals. You see, Callas knew, perhaps instinctively, all that the conservatorio cannot teach.

He also told me an anecdote confirmed, reluctantly but with amusement, by Callas herself in 1973. During the stage rehearsals of *Parsifal* Serafin noticed that Maria, who knew the music well and always followed the composer's instructions meticulously, avoided rather cunningly giving Parsifal the prolonged kiss on the lips that Wagner specifies for Kundry. Serafin waited until the last rehearsal, feeling confident that eventually Maria would do it. But she did not and Serafin stopped the rehearsal, walked on to the stage and, pretending to ignore Maria's presence gave Hans Beirer, the Parsifal, the required kiss. He then turned round and in a mock-brusque tone said 'Listen, Maria, if I can kiss him surely you can too.' Everybody laughed and Maria managed it. Callas admitted that she had always been rather shy. At this time she was only twenty-five years old 'and Beirer was such a gorgeous man and all those people watching', made it very difficult for her to kiss him. 'Fortunately dear old Serafin, that sly fox, broke the ice and put me right as always.'

Altogether the eighteen months Callas had so far spent in Italy were certainly eventful. She had been desperately disillusioned during the three months after her début in Verona when she could not find work and particularly when she was turned down by La Scala. But from the moment she was engaged for *Tristan und Isolde* and began her close association with Serafin she again found her purpose in life. Henceforth, though not with ease, her extremely hard work and Serafin's guidance enabled her to achieve consistent success in most of the Italian opera houses. Only La Scala, the dream of every singer, seemed oblivious of her existence.

The day before her last performance in *Parsifal* Callas gave her first Italian radio concert in Turin. Her programme consisted of 'Casta Diva', the 'Liebestod', 'Qui la voce' and 'O patria mia'. It was to prove of far-reaching significance, for not only was she heard by the Italian public at large, but her popular success prompted Cetra, the Italian recording company, to offer her a contract. Initially three 78 rpms of items she sang on the radio were to be recorded, then she would follow with complete operas. Thus began Callas's extraordinary recording career – one that was to take her art to all the corners of the world.

In her private life, though not quite secure, Maria was on the whole happier than she had ever been. Her love for Meneghini and his complete devotion to her gave her the moral support and

Maria with Meneghini shortly before their marriage, Verona, 1949.

strength to proceed with her career and life regardless of the inevitable obstacles. Meneghini faced strong opposition from his family: his brothers were against Maria, this foreign singer whom they refused to meet and accused of having turned Battista's head, making him behave like an imbecile. Writing about it in 1981 Meneghini said that the real motive behind his brother's disapproval of his marriage to Maria, or anybody else, was a fear of losing their share of the money he was making for the family 'and in the event of my death, they would not have been the sole beneficiaries of my estate'.

The situation was a little different with Meneghini's mother, who showed some understanding for her son's feelings. Even so, his family's hostility was undoubtedly the real cause of the delay in his marriage inasmuch as he was reluctant to break with his brothers, and to an extent with his mother who would have been forced to take sides with her remaining sons. There were, of course, other difficulties such as getting Maria's birth certificate (apparently the church authorities in Verona expected her to produce papers both from the United States and Greece) and the dispensation from the Vatican for Meneghini, a Roman Catholic, to marry a Greek Orthodox woman. Apart from this Maria and Meneghini were in perfect harmony and he never wavered in his devotion to her. However, the day came when Maria could wait no longer, whatever the obstacles. She was preparing to leave Italy alone (Meneghini's business affairs did not allow him to accompany her) for a very important engagement at the Teatro Colón, when she gave Meneghini an ultimatum that unless they were married within twenty-four hours she would not go to Buenos Aires. He obviously realized that she was deadly serious because what he had been unable to accomplish over a period of eighteen months he now, amazingly, resolved within hours: he surmounted all the obstacles and at 5 p.m. on 21 April 1949 went with Maria to the little church of the Filippini in Verona for their wedding. The ceremony, in fact, had to take place in the storeroom of the sacristy because Maria, not being a Catholic, could not be married in the church proper. Quickly, a small space was made near the altar of the storeroom and two large candles were lit. There, surrounded by broken pews, old banners and all sorts of detritus, the priest performed the ceremony and pronounced Battista and Maria husband and wife. Two friends who acted as witnesses were the only attendants.

At midnight Maria Meneghini Callas sailed alone from Genoa to Buenos Aires, where she would stay for three months.

1 In the opera's 167 years there have been few truly great Normas: Giuditta Pasta (the creator of the role), Maria Malibran, Giulia Grisi, Lilli Lehmann, Thérèse Tietjens, Rosa Ponselle and Maria Callas complete the short list.

CHAPTER FIVE

SUCCESS AND SQUABBLES IN LATIN AMERICA

T HE TEATRO COLÓN had long been an important theatre, with a visiting Italian contingent participating each year and Tullio Serafin, a regular guest, was looked upon by the Argentinians as the artistic driving force behind the opera seasons. In 1949 Serafin was taking with him the long-established favourite of the Colón, the baritone Carlo Galeffi, and the cream of the most promising young singers of Italy. Mario Del Monaco, Fedora Barbieri, Nicola Rossi-Lemeni, Elena Nicolai, Cesare Siepi, Mario Filippeschi and Maria Meneghini Callas were to be the stars, with the last-named appearing as Turandot, Norma and Aida, all three works to be conducted by Serafin.

It was the first long journey that Maria had made alone since she had met her husband and she was very depressed from the beginning. During the long sea voyage and the almost two months in Buenos Aires the twenty-five-year-old newly wed seems to have spent most of her free time writing to the husband she had left in Italy, constantly expressing her love for him and her longing to return to him: 'I thank God for finding such a companion in life as you . . . no woman has as much as I have. Thank you again for becoming my husband before I left . . . you have made me love you even more. No woman is happier than I am. . . . Above all you are the man of my dreams. My sole purpose in life is to make you the happiest and proudest husband in the world!'

After twenty days at sea the company arrived in Rio de Janeiro, the plan being to proceed to Buenos Aires by air. During their brief stay the directors of the opera house, who knew of Callas's success in Italy, asked her to sing Norma in Rio and Montevideo after her season in Buenos Aires was completed. Thinking of the husband she had left behind Maria, who was already counting the days until her return, refused all offers on the pretext that contractual obligations made it imperative for her to travel back to Italy.

In Buenos Aires the directors of the opera house at first wanted to open the season with *Aida*, with Delia Rigal in the title role. Rigal, a dramatic soprano, was very popular in her native

Buenos Aires but Serafin would not hear of it; the contract for this tour stipulated the guarantee that Maria Callas should open the season. Finally, she did, as Turandot, and made quite an impact on the public who were very much taken with her total involvement in her role. She held her own, singing opposite Del Monaco (Calaf) who was already established as a great favourite at the Colón. The critic of *La Prensa* was impressed with Callas's excellent dramatic expression but was somewhat bothered by 'a certain nervousness in her vocalization and a slight vocal indisposition ... although one could appreciate her marvellous middle voice and the facility of her upper register'.

All reservations vanished however, when Callas sang Norma, the role she had meticulously studied with Serafin and had sung in Florence during the previous year. The Argentinian public and critics discovered the excitement a dramatic soprano *d'agilità* could bring to such a role — *Norma* was a revelation, their enthusiasm knew no bounds and Callas became the rage of Buenos Aires overnight.

Writing to her husband after her success, Maria's immediate regret was that he was not with her to share such a triumph. She also revealed that on top of her unhappiness and loneliness in being away from him, some of her colleagues were rather hostile towards her. Only Serafin and his wife — and of the singers, Elena Nicolai and Cesare Siepi — were genuinely friendly and helpful. The others had seemed to resent her success even in anticipation. 'I am so upset by the deviousness of some of my colleagues,' Maria wrote. Del Monaco, who sang with her in *Turandot*, 'has been particularly unpleasant because his superiority was dampened when he sang with me [rather] than with that Rigal woman. ... I, for my part, have never treated badly any of my colleagues but after a very good rehearsal of *Norma*, when even the orchestra players applauded, the singers who were not taking part began to spread false rumours that I was ill and the opera should be substituted with another. I feel sorry for these louses! ... The just and great God has allowed me to win because I have never tried to cause harm to anyone and, of course, because I have worked very hard.'

After *Norma*, Callas sang a single Aida. In this role she was following Rigal, who at the time was not on good form and almost met with disaster on the high notes. Callas's Aida was not an unqualified success: some critics, as well as a relatively small section of the public, were disturbed by the way she occasionally produced 'ugly' sounds for the sake of dramatic expression for hitherto they had always expected a beautiful and smooth tone whatever the situation. There were also those who readily accepted Callas's performance as drama expressed in music, the true and only purpose of opera, and her overall success in Buenos Aires, notwithstanding some healthy controversy about her voice, was not in dispute. Before she departed, the management of the Colón offered her *I Puritani* and one other opera for the following season, but she was not prepared to sign a contract there and then.

On 14 July Meneghini met his wife's plane at Rome airport and they went to Venice for a brief, much-belated honeymoon. While Maria was in Buenos Aires Meneghini had seen that their apartment, built above his office in Verona, was ready. It was very comfortable, with a lovely view of the Arena, and for the next four months the Meneghinis continued to enjoy their extended honeymoon, perhaps the happiest period for both of them. Her fastidious decorating of the home gave her, for the first time in her life, a feeling of security as well as maturity, despite the fact that she was not quite twenty-six years old.

Apart from one engagement on 18 September when she sang Herod's daughter in Stradella's oratorio *San Giovanni Battista* at Perugia, Callas's performances began with *Nabucco* at the San Carlo in December. Her stirring characterization of Abigaille, the vengeful Babylonian Princess, in what was then a rarely performed opera, was a triumph. 'Maria Callas, a most talented dramatic soprano,' the critic of *Il Mattino* (Naples) wrote, 'portrayed a very proud Abigaille; the dramatic impact of her interpretation was rendered by her vocalization, her vitality and great insight into the character – her superb voice is homogeneous, pliable in the most subtle details throughout its remarkable register. Callas should only exercise more control on her high notes which sometimes sound a little sour.'

Maria Meneghini Callas at home in Verona.

95

With this success at an important theatre – in Italy generally considered second only to La Scala – Callas found herself in demand by other Italian opera houses. She followed with Norma at La Fenice and Aida at Brescia, but it was in Rome during February that she enthralled the audience with superb interpretations of Isolde and Norma in a series of five performances each over a period of forty days. Serafin conducted both works and the casts consisted of some of the best Italian singers of the period: Ebe Stignani, then the leading Italian mezzo-soprano, sang Adalgisa and Elena Nicolai Brangaene. Giulio Neri sang Oroveso, Galliano Masini Pollione and August Seider Tristan. In these performances Callas showed considerable development, which prompted the famous veteran tenor Giacomo Lauri-Volpi to describe her art most effusively: 'Her Norma is divine! . . . Voice, style, bearing, power of concentration and that vital pulsation of the spirit rise to unusual heights in this artist. . . . In the final act, this Norma's imploring voice came to me as art's purest joy.'

A concert on RAI Turin further increased her popularity, especially as she included in her programme for the first time excerpts from *La traviata* and *Il trovatore*. Almost immediately afterwards several Italian theatres, but still not La Scala, began preliminary negotiations with her for future engagements, as for the next few months she already had a rather busy schedule: Norma at Catania, Bellini's birthplace; Aida at the San Carlo; then her début in Mexico City the following May.

While she was at Catania, however, an invitation came quite out of the blue from La Scala: would she sing Aida in two performances during the Milan Fair in April? At first Callas was thrilled, but soon her enthusiasm was dampened when she discovered that in fact she would be replacing the indisposed Renata Tebaldi, who had originally been given the role. Nevertheless, she was sensible and modest enough to accept the offer. After all, she had considerable confidence in herself and once she was actually heard at La Scala – confirming, as it were, the reputation she had acquired throughout Italy – this could well lead to greater things. Her début at La Scala on 21 April 1950 before President Eunardi, several dignitaries, visitors to the Milan Fair and the Milanese public turned out to be a brilliant social affair. Artistically (the excellent cast included Del Monaco and Barbieri, with Franco Capuana as conductor) Callas's performance was controversial; the way she explored vocally Aida's human predicament was most moving, but the relative lack of velvet in her voice as compared with Tebaldi's, particularly in the aria 'O patria mia', was looked upon unfavourably.

Apart from two contradictory reviews, the press generally was non-committal and rather indifferent. The critic of *Il Tempo di Milano* admired Callas's 'exceptional musicianship, the intensity of her voice and the nobility of her phrasing that was further complemented by her ever alert stage presence'. *Corriere Lombardo* was explicitly damning: 'Undoubtedly Callas is endowed with temperament and fine musicianship, but her scale is uneven. Her method and vocal technique is old, her diction unclear, her high notes forced and her intonation not always secure.'

By far the most severe criticism of this Aida came from Franco Zeffirelli, the future opera producer and designer, who was later to be closely associated with Callas. Writing in his *Autobiography* (1986), Zeffirelli maintained that because of her longing to sing at La Scala she agreed to appear in a tired old production of *Aida*. She also misguidedly decided on this occasion that Aida, the enslaved princess ashamed of her situation, should only occasionally show her face which she kept wrapped in a veil. Furthermore, vocally she did not give the dramatic performance that her reputation had led the audience to expect. 'All the Milanese saw was this overweight Greek lady, peeping out from behind her trailing chiffon, and heard the unevenness, the changes of register between contralto and soprano which she thought helped reveal the sharpness of the character of the barbarian princess.'

Even so, the Meneghinis felt that at any moment La Scala would offer Maria a contract in her own right. However, for some unknown reason Antonio Ghiringhelli, the general administrator, not only offered nothing but did not even bother to pay the customary call on Callas at the end of her début performance. In fact, he visited the baritone Rafaelle de Falchi, whose dressing-room was next door to hers, but avoided her. The second performance found Callas more in her stride but the enigmatically silent Ghiringhelli remained aloof. It was impossible to guess what he really thought of her performance and the Meneghinis left Milan empty-handed.

A week later Callas recovered from her disappointment when she was acclaimed as Aida at the San Carlo and in early May she left for Mexico. Meneghini, owing to important business commitments, again could not accompany his wife, but as she was travelling by air they arranged to meet in Madrid on her return in eight weeks' time.

It was possible to travel to Mexico City via New York and Maria decided to interrupt her journey there, so that she could visit her parents. She had not seen them since she had sailed away to sing Gioconda in Italy three years before. Many things had happened in the interim. She was now an important, if not yet really famous, singer and happily married, but her pursuit of parental affection and appreciation continued. According to Meneghini, in 1948 Maria was moved to tears and could not thank him enough for sending her mother a telegram to inform her that her daughter was about to sing Isolde at La Fenice. This was only a few months after she had arrived in Italy and she was not yet married. Later in 1949 when she sang in Buenos Aires and could spare some money (although Meneghini provided for her from the beginning, Maria would accept help only for her basic needs), she immediately despatched one hundred dollars to her mother – all the currency the Bank of Argentina would then allow her to send out of the country.

During the flight to New York Maria met Giulietta Simionato, who was soon to become Italy's most important mezzo-soprano of her period; she too was on her way to Mexico, where she would be singing with Maria. Their friendship was instant and remained lifelong, and both singers were to know joint triumphs on many occasions.

Maria's parents were still feuding. Since Evangelia's return to New York in 1946 she had lived with her husband, though she was a long way from solving her marital problems. When Maria reached New York she found her mother in hospital with an eye infection and her father rather unwell with diabetes and heart trouble. However, as it was hoped that her mother would soon recover Maria invited her to Mexico City. Her father would receive a subsequent invitation at a later date when he was feeling better.

Antonio Caraza-Campos, the administrator of the Opera Nacional in Mexico, had engaged Callas on the recommendation of Cesare Siepi, who had enthused about her versatility and tremendous range, accompanied by unusual dramatic colour. Four operas were scheduled for Callas: *Norma*, *Aida*, *Tosca* and *Il trovatore* with Simionato participating in all of them except *Tosca*. As Carlos Diaz Du-Pond, the assistant administrator, was to reminisce years later, he was so moved by Callas's singing at the rehearsal of *Norma* that he immediately called Caraza-Campos to come and listen to her: 'She is the best dramatic coloratura I have heard in my life!; Apparently Caraza-Campos, who was very impressed, asked Maria if she would sing some of the music from *I Puritani* so that he could hear her E flat (Mexican audiences are crazy about high notes). But Maria promptly and not without some shrewdness answered that if Mr Caraza-Campos wanted to hear her E flat he could engage her for the following year to sing *I Puritani*.

On 23 May Callas made her Mexican début at the Palacio de las Bellas Artes as Norma. Simionato was singing her first Adalgisa, Kurt Baum was Pollione and Nicola Moscona, the Greek bass who in 1947 in New York could not find time to see Maria, was Oroveso. At first the public liked Maria to a degree, but there was no enthusiastic applause after 'Casta Diva'. However, as the performance went on and she produced some fabulous high notes, especially the D flat at the end of the second act, the audience was conquered. So were the critics, who immediately recognized the exceptional qualities of the new singer. The review in *Excelsior* described Callas as 'a surpreme soprano with an astonishing extension of voice; she has the very high notes, and even the staccatos, of a coloratura, but also the very low notes of a mezzo-soprano and even a real contralto. She enchanted us and if at the end of such a superb performance we were somewhat saddened, it was because we felt that perhaps we shall never again hear another comparable Norma in our lifetime.'

After Callas's dress rehearsal of her second opera, *Aida*, Caraza-Campos invited her and Simionato to his house. Du-Pond, who escorted the two singers, related how Caraza-Campos showed Callas an *Aida* score that a famous Mexican soprano of the previous century, Angela Peralta, had used and in which she had interpolated a high E flat at the end of the ensemble-finale of Act Two. 'If you give this high E flat,' he said to Maria, 'the public will go mad.' Maria was somewhat taken aback but with a broad smile answered, 'Impossible, Don Antonio; it is not written by Verdi and it is not nice. Besides I should ask permission from the conductor and my colleagues.' The matter did not go any further until after the first act of *Aida*. During the interval Moscona went to Maria's dressing-room and complained that Baum, the tenor, was holding on to his top notes. Maria, who had had a slight quarrel with Baum during the dress rehearsal of *Norma* (he was not well prepared for his role and was being belligerent), immediately sent a message to the other singers asking them if they would mind her singing the high E flat. Simionato and Robert Weede, the baritone who was singing Amonasro, were thrilled with the idea. The result was stupendous and the ovations were well beyond expectation. Maria wrote to her husband:

> *Aida* fared marvellously well. The public was ecstatic over Simionato and myself. So much so that the other singer had a stroke! . . . I am simply furious with that tenor Baum who is very insulting. He is angry with me because I took a high E flat at the end of the ensemble [Act Two finale]. His jealousy was so great (worse than any woman's) that I thought he wanted to kill me. ['I will never sing with you again and I shall see that you never sing at the Metropolitan,' Baum had screamed at Maria.] Anyway when he heard that I would refuse to sing with him again if he didn't apologize, he came to me before the second performance of *Aida* and asked me to forget what he had said. The skunk!

Callas and Baum did sing together again, in Mexico and elsewhere.

The critic of *El Universal* summed up the impact Callas made on the Mexican public. He wrote: 'Her triumph as Aida was complete . . . the audience was moved from the beginning and followed her through the first aria 'Ritorna vincitor' until the closing limpid phrases (initially she assumed the attitude of the submissive slave but soon she changed, as if she were remembering that she was an Ethiopian princess). After this enthusiastic and prolonged applause broke out — the audience felt that they were in the presence of a magnificent singer and began to call her in their ovations, soprano assoluta.'

Tosca and *Il trovatore* followed with equal success and the Mexicans hailed Callas as nothing less than a phenomenon.

Evangelia, who had recovered from her eye infection, arrived in Mexico City in time to admire her daughter in each of her four roles. Maria paid all her mother's expenses and in Mexico bought her a mink coat, several other presents and settled a $1000 debt that Evangelia had contracted in New York. Additionally, before Maria left Mexico — Evangelia stayed a few extra days on her own — she gave her $1000 so that she could keep herself for a year and also sent $500 to her father to cover her mother's recent hospital bills. Her great generosity towards her mother was at least in part a desperate effort to stop Evangelia and Georges separating. She was then very much against divorce and it was unthinkable that it should happen to her own parents.

Throughout her seven-week stay in Mexico City Maria almost made herself ill with worry over their problems. In her letters to her husband in Verona she generally attributed her tiredness, insomnia and other ailments to the awful Mexican climate and the hard work, as well as the separation from her husband. Although these were valid reasons, the basic cause of her unhappiness and worry at that period was her extreme concern at her mother's unwillingness to live with her father. Furthermore, Maria would in no way entertain the idea of Evangelia moving in with her; not only would this be encouraging her to abandon Georges but also in all probability she would have tried to take over the Meneghini household. Maria was embarrassed by the situation and instead of turning down this demand she ignored it and never gave her mother a direct refusal. In a letter to Battista (Mexico City, 19 May 1950) Maria unloaded her worries about her parents. She wrote: 'My mother wants to leave my father but I told her "How can you do this to him at a time when he is ill and old?" She also wants to come and live with us. May God forgive me but I want to live with you alone in our home. There is no way I would compromise my happiness and my right to be with you alone. Surely we both deserve this much. But I don't know how to explain this to my mother, that I do love her but with a different kind of love than I have for my husband.'

Not only did Evangelia shun all advice to reconcile herself with her husband, but two months after her visit to Mexico she wrote to her daughter asking for more money. Maria bluntly refused and again urged her to try and resolve their differences. But Evangelia was adamant and her demands for money became more aggressive.

Apart from the presents and all her expenses in Mexico City [Maria reiterated], I gave her practically all the money I earned in Mexico so that she would manage comfortably for a year. I was only left with two or three hundred dollars as I also repaid my godfather for the loan he made to me when I left New York for Italy and of course I paid for my own expenses – and I was happy and content with myself to have done all this. But when my mother, only a couple of months later, demanded more money, I got angry. At that time I had only been married a year and could not very well bring myself to keep on imposing upon my husband. The worst part of it was that my mother wanted to divorce my father who was old and infirm. That is why I was then fed up to the teeth with her.

What Maria avoided mentioning was that Meneghini was nowhere near as rich as he had often boasted.

On her return to Verona from Mexico Maria spent the whole summer with her husband. In September–October she gave two performances of *Tosca* in Bologna and Pisa, and one *Aida* in Rome. During that autumn a short festival of rarely performed as well as new operas was organized by the Amfiparnasso, an intellectual group, at the Teatro Eliseo in Rome. For the comic role of Donna Fiorilla in Rossini's *Il Turco in Italia*, an opera not heard anywhere for a hundred years, Maestro Cuccia and the conductor Gianandrea Gavazzeni turned to Callas, who was now undertaking a comic role for the first time — one that had nothing in common with her other heroines. Her triumph in *Il Turco in Italia* was no less important than her success in *I Puritani* had been the previous year.

Beneducci (*Opera*, February 1951) wrote that 'Maria Callas sang a *soprano leggera* role with the utmost ease in what one imagines was the style adopted by sopranos at the time this work was composed, making it extremely difficult to believe that she can be the perfect interpreter of both Turandot and Isolde. In Act One she astounded everybody by emitting a perfectly pitched high and soft E flat at the end of an attractive and vocally very difficult aria . . .'

But again La Scala, a theatre usually alert to artistic excellence, showed absolutely no sign of awareness and Callas, knowing she was being ignored, was enormously depressed. In these circumstances she turned her attention once again to Toscanini who, though he lived in America, often visited his native Italy. She felt that only if the great maestro liked her singing would the gates of La Scala open for her. It was, however, very difficult, if not impossible, to approach Toscanini, as she had discovered in 1946 when she was looking for work in New York. Even so, Callas's chance came in the most unexpected way.

Luigi Stefanotti, one of Callas's earliest admirers, told her that his dream in life was to hear her in an opera conducted by Toscanini. Apparently Stefanotti was often invited to Toscanini house and on one occasion spoke to him about Callas. Toscanini expressed the desire to hear her and also said that he had something in mind for her. Both Meneghini and Maria thought that Stefanotti, though well-meaning, was exaggerating, but he was not. A few days later, on 20 September, Wally Toscanini informed Callas by telegram that her father would like to hear her sing at his house in Milan.

At the audition the Meneghinis were surprised but delighted to find that Toscanini knew all about Callas, her extraordinary repertoire, vocal technique and artistry, and of her association with Serafin. However, he was annoyed to hear that Callas's absence from La Scala was not her own choice but, obviously, Ghiringhelli's. Meneghini then spoke of Ghiringhelli's insulting indifference towards Maria when she had substituted for Tebaldi in *Aida*, whereupon Toscanini contemptuously exclaimed in his inimitable manner, 'Ghiringhelli is an ignorant ass.'

It transpired later that he had been informed of Callas's capabilities by his old friend, the composer Vincenzo Tommasini, who in fact had suggested her as a possible Lady Macbeth. Toscanini was in Milan at that time looking for a suitable soprano for this role, as he was planning to present Verdi's *Macbeth* in 1951 on the occasion of the fiftieth anniversary of the composer's death. The opera was to be produced at La Scala but was first to be performed at Bussetto, where the composer had spent so much of his youth, near the tiny village of Le

Roncole, his birthplace. *Macbeth* would then be presented at La Scala, Florence, New York and possibly elsewhere.

Accompanied on the piano by Toscanini, Callas sang long excerpts from the first act of *Macbeth*. She so impressed him that there and then he told her that he had found in her what he had been looking for all his life. 'You have the right voice and you are the correct singer for this extraordinary role. I will do *Macbeth* with you.' Toscanini would now instruct Ghiringhelli to start planning for the production of *Macbeth* with Maria as prima donna.

A few days later Ghiringhelli wrote cordially to Callas, asking her to confirm her availability during August and September 1951. She complied, but *Macbeth*, conducted by Toscanini, never materialized even though the maestro did not lose heart about the project and the necessary financial support was secured, as well as arrangements for broadcasting the performance live.

Although no official reason was ever given, it became common knowledge that theatre politics were at the bottom of it. The principal conductor, a mainstay at La Scala since 1929, was the formidable Victor De Sabata (in 1953 he replaced Mario Labroca as musical and artistic director) whose interpretations, particularly of Verdi's music, had much of Toscanini's legendary incandescence. Maybe because of this, Toscanini did not like him and had for some time held him in disdain. Toscanini was widely considered, both by the general public and musicians, as no less than a god, his music-making and opinions sacred. De Sabata, also, at least in Italy, had a substantial and influential following, which included Ghiringhelli. The latter, a confirmed autocrat and a very wealthy man, in his strong position at La Scala needed De Sabata, but was also prepared to suffer Toscanini's insults and commands, so that he would maintain the great possible prestige in the Italian musical world.

A production of *Macbeth* conducted by Toscanini at Bussetto, then at La Scala during the Verdi commemoration year would positively have damaged, if not totally eclipsed, De Sabata's stature and undoubtedly this was the main reason that the Toscanini *Macbeth* did not take place. The deteriorating health of the eighty-five-year-old maestro was no more than a convenient pretext, as he conducted a celebrated all-Wagner concert at La Scala on 19 September 1952, less than three months before *Macbeth* was triumphantly staged with Callas, and De Sabata in the pit.

Callas's struggle to be engaged at La Scala did not end in September 1950, when she confirmed her availability for Toscanini's *Macbeth* in the following year. At first Toscanini suggested that she should sing Magda Sorel in Gian-Carlo Menotti's *The Consul*, which the composer was staging at La Scala in January 1951. She declined the offer, however, because she did not consider herself suitable to portray this modern character and also because it was a far from ideal role for her official début at the most important of the world's opera houses. She would only have sung this role if the occasion had guaranteed her entrée to La Scala as a permanent member of the company. Her audition with Menotti was most successful, but Ghiringhelli would only have her as a guest artist.

In the following April Ghiringhelli asked for Callas, but again to substitute for an indisposed Tebaldi in *Aida*. Remembering the way she had been treated on the previous occasion, Callas refused: if La Scala wanted her she would be delighted to sing, but only on the terms of a top-rank artist and not as an understudy.

Meanwhile she contributed to the Verdi celebrations by singing her first Violetta in *La traviata* in Florence. This role, which she had studied meticulously with Serafin, had captured her imagination and her portrayal of the consumptive courtesan who finds purification through personal sacrifice was already highly accomplished and moving. Later it was to deepen and achieve sublime heights. Callas followed with *Il trovatore* at the San Carlo where, despite the excellent cast – which included the redoubtable Giacomo Lauri-Volpi, Cloe Elmo and Paolo Silveri, Serafin as conductor and Gioacchino Forzano, another septuagenarian of long experience, as producer – the expected great promise did not quite materialize. From the start, Serafin disagreed strongly with Forzano and although they soon made it up publicly, the singers themselves did not establish complete rapport, especially in the ensembles with the conductor. In addition, Lauri-Volpi, a long-standing idol of the public, was now at the end of his career and in these performances he was vocally insecure. In 'Di quella pira', when the public expect high ringing notes, he was openly booed. These drawbacks did not affect Callas, who sang exquisitely and made Leonora a living character. The critics, however, more concerned on this occasion with theatre politics than with art, praised both Serafin and Forzano rather extravagantly and practically ignored the singers. Lauri-Volpi, always an artist of great integrity, felt he could not let this go by, not on his own account but because of Callas's artistic achievement. In an open letter to the press he protested strongly about 'the appalling indifference and lack of appreciation for Callas's magnificent singing'.

It was indeed some time before Callas's portrayal of Leonora would be acknowledged as a major contribution to Italian opera. 'I have never considered Leonora', Callas told me,

> to be secondary or overshadowed by the mezzo-soprano role of Azucena – a part, in fact,
> also offered to me, but which I did not want to sing. Do not misunderstand me. Azucena
> is a wonderful role especially when 'sung', not bellowed, but it is not for me. Only
> Leonora interests me. Let me add that vocally it is one of the most difficult. The fact that
> it is comparatively short makes it harder for her to dominate the drama. And she must,
> because everything in the plot revolves around her – she is the pivotal character in the
> opera. Azucena is central to what had happened before the curtain goes up.

The year 1951 was also the anniversary of the birth of the Sicilian composer Vincenzo Bellini, and Callas, who had already distinguished herself in *Norma* and *I Puritani*, sang Norma with success in Palermo. After performances of *La traviata* and *Aida* in the provinces she returned to Florence for her second contribution to the Verdi celebrations.

Florence holds its prestigious Maggio Musicale Fiorentino in May and June, and was this year opening with a rarely performed opera of the 'middle Verdi' period, *I vespri Siciliani*. Erich Kleiber, making his Italian début, conducted with meticulous care and love; the rapport between him and Callas in the leading role of Elena (Giorgio Bardi-Kokolios, Enzo Mascherini and Boris Christoff were also in the cast) was mutual. Apart from a slight indisposition at the first performance, she subsequently rose to top form and used her coloratura so dramatically that the audience were thrilled. Reporting in *Opera*, Giuseppe Pugliese said that 'Her dramatic flair was very much in evidence in the smooth cavatina and exhortatory cabaletta [Act One]. . . . At this performance her voice showed a tendency to lose quality in the forte passages (apart from a ringing top E at the end of the "Bolero"), but her soft singing in the duets of Acts Two and Four was exquisite, and the long and crystal-clear chromatic scale with which she ended her Act Four solo made a most brilliant effect.'

Lord Harewood, who heard Callas in a stage rehearsal, wrote about his impressions of her first entrance (*Opera*, November 1952):

Callas rehearsing her first entrance in Vespri, *that so impressed Lord Harewood.*

... a female figure – the Sicilian Duchess Elena – is seen slowly crossing the square. Doubtless the music and the production helped to spotlight Elena but, though she had not yet sung and was not even wearing her costume, one was straight away impressed by the natural dignity of her carriage, the air of quiet, innate authority which went with her every moment.

During the past year Toscanini, who had returned to the United States, never lost his enthusiasm for *Macbeth* with Callas and continued to enquire about it. Not surprisingly, the whole of Milan was following the progress, or its absence, of this project and at the same time began to wonder why Maria Callas, Toscanini's positive choice for an opera he had never conducted before, was not singing at La Scala. Eventually Ghiringhelli and his associates could no longer ignore the public's interest in her, since she was currently singing with great success in various Italian theatres but not in Milan. Nevertheless, it was Wally Toscanini who, acting on her father's wishes, finally prodded Ghiringhelli into engaging Callas.

After the première of *I vespri* in Florence, Ghiringhelli congratulated Callas by telegram. Several telephone calls followed and Maria agreed to meet him after her third performance of *I vespri*. Hardly had the applause died down when Ghiringhelli, who had been out front, appeared with open arms and contract in hand at Maria's dressing-room. La Scala was yielding at last to the successful prima donna. The invitation this time was a royal one. She was offered four leading roles: Constanze at La Scala's first ever production of Mozart's *Die Entführung aus dem Serail*, Norma, Elisabetta di Valois (*Don Carlos*) and Elena in *I vespri*, with which the forthcoming season at La Scala was opening on 7 December. It was a contract that any artist would go a long way to obtain and Callas was happy beyond description. However, she would not readily accept it unless they also allowed her to sing Violetta in *La traviata*, a role which she considered ideal to establish her reputation there. True though this was, Callas had an additional motive: Tebaldi had sung the role for them only months before without success. Here was a chance for Callas to show her supremacy, as people would be able to compare. Ghiringhelli, at the time a great supporter of Tebaldi whom he had in the company, almost certainly sensed Callas's motives and consequently embarked on a campaign to persuade her to sign the contract without making concrete plans for *Traviata*. Their verbal fencing continued and although by the time Callas left for Mexico they had agreed on dates for the operas offered she did not actually sign, because she was only given vague promises for *Traviata*.

In any case she had six very busy months before her official début at La Scala. At the Maggio she followed *I vespri* with Haydn's *Orfeo ed Euridice*, an opera written in 1791 but receiving its stage première in 1951 in Florence.[1] Callas created the role of Euridice (Tyge Tygesen sang Orfeo, Christoff Creonte and Kleiber conducted) with consummate art, expressing her emotions

through Haydn's classic florid style but with modern awareness. The reviews of the first performance were highly contrasting. The critic of *La Nazione* wrote: 'Callas used her colourful and
warm voice to portray with vitality the character of Euridice.' Newell Jenkins (*Musical America*), on
the other hand, found the staging inadequate, the ballet of the Bacchante in the last scene laugh-
able. 'Callas's voice was rich and beautiful, but was often uneven and sometimes tired. Certainly
the role was too heavy for her; but she sang the death aria in the second act with rare insight and
fine phrasing.'

Writing about the second and last performance, Howard Taubman (*New York Times*, 11 June
1951) thought 'Callas distinguished herself as Euridice … and could manage the florid style
with assurance. She has full control of the voice in soft singing, and she did coloratura passages
with delicacy and accuracy.'

A week after her *Orfeo* performances Maria, accompanied by her husband, left for her second season in Mexico. Meneghini now sold his share of the family business to his brothers and became
his wife's manager. This was their first long trip together and they were to stay away all summer.
Mexico City was the first stop, followed by São Paulo and Rio de Janeiro.

In Mexico City Callas scored enormous successes as Aida, with Del Monaco as Radames, and
Violetta with Cesare Valletti as Alfredo, both operas conducted by Oliviero de Fabritiis. As
Violetta she was particularly outstanding: the critics lavishly praised the beauty of her voice and
her overwhelming dramatic power, while the public went wild over her. 'How completely justified one is to call her Soprano Assoluta!' Junius wrote in *Excelsior*.

The Meneghinis then went on to São Paulo where Callas was to make her Brazilian début in
Aida and follow with single performances of *Norma* and *La traviata*. Brazil was not, however, to be
the happy place Mexico had been. From her first day there Maria fell ill – the climate and her
increasing weight caused her legs to swell, practically immobilizing her – and could not sing in
Aida. She recovered in time to make her début in *Norma* and also sing in *La traviata*, and her success in both works was unqualified. *Norma* was conducted by Antonino Votto, *La traviata* by
Serafin and in the cast were Giuseppe di Stefano as Alfredo and Tito Gibbi as Germont, two
singers appearing with Callas for the first time, who were to be especially associated with her in
the years to come.

The São Paulo opera season ran concurrently and in conjunction with the more important
one in Rio, where Barreto Pinto, a concert manager, assembled a most exciting cast consisting of
a number of Italy's leading singers, old and young. Callas was contracted to sing two performances each of *Norma*, *Tosca* and *La traviata*, all to be conducted by Votto, Serafin not being available. Renata Tebaldi was also engaged to sing in *La traviata*, *La bohème*, *Andrea Chénier* and *Aida*.
This young singer rose to stardom when Toscanini included her in the concert with which he

inaugurated the rebuilt La Scala in 1946. Three years later she joined the company there, and in the absence at the time of another formidable soprano, she soon established herself as the queen of La Scala, though as yet uncrowned. As we have seen, in 1950 Callas had substituted for her in *Aida* when she was indisposed.

The season in Rio opened during the last week of August with the then sixty-one-year-old celebrated tenor Beniamino Gigli and Elena Nicolai in Giordano's *Fedora*. Tebaldi, who had recently failed to please the Milanese with her Violetta at La Scala, made her Rio début in the same role and completely won over the Brazilian public. She became the talk of Rio until one week later, when Callas made her début in *Norma*. The audience gave her a prolonged standing ovation and at the second and last performance their excitement knew no bounds. The critics, too, saw in her a great singer with extraordinary dramatic powers. Franca wrote in the *Correio de Manhã*: 'Her art possesses all degrees of dramatic passion – a great singer, an extraordinary figure on the operatic scene.'

Despite this success Callas found herself in a highly competitive situation as in addition to Tebaldi she had also to contend with Elisabetta Barbato, who was already extremely popular in Rio and had a considerable fanatical following. Both Callas and Tebaldi were in a tense, irritable state of mind, though not initially on a personal level, but because the public – a small number of people, to be precise – were creating a strong atmosphere of rivalry. More fuel was put on the fire when Elena Rakowska quite openly and with little tact lost no opportunity in declaring her preference. Rakowska would tell off her husband while he calmly explained that the two singers were both wonderful in their own way – they had different voices, different repertoires and comparison between them was simply incongruous. Although Rakowska had to agree with this, she had a field day proclaiming Callas's supremacy after she sang Violetta in São Paulo. Such comments, which travel fast in the theatre world, and the fact that Callas would be joining the company at La Scala in the forthcoming season, upset Tebaldi very much. Unwisely she reacted by being cold and on occasion hostile towards Maria and her husband. The Meneghinis, who soon became aware of this change in Tebaldi's attitude, decided to ignore the whole thing, believing that it would fizzle out before long. Maria for her part may have been outspoken about artistic matters, and even enjoyed to some extent the rivalry that was thrust upon the two singers, but she never said anything against Tebaldi, whom she considered a friend. An event that followed, however, strained this friendship and later transformed it into a kind of long-standing feud. But the story is better told by the principal characters themselves: 'I believe that seldom between two woman of the same age and in the same profession can there be a friendship as fresh and spontaneous as that which occurred between us,' Callas related later (*Oggi*, 1957 and to me in the early 1970s). Apparently this friendship began in Venice. 'One night,' she continued, during the performance of *Tristan* at La Fenice [December 1947], while I was making up my dressing-room, I heard the door open unexpectedly and in the doorway stood the tall figure of Tebaldi, who was in Venice to sing in *La traviata* with Serafin. We knew one another only by sight (since a party at Verona in the previous August when I sang in *Gioconda* and she in *Faust*), but on this occasion we shook hands warmly and Renata addressed such spontaneous compliments to me that I was enchanted. '*Mamma mia*,' she exclaimed, 'if I had been obliged to go through such a tiring role they would have had to scoop me up with a spoon.'

My friendship with Renata became real affection a short time later in Rovigo, where she was singing in *Andrea Chénier* and I was singing Aida. At the end of my big aria 'O patria mia' I heard a distinct voice shout from one of the boxes, '*Brava, brava Maria!*' It was the unmistakable voice of Renata. Henceforth we became — I can sincerely say it — very dear friends. In our meetings, which were relatively frequent in those early days, we invariably discussed and exchanged advice, amongst other things on dress, coiffure and even repertoire. Afterwards, as our professional commitments increased, we usually met briefly, between one voyage and another, but always I think, or rather I feel sure, with reciprocal pleasure. She admired me for my dramatic strength and my physical endurance and I admired her *dolcissimo canto*.

However, the first collision between us occurred in Rio in 1951. We had not seen each other for some time and we were very happy to meet again, or so it seemed to me. Renata was with her mother and together with the mezzo-soprano Elena Nicolai and her husband and myself with my husband we often went to the delightful restaurants of Rio. Then one day, after I had made my début as Norma, Barreto Pinto — the administrator of the opera season, a rather simple man, but quite powerful in financial and political circles and who also had married one of the richest women in Brazil — asked his singers to take part in a benefit concert. We accepted and Renata proposed and we all agreed not to sing encores. To our great surprise, at the concert Renata was the only singer who gave not one but two encores. After the 'Ave Maria' (*Otello*) she sang 'La mamma morta' (*Andrea Chénier*) and then 'Vissi d'arte' (*Tosca*). I only sang 'Sempre libera' from *La traviata*. Although I felt badly about Renata's gesture, I soon got over it and considered it a childish caprice. Only later, during dinner (Nicolai and her husband were also dining with us) after the concert did I realize that my dear colleague and friend had changed in her attitude towards me, and that she could not hide a touch of bitterness every time she addressed me.

Meneghini told me in 1978 that the conversation on this occasion between Tebaldi and Callas became quite animated and centred on La Scala.

For some reason Tebaldi kept on saying that she had never been in her best form at La Scala and was trying to put Maria off that theatre. I could not understand what Tebaldi was really driving at when suddenly it crossed my mind that it was Maria's brilliant singing from *La traviata* at the benefit concert that worried her. You see Tebaldi had not been very successful in *La traviata* at La Scala during the previous season. It would, therefore, not have been in her interests if Maria sang this role at La Scala. So in order to change this incendiary topic of conversation, I nudged my wife with my elbow several times. Of course Maria understood and stopped but not before she answered Tebaldi rather sharply with words to the effect that perhaps it is a good idea for Tebaldi not to sing at La Scala too often. 'People get tired of you.'

'Anyway,' Callas felt, 'everything would have ended there and then at the dinner table with a superficial brisk exchange of words, if it had not been for the incident of *Tosca* that followed.' While Callas was singing Tosca a few people in the audience, in order to show their displeasure, shouted the name of Elisabetta Barbato. However, at the end of the performance the majority of the audience gave Callas a long and warm reception. Despite this, the following day Pinto told Callas that she was not to sing any more in subscription performances as she was *protestata* (a slang theatrical term meaning undesirable). 'At first I was speechless,' Callas said,

> but soon I realized what he was telling me and reacted strongly – unjust accusations always make me rebel. I really took exception to this and angrily I reminded him of his contractual obligations. Apart from the operas given only to subscribers there should be two non-subscription performances of *La traviata*, and also that they had to pay me for them whether they prevented me from singing or not. Pinto was absolutely mad. 'All right,' he said – he really had no choice – 'sing *Traviata* but I warn you now that no one will come to hear you.'
>
> Pinto could not have been more wrong as both performances were completely sold out. Nevertheless, he didn't give up and tried to annoy me in other ways. When I went to his office to collect my fees he rudely told me, 'For the awful performance you gave I should not pay anything.'

Callas was so annoyed that she grabbed the first object (Meneghini remembered that it was either a rather large inkstand or a paperweight) she could find on his desk to hurl at him but Meneghini took her by the arm and saved Pinto from getting his skull smashed. However, as soon as Pinto thought himself safe he resumed his rudeness to Callas and also said that he would have her arrested for threatening him.

'I really must put a stop to this,' Callas shouted and pushing Meneghini aside hurled herself at Pinto, striking him in the stomach with her knee. Pinto, who practically fainted (the young and heavily built Callas was then quite strong), decided not to take any further action. He promptly had delivered at Callas's hotel her full fees as stipulated in her contract and two air tickets for Italy. Whereas Meneghini, who was scared out of his wits, feared that the powerful Pinto might well have them arrested, Callas only regretted that she did not, after all, break his head. Anyway, the Meneghinis were glad to leave Rio, Maria vowing never to sing in Brazil again as long as there were people like Pinto around.

According to Meneghini, Pinto, a strange and difficult man, would unpredictably change the singers and even the operas to be performed at the last minute if something or somebody upset him. No one dared contradict this absolute despot. At Callas's first *Traviata* Pinto was so annoyed with Votto, the conductor, for a trivial reason (Votto placed two of his guests at the back of Pinto's box) that he instantly fired him only a few minutes before the performance. He then ordered Nino Gaioni to take over.

But to continue Callas's Brazilian saga: 'This unpleasant episode of my career,' she further elaborated,

> was unfortunately tied to another bitter disappointment. As I have said, while I was
> singing *Tosca* in Rio, Tebaldi was singing in *Andrea Chénier* in São Paulo. Naturally having
> been *protestata* — and in such a manner — I was curious to find out who was to replace me in
> *Tosca*. To my sorrow I learned that Renata, the singer I had always considered my good
> friend, was taking over. They said that Tebaldi had ordered copies of the costumes I wore
> in *Tosca*, and from the same dressmaker too; not only that, but she had gone to try them
> on before leaving for São Paulo, that is, when no one could have predicted or known that
> I would be *protestata*.

Tebaldi's version is completely different. She refuted almost everything Callas had said and gave her own explanation about minor points of the affair. 'And why speak of hatred', Tebaldi declared, 'when there has never been any love between us, and why speak of enemies if we have never been friends?'

According to Tebaldi, she first met Callas at a party given at Castello Romano in Verona. Tebaldi did not like Callas's physical appearance and only a few polite words were exchanged between them. There was certainly no love at first sight. When they subsequently met in Venice Renata did go to see Maria in her dressing-room and after she complimented her on her performance Maria introduced her to Meneghini and told her in a most patronizing manner: 'I wish you too would find such a wonderful husband.'

Later, at Rovigo, although Tebaldi did shout '*Brava, brava Maria!*' she did not feel enthusiastic enough to go backstage to congratulate Callas on her performance. About their meeting in Rio

Tebaldi insisted that she never proposed 'not to sing any encores. Besides all the singers knew that on such an occasion they were expected to give encores.' (It may be noted that only Tebaldi gave encores in this concert.) She also insisted that it was Callas who brought up the subject of her unsuccessful *Traviata* at La Scala, not at dinner after the concert in Rio but on another evening several days before.

As for the *Tosca* performance, Tebaldi professed not to have known anything about it. She was simply asked to sing and did so, and the costumes were made within twenty-four hours. No preparation had begun before Callas had sung in *Tosca*.

This incident that broke the friendship between the two singers (at least on Callas's part, as Tebaldi denied the existence of any relationship) assumed exaggerated dimensions later in Italy when both press and public, always ready to enjoy rivalry between two successful artists, took over completely.

1 *Orfeo ed Euridice* was first performed complete for a recording in Vienna in 1950.

CHAPTER SIX

THE PASSIONATE PILGRIM
ATTAINS LA SCALA

Milan is Italy's largest city and her industrial capital, whose contribution to the nation's economy is by far the greatest in the country. Although it offers little in the way of antiquities as compared with Rome, the eternal city and Italian metropolis, Milan has a trump card in possessing the most famous opera house in the world, the Teatro alla Scala, generally known as La Scala. The theatre, ordered by Empress Maria Theresa, Duchess of Milan, and designed by Giuseppe Piermarini, was built on the site previously occupied by the church of Santa Maria alla Scala (founded by Regina della Scala, wife of Duke Barnabò Visconti of Milan in 1381) for the purpose of replacing the Teatro Regio-Ducale which stood on a site nearby and was burned down in 1776.

The inauguration of the new theatre took place in 1778 with Salieri's *Europa riconosciuta*. All the important Italian composers wrote for La Scala, which has always been the touchstone, the ultimate goal, of all singers. Arturo Toscanini (1867–1957), the most influential conductor of the twentieth century, raised the standard at La Scala to that of premier opera house in the world. His first period there was 1898–1903, then 1906–08 and later 1921–9, when he left because of his vehement objections to Mussolini's Fascist regime.

Badly bombed during the war (August 1943), the theatre was rebuilt and inaugurated on 11 May 1946 with a concert conducted by Toscanini who, in response to the insistent appeals of his countrymen, returned from his long exile. The programme, consisting of music by Rossini, Verdi, Boito and Puccini, was performed by the veteran singers Mariano Stabile and Tancredi Pasero, and the young soprano Renata Tebaldi. The opera season then opened with *Nabucco* on 26 December 1946, the traditional St Stephen's Day. It was conducted by Tullio Serafin, who had been at La Scala in 1902 as Toscanini's assistant and had made his début as conductor in December 1910. After an outstanding career both in Europe and America, Serafin returned to La Scala in 1946 but only stayed there for two seasons. The reasons for his leaving were never made public, but it was thought, with good cause, that the great conductor whose artistic ability and sincerity were indubitable would not gladly entertain artistic ignoramuses like Ghiringhelli, who never saw eye to eye with Serafin.

Born in the Italian town of Brunello, Ghiringhelli (1903–79), a leather manufacturer, came from a factory-owning family who made their money during the Second World War. He was a very private person without real friends. A man in Milan who knew him in his teens told me a little about him: an accident in his youth, when a horse kicked him, rendered him impotent, which stopped him from getting married. Apart from being a Freemason (at that period an illegal society in Italy) he had no other interests outside his work at La Scala where, after the Italian liberation in 1945, he was engaged by Antonio Greppi, the mayor of Milan, first as a supervisor for the rebuilding of the bombed theatre, then as general administrator. So great was his love for and devotion to La Scala that he never accepted any form of payment for his services.

Although Ghiringhelli had had a higher education, studying law in Genoa, his lack of culture was such that if obliged to give an opinion on an artistic matter he would often make a gaffe. He also knew almost nothing about music, nor was he interested – La Scala's musical integrity was in any case ensured by Mario Labroca, Serafin's successor, Franco Capuana and Victor De Sabata. It was said of Ghiringhelli that he very rarely saw an opera performance to its end and ran the affairs of La Scala like an absolute dictator; his staff privately referred to him as the Mikado and were in constant fear of him. He was, however, an outstanding, very shrewd and capable administrator. During his reign at La Scala, which ended in 1971[1] when he retired on account of serious health problems, he achieved a golden age: great singers, conductors, producers and designers were brought together to give opera a new lease of life – a new public, the middle class in particular, were attracted to La Scala.

Ghiringhelli was also instrumental in the building of a small second theatre, the Piccola Scala, and he developed the ballet school and founded conservatories for young singers and stage designers. His twenty-seven years at La Scala can with good reason be called the Ghiringhelli era. La Scala was in excellent financial health and it was thought by some that he had on more than one occasion footed the bills when promised funds failed to arrive.

As with employees, so with artists, he was ruthless and had no ethics. If he thought he needed somebody who would be good box-office he would treat him or her wonderfully, but only as long as that person was useful and obedient. Otherwise they would be dropped. Tebaldi became his first favourite because, as we have seen, in 1946 Toscanini, considering her to be the most promising young Italian singer, chose her to sing at the inaugural concert at La Scala, a great honour indeed. He also said of her: 'She has the voice of an angel.' Callas arrived on the scene in 1947. She was not Italian and therefore her credentials, as far as Ghiringhelli was concerned, were suspect, if not downright unacceptable. The fact that she was a protégée of Serafin, who had left La Scala for the reasons mentioned above, was against her. These theatre politics may also have had something to do with Labroca's rejection of Callas at her La Scala audition in 1947, for it is difficult to believe that he would otherwise have dismissed her without even a second hearing. She herself felt that both Ghiringhelli and Labroca were against Serafin. Meneghini also wrote that although Toscanini was not surprised that Ghiringhelli, being such an ass, had not engaged Callas, he thought Labroca's rejection strange because the latter was a musician and a good judge of voices.

Even after Toscanini chose Callas for his putative *Macbeth* at La Scala, Ghiringhelli was for a long time prepared only reluctantly to have her as a guest artist to substitute for an indisposed Tebaldi. He did not want to engage Callas on a permanent basis at the premier Italian opera house. In a perceptive assessment of Ghiringhelli's (and others') initially belligerent attitude towards her, Zeffirelli wrote in his *Autobiography*: 'Ghiringhelli couldn't handle her; he was afraid of what she represented, a singer with a mind and a vision of what opera could be far beyond his, or in fact anyone else's, conception at that time.'

Here we must digress to explain why Callas became the most controversial operatic artist of her period and, by general consensus, of the twentieth century. Musical history suggests that she would have been so in any age. However, it is first necessary to define opera and the singer's relationship and obligation towards the art.

Opera was born in Florence at the end of the sixteenth century when Italian artists formed an intellectual club, the Camerata, with the aim of re-creating the music of the Greek tragedies. The exact nature of this music is a matter for conjecture, this form of drama having disappeared for hundreds of years after the collapse of Graeco-Roman civilization. Was it simply incidental music with songs, or was all the dialogue sung? Without any evidence, the Camerata opted for the latter mode. Consequently opera, as we know it, is drama expressed in music and not glorification of sound *per se*; if the words are not given a deeper meaning, an abstract dimension, by means of the music, there is no reason why they should not be left as they are. All operatic composers worth their salt strive to write dramatic music and do not create their characters by accident. Consequently opera singers should at all times be singing actors if they are to identify with the characters they are portraying, which they must.

The singing voice, which uses both words and music, is endowed with heart, soul and brain, and when not abusing its capabilities is fully equipped to convey every form of emotion and information. But without the necessary technique no singer can hope to develop complete powers of expression, inarguably the *raison d'être* of this art. If this goal is not achieved the development of opera will decelerate, deteriorate and eventually die a natural death.

In order to understand the advent of Maria Callas – a landmark in the history of opera – and how it has influenced her contemporaries as well as her successors, one must first consider the period immediately before and during the beginning of her career. By the middle of the 1930s opera had lost most of its splendour. There were no new acclaimed opera composers and few singers endowed with genius to inject new life – a necessity for the survival of the art. Puccini was dead, as were the great singing actors Feodor Chaliapin (1873–1938) and Claudia Muzio (1889–1936). Rosa Ponselle (1897–1981) had retired and Kirsten Flagstad (1895–1962) was only beginning to find her true medium in her magnificent Wagnerian portrayals. Opera became more of a 'vaudeville de luxe' than drama expressed in music and was deprived of so much of its earlier esteem that it ran the risk of being almost completely misunderstood.

During this period the world found a great deal of enchantment in the exquisitely lyrical singing of Beniamino Gigli (1890–1957), Jussi Björling (1911–60) and Tito Schipa (1889–1965), three honourable representatives of the art form who still kept it alive, albeit at a relatively lame pace from the acting point of view. There were of course important singers among the women: Gina Cigna (1900–), Maria Caniglia (1905–79), Zinka Milanov (1906–89) and others could often be exciting, though from various reports and from some personal experience not really moving, possibly because, whatever their vocal techniques, their rudimentary physical acting did not serve fully the dramatic demands of their roles. Above all, they might well have lacked that touch of genius that enables an artist to capture the imagination of today's more demanding audiences.

Even though the arrival of Callas, first in Athens during the early 1940s and then in Italy in 1947, made some impact, both the quality of her soprano voice and her style of singing appeared anachronistic to their age: her voice did not correspond to the categories into which voices are divided today – light, lyric or dramatic – yet it encompassed all these categories. Not since the early part of the nineteenth century, when Isabella Colbran (1785–1845), Giuditta Pasta (1797–1865), Maria Malibran (1808–36) and some of their successors were extolled for their amazing versatility and acting talent in Rossini, Donizetti, Bellini and later the young Verdi, had there been such a voice. By the middle of the nineteenth century composers began to write roles with simplified vocal demands so that artists could cope by being light, lyric or dramatic sopranos, though often more than one type was required in the same opera and it is not particularly rare for one singer to combine two of these vocal qualities such as lyric and dramatic or light and lyric. The exceptional case, almost a phenomenon in our times, remains the dramatic soprano with great flexibility of voice and the ability to sing coloratura expressively best described as a dramatic soprano *d'agilità*.

As Callas was precisely such a singer it is not surprising that among all her accomplished colleagues in the early 1950s she led the way and, in short, began a new chapter in musical history. This is generally the case when an artist combines extraordinary natural gifts with a capacity for hard work and thereby with insight and genius creates or re-creates something outstandingly different. Thus Callas at first appeared to the world as a modern singer and this led to the arguments that surrounded her. To analyse this controversy one should first put the public 'on trial' and, for practical purposes, consider three representative groups.

A rather large faction revels almost entirely in the absolute purity of sound, their sole criterion being the degree of sweetness and smoothness (sometimes referred to as velvet), however inappropriate, the brilliance of the high notes, and flexibility allied to mechanical accuracy but devoid of stridency at any price and in any situation. Moreover, this faction has little interest in the words and any degree of dramatic expression is accepted as a luxury, but only if it does not interfere with 'beautiful' tone.

People with this approach (at its extreme, a form of introverted philistinism) found Callas's voice, and particularly the way she used it uncompromisingly to express real human emotions, very disturbing – indeed she was accused of violating the traditions of vocal art. In actuality they mistake vocal technique (in itself a facility) for art. The ability to vocalize the notes should be taken for granted and even the most accomplished opera singer will achieve nothing if unable to apply his or her technique to bring a character to life. Instead, such singing often becomes counterproductive and belongs more to the circus than to the theatre. A parallel may be drawn by appraising ballet merely on its acrobatic and contortionist aspects. Neither Galina Ulanova, Margot Fonteyn nor Rudolph Nureyev could or wanted to outdo circus acrobats. By the same token, opera must always be drama expressed in music, not a sterile and ephemeral creation.

Others, at first a minority, understood Callas's voice and the way she used it, and were moved by the truth of her musical interpretations. This faction's appreciation of art, built upon intrinsic knowledge, centres on the varying shades of expression and colour which, through music and words, convincingly bring a character to life; a feat which is true beauty, satisfying both the senses and the intellect, and can only be attained by applying astutely developed technique.

A third faction may not really hold an opinion but, when confronted with something beyond their comprehension, disguise their ignorance with an air of bogus superiority by taking a fanatical stand in favour or against. They are futile and they need not detain us.

With the public's general approach in mind, it is constructive to put Callas the artist on trial, or more precisely to assess her example. Her talent was basically musical. Everything that she did sprang from this source and was primarily conveyed through the medium of her singing voice. Later she developed and refined acting until her physical movements became one with the music. Even though her voice was a natural gift and her acting instinctive to a degree, the manner in which she used these talents was the result of very hard work – her training was long and laborious.

Returning to Callas and La Scala, Ghiringhelli was soon forced to change his ideas. She was rapidly becoming an important asset in the musical world and above all she began to generate the kind of excitement that creates universal interest. Consequently the time came when he had to take this into account, if only to avoid accusations of missing out on the mainstream of contemporary operatic developments. Furthermore, Toscanini still wanted her at La Scala; the final pressure was, in fact, put on Ghiringhelli by Wally Toscanini, who by 1951 was already becoming an influential person in the affairs of the opera house, in some ways representing her ageing father.

Hardly had the Meneghinis returned from Brazil at the end of September when Ghiringhelli, accompanied by Luigi Oldani – his administrator – and a lawyer, was on their doorstep in Verona, anxiously begging Callas to sign a contract for the forthcoming season due to open in 7 December, the feast day of St Ambrose, patron saint of Milan.[2] It has, of course, always been considered a great honour for the artists chosen to sing on such a night. When Maria realized that Ghiringhelli was continuing in the same vein as at their last meeting before she left for Mexico, that is excluding *Traviata*, she politely thanked him and sent him on his way. 'Perhaps we can recommence our conversation next year,' she said, as the three dumbfounded men followed her to the door. Not quite done for, Ghiringhelli returned, declaring that as he really wanted Callas to open the forthcoming season at La Scala he would try his best to make it possible that she also sang in *La traviata* during her first season there.

The 1951–2 season at La Scala opened with a spectacular production of *I vespri Siciliani*. Apart from Eugene Conley, a new tenor, and Victor De Sabata, the famous conductor and La Scala's artistic director, the rest of the cast were the same as in the Florence performances a few months earlier. Callas sang the leading role of Elena and took the Milanese audience by storm. Furthermore, at rehearsal she impressed her colleagues immensely; her complete dedication to every detail of the score, her extensive vocal range, and above all the meaning and excitement with which she imbued every phrase, whether recitative or aria, came as a revelation even to such a disciplined company. The critics also received the new soprano enthusiastically. Franco Abbiati (*Corriere della Sera*) described Callas's throat as 'miraculous and the prodigious extension of her middle and low register is full of incandescent beauty. Her vocal technique and agility are more than rare – they are unique.' Thus Callas auspiciously began her association with a theatre where she was to know her greatest triumphs.

Even so, her success in *I vespri*, repeated in all the seven performances given, did not deter her from bringing up the *Traviata* affair. When Ghiringhelli again resorted to his old evasive tactics Callas gave him an ultimatum: unless she received a conclusive answer about *Traviata* she would not sing Norma a few days later. More arguments followed, Ghiringhelli admitting in the end that he had made a mistake but promising to mount a splendid *Traviata* for her in the next season, as well as paying her for the performances that did not materialize in the current one. Fearing that Maria would not accept Ghiringhelli's compromise and that she would refuse to sing, thereby causing a scandal and harming her career, Meneghini wisely intervened and saved the situation.

With an excellent cast which included Ebe Stignani, the reigning Italian mezzo-soprano, the tenor Gino Penno, Nicola Rossi-Lemeni and conductor Franco Ghione, Callas sang Norma, the role she was already most closely associated with. She was on top form, electrifying the Milanese who filled the theatre to capacity. In many ways her achievement in *Norma* was greater than in *I vespri* because the former is a better work by far and its protagonist, if capable, has every opportunity to be moving as well as impressive, both vocally and dramatically. Newell Jenkins (*Musical America*) called Callas after her Norma

not only Italy's finest dramatic-lyric soprano but also an actress of exceptional gifts. She electrified the audience by her very presence even before singing a note. Once she began to sing, each phrase came out effortlessly, and the listeners knew from the first tone of a phrase that she felt instinctively as well as consciously just where and how that phrase would end. . . . Her agility was breath-taking. Hers is not a light voice, but she negotiated the most difficult coloratura without batting an eye, and her downward glissandi made cold shivers run up and down the hearer's spine. There was occasionally a slight tendency to shrillness and hardness on the high notes, although her pitch was faultless.

After eight performances of *Norma* Callas gave a dazzling concert on RAI, the Rome radio station, singing for the first time arias from *Lucia di Lammermoor*, Verdi's *Macbeth* and Delibes's *Lakmé*, as well as from *Nabucco*. The contrast of these excerpts is remarkable and Callas reaffirmed, as it were, that her extraordinary versatility was based on sound foundations and was, at the time, unique. A series of *Traviatas* at Catania followed before she returned for her third and last role in her first season at La Scala.

Mozart's operas have never been very popular with Italians. *Die Entführung aus dem Serail*, composed in 1782, was having its first ever production in Italy at La Scala in 1952. Given in Italian as *Il ratto dal serraglio*, it scored a critical as well as a popular success. This was primarily due to the distinguished cast which included the *basso buffo* Salvatore Baccaloni as Osmin and Callas as Constanze. Jonel Perlea was the conductor. Callas mastered the difficult role and sang with expressive bravura which delighted the highly critical Milanese audience. Peter Dragadze reported in *Opera*: 'Maria Callas scored yet another triumph in the part of Constanze, which, even though it was completely different from the heavier *spinto* parts she has been singing at La Scala lately, was rendered with delicacy and feeling, reaching a climax in the difficult aria ['Martern aller Arten'] during the second act'.

The success of her first season was undeniable and Callas had every reason to be happy, despite the fact that she was not allowed to sing Violetta, the role that would have provided direct comparison with Renata Tebaldi, the established favourite there and consequently of the whole of Italy. Undoubtedly Tebaldi, who had also been successful at La Scala during the current season in Boito's *Mefistofele* and Verdi's *Falstaff*, offered strong competition whatever some thought of as her shortcomings and Callas did not take this lightly. Nevertheless, both singers were very serious about their work and their rivalry was a healthy one as long as it rested on artistic achievement.

Be that as it may, as a result of their Rio feud, of which exaggerated news reached Milan in no time, the Milanese formed two camps. Generally speaking the Callasiani claimed that they were capable of appreciating the finer forms of art when opera is drama expressed in music. After all, they claimed, this is the *raison d'être* of opera. On the other hand, and with equal fanaticism, the Tebaldiani declared that the smooth velvet in their idol's voice was all they needed to ravish their senses.

There were, of course, other favourites but their glitter was somewhat dimmed with the arrival first of Tebaldi and then of Callas. Margherita Carosio was still in her prime and had a faithful following. Even the young and promising though rather limited Rosanna Carteri had a number of votes from the public. There was also the long-established 'tower of vocal strength', Ebe Stignani, who not only had a personal triumph as Adalgisa to Callas's Norma, but whose singing, if not her physical acting, as Santuzza (*Cavalleria rusticana*) and Eboli (*Don Carlos*) in the same season was truly memorable.

At this stage of Callas's career — artistic mission is a better description — what was even more important than La Scala and all that this august theatre represented, was the fact that not only the highly qualified musicians but to some extent the general public, too, were realizing that her achievements went beyond those of an exciting and moving performer. Her interpretations were endowed with creative genius and as such, her contribution to the evolution of operatic culture was influential.

Recalling this period of her career to me, Callas said

I was over the moon when Siciliani, together with Serafin of course, asked me to sing the title role in Rossini's *Armida*, an opera that had not been performed anywhere for almost 120 years.[3] The reason why I accepted to learn it in a matter of six or seven days (that is including the dress rehearsal) was because Serafin, that endearing, sly fox, persuaded me, quite easily I may add, that I could and should do it. I believe that the primary reason for the virtual disappearance of Rossini's *opere serie* (at that period only two or three of his comedies were really performed) was the unavailability of singers, both female and male, who could put the numerous florid passages at the service of dramatic expression. So it was a step forward and *Armida* opened the way to rediscover an all but lost repertoire.

Hence a few days after Callas completed her performances at La Scala she rushed to Florence to prepare Armida, her contribution to the Maggio Musicale Fiorentino which was that year paying homage to Rossini by producing six of his operas: *Le comte Ory, Guillaume Tell, La pietra del paragone, La scala di seta, Tancredi* and *Armida*. Her success was phenomenal both with the public and the critics.

Newell Jenkins (*Musical America*) marvelled at Callas's virtuosity. He wrote: 'One can readily believe that no one today save Maria Callas, undisputedly the finest woman singer on the Italian stage, could possibly negotiate the incredibly difficult part and make it sound like music.'

Andrew Porter (*Opera*, July 1952) was more constructive in his review:

It is possible to feel that the phrases beneath the florid passages are far too overlaid with ornament; but it was impossible to regret it when Maria Callas was singing them . . . she must be one of the most exciting singers on the stage today. Her presence is imperious, her coloratura not piping and pretty, but powerful and dramatic. It must be noted that a nasty edge crept into the tone from time to time; but when she sailed up a two-octave chromatic scale and cascaded down again the effect was electrifying. . . . But whenever tenderness and sensuous charm were required, she was less moving. This seems to be her present limitation; it may well disappear quite soon.

Overlapping with her last Armida, Callas also gave three performances of *I Puritani* in Rome, thereby confirming that her achievements were the result of real talent.

It had been a most successful and busy year, and apart from the unpleasantness in Brazil, which Maria put behind her, quite a happy one as far as her career was concerned. In other respects the picture was not so pleasant. Although her marriage was in itself a great success, the devotion between her husband and herself being genuinely mutual, Meneghini's brothers continued their belligerence, stubbornly refusing to accept Maria, the foreigner, into their family. Meneghini wrote in *Maria Callas mia moglie* that his marriage further aggravated his brothers' contempt for Maria and 'as our apartment in Verona was above the office of the family business . . . if any of my brothers met my wife on the stairs, they would always ignore her. . . . When once Maria, coming down the stairs, lost her footing and fell, one of my brothers who witnessed the accident did nothing about it but merely shouted, "She is so hopeless that she is incapable of even walking down the stairs."'

Nevertheless, Maria mustered enough strength from the security she had found in her marriage, and in her art, to put this distressing state of affairs out of her mind. What she could not dismiss was the precarious relationship between her parents who, although still officially married, in effect no longer lived together. Her mother, having again returned to Athens, was

Backstage before a performance of I Puritani *at the Comunale, Florence, 1952. Callas and Conley wish each other luck: 'Break a leg!'*

threatening to sue her husband for maintenance. Maria did not take sides but in her letters she had some harsh words for both of them. She took her father to task for driving her mother away with more than a little help from Miss Papajohn. At the same time she scolded her mother for continually nagging her husband and not exercising even a little diplomacy and patience to save her marriage.

However, as her father was alone and she had promised him an invitation, Maria asked him to join her and her husband in Mexico City, where she would be singing during June and July. The change could only do him good and it might, with luck, help him to put his house in order. Furthermore, the trip would provide a chance for her father to meet his son-in-law whom he had not yet seen. Deep in Maria's heart there was also an ulterior motive. Her father, a very conservative man, had always had ambiguous opinions about the stage and had never really believed that his daughter would one day be a famous prima donna. If he did, he certainly had not shown it, nor had he given her any encouragement. Now for the first time he could see for himself and perhaps the experience would make him change his view. As it happened Kalogeropoulos was so much taken with seeing his daughter in performance that his reservations about the stage vanished. His pride in Maria even made him forget, for the moment, his marital problems and he returned to New York a happier man, at least for a while.

For her third consecutive season in Mexico City Callas was to sing in five operas: *I Puritani*, *La traviata*, *Tosca*, *Lucia di Lammermooor* and *Rigoletto*, the last two for the first time anywhere. Giuseppe di Stefano, the young and most promising Italian lyric tenor, was engaged for all her performances. They had sung a single *Traviata* together in São Paulo in the previous year but it was now, during the rehearsals of *I Puritani*, that they really became acquainted and it could be said that the foundations were laid for what was to become the most celebrated duo of their time. In the years that followed they were to sing together in many opera houses and also to feature on ten complete opera recordings. With the exception of *Rigoletto*, their success in Mexico City was great. As Lucia, Callas had an unqualified triumph. The Mexican public were the first in the twentieth century to hear a dramatic soprano capable of executing Lucia's florid music with the utmost ease. This was a notable characterization from the beginning and one that was subsequently perfected with various refinements.

Referring to the 'mad scene' in *Lucia*, Callas commented that she disliked violence as she found it artistically inefficient:

> The suggestion of the action in such cases is by far more expressive and moving than the exhibition of it. I always eliminated the knife in this scene because I thought it was a useless and old-fashioned business – the action could get in the way of the art and this kind of realism would interfere with the truth.

The first performance of *Rigoletto* came close to disaster: the company appeared without a full rehearsal, the orchestra were at their worst, stage direction practically non-existent and the singers, including Callas who had to learn her part, the role of Gilda, in record time and between rehearsals and performances of other roles, were feeling far from confident. The second and last performance was a great improvement inasmuch as the singers and orchestra were more of a team. On arrival in Mexico City Callas, who realized that there would not be sufficient time for preparation, especially for a role she had never sung before, failed to have the opera changed. The management simply reminded her that as the highest-paid singer ever engaged in Mexico she was expected to carry out her contractual obligations.

Amid this wreckage, the freshness of Callas's revelatory interpretation – circumstances change Gilda from an adolescent into a woman overnight – was at the time widely misunderstood, mainly because of the long and wrong association of the role with light coloratura soprano voices. Solomon Kahan (*Musical America*, September 1952) described this *Rigoletto* as 'a pedestrian performance ... and Miss Callas's Gilda, not an ideal role for her, did not improve the situation.'

Although she never sang Gilda on stage again, Callas made her mark and to some extent instigated a re-evaluation of this role. Her recording of the opera in 1955 as well as a 'pirate' recording of one of her stage performances proved influential in understanding the character of the at first virginal though by no means insipid Gilda. In one of her master classes (Juilliard, New York, 1972) Callas told a young soprano who sang 'Caro nome' that 'Gilda is a girl passionately in love. She is a virgin but do not make her too cute. Remember what happens to her later; she sacrifices herself for love.'

During their time in Mexico City Maria and di Stefano became the best of friends but at their last performance of *Tosca* a small misunderstanding on his part temporarily upset this relationship. Maria sang a superb Tosca and di Stefano, too, in glorious voice as Cavaradossi, gave of his best. At the end of the evening when Maria was given a standing ovation the orchestra played 'Las golondrinas' ('The Swallows'), a Mexican farewell song traditionally reserved for outstanding artists who are leaving to wish them a speedy return. Maria, moved by the occasion, was in tears kneeling on the stage while the audience sang their farewell. Feeling offended that he had been excluded from this demonstration di Stefano, in a moment of anger, exclaimed that he would never sing with Maria again – a threat, it must be added, which was not carried out. However, the Mexicans could not have predicted at the time that their adored swallow was flying away to other climes for good: Callas's international fame began and her return to Mexico never happened. None the less, the Mexicans always remembered with affection that this extraordinary artist gave them a substantial share of her early career.

The Meneghinis returned to Verona during the first week of July in time for Maria to prepare for her next assignment. The 1952 season at the Arena was opening with *La Gioconda* and she was returning to the scene of her Italian début to sing the same role. She had now acquired artistic stature inasmuch as she brought new ideas and excitement to the operatic stage and although it cannot be claimed that all her performances so far were unqualified triumphs she had never yet had a failure.

As Maria walked on to the vast stage of the Arena to face the thousands of people, for a moment time stood still and she knew that all had not been in vain. Serafin was missing (Votto conducted her performances on this occasion) but the other gentleman of Verona, her husband, was very much present, reliving with her many sweet memories – their first meeting followed by the day trip to Venice, their falling in love and their marriage. The hardships of not finding work and La Scala's first dismissal of her during those dreadful three months after *La Gioconda* were now truly forgotten. The success of her second Gioconda and of Violetta which followed at the Arena, enthused the Veronese to fever pitch, as they now claimed Callas as their own creation.

After the Arena performances Callas had two clear months before her next engagement. She had of course to study new roles and also to have some rest. In October she was very happy to have her sister Iakinthy stay with her for a fortnight. They had not seen each other since Maria left Greece for America over seven years before. Maria was now a famous prima donna and a very happily married woman. On the other hand Iakinthy, who continued to live in Athens, was unmarried and did not seem to have accomplished much with her life. The reunion was not an entirely happy time for the two sisters. Maybe Maria tried too hard to please Iakinthy who to some extent misunderstood her intentions as boastful and patronizing; perhaps she was too anxious to show off her loving husband. Nevertheless, good spirits prevailed and they parted on an amicable note.

The Royal Opera House Covent Garden in London first invited Callas to sing in *Norma* during June 1952 (the opera had not been heard in the English capital since Rosa Ponselle, the last of the great Normas, sang it in 1929). But as Callas was then appearing in Mexico City her Covent Garden dates were postponed to the following November. Her début as Norma in London, her first European capital outside Greece and Italy, took place on 8 November 1952. The cast included Mirto Picchi (Pollione), Stignani (Adalgisa), Giacomo Vaghi (Oroveso) and in the comprimario role of Clotilde Joan Sutherland, a young Australian soprano later destined for international acclaim. Vittorio Gui was the conductor.

Callas created a sensation, giving London, with the participation of Stignani, what was considered its most noteworthy post-war operatic performance. The British critics immediately saw in her a greatness that seemed to make other contemporary sopranos appear almost insignificant. Not that her voice was considered flawless, but the way she used her vocal resources to express Norma's inner emotions was pure genius.

Cecil Smith wrote in *Opera* that 'Callas's fioriture were fabulous. The chromatic glissandi held no terrors for her in the cadenza at the end of "Casta Diva". Nor did the superhuman leap from middle F to a forte high C. One of the most stunning moments came at the end of the stretta to the Act Two trio [the performance was given in three acts], when she held for twelve beats a stupendous, free high D. From this point onwards Callas held her audience in abject slavery. She rewarded them by never letting them down, and by reaching a peak of eloquence in the infinitely moving closing scene of the opera.'

Andrew Porter's evaluation of this Norma (*Musical Times*, January 1953) was even more instructive: 'Callas is the Norma of our day, as Ponselle and Grisi were of theirs. . . . She is surely the most exciting singer on the stage today. Her virtues? Great range and power, prime necessities. A great range of vocal colour, allied to an exceptional dramatic understanding. Tones which are affecting and tones which are thrilling. An imposing presence, a wealth of gesture and physical expression, and command of the stage rarely found today in any actress. . . . To be sure, there were one or two moments when the tone became less beautiful, a shade nasal. But these could hardly detract from a superb assumption.'

Still there was one critic who would not surrender unconditionally. Ernest Newman, in the Covent Garden foyer after the performance, found himself surrounded by a crowd of people who wanted to hear his opinion. After all, he was the oldest music critic in London and the only one who had heard some of the great Normas of the past. Newman said very little: 'She [Callas] is wonderful, truly wonderful.' And then, raising his umbrella, he said in a rather high-pitched voice: 'But she is not a Ponselle!'

Meanwhile St Ambrose's Day was approaching and Maria rushed to Milan to begin rehearsals for *Macbeth*, the opera with which La Scala was opening its new season and the one in which she had nearly sung for Toscanini. De Sabata was the conductor and Enzo Mascherini sang the title role. The exceptionally difficult leading roles and the necessary expense of production have prevented it from being performed often. Although the libretto follows Shakespeare, in the opera it is Lady Macbeth who is the main protagonist, with Macbeth remaining a secondary figure. As Lady Macbeth Callas reached great heights both vocally and dramatically. In the sleep-walking scene – the climax of her art – she incited tremendous enthusiasm in the audience. Her achievement is best described by referring to the composer's meticulous instructions as to how the role of Lady Macbeth should be performed: 'I would like Lady Macbeth to look ugly and evil . . . her voice harsh, hollow, stifled . . . some passages must not even be sung, but acted and declaimed with a veiled, dark voice . . . in fact the voice of the very devil.'

'Perhaps no other opera', Teodoro Celli (*Corriere Lombardo*) declared, 'can be considered such a "natural" for Callas as *Macbeth*. Verdi did not accept a soprano with a lovely voice so that he could use Barbieri-Nini, a great actress capable of imbuing her voice with "diabolical" sounds. This should have been taken into serious account by those two or three misguided persons in the audience who with prearranged hisses tried to harass the singer after the great sleep-walking scene. However, their effort misfired with the result that it transformed what would have been enthusiastic applause into a triumphant, interminable ovation.'

Moreover, Callas's consummate art convinced La Scala that it was now possible to revive operas hitherto neglected because of the lack of suitable interpreters.

Macbeth was immediately followed by *La Gioconda*. Despite the presence of Callas, who was at the time generally hailed as the best exponent of the eponymous heroine, and an excellent cast which included Stignani and di Stefano the performance on the whole fell somewhat flat. It was a lifeless production and Votto, who conducted, did little to raise the temperature.

After a few performances of *La traviata* in Venice and Rome, Callas sang Leonora in *Il trovatore*, her third and last role in the season at La Scala. Except for the two controversial *Aidas* when she substituted for Tebaldi, she had so far only appeared in operas that were comparatively rarely performed. With *Il trovatore* Callas, on top form, threw new light on one of the most popular operas in the world. 'This *Trovatore*', Dragadze wrote in *Opera*, 'was worth waiting for due to the unforgettable singing of Leonora and Azucena taken by Maria Callas and Ebe Stignani. Callas again passed a difficult test and showed once more her artistic intelligence, her exceptional gifts as a singer and the fact that she possesses a vocal technique second to none. Her handling of the dramatic content of her part was a masterpiece of artistry.'

It had been a most exciting season and in many ways a crucial one for Callas. Her success was not confined to La Scala but was happening elsewhere almost simultaneously. *Norma*, *Lucia*, *Traviata* in several Italian opera houses, *Aida*, *Norma* and *Il trovatore* at Covent Garden were never less than interestingly stimulating performances, sometimes creating a healthy controversy, at others scaling great vocal and dramatic heights. Her most controversial interpretation was that of Violetta in Rome, which defied and in some cases modified certain conventions, and drew a storm of disapproval from many of the traditionalists. Others declared this 'new' Violetta divine and a living characterization according to modern sensibility.

The London performances were given in early summer during the celebrations for the coronation of Queen Elizabeth II. Although Covent Garden had commissioned Benjamin Britten to write a new opera for the occasion, *Gloriana*, they also planned a gala season of Italian opera in which Callas, the unforgettable Norma of the previous year, would be the star. Giulietta Simionato, who was making her London début, sang the mezzo-soprano roles in all Callas's performances.

On 4 June, two days after the coronation, Callas sang in her first London *Aida*. It was a memorable occasion, even though the performances (particularly the first), conducted by Sir John Barbirolli, were under-rehearsed and the production rather parochial. But to the ears of the British critics Callas was a controversial Aida.

Andrew Porter's review (*Opera*, July 1953) was again the most instructive:

Callas was thrilling in the Grand Finale of the Triumph Scene, splendid in the Nile duets and final duet. The two arias were less satisfactory; she often sacrificed a smooth line, and disconcertingly changed vocal colour. . . . But what exquisite things she does. How beautifully she caressed the phrases (in the final duet) starting 'Vedi? di morte d'angelo', touching gently the notes marked staccato, ravishing the ear with the downward portamento from the high B flat (a steady, sweet one here). It is foolish to be grudging about this performance.

A fortnight later Callas sang Norma, which in several ways surpassed her earlier performances of this opera. Simionato, at the top of her powers and looking considerably younger than Stignani in this role, made a more convincing Adalgisa and consequently the opera was better balanced. Furthermore, because Simionato at that stage of her career could sing the duets with Norma in the original higher key (Stignani could not), Callas also sang 'Casta Diva' in the original key – G instead of F – which suited her voice better. 'Mme Callas's singing', *The Times* reported, 'is remarkable not only for its technical accomplishments but for its great wealth of expressive colour. She carried the whole opera with authority, having sharpened and amplified the character of the Priestess. In recitative her voice has an edge, in "Casta Diva" her line is suave with beautiful mezza voce, in moments of excitement or climax it becomes brilliant.'

Il trovatore followed and despite the inadequacies of the production Callas made even the oldest opera-goers, as at La Scala, feel as if they were hearing this familiar and popular music for the first time. As Cecil Smith (*Opera*) described, 'her voice – or, rather the use of it – was a source of unending amazement. For once we heard the trills fully executed, the scales and arpeggios tonally full-bodied but rhythmically bouncing and alert, the portamentos and long-breathed phrases fully supported and exquisitely inflected. The spectacular ovation after "D'amor sull'ali rosee" in the last act was still less than the soprano deserved . . .'

Notwithstanding these successes, Callas's greatest achievement at the time was her unique portrayal of the title role in Cherubini's *Medea* (1797). In addition to melodic purity, the opera has much originality both in the vocal line and orchestration and a classic tragic grandeur. Above all, its impeccable musical pace and masterly architecture elevates it from the academic workshop to the realm of art. Both Beethoven and Puccini declared *Medea* a masterpiece. The nineteenth-century English critic Chorley wrote that the role of Medea needed an '[Angelica] Catalani with a voice, as it were, like a clarion, and a frame of adamant and gold, capable of undergoing the strain and fatigue of such a long display of unmeasured emotion. And, after the compass and lungs of a Catalani are found, we must then ask for [Giuditta] Pasta's grandeur of expression and statuesque bearing, and withering scorn and fearful vengeance, and maternal remorse, ere the creation of the composer can be rightly filled up.'

After years of neglect because of casting difficulties (the Italian première at La Scala in 1909 with Ester Mazzoleni as Medea was a failure), Callas, the kind of singing actress that Chorley dreamed of, succeeded in bringing this amazing heroine to life. It was Siciliani's idea to resurrect this opera, as had been the case with *Armida* and *Orfeo ed Euridice* in previous seasons, at the Maggio Musicale. Apparently Callas learned the fiendishly difficult role in eight days and, although she was later to perfect her original interpretation, Medea provided her with yet another triumph from the beginning.

'*Medea* is only possible if the protagonist can carry the tremendous burden of her role,'[4]

Teodoro Celli commented in *Corriere Lombardo*. 'Last evening Maria Callas was amazing as Medea. She is a great singer and a tragedienne of remarkable power, bringing to the sorceress a sinister quality of voice – a savage intensity in her lower register, a terribly penetrating quality in her high register. But Medea the lover also had heart-rending tones and Medea the mother was very moving. In short, her expressive powers went beyond the notes to reach the monumental character of this woman, this legend, though at all times remaining faithful to the composer with devotion and humility.'

In 1953 Verona was celebrating the fortieth anniversary of the opera performances at the Arena and Callas sang Aida to open the season. The forty-year-older Tullio Serafin was again conducting the opera with which he had inaugurated the festival at the Arena in 1913. Callas also sang in *Il trovatore*, after which she spent time making recordings.

The most perceptive summing up of her achievement during that year was made by Giacomo Lauri-Volpi, the Edgardo to her Lucia in Florence. He wrote: 'This young artist, with her ability to rouse the multitudes, may yet lead the lyric theatre to a new golden age of singing.'

After her recordings (*Cavalleria rusticana*, *Tosca* and *La traviata*) were completed, only part of September and October were left free for a much-needed rest – a luxury that she could not afford easily at that stage of her career. Having virtually no private life, the Meneghinis made the most of their holiday, with Maria playing the role of housewife, cooking for her husband and entertaining a few friends.

Soon she would be embarking on an even more strenuous and enterprising year, and would have to work hard in order to win the accolade of 'Queen of La Scala', even though she was undoubtedly already the most interesting and exciting artist there. Tebaldi, too, was still quite a favourite and paradoxically as Callas's admirers increased so did hers. Except for an abortive effort by Tebaldi's followers to ruin Callas's sleep-walking scene in *Macbeth*, nothing much else happened. But as yet the rivalry between the two singers was not clearly evident, because Ghiringhelli had arranged Callas's appearances during the first part of the season and Tebaldi's during the second. However, by the 1953–4 season Ghiringhelli was obliged to give full consideration to Tebaldi. As Callas had opened two consecutive seasons the honour was now extended to Tebaldi, with both artists appearing during the same period. La Scala was, as it were, dividing its kingdom between two queens, albeit as yet with neither crowned. For the opening Tebaldi would sing the title role in Catalani's very rarely performed *La Wally*, to commemorate the sixtieth anniversary of the composer's death. She would then follow with Desdemona (*Otello*), Tatyana (*Evgeny Onegin*) and Tosca.

The plans for Callas, more enterprisingly ambitious, included four diverse operas: *Lucia di Lammermoor*, Gluck's *Alceste* and *Don Carlos* were to be given, the first two to be new productions expressly mounted for her. Furthermore, they planned to unearth an interesting rarity. The example given by Florence in presenting Callas in roles that had long been forgotten did not go unnoticed and after careful consideration La Scala's choice fell on Alessandro Scarlatti's *Mitridate Eupatore* (1707).

Apart from the artistic excitement aroused by these plans, anticipation also ran very high in Milan for slightly different reasons. The Milanese were by and large more concerned with the possible rivalry between Callas and Tebaldi than were the two prospective queens themselves; undoubtedly they were both very serious artists and their work came first, but as the opening night of the season drew closer the excitement between the divided public rose uncomfortably high. The music critic Emilio Radius sensed this and, writing in *L'Europeo*, stressed the importance that the two singers would be bringing to the art of opera, where there was ample room for both of them. However, the whole point of the article was a well-considered suggestion that they should greet each other in public and have a great handshake thus focusing attention solely on their considerable artistic merits.

La Wally was only fairly successful inasmuch as the virtually unknown work, first performed in 1892, offered little to a 1950s audience that had not in the meantime been better done by Puccini. The strong cast – Tebaldi (Wally), Del Monaco (Hagenbach) and Giangiacomo Guelfi (Gellner), with Carlo Maria Giulini conducting – did very well and, if Tebaldi's singing could have been more exciting it was none the less very beautiful. The evening, however, was memorable, though for extraneous reasons. Arturo Toscanini was in the theatre and as all Milan knew he liked Tebaldi very much. This in itself was sufficient to generate enthusiasm on such a night. Moreover, Toscanini had been a great friend of Catalani: he had conducted the première of *La Wally* at La Scala and he had even named one of his daughters Wally.

There was another member of the audience who attracted enormous attention. Callas, following Radius's advice, showed her goodwill by coming to the theatre. Sitting with her husband in Ghiringhelli's box, she applauded Tebaldi enthusiastically and was very complimentary about her. Everybody in the audience knew of her conciliatory gesture but Tebaldi chose to ignore her presence and gave no recognition whatsoever to what was, in effect, an offer of friendship.

Three evenings after *La Wally* Callas appeared in the second production of the season, though not in *Mitridate Eupatore* as originally announced but in *Medea*. It was a last-minute substitution as only a month before Ghiringhelli and his associates felt that La Scala's projected repertoire during the first six weeks of the season (*Mitridate* was to be followed with *Rigoletto*) was rather inconsequential. What was really at the back of their minds was the sensational success of Callas's Medea in Florence six months earlier and they considered it imperative for La Scala to match the enterprising spirit of the Maggio Musicale that unearthed such a great work for the right interpreter.

When Callas was sounded out about it she agreed immediately. Recalling this event later, she told me: 'It is not that I did not want to sing in *Mitridate* but at that period, having recently discovered the wonderful *Medea*, I was anxious to do it at La Scala because it would have provided me with great possibilities. You must remember that although I had already been successful at La Scala, I was not yet firmly established there in the way I aspired. Thank God we were lucky to have found Leonard Bernstein to conduct this difficult and, at that time, unfamiliar score.'

Whatever the case, La Scala's decision to scrap its plans for *Mitridate* in favour of the new discovery was very courageous, to put it mildly. Margherita Wallman, the producer of *Medea*, was not at all exaggerating when she said later, recalling the situation, 'We really had nothing and had to begin from scratch.' The Florence sets were not up to La Scala's standards and therefore could not be borrowed and Victor De Sabata, who would have been ideal to conduct the opera, fell ill with heart trouble – he was, in fact, never to conduct opera again. Furthermore, Gui, who had conducted *Medea* in Florence, was unavailable because of other engagements. In the face of such adverse conditions La Scala promptly took a gamble which paid off. The painter Salvatore Fiume, with hardly any experience in stage design, quickly produced imaginative sets that accentuated the primitive, verging on the savage, character of Medea. The choice of conductor was an even bigger gamble.

While Ghiringhelli was at his wits' end, having no one he could rely on, Callas suddenly came up with an idea: she had listened to an orchestral concert on the radio only a few evenings before and although she did not know who the conductor was she was very impressed and felt confident that he would be ideal for *Medea*. Ghiringhelli discovered him to be Leonard Bernstein, a young American who was at the time completing a concert tour of Italy. As he was unknown in Italy Ghiringhelli did not want to engage him, but on Callas's insistence he reluctantly got in touch. Bernstein's only previous experience in opera was conducting Benjamin Britten's *Peter Grimes* at Tanglewood in the United States and, as he was totally unfamiliar with the score of *Medea*, he would not accept the assignment. What really put Bernstein off was a group of acquaintances, acting out of jealousy, who convinced him that Callas was an impossible woman to work with, creating terrible scenes when she could not have her way. At this point she took over and after a lengthy telephone conversation Bernstein happily accepted.

The hard work and enthusiasm that everybody concerned put in – only five full days of rehearsal on stage were available – paid off well. Bernstein did wonders with the orchestra and the cast which included Penno (Jason), Barbieri (Neris) and Modesti (Creon) rose to the occasion. Callas surpassed herself as Medea and the Milanese gave her a ten-minute standing ovation after her first aria 'Dei tuoi figli la madre'. At the end of the performance a large number of people waited late into the night to see her outside the theatre. The critics, too, were unanimous in their praise, Teodoro Celli (*Oggi*) comparing Callas's vocal mastery of both technique and style with that of the legendary Maria Malibran. But it was Bernstein's remark that described completely the general feeling. 'This woman', Bernstein declared, 'generates pure electricity on the stage. In *Medea* she is a power-station.'

With this *Medea*, which received international press coverage, Callas most decidedly won the first round in her comparison with Tebaldi, though it was a little premature as yet to speculate as to who would win the crown. Even so, their rivalry began in earnest through their respective followers, the fanatics among whom would not miss an opportunity to cheer their idol excessively and to jeer at her rival. For the time being, neither singer expressed her opinion on this issue.

According to Meneghini Tebaldi, who had ignored Callas's presence three evenings before at the performance of *La Wally*, did come to hear *Medea*. However, at the first interval when Callas was given a lengthy and tumultuous ovation, Meneghini saw Tebaldi preparing to leave the theatre. She was rather put off, seeing him face to face, and when he greeted her she responded curtly and hurried away.

After *Medea* Callas sang in *Il trovatore* in Rome just before Christmas. These were strangely melodramatic performances despite the fact that the cast on paper was difficult to improve upon: on this occasion the sixty-year-old Lauri-Volpi held his high notes to the point of choking, Gabriele Santini, the conductor, failed to exercise his authority and, to cap it all, Barbieri was taken ill during the performance and had to be replaced by Miriam Pirazzini. Only Callas emerged unscathed from this near disaster, the critics aptly describing her triumph: 'The voice of Callas was heard in all its admirable purity, radiantly rising like a stem from a bloody battlefield. … At other times, better for music, Maria Callas would have been the most famous woman in Europe.' (*L' Europeo*, December 1953)

The Meneghinis spent a brief but very happy Christmas holiday at their home in Verona before Maria returned to Milan in the first week of January to start rehearsals for the second round at La Scala. She was to appear in a new production of *Lucia di Lammermoor* conducted and staged by Herbert von Karajan. A delectable cast that included Giuseppe di Stefano, Rolando Panerai and Giuseppe Modesti, all at the height of their vocal powers, was assembled. The sets were to be designed by Nicola Benois, who opted out when he became aware of the producer's unorthodox intentions. Karajan wanted the sets to be rather bare with stylized outlines and above all dimly lit so that gloom would permeate the stage. Eventually, Gianni Ratto achieved this under Karajan's constant guidance. It was certainly not a production to please everybody and reactions were varied, but there was nothing controversial about the performance which was given on 18 January. 'La Scala in delirium – A rain of red carnations – Four minutes of applause after the first part of the mad scene,' was *La Notte's* concise description. 'She remains', Cynthia Jolly reported in *Opera News*, 'more strongly herself with every performance she gives, yet penetrates always more perceptively into the role at hand. … Callas's supremacy among present-day sopranos lies in no mechanical perfection but in a magnificently tempered artistic courage, breath-taking security and agility, phrasing and stage-poise: and in a heart-rending poignancy of timbre which is quite unforgettable.'

For Callas it was a personal triumph without precedent. The ovations that she received were indeed delirious; floral tributes were scattered across the stage and many considered her Lucia the greatest they had ever heard. The tension she created in the famous mad scene was so moving – the ingenious lighting enhanced Callas's dramatic depth – that the audience, as an emotional release, interrupted her scene with a prolonged standing ovation.

A few days after this triumph, her second at La Scala within the first two months of the season and in very diverse works, she repeated both Medea and Lucia at La Fenice. Moreover, she sang her first Italian Tosca in Genoa before returning to La Scala for two further new roles.

Following the success of *Medea*, which was even bigger than in Florence, La Scala confidently proceeded with Gluck's *Alceste*, their own rarity for Callas. Apart from his *Orfeo ed Euridice*, which had usually been conducted by Toscanini, only single productions of his *Armide* and *Ifigenia in Tauris* appear up to 1953 in the annals of the house. Although the Italians in general are very musical people and do appreciate Gluck's work, it does not really speak directly to their hearts in the way that the Italian composers often do. The same applies to Mozart. As it turned out – and La Scala is usually right in its big experiments – Alceste suited Callas ideally; she captured the spirit of the music and very movingly conveyed the noble humanity of this classic heroine.

It was the first occasion on which Callas was appearing in Milan in a 'static' role, where the action of the plot is almost all in the mind. She loved the part: the music, particularly Gluck's recitatives, was a constant joy and her attempts to find the right inflexions for dramatic expression as Alceste journeys through slender hope, despair and elation – the apotheosis of conjugal love – proved a satisfying experience. Callas was at that time a model of the devoted wife and Alceste was Greek.

In the mid-1960s, Callas told me that Alceste remained her favourite Greek heroine. When she portrayed Ifigenia (*Ifigenia in Tauris*), who is also Greek, she felt that, 'As the production was set in a different period, the staging took away part of her Greekness. My other Greek character, Smaragda [*Ho Protomastoras*], was all right, but she was not a woman from antiquity, the type who appeals to me.'

Mario Quaglia (*Corriere del Teatro*) described Callas's Greek Queen Alceste as 'stupendous, achieving this by skilfully and exquisitely adapting her voice to the demands of the role; she was profoundly moving in dramatic scenes, tender in emotional moments'. Artistically, *Alceste* was an unqualified success, though confined to the relatively few – they would have been fewer without Callas in the cast.

Concurrently with *Alceste* she began a series of performances of *Don Carlos*, an opera that readily does capture the imagination of Italian audiences. The first performance was a gala given to coincide with the opening of the Milan Fair and the large cast that the opera requires was carefully selected: Rossi-Lemeni and Paolo Silveri as King Philip and Posa respectively, Stignani as Eboli. Only Mario Ortica as Don Carlos was no more than competent. Callas was singing the part of Elisabetta di Valois for the first time — she had learned it in 1950 but did not sing it in Naples because of the jaundice she had contracted at the time. Although it was generally accepted that she made a regal queen, both vocally and physically, and expressed deeply the predicaments of the tragic heroine, some felt that a certain sweetness and softness in moments of abandon eluded her. Others attributed the lack of tenderness to the emotional restraint that is demanded of the queen.

Thus ended Callas's exciting second season at La Scala where Tebaldi, on top form, also did well as Desdemona, Tatyana and Tosca. The success of both singers, during the same season and with their performances practically alternating, encouraged their respective followers to join forces with the press, which also took sides, and declare their little war against one another. Both factions, in which neither singer was personally involved, were equally fanatical and given the opportunity they would try, albeit without significant success, to cause disturbances at the rival's performances. The press went further. Not only did they keep this feud alive in Milan but also everywhere else where Callas or Tebaldi was performing.

Before long the claque, always ready to exploit such situations, took up the matter. A claque is a group of people best described as professional applauders. It dates from the beginning of opera and still exists in many countries. Admittedly, some applause at certain times could be encouraging for any artist and in fact some do pay a claque for it, though neither Callas nor Tebaldi is known to have employed this kind of service. Consequently it was easy game for anybody to direct the hostility of the claque against either of them. Fortunately, however, there are more often than not enough people with genuine appreciation for art to stop the claque from getting out of hand, even though the artist concerned may be greatly upset by their destructive tactics.

The 1953–4 season at La Scala, which became in effect a tournament between two highly accomplished singers, ended on a high note. Even though no definitive victor emerged, artistic standards were raised, which influenced other theatres. For the moment the Milanese looked forward to the next season at La Scala with great anticipation: not only would it have a great deal to live up to but it could also prove to be decisive.

In the interim another kind of battle in Callas's life was coming to a victorious conclusion; in fifteen months she succeeded in reducing her weight permanently from 100 to 60 kilos. This dramatic weight loss, which she accomplished without withdrawing from her numerous stage performances and amazingly without any side effects (her skin remained smooth and taut), created a furore. For a long time the international press gave its own incredible versions about Callas's mysterious transformation. These stretched from starvation to ingesting a tapeworm and employing other secret therapies that amounted to sorcery. At the same time she was also bombarded with fantastic offers from clinics for exclusive rights to her precious secret. She had no secret formula. 'If I had a reducing system, don't you think I could become the richest woman in the world?' was her only comment.

The issue of Callas's dramatic loss of weight was further confused by her mother who later, when all communication with her daughter had ceased, misconstrued all the facts. The truth of the matter was that, contrary to what Evangelia asserted with such assurance, Maria as a child was thin and did not devour huge quantities of food. Her photographs up to the age of thirteen in America confirm the fact. On arrival in Greece, she began to gain weight rapidly – not because of over-eating but apparently as a result of a rather odd medical treatment for a form of acne, which prescribed whipped eggs with full-cream milk and other fatty food as a basic diet. Before long a non-specific glandular disorder was also diagnosed, most probably induced by the diet. In any case as nothing was done about her weight and although she ate only normal quantities of the food prescribed, not surprisingly she very quickly became fat. At that period her mother showed no interest in her young daughter's problem, a piece of negligence which may explain why Evangelia later blamed this state of affairs on Maria's childhood gluttony. As for the pimples, they disappeared from Maria's face within three or four years but she was only really rid of those on her back and cured of the glandular disorder at the end of 1954, when she had lost her excess poundage.

Callas herself said that after the treatment in Greece she began to put on weight for no apparent reason. Seeing her fat, people would jump to the conclusion that she was stuffing herself with food, which was not so. Besides, during the long years of the occupation it was not possible to overeat even had she wanted to. As we have seen, for three months she lived entirely on cabbage and tomatoes. When she returned to America in 1945 she weighed 100 kilos which she managed, by keeping to a strict diet for about two years, to reduce to 85 kilos. In Italy she tried several diets but without much success and after her operation for appendicitis she began again, inexplicably, to gain weight, reaching the 100-kilo mark by the beginning of 1953.

It was left to Meneghini to provide an explanation of sorts of his wife's extraordinary loss of weight. In *Maria Callas mia moglie* he related how one evening in Milan in the autumn of 1953 Maria summoned him to return immediately to their hotel. Flabbergasted by the inexplicable urgency of the call, Meneghini was further alarmed by his wife's strongly agitated declaration, 'I have killed it, I have killed it.' She then explained that while she was having a bath she had discharged a section of a tapeworm.

With medical treatment, two days later Maria was able to eradicate this common parasite from her system. From then on, Meneghini maintained, Maria, who continued to diet in the same way as before, began to slim easily and constantly. 'We concluded with the doctor that whereas with most people a tapeworm usually causes a loss of weight, in Maria it had the reverse effect. Once she was rid of it her fat began to melt away.' No other explanation was ever given. In fact, Meneghini somewhat weakened his conclusion by also saying, 'Not even I, who lived with her day and night, was able to discover precisely how she lost weight.'

I have never found a doctor to agree with Meneghini's verdict, reached with his doctor, that the tapeworm had the reverse effect on Maria. The only reasonable explanation of the saga is the diet she was prescribed in Greece for her acne and for the glandular disorder perhaps sparked by this diet and further worsened by the tapeworm which she may well have contracted during the terrible conditions in occupied Greece. Eventually, with the eradication of the tapeworm, her system itself overcame the glandular disorder, the most probable culprit of her weight problem.

If I have dwelled on this episode it is not for its own sake but because its advent was a major influence on the personality of both the woman and the artist. The change in her was fundamental. The tall, heavy girl, often clumsy and with a funny walk (when Walter Legge, the recording director, first knew her in 1950 he described her gait as that of a sailor who had been at sea for a very long time) became the elegant young woman and with the new clothes she was able to wear one of the best-dressed women in the world. As she no longer suffered from poor circulation the swelling of her ankles stopped and her skin affliction cleared up without trace.

Moreover, Meneghini testified that his wife's highly impulsive temperament underwent a drastic change. Previously she would, under provocation, go into a rage and even become violent. He recounted an incident in Rio de Janeiro: when one morning Maria asked for breakfast in her hotel room (Meneghini had gone out to buy newspapers), the waiter, finding her alone and in her dressing-gown, tried to grab her breasts. She was so enraged by this harassment that after punching the man she got hold of him and flung him down with such force that he hurt his head badly on the knob of the door and nearly died. And then there was the other episode, already mentioned, with Pinto also in Brazil. What Meneghini wanted to explain was that after Maria slimmed down she became calmer, more cheerful, no longer weak and drowsy, and as her stamina increased she was able to work at a faster pace.

Gratifying though her physical transformation was — she had after all become a swan — it was the effect it had on her character that was of even greater significance. Along with her excessive weight she also lost the inferiority complex she had had about her appearance. Henceforth her appearance not only became an added feature of her art but the uninhibited use of her body much enhanced her stage characterizations.

In the summer of 1954, weighing about forty per cent less than she had, Callas gave two performances as Leonora (*La forza del destino*) at Ravenna and then sang a new role, that of

Callas with friends at a restaurant in Verona, summer 1954, after her performance in
Mefistofele *at the Arena.*

Margherita in Boito's *Mefistofele* at the Arena di Verona. Rossi-Lemeni was Mephistopheles and Ferruccio Tagliavini Faust. Votto conducted. Despite the vast stage and the rather spectacular production, Callas was able (her new figure and refined movements contributing a great deal) to imbue her portrayal of the hapless woman destroyed by destiny with moving humanity.

The rest of the summer was taken up with recordings and a single performance of *Lucia di Lammermoor* at Bergamo, Donizetti's birthplace. After a three-week holiday Maria and her husband prepared for their journey to the United States. The young girl who had sung excerpts from *HMS Pinafore* at her graduation in New York and eight years later had failed completely to find work there was now returning to the country of her birth as a famous prima donna – but full of apprehension none the less.

1   Shortly before retirement, Ghiringhelli was accused of embezzlement, in the wake of allegations by the baritone Giuseppe Zecchillo, but was unconditionally acquitted on all counts.
2   The first occasion when the season opened on this date instead of the hitherto traditional St Stephen's Day.
3   First performed in 1817, *Armida* was only notably revived in 1835 and then disappeared altogether until the Maggio resurrected it in 1952.
4   There is indeed a story that Madame Scio (Julie-Angélique Legrand), the creator of the role of Medea, died from consumption brought about by her singing this opera.

CHAPTER SEVEN

CRUSADE TO THE NEW WORLD

I N 1953 CAROL FOX, Laurence V. Kelly and Nicola Rescigno, three able young people, came together to establish an opera company in Chicago which would be worthy of the city's memorable operatic past. Carol Fox had studied singing in Europe but on her return home realized her limitations and decided instead to become a manager and revive Chicago's opera which had ceased to function over twenty years before. With the help of her former vocal coach, Nicola Rescigno, a promising young conductor of Italian origin and a former protégé of Giorgio Polacco, a distinguished conductor, she set about her difficult task. She also met the dynamic businessman and operamane Laurence Kelly, who joined them in forming the company which they named the Lyric Theater of Chicago. Local feeling was most encouraging but in order to get real support for their ambitious venture the trio had to prove themselves initially. This they did by staging two most successful performances of *Don Giovanni* on 5 and 7 February 1954 with Rossi-Lemeni in the title role and Eleanor Steber as Donna Anna. Bidu Sayão, Irene Jordan and Leopold Simoneau completed the cast, who worked more for love than money. Rescigno conducted the orchestra which was mainly composed of members of the Chicago Symphony. This achievement enabled Fox and Kelly to obtain enough financial support to go ahead with their plans. They also gained access to an enormous quantity of sets and costumes accumulated by the city's previous resident opera companies.

Wasting no time, the enterprising Fox went to Italy where she was able to instil enough enthusiasm in Tito Gobbi, Giuseppe di Stefano and Giulietta Simionato to join the Lyric Theater for its first season the following autumn. This, though no mean achievement, was not sufficient for Carol Fox. Ever since she had seen Callas in *La Gioconda* at the Arena di Verona in 1947 she could not get her out of her mind and had followed her career closely. In fact, Fox and Kelly had already asked Ettore Verna, a Milanese agent, to sound out Callas with a view to her appearing at the new, budding opera company in Chicago, but they got no response; Callas paid little attention and not without reason, for she had not forgotten Bagarozy's disastrous efforts

Total dedication. Callas recording Norma in 1954

seven years before. However, when Fox visited the Meneghinis in Verona Maria began to see things differently. The two women got along well from the beginning. They both knew what they wanted and with little ado Maria – choosing her own repertoire – agreed to open the season in Chicago with *Norma*. *La traviata* and *Lucia di Lammermoor* would follow, each opera to be given twice. Neither Kelly nor Rescigno could believe their ears when Fox returned to Chicago with the biggest trump card in her pocket. In reality the three of them felt they would believe it when they heard it. It was left to critic Claudia Cassidy to put Fox, Kelly and Rescigno in perspective: 'Their necks were out so far they must at times have thought the chopping block inevitable.'

Surrounded by a bevy of photographers and reporters Callas, on arrival in Chicago, was surprisingly calm and very much in tune with the spirit of the occasion. She chatted with newspapermen and her unpretentious manner completely disarmed them. Within minutes of her arrival Maria, considering herself a member of a young and promising team, showed her own enthusiasm about reviving opera in Chicago. 'Where is the maestro? When do we start work?' were her first pressing questions. And indeed she soon began, rehearsing *Norma* and frequently exchanging views with her colleagues. She repeated the long and taxing 'Casta Diva' nine times so that she would achieve a perfect balance with the chorus in the large auditorium. With her hard work she set an example to everybody else.

Her American début on 1 November 1954 as Norma was a triumph that surpassed even Chicago's expectations of her, the huge audience (Giovanni Martinelli, Eva Turner, Rosa Raisa,

Edith Mason and other famous singers of Chicago's glorious past were also present) unreservedly acclaiming her 'queen of opera'. On the following day the critics unanimously endorsed the public's enthusiasm. Claudia Cassidy declared, 'This would have been an extraordinary performance in any opera house. It was serenely, handsomely staged, its musical pulse was so warmly secure you could quickly take it for granted, and it was magnificently sung. For my money, Callas was not only up to specification, she surpassed them. So did Simionato, the Adalgisa, who with her made the great duet, "Mira o Norma", something to tell your grandchildren about.'

The critic of *Musical America* was no less enthusiastic. He wrote: 'Callas's voice is excitingly big, vividly coloured and meticulously schooled. She moulds a line as deftly as she tosses off cruelly difficult ornamentations in the highest register. And she brings to everything a passion, a profile of character and a youthful beauty that are rare in our lyric theatre. It is possible to find flaws in Miss Callas's technique – an occasional spread tone in the high fortissimi; a troublesome tremolo in pianissimo. But the net effect is what counts, and that is grand opera singing in the grandest manner. . . . It was a great night for Chicago. It may prove an even greater night for opera in America.'

Chicago's admiration of Callas was not confined to her stage appearances alone, nor was the excitement confined to Chicago. The numerous reporters who gathered there from every corner of the United States did not find the tempestuous and catankerous woman she was rumoured to be, but a charming, patient, intelligent human being, and they all took her to their hearts as an American girl who had made good. Maria lived up to all this adulation when it was spread around that she had set up home at the Ambassador West Hotel where she found time to cook her husband's favourite dishes for him. Furthermore, she had invited her father to Chicago. She had not seen him since the time they had spent together in Mexico City two years before, Kalogeropoulos was now living alone in New York and Maria was in effect the only tie he had with his family. The same could almost be said for Maria, and father and daughter were happy about the reunion; he was extremely proud of her.

Amid this happy and exciting atmosphere Richard Eddie Bagarozy, the man who seven years previously had failed to give Chicago an opera company, suddenly and unexpectedly resurfaced. On 4 November, the day before Callas's second performance of *Norma*, Bagarozy filed a suit against her demanding $300,000 royalties in arrears owed to him as her sole general agent. He maintained that in June 1947 before her departure from America to Verona, he acted as Callas's agent in her contract for her performances in *La Gioconda* at the Arena and that she also signed another standard contract entitling him to ten per cent of all the gross earnings from her singing for a period of ten years. Bagarozy in return undertook, at his own expense, to use his best efforts, including the necessary publicity, for her to make the proper contacts to build and further promote her career.

Callas's prompt reaction was to deny the claim on the grounds that her contract with

Bagarozy was signed under duress and that by doing absolutely nothing to promote her career in any way he had failed to carry out his contractual obligations. In her eyes the validity of such a contract rested entirely on the agent's ability and successful efforts to secure engagements for his client. Meneghini, who was familiar with Bagarozy's contract, also considered it null and void. Moreover, he knew that in Verona Maria was required to sign again her Arena contract, which in any case was not procured by Bagarozy in the first place.

Once they had put themselves in this frame of mind the Meneghinis were not very perturbed by Bagarozy's threats. Callas was fully aware of her priorities, which dictated complete dedication to her work – immediately after her Chicago performances she would be embarking on a most strenuous season at La Scala. She knew she must not allow her powers of concentration to deteriorate and therefore opted against counter-attack. For the moment she would be prudent in not playing into his hands, should he try to serve her with a summons. Adopting this line of action she also succeeded, at least for some time to come, in not letting this unexpected episode (which, as yet, was not effectively publicized) to wreck her hitherto mutual love affair with the Chicago public.

Three days after her Norma Callas gave Chicago a memorable Violetta. Maybe because of the popularity of this much-loved opera both the public and critics thought her vocal acting even more outstanding than in *Norma*. Seymour Raven (*Chicago Tribune*) commented that 'Callas, in a total transformation from the personality of last week's Norma, revealed further the depth with which she has studied her roles. . . . Her acting reinforced last week's impression that she is a brilliant stage personality. The impact of other singers' lines is noticeable in her reactions. She elevates Alfredo and Giorgio Germont so that they "take it from there". It is small wonder that her singing, ranging from "Ah, fors'e lui" and "Sempre libera" to a heart crushing "Addio del passato" is red with the blood of dramatic music, pumped by the pulse of Giuseppe Verdi.'

Another critic was so stunned by Callas's artistic versatility that he found it almost unnatural to accept two equally haunting but entirely different images that she had so marvellously established within a few days. James Hinton (*Opera*) proclaimed: 'the idea of Callas mounting a pyre whose construction and lighting she had herself ordered is quite believable. But belief in the idea of Callas lying poor and neglected in a furnished room is too much to ask of any audience!'

There were still more revelations in store for Chicago. In her third role as Lucia Callas made this beloved romantic heroine a living human being. The critic (*Opera*, December 1954) found Callas

in virtually flawless voice, her singing throughout almost unbelievable lovely, with the tone always clean and forward, the phrasing aristocratic, and the execution of coloratura phenomenally crisp and well articulated. . . . After Callas I cannot imagine why anyone would prefer a conventionally cool coloratura voice, except out of sheer perversity. It was not so much the mere size of the voice that told. . . . It was the play of colour and the sense of reserve power that could be brought to bear — and was brought to bear — in climaxes. . . . Her performance was almost painfully exciting to hear, and after the first section of the mad scene the audience finally boiled over and interrupted the performance with a three-minute standing ovation — not mannerly, perhaps, but a physical release so necessary.

Thus ended the first season of Callas's happy liaison with Chicago. 'I will return next year if the right repertoire can be agreed upon,' were her parting words. Meanwhile Cassidy summed up the occasion: 'Callas came, sang and conquered and she left behind an adoring public, still a little stunned by it all.'

Back in Milan Callas began rehearsals immediately as in just three weeks' time she would be opening the 1954–6 season at La Scala with Spontini's *La vestale*. She would then follow with four other roles (three for the first time) in a season that was to prove her busiest, most varied and the most decisive in proclaiming her the absolute queen of La Scala. But more about this after Callas's return to Chicago and Bagarozy's further exploits. In the meantime Meneghini's Italian solicitors advised him that the Bagarozy contract was not as invalid as he had allowed himself to believe.

At the beginning of March, Fox, Kelly and Rescigno arrived in Milan with an open contract in hand. Maria was delighted to see her good friends but although there were no problems with repertoire, or the other singers who would be appearing with her, or her fees, she was reluctant to sign. What really worried her was Bagarozy's manoeuvres. Once this point was settled, inasmuch as the management of the Lyric Theater undertook in writing to protect her and her husband from any Bagarozy tactics such as legal proceedings and any form of harassment, she signed. Then, turning to Kelly, a smiling Maria rather mischievously said: 'You should sign up Renata Tebaldi. Then your audiences will have the opportunity to compare us and your season will be even more successful.' (During this season at La Scala Tebaldi only sang in *La forza del destino*, evidently losing ground rapidly to Callas's dominance.)

Incredible as it may seem, Kelly did just that and surprisingly Tebaldi accepted. Di Stefano, Jussi Björling, Gobbi, Ettore Bastianini, Weede, Stignani, Astrid Varnay, Rossi-Lemeni and Rosanna Carteri made up the remarkable cast of the forthcoming season at the Lyric Theatre. Callas would open the season with *I Puritani*, to be followed by *Il trovatore* and *Madama Butterfly* and literally alternate her performance with Tebaldi, who was engaged for *Aida* and *La bohème*. Carteri would only be appearing in *Faust*. Fox and Kelly certainly accomplished a grand *coup de théâtre* and it was only their second season; there were many who looked askance and murmured, 'You've got both!' meaning Callas and Tebaldi. In fact both prima donnas arrived in Chicago amid great excitement; both had many admirers and all their performances had already been sold out.

Maria, more glamorous than ever in her new magnificent dresses by Biki of Milan, reached Chicago as anxious as all the other singers to co-operate in every possible way to make the season a success. Undoubtedly a considerable sense of the rivalry between Callas and Tebaldi existed among the public, to whom the two were household names, but the Chicagoans proved themselves worthy: unlike in Milan, there was never any deliberate attempt to ruin the performances or cause annoyance to either of them. Both singers used the same dressing-room on alternate nights and managed to avoid each other completely. Tebaldi never mentioned Callas publicly and did not attend any of her performances. Callas, on the other hand, went to hear Tebaldi and quite openly praised her. 'Renata is in very good voice tonight,' Maria said of Tebaldi's Aida.

The Lyric Theater launched its second season (1955) with Callas as Elvira in *I Puritani*, at the time a completely unknown opera outside Italy. A prolonged standing ovation greeted her on her first entrance calling her divina and by the end of the performance the audience were frantic in their enthusiasm. Di Stefano, Bastianini and Rossi-Lemeni were also in excellent form. 'It was fantastic', Cassidy wrote (*Chicago Tribune*), 'to see Callas make Elvira a totally different creature from her Lucia ... the glint in Elvira's eyes, the dark hair, the lovely hands – you can't take your eyes off her. And her singing is magnificent.'

Howard Tulley in *Musical America* was even more eulogistic: 'Her acting in song, movement, and gesture was memorable; no mistake about it, she is the premier singing actress of today.'

The critics, however, though unanimous in their praise of the singers, had reservations about the opera which was found to be a bit of a dead weight. There was also some criticism of Rescigno, who had conducted with enthusiasm but not always with discretion.

On the following night Tebaldi received her own share of admiration as Aida; she, too, was very well partnered with Astrid Varnay and Tito Gobbi. However, the real star of the evening, the driving force, was Tullio Serafin who conducted with impeccable style.

Il trovatore followed, with Callas, Stignani, Björling and Bastianini, a unique cast at this time. Rescigno was also an inspired conductor and the performance proved a masterpiece. Callas's Leonora was appropriately highly aristocratic both in voice and appearance. 'Not in many a long year has Chicago had a *Trovatore* to rival that of November 5, with Maria Callas,' Claudia Cassidy (*Opera*, March 1956) declared. 'If you were to insist that the two *Puritanis* earlier in the week stole some of the lustre of Callas's "Tacea la notte", that could be true. But she sang it superbly in line and style, and her fourth act was a wonder. Her aria was so breath-takingly beautiful it stopped the show, yet so much a part of the vocal splendours of this exquisitely Spanish Leonora that it was the poignant climax of the whole.'

However hard the critics competed with each other in their fervent eulogies, it was Björling, one of the best tenors of his period and the Manrico in *Il trovatore*, who paid Callas the most memorable compliment. 'Her Leonora is perfection,' he declared. 'I have heard the role sung often, but never was there a better one than hers.'

Callas's last offering to Chicago was her first appearance in a role she had once turned down because of her excessive weight: there was no obstacle now and she created a youthful and fragile Cio-Cio-San in Puccini's *Madama Butterfly*. The Japanese Hizi Koyke, herself a highly accomplished Butterfly of the previous generation, staged the opera. For many Callas succeeded admirably, for others her movements, but not her singing, appeared to have been somewhat contrived, even a little exaggerated. This is of course a matter of opinion, though it must be added that the authentic can sometimes defy the artificial which has hitherto been the more usual. The character of the fifteen-year-old heroine who grows up prematurely and rises to great dramatic heights ending with suicide is an almost impossible challenge to bring off both physically and vocally.

'It was a fascinating performance in some of the old Chicago Opera's loveliest settings,' Claudia Cassidy (*Opera*, March 1956) wrote. 'For that full-throated, soaring ardour was seldom heard from the stage. This was an intimate *Butterfly*, brushed almost from the start by the shadow of tragedy to come. . . . Callas had worked out the complicated and taxing role to its geisha fingertips. My own regard for her talents goes higher than that. As a decoration she was exquisite. As a tragic actress, she had the unerring simplicity, the poignant power of that thrust to the heart of the score. But in the first scene she missed the diminutive mood, which is that Butterfly's essence. This was charming make-believe, but it was not Cio-Cio-San, nor was it the ultimate Callas.'

The *Chicago Daily News* thought Callas did bring it off describing her 'as if she were a fully trained member of the Kabuki, Japan's national theatre. After the crucial first act,' the critic continued, 'she handled Butterfly's transformation into a woman, matured in despair and suffering, with penetrating insight. Her characterization grew, increasing powerfully, as the opera moved inexorably toward its heart-breaking climax.'

Interestingly, baritone John Modenos told me that

I felt I was seeing the opera, which I thought I knew so well, for the first time. Callas's performance was all of a piece. Everything was completely integrated in the drama. Her first act was successful, but only when watched from a distance. The Chicago Opera is a huge auditorium with 3600 seats and Callas had to assume slightly exaggerated coyness to be convincing to more than half the audience. This Butterfly would have been ideal in a smaller house, where the fascinating subtleties of Callas's physical acting would have been fully appreciated.

After Callas's second and last Butterfly, public demand to see her again was so pressing that the management persuaded her to stay for a third performance on 17 November. There was an ulterior reason for this special anxiety to hear Callas at least once more; she had just signed a contract to open the 1956 season at the Metropolitan Opera in New York and it was common knowledge that conflicting dates would make it impossible for her to appear during the following season in Chicago. The theatre was packed to capacity for the evening. It was an occasion when emotions reached their zenith, on and off the stage. The audience, many in tears, were exhausted by their applause while Maria, still under the spell of the Japanese girl who had committed hara-kiri, waved a last affectionate goodbye.

However, when she left the stage, she walked into a reception of a different kind: the county sheriff, accompanied by ten policemen, served her with a summons brought by Bagarozy making her liable for court action. The management of the theatre seemed to have kept their promise to protect her, as agreed in Callas's contract. In fact, during the season the process-servers had already come close to accomplishing their task: after the last performance of *Il trovatore* Maria evaded them by leaving the theatre in the freight lift with the help of Water Legge and Dario Soria (two directors of Angel Records) and Carol Fox. Taking no chances, Maria spent the night at the flat of Fox's mother. With the excitement of her final performance, however, the backstage guard was momentarily dropped and the process-servers succeeded in pushing the summons into Maria's kimono, thus establishing bodily contact with the defendant as is legally required. The sum of money claimed was again $300,000. At first Maria was dumbfounded. The whole thing seemed like a trap. Feeling betrayed she exploded: 'Chicago will be sorry for this. I will never sing here again.' Her fury spent, she then burst into tears. It was like the sad ending to a most wonderful friendship. Carol Fox and Laurence Kelly stood by equally dumbfounded and feeling completely helpless, while Maria and her husband secluded themselves in her dressing-room.

There is a possibility that the sheriff gained access with the help of some disgruntled factions within the theatre staff who were very upset about Callas signing with the rival Metropolitan and thereby deserting Chicago. It is also not out of the question that Carol Fox herself was behind the ambush – Kelly always believed that Fox acted out of spite, because Callas would not be returning to her theatre, but he lacked proof for his theory and, only a year later, his own collaboration with Fox ended acrimoniously.

Losing no time, the press made a scandal out of this unfortunate incident which was not confined to the events at Chicago but spread in completely different directions and dimensions. At the very moment when Callas was most outraged a photograph was taken (a bevy of photographers also appeared out of nowhere when the sheriff served the summons) showing her face in an exaggerated form (almost in a caricature) of fury. Not only was the picture widely published in the United States but various stories were invented to match it. Always taking it for granted that a famous prima donna must be very temperamental, they fabricated feasible *mises-en-scène* in their sensational news columns. Some said she was brought up in the slums of Brooklyn, others contradictorily placed her in Manhattan's Hell's Kitchen, by then a notoriously squalid neighbourhood.[1] The Chicagoans continued for several days to discuss and argue about their lost love. While stories were invented, facts embroidered most imaginatively, Claudia Cassidy again kept her head: 'Callas is still a star. . . . Skip the rest. It's not worth the trouble of denying.'

The following day the Meneghinis, upset and disappointed, left Chicago for Milan, while solicitors were employed to file a countersuit against Bagarozy. In her defence to the court – Callas wrote it herself – not only did she reject Bagarozy's claim (for the reasons already mentioned) but she also accused him of dishonesty in no uncertain terms: he took a cheque for $1000 – the money Maria had borrowed, as we know, from her godfather for the journey to Italy – boasting that he would procure her a boat ticket at a discount price. Bagarozy also bought two other tickets with Callas's money, one for his wife, the second for another woman. The miseries of the voyage have already been described. 'When I arrived in Italy,' Callas explained in her defence,

> I was expected to get by on fifty dollars. Bagarozy had promised to send me the money in Italy but he never did – my ticket surely cost much less than $1000.
>
> I know I was stupid to place my trust in Bagarozy, but I was young and I imagined he would feel sorry for me after the collapse of the opera season in Chicago. . . . It is for Bagarozy to prove that he is an honourable man as he claims he is. Not only was he responsible for the disastrous Chicago opera season which was to have taken place in 1946, but he has also a record of having been accused of fraud three times.

At this stage of the proceedings Callas seemed to have made a favourable impression on the court, as her defence carried a great deal of credibility, and the Meneghini's hopes of winning their case were considerably boosted. However, as judgement was about to be delivered in 1956, while Callas was preparing for her Metropolitan début, Bagarozy promptly and without warning played his trump card, producing three letters she had written to him during her first four months in Verona. These were dated 20 August, 2 September and 25 October 1947, and Bagarozy lodged them as exhibits in his lawsuit in a successful effort to discredit Callas's statement that she had been forced to sign the contract.

It is quite evident from these letters, which throw new light on Callas's character – she writes as a close, intimate friend as well as a client – that in America there had existed an emotional involvement between her and Bagarozy, though it is not known how deep or genuine on either side this relationship had been. At times she sounds like a precocious schoolgirl who has a crush on her teacher but this attitude, at the time they were written, is little more than a veneer of faithfulness; if one reads these very affectionate letters carefully between the lines, Callas was really ending her relationship with Bagarozy; with masterful diplomacy she asks him for advice about both her career and her personal life, specifically about her relationship with Meneghini. Most significantly she finds an opportunity to tell Bagarozy how close is the friendship between her and his wife: 'After two months of waiting,' Callas begins her first letter,[2] 'at last we received your letter. It is very natural for me to say "we" because Louise and I are now like one person.' Then at first she suggests that there was a reason for not writing to him earlier – 'In fact I did write a very long letter but I decided at the last minute not to post it' – but she makes a point of reassuring him that she 'does not at all subscribe to the saying "out of sight, out of mind"' and follows by mentioning Meneghini in glowing, loving terms, at the same time asking Bagarozy's advice about him:

I thank God for giving me this angel of a man. . . . He is fifty-two years old but in good shape in every respect. We are the same person and there is perfect mutual understanding between us. After all, it is love and happiness that is most important in life. . . . For the first time in my life I feel secure. Nevertheless, I assure you that if eventually I marry him, it will be after I have given the matter my utmost consideration. . . . But I have, at last, found the right man and if I turn him down, I know I will regret it for the rest of my life. He can give me all I could possibly want and he adores me. . . . It is something greater than love that exists between us.

As you are an intelligent man and unselfish, please do advise me what to do. . . . Do not misunderstand me. My feelings for you are still the same as when I left you. Write to me without delay. Be direct and in humour, not as my manager but as Eddie, my friend. . . . Do read all this long letter without getting cross and try to remember as I do, only the beautiful moments we shared, not the ugly ones. I am always happy to have a dear friend like you and I never tire of loving you both [Eddie and Louise]. You must believe me. I shall be anxiously awaiting your letter and hoping that I will always be your Maria.

On 2 September Maria wrote again to Bagarozy before receiving his answer to her first letter. It is not clear whether she really lost heart about Meneghini or as she had not heard Bagarozy's views about him, was now arguably playing down the seriousness of her relationship. Strangely she seems to give considerable importance to Bagarozy's feelings, whatever they were, as well as seeking his approval for her marriage to Meneghini. She writes:

After a great deal of thought, I have come to the conclusion that it would be silly to get married now to Meneghini, even though I love him. He is still with me, a rich and powerful man who can give me security so that I can sing only when and where I please.

Do you think I should accept the offer to sing *Norma* and *Forza* in Barcelona in November?

My treasure, continue with your work. I am so happy for you and never think that I will ever forget you. Only circumstances make me behave indifferently. . . . Maria is constant, not like others and this despite the fact that you have been very abrupt during the months before my departure. I said nothing about it at the time and I am still faithful to you.

Please write to me immediately and answer everything . . . and one more favour, please: do not gossip about my affairs and private life with our friends. I will not like that at all.

In her third and last letter of 25 October, by which time she had heard several times from Bagarozy, Maria returned to the same subject, her devotion to Meneghini:

What a sweetheart he is. He is so full of lovely little gestures, the kind that I always wanted but which you could not understand. These things, dear, are not contrived. They simply happen naturally by both sides. Battista and I are made for each other. The only obstacle is that he is getting on in years and I am absurdly young. I say absurdly because you know how mature I am both mentally and emotionally . . .

I am sending this very long letter with a big kiss on the cheeks and perhaps one on your sweet and attractive mouth, but I will not as this would make me appear unfaithful to Battista and that is too dangerous. So no kiss on the mouth but one on the forehead. See you soon Eddie and please don't forget me.

These letters were also a revelation to Meneghini who, other than seeing his wife's actual contract with Bagarozy, had no idea of her involvement with him. Nor did he know that Bagarozy took Maria's $1000 and failed to return the balance after her ticket was paid for. In fact in *Maria Callas mia moglie* Meneghini said that as he was puzzled at Maria signing a contract with Bagarozy, apparently before she signed with Zenatello, he asked her about it several times during the first months of their relationship. Maria never gave Meneghini a precise explanation, saying only that she signed without thinking and also because of her ignorance of legal contracts and other such matters. After these letters were produced the Meneghinis wisely settled the lawsuit out of court in November 1957, the amount of money paid to Bagarozy never being disclosed. No other letters were produced by Bagarozy; if Callas had written to him any more, they almost certainly would have turned up. She probably fell for him, for his charm and perhaps above all the support and protection that, as an agent, he promised. His actions reveal an opportunistic nature: he took full advantage of Maria's feelings for him and coaxed her into signing a ridiculous contract with him.

Obviously Bagarozy had a compelling personality. Even after his disastrous failure to launch the new opera company not only Callas, who could be considered a special case because of her particular relationship with him, but also Nicola Rossi-Lemeni remained his clients: the moment they were both engaged, through their own efforts, to sing in *La Gioconda* at the Arena di Verona they asked Bagarozy to negotiate their contracts. Bagarozy's true feelings for Callas, other than those for her money, are not known.

Apart from the three 1947 letters already mentioned, Callas's only subsequent contact with the Bagarozys, until the 1954 lawsuit, was in January 1948 when Louise Caselotti visited her in her dressing-room at La Fenice after her performance as Turandot. It was not an altogether happy meeting because Callas on this occasion took exception to Caselotti's unsolicited criticism of her singing. Perhaps she used this as a further pretext to break her friendship with the Bagarozys, especially as her relationship with Meneghini was becoming more securely established. In July 1948 Bagarozy went to Rome to bring his wife back to America. According to Callas's mother, who was told this by Caselotti, Bagarozy tried to see Maria, who was singing Turandot at the Terme di Caracalla in Rome, but she had left for Verona by an earlier plane so that they would not meet.

Bagarozy featured only briefly in my conversations with Callas in 1977. I asked her if it were true that a tape existed of her outstanding Leonora (*Il trovatore*) which she sang with Jussi Björling in Chicago. She did not know. I then remarked on the coincidence that she had made her American début in Chicago, the city where she nearly sang in 1947 with Bagarozy's opera company. 'Life', she said, 'is unpredictable. Had I sung Turandot in Chicago I would not have sung that year in Verona, I would not have met Serafin and certainly not Meneghini. Only God knows what course, if any, my career would have taken.' At this point our conversation turned specifically to Bagarozy. She referred to him without any emotion as Eddie:

> He was very wrong to try to extort money from me. The whole thing amounted to
> blackmail. Even though Battista then looked after my finances, in 1957 I saw to it that the
> matter was settled out of court. Eddie was happy with the relatively modest sum he
> received. Anyway I was relieved, as I hate to be a courtroom character. Battista was also
> very happy that this unfortunate dispute was resolved. Only he was upset for some time
> afterwards for parting with the money, my own money. Well, such is life!

Callas did not disclose the amount of money she paid and, as for Bagarozy's attempt to blackmail her, she was obviously referring to the three letters he eventually produced as exhibits, but which were shown only to Meneghini and not to the press. Meneghini, though not giving a figure, wrote that Bagarozy was paid a fortune. Speaking for myself – this is little more than a guess based on Callas's attitude when she referred to Bagarozy – I would say that she paid him about $40,000 (rather more than ten per cent of what he asked), roughly constituting a royalty on her earnings in the United States until 1957, the year her contract with him expired. A year later Bagarozy died in a car crash in New York.

Concurrently with this disrupting episode, Callas's career took wing; her artistic achievements progressively climbed higher and she began to impress on her contemporaries that opera is uncompromisingly drama expressed in music. Inevitably, more tears would have to be shed before reaching but not conquering the ever-elusive highest peak.

1   In 1929 Kalogeropoulos's drugstore in Hell's Kitchen lasted six months. Maria was then under six years old.
2   Meneghini showed me copies of the letters and other documents. These were later published in his book which he had originally asked me to ghost.

NABUCCO

Opera in four parts by Verdi; libretto by Solera. First performed at La Scala on 9 March 1842.
Callas sang Abigaille in *Nabucco* three times at the San Carlo, Naples, in December 1949.

Part I: *Inside the Temple of Solomon, Jerusalem.* Abigaille (Callas), elder daughter of the Babylonian King Nabucco, and her troop of Babylonian soldiers, disguised as Hebrews, capture the temple.

Below Callas's electrifying entrance established Abigaille's dauntless character: the bitter sarcasm of 'Prode guerrier' ('Brave warrior') when she contemptuously taunts Ismaele and Fenena; the transitory tenderness when she vainly pleads with Ismaele for his love; her fury vowing to obliterate the Hebrews.

Above Part 2: *An apartment in Nabucco's palace in Babylon.* Having discovered that she is not Nabucco's daughter but a born slave, Abigaille swears to depose Nabucco and usurp the throne herself.

Callas's interpretation of this scene, the touchstone of Abigaille's role, remains unsurpassed. 'Ben io t'invenni, o fatal scritto' ('I am happy to find the fatal document') had the impact of a thunderbolt, yet every note, as well as the two-octave drop on the final word 'sdegno' ('anger'), maintained the dexterity of a virtuoso instrumentalist. The calm after the storm was even more amazing in 'Anch'io dischiuso un giorno ebbi alla gioia il core' ('My heart, too, was once opened to happiness') when Callas so movingly revealed the Amazonian Abigaille's vulnerability – her unrequited love for Ismaele. And when Abigaille's avenging nature again gets the better of her, 'Salgo già del trono aurato lo sgabello insanguinato' ('I will sit on the bloodstained throne'), the urgency in Callas's voice betrayed great anxiety – an integral part of the drama.

152

Part 3: *The throne room in Nabucco's palace in Babylon.* As custodian of the throne, Abigaille forces Nabucco to sign death warrants for all rebels including his daughter Fenena.

In her confrontation with Nabucco, Callas's voice became more exuberant and secure, the earlier anxiety replaced with an air of triumph.

153

TURANDOT

Opera in three acts by Puccini; libretto by Adami and Simoni. First performed at La Scala on 25 April 1926.

Callas first sang Turandot at La Fenice in January 1948 and last at the Teatro Colòn, Buenos Aires, in June 1949, a total of twenty-four performances.

Left Act 2: *A vast square in front of the Imperial Palace, Peking.* Princess Turandot explains to the unknown Prince (Soler) that the reason for the contest is to vindicate an ancient ancestress's murder; she will only marry the Prince who solves her three riddles – the penalty of failure being death.

With a blend of imperiousness and coldness, Callas narrated in 'In questa reggia' ('In this kingdom') how Princess Lo-u-ling was murdered. Exceptionally, she employed an introspectively telling mezza-voce in 'Lo-u-ling ava dolce e serena' ('Sweet and noble Lo-u-ling') which induced a visionary effect. Reaffirming her vow of revenge, Callas's voice became increasingly agitated, culminating with menacing rancour in 'Gli enigmi sono tre, la morte è una' ('The riddles are three, death comes but once') (Teatro Colòn, Buenos Aires, 1949).

Below Act 3: *The garden of the Palace. It is night.* Turandot interrogates, under torture, the slave Liù (Rizzieri), who stabs herself rather than reveal the identity of the Prince – the answer to his riddle. Timur (Carmassi) laments Liù's death.

Callas subtly conveyed the beginning of Turandot's change of heart: the ice began to melt when Liù said it was love that gave her strength (La Fenice, Venice, 1948).

IL TROVATORE

Opera in four parts by Verdi; libretto by Cammarano (completed after his death by Bardare). First performed at the Teatro Apollo, Rome, on 19 January 1853.

Callas first sang Leonora in *Il trovatore* in Mexico City in June 1950 and last in Chicago in November 1955, a total of twenty performances.

Callas as the Duchess Leonora (La Scala, 1953).

Left Part 1: *The gardens of the royal palace of Aliaferia, Saragossa. It is night.* In the darkness, Leonora at first mistakes Count di Luna (Silveri), who is also in love with her, for her troubadour, Manrico (Lauri-Volpi). When she sides with the troubadour the Count's jealousy pushes him to fight Manrico, who is also an outlaw. Leonora fails to stop them and Manrico escapes, wounded (San Carlo, 1951).

Below Part 2: *The courtyard of the Jerusalem Convent.* Believing Manrico dead, Leonora plans to enter the convent. When the Count and his soldiers try to abduct her Manrico (Penno) and his men intervene and Leonora leaves with them (La Scala, 1953).

Below Part 4: *Outside the tower where Manrico is imprisoned. It is a dark night.* After brooding over a desperate plan to save Manrico, Leonora expresses her undying love for him. A bell tolls and the chanting of the 'Miserere' horrifies her, until Manrico is heard bidding a loving farewell.

Callas's musical perception and alertness remain unsurpassed: the freedom and authority of 'Timor di me?' ('Fear for me?'), the lyrical eloquence and melancholy of 'D'amor sull'ali rosee' ('Borne on the rosy wings of love'), the trills on 'rosee' and 'dolente' conveying Leonora's painful anxiety with the ardent poignancy of a virtuoso violinist.

The 'Miserere' was full of foreboding, Callas's timbre and style appropriately changing from the lyric to the dramatic – a vocal feat.

Leonora offers herself to the Count for Manrico's freedom. The count accepts, but Leonora secretly takes poison from her ring.

The echo of Callas's plea 'Salva il Trovator' ('Save the troubadour'), the humanity of her utterance 'Conte' became an almost living emotion that lingers on. 'Vivra! Contende il giubilo' ('He lives! Oh God, I now thank you') with its breath-taking cascades of notes was a striking example of how dramatic the true *bel canto* school of singing can be.

Above Part 3: *The Castle of Castellor.* Manrico (Lauri-Volpi) and Leonora are about to be married, even though they are besieged by the Count's forces. Their wedding is deferred and when Manrico rushes to rescue Azucena, his mother, who is to be burned at the stake by the Count, he is captured (San Carlo, 1951).

I VESPRI SICILIANI

Opera in four acts by Verdi; libretto in French by Scribe and Duveyrier, in Italian it was anonymously translated. First performed as *Les vêpres siciliennes* at the Paris Opéra on 13 June 1855.

Callas first sang the role of Elena in *I vespri* at the 1951 Maggio Musicale Fiorentino and last at La Scala (her official début) in December 1951, a total of eleven performances.

Act I: *The great square in Palermo.* The Duchess Elena (Callas) is ordered by French soldiers to entertain them. She obliges with a ballad, subtly using its words to inspire the Sicilians who break into riot and fall on the soldiers. Montforte, the French Governor, averts the fight.

Callas began her song with deceptive calm, but artfully stressed the double meaning of the revolutionary phrase 'Il vostro fato è in vostra man' ('Your fate is in your hands'), making a tremendous impact when repeated. She maintained the tension in 'Coraggio ... del mare audaci figli' ('Courage ... brave sons of the sea'), which began lyrically but suddenly turned into an electrifying patriotic demonstration (La Scala, 1951).

Right Act 2: *A valley by the sea near Palermo.* Elena and Arrigo (Conley) have joined forces with Procida, the Sicilian patriot, who has just returned from exile. This raises Elena's hope that she may find in Arrigo the avenger of her brother's death.

Below Act 4: *The courtyard of a fortress used as a prison.* The imprisoned Elena and Procida (Christoff) reject Arrigo as a traitor until he explains publicly that Montforte is his father. Montforte frees the prisoners just before their execution.

Callas expressed Elena's conflicting feelings primarily in musical terms: her initial scorn at the presumed traitor was underlined with dismissive anger, her forgiveness reaching sublime heights of eloquence: 'Io t'amo! e questo accento fa lieto il mio morir!' ('I love you! Now I can die happy') was both lyrical and impassioned and carried a certain nostalgic sadness.

Right Act 5: *The gardens of Montforte's palace.* Elena is dressed for her wedding: 'Merce, dilette amiche, di quei leggiadri fior' ('Beloved friends, thank you for your beautiful flowers').

Callas sang this bolero with exemplary virtuosity and deft freshness. She made it less of a divertissement than it is, and more of a moment of happy repose. Elena emerges as a more human character.

Below Arrigo (Bardi-Kokolios) and Elena swear eternal love just before their wedding (Maggio, 1951).

DIE ENTFÜHRUNG AUS DEM SERAIL (IL RATTO DAL SERRAGLIO)

Opera in three acts by Mozart; libretto by Gottlob Stephanie. First performed at the Burgtheater, Vienna, on 16 July 1782.

Callas sang Constanze in *Die Entführung* four times at La Scala in 1952.

Act I: *The square in front of Pasha Selim's country palace.* Having genuinely fallen in love with Constanze (Callas), the slave he had bought, Selim (Bernardi – speaking role) proposes to her courteously. Constanze appreciates Selim's nobility of character but she will remain faithful to the man she once loved: 'Ach ich liebte, war so glücklich, kannte nicht der Liebe Schmerz' ('Ah, once in loving I was so happy but then I knew nothing of love's cruel pain'). Her constancy further stimulates Selim's love for her.

Above Act 2: *The garden in Pasha Selim's palace.* Constanze grieves for her beloved Belmonte who was torn away from her when they were abducted by pirates.

In 'Traurigkeit ward mir zum Lose, weil ich dir entrissen bin' ('Without my beloved only sadness is left for me') Callas's consummate dramatic singing encapsulated Constanze's plight: her lost love, her nostalgia for past happy times, all underlaid in turn with desperation and hope – very rarely was grief more sublimely expressed.

Left Blonde (Menotti), also a slave, tries to comfort Constanze, her mistress, with the hope that Belmonte will rescue them.

Above Again Selim woos Constanze – with some peremptoriness, threatening torture if she does not respond – but she readily rejects him.

During the orchestral prelude to 'Martern aller Arten, mögen meiner warten, ich verlache Qual und Pein' ('Even if all kinds of torture are inflicted on me I shall ignore the pain and suffering') Callas, using only facial expressions, predisposed the audience to Constanze's extreme hardship. Her wide-ranging dramatic bravura singing – like a soloist in an instrumental concerto – consistently maintained its urgency with some new musical revelation; what in actuality is a concert aria became an intregral part of the drama as she went through the gamut of emotion – her courageous defiance followed by menace, subsequently changing to pleading.

Right Act 3: *A space in the palace grounds overlooking the sea. It is midnight.* Constanze's and Belmonte's escape proves abortive.

ORFEO ED EURIDICE

Opera in four acts by Josef Haydn; libretto by Badini. First performed complete for a recording in Vienna in 1950 and on stage at the Teatro della Pergola, Florence (Maggio Musicale Fiorentino) on 9 June 1951 with Tyge Tygesen as Orfeo, Maria Callas as Euridice and Boris Christoff as Creonte. Callas sang Euridice twice.

Act I: *A rocky shore near the edge of a dark forest.* In order to avoid marriage to Arideo, Princess Euridice (Callas), who is in love with Orfeo, has left the palace of her father, King Creonte.

   In 'Sventurata . . . Filomena abbandonata sparge all'aure i suoi lamenti' ('I am grief-stricken . . . The forsaken nightingale laments only to the breeze'), Callas conveyed Euridice's distress and hopelessness, and suggested, by way of the florid passages, the tragedy to come. As Euridice is about to be sacrificed on the stake by savages, Orfeo (Tygesen) intervenes: the beauty of his singing accompanied by himself on the lyre so charms the savages that they allow Euridice to go free.

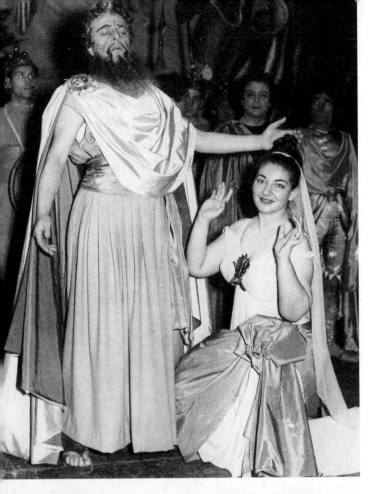

Left *A room at Creonte's palace.* Creonte (Christoff) is so happy to learn from a messenger of Euridice's miraculous rescue that he blesses her marriage to Orfeo.

Below Act 2: *A tranquil meadow by a brook.* Orfeo and Euridice are expressing their love for one another when some disturbance in the palace interrupts their idyllic happiness. While Orfeo runs to fend off any intruders, Arideo's men attempt to kidnap Euridice. She tries to escape but steps on a snake and is fatally bitten. Orfeo finds her dead.

Callas's tender expressions of love for Orfeo – after she was bitten by the snake – became a poignant cry in 'Del mio core il voto estremo dello sposo io so che sia' ('My only concern is to know my husband's fate'). The simplicity of her singing of this rather short melody, the highlight of the opera, was a masterpiece of dramatic understatement; one felt the poison of the snake spreading through Euridice's body.

Act 4: *Hades.* Orfeo crosses the river Styx where, after many trials with the Furies, Pluto allows him to land in Hades. The spirits bring Euridice, covered with a veil, and allow him to take her on condition that Orfeo will not look at her until they reach sunlight, otherwise he will lose her. He obeys and only touches Euridice but when she, unaware of any condition, unveils herself, he cannot resist looking at her, dooming the lovers to be parted forever.

ARMIDA

Opera seria in three acts by Rossini; libretto by Giovanni Federico Schmidt. First performed at Teatro San Carlo, Naples, on 11 November 1817.

Callas sang Armida three times at the Maggio in 1952.

Act I: *The Crusaders' camp on the outskirts of Jerusalem.* With the pretext that she needs help, Armida (Callas) succeeds in reawakening in Rinaldo (Albanese) his love for her.

In 'Amor! possente nome' ('Love! O powerful name'), one of the most erotic duets in Italian opera, Callas was at her most lyrical – her voice lightened and assumed a highly seductive tone – confirming to a degree Stendhal's statement that this music creates physical excitement.

Act 2: *A horrid forest.* Rinaldo followed Armida to the horrid forest which she transforms into a magic garden with a magnificent palace in it. She then proceeds to seduce him.

In the highly intricate aria, 'D'amor al dolce impero' ('Love is sweet and triumphant'), Callas surpassed herself as a singer whose exemplary vocal technique was completely at the service of dramatic expression: technical bravura (including three interpolated high Ds in the embellishments) linked with strands of sensuous melody to portray the enchantress convincingly.

RIGOLETTO

Opera in three acts by Verdi; libretto by Piave. First performed at La Fenice, Venice, on 11 March 1851. Callas sang Gilda in *Rigoletto* twice in Mexico City in June 1952.

Act I: *The courtyard of Rigoletto's house.* Callas portrayed Gilda as the orphan girl who longed for something more than paternal affection. When the Duke (di Stefano) appears out of nowhere (he tells her that he is Gualtier Maldè, a poor student), Callas conveyed, through a youthful, lyrical voice but with dramatic undertones, a mixture of fear and joy. As the initial touch of coldness thawed, her tone became warmer, almost submissive. It was as if she had waited for this moment all her life.

Above Gilda weaves fantasies round the name of the young man: 'Gualtier Maldè! caro nome che il mio cor festi primo palpitar' ('This dear name which first moved my heart'). Meanwhile courtiers have gathered outside the house intending to abduct Gilda, believing her to be Rigoletto's mistress.

With spontaneity and abandon – trills were appropriately integrated – Callas expressed the internal turmoil which occurs at the magical, indescribable moment when the sensation of romantic love is first experienced.

Left Act 3: *A desolate inn in the bank of the River Mincio outside Mantua.* Rigoletto has commissioned Sparafucile to have the Duke lured to the inn by Maddalena and then to kill him. While the Duke flirts with Maddalena (Garcia) inside the inn, Rigoletto and Gilda watch them from the outside, he threatening vengeance, she despairing at witnessing her lover's blatant unfaithfulness: 'Bella figlia dell'amore' ('Beautiful daughter of love').

PART THREE

La Divina

CHAPTER EIGHT

THE YEARS OF TRIUMPH ...
AND VISCONTI

W HEN CALLAS OPENED the 1954–5 season at La Scala with Spontini's *La vestale* she embarked on her most crucial year, which raised her artistic stature significantly. In her efforts to achieve this a new man, Luchino Visconti (1906–76), came into her life. As a director, he was in his own way a central force, though of a different nature from Elvira de Hidalgo and Tullio Serafin. His strength lay in his great operatic culture, which enabled him to understand from the beginning that Callas, an artist of genius, expressed all her emotions convincingly through music. He therefore did not set out to teach her, but instead guided her to refine her already accomplished physical acting abilities – eventually her expressive powers developed to such an extent as to shine in the realm of art that conceals art.

Their collaboration – from which both partners benefited equally – set new standards in the production of opera. Visconti produced his first five operas, *La vestale* (1954), *La sonnambula* (1955), *La traviata* (1955), *Anna Bolena* (1957) and *Ifigenia in Tauris* (1957), expressly for Callas at La Scala. But before their achievement is discussed it is worth probing into the persona of this extraordinary man, unarguably original and often possessing instinctive genius.

The third son of seven children, Luchino was born in the family palace in Milan. His father, Giuseppe Visconti Duke of Modrone (the dukedom was bestowed on the Viscontis by Napoleon), belonged to a very old aristocratic family claiming descent from Charlemagne. His mother, Carla Erba, came from peasant stock on the side of her father, Luigi Erba, who inherited great wealth through his brother's pharmaceutical company and married into the aristocracy, his wife being the daughter of Countess Anna Brivio. Luchino, whose love for all his family never waned, particularly adored his mother, one of the most beautiful women of her generation who most decisively influenced him in his interests and tastes during his formative years.

The Viscontis were also very musical and highly cultured and, like all prominent and wealthy Milanese families, always took a great interest in the maintenance of La Scala.

In the 1930s Luchino's decision to live in Paris crucially influenced his adult life and career. The wealthy and aristocratic playboy, who had hitherto flirted with Fascism and Nazism, became the dedicated artist, a practising homosexual and a socialist, later joining the Italian Communist Party and becoming a Resistance hero in the war. It was also in Paris that he developed a passion for the cinema (while working as assistant to Jean Renoir) and the theatre, though not as an actor but as a producer and stage/costume designer. In 1942, he made his mark with his first film, *Ossessione*, which brought neo-realism to the screen.

Some of his most important motion pictures were *Senso* (1954), *Il Gattopardo* (1963), *La Caduta degli Dei* (1969), *Morte a Venezia* (1971) and his last work *L'Innocente* (1976). His numerous theatre productions, which after 1954 included opera, were equally famous and varied. After his association with Callas ended, in practice with *Ifigenia in Tauris*, Visconti produced several operas for Covent Garden, Rome Opera, Spoleto, the Bolshoi and Vienna.

At his best Visconti's greatest accomplishment as a director was his extraordinary ability to express the past with passion and authenticity, but in a modern idiom. He achieved this by discovering the knot in an actor's personality and then providing the impetus for that actor to liberate and re-educate him- or herself appropriately.

Visconti first saw Callas in February 1949 when she sung Kundry (*Parsifal*) in Rome. His admiration was instant and soon turned into infatuation. The following year she sang in Rossini's *Il Turco in Italia* at the Teatro Eliseo in Rome. These performances were organized, as we have seen, by the 'Amfiparnasso', Visconti being one of the sponsors. The Meneghinis met Visconti briefly on social occasions and though he often sent Callas flowers and congratulatory telegrams when she sang, he was still a mere acquaintance. Undoubtedly Visconti's admiration of Callas at first sight was genuine and awakened in him the ambition to venture into opera production, ideally with her. In the very early 1950s, however, neither she nor he was famous enough (Visconti had done nothing in opera and though his films and theatre productions were most promising they were still at an experimental stage) for the opera houses readily to accept such a collaboration. Nevertheless, in 1951 Visconti almost persuaded the Rome Opera to consider him for one production. Unfortunately they offered Leoncavallo's *Zaza*, which Callas turned down without knowledge of the possibility of working with Visconti as director. For his part he had little admiration for Leoncavallo's music and stated that he would direct only if Callas were a protagonist.

After she made her successful début at La Scala as Elena (*I vespri Siciliani*) on 7 December 1951, Visconti's flowers and telegrams became more frequent and he expressed his fervent hope of working with her. According to Meneghini, he and his wife turned into friends rather than acquaintances of Visconti's inasmuch as Callas began, albeit infrequently, to discuss opera with him. In the next two years, by which time she was established at La Scala, Visconti became very anxious to direct his first opera for her there and she was favourably inclined. The best source of information as to how this collaboration came to fruition was supplied by Meneghini, who played a constructive part.

For almost three years Visconti failed to persuade Ghiringhelli to engage him as a producer, even though he boasted that he had Toscanini's support. At the time it was rumoured that Toscanini had in fact wanted Visconti to produce *Falstaff*, the opera the old maestro was planning to conduct for the inauguration of Piccola Scala, then under construction. As this projected *Falstaff* never materialized and Visconti's claim cannot be corroborated, it is impossible to know to what extent, if any, Toscanini recommended him. Meneghini stated that he and his wife never lost an opportunity to recommend him to Ghiringhelli, who apparently found Visconti objectionable as a man. Nevertheless, in 1951 Ghiringhelli had no option but to engage Visconti, though not to produce opera, but to write the scenario and produce *Mario e il mago*, a 'choreographic action' with ballet and vocal music, based on a Thomas Mann short story. Visconti was an indispensable party to the contract for the production of *Mario* because his brother-in-law, Franco Mannino, composed the music and Leonide Massine was choreographer.

Mario, however, was cancelled[1] shortly before its dress rehearsal in April 1954. The stormy reception Peragallo's modern opera *Gita in campagna* (*A Drive in the Country*) had received only a few days before (the hostility of the audience got out of hand when a motor car appeared on the stage with the two leading singers performing a striptease in it) convinced the management against taking a further risk when they realized that Visconti would be having bicycles in his production. This was a big blow but it did not quench Visconti's determination to produce opera for Callas at La Scala. He also realized that his only hope of accomplishing such a project clearly depended on her support. She seemed, however, inaccessible to him so he began to write and telephone Meneghini, who appeared quite responsive.

Meneghini told me that he took the initiative to keep in touch with Visconti because he could be of great benefit to Maria. During that period she was well established in Italy, had good conductors and offers from several important theatres all over the world. What she needed was an enterprising director to inject fresh life into opera production and Visconti was the obvious choice. However, the matter rested with Ghiringhelli and the Meneghinis remembered all too well what they had been through with him before he engaged Maria. But now Ghiringhelli was their friend and was devoted to her to the extent that he even began to neglect Tebaldi, his ex-protégée. Consequently Callas was in a position to exert considerable influence over him. Meneghini showed me Visconti's letters to him and read aloud excerpts from them as evidence that at the time only he and Callas were Visconti's link with La Scala. (The Meneghinis were never convinced that Visconti really had Toscanini's support.)

Writing to the Meneghinis in May 1954, Visconti enquired first about Maria's recent performances and then mentioned the cancellation of *Mario e il mago*, commenting that even though the matter was satisfactorily settled, both artistically and financially, the incident still upset and disgusted him ...

Despite this, Ghiringhelli was still prepared to make grand promises to me: *Norma* for the inauguration of the season or *Un ballo in maschera* conducted by Toscanini. This sounds to me like wishful thinking on La Scala's part. I hardly believe any of it. ... As far as I am concerned, if I am to produce opera at La Scala, I would naturally like to work with Maria. Will she sing in *Ballo*? Will they do *Norma* for her as well? If not, will she sing in *Sonnambula*? ... And what is happening about *Traviata*? Is it cancelled, or could it be performed during March and April 1955?

Please forgive me for so many questions. ... I am always cherishing the prospect and hope of working with Maria. Without Maria, I will not be at all interested in working at La Scala. Please answer my letter ...

As always, faithfully,

Luchino.

According to Meneghini, a month later Visconti still knew nothing definite about being engaged to direct opera at La Scala. He continued to express his passionate hope of directing Callas in *La sonnambula*, with the idea of having Bernstein as conductor, a most interesting prospect:

Maria in *Sonnambula* (and what a marvellous Bellini opera *Sonnambula* is) has appealed to me for a very long time (as well as in other Bellini operas; don't misunderstand me Maria!). Of course *Traviata* is *Traviata* and I have already said enough about it. Speak to Oldani [the general secretary of La Scala] about this, and then we shall see what develops.

My warmest greetings to Maria and to you a friendly handshake,

Luchino.

Visconti's letters, addressed to Meneghini, continued in the same vein. Above all, he wanted to make his début as director at La Scala with Callas in *La traviata*. He had seen her in this opera in Florence and became obsessed with her Violetta. 'Eventually,' Meneghini wrote in his book, 'I was in a position to inform Visconti that Ghiringhelli was agreeable for him to direct Maria at La Scala.' Apparently no one from the management of the theatre said anything to Visconti personally in the first instance. He was, naturally, offended but the prospect of working at last with Maria made everything else seem insignificant.

La Scala's plan was for him to direct her in Spontini's *La vestale* to open the 1954–5 season and then follow with *La sonnambula* and *La traviata* for her later. Initially, however, Ghiringhelli commissioned Visconti only for *La vestale*, obviously in order to try him out first, giving him a verbal promise for the other two operas.

Almost certainly, Callas was instrumental in Visconti's engagement, since her great success had given her strong negotiating power. She particularly wanted him to produce *La traviata* which at long last Ghiringhelli, no longer prevented by any loyalties towards Tebaldi, could not – nor did he want to – postpone any further. In fact Callas also asked to sing Donna Fiorilla in *Il Turco in Italia* during the same season, to be directed by the young Franco Zeffirelli who had just made a successful début at La Scala with *La Cenerentola*.

Zeffirelli recorded in his *Autobiography* that after this Ghiringhelli told him that Maria Callas, tired of singing only the great tragic roles, wished to do something lighter from time to time. 'You can imagine my joy when he told me that Maria wanted to sing Donna Fiorilla and had specifically asked that I should direct her.'

It is not clear whose idea it was to stage *La vestale*, a rarely performed and expensive work – the production at La Scala cost over $150,000. Callas later told me that she too did not know for sure how the notion originated. She had first heard of the role of Giulia in *La vestale* from Serafin many years before while she was studying Norma with him, but forgot all about it. Early in 1954 she had accidentally come across the score: 'I liked the part with its wonderful situations. Giulia fired my imagination. I may be mistaken but as far as I remember La Scala apparently wanted to stage this opera in 1951, the hundredth anniversary of Spontini's death, but could not find the right Giulia.'[2]

The new partnership of Callas and Visconti drew great anticipation from the Milanese, even though most of them knew practically nothing about *La vestale*. Also, the unexpected presence of Toscanini (he was the last to have conducted *La vestale* at La Scala in 1927) during rehearsals further augmented public interest. Toscanini's personal relationship with Victor De Sabata, La Scala's musical director, having been restored he was again, after twenty years, showing interest in the house's activities. At rehearsals he would discuss with the conductor, Antonio Votto, and Callas some of the finer points of the work. The celebrated maestro was in high spirits, greeting Maria with 'Where has all that weight gone? You have become so pretty!'

La vestale was a great success. Callas, for whose vocal gifts Giulia provided an ideal vehicle, and Franco Corelli, making his début at La Scala as Licinio, had personal triumphs. Toscanini approved and applauded fervently. When Maria was greeted with red carnations at the end of the second act she presented one to Toscanini, who was sitting inconspicuously in the proscenium box, whereupon the enthusiastic audience turned their attention to the maestro with deafening cries of 'Viva Toscanini'.

Piero Zuffi's sets and costumes, though superb (Visconti made him redo the sketches at least twenty times), upset some critics who found them by and large out of period. This was deliberate. Visconti believed that opera should be produced in the period when the music was composed and not in that of the libretto – an original practice at the time that was later to be

Visconti and Maria rehearsing.

Callas doing the gesture.

adopted widely. He gave *La vestale* a First Empire setting, finding in the music a parallel with the neo-classical style of Andrea Appiani's (1754–1817) paintings with their cold colours – like white marble in the moonlight. For the singers' gestures he drew on the pictures of the French painter Jacques-Louis David (1748–1825) and also had the stage of La Scala extended so that the singers could perform at the proscenium, as was the custom in Spontini's day.

Peter Hoffer (*Music & Musicians*) wrote that 'the role of Giulia is perfect for Callas, covering the entire vocal range and allowing much freedom for acting. She also looked superb. It is a pleasure to watch her, and one begins to believe at last in the action on the stage.'

Zeffirelli's perceptive and unbiased opinion of the performance (at the time he was at loggerheads with Visconti, his ex-closest friend) is also most illuminating: 'Luchino had been much praised partly for the stunning setting with its mighty columns and sweeping pageantry, but mostly for the way that he had drawn a performance out of Maria that had previously merely been glimpsed. ... He gave her gestures drawn from neo-classical paintings that she used to give another dimension to the action. ... Maria, the new slim woman, both looked and sounded magnificent. ... Corelli was absolutely magnificent and one cannot expect to see a couple like them again.'

Despite the many accomplishments of the performance *La vestale* did not enter the standard repertoire, its outdated libretto proving an insurmountable drawback.

After it La Scala planned to give *Il trovatore* with Callas, Del Monaco, Stignani and Aldo Protti. However, six days before the performance, announced for 8 January 1955, Del Monaco unexpectedly asked for the opera to be changed to *Andrea Chénier*; he was not well enough to sing Manrico in *Il trovatore* but could manage Chénier. Having no choice at the eleventh hour, Ghiringhelli agreed to make the substitution.

Del Monaco's alleged indisposition was the least of his worries. With *Il trovatore* Callas, who had just triumphed in *La vestale*, would again almost certainly have been the success of the evening as Leonora, a role in which she had already distinguished herself. On the other hand, *Andrea Chénier* really belongs to the tenor protagonist and was one that Del Monaco had excelled in. But his ulterior motive was that Callas for a thousand prudent reasons would, he thought, turn down the role of Maddalena in *Chénier*. La Scala would then almost certainly ask Tebaldi, the reigning Maddalena, for whom in fact the existing production of this work had been successfully mounted in 1948.

Nevertheless, Callas did accept, though on condition that La Scala publicized the reason for the change. She obviously saw the whole issue as a challenge she was willing to meet, while at the same time helping the house through a crisis, even though Maddalena did not offer her special vocal scope in any way comparable with Leonora's. But it gave her the opportunity – and at the time this was of paramount importance to her – to show what she could do with a role in which Tebaldi, her only rival, was apparently famous. The fact that she had only five days to learn it did not worry her unduly. She was rather tired, having in the preceding six months recorded *La forza del destino*, *Il Turco in Italia* and two recitals, appeared in *Norma*, *Lucia di Lammermoor*, *La traviata* and *La vestale* and given a radio concert. Maddalena's rather short role, basically consisting of an aria and two duets (Callas had already recorded the aria), is vocally much easier than Leonora's very demanding part.

Even so, the work she had to put into it, learning and rehearsing the role within a few days, found her at the opening performance below her best form, especially in the first act where her vocal resources were strained in an effort to portray the superficiality of the character by musical means – a valid attempt, though the means were not provided by the composer. When he did provide them Callas was incomparable, singing with the utmost musicianship. Her all-round characterization, notwithstanding the vocal strain mentioned, was a revelation – worlds away from the usual soprano who belts out the music, passing off this manner of singing as animal power and realistic drama. Later Callas told me that she found Maddalena interesting in the way she develops from a frivolous and superficial girl to a serious and dignified woman. 'Above all she is capable of the ultimate sacrifice.'

Tebaldi's partisans, however, were not prepared to accept Callas, whom they accused of

Callas during a break from rehearsals (La vestale) *with De Sabata. Toscanini is talking to Votto.*

usurping her rival's best role in her scheme to drive her away from La Scala. Inexplicably, Tebaldi was only scheduled to appear in *La forza del destino* in the current season. The Tebaldiani found their opportunity when Callas's voice momentarily wobbled on a high note – their booing and hissing, further intensified by the claque, was not immediate but came at the end of her big aria 'La mamma morta', Maddalena's climactic scene and in which Callas was very moving.[3] There followed a rowdy scene (in the gallery) when Callas's partisans responded with thunderous applause, some almost coming to blows with the perpetrators of the disturbance. Callas, who maintained her composure, went on to give an exciting performance, winning the battle in the end, for there were enough people in the theatre apart from the critics who appreciated her art.

The much talked-about unsteady note, a B flat, did not occur in subsequent performances. Riccardo Malipiero (*Opera*, March 1955) thought Callas rather wasted in this opera though 'she sustained her role with dignity none the less'.

Interestingly, Mario Quaglia, reviewing the third performance in *Corriere del Teatro*, praised Callas unreservedly. He wrote: 'she brought to the role a delicately sensual abandon, producing her rich and big voice with admirable artistry throughout its wide range.' Also Signora Giordano, the composer's widow, warmly congratulated both Callas and Del Monaco. Subsequent performances found Callas in steadier voice, but after the scheduled six performances she dropped the role for good.

This was the first time the two warring factions clashed publicly, although the artists concerned maintained their silence. Strangely, the Callasiani did not cause much trouble when Tebaldi was singing. A man in Milan, who seemed to be leader of a group of Callas fanatics, told me at the time when Tebaldi was singing in *Forza* at La Scala that there was really no point in wasting their energies to tell the world how boring the lovely sounding soprano was. This attitude goes some way to explain the hostility of the two factions whose motives were more personal than artistic inasmuch as they were searching to find their own identity. The hostility was primarily directed at Callas because she was an artist with a vision and, like all innovators, was daring and uncompromising in her dedication to art.

Concurrently with *Andrea Chénier*, Callas also sang three performances of *Medea* in Rome, where Wallmann's La Scala production was transferred, but apart from Barbieri with a new cast. Francesco Albanese was the new Jason, Boris Christoff the Creon and Gabriele Santini the conductor. In Rome, too, the Tebaldi partisans, reinforced by the local claque (Callas refused to pay them anything), showed their hostility to her by making noises to divert attention from the stage. Her Medea, however, was such a triumph that the thunderous applause drowned the hostile racket. Nevertheless, she had to cope with further enmity from another quarter. Her insistence on having many rehearsals in order to achieve perfection in movement and co-operation with the other singers caused resentment in some of her colleagues. At the end of the performance, when the audience was clamouring for more curtain calls from Callas, Boris Christoff, who had had a disagreement with her during rehearsals, blocked her bodily from making a solo bow. 'Either we all go out or nobody does,' he told her brusquely.

'Why don't you listen to whom they are calling. They are certainly not calling for you,' Callas promptly replied as she pushed her way to the stage amid enthusiastic acclamation by the audience, who would not leave the theatre.

There was no hostility from any of the critics, who observed a further development in her portrayal of Medea. 'A truly stupendous characterization. ... There is something strangely magical in her voice, a kind of vocal alchemy ...' Giorgio Vigolo declared in *Il Mondo.*

Her achievement was most rewarding, which made the brickbats she was inciting from some of the public as well as colleagues all the more incomprehensible to her; she had never said or done anything against Tebaldi and any argument she might have had with colleagues centred strictly on artistic values. None the less, this disagreeable atmosphere and the extremely hard work she was putting into her performances began to cause her great strain. On her return to Milan she managed her two last performances of *Andrea Chénier* before falling ill with exhaustion. A painful carbuncle at the back of her neck forced her to postpone for two weeks her forthcoming appearances in a new role, Amina in *La sonnambula,* which Visconti was producing for her at La Scala.

Eventually *La sonnambula,* with a splendid cast, reached the stage on 5 March. The stylish tenor Cesare Valletti sang Elvino – a part written for the great Gian Battista Rubini – Modesti was Rodolfo (Nicola Zaccaria taking up the role in later performances) and Bernstein returned to conduct.

Visconti and his designer Piero Tosi opted for a production which was basically a series of *tableaux vivants* with touches of realism and considerable artistic licence: Amina uses the same footbridge for her first entrance (arriving for her betrothal) and her sleepwalking on the following day when this footbridge with its rotten planks is supposed to be dangerous; the new moon in the first scene becomes the full moon overnight in the next scene and so forth. Yet Visconti's production was enormously successful and appeared absolutely valid: the still pictures he created (no mill-wheel turning) were like pages from an old-fashioned album, in perfect harmony with the music.

Callas worked wonders with the role of Amina. Her svelte new figure, youthful charm and graceful movements produced a superb portrayal of this engaging character. On her first appearance on stage the audience was dazzled to see this prima donna, who had impressed so much with her classic Norma, her ferocious Medea and several other weighty characters, looking like a ballerina, exquisitely dressed (by Piero Tosi who also designed the most attractive and original sets) – immediately reminiscent of the young Margot Fonteyn in *Giselle* and at the same time

Callas teaches Bernstein, her conductor in La sonnambula, *how to sleepwalk.*

singing like an 'angel'. Here at last was a Bellinian who could sing both Norma and Amina like the legendary Giuditta Pasta, for whom Bellini wrote these two completely different roles. Though much of the joy lay in watching Callas embody Amina, it was basically her treatment of Bellini's lyrical but deceptively simple music that enabled her to reach the greatest heights of poetry: her portrayal of the charming sleepwalker was spellbinding.

Bernstein described the production (*Opera News*) as 'something marvellous, the closest to a perfect opera performance I've ever witnessed. The time expended on its preparation – the care, the choices that were made, the work Maria and I did together on cadenzas and embellishments and ornamentation – was enormous. . . . And Callas was just glorious.' To me, Bernstein said that Callas sang as if she were the first instrument of the orchestra – at times she was the violin, the viola, the flute. 'In fact there were moments I felt that I was singing the role myself and was dubbed with her voice. Remember I was the conductor.'

In his review Riccardo Malipiero (*Opera*, May 1955) said that 'Bernstein lingered dangerously over certain parts of the work, and pushed rather too impetuously in others . . . but nevertheless succeeded in revealing the beauty of a score which normally receives but scant attention. Callas's Amina had something of the same quality; she is, as all know, a great artist and a perfect actress, and despite the strange lapses from her astounding vocal best, it was impossible not to yield to her Amina.'

Before the *Sonnambula* performances were over, Callas repeated at La Scala her early Roman success: the comic role of Donna Fiorilla in *Il Turco In Italia*. The opera was now produced and designed amusingly and with gusto by Zeffirelli, who had been assistant stage director to Gerardo Guerrieri for the Eliseo performances in Rome in 1951. This was the first time that Milan was to see Callas in a comic role, an aspect that not many would readily associate with her. Zeffirelli who, like Visconti, understood her well from the beginning – and she, in turn, understood him – explained some time later one of the interesting and constructive methods he employed during the production of *Il Turco*. 'In those days,' he said, 'Maria was not amusing or frivolous. In fact she was always taking herself too seriously' and in order to bring Fiorilla to life he invented some byplay for her. Everybody knew that she had a passion for jewellery, so for the scene when she meets the Turk (Rossi-Lemeni) 'I had him loaded with jewels – a vision out of the Arabian Nights – and told Maria not to be frightened but fascinated by this new fool with his splendid ornaments. Whenever the Turk offered her his hand Maria would take it and exam-

Backstage after a performance of La sonnambula *at La Scala in 1955.*
Ghiringhelli endorses how much Elisabeth Schwarzkopf and
Callas resemble each other.

Recording La sonnambula, *Milan, 1955: Ratti, Zaccaria, Monti, Callas.*

ine his rings. In the end it was she who was loaded with precious stones. She was adorable doing it, really very funny. . . . She overacted splendidly, for that was what was wanted. The audience loved it.'

Callas, who was by then as slim as a sylph, and had acquired great elegance and charm, proved in *Il Turco* that the hitherto acclaimed tragedienne was also a great comedienne. Her delightful versatility – Fiorilla was memorably scintillating – captured the imagination of the Milanese to such an extent that when she alternated *Sonnambula* with *Il Turco* on two successive evenings there were many who could not believe they were watching the same woman.

Peter Hoffer (*Music & Musicians*, June 1955) described Zeffirelli's production of *Il Turco* as superb, the performance a triumph. 'Maria Callas was brilliant – looking delightful, singing and acting magnificently with the finesse and subtlety and technical and artistic ability that usually one only dreams of.'

With the performance of *Il Turco* over there followed three weeks of fastidious rehearsals for Visconti's new production of *La traviata* with Callas, di Stefano and Bastianini in the principal roles and Carlo Maria Giulini conducting. For Callas and Visconti, this *Traviata* was like a dream come true. They both in their way had been obsessed with the idea of performing it at La Scala and now would not spare themselves in their effort to achieve perfection. It was, however, a for-midable challenge. Visconti was tackling only his third – though his first popular – opera and Callas, notwithstanding her success in this role several times in other theatres, knew that memories of Claudia Muzio and Toti dal Monte (1893–1975) were still vivid in the hearts of the Milanese. Above all, however, she was aware that this was the time when the whole of Milan would compare her directly with Tebaldi and finally choose their queen.

During the rehearsal period I called on Maria to collect a parcel she was sending to Elvira de Hidalgo in Athens. Waiting for a few minutes in the hall, I could hear her discussing the role of Violetta with somebody. The little I could understand was most fascinating. Presently she appeared, wearing a stunning scarlet dress (Violetta's costume in the second act of *Traviata* – she always wore new costumes at home so that she would get used to them) and escorting to the door a charming old lady, short and rather plump, carrying a beautiful parasol. It was Toti dal Monte, a completely different singer in voice and temperament from Callas. And yet Maria considered it important and beneficial to have discussed Violetta with her. There was more to her interest than met the eye. When dal Monte sang this role in the late 1930s the Milanese were moved to tears.

For complete success the role of Violetta, Verdi's loveliest female creation, essentially

Zeffirelli rehearsing Callas in Il Turco.

requires a dramatic soprano *d'agilità* with an intense voice, which can be scaled down almost to a whisper when required and be capable of a wide range of expression: she must possess exceptional coloratura technique in the first act, be a lyric spinto in the second and in the third a dramatic soprano, a tragedienne. Moreover, she must have the *physique du rôle* – a fat and inelegant Violetta is never a convincing consumptive demi-mondaine.

Visconti declared that he staged this *Traviata* exclusively for Callas,

in order to serve her, for one must serve a Callas. Lila [de Nobili], my designer, and I changed the period of the libretto to the *fin de siècle*, about 1875 (the social imperatives of the libretto remained valid) because Maria would look wonderful in costumes of that period. She was tall and slim, and in a dress with a tight bodice, a bustle and a long train she would make a perfect picture. Moreover the updated *mise-en-scène* would enable her exceptional dramatic talent to have greater scope for fulfilment.

The black, gold and red set of Violetta's salon in the first scene, with her in black satin and carrying a bouquet of violets, established an ambiance of luxury and decadent gaiety, as well as suggesting the inevitable doom of the heroine. The second act, set in the garden with various shades of blue and green, conveyed tranquil domesticity. Violetta's creamy white dress adorned with light-green ribbons and lace was modelled on Sarah Bernhardt's dress in *La Dame aux camélias*. Flora's party, set in a winter garden of lush tropical plants, created an atmosphere of torrid heat. Dressed in scarlet satin, Violetta became a courtesan again. In the final scene Violetta's bedroom had only a chair, a dressing-table and a bed left. At curtain rise, as she lay dying, porters were seen removing the last of the other objects for auction to pay her debts. In my direction I sought to make Callas a little of Eleonora Duse, a little of Rachel, a little of Sarah Bernhardt. But more than anyone, I thought of Duse.

To the majority of the audience, however, Callas was reminiscent of the divine Greta Garbo in *Camille*, the film version of Dumas's *La Dame aux camélias*, the novel and play from which the libretto of *La traviata* is derived. The production became an artistic landmark. It evoked the romantic atmosphere of the *belle époque* with such realism or, to be precise, illusion of realism that it transcended the realm of art and became a living world.

In this remarkable creation Callas eschewed the conventional series of irrelevant exhibitionistic effects committed by some interpreters and bequeathed to inartistic performers. Instead she penetrated to the roots of the character, explored it and gave it back afresh, according to contemporary mores and without compromise, as Verdi had conceived it. Her portrayal was a miracle of fusion of words, music and movement – a living emotion. At the end of the performance the exultant audience gave her an ovation, whereupon at Giulini's instigation Maria took another solo curtain-call. This proved to be the last straw for di Stefano. He rushed to his dressing-room, then left the theatre, the production and Milan. Trouble had started earlier when he thought it ridiculously unnecessary to have so many rehearsals and pay so much attention to every detail. He maintained that an opera singer really only has to sing. When he began to arrive late for rehearsal or sometimes not to appear at all, Maria felt upset and offended: 'It is a lack of respect, a lack of regard, for me and also for Visconti.' On the other hand, Visconti ignored di Stefano's insubordination. 'As far as I am concerned, the fool can go to hell,' he told Maria. 'It is his loss if he does not learn anything. If he continues to be late I will act his scenes with you myself.'

Di Stefano's pig-headedness was really his way of concealing his jealousy and resentment of the adulation that was lavished on Callas on her sensational success. Consequently he felt eclipsed and it was convenient to blame Visconti for everything. A few months later Visconti turned down La Scala's offer to direct *Aida* with di Stefano and Antonietta Stella. 'I will not waste a single minute even to suggest the minutest thing to that conceited di Stefano,' Visconti wrote to Meneghini. 'His unprofessionalism annoys me intensely. He thinks he knows everything. Good for him. I am only interested in art and not in vulgar ham performers.'

In subsequent *Traviatas* – there were only three more in the season – di Stefano was replaced by Giacinto Pradelli. Surprisingly, Callas's detractors, even Tebaldi's partisans, kept a rather low profile. They were in all probability stunned by Callas's exciting and deeply moving portrayal of this lovable character and the magnificent staging of the opera. Only once, at the end of the performance a bunch of radishes and cabbage leaves was thrown on to the stage for her. Thinking that it was a bouquet of flowers the very short-sighted Callas picked it up. As soon as she realized what it was, she sniffed it pointedly but with disarming grace and then, with a radiant smile, expressed her thanks for the appetizing salad offered her. Her sense of humour turned this highly disrespectful gesture to her advantage and succeeded in endearing her further to the amused audience.

At the third performance, however, Callas's detractors struck in a more effective way. Just as she was about to embark on the brilliant cabaletta 'Sempre libera' (at this moment Callas kicked her slippers in the air and with a provocative movement of her pelvis sat on the table) which closes the first act, a noisy demonstration broke out at the crucial moment when the singer's voice is at its most exposed. 'This is a scandal,' somebody from the gallery shouted. The disturbance was so unexpected and diverting that it shocked Callas, her performance coming to a standstill. For a few long seconds one could hear the ominous silence in the large and crowded theatre as Callas, a person who normally thrived on challenges, pulled herself together, moved forward to the footlights and sang directly to the audience, imbuing the difficult cabaletta with extraordinary dramatic brilliance. It was a stupendous, unique *tour de force*. Still feeling defiant, Maria insisted on a solo curtain call, 'They are hissing up there like snakes,' she exclaimed to people standing in the wings. 'They are after my blood.' When she reappeared on the stage, again near the footlights, at first looking somewhat contemptuous, there were some catcalls but these were quickly drowned by resounding applause and '*bravas*', the true homage the audience paid her. Her contempt changed: a single tear trickled down her face, then a warm smile broke across her face.

The critics were by and large in favour of her portrayal but at first generally accused Visconti of 'defiling Verdi's creation'. The review in *24 Ore* summed up concisely the consensus on the protagonist's and producer's contribution: '... this aristocrat [Callas] of the vocal and dramatic art who has restored to the work its passionate aura, its pullulating atmosphere of anguish, the very qualities of which the producer [Visconti] did his utmost to deprive the performance.'

In time, both Callas's and Visconti's achievement in *La traviata* became a cornerstone for interpreters of this most beloved role and for future producers. Visconti himself was fully aware from the beginning of the new standards Callas had set in his production, which he always considered his masterwork. When a few years later he was prompted by friends, in my presence, he unhesitantly proclaimed that 'Maria's Violetta has already influenced, more or less, all the Violettas that followed. At first, but not immediately, they took a little from her characterization. (Never underestimate human arrogance.) After a time, when the danger of direct comparison had some-

Callas, Visconti, Meneghini and a friend at a restaurant in Milan after a performance of
La traviata *at La Scala in 1955.*

what abated they took quite a lot more. In another few years they will take everything. One hopes they will rise above the level of mediocrity and caricature.'

All in all, these performances of *La traviata* were highly rewarding for Callas, an artist who deep down, and contrary to that feigned extrovert nonchalance that was often wrongly taken for arrogance, cared enormously whether she was loved and appreciated. She herself had always put artistic integrity above all else, even when the odds were stacked heavily against her. The hostility of some of the public and of her colleagues, di Stefano's at this time, was incomprehensible to her, though very hurtful none the less.

Life naturally was made easier for Maria with her husband by her side to provide the necessary reassurances and encouragement in the desperate hours of loneliness and need. She had been married for five years and the moral as well as the financial support at the very beginning undoubtedly gave her the necessary strength to pursue her vocation. For her part she remained a devoted wife with unquestionable respect for her husband, her master in all things other than artistic.

Although the Meneghinis initially had a comfortable flat in Verona they could spend only very little time there as Maria's engagements were increasing constantly. Immediately after her début at La Scala they also kept a suite at the Grand Hotel in Milan, which is located very near the theatre. By 1955 when Callas was securely established there, they moved permanently to Milan, where they bought their first house. No. 44 via Buonarroti Michelangelo was to become Maria's castle, which she took great pride in decorating sumptuously. She also set about perfecting her role as housewife. Meneghini, obviously his wife's most appropriate critic for this role, has left us with information that provides considerable insight into her character, view of everyday life and, interestingly, her attitude to and relationship with her subordinates.

'No two people', Meneghini told me and also wrote years after his marriage to Maria had ended, 'were ever so blissfully happy as Maria and I were in our Milan home. She was simply happy to be near me. As I always woke up very early she insisted that I would be with her by nine before the maid brought her coffee. After her "good morning" greetings and enquiries about my well-being we would discuss the plans for the day. I always helped her dress with the greatest mutual pleasure, brushed her hair and even did her pedicures.'

Meneghini's disclosures should in no way imply any undue passivity on his part. In spite of, or perhaps because of, her mother's belligerence towards her father, Maria had steadfastly old-fashioned ideas about family life and a sense of duty in general. In her eyes Battista was unequivocally the master of the house and she put him on a pedestal of high respect.

'In the running of our home,' Meneghini elaborated, 'Maria was just as disciplined and fastidious as in the preparation of her roles. She expected and received the same sense of duty from our several servants. Her rules had to be obeyed. She demanded that the servants should respect

Maria with her dog Toy at home in Verona, 1955.

each other and maintain absolute cleanliness without fail of everything and everybody including themselves, and be properly dressed at all times. They must never violate their masters' privacy or exercise the slightest disrespect and always show maximum, genuine not artificial, courtesy and so forth.' Meneghini also added that Maria's rigid rules worked extremely well in practice because her own humanity was so great that their servants loved her and would never leave her.

Having settled in her new home, Maria was overjoyed to see Elvira de Hidalgo who came to Milan to be with her brother, a permanent resident there. Unfortunately Hidalgo could not arrive in time for *La traviata* because she had been teaching at the Ankara Conservatoire. But she was with her beloved pupil for the preparation of her summer engagements: a concert performance of *Norma* for RAI, Rome, and the recordings of *Madama Butterfly* and *Rigoletto*. Later in September Hidalgo, who had herself been a distinguished Lucia, participated in the rehearsals of *Lucia di Lammermoor* at La Scala, giving constructive advice to all the cast. Nicola Zaccaria told me that they were moved to tears when the sixty-three-year-old Hidalgo sang to demonstrate fine points of the score.

La Scala was taking its production of *Lucia* to the Berlin Festival for two performances, when Callas would repeat her great success in the title role again under the baton of Herbert von Karajan. Except for Modesti, who was replaced by Zaccaria, the rest of the cast were the same as in Milan. The Berliners treated these appearances with great enthusiasm and anticipation. Toscanini's visit in the spring of 1929 with the La Scala company performing *Falstaff, Aida, Rigoletto, Il trovatore, Manon Lescaut* and *Lucia di Lammermoor* (with Toti dal Monte and Aureliano Pertile in the principal roles) and conquering the hearts of all Berlin was still within living memory and among those who had been vanquished was Karajan. Then a twenty-one-year-old music student, he apparently walked for many miles to get to Berlin for the event and never forgot the musical magic he experienced, later striving to re-create it.

Callas sang on top form and, together with the dramatic powers that she combined in a masterly way with her extraordinary musical technique, she too had Berlin at her feet. All the other singers gave of their best, di Stefano scoring a personal triumph and Karajan surpassing himself. Such was the excitement of the audience that the celebrated sextet 'Chi mi frena?' in Act Two had to be repeated. Henceforth the Berliners would have a new standard for comparison. 'Callas made it clear to us what song and art can be,' *Der Tagesspiegel* wrote. 'This was no mere virtuosity but an all-encompassing characterization which turns the voice into an instrument of unlimited expressiveness. One does not quite know what to single out in her portrayal because it was absolutely complete, with her incomparable magic, her pale beauty. ... There were masses of flowers, endless cheering, unprecedented applause.' After the performance, while the artists went to celebrate at a party given by the Italian Embassy, the Berliners crowded the city's bars until the early hours – the arrests for drunken behaviour broke a new record in the city.

With the triumphant interlude in Berlin over, Maria and her husband returned to Milan, where she had only two weeks to prepare for her second season in Chicago. Her extraordinary success there that ended in what she herself described as a great betrayal has already been recounted in the previous chapter.

For Callas it had been a whole year of glorious artistic achievement and considerable fulfilment. There were also other things to be thankful for: her devoted husband and her lovely home meant a great deal to her. However, peace of mind eluded her as a darker view of life dominated her feelings: the hostility of some of her colleagues and indeed a section of the public, Bagarozy's exploitation attempt and the way she was let down in Chicago by people she believed were genuine friends, depressed and hurt her deeply.

She was further exasperated when on arrival in Milan from Chicago advertisements in newspapers and magazines claimed with an air of assumed authority that the key to Callas's miraculous slimming was her steady diet of Pantanella's spaghetti, now renamed 'psychological spaghetti'. At the same time the Chicago picture showing her face contorted with fury was being published world-wide with various improvised stories to match, thus giving a misleading impression of her character. Henceforth it was easy for her to be labelled an obstreperous and egotistical ogre. Her detractors now increased to include ordinary people who had no particular interest in opera nor were in any way concerned with artistic achievement. They simply begrudged her success in much the same way a man who becomes rich is often resented for it without specific reason. It was in this hostile atmosphere that Maria, strongly encouraged by her husband, filed a counter-suit to Bagarozy's demands and a writ against Pantanella. Even though Callas eventually won the 'battle of the spaghetti' and was awarded damages four years later, the excessive publicity she received at this time (the 'battle' assumed a further newsworthy dimension when it was discovered that 'Pantanella' was Prince Marcantonio Pacelli, Pope Pius XII's cousin), also connected with the Chicago photograph, was unfair to her: she was accused of seeking publicity relentlessly and the dice were further loaded against her in her feud with Tebaldi and in any other confrontation, however trifling, with her colleagues. Part of the blame that landed her in this precarious situation must be put on Meneghini. He was clearly misguided in advocating legal action against Pantanella when the matter could have been settled privately. But as he was to prove later on several occasions, despite the fact that he would always act in good faith, he lacked the elementary diplomacy required in these matters.

Maria and Battista on a short, secret holiday in Greece, early summer, 1955.

In this depressing frame of mind, the otherwise triumphant thirty-two-year-old Maria Callas threw herself into hard work. She had only two weeks after returning from Chicago to rehearse the new production of *Norma* with which La Scala was opening its doors for the coming season. Her extraordinary success the year before prompted Ghiringhelli to reaffirm La Scala's artistic superiority; the first performance of *Norma* was given as a special gala attended by President Gronchi and other dignitaries. The assembled cast was the best possible at the time and they lived up to expectations. Simionato was already established as the supreme Adalgisa, having earned the mantle from Stignani, and Del Monaco was indisputably the greatest Pollione of his time when he chose to restrain himself from vocal exhibitionism. Oroveso was sung by Nicola Zaccaria, a rising young Greek bass who showed exceptional feeling and style, particularly for Bellini's music. Votto conducted with finesse and was far more interesting than usual.

Callas again gave a great portrayal of the tragic Druid priestess. In many ways she was vocally remarkable, coming as close as possible to perfection in this role. Some detected a slight strain, but it was not a vocal one. Perhaps she concentrated too much on her vocalization of the exacting 'Casta Diva' and having succeeded completely from a technical point of view, her singing, if judged by exalted standards, was not as inspired as one would have expected from her. However, she subsequently rose to great dramatic heights, possibly her greatest moment was in the confession scene 'Son io' in the last act. Some of the audience cried, others expressed their admiration verbally without clapping and the adversaries, the 'hissing snakes' as Maria had called them, were reduced to a cowed silence. One of them found his voice at the end of the performance: in an emotional outburst he preached to his friends how he had on that night been converted to the artistry of Callas. He had, he said, suddenly found his hearing and discovered that he had both a heart and a soul.

'Watching her perform is hard on Maria Callas's adversaries,' Radius said in his review. They may have remained silent in the theatre but elsewhere they were spreading rumours that Callas and Del Monaco were at daggers drawn backstage — no smoke without fire in this case. At the final rehearsals, Del Monaco demanded from Ghiringhelli that he should not allow solo curtain calls at the première for any of the singers, otherwise he would leave the cast. This was observed without incident. In subsequent performances (nine were given) there was some sparse hissing and even a few catcalls, mainly during Callas's curtain-calls, but these were promptly silenced by prolonged clamorous applause.

What the applause could not hush was the backstage squabble between Del Monaco and Callas during the last performance. Determined to score over her, whose superb portrayal of Norma was driving the audience to a frenzy of excitement, Del Monaco saw to it that the claque would give him extra support. Indeed, after his big scene in the first act (Pollione's first appearance on the stage precedes Norma's) Del Monaco received a prolonged and exaggerated ovation clearly instigated by the claque in the gallery. The ever-watchful Meneghini took exception to this and in the interval confronted the chief of the claque for such ridiculously partisan behaviour engineered to take the limelight away from his wife. Meneghini's intervention in something he could not effectively prove was an obvious blunder. The worst thing was that his mistakes were beginning to be motivated by his wife's fame, which was rapidly going to his own head. The claque chief immediately informed Del Monaco, who angrily shouted at Meneghini: 'You must get it into your head that you and your wife do not own La Scala. The audience applauds those who deserve applause.' Del Monaco then began to yell and harass Maria whenever she was backstage, especially during the first scene of the last act in which neither of them appears. Though furious with him, Maria controlled herself and would not answer him until the end of the performance when, between curtain-calls, they began to argue in earnest, yelling and accusing each other of being an unworthy colleague, lacking even the rudiments of good breeding and vowing never to sing together again.

Having acquired fame as the leading Italian tenor in his country and abroad before Callas, Del Monaco viewed her as the most dangerous threat to his supremacy. Excellent though he was, he knew that he could not displace her artistically so he sought to take advantage of her growing unpopularity as a person. Two days after this fracas he tried to turn the whole thing into a polemic through the press. He professed that as he was leaving the stage at the finale of *Norma* Maria kicked him: 'Dumbfounded, I stopped to rub my painful calf but by the time I could return to the stage for my curtain-call Callas had usurped all the applause.'

Normally, Del Monaco's accusations would merely have amused the public, but in that climate Callas's personal reputation was not very positive because of misconstrued incidents such as the Chicago photograph, di Stefano's walk-out from *La traviata* and Tebaldi's conspicuous absence from La Scala. The outcome of this rather childish incident was that Maria made more enemies, although Del Monaco made no new friends. Whereas it is possible to justify to some extent his argument with Meneghini, his subsequent behaviour towards his colleague during the performance was totally indefensible. A woman watching this *Norma* from the wings later told me that Del Monaco, for no apparent reason, seized every opportunity to yell at Maria who hardly answered back until it was over, when she gave as good as, and better than, she got. The eyewitness could not say for sure whether Maria kicked Del Monaco but added that as he was so offensive and vulgar she should have kicked him herself if she had got the chance.

Ten days after *Norma* Callas began a series of seventeen performances of the controversial Visconti *Traviata* at La Scala — an unprecedented number even for such a popular opera. Gianni Raimondi was the new Alfredo and Giulini again conducted. Although both the Italian and visiting critics were praising Callas's Violetta unreservedly some, Teodoro Celli in particular, would not give Visconti's production unqualified approval — this rethinking of *La traviata* continued to be too revolutionary for them. The public, on the other hand, which included a large number from other parts of Europe and from America, stirred by both Callas's inspired portrayal and Visconti's innovatory and vital production, flocked to see all the performances. Her Violetta continually gained in expression until the audiences became obsessed with her. Moreover, with her unique characterizations which remained faithful to the concept of the composer but adapted to modern ways, Callas lured to La Scala new, younger opera-lovers. Nevertheless, the 'hissing snakes', though relatively few, were also frequently present ready to whistle or hurl a catcall at her. They never succeeded in ruining the performance and generally their efforts were counter-productive: she gained more sympathy. She was of course very upset but never talked about it; her philosophy was to fight through her art – the only weapon she really knew how to handle.

Meneghini thought differently. He began to throw his weight around with the management of the theatre and everybody who would listen: 'Maria does not need La Scala or its money,' he constantly proclaimed. 'I will not let my wife continue with her career if this sort of thing does not stop. It is a gross indignity.' As it was not La Scala's fault Meneghini's protestations fell on deaf ears.

Despite Visconti's sensational success with *La vestale*, *La sonnambula* and *La traviata* during the previous season, at present only *La traviata*, albeit in an unusual number of performances, was revived. Nor did they offer him a new production. The reason for this was that at that period he was not willing to work on any opera without Callas in the cast and none of the three other operas (only two, in fact, were given new productions) she was appearing in at that time was offered to him. *Norma*, which had opened the season, was produced by Margherita Wallmann.

Concurrently with *La traviata*, Callas sang in five performances of *Il barbiere di Siviglia*. Notwithstanding the great agility throughout her vocal range, rich and telling lower register and ability to impart deep meaning in recitatives, all basic prerequisites for an ideal Rosina in *Il barbiere*, Callas fell far short of ideal. Her personality for once proved too powerful to adapt or sub-due, with the result that her characterization was that of a charmless shrew who 'knows the ropes', rather than the vivacious *ingénue* she ought to be. There were further repercussions. Although her singing was generally satisfactory, some stridency, particularly in the upper register, was not always employed in the service of dramatic expression thereby accentuating her overpow-ering excitability to the point of unwittingly stealing the show from Figaro – sung by the power-ful artist Tito Gobbi – who must remain the central character of the plot. Instead, Rosina was controlling the situations and this upset the balance of the work significantly. Even so, Callas could have redeemed her characterization, however misguided, had she shown some of her usual insight for the style of the music, as she had so admirably done in Rossini's other comedy *Il Turco in Italia*. Rosina was Callas's only failure on-stage.

Claudio Sartori (*Opera*, April 1956) wrote that 'Callas made an excitable, nervous, overpower-

Not content with their farcical tactics, Callas, Gobbi and Rossi-Lemen gave little side-shows during rehearsal breaks of Il barbiere *at* La Scala.

ing Rosina, and her familiar vocal unevenness made one regret, rather than forget, the great inter-preters of the past. After singing a wonderful "Calumny" aria, Rossi-Lemeni lapsed into farce. Gobbi made a generous Figaro, but the success of the evening was the Almaviva of the young tenor Luigi Alva.'

This production was not a great success when it was first indifferently staged in 1952 by Carlo Piccinato. Nevertheless, the present revival with a highly experienced cast – which further included Melchiore Luise as Bartolo – would not have been such a failure had it at least been properly rehearsed. But it was not. Giulini, who conducted the performances, was unwell at the time and as it was then too late to find a substitute, and inexplicably whoever was assigned to rehearse the production had failed to appear, there were no general stage-rehearsals; the singers had more or less to improvise their movements, with the result that they sometimes resorted to farce.

Not unexpectedly, Callas's adversaries found their booing voices but there were also in the theatre those who were prepared to support her against the 'hissing snakes'. One such occasion, when in fact her supporters dominated her detractors, occurred at the end of the lesson scene. After she sang her aria well enough, her music teacher praises her with '*Bella voce, bravissima*'

('What a lovely voice, bravo') whereupon many from the audience, as a token of their own appreciation, endorsed his statement by giving her an ovation that stopped the performance for a few minutes and squashed the loud, ugly noises of the adversaries.

Several years later, after she had stopped singing, Callas acknowledged to me that her stage performances in *Il barbiere* had simply misfired:

> Perhaps I tried too hard. Afterwards, before I recorded the opera, Hidalgo, my teacher, helped me to put the role in a better perspective. Thinking back on it, perhaps I should have done it again. In fact Larry [Laurence Kelly] was begging me to sing in *Il barbiere* at Dallas in 1958 or 1959 but I must confess I was not in the mood to sing this role again on the stage. The necessary enthusiasm, the commitment, was not there. It was not the music – my interest in the character was ephemeral. Rosina was a passing fancy. But surely you do give me some credit for my recorded performance![4]

Hidalgo, herself a very famous Rosina of the past, felt that for once Callas had failed on-stage: 'I am not criticizing her singing from a purely technical point of view. Maria can sing any-thing. It was the personality of her Rosina that was so wrong, and those awful costumes [by Mario Vellani Marchi], particularly the yellow, did not suit Maria.'

The outcome of the *Barbiere* performances was that Callas made more enemies and, more sig-nificantly, began to feel that she was in some way being persecuted. Nevertheless, her inborn spirit of meeting a challenge was aroused and putting the failure of her Rosina behind her she looked forward to the immediate future: three performances of *Lucia di Lammermoor* at the San Carlo. There was another incentive that reinvigorated her confidence. In Naples her path again converged with that of Renata Tebaldi who, having just completed her second season at the Metropolitan, was singing in Rossini's *Guillaume Tell*. Their performances alternated and both sopranos were successful in their respective roles. As in Chicago, they kept out of each other's way. There were, to be sure, the usual arguments about them but these were confined to the audi-ence, without causing any appreciable interference behind the scenes. Despite slight vocal strain Callas managed to give memorable all-round performances, her first after a five-year absence from the San Carlo. The Neapolitans were thrilled to have her back, for they knew they had appreciated her long before Milan did.

Tebaldi then went to Florence to open the Maggio Musicale with *La traviata* and Callas returned to La Scala for eight performances of the same opera. Unlike at the San Carlo – where their respective roles were not common to their repertoires – the two singers, now both appear-ing in *La traviata* over the same period, were open to direct comparison; it made no difference that they were in different theatres. In fact, quite a number of people were commuting from Milan and Florence and vice versa on nights when the performances did not clash. On one of those nights Maria also went to Florence to hear Tebaldi but except for the director of the theatre and a couple of friends who drove her in a small Volkswagen, nobody else was aware of her presence. She made no comments about Tebaldi's performance, nor did she go to see her afterwards. What really interested Callas at that time was to find out for herself the public's reaction to a conventional portrayal of Violetta, which Tebaldi's was. Much to her amazement, Tebaldi too had her share of adversaries who behaved just as badly as her own. Maria returned to Milan on that evening further disillusioned with human nature. Later she also heard that on another night several Callas fanatics caused so much disturbance, particularly in the first act of *Traviata* – Tebaldi's weakest scenes – that she all but came to a standstill. The Callasiani maintained, in their unreasonable way, that Tebaldi should not have been so bold as to appear in a role with which Maria worked wonders.

Callas's success as Lucia in Naples and almost certainly her Florence visit which helped her in an indirect way to ignore her detractors, enabled her to get back into her stride, and with her final *Traviatas* she attained divine heights. Even her enemies remained almost silent. Recalling this period many years later, when she no longer sang in opera, she told me that in these latter *Traviatas* at La Scala she had found redemption. It was no longer of much consequence to her if some idiot was being tiresome. 'As long as I was able to give of my best both the people and the critics appreciated me – that was important to me.'

La Scala ended its season with a new production of Giordano's rarely performed *Fedora*, mounted expressly for Callas. Colautti's libretto of *Fedora* is based on Sardou's play, written as a vehicle for the great Sarah Bernhardt. This is what prompted La Scala in the first place to produce this verismo opera for a great singing actress such as Callas. Her earlier appearance during the previous season in *Andrea Chénier*, also a verismo opera by Giordano, was, as we have seen, unscheduled but controversial none the less; a portrayal which expressed the drama primarily through music had upset many and thrilled others. Now her detractors, whose hostility had been dampened by her transcendent Violetta which healed to a degree the wounds opened by *Il barbiere*, convinced themselves in advance that Callas was not really suited to verismo opera, the type of music that was Tebaldi's speciality. They alleged that great realism expressed through elaborate orchestration and vocal music which was not conventionally melodious was simply not Callas's *métier*.

The first night was unjustly stormy. The considerable hissing and whistling, albeit from very few, was misguided, for she gave a memorable performance both vocally and dramatically, maintaining the integrity of the heroine, the only way to bring her to life. By and large the audience and some of the critics were left spellbound. Others considered *Fedora* a qualified success, their verdict centring more on the production by Tatiana Pavlova and even more on Benois's sets, rather than on Callas's portrayal. At worst, she was 'criticized' for being a greater actress than a singer – a point of view that betrays ignorance, especially for verismo opera. In fact Pavlova, an actress famous both in Russia and Italy, inspired Callas to achieve great dramatic heights – the Greek Orthodox woman became, on the stage, Russian in heart and soul. Benois explained to me that with his inauthentic sets for the Russian Act I, he deliberately depicted a fictitious Russia. 'I combined several elements of life before the Revolution, all, including the costumes, painted in vivid colours which created a more appropriate atmosphere than imaginary, and Callas looked superb. *Fedora* is an opera so evidently based on theatrical effect.'

Years later, Gavazzeni, the conductor of this *Fedora*, prompted by friends, reminisced about these performances. As far as he was concerned Callas had an unqualified triumph:

Her singing (and I will refrain from commenting on her superb physical acting) had all the colour and expression imaginable. She proved all the adverse critics wrong and with the public she scored a truly personal triumph. The reason for the initial reservations of some critics was because they were then witnessing, as indeed they had, though within a narrower scope, in Callas's Maddalena [*Andrea Chénier*], a different approach to verismo opera – one which with uncommon musical discipline and style and with a thousand different vocal colours conveyed the essence of the drama with unquestionable integrity.

For *Fedora* Callas and Franco Corelli, who sang Loris, worked closely together for three weeks to achieve perfection. 'She was so involved in the whole work', Corelli recalled later, 'that she made me involved too. I felt it was my duty to respond and work harder than ever before.'

Notwithstanding the failure of *Il barbiere di Siviglia*, with *Fedora* Callas completed another triumphant season at La Scala, and already the Milanese, and indeed much of the operatic world, were talking of a new golden age. For this, no small achievement, a great deal of the credit must be given to Ghiringhelli who, despite his inhumanity and complete lack of sensitivity and even his artistic ignorance, skilfully made it possible for outstanding artists – singers, conductors, producers and designers – to work together, perhaps for the first time constructively, so that opera could again become drama expressed in music.

A week after *Fedora* La Scala proudly took its production of *Lucia di Lammermoor* to Vienna for three performances in the rebuilt Staatsoper which was celebrating its inaugural season. Here, too, Toscanini in 1929, just before he took the La Scala company to Berlin, had presented *Falstaff* and *Lucia* with the same principals – a memory the Viennese treasured. Now Karajan, with the same cast as in Berlin during the previous year, took Vienna by storm. It was estimated that twelve thousand people, controlled by the better part of the city's police force, fought over the six thousand seats available for the three performances. Callas sang Lucia for the highly critical Viennese and the performances as a whole surpassed all expectations. Henceforth Vienna, like Berlin, had a new standard to go by.

The press was also beside itself. 'What a voice, what art and what intensity!' *Bild Telegraf* wrote about Callas, while *Neues Österreich* considered her a phenomenon: 'Her technique is stupendous,' it went on, 'her musical phrasing exemplary. ... In the higher register, her voice often became similar in tone to that of a flute and there were times in the mad scene which resembled a duet of flutes.'

After the performance the crowds outside the theatre were unprecedented, the jubilations in the bars and restaurants lasting until the early hours of the morning. The Meneghinis celebrated Maria's victory with friends in a typical Viennese café with wine, music and song. Incredible as it may seem, Maria felt like singing; it was daylight when she returned to her hotel.

With the Viennese interlude over Maria and her husband took a well-earned rest for the whole of July. Some of the time was spent on the island of Ischia, where they visited their friend the eminent composer William Walton. A great admirer of Callas, Walton originally wanted her to create the role of Cressida in his opera *Troilus and Cressida*, which had its première at Covent Garden in December 1954. She considered it but did not think herself suited to the role. It was eventually given to Magda László.

Two months of recording engagements and a concert for RAI in Milan followed, before Maria concentrated on her forthcoming visit to New York for her début at the Metropolitan. She had already triumphed in all the major theatres of the Western world except that of her home town. She was fully aware of the atmosphere of enormous anticipation awaiting her there.

1   *Mario e il mago* was eventually produced at La Scala in 1956. Although an artistic success, it was never revived.
2   Since Spontini's death in 1851 *La vestale*'s notable revivals were in 1924 at the Metropolitan, New York, for Rosa Ponselle and in 1927, 1954 and 1994 at La Scala.
3   Callas's recording of this aria made the international popular charts, after it featured in the film *Philadelphia*.
4   When Callas recorded the complete opera in February 1957, a year after her stage performances, she was vocally in very good form, singing with gusto and superb style, capturing the simple charm of the *ingénue* (see discography).

CHAPTER NINE

THE METROPOLITAN

THE FIRST HOME for opera in New York was the Academy of Music, until a number of rich businessmen got together to finance a new opera house to be built on Broadway between 39th and 40th Streets. Since the erection of the Metropolitan, first the old building and now the new, the company has always claimed, with good reason, that in no other house have so many stars been assembled. The pursuit of stars – particularly in the performing arts – especially, but not by any means exclusively in America where, after all, Hollywood was invented, has become an obsession. Paradoxically, at the commencement of their terms of office several managers of the Met have said, even solemnly promised, that they would do away with the star system in favour of a more homogeneous ensemble. None has really achieved this. Even Toscanini, a titan among artistic directors, did not succeed fully, though he came closest to amalgamating the star and ensemble systems. His confrontation with Geraldine Farrar (1882–1967) during the 1908 season describes well the situation that generally prevailed. When, at rehearsals, Farrar declared herself a star, the celebrated conductor reminded her that stars only exist in heaven. Not to be put down, the soprano answered defiantly that though this was true enough, 'there is also a human constellation that treads the Metropolitan boards to the renown of this institution and the gratification of the public; not to mention the box-office.'

In 1950 the Viennese Rudolf Bing (1902–97) succeeded Edward Johnson as general manager of the Metropolitan. He had begun his career running a concert agency in Vienna and, after holding appointments in Darmstadt and Berlin, in 1936 was made general manager of John Christie's newly created Festival of Opera at Glyndebourne near the south coast of England. Ten years later he became a naturalized British subject and was one of the founders of the Edinburgh Festival, which he directed from 1947 to 1949. An authoritarian – in some ways not unlike Ghiringhelli at La Scala – Bing went on to become the all-powerful manager of the Metropolitan. He, too, hated the word 'star' but liked, as he said in later years, 'a superb artistic personality who can catch an audience both off and on the stage' – in other words, a variation on the same theme. Bing, moreover, felt strongly that all singers, however great, should consider themselves highly honoured to be given the chance of a possible engagement at the Metropolitan.

He first heard of Callas, a young rising star, in 1950 just before he took up his New York appointment. When, shortly afterwards, her success in Italy and at the Teatro Colón was verified by Erich Engel of the Vienna State Opera, Bing promptly began negotiations through Liduino Bonardi, a Milanese agent, with a view to engaging her for the 1951–2 season.

At first there was some bargaining about fees, although Callas was more concerned with the choice of operas, particularly that of her début. She had reluctantly agreed to open with *Aida*, but on condition that she would follow with one or two operas to be chosen from among *Norma*, *Puritani*, *Traviata* or *Trovatore*. After an exchange of negative telegrams, negotiations reached an impasse. Bing would not agree to any of Callas's demands; he refused to pay for Meneghini's transport to New York and had no plans to mount any of the four specified operas during that season. Furthermore, it was imperative that arrangements for the company's tour and concrete plans for the subsequent season be made in advance – conditions which Callas was unwilling to accept.

Meanwhile, however, news of Callas's continued success and Toscanini's approval of her reached the United States and Bing, worried that another American company might engage her first, hurried to the Maggio Musicale Fiorentino in May 1951 to hear her in person in *I vespri Siciliani*. He later wrote in his autobiography *5000 Nights at the Opera* (1972) that 'the lady I saw in Florence in spring 1951 bore only a slight relationship to the Maria Callas who became world-famous. She was monstrously fat and awkward. . . . She had no doubt remarkable material but had still a lot to learn before she could be a star at the Met. We had quite a friendly discussion but did not get very far . . .'

Despite his allegedly serious reservations, a few months later, Bing met Callas's demands, both financial and artistic, and offered her *La traviata* for the 1952–3 season. Apparently this venture again fell through because Meneghini could not obtain a visa for the United States and Maria would not go without him. Meneghini explained that as at the time he was only managing his wife's affairs, the American embassy considered him officially unemployed and with Maria being an American citizen it was feared that he might remain in America as an immigrant looking for work. However real this obstacle may have been, it was not insurmountable. At the time other considerations occupied the Meneghinis and they knew their priorities. Callas had made her successful début at La Scala with *I vespri* and had gone on to sing other roles. Her immediate concern was to establish herself there as principal prima donna. Had she gone to the Metropolitan, she would not have been able to open the 1952–3 season at La Scala with *Macbeth*. The Met would have to wait. Besides, she had not completely forgotten Edward Johnson's treatment of her in 1946 and although she thought Bing rather sweet, his polite arrogance at times made her feel combative. None the less the Metropolitan was her biggest goal after La Scala and she would be very happy to sing there, but only when she was ready and all the elements were conducive to her success. During this period Bing had to be content with Renata Tebaldi, whose Leonora (*La forza del destino*) had impressed him greatly.

Two years later, in May 1953, Bing heard Callas in *Medea* at the Maggio Musicale and, although once more there were discussions, no agreement could be reached. By the summer of 1954, when Callas had lost weight and was transformed into a svelte and elegant woman, virtually overnight, she became very well known in America through various magazine articles. Losing no time, Bing reopened negotiations through his agent in Italy, Roberto Bauer. He was now offering *Traviata*, *Cavalleria rusticana* and *Tosca*, and a further choice of at least two roles from *Aida*, *La Gioconda*, *Un ballo in maschera* and *Andrea Chénier*. 'I would not like to have to pay her more than $750 per performance,' Bing stipulated, 'but if she at least agrees – finally and irrevocably and without any stings attached as to visas for husbands, friends or concubines – I would be prepared to go up to $800 per performance …'

Although this fee was well below that which Callas commanded at the time in all other theatres, the main issues as far as she was concerned were repertoire and artistic standards. On the other hand Meneghini, who in fact dealt with the financial side of his wife's career, constantly pressed for very high fees. He was keen to point out that the Metropolitan did not owe its great prestige to Bing but to the artists who sang there. Bing, equally averse to Meneghini, intimated that his avarice might well eventually wreck his wife's career. At one point Meneghini declared, 'My wife will not sing at the Metropolitan as long as Mr Bing runs it. It is his loss.' He then sprang on him that Maria had signed a contract with the Lyric Opera of Chicago for two seasons beginning in November 1954 for a fee of $2000 a performance, to be increased to $2500 in the second year. 'When Bing heard this,' Meneghini later wrote in his book, 'he nearly had a heart attack. I then advised him that as he could not afford Callas, he had better forget her. Besides, Callas did not need the Metropolitan.' Running out of arguments, Bing cynically remarked that Maria wanted more money than the president of the United States earned. Promptly offering to stand down, Maria urged, 'Let him sing then!'

Undeterred by these turbulent negotiations, Bing never lost interest in Callas. Furthermore, as her triumphs at La Scala, Chicago and other theatres continued, the music lovers of New York became impatient and highly critical of the Met's failure to engage her. In the spring of 1955 Bing approached Callas once more. His arrogance had disappeared and Maria, against her husband's advice, agreed to sing at the Metropolitan for $1000 a performance. But as she was expected to open the 1956–7 season with *Lucia di Lammermoor* and follow with the Queen of Night (*The Magic Flute*) in English, her agreement remained a verbal one, at least for the moment. Callas had serious doubts that she could do her best in *Lucia* under the baton of Fausto Cleva and refused absolutely to sing in an English-language *Magic Flute*. After all, she had turned down Johnson's *Fidelio* in English at a time when she was really desperate for work. There was another reason why she did not sign the contract immediately, though she was confident enough that Bing would eventually comply with her choice of roles: Meneghini, who wanted further to deflate Bing's ego, had persuaded her to wait. 'Let's make Bing', he told her, 'a little anxious for it by keeping him on tenterhooks for a while. It will do him good.'

Be that as it may, in the autumn of 1955, while Callas was singing in Chicago, all her differences with the Metropolitan were ironed out. Bing and his assistant manager, Francis Robinson, arrived in Chicago and accomplished their mission. 'To sign this contract,' Bing later said, 'we had to take the mountain to Mahomet. Also the roles changed. She would open with *Norma* and then sing *Tosca* and *Lucia*, twelve performances in all over the nine weeks of her stay.'

Maria and her husband arrived in New York on 13 October 1956. This time Georges Kalogeropoulos had no difficulty in recognizing his daughter at the airport as he had done when Maria arrived from Athens after the war. She was now the biggest star in the operatic world and already the box-office receipts at the Metropolitan exceeded the unprecedented amount of $75,000 for her opening night; this was a far cry from the young girl who had sung at her graduation in 1937 and left New York for Greece. Dario Soria of EMI's Angel Records, Francis Robinson and a lawyer were also there to receive her. Bagarozy, who had filed suit against her during the previous year in Chicago, had now done the same in New York's Supreme Court, with warrants of attachment served on the Metropolitan Opera and Angel Records. Bing's proposal to deposit Callas's fees for her appearances in a Swiss bank, so that Bagarozy would have no access to this money, was rejected by Meneghini; he demanded that his wife's fee be paid in cash, just before the commencement of each performance.

For the moment, however, any embarrassment of process-servers was wisely avoided by Maria's decision to receive a summons at her hotel on the following day. 'I am fully confident in American justice,' she calmly told the press. 'Writs of attachment and other such actions do not frighten me. I am simply and patiently awaiting an American judge to pass the final ruling on this boring affair.' This was not the only tiresome incident to greet her in New York. Apart from her impending début in the city where she was born, the enormous publicity that surrounded her was by and large more hostile than friendly.

It is one of human nature's failings that very great success and achievement can often arouse jealousy. Callas had become the queen of the august La Scala, not to mention most of the other major theatres in the world. In the eyes of many New Yorkers she had also sinned by appearing in Chicago first and, worse still, had triumphed there. Furthermore, the audience at the Metropolitan, as in most opera houses, had their favourites and many would not allow themselves to hear another singer with an open mind, especially an exceptional one who was consequently a stronger rival to their darlings. In New York there was already the long-standing Zinka Milanov who, although past her peak, had a great following. In the two previous seasons,

Tebaldi had also become extremely popular. Being a similar type of singer to Milanov, but younger and not so experienced, Tebaldi found it easier to be accepted; in a sense she was looked upon as a successor rather than a rival to the older singer. On the other hand, Milanov never for a moment considered herself a whit less important than all the sopranos in the world put together.

During her first days in New York Maria gave very few interviews. Always accompanied by her husband and Francis Robinson on such occasions, she appeared very calm and in good spirits. She answered questions simply and sincerely, yet even unimportant matters were frequently misconstrued. 'Madame Callas,' a lady reporter said, 'you were born in the United States, brought up in Greece and now you are practically Italian. What language do you think in?'

'I usually think in Greek,' Maria answered, 'but do you know I always count in English' – a very normal habit when one has learned arithmetic in English, as Maria had done. However, she was duly reported as confining her answer to 'I count in English', thus confirming, wrongly, that she was interested in money above all else. What before long really worried her, and this she could not ignore, were artistic standards. She became very tense when she discovered at the first stage rehearsals how dated the Metropolitan *Norma* settings were and how seriously they clashed with her own specially designed costumes. Worse still, the allotted rehearsal time was far below that which she considered necessary for perfection. Even so, these were to prove the least of her worries; the storm, which had been gathering since her Metropolitan début was announced almost a year before, would suddenly break with devastating effect.

On the day of the *Norma* dress rehearsal, two days before the première, *Time* magazine published a four-page article on Callas. Her portrait, commissioned by *Time* and painted by Henry Koerner during the previous spring in Milan, was used on the magazine's cover, a recognized symbol of international status. The article praised Callas's technical prowess, the instinctive dramatic qualities of her voice and all the other virtues of her art, but then proceeded with a vicious attack on her character. Lengthy biographical notes, in which facts were at best knowingly misconstrued and embroidered, were used to put before the public a woman of singular ruthlessness, who 'took her resentments out on the people around her'. Although nothing in the article was really true, but only an amalgamation of some facts distorted with out-of-context remarks made by her at some time, plus a great deal of malicious fiction, it served to establish a horribly inhuman picture of Maria Callas. Furthermore, it provided the basis for several future writers who not only used it selectively but passed misguidedly conclusive judgement on her in later years, without her point of view ever being taken into account.

But to return to the article on the eve of her Metropolitan début: after Callas's undisputed artistic merit was mentioned, she was accused of ruthless, unprofessional conduct towards her colleagues. 'On-stage,' the article alleged, 'Callas's thirst for personal acclaim is insatiable. She grabs solo curtain calls whenever she can, even after another singer's big scene.' Her backstage feud with Boris Christoff in Rome was mentioned, naturally presenting Maria as the villain. The piece also quoted di Stefano: 'I'm never going to sing opera with her again, and that's final.' This statement was further reinforced with 'the day will come when Maria will have to sing by herself', conveniently attributed to an anonymous 'close acquaintance' of Callas.

As we have seen, di Stefano was unjustly annoyed with Maria on the first night of *La traviata* at La Scala, but that was in May 1955. In September of the same year he recorded *Rigoletto* with her and later in the month sang *Lucia* with her in Berlin. He continued to work with her both on the stage and in recordings. So much for the article's credibility. There was no mention of Callas's backstage brawl with Del Monaco at La Scala during the previous January. He was now scheduled to join her in *Norma* at the Metropolitan and when approached by the magazine had sent them away. Del Monaco might have said harsh words and behaved badly in his quarrel with Maria, but before the year was out he spoke very sensibly about it in another interview, after he had sung with her at the Met: 'Much has been said about the obstreperous clash between us in January 1956, whereas nothing is said about other aspects of our artistic collaboration in various theatres, which show sincere mutual respect. One must look at both sides of the coin.'

Time then concentrated on Callas's relationship with Renata Tebaldi, who was concurrently appearing at the Lyric Theater in Chicago. After proclaiming that she had been Callas's first victim, Tebaldi was rather extravagantly described as the 'possessor of a voice of creamy softness, musicianship of delicate sensibility, and a temperament to match. She was no match for Callas. From the beginning the two women glowered. Tebaldi stayed away from Callas's performances; Callas, on the warpath, sat in a prominent box at Tebaldi's, ostentatiously cheered and watched her rival start to tremble.' Finally Callas was quoted as saying 'When I'm angry, I can do no wrong. I sing and act like someone possessed. She's [Tebaldi] got no backbone. She's not like Callas.' This part of the article concluded: 'Year after year she [Tebaldi] reduced her appearances, until last year she was absent entirely from La Scala, and Callas held the field with thirty-seven performances.'

It continued with another of Callas's ruthless actions. The allegation was that she broke with Tullio Serafin, 'the maestro who helped her first and most', because he dared record *La traviata* with another soprano. Consequently, it stated, 'Serafin is no longer engaged to conduct her and moreover other singers are now mysteriously unable to sing under him.' Lastly the article dealt its meanest blow, citing Serafin describing Callas: 'She is like a devil with evil instincts, and implying that Callas's counter-comment was 'I understand hate; I respect revenge. You have to defend yourself. You have to be strong, very, very strong.' Clearly this scandalously libellous accusation, based on a minute grain of truth, was designed to expose her insatiable ruthlessness

A small digression can easily remove the 'grand guignol' aspects of the incident and put it in its true perspective. Soon after Callas's sensational success in *La traviata* at La Scala in 1956, EMI wanted to record the opera with her and di Stefano, with Serafin as conductor. However, as Callas had already recorded the same opera for Cetra she could not, under the terms of her contract, re-record it for another company until 1957. In the circumstances EMI, anxious to publish a *Traviata* recording without delay for commercial reasons, replaced Callas with Antonietta Stella. Callas was very upset about this at the time and, as she told me much later, her first reaction was to blame Serafin, the man she never stopped venerating, for not waiting a year until she would have been free to make the recording. 'Sure, I was upset and annoyed. I had studied the opera with Serafin and it has, if I may say so, been from the beginning one of my greatest successes. Neither the recording nor some of the other singers on the Cetra *Traviata* were at their best and more importantly I had afterwards improved as a singer generally and developed by interpretation particularly. That is all. I never said those monstrous things against Serafin that were reported and neither did he.'

While it was my intention to ask Serafin about this incident, when I had the opportunity I changed my mind. In the course of our conversation I was absolutely convinced that he would never have said what *Time* reported about Callas or anybody else and it would have been an indignity even to enquire about it. Moreover, it soon became obvious that *Time* was misinformed, or chose to be, when it said that Callas had banished Serafin from conducting her. After the *Traviata* recording he did not do so for about a year, because during this period she was singing at La Scala and the Metropolitan, who had their own conductors. She also sang in Chicago where her performances were conducted, as in the previous season, by Rescigno. When Tebaldi agreed to sing in the same season, Rescigno invited Serafin to conduct her performances, and perhaps this was as misconstrued as Callas not wanting him. Furthermore Serafin, at the time in his seventy-ninth year, had also begun to cut down on his engagements. Nevertheless, as soon as Callas was available, he conducted her in *Lucia* for RAI, Rome in June 1957 and followed on with recordings of *Turandot*, *Manon Lescaut* and *Medea*.

While the allegations were damaging to Callas, they surely could not be completely credible to everybody and the hostility they created would thus inevitably prove ephemeral. The worst result of the article, creating far-reaching ill will against Callas, was the discovery of her mother by the press. Having separated from her husband, Evangelia was now living in Athens. Not only had she not seen Maria since the time they spent together in Mexico City in 1951, but her uncompromising attitude and further demands for money eventually brought all communication between mother and daughter to a halt.

Now *Time*, having failed to get any response whatsoever from Maria's father as far as his family's affairs were concerned, traced Evangelia, who was delighted to give interviews. The present article condemned Maria for turning 'bitterly against her mother', then quoted her as saying that

'"I'll never forgive her [Evangelia] for taking my childhood away. During all the years I should have been playing and growing up, I was singing or making money."' Evangelia's accusations were even more devastating. She said that when, in 1951, she wrote to her daughter asking for $100 '"for my daily bread"', she was told: '"Do not come to us with your troubles. I can't give you anything. Money does not grow on trees. . . . I have to 'scream' for my living, and you are young enough to work, too. If you can't make enough money to live on, you had better jump in the river and drown yourself."'

Both Evangelia and Iakinthy confirmed the existence of this letter, but omitted to mention how seriously provoked Maria was by her mother's selfish demands. Almost certainly, Iakinthy was not aware that only two months earlier Maria had provided generously for Evangelia. Moreover Evangelia, in her statement to *Time*, changed her request for quite a lot of money as well as moving in with the Meneghini household to the melodramatic plea '$100 for my daily bread' – a sly pretext to get her own back when her original demands fell on deaf ears. Inarguably Evangelia maintained that her daughter, a famous prima donna, was earning millions as well as being married to a millionaire. In her paranoia she convinced herself that by rights she too should be provided with a millionaire's life-style.

Neither Maria nor her father endorsed Evangelia's accusations, nor did they discuss their family publicly. On the other hand, Evangelia's vitriolic charges could not have been more destructive for Maria's public image – undoubtedly a far-reaching blow had been dealt. Evangelia's tactics were ill advised as in such cases there is seldom, if ever, any solace to be found in the press: only greater misery is caused. The world at large, however, usually takes such libellous statements at face value; whereas a prima donna's temperamental behaviour and the like may well be forgiven, it is unlikely that her repudiation of her mother will be.

Maria was so distressed that her initial reaction was to return to Italy immediately, rather than make her Metropolitan début before what she imagined would be an indoctrinated audience. But as usual good sense prevailed; she became incensed in the face of hostility (this is what she meant when she had said 'When I'm angry I can do no wrong') and instead of running away, stood her ground firmly, ready to fight using her art as a weapon. She had learned to be a fighter when she was so unfairly dismissed by the Athens Opera in 1945. Meneghini testified that although his wife was very sensitive to unjust accusations, she was never dispirited. On the contrary, she would before long become inspired by them.

Nevertheless, the two days before opening night were nerve-racking. Apart from the article, which she thought grossly unfair, the heat and dryness of that October's Indian summer in New York were affecting her voice. During these turbulent times Bing stood by her like a good and comforting friend. 'He was helpful and kind without being gushing,' Maria later said. It may have taken quite a time for her to sign the contract with the Met but one must bear in mind that

Bing was primarily negotiating with Meneghini and the two men could not stand one another. From the moment Maria arrived in New York Bing was very amicably disposed towards her. Later, he wrote in his autobiography,

> We gave Miss Callas treatment no other artist has ever received. . . . What almost everything written about her fails to catch is the girlishness, the innocent dependence on others that was so strong a part of her personality when she did not feel she had to be wary. Her letters to me in 1955 and 1956 are full of these moments. 'Is New York', she wrote, 'anxious to hear me?' Indeed it was: her opening night was undoubtedly the most exciting of all such in my time at the Metropolitan.

Evidently Callas's relationship with Bing at the time she became a member of the Metropolitan Opera began most auspiciously. Not so, however, her first performance – the rather cool reception she was given on her stage entrance was no vote of the audience's confidence in her. Callas, clearly very much on edge, began Norma's great first scene, which includes the celebrated 'Casta Diva', somewhat unevenly. Only intermittently did the magic of her expressive powers manifest itself. It was a different story after the first act, when her performance suddenly came to life. An incident during the interval almost certainly played a great part in this.

A couple of minutes before the curtain was raised for the second act a bejewelled Zinka Milanov ostentatiously strolled down the aisle to take her seat, attracting as much attention as she could from her admirers, who applauded her rather extravagantly. Milanov often employed these tactics when a rival was appearing at the Met. Apparently on this occasion she came late so that she might be spared the 'horrors' of the 'Casta Diva', though conveniently choosing to forget that her performance in that very same production of *Norma* was a disaster in 1954. Her antagonism was considerably undermined when, four weeks later, she sang with little success in a new production of Verdi's *Ernani*, merely confirming that 'early' Verdi and 'late' Milanov was not a good mixture.

Recalling the *Norma* occasion at my instigation, Meneghini said that Maria, who had already taken her position on-stage, heard Milanov's brouhaha in the stalls. 'When she realized what this was all about, she walked towards the wings where I was standing. "Poor Milanov," she told me, "I guess she owes it to herself to have, by hook or by crook, an ovation for her Norma. Pity she is only successful off-stage."' Meneghini then said that he noticed a bitter-sweet smile at the corner of his wife's mouth and knew, to his delight, that Maria had already planted her feet in firm ground and was ready to meet any challenge.

This was precisely what followed. The performance, which had begun rather coolly, was now ablaze, thrilling and moving the audience by turns. At the end, during the sixteen curtain-calls that were demanded by the public many flowers were thrown. Callas had won an important battle and she knew it. 'I guess it is hardest to be accepted in your home town,' she exclaimed between curtain-calls. She was deeply moved and on the brink of tears as she gathered roses and presented them to her fellow artists – then an unusual gesture which further impressed the audience. At the next curtain-call Del Monaco (Pollione) and Siepi (Oroveso) also showed their feelings in the best way they could; ignoring the Metropolitan's regulation, which banned solo curtain-calls, they pushed Maria on to the stage, leaving her alone to receive the ovation that was her due.

After the performance a glittering party, given by Angel Records in Maria's honour, awaited the Meneghinis at the Ambassador Hotel – an excellent way for any artist, however exhausted, to unwind. Apart from the principals of *Norma*, other members of the Metropolitan and famous singers of previous generations – Giovanni Martinelli, himself a great Pollione, and Gladys Swarthout – the guests included a considerable tranche of the artistic, diplomatic and social worlds. Wally Toscanini and Marlene Dietrich, a long-standing admirer of Callas (Dietrich had prepared a special soup – reducing eight pounds of beef into a bouillon – to keep up Maria's strength during rehearsals), were also there to greet New York's new star. It was a great occasion, too, for Georges Kalogeropoulos, who could not take his eyes off his daughter.

In spite of all this adulation, Maria herself was not completely satisfied with her début performance. 'Now that this is over I can relax and get down to work,' she said. She did neither, as it turned out. Some continuing hostility from the media and the unusually dry weather that affected her throat still played on her nerves to the point that she felt too exhausted to sing her second performance, a Saturday matinée. 'I literally ran to her room,' Bing later recalled in his autobiography, 'and found her genuinely ill, with Meneghini and a doctor in solicitous attendance ... after a few encouraging words from me she agreed to go on, saving us from what would have been a riot.' It would seem that Callas's indisposition was not as physical as she thought and although she had not yet found her best form she none the less gave a creditable portrayal of this most demanding of roles. Bing also mentioned: 'It was at the close of this performance that some idiot threw radishes on the stage; fortunately Miss Callas was so shortsighted she thought they were tea roses.' Obviously this 'idiot', having heard of the Milanese vegetable incident at the end of *La traviata* during the previous season, had tried to imitate his Italian counterpart. Each in his own misguided way misfired.

Callas was in better form for the remaining four performances of *Norma*. In the last two (the second was given in Philadelphia) Kurt Baum and Nicola Moscona replaced Del Monaco and Siepi respectively. The Mexican episode, when Baum had vowed to prevent her from appearing at the Met, let along sing with her, was completely forgotten and she responded well to his courtesy.

The *Norma* reviews, however, refer to the first performance: Howard Taubman (*New York*

Times) found Callas's voice 'puzzling. Occasionally it gives the impression of having been formed out of sheer will power rather than natural endowments. . . . Miss Callas may be forgiven a lack of velvet in parts of her range. She is brave to do Norma at all. She brings sufficient dramatic and musical values to her performance to make it an interesting one.'

Other critics thought differently, showing a better understanding of what opera is all about. Summing up Callas's Metropolitan début, Ericson and Milburn (*Opera Annual*, No. 4) wrote that 'She immediately established herself as a magnetic and fascinating personality with a voice of unique timbre ... an actress with an original and subtle style. Since she had been preceded by such a fabulous reputation, the fact that her singing was not perfect was, perhaps, overstressed and took some time getting used to, but there was no denying that Miss Callas was a remarkable artist whose interpretations were worth seeing even when one disagreed with them.'

Tosca followed and in Callas's hands the familiar opera became a much more interesting affair than it usually was at the Met. For this, credit must also be given to Giuseppe Campora (Cavaradossi) and George London (Scarpia) and to Dimitri Mitropoulos, the conductor, who brought tremendous excitement to the orchestra.

The most concise summing-up of this Tosca came from Irving Kolodin (*Saturday Review*) who wrote, 'There may be sound basis for arguing which singer, of all contemporaries, is the most voluptuous sounding Tosca, the most ample in vocal volume, the most unwilling partner to Scarpia's intentions, but Callas strikes me as the most credible Tosca of our time. She sings her music with the instincts of an actress and phrases her acting with the instincts of a fine musician.'

Almost as rewarding was Lucia, Callas's third and last role during this season – indisputably a *tour de force* for a soprano who had just sung Norma and Tosca. As in many other theatres, her stunning portrayal revealed the great dramatic possibilities of the work and for many the opera made sense for the first time, even though the Metropolitan's production was shabby and dull; Callas aptly described the sets of her first scene as 'a monstrous well which covers half of the stage and looks no more romantic than an oil tank'.

The majority of the critics gave her performance as a whole their unqualified praise. R. Sabin (*Musical America*) wrote that 'Her singing was at its best in passages which were fluid in tempo. . . . If she hurried phrases and skimmed over the tones a bit, she none the less sang several such passages in the mad scene with virtuosic flexibility and smoothness.' Kolodin in the *Saturday Review* singled out the mad scene: 'Here, instead of indulging in useless wanderings about the stage with the surface suggestions of dementia, Miss Callas concentrated on interpreting the words with a simplicity and power that absorbed the attention of the capacity audience. When she finished "Ardon gl'incensi", sung with steady accuracy, a full measure of musical meaning, and strongly executed embellishments, the roar of applause was house-wide.'

On 26 November Tebaldi wrote an open letter to *Time* protesting at Callas's allegations against her, which the magazine had recently published: 'The Signora Callas', Tebaldi wrote, 'admits to being a woman of character and says that I have no backbone. I reply: "I have one great thing that she has not – a heart!" That I actually trembled when I knew she was present at a performance of mine is utterly ridiculous. It was not the Signora who caused me to stay away from La Scala; I sang there before she did, and considered myself a *Creatura della Scala*. I stayed away of my own free will because an atmosphere not at all pleasant had been created there.'

It must be mentioned that Tebaldi was already a popular singer in the United States with several fan clubs. The day after her letter was published Callas sang Norma in Philadelphia where a square had been renamed Renata Tebaldi Square.

Tebaldi's letter dismayed Maria. She had not made those remarks, which were seemingly fabricated by the press so that the feud between two prominent singers might be rekindled. She remained silent, which was perhaps a mistake. The problem was that public relations were not within Meneghini's compass and no one else was ever engaged for this job, so essential in a famous artist's career. Consequently, at the time many interpreted Maria's silence as proof of her guilt and the dice continued to be loaded against her.

An incident that happened in the second performance of *Lucia* was even more distressing. Baritone Enzo Sordello (Ashton) held an unwritten high note interminably and long after Callas had appropriately released her high D at the end of their duet which closes the second act. His intention was to make game of Callas, who in this situation would appear short of breath, and encourage applause for himself. '*Basta* [enough]!' Maria told him in an aside. 'You will never sing with me again.' Well prepared for a confrontation Sordello growled. 'And I will kill you.'

Sordello was a very arrogant man whose only qualification was his lovely voice which, however, lacked any appreciable degree of dramatic artistry. Having been praised by the critics for its quality, he immediately tried to cash in by provoking a quarrel with Callas. He misfired badly because after the performance she ignored him completely and issued an ultimatum to Bing: 'Either he goes, or I go.' At first, Bing did not believe Maria was serious, until she failed to turn up at the theatre for the subsequent performance. In the meantime Dolores Wilson sang Lucia in this performance, much to the consternation of the audience who created havoc in the theatre when told that they were not entitled to a refund. It took the intervention of the police to restore order so that the performance could commence some forty-five minutes late.

For the remaining two *Lucias* Bing replaced Sordello with Frank Valentino. When Sordello became very insulting, Bing instantly ordered the cancellation of the remainder of his Metropolitan contract. Bing explained that his decision to fire Sordello was not only because of his behaviour to Callas but also because all along he had been uncooperative and insubordinate in the extreme with Fausto Cleva, the conductor.

The majority of the press turned the story entirely into a Callas scandal: she could not cope with the high note and kicked the poor baritone, calling him a bastard for not letting her get away with it. Callas's subsequent cancellation of her performance added more credibility to press allegations that she was a tempestuous person, totally responsible for Sordello's dismissal from the Metropolitan.

Wasting no time, Sordello went after as much publicity as he could; he made front-page news shown tearing up her photograph. When Maria was leaving New York Sordello, who had booked on the same flight, waited for her at the airport. He was accompanied by a band of photographers ready to capture every facet of their meeting. It was just before Christmas and Maria responded to his seasonal greetings but refused, rather disdainfully, a handshake intended to show that there were no hard feelings between them. 'For that you must first apologize publicly', Maria told him, 'for all the things you said about me in the past few days.'

'That is not possible,' Sordello answered.

Maria then simply shrugged her shoulders and said to the photographers (who had already captured her refusal to shake Sordello's hand), 'I don't like this man taking advantage of my publicity.'

Unfortunately for Maria, Sordello did just that: the airport photograph was more effectively publicized in America and Europe than Sordello's picture-shredding one.

What kept the arguments and controversy about Callas alive during the season in New York, apart from unforeseen incidents, was the vitriolic Elsa Maxwell, the notorious gossip columnist generally known as the 'Hollywood witch'. An exceptionally shrewd and insincere woman, Maxwell had at first made a living playing the piano in cinemas for silent films. After the First World War she moved to Europe, where she played at parties and clubs, and sang Broadway hits, as well as her own songs. She made her grand entrée into the world of café society through Prince Aly Khan, son of the Aga Khan, with whom she struck up a friendship in 1947. Thereafter, having discovered the knack of manipulating other people's lives and money provided they were very rich or very famous, she became the confidante and often champion of many in this milieu. Moreover, in due course she established herself as an extraordinary party giver, or party organizer to be precise, for the rich and idle usually referred to as the Jet Set. 'I have been called a parasite for accepting the largesse of the wealthy,' Maxwell wrote in her autobiography (*R.S.V.P.*, 1954), 'but I contributed as much, at least, as I received. I had imagination and they had the money, a fair exchange of the commodity possessed by each side in great abundance.'

In the early fifties Maxwell became the best-known gossip journalist in America through the extensive syndication of her popular articles and her regular radio and television programmes. Occasionally she would turn theatre and opera critic of sorts and, in spite or because of the violent likes or dislikes expressed in a pseudo-sociological fashion in her reviews, she exerted considerable influence on public opinion at large.

At the time of Callas's New York début Maxwell was seventy-three years old, short and plump, and described by Meneghini as 'the ugliest woman I have ever seen'. Others compared her with a spinster hyena. A committed partisan and friend of Renata Tebaldi, Maxwell was well aware of her idol's long-standing feud with Callas. She had already written derogatory articles about Maria when she sang in Chicago. These were, however, ineffective as at the time Callas's unqualified triumphs reduced Maxwell's grumbling to a voice in the wilderness. It was different in New York, especially with the hostile atmosphere the *Time* article had created. Now very much on her mettle, Maxwell prepared to attack Callas, both the artist and the woman, on every count. About her Norma, Maxwell declared that 'the great Callas left me cold' and for *Tosca* her attack was directed at Maria's character, ludicrously referring to her as the 'devious diva whose jealousy of George London (Scarpia) was evident by the way she knifed him at the end of the second act'.

Maxwell was not the only one who tried to invent such idiotic though malicious gossip about Callas's attitude to London. Other writers did as much after Callas and London performed part of the second act of *Tosca* on television. London exposed the lie in his article 'Prima donnas I have sung against'. He wrote:

> Callas was a most co-operative colleague. At one point, during dress rehearsal, after she had 'murdered' me, I fell too close to the desk and she couldn't pass to cross the stage and pick up the two candelabra. . . . Callas laughingly stopped and announced to the director, 'There are just too many legs around here.' We all had a good laugh. . . . Yet the day after the broadcast many newspapers reported that Mme Callas and I had had a tiff during our rehearsal. I tried to tell my friends this was just not so. But I finally gave up. . . . They [friends and press] want her to be tempestuous and fiery, and that is the way it is going to be.

Even so, Maxwell continued her bizarre review of *Lucia*: 'I confess the great Callas's acting in the mad scene left me completely unmoved. But I think she sang the aria in the first act beautifully. I was intrigued by the red wig she wore through the first two acts but in the mad scene she came on as a platinum blonde. Why this change of colour? What did it mean to this egocentric extrovert?'

As Maxwell's scurrilous attacks continued in the press, on radio and on television, Meneghini was vainly racking his brains to find a way to 'shut the "ugliest woman" up'. He was at the end of his tether when one day during their last week in New York Maria told her husband to stop worrying about this matter and leave everything to her. Three days later she applied her strategy at a benefit dinner dance held in aid of the American Hellenic Warfare Fund at the Waldorf Astoria. The Meneghinis were the guests of Spyros Skouras, the film magnate. After dinner

Maria surprised her husband by asking Skouras to introduce her to Elsa Maxwell. There is no denying that she was determined to beat Maxwell at her own game and was prepared to use any means at her disposal for this purpose. The two women appeared to be pleased with one another and in fact spent the rest of the evening together.

The next day Maxwell immortalized this meeting in her column, retelling verbatim much of their conversation. 'Madame Callas,' she had apparently said, 'I would have imagined myself to be the last person on earth that you would have wished to meet.'

'On the contrary,' Maria answered, 'you are the first one I wish to meet because, aside from your opinion of my voice, I esteem you as a lady of honesty who is devoted to telling the truth.'

'When I looked into her amazing eyes,' Maxwell wrote, 'which are brilliant, beautiful and hypnotic, I realized she is an extraordinary person.'

From then on there was, as if by magic, a radical change of tune in Maxwell's articles. They were now devoted to exalting Callas's artistry and defending her from her enemies. Furthermore, Tebaldi was all but banished from the revised Maxwell pecking order. Meneghini said that once her articles became favourable Maria was inundated with invitations to appear on television, attend balls and all kinds of social functions. 'The friendship of the "Hollywood witch" proved invaluable.'

Undoubtedly Maria made a conquest, though little did she realize at the time that she had bitten off a great deal more than she could chew; Maxwell fell head over heels in love with her and henceforth followed her everywhere.

Callas completed her first Metropolitan season on 19 December. Although she was not in best voice for every performance, all in all she had been successful; the ultimate Callas was yet to come in the next season. Before leaving New York on 21 December she discussed her return with Bing. They later agreed by letter that she would sing in *La traviata*, *Lucia* and *Tosca* in February 1958.

'She held the contract ten weeks before signing it, shortening my life,' Bing later noted in his autobiography.

NORMA

Opera in two acts by Bellini; libretto by Romani. First performed at La Scala on 26 December 1831.

Callas first sang Norma in November 1948 in Florence and last in May 1965 at the Paris Opéra, a total of eighty-four performances.

Right Act I: *The sacred grove of the Druids.* Norma (Callas), the High Priestess, rebukes the Druids for their impatience to fight their Roman oppressors – Rome will fall through its own decadence.

Callas's authority and grandeur in 'Sediziose voci' ('Seditious voices') characterized Norma's incendiary disposition. After cutting the sacred mistletoe the moon shines forth and Callas prays for peace: 'Casta Diva' ('Chaste Goddess'), with its oriental mysticism, possesses a vigour all of its own, and with a veiled tone Callas conveyed an uncanny combination of chastity and eroticism. Her real mystery was manifested when by some entrancing alchemy the florid phrases floated above the choral background expressing in wordless ecstasy Norma's divine side.

In 'Ah! Bello a me ritorna' ('Ah, when will my beloved return') Callas assumed sensual accents, privately vowing to avert the danger from Pollione, the Roman Proconsul and her clandestine lover, as a counterpoint to the angry sentiment of the Druids, who are demanding his death (La Scala, 1955).

Left *Outside Norma's dwelling where she secretly keeps her two sons.* The novice priestess Adalgisa (Simionato) confides in Norma, her friend and superior, her sacrilegious love for a Roman and begs to be released from her vows.

Remembering Norma's similar situation, Callas fell into a reverie, 'Oh, rimembranza' ('Oh, how I remember'), wistfully reliving the emotion of being loved by Pollione, until she discovers that Adalgisa's lover *is* Pollione.

Below *Inside Norma's dwelling.* Norma confronts the faithless Pollione (Corelli).

Callas, now the wronged mother, the scorned woman, charged the cascades of coloratura with utter contempt: 'Tremi tu? E per chi? . . . Trema per te, fellon! Pei figli tuoi, trema per me, fellon! ('You are trembling! For whom? . . . Tremble for yourself, for your children, for me, traitor!') (Paris Opéra, 1964).

Above With an inner vitality which never vacillates, Callas and Simionato raised 'Mira o Norma' ('You see Norma'), the most celebrated duet in Italian opera, to a rare theatrical experience. The rondo 'Sì, fino all ore' ('For the rest of my days') marks the reconciliation of the two women. United they will face adversity together (La Scala, 1955).

The Temple of Irminsul. Callas declared war against the Romans, 'Guerra! Strage! Sterminio!' ('War, pillage, death!') with electrifying rage. When she confronted Pollione (Del Monaco), now a prisoner, Norma's fury, vindictiveness, anguish and eventual despair were passionately depicted in their climactic duet 'In mia man' alfin tu sei' ('At last you are in my hands').

Left Finally the diminuendo on 'Son Io' ('It is I') at her confession that she is the guilty priestess personified the complete collapse of a human being who knows that death is the only absolution. (Covent Garden, 1956)

Opposite Pleading with Oroveso (Zaccaria), Norma's father, Callas's pathos in 'Ah padre, abbi di lor pietà!' ('Father, your pity for my children!') culminated in a 'shriek' of despair on 'pietà'. After her father showed compassion, Callas reached transcendent eloquence and harmony: through Norma's wretchedness shone the realisation of her complete purification. Recognising her greatness, Pollione, his love rekindled, joins her on the funeral pyre, both accepting their punishment for the sacrilege committed.

Above left and right
Callas as Norma
(Epidaurus, 1960).

Right Callas as Norma
(Teatro Massimo Bellini,
Catania, 1951).

MADAMA BUTTERFLY

Opera in two acts by Puccini; libretto by Giacosa and Illica. First performed at La Scala on 17 February 1904.
Callas sang Butterfly three times in Chicago in 1955.

Act I: *A small Japanese house on a hill facing the harbour of Nagasaki.* Butterfly (Callas), a young geisha, arrives for her wedding to Pinkerton (di Stefano), an American sailor.

For some, Callas succeeded in scaling down both her personality and voice to present, with artless charm, a child-like Butterfly, innocent, naïve and devoted to the man of her dreams. For others, it was no more than make-believe – accomplished but not entirely convincing. Both factions were right: Butterfly remains to her death both child and woman – more of a child at the beginning, more of a woman later on.

Left Act 2: *Butterfly's living-room.* Three years after her wedding and Pinkerton's departure, Butterfly describes to her maid Suzuki the moment when her husband will return: 'Un bel dì vedremo . . . e poi la nave appare' ('One fine day . . . the ship will appear').

Callas's narration, at first in nostalgic pianissimo, became introspective as she thought of those intimate moments when husband and wife would be reunited. As her fears grew (Pinkerton might not return), the intensity of her voice increased, culminating in a self-reassuring emotional outburst: 'Io con sicura fede l'aspetto' ('He will return, I know it').

Right In vain Sharpless (Weede) tries to read Pinkerton's letter to Butterfly, who is so excited that she constantly interrupts him. Eventually realising the gravity of her situation, her excitement changes to dismay: 'Tornar a diventir la gente col cantar, oppur, meglio, morire' ('Either again entertain people with my songs or, better, to die').

MACBETH

Opera in four acts by Verdi; the libretto, which is after Shakespeare's tragedy, was prepared in prose by Verdi and put into verse by Piave, with additions by Andrea Maffei. First performed at the Teatro della Pergola, Florence, on 14 March 1847.

Callas sang Lady Macbeth five times at La Scala in 1952.

Left Act I: *The great hall in Macbeth's castle.* A letter from her husband informs Lady Macbeth (Callas) of the witches' prophecies: that Macbeth will become Thane of Cawdor is already fulfilled; the other is that he will be King of Scotland.

Callas's idea of declaiming the words of the note slowly, as if it were difficult to understand them, proved too subtle in the theatre. When she determined to strengthen her husband's will to gain the throne by murdering King Duncan, the full-bodied tone of her singing was appropriately hard and cold, invested with magic authority and brooding single-mindedness – a total expression of power: 'Or tutti sorgete ministri infernali ('All you infernal ministers arise').

Below After killing the sleeping Duncan, Macbeth (Mascherini) is so distraught that Lady Macbeth has to return the blood-stained dagger to the murdered King's chamber herself.

She began in almost hushed tones, which betrayed her own fears. Then Callas's voice acquired a reassuring firmness in her effort to build up Macbeth's confidence: 'Le sue guardie insanguinate . . . Che l'accusa in lor ricada' ('Smear the grooms with blood . . . The blame will fall on them').

Act 2: *The Banqueting Hall in Macbeth's castle.* The Lords hail the Macbeths as their monarchs. She begins a rousing song 'Si colmi il calice' ('Fill the goblet') until Macbeth, who imagines he sees Banquo's ghost, protests that he was not responsible for his death. Lady Macbeth sings a second verse, but the ghost reappears to Macbeth who practically confesses his guilt.

Callas sang the first verse incisively and cheerfully, underlining its jauntiness with an irony that created an atmosphere of weird, almost spooky, anticipation. Rallying Macbeth, the dauntless hostess put a nervous pressure on the words 'Chi morì tornar non può' ('The dead do not return') and an artificial gaiety devoid of grace.

Act 4: *The great hall in Macbeth's castle.* Entering in a hushed, claustrophobic atmosphere the haunted Lady Macbeth, sleepwalking, is now mentally unbalanced.

Callas rubbed her hands as if to wash them before she began in mournful pianissimo and veiled tone as though produced through clenched teeth – terror and guilt with underlying disgust – 'Chi poteva in quel vegliardo tanto sangue immaginar?' ('Who would have thought the old man had so much blood?') A dark intensity, followed by resignation (the child in Lady Macbeth begins to accept her guilt) imbued her voice in 'Arabia intera rimedar si piccol mano' ('All the perfumes of Arabia cannot cleanse this little hand'). With the softest sensual voice, rising to D flat to drop an octave on the final note in 'Andiam, Macbetto' ('Let us go, Macbeth') Callas sleepwalked to her death (falling over a parapet), after she had come to terms with her conscience and, in her mind, was reconciled to her husband.

In this, the denouement of the opera, Callas reached the zenith of her art – she gave the words an abstract dimension, superbly descriptive – through a wealth of vocal coloration as she conveyed how Lady Macbeth's unhinged mind desperately tries to change the pattern of the mood in her subconsciousness, culminating in the moment of catharsis.

ALCESTE

Opera in three acts by Gluck; libretto in Italian by Calzabigi. First performed at the Burgtheater, Vienna, on 26 December 1767.

Callas sang Alceste four times at La Scala in 1954.

Act I: *The Temple of Apollo in Pherae, Thessaly.* Alceste (Callas) laments with her people the imminent death of her husband, King Admetus.

Offering gifts and prayer, 'O Dei, del mio fato tiranno' ('Oh Gods, see me humbled before you'), Callas unveiled most tellingly the soul of the young queen through a variety of vocal colours. As her fears grew, so did the urgency of her singing, culminating in an outburst of despair: life is meaningless without her husband. There was also something sublime in the way she obeyed the High Priest — he indicated the lower steps of the altar where she must bow her royal head.

Left When the oracle decrees that the King must die that day if no volunteer gives his life for him Alceste offers herself. In 'Divinità infernal' ('Infernal Gods') she does not ask for pity; if she takes from the gods a beloved husband, she gives them in return a beloved wife.

Callas's initial agitation came from within, as if she had been stabbed by an invisible knife. Hopelessness and desolation followed, gradually changing to strength, until the thought of her children almost broke her heroic decision. But her resolution was unshakeable. Her voice gained in vibrancy without losing any of the ecstatic poetry as she pronounced her vow to the gods; repeating a tremolo that the orchestra applies on some notes, Callas achieved incomparable dramatic grandeur.

Below left and right Act 2: *A room in Admetus's palace.* Admetus's (Gavarini) health has been suddenly restored. Alceste evades his searching questions until the time approaches for her death.

With a 'veiled' tone on certain notes and poignant gestures, Callas surpassed herself with her portrayal of despair, tenderness, mourning and dismay. She was intensely moving when she told her husband that the gods knew how much she loved him: the 'tears in her voice' were heard, the power of conjugal love felt and the Alceste of antiquity became a living woman.

DON CARLOS

Opera in five acts by Verdi; libretto in French by Méry and Camille du Locle. First performed at the Paris Opéra on 11 March 1867 and in Italian, translated by Angelo Zanardini, at La Scala on 10 January 1884.

Callas sang Elisabetta in *Don Carlos* five times at La Scala in 1954.

Below left Act 1: *A garden outside the cloister of the monastery of San Yuste.* Callas as Queen Elisabetta di Valois. When King Philip (Rossi-Lemeni) finds his Queen unattended (contrary to royal decree), he orders her French lady-in-waiting back to France.

Below right The sweet and dignified queen was revealed in Callas's farewell, 'Non pianger, mia compagna' ('Do not weep, my dear companion'). It was so deeply and simply felt that it conveyed the Queen's own longing for her native France.

Above Act 2: *A large square in front of the Cathedral in Madrid.* During an *auto-da-fé* in which heretics are to die at the stake, the King's son Don Carlos (Ortica), leading Flemish deputies (and having the support of the court, including Elisabetta and Rodrigo – Mascherini, left back – as well as the people), begs the King, in vain, to end the persecutions in Flanders. Carlos then asks for the governorship of Flanders. The King refuses brusquely and orders the arrest of the Flemish deputies, whereupon Carlos draws his sword, vowing to become the saviour of Flanders. When the guards defy the King's command to disarm Don Carlos, Rodrigo does so and saves the situation.

Right Act 3: *The King's study in Madrid.* The King discovers his son's portrait in his wife's jewel box and accuses her of adultery, even though she was betrothed to Carlos before her marriage.

Above Following her husband's accusations, Elisabetta faints and the King calls for help, whereupon Princess Eboli (Stignani) and Rodrigo appear. When Rodrigo reproaches the King for lack of self-control. he is overcome with remorse, and accepts his wife's innocence. The repentant Eboli confesses to Elisabetta that her own unrequited love for Carlos drove her to send the jewel box to the King. She had earlier been the King's mistress. Elisabetta forgives her but orders her to choose, by morning, either exile or a nunnery.

Right *The cloisters of San Yuste. A moonlit night.* Elisabetta, waiting for Carlos, meditates at the tomb of Charles V: 'Tu che le vanità conoscesti del mondo' ('You who knew the vanities of the world').

Callas brought dramatic grandeur to her introspective monologue and moving resignation as she recalled her brief moment of happiness with Carlos at Fontainebleau. When Carlos appears and tells her that he will go to Flanders to be the people's saviour, they part not as lovers but mother and son.

MEFISTOFELE

Opera in prologue, four acts and epilogue by Arrigo Boito; libretto by the composer. First performed at La Scala on 5 March 1868.

Callas sang Margherita in *Mefistofele* three times at the Arena di Verona in July 1954.

Right Act 2: *Martha's Garden.* Rejuvenated as a handsome young knight under the alias of Enrico, Faust (di Stefano) declares his love to Margherita (Callas). He evades her questions about religion and provides her with a sleeping potion to give to her mother; Margherita will then be able to meet him later that night.

Below Act 3: *A prison cell.* Margherita, condemned to death for poisoning her mother with the sleeping potion and strangling her child, has lost her reason: 'L'altra notte il fondo al mare il mio bimbo hanno gittato' ('The other night my baby was thrown to the bottom of the sea').

Callas's committed interpretation of this mad scene was true drama in music; a case where the melodic line with rich colours is fully sustained throughout a wide range of expression. One felt the freezing but eloquent emotion of 'L'aura e fredda, il carcer fosco, e la mesta anima mia' ('The air is cold, the prison dark and my soul full of sorrow').

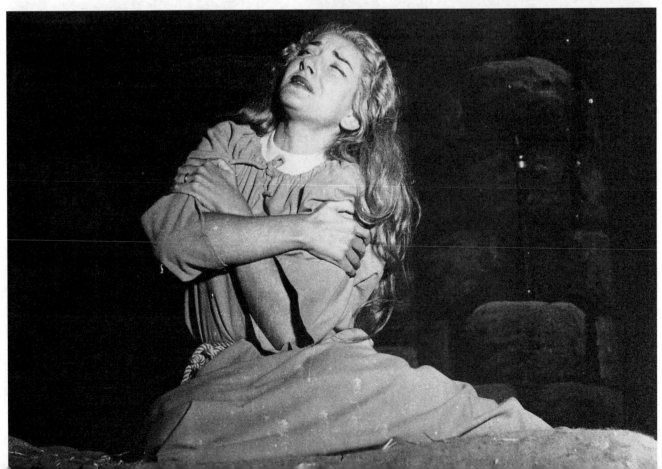

IL TURCO IN ITALIA

Opera in two acts by Rossini; libretto by Romani. First performed at La Scala on 14 August 1814.

Callas first sang Donna Fiorilla in *Il Turco* at the Teatro Eliseo, Rome, in October 1950 and last at La Scala in May 1955, a total of nine performances.

Above Act I: *The quayside in Naples.* Donna Fiorilla (Callas) preaches in favour of infidelity to her friends: 'Non si dà follia maggiore dell'amare un solo oggetto' ('It is a great folly to love only a single object [man]').

Callas's singing was light, deceptively simple and by understating her outrageous declarations, her chuckling merriment, the mischievous vixen acquired that frivolous charm that enables one to get away with anything (La Scala, 1955).

Right Fiorilla flirts with Selim, the Turk (Rossi–Lemeni), at first sight. She is thrilled by his bejewelled fingers and before oong, the two of them wander off arm in arm.

There was calculated coyness in Callas's suggestive exchanges with the Turk, but she was more down to earth in her aside 'E già ferito. E' nella rete' ('He is already caught in my net').

Left Fiorilla entertains the Turk at home. Infused with provocative vitality, Callas affected incredulity at the Turk's advances which, in fact, she herself had instigated – the vivid coloration of her voice rendered each repeat more memorable, while the blatant exhibition of her femininity enhanced with gusto her hilarious efforts to seduce a master seducer: 'Siete Turchi: non vi credo, cento donne intorno avete' ('You Turks have a hundred women').

Right When Don Geronio (Calabrese), her elderly husband, interrupts her *tête-à-tête*, she calmly exclaims: 'Vi calmate è mio marito' ('Do not worry, it's only my husband'). The Turk does leave but not before he has made another assignation with Fiorilla.

The hen-pecked Geronio then attempts to be firm with his wife, she counter-attacks by feigning tenderness and feeling sorry for herself.

Callas expressed her 'crocodile' tears by brilliant vocal inflexions until she resumed the hen-pecking, when her tone became strident and defiant: 'Per punirvi ... mille amanti ... divertimi in liberta' ('I shall punish you with a hundred lovers with whom I shall go mad').

Arriving for her
assignation with the
Turk, Fiorilla is
perturbed to find
Zaida (Gardino) there.
The two women
squabble, at one
moment Fiorilla takes
off her shoe to hit
Zaida, but eventually
the Turk, assisted by
Geronio, averts a
possible scuffle.

PART FOUR

Prima Donna Assoluta

CHAPTER TEN

RIVALS AND RECRIMINATIONS

W HEREAS LA SCALA provided Callas's spiritual home, the Metropolitan established her at the end of 1956 as one of the most famous and widely known artists in the world, but international acclaim brought her a great deal of unhappiness. The price of fame does not, as is the way of the world, make exceptions and Callas too had to pay it. She lost her rights to privacy; her elementary claim to personal freedom seemed to have been taken over by both press and public, who declared themselves qualified to pass judgement on her every action, whether it had to do with the theatre or everyday life.

Whatever she said promptly appeared in the media, more often than not misquoted, speculated upon and psychoanalysed by self-appointed experts in their pursuit for hidden meanings and motives. If she dared to say she was unwell or to cut down her engagements she was accused, without trial, of being capricious and publicity seeking. When, years later, Meneghini wrote about this period of his life with Callas he said that his wife, who had for years been subjected to extreme pressure in her work and was by nature a restless person, felt shattered in this situation not of her making. She was at the same time fuming with indignation, for such was her rebellious nature in the face of injustice, whether it affected her personally or not.

As we shall see, 1957 was to prove a crucial year for Callas. Artistically she reached the pinnacle of her art, often achieving complete fusion of all the sources of expression to be found in a human being. Her portrayals became almost artistic miracles. In other ways the picture was not so successful. It was at this period that the seeds were sown for events that would eventually deprive her of her peace of mind and all but ruin her life. There was nobody to give her a protecting hand; her hitherto beloved husband was not only to prove incapable of handling adverse situations, but his misguided philosophy of measuring achievement by money also often led him to escalate and sometimes even create hostility.

After Callas's engagements in New York were over the Meneghinis, longing for the peace of their home, arrived in Milan on 22 December to spend Christmas there. However, all they could do to avoid the battery of reporters and photographers that besieged them was to barricade themselves in for the whole holiday. The Italian as well as the rest of the European press generally were familiar with the picture of Callas with Sordello at the airport in New York. Furthermore, the recent *Time* article in the United States had rudely re-awakened her long-standing alleged feud with Tebaldi, brought to the fore her supposed resentment towards Serafin of all people and above all, made public for the first time her bad relationship with her mother. Callas's feelings about the numerous questions hurled at her were ignored: the press were determined to give their own interpretation and were continually denigrating her.

In the meantime, while she was in New York the season at La Scala had opened with *Aida* starring Antonietta Stella and di Stefano. Neither the production (originally turned down by Visconti) nor the performances were very successful. Most of the audiences wanted Callas and the excitement she always brought to the scene. Even her adversaries realized what they were missing, compared with what they were getting. Before long, however, Maria, in an article published in *Oggi*, confirmed to the Milanese that after a concert in Chicago and *Norma* at Covent Garden, 'I shall be returning to La Scala to sing in *La sonnambula*, *Anna Bolena* and *Ifigenia in Tauris*.' Influenced by the rather hostile section of the media, Callas added ill-advisedly, 'I know that my enemies are waiting for me, but I shall fight them in the best way I can. Above all I will not disappoint my public which, I know, loves me, and whose esteem and admiration I am determined to maintain.'

Even though the last part of her statement was redeeming to a degree, the overall impression she gave was that she was openly on the warpath, confirming by this seemingly aggressive attitude that there could well be some truth in the numerous allegations against her — that there was indeed no smoke without fire. She was much more tactful when she eventually clarified her position towards Tebaldi. 'It is simply not true', Callas professed,

that I told the *Time* correspondent that 'Renata is not like Callas; she has no backbone'. This offending phrase was in fact attributed to a third party and not to me. I cannot understand why Tebaldi took exception to these innocuous words. How should I react to an article that violated my private relationship with my mother? And what about Renata's accusation, publicly thrown at me, of 'lacking a heart'? But I am glad that, at last, Tebaldi confessed that she left La Scala because she found its atmosphere stifling and not because, as I have been until recently accused, I drove her away with my diabolical arts.

I should also like to say that if I followed her performances with attention, I did so only to discover in every detail how Renata sang; and I am deeply sorry to hear the ridiculous accusations flung at me that I went to 'intimidate' her. The public, Renata, and even more, the people with whom she associates, cannot understand that I — and I am not at all ashamed of it – will always find something to learn in the voices of all my colleagues, not only the famous ones like Tebaldi, but also the humble and mediocre ones. And I, who have tortured myself hour after hour in search of continuous improvement, shall never give up listening to the singing of my colleagues.

It is probable that Callas may have had some ulterior motives when she made these generous comments about Tebaldi, for at that time she could not risk public opinion turning against her further than it had already. But however much the press and public may have been responsible for their alleged feud, it is undoubtedly true that some professional jealousy existed between the two women. Even though Tebaldi may have fallen short in dramatic expression and perhaps could not generate the excitement that Callas's performances always did, she ravished many ears with her velvety voice and had a considerable following – large enough to cause Callas to believe that, at least in Italy where she was a foreigner, she might lose the contest for the title of prima donna assoluta to the Italian singer.

Exasperated by the constant pestering of the media, who were enquiring provocatively whether the two singers were rivals, Callas commented confidently but soberly: 'Our repertoire is different. Should there come a time when Tebaldi sings *Sonnambula*, *Lucia*, *Gioconda* and then goes on to *Medea*, *Norma* and *Macbeth*, then there will be scope for possible comparison. Well, it's like comparing champagne with cognac.' 'No, coca-cola!' a reporter promptly added and the maliciously amusing phrase was henceforth wrongly attributed to Callas herself.

Tebaldi retaliated by referring to Callas's dramatic loss of weight in 1954: 'Callas did lose all her fat but she also lost her voice with it.'

During the previous autumn when Callas had had to testify in the Bagarozy suit in Chicago again, she also accepted an invitation to give a benefit concert there on 15 January 1957. The concert was organized by the Alliance Française for Hungarian Relief and it was in her interests to show goodwill towards a city where she had not so long ago sworn never to sing again. Nevertheless, she still remained adamant that she would not sing for the Lyric Opera, where she felt that her great friends the management had let her down so appallingly.

On their way to Chicago the Meneghinis stopped in New York for a couple of days, so that they could attend the glittering annual costumed ball (a regal pageant) at the Waldorf Astoria given as a benefit for the Hospitalized Veterans Service. Dressed as the Egyptian Empress Hatshepsut, Maria made a sensational entrance, bejewelled with magnificent emeralds valued at a million dollars lent by Harry Winston. Elsa Maxwell, who was there to meet her new friend, wasted no time in telling the world through her social column that, 'It seems Maria and I are

Callas as the Empress Hatshepsut at the costume
ball in New York.

going to be friends', and then, as if in a postscript, a solitary statement that she still loved the golden voice of Tebaldi. Four days later Maxwell rushed to Chicago to attend Maria's concert.

Expectation for Callas's return to Chicago ran very high, especially as the concert was to be under the baton of the acclaimed Austrian conductor Karl Böhm. However, at the very first rehearsal Callas and Böhm disagreed strongly about the tempo of 'Ah! non credea mirarti' from *La sonnambula*. Neither of them would budge, whereupon Böhm, exclaiming that he was not merely an accompanist, walked out, leaving Callas and the orchestra without a conductor. To make things worse Callas asked for Fausto Cleva, who had recently conducted her at the Metropolitan, to replace Böhm. This created another situation because Cleva, who had been artistic director at the Lyric Opera, was not popular in Chicago. While the international press was blaming the 'capricious' Callas entirely for Böhm's flight from the scene, the concert management in Chicago capitulated to her wishes at the eleventh hour and engaged Cleva. Writing about this crisis, Meneghini described it as very difficult for everybody except Maria who, para-doxically, treated it as the kind of challenge, which as a rule stimulated her to surpass herself. The concert was an unqualified success. Excerpts from *Norma*, *Il trovatore* and *Lucia di Lammermoor*

241

brought back memories and tears, and two contrasting arias from *La sonnambula* and *Turandot*, both new to Chicago, further incited the public to frantic excitement.

Before her return to La Scala, Callas went to London at the end of January where she had two performance of *Norma* at Covent Garden, followed by a recording of *Il barbiere di Siviglia*. She was returning to Covent Garden after an absence of over four years, this time slim and elegant almost beyond recognition, but very well remembered. The press devoted considerable space to her arrival and the preparations for her performances, which were sold out on the first day of booking. Nevertheless, concurrently with this high expectation there was also some apprehension as to whether this extraordinary artist would live up to her previous outstanding portrayals of the same role, one which other contemporary singers were as yet reluctant to tackle. What precipitated the apprehension was that the reports of her début season at the Metropolitan were not unqualified raves and the rumours that her dramatic loss of weight in 1954, which had transformed her into a 'swan', had taken its toll on her voice.

But all fears vanished on the first night. In fact, word had got around after the dress rehearsal of *Norma* two days previously that Callas's voice had indeed changed, but for the better; it had become a closer-knit and more even instrument and above all, her singing displayed a newly found meaningful beauty, particularly evident in the 'Casta Diva', which she now sang with unique, mysterious inspiration. Furthermore, her overall interpretation of the Druid priestess had acquired greater intensity yet more simplicity and naturalness, culminating in a memorably moving performance.

The other principals were also successful. Ebe Stignani (Adalgisa) was still a 'tower of strength', Nicola Zaccaria (Oroveso) impressed greatly with the nobility of his voice and stage presence. Only Giuseppe Vertecchi (Pollione), who replaced an indisposed Renato Gavarini, was no more than adequate. John Pritchard, who had conducted Callas in *Norma* at Covent Garden in 1953, was again the most considerate and stimulating maestro. Such was the frenzy of the public's excitement at the second and last performance that an encore of the second part of the Norma–Adalgisa duet 'Mira o Norma' had to be granted. This gave Covent Garden its first encore since 1932, Callas her first ever and Stignani her first in *Norma*. It was a triumphant return to London and she not only lived up to expectations but surpassed them. *The Times* wrote of her:

> . . . Her singing is still glorious, at once epic and pathetic in effect. Her breath control is still astonishing, enabling her to draw out a legato as suave as that of the finest instrumentalist, subtly shaded but always even in quantity. Fioritura never sounds vacuous when she sings it. . . . most expressive of all are the descending chromatic scales which are so characteristic of Norma's music, and which she weighs with a curious, highly individual

melancholy that stabs at the heart. Her historic presentation of the role is of the art which conceals art. . . . No one in the world can sing with so much power and intensity.

Callas continued to be on top form at La Scala where at the beginning of March she sang Amina in a revival of Visconti's production of *La sonnambula*. Her achievement in this role was even greater than in the previous season. Writing in *Oggi*, Teodoro Celli said that 'Callas has not so much restored to Bellini's Amina attitudes, movements and voice, but soul; she found revelatory expression not only in the flowing melodies but in the slightest bits of recitative; she even found two ways of expression, one for Amina awake and aware of herself and the other for Amina rapt in her painful drowsiness.'

La Scala then mounted expressly for Callas a sumptuous new production, directed by Visconti, of Donizetti's *Anna Bolena*. The opera was unfamiliar even to Italian audiences until Callas sang in it on 14 April, officially coinciding with the opening of the Milan Fair.[1] Previous revivals of the work (which dates from 1830) in Italy were at Leghorn in August 1881 and at Bergamo, Donizetti's birthplace, in October 1956. The latter revival, sung by young, inexperienced but talented artists, made it obvious that here was an important opera in need of a great singer as protagonist. For *Anna Bolena* La Scala assembled an excellent supporting cast which included Giulietta Simionato (Giovanna Seymour), Rossi-Lemeni (Enrico VIII) and Gianni Raimondi (Percy). Gavazzeni, one of the most illustrious Donizetti scholars was the conductor. 'After the Bergamo *Anna Bolena*,' he reminisced many years later,

we recognized there and then that this opera would make an ideal vehicle for Callas, both musically and theatrically.

This *Anna Bolena* became a complete realization of ideal collaboration between stage and music – and into this ideal Callas's personality fitted perfectly. It was also the peak of my career in the theatre, after which I should have retired. I did not but I never reached that peak again.

Visconti's production had remarkable atmosphere. 'My designer Nicola Benois and I', Visconti said to Ardoin and Fitzgerald (quoted in their book *Callas*) and later to me, 'chose black, white and "London" grey for the sets. The huge portraits on the broad staircase at Windsor Castle, down which Callas made her first entrance, and the colourful costumes augmented the sombre sets. Seymour, the King's new love, wore red, the guards red and yellow. Anna was in all shades and nuances in blue. Her enormous jewels matched her eyes, her strong features, her stature.'

Having given new life to *Lucia di Lammermoor* – the only tragic Donizetti opera that had for many years been in the international repertoire – Callas proved with *Anna Bolena* that he is a dramatic composer to be reckoned with.

The critics were unanimous in their praise of the performance in general and of Callas in particular. 'As Anna, Callas reminded us of her great performances of Medea and Norma,' the critic of *Corriere della Sera* wrote. 'Her vibrant voice, the artistry of her song, stage comportment and magnificent stylization, all make her portrayal unrivalled today.'

Writing in *Opera*, Desmond Shawe-Taylor also expressed his admiration for Callas: 'The soft cavatina of recollection in her first scene "Come innocente giovane", which suited Callas to perfection, provided her with the first of many triumphs during the evening ...' Interestingly, he ended his review with the comment, 'Could *Anna Bolena* enter the international repertory? With Callas, yes; without her, or some comparable soprano of whom as yet there is no sign, no.'

Anna Bolena found Callas at the summit of her powers both as a unique vocalist and a tragedienne of the first order – an aristocrat among artists. Throughout the opera she distinguished between Anna's public and personal lives. She realized this by means of subtle intonation, variegated timbre (now regal, now grave, now frantic) and electrifying force, applied with unfailing discipline and economy in her masterly characterization of the 'Tragic Queen' of England, the 'Rose without a thorn'. Her portrayal was a summation of her art, which happens at that undefinable moment in a great artist's career – life is perhaps more accurate – when the fusion of

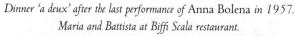

Dinner 'a deux' after the last performance of Anna Bolena *in 1957.*
Maria and Battista at Biffi Scala restaurant.

technique, expression, both vocal and physical, and all the other intangible qualities achieve as perfect a balance as nature will allow. Indisputably, this production of *Anna Bolena* went down in history as one of La Scala's major achievements.

All seven performances were complete sell-outs and public enthusiasm was unrestrained. There were no more distracting noises and for the moment nobody was after Maria's blood — the 'hissing snakes' having gone into hibernation. Both Tebaldi and Sordello were forgotten, as if they had never crossed Callas's path, as was her mother and any would-be rival. Instead, she was fêted with exclamations of '*brava Divina!*' — her solo curtain-calls at the end of the performance extended for almost half an hour, with one voice from somewhere in the theatre proclaiming: 'This woman sings like an orchestra.'

Nevertheless, hardly had the cheers for *Bolena* died down, when early in May the Italian press, taking its lead from their Austrian colleagues, began to blow out of proportion a 'new Callas Scandal'. When singing Lucia in Vienna during the previous June, she had agreed with Karajan to give seven performances of *La traviata* there in the following June. Apparently Callas asked for a higher fee than the one she had received for Lucia and Karajan readily agreed. However, when in May 1957 the contract arrived her fee was not increased. Despite his earlier promise, Karajan now bluntly refused any increase and as Callas had not signed the contract under these conditions her performances in Vienna were cancelled. The press concocted a wilder version: Maria had quarrelled with Karajan and when he refused to pay her more money she told him, 'Sing *Traviata* yourself.' He then retaliated by tearing up her contract before her eyes ... and so forth. An outcry followed in the press about her scandalous greed for money. What really happened had very little to do with Maria, who always left financial considerations to her husband. She never had the time, nor did she wish to concern herself with such matters. On this occasion, during the press furore directed against her, Callas was completely involved in rehearsals for a new production of Gluck's *Ifigenia in Tauris* at La Scala.

For the Vienna *Traviatas* Meneghini demanded $2100 per performance against the opera house's offer of $1600. Both sides regretted the cancellation. Callas could have saved the situation had she really wanted to but as at the time, apart from *Ifigenia*, she had already signed contracts for an unusually tight schedule she simply let Vienna go. Once again her reaction, partially influenced by her husband's misguided belief that money was the true barometer of achievement, succeeded in adding yet another wart to her character. She was never to sing in Vienna again. Elsa Maxwell, who was in Milan at Maria's invitation to attend *Anna Bolena* and *Ifigenia in Tauris* promptly defended her idol from the 'dictatorial' Karajan: 'Someone, somewhere,' she wrote in her gossip column, 'is spreading poison about one of the most touching individuals I have ever known. I am going to track them down wherever they may be. Nothing can destroy the supreme art of Maria Callas.'

La Scala had planned originally that after *Anna Bolena* Visconti would also direct Callas in

Zandonai's *Francesca da Rimini*. For technical reasons, however, the production was postponed and replaced with *Ifigenia in Tauris*, for which Visconti teamed up with Benois to produce Callas's fifth heroine under his direction. Nino Sanzogno conducted and the cast included Dino Dondi and Francesco Albanese. Though a splendid affair, the production could only be given four times as it was the end of the season. Visconti and Benois approached the opera, which is based on an ancient Greek legend, in an anachronistic way – the single set being after the Bibienas, the designers of Gluck's period, and the costumes inspired by the paintings of Tiepolo – yet the result was in perfect harmony with the music.

As in Gluck's *Alceste*, Callas sang *Ifigenia*, a role that vocally lay very comfortably in her middle register, with impeccable style and taste. The plot deals with the endeavours of the Greek Ifigenia, now a Scythian priestess, to put an end to human sacrifices. Even though it is devoid of sexual love Callas, with her dramatic abilities, maintained the interest and was very moving, reaching great heights in the recognition scene.

Visconti's comments are particularly interesting:

> Although Maria did not agree with my conception of the work, she did exactly what I asked. 'Why are you doing it like this?' she enquired. 'It's a Greek story and I'm a Greek woman, so I want to look Greek on-stage!' I answered. 'You are referring to a Greece that is too far off, my dear. This opera must look like a Tiepolo fresco come to life.' But whatever Maria felt about *Ifigenia*, in my opinion it was the most beautiful production we did together.

Generally speaking, Italian audiences are not enthused by Gluck's music, but they liked *Ifigenia* because of Callas. The critics were more appreciative, praising its style and good taste. Eugenio Gara had reservations about Visconti's staging which in his opinion took away something from Gluck's forceful drama. 'Callas, however,' he pointed out, 'remained with Gluck all the time. She was a vibrant and impetuous Ifigenia while the others tended to pastoralize.'

Lionel Dunlop (*Opera*, August 1957) thought that 'With her noble dignity of bearing and authoritative command of the stage, Callas as the humane priestess of the barbaric Scythians who would see an end to their human sacrifices was a constant and exciting joy. She is in fine vocal state at present.'

Thus Callas's sixth season at La Scala, with twenty productions to her credit, ended – happily – on a high note; at the completion of her performances President Gronchi bestowed on her the honorary title of Commendatore, one which very few women have ever received, for her services to Italian opera.

No one knew, however, not even Callas or Visconti themselves, that *Ifigenia* was to be their last collaboration. The projected Callas–Visconti *Francesca da Rimini* was eventually performed in

May 1959 with Magda Olivero in the title role and produced by Carlo Maestrini, for Callas had already left the La Scala company. On four other occasions Visconti was scheduled to produce opera for Callas: *Poliuto* for La Scala in 1960, *Il trovatore* at Covent Garden in 1963 and *La traviata* and *Medea* at the Paris Opéra in 1969. Apart from *Poliuto*, from which Visconti withdrew, with the result that it was directed instead by Herbert Graf, all the others proved abortive due to her reluctance to sing.

Throughout the period of the Callas–Visconti collaboration, which yielded five exceptional productions, it was generally taken for granted that the extraordinary artistic rapport between them also extended to their private lives. The press, particularly women's magazines, romanticized the personal relationship between the great singer and the eminent director, implying that Callas was in love with Visconti but without actually suggesting a sexual affair. This was left to those who always profess to be in the know about the love affairs of the rich and famous: it was spread around that Maria and Luchino were caught in amorous embraces, kissing passionately in her dressing-room, particularly during the period when she was appearing in *Anna Bolena*. The gossip, it must be said, was always carefully qualified in the end as nothing more than hearsay – nobody ever admitted to having eyewitnessed anything.

Nevertheless, a great deal of credence was given to the tales by Visconti himself who, on several occasions during the three years of their active collaboration, paid homage to Callas, sometimes obsessively, both as an incomparable artist and an enchantingly captivating woman. She, on the other hand, only referred to Visconti the director with humility and gratitude. Nothing describes their artistic relationship better than their reciprocal statements, at the time of their major triumphs of *La traviata* or *Anna Bolena*, that they had learned from each other. She never spoke publicly about Visconti the man, nor did she ever hint at the existence of any affection, let alone love, on her part. Yet people jumped to other conclusions. As, in the mid-1950s, Maria was still a very young woman married to a man thirty years her senior (Meneghini was in his early sixties), it was asserted that she found an outlet for her inevitable sexual frustration in her art – achieving this through Visconti, though only emotionally. Nobody dared to suggest that she was committing adultery with the homosexual Visconti for fear of the libel risk.

The truth of the matter is that Callas's personal relationship with Visconti was very different from what people imagined. Their artistic collaboration and triumphs were of course undeniable, but on a personal level things were distorted out of all recognition. Even years later, some writers continued to declare that Callas was in love with him and was often very jealous when he paid attention to handsome men. This seems to have originated from Visconti himself, who on occasion could not stop himself from talking about it and whom Ardoin and Fitzgerald quote in good faith in their book *Callas* (1974): 'At some point during the rehearsals of *La vestale* in 1954,

Maria began to fall in love with me. It was a stupid thing, all in her mind, but like so many Greeks, she has a possessive streak, and there were many terrible jealous scenes. She hated Corelli [the tenor in *La vestale*] because he was handsome. . . . She was always watching to see I didn't give him more attention than I gave her. . . . The simple fact was, because of this crazy infatuation, she wanted to have me command her every step.'

Later, Visconti related to a few people a bizarre story (also published in *Callas*), which he alleged happened during the last interval of the *Traviata* he had produced for Callas at La Scala in 1955 and 1956. Apparently he stopped by the theatre to say goodbye to her and after long and sweet farewells he went to a local restaurant, the Biffi Scala. Presently Maria followed him there in full stage make-up, her red ballgown half covered by a cloak. 'Fool! Go away. What do you want coming here dressed like that?' he chided her. But when the sad Maria embraced him saying that she wanted to see him once more, Visconti felt: 'how could anyone not lose his heart to her. But the incident could have been quite scandalous — suppose Maria had changed her costume and come to the restaurant in the nightdress Violetta wears in the last act!'

It must be added that these incredible statements were made in the early 1970s and from what we now know about the Visconti–Callas collaboration during the 1950s he was perhaps getting his own back. On closer examination a different aspect of this relationship emerges. My attempt to put the record straight is based on conversations with Callas in 1977, with Meneghini in 1978 (as well as what he later published in his articles and his book), with Visconti and on my own experience and observation — I saw the five works they did together and had been present at a few stage rehearsals.

To begin with, Visconti himself had in the past (see page 186) spoken differently about the nature of his artistic collaboration with Callas; what he said was in direct contradiction to his other, later statement — albeit not a public one — that Callas obeyed his commands slavishly because of her infatuation with him. Similarly his claim (again attributed to him in later years) that he had transformed a fat and clumsy Callas into a svelte and distinguished actress could not, according to both circumstantial and documentary evidence, be true. What he did say to me personally was very different: 'Even before I worked with her, before I knew her, I had been her greatest admirer for several years — since the time she sang Kundry and Norma in Rome; I always had the same box near the stage and applauded her like a mad fanatic. She was fat then, but beautiful on the stage. I loved her fatness which gave her a commanding stature and great distinction. Her gestures — and what marvellous gestures they were — which she learned on her own, simply thrilled you. My contribution afterwards was to refine and together with her develop her physical acting.'

When I saw Visconti a few months before he died in 1976 (he had earlier suffered a stroke which partly paralysed him) he spoke fondly of Callas. My main purpose was to benefit from his

248

advice on photographs I was planning to use and to ask him if he would write a preface to one of my books. Although I first met him in the mid-1950s I subsequently only spoke to him on a few occasions. I always found him pleasant and helpful. He was moved to tears when he saw photographs of Maria in *Traviata*. However, he evaded my question – really a hint – about Callas running after him to the Biffi Scala restaurant, but instead mentioned another little anecdote. So close was their artistic collaboration in *Traviata* (and he stressed the word artistic) that Maria wanted him to be near her till the last second before the performance. 'Maria insisted that I should stay on-stage with her, even during the prelude to Act One. It was so difficult to deny her anything. But one evening it got so close that I was afraid the curtain would go up with me still on-stage. I cried out, "Maria, I must go. What will the Milanese say when they see me with these *putane* [vulgar word for whores] around me?" [Visconti was referring to Violetta's friends in the opera.] Then I ran away and made it by the skin of my teeth. But I loved every minute of it.'

After a pause he reminisced about Maria's greatness which made her characterizations seem like 'living emotions. We shall never see the like of her, not in our lifetime.' For a moment Visconti lamented the fact that there was really no satisfactory visual record of Callas in opera (generally he hated opera on film, particularly television) but felt we should all be grateful for her recordings which would comfort us in our old age, for if one listened well a great deal of her visual greatness, her aura, would emerge from her voice. He said nothing disparaging of Callas the woman and nothing about her so-called jealousy or infatuation for him.

In 1977 I mentioned Visconti to Callas, believing, or more precisely taking it for granted like many other people, that she was fond of the man. At first she commented specifically and at some length on the great director. 'Yes,' she said,

I enjoyed working with him immensely. His intelligence, knowledge of detail and insight into a character and particularly period were incredible. But with this gift – and it was to a great extent a gift – he would not have accomplished all that much had he not also been able to use it constructively. The producer's work in opera is the least creative contribution. Visconti never did things for you but would discuss everything in great detail, argue about it if necessary and when a reasonable conclusion was reached, he would leave you to your own devices – and I am speaking for myself. He knew better than to try to use me as a marionette. Besides, that would never have worked and there was much artistic respect between us. On the whole, I can say, we agreed on most things in the theatre. Except for *Ifigenia*, we were in harmony about the basic conception of the other four women I portrayed under his direction. Above all, however, the lifeblood of our artistic collaboration was our mutual belief that in opera the stage characterization is the natural outcome of the music. Our disagreements were not about crucial things and we fought our battles on our own, never *vis-à-vis*.

Sensing my great curiosity about these battles, Callas gave some examples:

You remember the last act of *Traviata*? Well, he insisted that in the final scene I should wear a hat and die in it. I protested, because at that point in the opera I felt quite ridiculous and disconcerted with the hat; and frankly why should I wear it? The hat had nothing to contribute. He thought differently and could have given reasons for Violetta to die in Brünnhilde's shield, let alone a chic hat. When I realized that he was adamant about this I was equally furious, but I thought it would be foolish and not to my advantage to quarrel with him. So I controlled my temper, said nothing more about it (Luchino was stunned by my silence) and decided to settle the matter diplomatically. In the performance I simply let the hat fall to the floor. Apparently he was fuming with anger, but not to my face, and I tactfully avoided discussing the matter any further. I lost his blessed hat in the same way at every performance.

There were other disconcerting things. For instance he would spend a whole day of precious rehearsal time deciding on the right hankerchief or the right parasol. Of course afterwards all these sound trivial and really they were. But at the time you are exhausted from the great strain you put on yourself and worried to death that the situation may be damaging. It is the same if there is acrimony with your fellow singers or the conductor because they are directly involved in what you are trying to do. What perturbed me most at the time with Visconti was my inability to understand how a man of great intelligence could be excessively pedantic in matters of so little importance. A few years later, after my last opera with him, a friend who had known the Visconti family for forty years told me that Luchino's love for his mother was pathological and that he always brought something associated with her into all his productions. I think this explains the handkerchief, the parasol, the hat and so forth.

If I have dwelt on these seeming trivialities it is because they, perhaps paradoxically, put into sharper focus Visconti's ingenuity as a director; he helped an artist (and I am talking about myself exclusively) to form her ideas about movement on the stage in conjunction with everybody else involved and within the specified environment. (Before the producers descended upon us, the composer himself usually did all that as well.) This is, unarguably, only one factor in acting in opera where, unlike in the straight theatre, you have the all-important music. The rest, though of importance is really subordinate to your ability to interpret the music. In short — how you act with your voice. I said subordinate, not insignificant. The visual aspect is of paramount importance in everything when you are dealing with human beings but as such in isolation, it becomes superfluous and meaningless before too long. Visconti knew and believed this. That is where his greatness had its foundation. As I always said, I enjoyed working with him. His contribution was very valuable but it was not unshared. What about the conductor and the singers? We are talking about opera, not some kind of pageant. I have also worked with other directors who have in their way been exceptional. Zeffirelli, too, often had good, constructive ideas. And what about the *Medea* that Minotis directed [at Dallas, Covent Garden, Epidaurus, La Scala]? I enjoyed working with them and others too. But remember, however good an idea is, it is useless if not performed well. In other words it all depends on how you do it. Have you not seen singers who copy, even fastidiously, something that has been a very great success, but make a ridiculous caricature of it?

I am going to say only one more thing. I object strongly to the habit of referring to, say, *Traviata* or any other opera as if it belongs to the producer. It does not belong to me either. You can say Callas in *Traviata* was good, bad or indifferent. That is all. Even if there were fifty Viscontis and fifty Callases (God forbid!) *Traviata* is and always will be Verdi's and, if you like, Piave's, the librettist. We are, and we must never forget it, interpreters and our duty is to serve the composer and art with respect. The moment we get too big for our boots, we are really finished.

With all I have said, I am in no way trying to minimize the producer's contribution, especially Visconti's. On the contrary he was a great artist in his medium. But for heaven's sake let's keep things in a logical perspective!

After diverting the conversation to other things of no particular significance, I suddenly realized that Maria had not said anything about Visconti the man. Although a great deal about her love and devotion for Visconti had been written and talked about, even by him, there had been nothing from her. My second attempt to bring Visconti the man into the conversation was more successful. As usual when confronted with an awkward personal question, Callas played for time by being first silent and then speaking about something interesting but absolutely irrelevant. Afterwards, casually but firmly, she said: 'I had no time for him.' Aware of my obvious surprise she took my hand and in a mock-serious manner told me that perhaps I had read too many magazines.

She was amazed to read that Visconti had said she was in love with him and other such nonsense. 'Anyway it is really too ridiculous even to talk about it,' she said rather flippantly. 'You will have to accept a simple "NO" in capital letters for my answer. I cannot do better. And remember I am never theatrical in life. I do not dramatize my behaviour with other human beings. Decorum has always been fundamental in my life and I have never acted like a silly little girl who makes a fool of herself and thinks she is romantic.'

Maria was undoubtedly referring to the alleged Biffi Scala scene: she was clearly irritated by it and considered it too humiliating to have to repudiate it directly. Regarding Corelli, she then emphatically said that she had always liked and respected him, which is very different from being jealous of him. In fact she had been instrumental in getting him to La Scala to sing with her in *La vestale*. The same more or less applied to Leonard Bernstein. She was proud to have succeeded in 1953 in persuading Ghiringhelli to engage him to conduct her *Medea* performances. 'You see,' Maria said, putting an end to the subject, 'I appreciate Corelli and Bernstein both as colleagues and friends, which puts them in a different category from Visconti. If I ever hinted at any disapproval of Corelli and Bernstein in associating with Visconti outside the theatre it was not out of jealousy of any kind. Let us say I felt that my friends would have been better off without the friendship and influence of Visconti the man.'

Responding to my inferences, Maria also said that she did not dislike Luchino (she began to refer to him by his Christian name) because of his homosexuality:

We are talking of other times when the world was rather ignorant of such things. There was also a great deal of hypocrisy. If you did not like a person his homosexuality would be a disgusting and unforgivable sin. On the other hand, if you liked the person you could well consider his homosexuality to be an unfortunate phase, hopefully a passing one. But I must come to the point. At first Luchino's homosexuality shocked me but I can say even in the short run my feelings about the man would have been the same if he were one hundred per cent heterosexual. Fortunately, I did get over my prejudices and not too late in life. The sexuality of any man or woman should be immaterial, as long as it does not affect you personally; love between two men or two women has always existed and always will in every part of the world. It is, as with most things in life, under what circumstances and how it is carried out that is necessarily important. If I have appeared at times in the past, the distant past, less than tolerant of such matters my only excuse is that it must be attributed to the superficiality of youth. Alas! Wisdom and tolerance have to be acquired, for they are seldom found in the young. I always had a great admiration for Visconti, the talented director, so let's leave it at that.

It was left to Meneghini to fill in the gaps and put his wife's personal relationship with Visconti in proper perspective. Without ever disclosing to him that I had discussed Visconti with Callas, in 1978 he brought up the subject himself. He was upset that such ridiculous gossip had been published about them. 'Not only was Maria never in love nor infatuated with Visconti,' Meneghini declared, but she strongly disliked the man in no uncertain terms. Whereas his admiration and affection for Maria became more intense as they worked together and got to know each other better, her aversion for him increased. His foul language, the derogatory way he referred to women in general and his crude manners, all despite his aristocratic background and impressive appearance, were totally unacceptable to her. He would often use obscene words as epithets to various people he mentioned in his conversation. On such occasions Maria was utterly disgusted and told him that she would throw up if he did not stop. Visconti's excuse was that people are stupid fools and can only understand this kind of language. Maria would then reprove him further, telling him to go and talk in that way to those stupid fools' faces and save us from more nausea. What appeased Maria on such occasions was the switching of their conversation to opera. She did admire his artistic talent and as she felt that something useful for her could well materialize if she worked with him, she agreed with my suggestion that I, not she, would keep up our connection with Visconti.

So you see, [Meneghini continued with an air of greater confidence] Maria could not possibly have been in love with the man. Her admiration of his artistic talent was completely another matter. As long as they were working together in the theatre and she felt that she could profit from his mind she was prepared even to be, albeit in some detached way, affectionate towards him. In matters that concerned her art she would try to get the most out of anybody. She would be a 'sponge' – her word, not mine. That is why, I suppose, some people said that she was in love with him. Be that as it may, I can tell you categorically that had Visconti not been a talented director Maria would not have entertained his company at all.

I must admit that Maria's mentality was a little unusual in her judgement of people or situations. She simply relied on her instinct which often prevented her being objective inasmuch as she found it impossible to corelate with a person who possessed some trait that offended her sensibilities. With time her aversion to Visconti became even stronger. She just did not want him near her as even his scent and breath annoyed her. His blatant homosexuality and his coarse language to other artists in the theatre disgusted her. Maria told me that 'if Visconti ever dares apply one of his foul epithets to me, I will punch his mouth so hard that his teeth will drop out'. In their work, Maria's attitude to him was absolutely professional and they got on very well together. But once she had finished working with him in the theatre she never wanted to see him at other times. She would not invite him to her house. We went out to dinner with him a few times but only once to his house in Rome.

This alone makes Visconti's story about Callas running after him to the Biffi Scala quite absurd. Furthermore, Maria would have had no time to go to the restaurant even had she wanted to. She needed the interval to change a difficult costume and make-up, and also to prepare herself emotionally for a very taxing last act. Although the restaurant is in the same building she would have required considerable time to get out of the theatre and walk along the street (via Filodrammatici) – about seventy metres – and make the return journey to her dressing-room to prepare to go on-stage. Meneghini could not understand Visconti's motives for fabricating such a tale. It is quite possible that Visconti was furious with Maria after she made the film *Medea* with Pasolini in 1970. His jealousy of anything like that knew no bounds because he would convince himself that nobody could 'serve' Callas better than he.

'And there is another odd thing about this bizarre story,' Meneghini added.

Why would Visconti want to ridicule Maria by completing his scenario with the possibility that, had Maria changed her costume for the last act, she would have gone to the restaurant in Violetta's nightdress? Visconti may have been very vain but this remark does not enhance his vanity in any way and he was a very intelligent man – at least I would like to think so. You see, I knew him as a man better than Maria did. Outside the theatre it was I, not she, who was a friend of his.

On the other hand it was evident that from the beginning Visconti was infatuated with Maria. He wrote to her frequently, but as she never answered he later addressed his letters to Meneghini, who also took his numerous telephone calls. His letter dated May 1954 began, 'I also address this letter to Battista because I do know that Maria will not even read it, and if I ever get an answer it will come from Battista.' On one occasion Visconti, carried away by his infatuation for Callas, wrote to Meneghini that he would be the happiest man if they employed him as their gardener; he could then be near Maria and hear her sing every day.

'After Maria's first season with Visconti in 1955,' Meneghini elaborated, 'apart from seeing him once in that summer, it was eighteen months later when rehearsals for *Anna Bolena* began that we saw him again. During this intervening period Visconti continued to write to me always complaining of not seeing us; he would either just miss us or we would miss him. Feeling very sad about it, he wrote, "It must be destiny . . . fate!" It was, in fact, Maria herself who tried her best to avoid him.'

I   With *Anna Bolena*, his twenty-ninth opera, Donizetti established himself as an important operatic composer. It is dramatically very effective, with an originality of style expressed in beautiful melody. Romani's libretto is well constructed and the characters are realistically drawn.

• CHAPTER ELEVEN •

SCANDALS

T HREE WEEKS AFTER the season at La Scala closed with *Ifigenia in Tauris* the company planned to give two performances of *La sonnambula* with Callas as Amina at the newly rebuilt Cologne Opera House. La Scala would also be participating at the Edinburgh Festival in August, when Callas would appear in the same opera.

With such a strenuous schedule before her and already feeling tense and tired Callas, after *Ifigenia*, took a three-day holiday in Paris. Some time was spent visiting fashion salons, an excellent diversion for a hard-working opera singer, especially for one who had become, after her dramatic weight loss, so elegant. Time was also spent with Elsa Maxwell, who followed Maria almost everywhere. In Paris Maxwell felt very much on her own ground having adopted the city, since the days before the war when she lived there, as her second home town. Now, with great excitement and delight, she took the chance to show off Maria to her friends: the Rothschilds, the Duke and Duchess of Windsor, Prince Aly Khan and several members of exiled royalty were on their part delighted to meet Maria Callas, the celebrated prima donna. Maxwell's 'conducted tour' of the French capital for Maria further included dinner at Maxim's and a visit to the races. All this socializing was a new experience for Maria, who enjoyed it up to a point. When she was pressed to return to Paris for a party Maxwell was organizing later in the month she declined the invitation without any hesitation. She might have discovered the pleasure of parties and such diversions, but she felt from the beginning that this kind of life had little appeal to her. Be that as it may, before the Meneghinis left Paris they promised to be at a grand party the tenacious Maxwell would be organizing in Maria's honour in Venice on 3 September.

During the next two weeks Callas gave a concert in Zurich and sang Lucia in a concert performance for RAI, Rome where she was delighted to have Serafin as her conductor. She then gave Amina in Cologne, scoring a great success both with the public and the critics, although Bellini's music was at that time not well known in Germany; having been in the audience I know that they were so impressed that they went home feeling they had been present at one of the great theatrical experiences of the era.

After Cologne Callas spent the following three weeks in Milan, recording two Puccini operas whose heroines could not be more different from Amina. The first was Manon (*Manon Lescaut*), a new role she had never sung on-stage, the second the very taxing title role in *Turandot*. Serafin conducted both, di Stefano was the tenor in *Manon Lescaut*, Eugenio Fernandi in *Turandot*, in which the famous soprano Elisabeth Schwarzkopf sang Liù. The collaboration of the two ladies could not have been more amicable. It gave them the opportunity to get to know each other better and become great friends.

Impresarios from Greece had been trying for some time to engage Callas for the Athens Festival. She was very willing to sing for her compatriots but her numerous commitments had so far made it impossible. However, while singing in *Norma* at Covent Garden during the previous February and again approached, she decided to forgo her only holiday so that she could give two concerts in Athens at the beginning of August. This was to mark her return to the land of her forefathers and she was anxious to succeed and show her countrymen that the great fame she had acquired was real. But Maria soon discovered that her path was not altogether smooth. When the contract was produced for her signature, some time in late spring, she immediately expressed the wish to donate her fees to the promotion of the festival. Surprisingly, the organizers bluntly turned down her well-meant suggestion. The Athens Festival, they declared rather patronizingly, needed neither her subsidy nor her charity. Such an uncalled-for rebuff of what was indisputably a most generous gesture on Callas's part was incomprehensible though very hurtful and offensive to her. Presently, however, Callas retaliated: 'Fine,' she told them firmly. 'I shall be very happy indeed to keep my fees.' She then demanded the same top stipend she had been receiving in the United States. Forced to eat humble pie, the shocked organizers did not risk further argument.

Once again Maria's compatriots had managed to upset her. It was evidently beyond her comprehension that some Greeks, often with superficial obstinacy, were reluctant to acknowledge great achievement in a fellow countrywoman which they would readily have accepted in a foreigner. Nevertheless, she decided to shrug off the insult. Twelve difficult, glorious and rewarding years had passed since she had left Greece. All that really mattered now was that she was returning to sing in the ancient theatre of Herodes Atticus where once she had triumphed in *Fidelio*. Would she do so again?

There were further obstacles in her way. Immediately after she had completed her recordings of the two Puccini operas and was preparing to leave for Athens she fell ill with exhaustion. Her doctor prescribed absolute rest for a few weeks but she would not hear of it. The Meneghinis arrived in Athens on 28 July, to find exceptionally hot and windy weather, and an unbearable dryness which, as always, affected Maria's voice. She was very nervous and, when she felt at the rehearsal that her voice was not responding, asked for a substitute to be found – a proposal that was dismissed out of hand. Meneghini later recalled that although Maria felt by no means well (her Greek doctor diagnosed a slightly inflamed vocal chord) she would in all possibility have sung, had it not been for the appalling attitude of the festival organizers. Behind their belliger-

256

ence was their miscalculated response to Callas's offer to donate her fees and now of course they had to pay a very high price for her services. 'If I am not physically well enough,' Callas announced, 'I do not appear before the public so that I can collect my fee. That would be dishonest.' Consequently she did not give her first concert.

Unwisely, the organizers announced the cancellation only an hour before the start, thus further enraging the public against Callas. Loud voices were heard claiming that her indisposition was due to 'cold feet' rather than 'dry throat'. From then on the press took over to publicize the organizers' dishonest grumblings about her demand for exorbitant fees, her ghastly relationship with her mother and sister – who apparently at Maria's stipulation had been sent off to New York. On top of this outrage, the issue promptly assumed political connotations: the opposition party bluntly accused Karamanlis's government of mismanaging tax-payers' money when they approved Callas's fees. There was no mention of her initial offer to sing for nothing. One other rumour was spread around that this egocentric woman refused to sing because Queen Frederica would not do her the honour of attending her concert.

In the face of such hostility, which was beyond her comprehension, Callas was both exasperated and dismayed and would have left Athens immediately and without singing at all, had not Meneghini's ingenuity been used, for once, constructively; of course it would not have been in his interests to lose Maria's fees and being familiar with his wife's mentality, he shrewdly prodded her to consider the whole affair a personal challenge – the only effective stimulus for Callas to rise to any occasion.

On 5 August Maria, in a superb dress and tastefully resplendent jewels, faced a very antagonistic audience which crowded into the huge theatre of Herodes Atticus. After the orchestra had played the opening piece and she was about to begin her first aria 'Pace, mio Dio' (*La forza del destino*), a loud voice from the audience was heard repeating the word 'shame'. But all doubt and resentment were quickly dispelled when Maria started to sing. It was clear that she was appreciated and, in spite of everything, accepted by her own people; for the moment the power of her art demolished all prejudice against her, or so it seemed.

Her teacher, Elvira de Hidalgo, sitting quite near the stage, shed a few tears when her beloved pupil, the 'plump girl, who was nervously biting her finger-nails waiting for her audition', began to sing. Maria's programme was strenuous and diverse: arias were included from *Forza*, *Il trovatore*, *Lucia di Lammermoor*, *Tristan und Isolde* and Ophelia's mad scene from Thomas's *Hamlet*. At the end of the concert the applause reached unprecedented heights for Athens. Apparently it could be heard for miles from the open-air theatre. There were many requests from the audience to hear something from *Norma* but the absence of a chorus decided Callas not to sign the 'Casta Diva', the only aria from the opera that would be suitable for the concert performance. Then Prime Minister Karamanlis made a special request: he was fully aware of Maria's exhaustion but could not help ask-

*Maria shares a joke with her teacher, Hidalgo, during a rehearsal break
of her concert at Herodes Atticus theatre.*

ing to hear that divine voice again, whereupon she repeated the second part of Ophelia's mad scene.

Callas's return to Athens, treated at the beginning almost like a declaration of war, ended in triumph. She knew that she had won her battle through her art. Subsequently she was besieged by everybody anxious to pay tribute to her. The festival organizers also came to apologize for not making her return to Greece (now referring to it as an historic event) easier and above all to invite her back. 'Never again,' Callas exclaimed.

When she returned to Milan, her nervous exhaustion, further aggravated by the terrible emotional strain she had suffered in Athens, became more pronounced. It was against her doctor's orders as well as her husband's advice that Callas left, a week later, with the La Scala company to appear in four performances of *La sonnambula* at the Edinburgh Festival.

La Scala were also taking Cimarosa's *Il matrimonio segreto* (a production from Piccola Scala's repertoire), *Il Turco in Italia* and Donizetti's *L'elisir d'amore*. Nicola Monti and Nicola Zaccaria were Callas's partners in *La sonnambula*, which was conducted by Antonino Votto. Originally it was planned that the brilliant Guido Cantelli (1920–56), a protégé of Toscanini, was to conduct

258

these performances. His untimely death in an air crash during the previous November, only a few days after the confirmation of his appointment as musical director of La Scala, ended a most promising career.

The opening performance at the King's Theatre found Callas in rather poor voice and the stage lighting was functioning so badly that it nearly wrecked the production. There was a substantial improvement in the second performance but on the third evening she was so unwell that she pulled through primarily by means of her extraordinary dramatic powers. Meanwhile an extra fifth performance with Callas was announced without even consulting her. Despite her doctor's advice to withdraw immediately Maria, once more faced with a challenge, summoned all her resources and gave her agreed fourth performance, which turned out to be the most successful: Amina came to life and Callas was unequivocally declared the 'diva of the festival'. What gave her the impetus to sing in this performance was not only her contractual obligation but also the responsibility she felt towards her public, to whom she had not given of her best in the previous three performances. She could not, however, sing in the extra fifth performance and left Edinburgh for home.

Harold Rosenthal (*Opera*, October 1957) wrote that Callas in her last performance was 'in excellent voice ... the musicianship, intelligence and intensity with which she invests her roles were in evidence throughout the evening. ... Dramatically her interpretation was a *tour de force*: by her very nature Miss Callas is an imperious figure ... and yet although Amina is a Giselle-like figure, the soprano was able by her personality to make us believe in the figure she created.'

While the Meneghinis were travelling back to Italy, completely unaware that Maria had either let anybody down or had in any way reneged on her contract, the press bluntly described her departure from the festival as another walk-out which La Scala, incredibly, was unable to explain. By the time she reached Milan, most of Europe and the whole of Italy were informed that she had let down the theatre that made her – an unforgivable sin in any circumstances. These accusations stunned her but, believing that the management of La Scala was bound in due course to deny the preposterous allegations of the press, she herself said nothing about it. She was in any case far from well. However, this lack of action on her part, which must have seemed sensible at the time, was to work against her.

It was later in 1959, by which time Callas had broken with La Scala, that she spoke of this affair to *Life* magazine – and eventually to me. Her version is enlightening, was supported by documentary fact and puts the record straight: 'My agreement with La Scala', Callas testified,

> stipulated that I should be in Edinburgh between 17 and 30 August 1957, during which period I was contracted to sing in four performances of *La sonnambula*.
>
> Earlier there had been talk that I might also sing in *Il Turco in Italia* but I declined the

offer. What with my Metropolitan début, the demanding schedule at La Scala before me and so forth, I was beginning to feel the strain of overwork. The sensible thing to do was to cut down the number of performances, not the ones I had agreed to give but any new offers. The Athens concerts were a special case. I had already been asked several times and naturally I was very keen to sing in Greece. Had I turned them down again it would have meant that we would have to wait for another year, for the next festival. Well, I did go and tried to do the right thing, even though my compatriots then decided to rebuff me on every count.

But to return to the Edinburgh Festival. In August of that year I felt so worn out that my doctor Arnaldo Semeraro of Milan certified on 7 August that 'Callas has symptoms of nervous exhaustion to a serious degree, caused by overwork and fatigue. I prescribe a period of complete rest for not less than thirty days.'

After La Scala was informed of this situation Oldani, the general secretary of the theatre (incidentally Ghiringhelli, the director, did not go to Edinburgh), would not hear of it. He said that it would be better for La Scala not to go at all than to go without me, for the guarantee of my name had been the basis for the contract. However, La Scala believed that apparently I could perform miracles. What gave me strength and made me agree to go to Edinburgh against my doctor's and my husband's strenuous advice was Oldani's moving statement: 'La Scala will be forever grateful to you, Maria, for all your work and sacrifice and especially for this latest gesture.' Little did I know that this eternal gratitude was not as eternal as all that.

When Robert Ponsonby, then artistic director of the Edinburgh Festival, learned the date of my departure, he asked me how I could possibly do such a terrible thing when I still had to sing a fifth performance. I simply produced my agreement with La Scala and he was flabbergasted that he had been told nothing about it. He then rushed to Oldani and indignantly demanded an immediate explanation.

Before long Oldani was begging me, 'Maria, you must save La Scala.' Well, I was not in a position to save anybody. I was far too tense and exhausted to grant Oldani's request to save La Scala with a fifth performance, which of course he was asking only as a favour and not because I was in any way obligated. Nothing at the time hinted that I was letting anybody down and I was acting in good faith when I agreed, for La Scala's sake, that it could be said I was unable to sing the fifth performance because of indisposition certified to by a doctor.

On the afternoon I left Edinburgh, the mayor [the Lord Provost of Edinburgh] and his wife came to say goodbye to me at my hotel, scarcely the normal procedure if one is breaking a contract and fleeing the country.

Before leaving Edinburgh Callas told the press that Renata Scotto (who was in fact originally engaged by La Scala for the fifth performance) 'is a fine young singer who will cover herself with glory'.

In this frame of mind and suffering from nervous exhaustion, Callas sought relaxation at the party Elsa Maxwell was giving in her honour in Venice on 3 September, the very same day that the fifth *La sonnambula* was performed in Edinburgh. The party, which lasted for four days, began in grand style in the ballroom of the Danieli Excelsior Hotel in Venice and continued on the Lido beach during the day and various cafés and hotels at night. Among the great number of guests (some estimated them as around 180) there were the usual Maxwell associates which included several princes and princesses, millionaires, film stars, a few musicians (on this occasion Arthur Rubinstein), Aristotle Onassis, the Greek shipping magnate, and his wife Tina, and various other socialites.

Callas's party-going, though in her eyes a very normal way to relax and get herself in good shape, proved a dangerous step and was to have serious repercussions. Throughout the long party Maxwell was in seventh heaven. At last she could count her beloved Maria as part, indeed the principal member, of her international family, as she often referred to her friends. There is no denying that Maria, too, enjoyed herself at the party, such a pleasant novelty for her. She believed it could only do her good, to get her out of herself for a bit, before embarking on her next engagements. But things seldom work out that smoothly. The press with their photographers soon gathered in Venice (the annual Film Festival was also on) and, seeing Callas looking absolutely radiant and having a great time dancing at the party, were not prepared to believe for a moment that this woman had fled the Edinburgh Festival for health reasons.

The final blow to Callas's credibility was given by Maxwell herself. Never one to miss out on publicity, this time she surpassed even herself. 'I have never given a better dinner and ball in my life,' she wrote in her column. 'It had a flare of such joy and happiness. Even two princesses who hated each other were found exchanging smiles. … I have had many presents in my life but I have never had any star before give up a performance in an opera house because she felt she was breaking her word to a friend.'

Moreover Maxwell, at the moment during the party when her happiness was at its zenith, told the press that Maria had been singing the blues and other popular songs, namely 'Stormy Weather', to her piano accompaniment. Now she could call herself Maria Callas's accompanist. This was either a deliberately gross exaggeration, or a figment of Maxwell's imagination. All that happened was that when Maxwell was playing the piano and singing, something she often did, Maria, who was sitting nearby, was apparently heard humming the tune of 'Stormy Weather'. Whatever the case, Maxwell's reportage provided all the ammunition the press needed to blow up the whole affair into a large-scale scandal that destroyed any intention the public might have had of giving Callas the benefit of the doubt. It also provided Ghiringhelli with heavy guns for the next act of the encounter.

After the Venetian festivities the Meneghinis returned to their home in Milan. Maria's depression and exhaustion were far from cured. Doctors were called in and after several tests considerable organic loss of energy was diagnosed. A second opinion confirmed that she was really ill and it was imperative that she should rest. However, for Callas this was not as simple as it seemed: she was eagerly expected in San Francisco in three weeks' time to sing in *Lucia di Lammermoor* and *Macbeth*.

Although it was not in her nature to shy away from her responsibilities or a challenge in any circumstances, her recent experiences in Athens and Edinburgh somewhat shook her self-confidence and obliged her to question her outlook. She decided that henceforth she must no longer sing so often but relax more and learn to enjoy life outside the theatre. The writing was clearly on the wall. Nevertheless, because of the further deterioration of her health she was again in a most difficult, if not impossible, situation as far as her San Francisco engagement was concerned. Her own explanation (which she made known in 1959) of what developed into yet another Callas scandal was as follows:

> I was contracted to sing in San Francisco from 27 September to 10 November 1957, but on 1 September (the day I returned to Milan from Edinburgh) I cabled Kurt Herbert Adler, the general manager of the San Francisco Opera, warning him about my health and suggesting that he have a substitute ready, just in case. As my health did not improve with my brief holiday in Venice (if anything it had deteriorated), on my return to Milan on 7 September my doctors examined me again. The results of several tests decided my doctors to forbid me to leave Milan, explaining that I was no longer strong enough even to travel. On 12 September, two weeks away from the San Francisco opening, I notified Adler that for health reasons it would be impossible for me to be there on the set date. To help San Francisco and because I was really looking forward to singing there, I offered to go for the second month of the season. Hopefully, this arrangement would have given me time to recover my physical strength.

Adler, who had read that Callas abandoned the Edinburgh Festival on the grounds of ill health but was well enough to go to Elsa Maxwell's party, was most sceptical about her present indisposition.

'I then forwarded to Adler my medical reports,' Callas continued, 'but the answer was "come as of contract or not at all". Adler seemed to take the position that, having snubbed Edinburgh, I was now snubbing San Francisco. Obviously I was suffering the consequences of Edinburgh which was unfair to me. Had La Scala come clean about the true reasons why I did not sing the fifth *Sonnambula*, Adler would have believed me and I think would have agreed with my request for postponement.' The explanation and argument were true enough – but Callas omitted the fact that on the day she asked Adler for the postponement she began recording *Medea* in Milan.

In 1977 I brought up this incident, implying that, notwithstanding the Edinburgh injustice, perhaps she had pushed Adler too far, hardly leaving him any choice. The crux of the matter was that she could sing in Milan but not in San Francisco two weeks later. Maria took her time to comment. It was something, after all, that had happened nineteen years before. 'You are right,' she said eventually,

> but you see I was at the time faced with a dilemma. I was suffering from mental exhaustion, my doctor said I should not travel and public opinion was so much against me. Things would have been worse if I had cancelled the recording, which incidentally took a week to make in Milan and I did not have to travel. What I did wrong was to have gone to that blessed party in Venice though I must emphasize there was nothing deliberate about that. I simply believed that it would have done me good as I wanted, more than anyone else, to get over my ailments and carry out my contractual obligations. Well, the motive was right but the action was not. But remember, I did not cancel San Francisco. All I asked for was a postponement of two weeks so that I could get myself together. There was also another thing. Then I relied on my husband, who was obviously not a very good agent, to protect me. All artists need that. I am not trying to make excuses for the things I did wrong, but I will not be made a scapegoat either. I always tried to handle any situation responsibly. Sometimes I failed but it was not through want of trying.

Unlike the management of La Scala, who were the real culprits of the Edinburgh scandal, Adler was justified, in the circumstances, in not believing Callas. And what guarantee did he have that she would have sung in San Francisco on the alternative date she had requested? Even ignoring Maxwell's superficial but highly damaging prattle, the Venice party was not a token of Callas's best intentions and it did not take very long for Adler to be informed that his ailing prima donna was currently recording with electrifying vocal power the title role in *Medea* – one of the most difficult in the repertoire. Not only did Adler cancel Callas's contract (she was replaced by Leyla Gencer in *Lucia* and Leonie Rysanek in *Macbeth*) but he also referred the case to the board of AGMA (American Guild of Musical Artists) alleging breach of contract. An adverse ruling from the very powerful Guild could mean suspension for an artist, thus making it impossible to appear in the United States.

Throughout this stormy autumn Maria was also trying consistently to clear her name *vis-à-vis* the press's totally untrue allegations that followed her departure from the Edinburgh Festival. The facts were straightforward and she never imagined that her supportive gesture towards La Scala would have been used against her. Even before she left Edinburgh she had telephoned Ghiringhelli in Milan asking him to elucidate the situation. Despite his assurances that he would and his effusions of appreciation of her loyalty to art and La Scala, he did nothing about it.

The press continued the allegations in a most destructive way, especially when Callas returned to Milan from Venice, while her several telephone calls to Ghiringhelli were never answered and nobody at the theatre could tell her where he was. It was evident that he was avoiding her, hoping that with time the scandal would lose its potency. Meneghini later revealed that it was a miracle that during this terrible period Maria did not suffer a nervous breakdown, though she came very close to it every time the press criticized her about Edinburgh and Venice, and she could not locate Ghiringhelli anywhere. 'After Edinburgh,' Callas related,

> I was furious with La Scala and expected Ghiringhelli to clear my name. I had every right to demand this much, for I had been with La Scala six glorious years – I worked hard and sang everything. . . . Each year Ghiringhelli gave me a present: a silver bowl, a silver mirror, a chandelier, costumes and lots of sugared words and compliments. But now he would not speak up to defend me for Edinburgh. When my husband and I succeeded in seeing him on 17 October, seven long weeks after my return, he said that it was only justice to do as I asked. Although he solemnly promised to make, by 25 October, a formal statement that would have vindicated me, he did absolutely nothing about it. We managed to track him down again at the beginning of November. (Ghiringhelli went into hiding when he wanted to avoid anybody.) This time I demanded that he act immediately and in our presence he phoned Emilio Radius, editor of *Oggi*, the popular Italian magazine, asking him to send a reporter on the following day so that Ghiringhelli could exonerate me.
>
> I waited a month for Ghiringhelli to keep his promise, but he never did. Later Radius told me Ghiringhelli kept the reporter waiting two hours, then told him he had changed his mind and would not need him. By this time I was fed up to the teeth with Ghiringhelli's evasive tactics. So I changed my strategy and succeeded in getting Ghiringhelli to the offices of the mayor of Milan. There, before the mayor, Ghiringhelli and my husband finally agreed that I should write the story myself, at least in the first instance. I did so (*Oggi*, January 1958), praising La Scala for its excellence, explaining the confusion about the fifth performance and pointing out that in the previous six years I had postponed, because of illness, only two out of 157 performances and that I was not at all responsible for Edinburgh.

Thus Callas put the ball in Ghiringhelli's court. As he never returned it and no other statement came from La Scala, it was clear that he had tricked her into virtually demolishing her own case: her defence did not achieve the credibility it deserved. Moreover, before long, other serious issues came between them.

During the six weeks after she had recorded *Medea* Maria, apart from chasing Ghiringhelli, took a most beneficial rest at her home in Milan. She was still slightly underweight but happily got over her nervous exhaustion and although her case with AGMA and her argument with La Scala had not yet been resolved she looked forward none the less to singing again.

On 5 November the Meneghinis arrived in New York, where Maria appeared in court for her lawsuit against Bagarozy. Twelve days later the case (as already mentioned) was settled out of court. Callas was at the time in Dallas, rehearsing for the concert that was to inaugurate the newly founded Dallas Opera.

Carol Fox, Laurence Kelly and Nicola Rescigno, the directors of the Lyric Theater in Chicago, having managed successfully their first two seasons, were at loggerheads when contracts for 1956 came to be negotiated; the enormous deficit of the first two seasons and Fox's blunt refusal to grant Rescigno, the musical director, executive power over all artistic matters caused a split in the board that led to a courtroom dispute. Fox remained in power at Chicago while Kelly, with Rescigno as his artistic director, started a short celebrity opera season in Dallas. Kelly, who particularly appreciated and admired Callas's artistic gifts, was determined to lure her to his new opera house. He even offered her all three female leading roles in *Tales of Hoffmann*. 'My dear, would you pay me three fees?' was the playful answer. After several discussions, mainly on artistic matters, which all concluded agreeably, Callas was very happy to sing in Dallas. She was back in good form again and Dallas, where the slogan 'Dallas for Callas' was coined, gave her a reception fit for a queen. The concert, which was unusually taxing and very impressive, included arias from *Die Entführung aus dem Serail*, *La traviata*, *Macbeth* and the mad scenes from *I Puritani* and *Anna Bolena*. Dallas had discovered opera.

While there, Callas resolved another personal matter. It was exactly a year since the night of the ball in New York when she had set out to beat Elsa Maxwell at her own game and had succeeded with the first shot. Whereas Maria's motives were in the beginning entirely hypocritical, she could not at the same time help being a little amused by Maxwell's exuberance, wit and that insatiable desire to live a life of endless parties. She even enjoyed the novelty of the world to which Maxwell introduced her, but only as very occasional escapism – until Maxwell's acute egocentricity manifested itself and began to cause serious damage.

Many years later, after the death of both women, it emerged that Maxwell's calculated imprudence at the Venice party which was so damaging to Callas was in fact the last straw. Callas never commented publicly about her friendship with Maxwell but, as Meneghini related to me in

1978 and somewhat less explicitly in *Maria Callas mia moglie*, privately his wife was far from being responsive to this woman. Nor did she find in Maxwell a surrogate mother, as some writers alleged, because of Callas's estrangement from her own mother. There was more to it. 'When this friendship began,' Meneghini recalled,

> several people, who claimed that they knew of Maxwell's lesbian proclivities,[1] jumped to the conclusion that Callas must share the same sexual tendencies. Although these assertions proved to be true of Maxwell, I can categorically say, and I ought to know, they did not apply to my wife. She valued affectionate friendship with another woman but in an intellectual, not physical, sense. In April 1957 Maria invited Maxwell to attend *Anna Bolena* at La Scala. Maxwell, who readily though without cause construed much more in this 'normal' invitation, before long, with hardly any restraint or inhibition all but declared her great love (or infatuation, I am not sure which) for my wife. Afterwards Maxwell never stopped bombarding Maria with passionate love letters, overflowing with affection as well as a great deal of sadness and almost always further distorted with grotesque remarks which referred to lesbian relationships of other well-known people. Maria was so disgusted with these letters that her first reaction – and mine – was to break off all relations with this dangerously strange woman. However, knowing how influential Maxwell was at the time and more importantly how revengeful she might be, Maria decided on a different strategy; she would diplomatically and with utmost discretion convey to Maxwell that her feelings were not reciprocated.

As this plan needed time to be enforced, Maxwell wishfully misconstrued Maria's silence (during this period Callas was working very hard and also began to suffer from mental exhaustion) as a sign that their feelings were mutual. Her letters became even more nauseatingly intimate to the point where Maria refused to read them and passed them on to her husband unopened. These very long epistles were full of such effusions as 'Only your face and your smile, Maria, send me into ecstasy. . . . I do not dare reveal all my feelings for you for fear that you would think I am mad. I am not at all mad, Maria, but only a woman different from others.' Maxwell also telephoned Maria frequently and sometimes during the night to invite her to this or that party. All the Meneghinis had agreed, and this was at the beginning of their acquaintanceship with Maxwell, was to see her during their visit to Paris in June and attend the Venice party in September, not to please their importunate hostess but because it suited them to do so.

Maria next saw Maxwell in November at Dallas. 'By this time,' Meneghini declared, 'Maria had had enough of her and no longer cared how revengeful she might turn out to be.' During their return flight to New York (Maxwell promptly arranged to travel with Maria, Meneghini was busy elsewhere) harsh words were exchanged between them, the argument triggered off by

Maxwell's tiresome grumbling that Maria was not giving her the undivided attention that was her due. A member of the crew overheard them and told the press, which lost no time in reporting widely the ending of their alleged friendship. The reportage was not without veiled connotations that the relationship between them was more a love affair than an ordinary friendship.

Subsequently, Maxwell told Maria that 'if *Time* magazine asks about it, you must deny everything categorically, as I did', Maria did absolutely nothing about it and Maxwell, in the middle of December, wrote her a long, pathetic letter with bitchy, ambiguous contradictions in practically every other sentence:

> I feel compelled to write and thank you for being the innocent victim of the highest form
> of love that a human being can have for another. . . . It is I who terminated it or, more
> precisely, you who helped me to end it. . . . It brought you no happiness and, apart from a
> few marvellous moments, it brought me only profound misery. . . . You destroyed my love
> that day on the flight from Dallas. And yet I believe I almost touched your heart once or
> twice. . . . I do not mean to reproach you for anything, except for not crushing my feelings
> before it was too late. But this too is now forgotten. . . . I was and always will be your
> most eloquent defence lawyer – I stood up to your enemies, Maria, of which you have
> many!

Later, Maxwell informed Maria that she would be in Rome in January to see her in *Norma*: '. . . you must not think that I am coming so that I may get in touch with you . . .' At the same time she added that she hoped Maria would ask to see her. 'Oh, I do hope you are good [in *Norma*],' Maxwell continued bizarrely, 'because I am now in a state of such detachment that no friendship, old or new, could possibly tempt me again to lose my integrity as a critic. I probably will not see you during my stay in Rome . . . the fact remains that you are the greatest and most stimulating artist I have ever known . . . you are not the type of woman who is interested in friendships or affection of any kind, except with your husband.' There were no more letters or telephone calls from Maxwell. Henceforth her meetings with Maria were confined almost entirely to the opera house. She continued to praise Callas the artist to the skies but would also stab her in the back when she found the opportunity.

In 1961 I was asked to escort the seventy-eight-year-old Maxwell for the last hundred metres (motor cars cannot go beyond this point) to the theatre at Epidaurus where Callas was singing in *Medea*. She asked me a thousand questions about Maria and the dress rehearsal of *Medea* which had taken place two days previously. At one moment she reminisced about the ball in New York when Maria went as the Empress Hatshepsut. Maxwell could not hold back her tears and we stopped walking for a few minutes. She then smiled and exclaimed, 'On with the show!' Notwithstanding this woman's contradictory character, which oscillated between being a parasite (at times a dangerous one) and a 'source of life', I believed that she had fallen in love with Callas but totally lacked the nobility, let alone the elementary decency, for this highest form of feeling. The moment she realized she could not have her way, however selfish the issue, she would turn slyly vindictive, very often causing enormous damage.

Although the success of the Dallas concert lifted Maria's spirits considerably, her confidence was somewhat undermined when she returned to Milan to find that relations between her and La Scala were still at a low ebb. Ghiringhelli, who knew exactly where the fault lay in Edinburgh and had already agreed that Callas herself shoud explain it in *Oggi*, continued to be aloof. As the article had not yet been published and Ghiringhelli remained permanently silent, the public at large believed that their turbulent prima donna had indeed disgraced herself by letting La Scala down when she walked out of the festival to go to Elsa Maxwell's party in Venice.

Such was the general atmosphere – hostile to a degree – in Milan when Callas began rehearsals for *Un ballo in maschera* with which La Scala was opening its 1957–8 season. Physically she was feeling fit, despite her recent mental exhaustion and further loss of weight, which was down to 53 kilos. Before long, however, the tense atmosphere at the theatre and for that matter among the public began to play on her nerves and she, too, became tense and irritable during the rehearsals. This in turn strengthened the rumours which had been already circulating that there was a decline in her vocal powers. Ten years previously Callas had auditioned for the role of Amelia in *Ballo* at La Scala but Mario Labroca had turned her down. She recorded the opera in 1956 but it was only now that she was singing the role for the first time on stage to open her seventh season at La Scala, in a new production directed by Margherita Wallmann and designed by Nicola Benois. Di Stefano, Bastianini and Simionato completed the distinguished cast, and Gavazzeni conducted.

At the première all tension and resentment disappeared and the performance was hailed as one of the most exciting of a Verdi opera. Callas once again rose to the occasion, scoring a personal triumph. She looked stunning (her superb costumes, designed by Benois, were cut and fashioned at the atelier of Christian Dior in Paris) and sang magnificently, expressing her chaste love with tremendous passion and moving vulnerability.

Ernest Weerth (*Opera News*, January 1958) wrote that 'as soon as the turbulent Maria Meneghini Callas appeared, extravagantly costumed as ever, we realized that she had set her stamp on Amelia. She was in voice and sang superbly. Callas is never dull. . . . Her personality is without doubt the most imposing on the operatic stage today.'

It was like old times and the Milanese, who crowded all five performances, applauded her exultantly. Gavazzeni was also enthusiastic, extolling 'Callas's inner flame that generates her unique sense for the words in the opera where the music completely comes to life from the text'.

After completing her performances Maria and her husband spent a peaceful Christmas at their home in Milan. Now that most of the ice that lay between her and the public was thawing she felt relaxed and reasonably happy. She hoped that the forthcoming publication of her article in *Oggi* would serve to clear the air completely and her relationship with La Scala would once again be warm and inspiring. Had she finally weathered the rampages of the last few months? The signs seemed favourable and she looked forward confidently; it did not even cross her mind that this was merely a lull before incredible storms.

---

1   In her autobiography *R.S.V.P.* Maxwell presented herself as totally asexual, professing that she never felt any sexual impulse for man or woman: 'I discovered when I was sixteen that I could not permit myself even to be kissed by a man.'

CHAPTER TWELVE

MORE SCANDALS: THE BREAK WITH ROME AND LA SCALA

AFTER THEIR SHORT but most agreeable Christmas at home the Meneghinis left Milan on 27 December for Rome, where Maria was eagerly awaited; she was to open the season with a gala performance of *Norma* before President Gronchi and other dignitaries.

It had been five years since Callas had sung Norma in Rome and now, by coincidence, the same cast was reassembled: Corelli was Pollione, Barbieri Adalgisa and Giulio Neri Oroveso. The conductor was Gabriele Santini. The first rehearsal on 29 December did not fare very well – not artistically, for all the singers seemed quite happy, but because of the absence of any heating in the theatre during a cold winter. The cast's complaints and requests to turn on the heating during rehearsals fell on deaf ears – even when Barbieri on the following day went down with influenza and was replaced by Miriam Pirazzini. Maria, who was fine before this rehearsal, also developed slight trouble with her throat, but she took good care of herself by resting and felt all right at the dress rehearsal on 31 December.

On that same evening she also sang 'Casta Diva' live on Italian television with success, then saw the New Year in with one glass of champagne at the Circolo degli Sacchi, a Roman night-club, where she stayed until 1 a.m. Although Callas's activities on New Year's Eve were perfectly normal, her night-club visit would never have been mentioned again, if it had not been for the fact that she woke up next morning, the day before the actual performance, to discover that she was practically voiceless. Being New Year's Day, a throat specialist was found only with the greatest difficulty and at the same time the theatre was informed of the situation. Sanpaoli, the artistic director of the Rome Opera, would not even hear of having a substitute ready just in case. 'Impossible,' he said, 'this is no ordinary performance. It is a special gala and the public has paid to hear Callas. The President of Italy and his wife will be there.' With the help of medical treatment Maria's condition improved considerably in the next twenty-four hours. Hopefully she continued the treatment and prayed for a miracle. One hour before the performance her doctor found her condition satisfactory. She may not have been on top form but in the circumstances she felt confident enough to carry out her engagement.

The theatre was packed to capacity with the most glittering audience that Rome could produce. Arrangements were also made for the performance to be broadcast live so that it could be heard throughout Italy. Callas began her great scene in the first act cautiously: the menacing phrases of the opening recitative were expressively if not loudly declaimed. In the ensuing aria some unsteadiness crept into her voice harming her high notes. Presently her lower notes were affected as well and Maria, who had always thrived on challenges, realized that this time she was fighting a losing battle. She gathered all her energies, her great technique and determination, and managed to get through the long and difficult scene – far from brilliantly, indeed barely adequately. The applause was rather lukewarm, but displeasure was expressed from the gallery when she almost cracked on the final note of the cabaletta at the conclusion of the scene. One voice rose above the shouting: 'Why don't go back to Milan? You have already cost us a million lire!'

When Callas left the stage for her dressing-room she discovered that her singing voice was not there. She could hardly speak and consequently was unable to continue her performance after the first act. Backstage, Carlo Latini, the superintendent of the theatre, the conductor, Wallmann who directed the production, and other close associates were trying to persuade Norma to return to her sacred shrine. They even suggested she should walk through the role, declaiming instead of singing. 'You are a great actress,' they kept telling her, 'and you are sure to bring it off.' They then appealed to her unshakeable artistic beliefs and her sense of duty and gratitude towards Italy, the country that helped her to find self-fulfilment as well as fame. Meneghini, who understood the gravity of the situation perfectly and had not lost sight of her responsibilities, would have done anything possible to enable her to finish the performance.

There was no second or third act that evening as the theatre had never even considered an understudy – the usual practice virtually everywhere – nor could they find another soprano at such short notice to resolve the crisis. After an hour-long interval, first the President and then the audience were told that the performance had to be abandoned. Neither the management nor Meneghini, who was after all his wife's manager, nor even, as a last resort on such a special night, Callas herself, appeared to offer any explanation to the long-suffering audience. Instead, through loudspeakers, the public were merely told that 'the management of the theatre is forced to suspend tonight's performance for reasons which are absolutely beyond its control'. The announcement was greeted with a violent demonstration against Callas. Without another thought a large number of people blamed her egotistic character and pique at not being sufficiently enthusiastically applauded as the cause of her walk-out. After a rather long spate of angry shouts and catcalls, 'This is Rome, not Milan and not Edinburgh', a rather large crowd gathered outside the stage door, presumably to lynch the woman who had dared to insult the Romans and their President.

Eventually Maria, carried by Meneghini, left through an underground passage that connects the theatre to the Hotel Quirinale where she was staying. The demonstrators also moved to the hotel where a sizeable group of extremists, standing under the windows of her rooms, continued their curses and insults throughout the night. Elsa Maxwell, who rushed to comfort Callas, found time to speak to the press. 'You Romans,' she chided the reporters who crowded the foyer, 'you are still behaving like your barbarian ancestors. Can't you understand that Mme Callas is ill?' And then Maxwell added quite gratuitously in her inimitable way, 'Of course she had no business staying up late in night-clubs before an important performance.'

Not surprisingly, the Italian press (and before long their international cohorts) blew up the situation into a large national scandal, blaming Callas for everything. All sorts of stories which added fuel to the fire were invented, basically implying that she had not lost her voice but had walked out because her applause was not overwhelming. Other versions had it that Callas did lose her voice because she had been celebrating the New Year irresponsibly at various all-night parties. *Il Giorno* was much more explicitly insulting, albeit totally wrong on every count: 'This second-rate artist,' the ill-informed reporter wrote, 'Italian by marriage, Milanese because of the baseless veneration she enjoys from a section of the audience at La Scala and of international fame due to her dangerous association with Elsa Maxwell, has for a number of years followed a path of melodramatic intemperance. The present episode shows that Callas is, in addition, an ungracious performer without a grain of discipline and propriety.'

The press generally continued its attack for several days, while in the Italian parliament she was denounced for her gross insult to the President. Moreover, the Prefect of Rome granted the Opera House an order to stop her from singing in the remaining three performances of *Norma* for which she had been contracted, as well as banning her from entering the theatre. When she protested against this decision, which constituted a breach of human rights, she was told that the theatre was merely taking precautionary measures to protect her: it was highly probable that, had she reappeared on the Rome stage so soon after her 'scandalous' behaviour, the public would riot and no responsible theatre management could risk that.

Two days later the Rome Opera House, which originally claimed that it could not provide an understudy for Callas (an understudy had been provided for Barbieri), presented another gala performance of *Norma* with the Italian soprano Anita Cerquetti in the title role. When a week later Callas recovered her voice but was not allowed to give the remaining two scheduled performances she sued the Opera House, claiming payment of the corresponding fees due to her. The opera promptly placed a counter-suit for $13,000 on the grounds that Callas's walk-out was unjustified. It took the Roman Supreme Court of Appeals fourteen years to reach a decision. In April 1971 the counter-suit was dismissed and Callas was awarded $1600 in lost fees, plus her costs. There was, however, hardly any mention of the verdict in the press. By 1971 she had already been in retirement from the stage for six years and the public no longer cared whether she had been guilty or not. At the time of the scandal Callas provided medical reports to prove her physical illness and, having sent her apologies to President Gronchi, she thought it unnecessary to comment further. However, much later, in an interview with Kenneth Harris (*Observer*, 1970), she spoke of the incident:

> Some people said that I left the performance because of rudeness from a section of the audience. Anyone who knows me knows this is ridiculous. Hisses and yells do not frighten me, for I am fully aware of the enmity of claques. When my enemies stop hissing, I'll know I've failed. They only make me furious, make me want to sing better than ever to drive the rudeness down their throats. More than anybody else, I wanted to sing and complete the performance, but that night in Rome I was unable to sing. . . . Many singers have had colds, and many of them have been substituted for even during the performance. It happens all the time. The opera house must either have a substitute ready, or else it must take the responsibility. Rome did neither . . .
>
> In the morning a doctor sent by the opera house examined me and reported that I had bronchitis and tracheitis but could possibly sing again in five or six days. The President's wife telephoned and said, 'Tell Maria we know she was sick and could not continue.' Unfortunately she did not say that to the newspapers. The press demanded pictures of me sick in bed, but I am a serious artist, not a soubrette, and I do not pose for pictures in bed. I refused, and the newspapers decided that it would be more interesting to imply that I was perfectly healthy but had lost my nerve because of the insults. . . . My name was seriously damaged by this unjust incident.

'For a time,' Callas later told me, 'I was terribly unhappy and hurt by the unkindness and the unfairness — in the papers I read nothing but insults. Eventually I did find justice and cleared my name. I do not mean the damages I received. That money went to charity immediately.'

But to return to the turbulent days of the scandal. Having been barred from singing, Maria could find no reason whatever to remain in Rome. The Meneghinis were now anxious to go back to the peace and privacy of their home. The recent events had been most trying for Maria and a rest was essential. She never imagined, especially after Edinburgh, that she could possibly be involved in another scandal of such monstrous magnitude in Rome. Even so she was determined to go on and prove to the world that she was not the ogre she had been made out to be.

Apart from appearances at La Scala in the spring, she had no other engagements in Italy. Her return to Milan, however, was treated with stony silence by La Scala, obviously reflecting Ghiringhelli's complete lack of solidarity with Maria. None the less, there was significant compensation from other quarters: the hundreds of letters from friends and admirers, all expressing their profound sympathy for her Roman misfortune, were the most effective antidote to her unhappiness. It was the unfairness of Rome that distressed her and she could not quite fathom how, with such honourable intentions, she had landed herself in this incredible mess. Furthermore, the imminent AGMA decision was looming over her and if unfavourable she almost certainly would not be able to sing in the United States. Bing had warned her that 'If AGMA should terminate your membership or suspend you for any period of time, your Metropolitan appearances will probably be impossible. I need not tell you how terribly upsetting this would be, not only to our whole repertory planning but also personally to me. I was looking forward so much to your return ... hoping for your new immense success which would really then have established you finally.'

Before her Metropolitan performances Callas was due to give a concert in Chicago. On their way there the Meneghinis stopped briefly in Paris to attend a dinner at Maxim's that Pathe Marconi (EMI's French counterpart) was giving in Maria's honour. It was a happy occasion described by her, who still had the Roman tribulations on her mind, as very thoughtful. 'In Rome', she said, 'it was not so easy to know who my friends are. It is very easy in Paris. I am grateful to all those who believed me and defended me.'

The concert on 22 January was again a benefit for the Alliance Française. The programme consisted of arias and scenes from operas that she had not sung previously in Chicago: she began with 'Non mi dir' from *Don Giovanni* and followed with excerpts from *Macbeth*, *Il barbiere di Siviglia*, *Mefistofele*, *Hamlet* and *Nabucco*. Cassidy found Callas 'in full glory' and the audience gave her a prolonged standing ovation before and at the end of the concert — a most gratifying balm after her traumatic Roman experience. Fortified by her success and above all by the appreciation of the public, Callas left for New York.

Her appearance there on a nationwide television interview with Edward R. Murrow proved an excellent idea: the American public saw for itself that this woman was moderate, good-humoured, modest and above all totally serious about her art — a very different image from the one that had been created by rumours and by the press. There was, however, still one hurdle to jump before she could begin her performances at the Metropolitan announced for 6 February.

On 26 January the board of AGMA, which had in the meantime conducted its own investigation, listened to testimony by both Adler and Callas. For almost three hours she argued her case personally before the jury of twenty people. The board concluded that although she had been in breach of her contract, the mitigating circumstances of her ill health (supported with

Callas is shown the renowned wine cellars of the restaurant
'La Tour d'Argent' in Paris.

valid medical certificates) and her correct behaviour, were in her favour: she was discharged with a reprimand and was free to start work in the United States.

The first rehearsal of *La traviata* at the Metropolitan, however, upset and disappointed her; no stage rehearsal apart from the dress was allotted. Being completely unfamiliar with the production Callas could only study it from photographs and then go through it alone on a terrace, with chalk marks and elementary props to mark distances on-stage. This created another problem. Because of her myopia she was terrified of misjudging distances. In fact, at the dress rehearsal she did have an accident. When the sick Violetta tries to get up out of bed in the last act Maria did not know that there was a little step by it and she stumbled. Those present thought the fall was part of her interpretation. She thought herself fortunate that she was not hurt.

The opening night found her in excellent voice and she was able to give the very appreciative audience an incomparable Violetta. So much so, that many felt they were hearing this familiar role for the first time. The applause at the end of the performance lasted half an hour, with

Callas taking ten solo curtain-calls. 'I am numb, numb. I still can't believe it's finally happened' (meaning that at last she had scored the success at the Met that she thought herself capable of), she murmured as she left the stage for the last time to fall into the arms of her husband and her father, who were standing in the wings.

Lucia di Lammermoor followed and it was equally successful; the audience were in turn moved and electrified. Irving Kolodin, summing up these last two performances in the *Saturday Review*, said of her Violetta: 'She commands the attention of all who regard opera as something more than a concert in costume' and for *Lucia*, 'She sang Donizetti's music with a comprehension of musical meaning usually reserved for the best players of Chopin's Nocturnes.' *Time* described her performance in *La traviata* as having 'warmth and purity in the lower and middle registers, edginess and wobble in the upper ones. But she infused the character of Violetta with ardency, hectic gaiety and a dampened passion that flickered through the role like a wayward fever. Her deathbed agonies had the quiet poignancy and the ring of truth that so often evade lesser artists.'

Callas's third and last role was in *Tosca*, with Richard Tucker and George London. Dimitri Mitropoulos was, as in the previous season, conducting. He collaborated so completely with the singers that the result was an artistic triumph. 'To this reviewer,' Taubman (*New York Times*) concluded, 'who heard her in one of last season's *Toscas*, her performance last night had more concentration and fire. It was comparatively underplayed and pallid a year ago. But this time it grew out

Rudolf Bing greeting his sublime Violetta at the end of La traviata *at the Metropolitan, 1958.*

of an inner flame. Not that Miss Callas exaggerated. But she performed as if every faculty was alert and engaged.'

If New York had had any reservations about Callas from her previous season they all vanished and her conquest of the city was complete. How she felt is best described in her own words: 'I returned to America to sing, first in Chicago, then at the Metropolitan. At both places, the first time I appeared on the stage wondering how I would be received after the destructive publicity, the public gave me an ovation before I sang a single note. Both times the ovations went on and on until I asked myself, how can I ever sing well enough to thank them? I will never forget those tributes given me for the rest of my life.'

During the seven weeks Callas spent in New York she saw a great deal of her father, who never missed any of her performances and also took part in some of her interviews. Kalogeropoulos, who had divorced his wife during the previous year, had no contact with her even though she had left Greece to live again in New York. Some of Evangelia's Greek friends tried to reconcile mother and daughter but Maria was not interested even in discussing it. This line of action or, more correctly, inaction was rather hard. Whatever the past, time should cure most ills and should also have done so for her. But Maria's good intentions, albeit not many, usually proved stillborn, destroyed by her mother. Always insatiably eager to get into the papers, Evangelia would lose no opportunity to run down her daughter. As her mother, she enjoyed a strong position but as nearly always happens with people who trade on their children, she often went too far and weakened, if not lost altogether, her credibility. Maria and her father took a diametrically opposite stance, remaining silent about their family's private affairs. Pressed by interviewers, Kalogeropoulos, who was by nature a very reserved man, acknowledged that a mutual love had always existed between him and his daughter. Adopting this conservative attitude, father and daughter highly impressed the American public when they appeared together on Hy Gardner's television chat show. Gardner, writing in the *Herald Tribune* about his first meeting with Callas at a luncheon given by Harry Sell, the publisher, reproduced his conversation with her: '"You seem like a perfectly normal, nice woman. Why have so many people, including myself, been influenced to believe otherwise by the bitter press you've had? Don't you think you ought to hire a public relations man?"

'"I don't see any reason why I should employ anyone to defend me. I am an artist. What I have to say, I sing. Greeks never stop fighting for what they know is right and fair."'

Gardner ended his column with: 'I went to lunch expecting to meet a cold, tempestuous but talented female ogre and found instead a warm, sincere, handsome and down-to-earth human being, a real live doll.'

Before Maria left New York she signed a contract to appear at the Metropolitan during the following season in *Macbeth*, *La traviata* and *Tosca*. *Macbeth* would be a new production. She also agreed to go on tour, though reluctantly, as Bing later said.

The great success of Callas's performances, especially in America, where her public image at last began to resemble her real self, helped significantly to alleviate her insufferable depression during the recent turbulent times. Furthermore, during her absence from Italy her own version of the Edinburgh affair was published in Milan and on the strength of this she hoped to find a favourable climate on her return home. Her optimism was shattered almost immediately. The attitude of a rather large section of the Milanese public towards her was generally so hostile that it amounted to hatred. Taking the press's accusations of Callas as gospel truth, they maintained that in both Edinburgh and Rome she was not really ill – in Rome she had deliberately set out to insult the President as well as the public when she refused to finish the performance. What was more, Ghiringhelli now made himself completely inaccessible to her and in fact went out of his way to avoid meeting her on one occasion, blatantly ignoring her presence at the Biffi. After this they were no longer on speaking terms, although her imminent scheduled appearances at La Scala were not affected.

'In spite of all the hostility I had encountered on my return to Milan,' Callas later recalled, 'I would not leave during the season and give La Scala the opportunity to say that "Callas has walked out – as usual". Not that I lacked provocation. I had been asked to sing *Anna Bolena* to open the Milan Fair on 12 April before President Gronchi. For some weeks there was obscure talk from La Scala about not knowing the exact date and circumstances of the performance, when all of a sudden I read in the newspapers that the Milan Fair would actually open with Pizzetti's *L'assassinio nella cattedrale*. I did not receive the courtesy of an explanation.'

The five performances of *Anna Bolena* were finally scheduled for 9, 13, 16, 19 and 23 April. On the evening of the first *Bolena* the square outside La Scala was filled with people, the majority of whom were noisy protesters. A great number of armed policemen were called to keep order outside the theatre, with a special patrol at the stage door. Plain-clothes policemen were also placed inside the theatre, even backstage. Accompanied by her husband, her maid, Bruna, and her butler, Maria arrived rather early. They were horrified at the presence of the constabulary and when Meneghini protested that they were not exactly criminals a theatre spokesman told him that the police were there for the security of Mme Callas – just in case any hooligans got out of hand.

The theatre was packed to capacity, but for the first two scenes the audience reacted to Callas with icy indifference as if she did not exist, despite the fact that during the previous season she had had one of the greatest triumphs of her career in this same opera and theatre. On the other hand, they went out of their way to applaud warmly all the other artists (Siepi as Henry VIII, Simionato as Seymour, Raimondi as Percy and Carturan as Smeaton). Callas was certainly a persecuted queen and was facing trial on and off the stage. But in the third-scene finale of the first act when the King wrongly accuses the Queen of adultery (in the opera Anne Boleyn is presented as being unequivocally innocent) and orders her arrest, the wronged Queen Maria was determined to win her real-life trial. As two guards came to seize her, following the King's order, Callas pushed them away and hurled herself at the footlights, throwing her lines directly at the audience: '*Giudici? ad Anna? Giudici. . . . Ah! segnata è la mia sorte, se mi accusa chi condanna. . . . Ma scolpata dopo morte a te darò*' ('Judges? For Anne? Judges? . . . Ah! My fate is decided if my accuser is also my judge. . . . But I will be defended after death, when I will be absolved'.) For a few moments the audience were stunned, then they went mad with applause. Maria was still their queen. She went on to give one of the most exciting and moving portrayals of her whole career. 'There was a new kind of sadness, a pathetic tenderness of pure Donizettian inspiration,' Eugenio Gara, the doyen of Italian music critics, said of this performance.

At the end of the opera the audience were calling Callas *divina* and any other eulogistic epithets they could think of. Word of her triumph and acquittal by the public inside the theatre had spread outside and when Maria left the police had now to protect her from the excessive cheering. Eventually she drove home, fully content with her unprecedented triumph; what was really important was the proof that she had found justice. And yet when she arrived home that night there was another dreadful disappointment awaiting her; the door and windows of her house were defaced with obscene graffiti and worse still, the gate was smeared with excrement. It was a bitter blow to find that other enemies had struck, even though she had won one big battle. In spite of these vicissitudes the majority of the Milanese were saying that in Milan the Roman incident would have been avoided. Everyone except the management of La Scala, which retained its full hostility, forgot their grievance against Callas. There was also another section of the population: the hooligans who, from the gallery at La Scala, tried to create disturbances and ruin the subsequent performances of *Anna Bolena* with catcalls and vulgar bellowing. However, the capacity audience at every performance silenced these louts, who continued their harassment outside the theatre: on one occasion the remains of a dead dog were put in Callas's car and the railings of her house were again smeared with excrement. The Meneghinis also received a number of obscene telephone calls at all hours and anonymous letters full of the foulest insults imaginable. The police were naturally informed, but as they failed to provide any effective protection Maria and her husband moved to their villa at Sirmione on Lake Garda.

This was a terrible situation made even more insufferable for Callas by the persistently hostile behaviour of the management of La Scala. Even though she had no grievance against her public (she felt strong enough to ignore the lunatics), she found it impossible as an artist to fulfil her vocation. Very soon it became clear to her that she had no alternative but to leave. In the meantime, however, she was under contract for another role – that of Imogene in Bellini's *Il pirata* –

which she would be singing for the first time.[1] She prepared it meticulously, working closely with the other singers, Franco Corelli and Ettore Bastianini, and with the conductor Antonino Votto. Five performances were scheduled, the first on 19 May.

The première found Callas rather slow to warm up but in the great mad scene she gave of her best. 'The work is exceptionally difficult to sing,' Peter Dragadze (*Musical America*) commented, 'accounting in part for its infrequent performances. Callas had a triumph second only to her unforgettable Medea. She brought the cold Milan audience to its feet, cheering and applauding almost hysterically for over 25 minutes after the mad scene.'

Claudio Sartori (*Opera*, August 1958) found 'Callas's interpretation flawless. Never perhaps has a singer been better adapted to her own means of expression to portray Imogene: and never avoided so well those strongly dramatic accents so as to limit herself almost entirely to the meaningful recitatives and to those lyrical mezza-voce sections, meditative and with slackened tempo, which have become a predominating characteristic of her interpretations . . .'

The second performance three days later was even more successful, with Callas getting into her stride from the beginning and thus bringing to life completely another Bellini heroine. On the following day she suffered from an acute attack of haemorrhoids that made it necessary,

Backstage at La Scala during a performance of Il pirata
in 1958. Meneghini comforts his 'persecuted' wife.

twenty-four hours later, to have an operation: 'I had to undergo a painful operation,' Maria revealed later. 'Only my doctors and a few close friends knew about it, for by then I had learned that Callas is not allowed to postpone a performance – or even to have a cold. For six days after the operation I was in pain, for I am allergic to strong pain-killers and cannot take them. I had no sleep and almost nothing to eat. On Sunday, the day after the operation, I sang *Il pirata*. On Wednesday I sang it again. Saturday was to be my final night and I hoped to create for the public and myself a last happy memory of our long association.'

By this time the rumours that Callas was leaving were widespread. Nobody was quite sure of the exact reason; the public was acclaiming her at every performance and Ghiringhelli made absolutely no comment about it. The end did come with the last performance of *Il pirata* on 31 May. 'For this special occasion,' Callas reminisced, 'several young men decided that they wanted to throw flowers to me at the end of the performance, and they asked permission. It was granted. But that night when they arrived with their flowers the order had been changed: no flowers were to be thrown. When I appeared on stage, the public applauded warmly. It was the beginning of a splendid performance.'

Indeed it was, for she sang with an intensity that thrilled and moved the audience by turn. In the mad scene, the finale of the opera, as Imogene grieves for the fate of her lover, now captured, Callas sang the words *'Vedete il palco funesto'* ('There, behold the fated scaffold') with a bitter smile at the corner of her mouth, her arms raised, pointing towards the proscenium box where Ghiringhelli was sitting, for all to see the cause of her departure. The word *'palco'* in Italian also means theatre box and this was the way the prima donna assoluta left the stage of the leading opera house, the theatre where she had known her greatest triumphs, the place she had always loved. At the end of the performance the audience, who understood her message perfectly, gave her an ovation lasting half an hour. It was a mixture of tears and cheering, voices rising with, 'Do not leave us Maria. Stay home.'

This, obviously, proved too much for Ghiringhelli. Infuriated by the cheering audience who turned their heads towards his box, he found an opportune moment to retaliate. Callas described his action:

> When the long ovation and curtain-calls were finished, and while I was still on stage with my friends and the audience still in the house, the great iron fire curtain was suddenly rung down. I know of no single act in the entire repertoire of operatic insults as brutal as this one. It is a blunt signal that says: 'The show is over, get out!' But in case I and my friends had missed the point, a fireman appeared on stage to say, 'By order of the theatre, the stage must be cleared.'

As I walked for the last time out of the theatre that had been my spiritual home for seven years, the young men were standing out in the street, throwing their flowers for me. They finally crowded around me to say goodbye and some policemen tried to disperse them. 'Please leave them in peace,' I said. 'They are my friends and do not mean any harm.'

They then walked her to her car and as she drove away she could no longer restrain her tears. On the following day Callas made a statement to the press: 'I will not be returning to La Scala as long as Ghiringhelli is there.'

Ghiringhelli's persistent aloofness allowed him but one curt comment about Callas's departure: 'Prima donnas may come and go, La Scala stays on for ever.'

Notwithstanding the trials and tribulations of these performances, Callas's portrayal of Imogene, her fourth and last Bellini heroine, was a significant triumph, confirming the renaissance of Bellini's music which she herself brought about and that continues to the present day. Commenting on Imogene, Callas said that 'She is a terrified women, she has suffered a lot, she has known love and has been torn away from it and is torn away from it again.'

Callas continued to speak fondly of the theatre: 'Each time I walk past La Scala, each time I pass that wonderful building, each time I think of an opera that I could do there, I am hurt. I wish I could go back. I would go back if I were promised that there would be courtesy, good manners, a willingness to discuss problems and solve them together. But I cannot return while Ghiringhelli is there. He could have come to me during that final season and said "Look we have had differences, but we need each other. Let us both try to work together again."'

Some time during the course of Callas's appearances in *Il pirata* she learned that neither La Scala nor any other Italian theatre would be engaging her in the foreseeable future – after the Rome scandal the Italian government instructed Ghiringhelli that once her scheduled performances of *Anna Bolena* and *Il pirata* were over he should on no account re-engage her. La Scala's plans to give performances in Brussels in the summer of 1958 were also abandoned. Meneghini revealed many years later that he found this out from the director of Théâtre de la Monnaie in Brussels, when he apparently tried to obtain confirmation of La Scala's participation in the World Fair season (1958) there. '"We will not come to Brussels," Ghiringhelli told him, "because the Italian government has instructed that Callas will not be granted permission to go on tour with La Scala."' In these circumstances she had no alternative but to resign. Had she chosen to stay she would not have been offered any engagements. Since the previous January all her enquiries about future plans (she no longer wrote to Ghiringhelli direct but addressed her letters to the 'Administration of La Scala') were answered by Ghiringhelli formally and evasively.

It is difficult to be certain about the Italian government's intervention. If true, it may explain Ghiringhelli's extraordinary behaviour towards Callas after January when he made himself inaccessible to her and, when unable to avoid her, blatantly ignored her. Furthermore, La Scala even cancelled the Brussels visit which was, as with Edinburgh, not possible without Callas's participation. There was a further motive behind Ghiringhelli's stance: the aftermath of the Rome scandal let him off the hook, as it were, from any explanation he owed regarding the fifth performance at the Edinburgh Festival.

The public, however, could not comprehend why things had come to such an impasse at La Scala that Callas was being forced to leave. At certain moments it seemed that the whole affair was temporary, that it would be resolved given a little time. But this was not the case. Not only was she to stay away for the next eighteen months, she was also to encounter further violent storms both in her career and in her private life.

---

1   *Il pirata*, which dates from 1827, remained popular until 1844. Except for performances in 1935 in Rome and in 1951 at Catania (the centenary of Bellini's death and 150th anniversary of his birth respectively), the opera had to wait until 1958 when La Scala staged it for Callas. It is now on the fringe of the repertoire.

CHAPTER THIRTEEN

AT WAR WITH THE METROPOLITAN

C ALLAS'S DRAMATIC EXIT from the Rome Opera House and a few months later from La Scala resulted, in effect, in her break with all state-subsidized theatres in Italy – a break, as Meneghini had found out, unofficially imposed by the government. While the Italian press was turning the 'double scandal' into a vehement polemic, Callas found solace in London, where she went for a series of performances.

On 10 June 1958, in the presence of Queen Elizabeth II, Prince Philip and several members of the royal family, ambassadors, government ministers and other distinguished politicians, men of letters and the general public, Covent Garden celebrated its centenary with a grand gala evening of opera and ballet. The singers were headed by Callas, Jon Vickers, Joan Sutherland, Blanche Thebom and others, the dancers by Margot Fonteyn and Michael Soames. The programme consisted of scenes from various ballets and operas, Callas's contribution being the mad scene from *I Puritani*. She was the star of the evening and the eight curtain-calls she received were unusually prolonged applause for such an occasion.

'If the timbre of her voice is unmistakable,' Grier wrote in the *Scotsman*, 'so too is the calibre of her artistry. . . . Hers was singing and mime such as one imagines the early nineteenth-century tradition had tried to foster.' Harold Rosenthal in *Opera* described Callas's performance as 'an example of consummate operatic singing and acting which held the audience spellbound'.

A few evenings later she delighted the British public by appearing on Granada Television's *Chelsea at Eight*, when she sang arias from *Tosca* and *Il barbiere di Siviglia*. Ten days after this she began a run of five performances (with Cesare Valletti and Mario Zanasi) of *La traviata* at Covent Garden. She was not in her best voice on the opening night inasmuch as her high notes in the first act were distinctly strident, but she recovered in the subsequent performances and, with her compelling dramatic force, most people felt that she had given London its best Violetta for many years.

'Her performance of Violetta,' Rosenthal wrote in *Opera*, 'no less than any other role, even when she is not singing at her best, represents a great interpretation, conceived as an organic whole, such as only comes our way very, very rarely ...' Peter Heyworth in the *Observer* also assessed Callas's portrayal as incomparable: 'She may have not done so with beauty of tone, but in almost every other aspect it was a performance of outstanding distinction and musicality, full of detail that again and again illuminated the part as though for the first time.'

With forthcoming engagements at the Dallas Civic Opera and the Metropolitan, as well as a series of concerts in the United States and Canada, the Meneghinis left London for their villa at Sirmione which at the time seemed to be the most peaceful place on earth.

Three months later in October Callas began her North American concert tour which was to take her to Birmingham, Atlanta, Montreal, Toronto, Washington DC, San Francisco and other cities. Her programme, which was the same throughout the tour, consisted of music as wide in range as it could be, both vocally and dramatically: from 'Tu che invoco' (*La vestale*) to Musetta's Waltz 'Quando me' n vo" (*La bohème*) and arias and scenes from *Macbeth*, *Il barbiere di Siviglia*, *Mefistofele* and *Hamlet*.

The Dallas Civic Opera's second season, though a short one, was most impressive. Apart from the Callas performances of *La traviata* and *Medea*, in themselves a great achievement for the company, *L'Italiana in Algeri* with the highly gifted young mezzo-soprano Teresa Berganza in the title role was also included.

La traviata was produced by Zeffirelli in a most original manner. Believing that Verdi conceived the prelude to the last act to be the same as the one to the first act but in a different key, he staged the entire opera in flashback: Violetta, seen on her death-bed during the first-act

Callas is besieged by the audience when she attends a performance of Turandot *at the Arena di Verona in 1958.*

prelude, is transformed into a young courtesan when the music of the opening party scene begins: she comes full circle in the end. The production worked well and Maria gave Dallas a unique characterization. 'She is that rarest of creatures, a genuine artist, by which we mean a musical intelligence first and foremost,' Raul Askew wrote in the *Dallas Morning News*. 'Roles are created to such fine degree that their impact as vocal communications will be remembered as long as great artistry is catalogued . . . her Violetta, a triumph of a complete art and not just of the sounds that can be made.'

In order to give an authentic style of classicism to *Medea*, which followed a week later, the Dallas Civic Opera, at Callas's instigation, engaged Alexis Minotis, the eminent actor-producer from Greece's National Theatre, to direct the work. Minotis had in the past staged and acted in many Greek tragedies, together with his wife, the acclaimed tragedienne Katina Paxinou. Yannis Tsarouchis, the talented Greek painter, designed the sets and costumes which were made from fabric woven in Greece. The dramatic tenor Jon Vickers (Jason), along with Nicola Zaccaria (Creon) and Berganza (Neris) completed the exceptional cast and Rescigno conducted. The Dallas Opera may have been just beginning but what they accomplished was of the highest standard. The productions were properly rehearsed and everybody concerned spared no effort in making the occasion an artistic success.

An original misunderstanding with Vickers brought Maria close to him. At their first rehearsal, which was also their first meeting, she appeared somewhat patronizing, telling Vickers where and how he should move and so forth. However, she got short change from him, for he promptly informed her that he had already had full coaching from the producer and that she would be more constructively helpful if instead she explained how she intended to play the scene. They both felt that they had met their match in one another. The ice was broken and without further ado they became the best of friends. 'She was a marvellous colleague, always inspiring you to surpass yourself,' was how Vickers afterwards described her. Even ten years later, after he had sung with her many times, he told me: 'You ask me about my experiences in my profession. My greatest experience is that I have sung with Callas.'

Having appreciated the young Berganza immediately, Maria went out of her way to rehearse and give her valuable advice in stagecraft, particularly for their scenes together. At the end of the performance it was Callas who was literally pushing (not kicking, as she was once accused by Del Monaco at La Scala) both Vickers and Berganza on to the stage to take solo curtain-calls.

This dedication and rapport among her colleagues, and no less with the management – a far cry from her recent experiences in Italy – boosted Callas into further exploration of the character of Medea. It was during the preparation of these performances that she added to her already accomplished portrayal of this accursed woman that extra dimension which creates the kind of living character modern audiences demand. Years later, after Minotis had directed her in three different productions of this opera, he told me that from the beginning he never ceased to be amazed by her instinctive ingenuity and resourcefulness. 'Certain movements', Minotis added, 'that took us years in the theatre to improvise and develop, were performed by her quite spontaneously. They simply came to her naturally. I cannot explain Maria's dramatic instincts, her genius, better.'

The Dallas *Medea*, which marked Callas's first assumption of the title role in America, was an unqualified triumph. Writing in *Theatre Arts*, Emily Coleman said that 'In no other performance of our experience, has her vocal production been steadier, her quality more rounded, her acting more plastic and yet tastefully contained within a dramatic framework.'

At this particular performance she was actually singing in dramatic circumstances, unconnected with *Medea*, that imbued her with the blend of strain and fury which often creates the most provocative challenges: less than six hours before the performance Bing had notified her by telegram that he had cancelled the contract for her appearances at the Metropolitan due to begin in a few weeks' time. Simultaneously with the telegram, the newspapers' front-page headlines announced: 'BING FIRES CALLAS!' The bone of contention between them which led to such drastic action was relatively unserious and could have been avoided. It is incredible, to say the least, that Bing, a very intelligent and capable administrator, allowed the situation to get out of hand.

For her third season at the Metropolitan Callas had signed a contract to sign in a new production of *Macbeth*, in *La traviata* and in *Tosca*, as well as going on tour with the company. Whereas she was perfectly happy to sing these roles in this order, Bing unexpectedly and only a few weeks before she was due in New York, insisted that she should appear first in *Macbeth* then in *La traviata* and then again in *Macbeth*, all within the space of a few days. (*Tosca* had been dropped a few months before, as was her participation in the tour.)

Because of the completely different voices required for each, Callas refused to sing the two roles in Bing's new order. He appreciated that Lady Macbeth is a much heaver role than Violetta but dismissed her concern. 'I did not worry about it too much,' he later wrote in his memoirs, 'because she had mixed Violetta and Medea, just as heavy as Lady Macbeth, in Dallas and she would be returning to Dallas to mix Medea with Lucia, which is even lighter than Violetta.' This is completely untrue. Callas did sing these roles in Dallas but they were never mixed as Bing conveniently states; she finished her Violettas in 1958 and her Lucias in 1959, before embarking on the Medeas in both seasons. Bing's offer to replace *La traviata* with *Lucia di Lammermoor*, but still in the same alternation with *Macbeth*, was absolutely pointless as it did not solve the problem. It was precisely this alternation that Callas objected to and which Bing deliberately ignored, shifting the emphasis entirely on to the type of role.

When Callas received Bing's initial telegram she was about to go on-stage for the first *Traviata* in Dallas. His greeting ended with: 'But why in Dallas?' Callas did not answer. The second telegram arrived on 6 November, during the dress rehearsal for *Medea* also in Dallas. It was in the form of an ultimatum in which Bing demanded Callas's immediate acceptance of the three *Lucias* instead of the three *Traviatas* but again in alternation with *Macbeth*. 'Prussian tactics,' Callas exclaimed and answered the telegram on the following day, refusing the *Lucias*. Before receiving her reply, or so he pretended had been the case, Bing sent a third telegram which arrived a few hours before the performance of *Medea*, notifying her that he had cancelled her contract. 'So Mr Bing cancels my contract and does it today. It might affect my Medea. Pray for me tonight,' Maria begged her friends.

Moreover, Bing's statement to the press deviated completely from the point at issue and concentrated impertinently on Callas's previous disagreements with other theatres, as well as remarking at this late hour that her artistry was controversial. The man who had appeared so sympathetic to Maria's trouble in Rome was now airing his own ego or was perhaps trying to justify his mishandling of the whole affair. 'I do not propose,' he stated,

> to enter into a public feud with Mme Callas since I am well aware that she has considerably greater competence and experience at that kind of thing than I have. . . . Although Mme Callas's artistic qualifications are a matter of violent controversy between her friends and foes, her reputation for projecting her undisputed histrionic talents into her business affairs is a matter of common knowledge. This, together with her insistence on a claimed right to alter or abrogate a contract at will or at whim, has finally led to the present situation, merely a repetition of the experience which nearly every major opera house has had in attempting to deal with her. . . . Mme Callas is constitutionally unable to fit into any organization not tailored to her own personality . . . the Metropolitan is nevertheless also grateful that the association is ended. . . . So, on with the season!

Meanwhile on a picture of Callas which decorated Bing's office an inscription appeared: 'You are fired, darling!' The identity of its author was soon to become an open secret – Bing himself. Afterwards, as if putting other people's words into his mouth, he wrote in his autobiography: 'Some of my associates later came to believe that Miss Callas was afraid of Lady Macbeth, a terrifying role rising to a D flat which of course she would have to sing herself (one could not imagine a chorister supplying a high note for Maria Callas).' With this statement Bing had, in effect, demolished his own case – this time, his notoriously sardonic wit misfired. The words he implied are completely unrelated to the dispute at issue and neither with the greatest stretch of the imagination nor plain bitchery could anyone suggest that there had ever been an occasion or even a rumour that a chorister, or anybody else, would sing Callas's high notes for her in any performance past or present. The cancellation of Callas's contract elicitated several diatribes against

Bing; Paul Hume, the music critic from Washington DC, demanded that he should resign and Harry Golden, the American essayist-philosopher, accused him of depriving the Metropolitan of such a sublime artist.

More hurt than angry, Callas gave her own version of her quarrel with the Metropolitan about five months later:

> I did not refuse to sing *Macbeth* and *Traviata*. On the contrary, I was delighted to sing, at last, in a new production – the first offered me at the Metropolitan – of *Macbeth*, an opera I had previously done well at La Scala. What I refused to do was to sing first *Macbeth*, then two *Traviatas*, then *Macbeth* again. Since I am the only soprano who sings both these roles, I think I am entitled to some opinion about what is and is not possible with them.
>
> For Lady Macbeth the voice should be heavy, thick and strong. The role, and therefore the voice, should have an atmosphere of darkness. Violetta, on the other hand, is a sick woman. I see the role, and therefore the voice, as fragile, weak and delicate. It is a trapeze part filled with sick pianissimo. To change from one of these roles to the other requires a complete change of voice. Bing was asking me to treat my voice first as a punch, then as a caress, then as a punch again. My voice is not an elevator which goes up and down. If I were at the beginning of my career I would have been forced to do it, but now I will not risk the strain and damage. It is asking far too much, really asking for trouble, both mentally and physically. When I tried to explain my case to Bing, he offered to substitute *Lucia* for *Traviata*, but since that is another trapeze part I am afraid he missed the point.

In spite of all her explanations, which are logical enough, Callas admitted that she still could not really understand Bing's behaviour in this matter. She thought that her difficulties with him might have had something to do with the fact that they could not agree on a programme for the next season in 1959–60.

> For the following winter Bing offered me three operas, namely the Met's old shabby production of *Norma*, the ancient *Lucia* in which the famous scene at the well is dominated by a monstrous well that covers half the stage and looks no more romantic than an oil tank, and *Il barbiere di Siviglia*, for which I simply could not work up any enthusiasm at that time. I told Bing that I would love to sing both *Norma* and *Lucia* for him but only if we could have new productions, long overdue. His answer was, 'Maria, if you sing, I can fill every seat with old productions.' I told him that I was delighted that because of me he earns for the Met a lot of money, but I suggested that he could do worse than spend some of this money on new productions so that I will not feel ashamed of them. I then suggested *Anna Bolena* (in place of *Il barbiere*), an opera in which I have had tremendous

success at La Scala. 'No,' Bing said, 'that is an old bore of an opera.' The fact that we could not agree on the 1959–60 season may have influenced Bing five months before in the cancellation of my contract.

Calling Bing a Prussian corporal in artistic matters, Callas summed up the situation, 'For him *Macbeth, Lucia, La sonnambula, Il barbiere, La Gioconda* are all neatly lined up, side by side, within the same category of interpretation.'

Nevertheless, in all fairness to Bing, though not in an attempt to absolve him from this unfortunate affair, Meneghini's share of skulduggery behind the scenes must be mentioned. As he himself revealed in *Maria Callas mia moglie* after Callas's death, Meneghini, though not the culprit in the disagreement with Bing, was at the very least guilty of acting as an *agent provocateur*. There had never been much love between Bing and the financially greedy Meneghini. As his wife became more and more famous, his interest in money increased. Callas did not have the time, nor was it in her nature, to involve herself in matters outside her artistic commitments. Had Meneghini in this case acted as an honest and tactful referee, the regrettable public duelling between Callas and Bing might well have been averted. Instead Meneghini threw spanners into the works to curtail any dialogue with Bing and thus provoked him into cancelling Callas's contract. Boasting of his entrepreneurial expertise, Meneghini confessed, 'I found out from concert promoters in Dallas that here was an opportunity for Maria to make a grand concert tour of the United States with fantastic financial returns, as well as with the participation of television.'

Unfortunately for Meneghini's lucrative plan, Maria had signed to sing at the Metropolitan and was therefore not free. When her justified disagreement with Bing arose Meneghini was delighted: 'It was necessary to exasperate him [Bing] to such a degree that he would cancel the contract himself. Bing could not stand the sight of me. He had described me as greedy and grasping and that only money was important to me. You can see how annoyed the "Prussian corporal" would be if outwitted by me.'

Meneghini also described another of his contests with Bing, which reveals further the lack of any rapport between them. Bing apparently was saying that Meneghini always insisted on being paid Maria's fee in cash, which he invariable counted before letting her go on stage. 'One day,' Bing said, 'I shall play a trick on that miser by paying him his wife's fee in single dollar bills. That will teach him a lesson.' When Meneghini heard about this he spread the word, so that it would reach Bing's ears, that he would make himself comfortable and forbid Maria to begin the performance before he had finished counting all that paper twice.

Of course, Bing cannot be acquitted of his misguided stubbornness in the affair of Callas's contract on the pretext that Meneghini was very tiresome, but without Meneghini adding fuel to the fire Bing might have shown more understanding of her artistic demands, which were, after all, not unreasonable. Even though Callas lost her contract with the Metropolitan, Meneghini's much-hoped-for lucrative concert tour never materialized: 'We did not get very far with it.'

Six months later Meneghini's goose which laid the golden eggs abandoned him, but it is only fair to mention that after Callas's death he did accept a great deal of the responsibility for his wife's disagreements. In fact, he exonerated her as a 'basically pacifist and tranquil woman'. Furthermore, he was anxious to tell me that Maria was never the stingy, demanding and even unbending woman she was at times made out to be. It was he who dealt with all financial matters and who demanded and obtained exorbitant fees for her performances, because according to his philosophy this was necessary for her fame as the world's premier singer.

Bing engaged Leonie Rysanek for the abortive Callas *Macbeth*. Many years later, he admitted in his memoirs that he had influenced the reception of the opera: 'I hired a claque to shout at Rysanek's entrance, "*Brava Callas!*" I counted on the American love for the underdog to resent this intervention, and to balance the scales a little for Rysanek.' His innovation did more harm to Callas than good to Rysanek; neither Bing nor the claqueur was blamed for this. It just added a little more obloquy to Callas's name.

All Maria's quarrels have been spectacular and undoubtedly in her determination to preserve her artistic beliefs she sometimes allowed other things, such as tact, to go by the board. 'Bing accused me of being difficult,' she said.

> Of course I am difficult, so are all serious, responsible artists. They've got to be. Bing did not have to take it out on me. I should not have paid for his problems with other artists as well.
>
> I will miss the Met public, which is among the finest in the world, eager to hear and appreciate something new on the rare occasions when it is offered. But I will not miss the Met productions with their scenery and costumes from the Middle Ages.
>
> I have lost some great opera houses and I regret it. I regret the misunderstandings and the occasional outright dishonesty and unfairness on the part of supposedly responsible men that have created these situations.
>
> When I have really said or done something, I take full responsibility. I am not an angel and do not pretend to be. That is not one of my roles. But I am not a devil, either. I am a woman and a serious artist, and I would like to be so judged.

Whatever the reasons, the Metropolitan was the fourth major opera house to dispense with her services. In the space of less than two years she had lost Vienna, Rome and La Scala. Nevertheless, following her break with the Metropolitan Callas was inundated with offers from various American companies. She only agreed to appear in *Il pirata* in concert performances at Carnegie Hall in New York, and in Washington DC, primarily because she liked the opera and had sung it at La Scala with enormous success. She also looked forward to showing Bing how much she was appreciated by the American public.

Since the spring of 1957, when Maria had begun to feel that the strain and fatigue of the preceding extremely hard-working years were catching up with her, she had decided to reduce drastically the number of her engagements. But because of previous commitments she was unable to do that soon enough and she paid for the consequences. In the final analysis the blow of losing the Metropolitan was very significant for her, especially as it struck within a few months after she was forced to leave La Scala. She was terribly unhappy and for the first time, as she revealed to me almost twenty years later, she began to question in her mind her husband's ability and wisdom in handling her affairs. Undoubtedly Meneghini had been acting in good faith, but was that enough? The thought of her career collapsing preoccupied her and she knew that the higher one has climbed, the deeper the fall will be. Additionally, she had discovered that Battista secretly had used a huge amount of her money to make investments in his own name. They had a row and although he talked his way out of the argument, her trust in his handling of her finances was never again restored completely. In fact, she tried secretly to find ways for her fees no longer to be paid to him or to be deposited in their joint account. But above all she tried, out of fear, to convince herself that her very personal feelings about her marriage were not damaged by her recent misfortunes and began to show her love for her husband more demonstratively in public than she had ever done before.

Her next engagement after Dallas was her début in Paris, where she sang in a gala concert on 19 December at the Opéra before René Coty, President of France. It was a benefit performance with the proceeds going to the Légion d'honneur. The glittering audience paid the highest prices ever charged at the Opéra and Callas also donated her $10,000 fee to the cause. For them she sang arias from *Norma*, *Il trovatore*, *Il barbiere di Siviglia* and then appeared in the complete second act of *Tosca* with Tito Gobbi as Scarpia and Albert Lance as Cavaradossi. She captivated the Parisians, who gave her standing ovations unprecedented in Paris within living memory. The performance was also televised complete throughout Europe. The love and devotion the French so warmly lavished on her boosted her self-confidence and once again she looked forward very much to singing in America.

She gave a concert in Philadelphia, before going to New York to sing in *Il pirata* for the New York American Opera Society. People turned out in their thousands to cheer her and a practically unknown Bellini opera. On the following day a citation by the Mayor of New York honoured her with the 'Freedom of the City', the place where she was born.

Apart from a week in March, when she recorded *Lucia di Lammermoor* in London, Callas spent the next three months with her husband mainly at Sirmione. In April the Meneghinis celebrated their tenth wedding anniversary in Paris, where a radiant Maria could not stop talking about the happiness she had found with her beloved husband. Her exaggerated efforts to tell the world how much she owed him were misconstrued a couple of years later, as a sign that she was already involved emotionally with another man and she was desperately trying to squash these dangerous feelings. The future, however, proved this to have been a superficial and groundless conclusion. What was rapidly coming between Callas and her husband at that stage of their lives was not another man but her career, inasmuch as the most famous opera singer in the world was barred from singing in four of the major opera houses. Although Meneghini was not the direct cause of this depressing state of affairs, he could be seriously criticized, none the less, for his misguided notion that money is the most important factor in every negotiation, a principle that rendered him incapable as an agent in handling the situations in which his wife (and client) had been involved. Even so, Callas still had Covent Garden, where all five performances of her *Medea* were sold out on the first day of booking six weeks earlier. After a spectacular concert tour in Spain and Germany, she arrived in London early in June.

Through an enterprising exchange scheme Covent Garden would put on Minotis's Dallas production of *Medea* while the Dallas Civic Opera would get in return Zeffirelli's Covent Garden production of *Lucia di Lammermoor*. This arrangement would make it possible for London to see Callas in *Medea* and afterwards for Dallas to see her in *Lucia*. The cast for *Medea* was the same with the exception of the heavily pregnant Berganza who was replaced by Fiorenza Cossotto. On 17 June London saw its first *Medea* in over ninety years. It was a powerful performance and the way Callas combined vocal and dramatic resources in her characterization of the highly complex heroine left the audience greatly impressed and moved.

The critic of *The Times* (18 June 1959) wrote: 'What Miss Callas does is to paint the character in strong colours by vocal inflexions that are pointed with significant gestures i.e., she is an operatic actress with the voice as her chief but not her only instrument. She was in good voice . . . with phrasing moulded to show every shift of emotion. It is this play of conflicting, oscillating, burning feelings that is the core of the opera and it is this fluctuation which Miss Callas can convey with unique art.'

Watching one of these performances of *Medea* from a secluded corner in the wings of Covent Garden, I was able to study closely the artist/woman at work and how she behaved towards her colleagues. After the opera had started I saw Callas's lithe figure, her cloak trailing behind her, coming alone from her dressing-room to wait for her first entrance. She seemed nervous and she gave me the impression that she was rather lost, whereupon she began to pray quietly and, oblivious of anyone present, crossing herself several times in the manner of the Greek Orthodox Church. This moving scene distracted my attention from the stage and I began to observe her unseen.

'A mysterious woman is outside the gates' ('*Fermo una donna a vostra soglie sta*'), they announce on the stage. Promptly Callas knocked gently on wood, presumably for luck, and then, sweeping up her cloak to cover her face to her eyes, heavily rimmed with black, as her first appearance demands, made her way on to the stage. Standing between two huge pillars, her eyes filled with what looked like implacable hatred, she raised her hand as the words '*Io Medea*' fell like a thunderbolt. She had already become Medea and I saw the transformation while time stood still, or so it seemed. The metamorphosis continued as she went through the gamut of emotions, at the same time carrying the tremendous burden of her long role to the end.

It must not be thought that Callas, who was consistently in character, was in some kind of trance. During the interval she was her natural self and in fact she helped Cossotto, who seemed to have some difficulty with the role of Neris: Maria rehearsed with her on-stage for about fifteen minutes, singing *sotto voce*. A few minutes later the performance began and there was nothing amiss. I was enthralled until the scene when Medea attempts to kill her children. At one moment Callas, brandishing the knife, her face twisted by anger and despair, came very close to me. She then turned round abruptly and threw the knife away. Knowing that she was so short-sighted (without her spectacles she could not see the conductor and she was unable to wear contact lenses) and that she has to find the knife later, I worried as I could not see it myself. Meanwhile Medea ran up the steps to the temple, cursed her enemies and right on time picked up the knife.[1]

At the end of the performance and after many curtain-calls, Maria wanted Jon Vickers (Jason) to take another on his own. He was reluctant to do so, even when Maria jokingly threatened to kick him on to the stage. Suddenly she pushed him and Vickers faced a cheering audience alone, while Maria in the wings was also applauding.

For some reason her maid was not there to help her back to her dressing-room. As she set off on her own, I followed her through the backstage labyrinth until she heard my footsteps, stopped round a corner and caught me with both hands. We were chattering about the performance when suddenly she raised her voice, accusing me of making her late: 'Do you realize that the Queen is waiting for me?' 'It is not the Queen but the Queen Mother,'[2] I informed her with a touch of smugness. Waving her hand rather extravagantly, Maria declared, 'Same thing, isn't it!' I then escorted her to her dressing-room.

After the first performance of *Medea* Aristotle Onassis and his wife Tina gave a sumptuous party at the Dorchester Hotel, with Callas as their guest of honour.

As already stated, the Meneghinis first met Onassis and his wife at the party Elsa Maxwell gave in Venice on 3 September 1957. There was nothing memorable about that meeting and Callas made no great impression on Onassis, nor he on her. He was merely courteous, without his usual exuberance, for during that period he and his wife were being very attentive to one another in public to squash rumours that their marriage was on the rocks. Onassis had been seeing other women and Maxwell particularly wanted him at the party to save Tina, her devoted friend, from further humiliation.

The second meeting was not until 19 December 1958 when Onassis and his wife saw Callas briefly in her dressing-room after she had sung at the gala concert for the Légion d'honneur at the Opéra in Paris. In April 1959 the two couples met again at the Venice house of Wally Toscanini, where Callas was the guest of honour at a party. On this occasion the Onassises went out of their way to endear themselves to the Meneghinis, inviting them for a cruise on their yacht, the *Christina*. Maria, however, declined the invitation politely: she was about to embark on a concert tour in Spain and Germany during the best part of May, and in June she would be singing Medea at Covent Garden and she could not turn her mind to anything else.

Reminiscing in 1978, Meneghini told me that Onassis's friendly behaviour towards them increased tremendously on the night Maria sang for President Coty and selected glitterati in Paris. 'He was really dazzled with such an audience paying homage to Maria unreservedly. Both he and his wife were full of Mediterranean charm and warmth when they called at Maria's dressing-room at the end of the concert to congratulate her. Maria, naturally, also received them warmly but indifferently. Her mind was still on her singing as she always needed time to unwind after a performance. But even later that night at our hotel, when I mentioned the Onassises, Maria made no comment, which meant our meeting with the Greeks was of no particular consequence.'

In Venice, where Maria had turned down their invitation for the cruise and mentioned her *Medea* performances in London, Onassis promptly responded, 'We shall be there.' And so he was. Seizing the opportunity presented by Callas's appearances in London and still having in his mind her triumph, both social and artistic, of the Paris concert, he sought to do something similar in London. Not only did he invite thirty people to the opening night of *Medea* (he obtained the tickets by paying astronomical prices on the black market), but he also gave a party at the Dorchester Hotel with Callas as guest of honour. The primary reason for this grand occasion was to serve as a demonstration of Anglo-Greek friendship, which was badly strained because of the Cypriot fight for independence. In fact, two years before, Onassis had sent one of his tankers to take Archbishop Makarios, the Cypriot leader, back to Cyprus on his release from the Seychelles where he had been exiled by the British. Onassis's guests for *Medea* included the Duchess of Kent and her daughter Princess Alexandra, Lady Churchill and her daughter Lady Soames, Sir Winston Churchill, Margot Fonteyn and other important people from the English aristocracy. Also invited were the whole cast of *Medea* in which, along with Callas, other illustrious Greeks were taking part: Minotis, an old friend of Onassis, was producing the opera, Tsarouchis designed the sets and costumes, Maria Hors the choreography and Zaccaria was singing the role of Creon.

Maria received Onassis's invitation a few days before she left Milan for London. Her first reaction was to decline as she had a series of performances to give and little time for diversions. However, by the time she arrived in London the publicity about the party had assumed such dimensions, and Meneghini was so much in favour of going, that in the end Maria gave in.

The Onassises surpassed themselves as hosts. Decorated entirely in pink, the Dorchester ball-room with two orchestras created an atmosphere of elegance and grandeur. When Callas made her entrance, after 1 a.m., all the guests stood and applauded her. It was a very enjoyable evening, which undoubtedly owed not a little to the infectious exuberance and prodigious hospitality of the host. Even so, after almost two hours Maria and her husband left at 3 a.m. She pleaded exhaustion as she had, after all, sung Medea earlier that evening. Just as she was leaving Onassis, who accompanied her to the exit of the hotel, repeated his invitation for the cruise. Maria responded with a wide, enigmatic smile and a promise to think about it.

The performances of *Medea* continued with enormous success and before leaving London Callas agreed to return to Covent Garden the following year. *Lucia* was very much on the cards for her, as was the possibility of borrowing the production of *Anna Bolena* from La Scala, so that London could witness one of Callas's unique portrayals. On her way home she gave a concert at the Holland Festival in Amsterdam, and also in Brussels, arriving at Sirmione on 15 July to begin a six-week holiday.

Following her doctor's advice to spend time by the sea, Maria planned to go the Lido in Venice for a month. However, the day after the Meneghinis arrived at Sirmione Onassis began to telephone them. Maria would not answer the calls, instructing her housekeeper to say that she was not there. Eventually, after several calls from the persistent Onassis, Meneghini spoke to him. The Onassises were pressing them to accept their invitation for a cruise, but Meneghini said that apart from everything else, he needed to be in constant touch with his mother, who was seriously ill. 'You will have no problem with that,' Onassis assured him. 'There are hundreds of radio telephones on the *Christina*.' Tina also came to the telephone and between them, husband and wife persuaded Meneghini to try and get Maria to join the cruise. 'We will have a great time. The Churchills, including Sir Winston will be on board,' Onassis added. Both of them then spoke to Maria and, together with Meneghini's support, they persuaded her.

Later on that day Maria had second thoughts, preferring to go to the Lido as originally planned. 'This invitation', Meneghini told her, 'is absolutely timely. The doctor has prescribed sea air and we cannot find that better than on a boat. It would be absurd for us to buy a boat and it is common knowledge that the *Christina* is very comfortable indeed. I do think we must go. If you find that you are not very happy with it, we can always leave at the first port and return home.' Maria ran out of excuses and within a week she had ordered a superb cruising wardrobe from Biki of Milan.

On 22 July the *Christina* sailed from Monte Carlo through calm as well as stormy seas. She took her distinguished guests through the Italian and Greek waters as far as Istanbul. None of the four principals was even remotely aware of what destiny had in store for them.

1   Two days later, a mutual Italian friend and I teased Maria that she was hanging around the stage, like a blind woman, looking for the knife. It took a few minutes and some comic demonstration of how she went about it (she was rather slow in such matters) for her to get the joke. After laughing heartily and sending herself up, she became serious and explained: 'Because I am "blind" my hearing is very good. I only had to hear the knife fall to know exactly where it was.'
2   The Queen Mother, who saw the performance, was that evening expecting Callas for dinner at Clarence House.

LA VESTALE

Opera in three acts by Spontini; libretto in French by Étienne de Jouy. First performed at the Paris Opéra on 16 December 1807.

Callas sang Giulia in *La vestale* five times at La Scala in 1954.

Act I: *The forum in Rome near the temple of Vesta. It is dawn.* The High Priestess (Stignani) informs Giulia (Callas), a vestal virgin, that she has been chosen to bestow the hero's wreath on Licinius in the forthcoming triumphal ceremony. She also warns her that sexual love is punishable by death.

Callas's responses were full of formal pathos: 'E l'amore un mostro' ('Love is a monster'). In 'Oh di funesta possa invincibil commando' ('Oh distressing day, I cannot control my feelings'), she expressed Giulia's inner struggle between love and duty – the scales weighing heavily on the side of love for Licinius – with a tenderness devoid of sentimentality.

Above Giulia places the golden wreath on Licinius (Corelli), who secretly persuades her to meet him later that evening at the temple so that they may elope.

Callas's whispered, yet resounding 'Sostenemi, o Numi!' ('Restrain me o Gods!') conveyed fully her decision in favour of love. The High Priestess is behind Giulia, the High Priest (Rossi-Lemeni) in the centre.

Left Act 2: *Inside the Temple of Vesta. It is night.* The High Priestess instructs Giulia to guard the everlasting sacred flame and reminds her of her chastity vows. Alone, Giulia again prays for strength to resist her love for Licinius.

The grave melody of 'Tu che invoco, cor orrore Dea tremenda' ('I appeal to you tremendous Goddess'), superbly sculpted by the composer like a Renaissance statue, became memorable through Callas's ability to express profound emotions with extraordinary though deceptive simplicity and perfect style.

Above Licinius breaks into the forbidden temple and urges Giulia to elope with him. As she almost succumbs, the sacred flame goes out. Giulia refuses to flee and Licinius leaves to seek help to save her from her inevitable fate.

Right Giulia refuses to name the man who was with her but admits her own guilt; her vestal decorations are removed and she is sentenced to be buried alive.

Callas's prayer for Licinius's safety, 'O Numi tutelar degli infelici' ('Oh Gods protect the unhappy'), a feat of vocal colours, achieved a stillness at once chaste and sensual, which is the personification of Giulia.

ANDREA CHÉNIER

Opera in four acts by Giordano; libretto by Illica. First performed at La Scala on 28 March 1896. Callas sang Maddalena six times at La Scala in January/February 1955.

Left and below Act I: *The ballroom at the chateau of Countess di Coigny.* When the poet Andrea Chénier (Del Monaco), a guest at the ball, refuses to recite a poem, Maddalena (Callas), the Countess's daughter, ironically provokes him. Chénier improvises 'Un dì all'azzuro spazio guardai, profondo' ('One day I looked at the boundless blue sky'). Contrasting the love and beauty of nature with the misery of underprivileged man, the poem becomes a revolutionary proclamation. Chénier ends by telling Maddalena not to scorn love, the divine gift of the world. She begs his forgiveness; the other guests are scandalised. The Abbé (Carlin) and Maddalena's mother (Amadini) are sitting on the right.

Act 3: *The Revolutionary Tribunal.* Maddalena visits her ex-servant Gérard (Protti), now a leader of the Tribunal, who has always secretly loved her. She repulses his advances and sadly recalls the destruction of her family during the Revolution: 'La mamma morta m'hanno alla porta della stanza mia' ('My mother was killed on the threshold of my room'). It was her love for Chénier that kept her alive. Even so, she now offers herself to Gérard if he will save Chénier, who has been arrested for anti-revolutionary activities. Deeply moved, Gérard agrees to save him, but presently it transpires that an enemy of Chénier has already prepared his trial, with the inevitable death sentence.

Callas brought to this aria an individuality and abandon that amounted to living emotion, primarily achieved through musical means.

IL BARBIERE DI SIVIGLIA

Opera in two acts by Rossini; libretto by Sterbini. First performed at the Teatro Argentina, Rome, on 20 February 1816.

Callas sang Rosina in *Il barbiere* five times at La Scala in 1956.

Left Act 1: *A drawing-room in Dr Bartolo's house in Seville.* Rosina (Callas) meditates that the man she only knows as Lindoro will be hers no matter what her awful guardian, Bartolo, may do. Her dreamy thoughts soon change to spirited self-eulogising: 'Io sono docile, son respettosa, sono obbediente, dolce amorosa' ('I am sweet and respectful, humble, obedient and most affectionate'). But, if anyone crosses her path, she can be a viper.

Callas's slight stridency, the uneven and inappropriate vocal colour suggested a scheming virago rather than a mischievous and charming *ingénue*.

Below The sly Rosina learns from Figaro (Gobbi) that Lindoro does love her: 'Dunque io son – tu non m'inganni?' ('Can it be true, dare I believe you?'). Figaro gives her a letter from the young man and suggests she answer it. Rosina protests, but surprises Figaro: 'Un biglietto? ecco lo qua' ('Write a letter? Well, here it is').

Callas was flirtatious, appropriately coy in her badinage with Figaro. The lightening of her voice, her jaunty laugh were those of a vivacious girl in love until she produced the letter, after which she turned shrewish and shifted the emphasis from Figaro – incongruously she had the whole situation wrapped up in her hands.

Left Rosina is more than a match for Bartolo (Luise) when he scolds her for writing letters. Her clever little lies further upset him while his warnings of punishment are totally ignored.

Below Count Almaviva (Alva) – Lindoro to Rosina – disguised as a drunken soldier has forced his way into Bartolo's house demanding to be billeted. He gives Rosina a note before Basilio (Rossi-Lemeni – centre), music teacher and Bartolo's friend, appears. The police arrive but the officer salutes the drunken soldier: the Count gloats over his fairly successful ruse and old Bartolo's helplessness.

Act 2: *The library of Dr Bartolo's house.* The Count poses as a teacher, sent by a supposedly ill Basilio to give Rosina her music lesson. Bartolo is fooled, Rosina is delighted and using words from the aria 'Contro un cor che accende amore' ('When a heart is glowing with love') teacher and pupil confirm their love for each other.

Although, by and large, Callas's interpretation was, in theory, well conceived, it was not fully successful in practice: she did provide some necessary appealing moments of repose, but the slight unevenness and unsteadiness in her singing somewhat marred the accomplishment.

MEDEA

Opera in three acts by Cherubini, with recitatives to replace the original spoken dialogue by Franz Lachner; libretto in French by François Benoit Hoffman, in Italian by Carlo Zangarini. First performed at the Théâtre Feydeau, Paris, on 13 March 1797.

Callas first sang Medea in Florence in 1953 and last at La Scala in 1962, a total of thirty-one performances

Act I: *King Creon's palace in Corinth.* The barbarian Colchian Princess Medea (Callas) arrives to reclaim her husband Jason: 'Io? Medea' ('I am Medea') falls like a thunderbolt, establishing, there and then, the ferocious side of Medea's character (Covent Garden, 1959).

Act 2: *Outside a wing of Creon's palace.*
Medea craftily pleads with Creon
(Zaccaria) to allow her to stay for her
children – Jason she can forget. Creon
urges her to leave if only for her own sake.
Moved at last, Creon grants Medea one
more day with her children: 'Date almen
per pietà un asilo a Medea' ('In pity at
least grant asylum to Medea').

Although Jason rejects Medea's pleading to see her children, she is secretly jubilant when she realises how much they mean to him. Using all her guile and duplicity, she persuades him to give way to her. There is, however, no elation in Medea's victory – Jason has been irrevocably lost to her.

Both vocally and physically, Callas became in turn the embodiment of wretchedness and supplication, suspense, jubilation and heart-break (La Scala, 1962).

When Jason leaves, Medea again thinks of revenge: 'Caro pagar dovrai ... D'amaro pianto a te sarò cagion' ('You will pay dearly ... with bitter tears') (Covent Garden, 1959).

Watching Jason's and Glauce's wedding ceremony, Medea vows to end this celebration: her gift to the bride, a poisonous diadem, will kill her.

Callas was filled with the wrath of an avenging Fury: 'Questa promessa un dì tu l'avesti per me! Amor, la mia vendetta appresta' ('Once he made the same promise to me. God of Love, hasten my vengeance') (La Scala, 1962).

Left Act 3: *A hill near Creon's palace. It is a stormy night.* Liberated from doubt, Medea resorts to sorcery.

A dark, venomous tone infused Callas's voice while, in a frenzy, she beat the ground: 'Numi, venite a me, inferni Dei' ('Infernal gods, come to my aid').

Below Medea repels her children and raises her dagger to slay them. She falters and, throwing the dagger away, embraces them lovingly.

A tenderness permeated Callas's voice, which now assumed great lyrical qualities: 'No, cari figli, no!' ('No! My dear sons, no!'). For a while she was at peace with herself.

Medea's fury gathers momentum and although her motherly feelings return once more, finally she rushes into the temple, where she slays her children.

When Callas appeared before Jason and the Corinthians, in a serpent-entwined chariot, her slain children lying at her feet, she released all the built-up tension of the world of the cursed woman, who at last finds redemption: 'A sacro fiume io vo' colà t'aspetta l'ombra mia' ('I go now to the Styx, the sacred river, where my shade will await you').

Callas's curtain call as Medea, with Simionato and Vickers, on 3 June 1962, was also her last at La Scala.

FEDORA

Opera in three acts by Giordano; libretto by Colautti. First performed at the Teatro Lirico, Milan, on 17 November 1898.

Callas sang Fedora six times at La Scala in May 1956.

Act I: *The drawing-room of Count Vladimir in St Petersburg.* On the eve of their wedding, Vladimir, the fiancé of Princess Fedora Romazov (Callas), is brought in unconscious; he was found shot in a hunting-lodge.

Callas's 'body language' presented a Russian aristocrat, anxious and imperial in manner and, looking at her fiancé's portrait, 'O grandi occhi lucenti di fede!' ('O shining eyes, so large, so truthful!'), a woman passionately in love. When Vladimir dies her tender feelings gave way to an anguished cry of vengeance.

Act 2: *A grand reception in Fedora's house in Paris. A few months later.* Believing Loris (Corelli) to be a nihilist and Vladimir's murderer, Fedora pressurizes him to admit that he has killed her fiancé. Loris refutes the charge half-heartedly and leaves, promising to return later that evening. News of an assassination attempt on the Tsar by nihilists breaks up the party. Before Loris returns, Fedora writes to Yariskin, Chief of Police in St Petersburg and Vladimir's father, of Loris's alleged confession.

In her effort to destroy Loris, Callas also betrayed, intermittently, her sexual attraction to him: 'Hola prova suprema . . . la confessione sua!' ('I now have absolute proof . . . his confession'). But on discovering the truth (Vladimir was the lover of Loris's wife and Loris shot him in self-defence), Callas admitted her love unreservedly: 'Loris, no parto più!' ('Loris, I will never leave you').

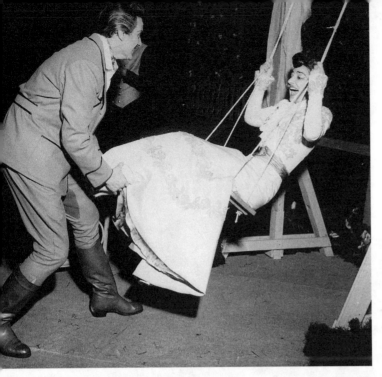

Act 3: *The garden of Fedora's villa by Lake Thun, Bernese Oberland.* Fedora and Loris have been living blissfully together for the past three months. Learning that his brother, who was arrested as a nihilist, was found dead in prison and that his mother also died from the shock, Loris curses the anonymous informer – a Russian woman domiciled in Paris.

Callas's pleading for this woman is so impassioned that Loris soon realises that Fedora herself was the informer; he repulses her violently but she takes poison before she can be prevented. Her dying words, 'Ho freddo . . . Loris ricaldami . . . T'amo!' ('I am so cold . . . Loris warm me . . . I love you'), as she received Loris's forgiveness, were unforgettable.

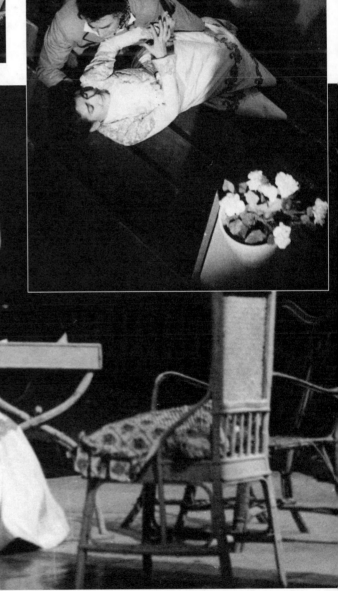

PART FIVE

Life Beyond Art

• CHAPTER FOURTEEN •

A FATED GREEK CRUISE AND ONASSIS

O N THE EVENING of 22 July the luxurious *Christina*, with her distinguished passengers, a crew of sixty and hosts who were anxious to provide their guests with every amenity, comfort and entertainment imaginable, sailed from Monte Carlo in an atmosphere of carefree jollity. Aboard this floating *sans souci* there existed a world which the Meneghinis presently discovered to be different from anything they had ever known. It was not so much the luxury, for they too were used to that, but the way that one lived only for oneself without a worry for past or present and, more significantly, no thought for the future, that made a profound impression on them, though in diametrically opposite ways. Maria responded immediately; the tension and nervous exhaustion that had been plaguing her during the last two years seemed to have vanished almost overnight and she was happy to grasp this freedom, this lightness that was there for the taking. For the moment, she even put aside her vocal problems which had first manifested themselves, albeit intermittently, at the time of her quarrels with the opera houses. Thus Maria began her voyage of self-discovery and with it gradually came an inner strength that liberated her from her absolute dependence on her husband for everything other than artistic matters, and before very long she stopped professing to herself and to everybody else that her feelings for Battista had not changed.

It was a different story for Meneghini who, despite his wife's companionship, though now less close, felt progressively more uncomfortable and taciturn; if he was not dozing he was grumbling to Maria that some of the other guests were slighting him. As he only spoke Italian – his French and English were minimal – and would not show much interest in anything that was going on, he may well have misunderstood the other guests' feelings towards him. But nothing would have mattered and he would have felt perfectly happy had his wife's undivided attention not been slackening day by day.

Something else played on his mind. On the morning of the day of their departure Elsa Maxwell, who was at Monte Carlo but not on the cruise, wrote a letter to Maria offering her unsolicited advice. As was the Meneghinis' rule Maria did not read the letter. However, this impertinent communication upset Meneghini not a little and he kept thinking about it as a possible ill omen. After wishing them a wonderful voyage and praising their host and his yacht rather extravagantly, Maxwell got to the point:

> You, Maria, are replacing Greta Garbo, who is much too old now for the *Christina*. Good luck. I never liked Garbo, but I loved you. Henceforth enjoy every moment. Take everything (this is the most discreet of arts). Give (this is the most important art) only all that you feel like giving: this is the true course of happiness which you will have to discover by yourself alone. . . . Now I have not even the desire to see you. The world is already saying that you only wanted to use me. I refuse to accept this. What little I have done for you, I did with my heart and soul and with my eyes wide open. . . . (PS Yesterday Ari and Tina invited me to dinner with you for tonight. I could not refuse).

'The first shock on the *Christina*', Meneghini later remarked rather facetiously, 'was seeing Onassis naked [presumably in a bathing costume]. He was so hairy that I thought he was a gorilla. Maria also laughed at this sight.' Nevertheless, Meneghini found Onassis a most considerate and pleasant host, who further impressed him enormously by his genuine veneration of Churchill; Onassis played cards with him and was always ready to assist the incontinent elder statesman with even his humblest needs. In order to take Churchill sightseeing in the places where the *Christina* stopped, Onassis had a special vehicle constructed which was kept on the yacht. Churchill would remain seated in it as it was lowered to shore.

Portofino and Capri were the first ports of call. Then the *Christina* sailed through the Isthmus of Corinth to Piraeus, stopping on the way for sightseeing. There were excursions to Corinth, Mycenae and the ancient theatre of Epidaurus where Callas sang a few phrases to test its legendary acoustics. On 4 August the *Christina* made an unscheduled call at Smyrna. Onassis wanted to show his guests his birthplace, though in the evening he took only Meneghini to dinner in the old port of the town so that he could see some of the dives which are steeped in local colour. They returned to the boat in the early hours of the morning with Onassis blind drunk. After Smyrna they sailed to Istanbul where the Turkish Prime Minster, Adnan Menderes, came on board to pay his respects to Churchill. On the following day, when the *Christina* was anchored in the Bay of Bosphorus, the Greek Premier, Constantine Karamanlis, and his wife also came to see Churchill and to be entertained to lunch.

It was here, too, that Meneghini completely misconstrued an event which caused him to consolidate the bottled-up feelings that he had had about his wife's somewhat changed disposition towards him. 'Destiny destroyed my life', Meneghini revealed many years later, 'the day the Patriarch Athenagoras[1] received Onassis and his guests. The Patriarch knew of both Onassis and

*Callas and Meneghini visiting the theatre at Epidaurus during
the 'fated' cruise on the* Christina.

Maria Callas. I do not know why, but speaking to them in Greek he blessed them together. The whole scene looked as if the Patriarch was performing a marriage ceremony.'

Of course there was absolutely nothing unusual or sinister in the Patriarch's actions. He naturally spoke to them in Greek. As they both belonged to the Greek Orthodox religion and at the time were two of Greek's most famous ambassadors (he called Callas the greatest singer, Onassis the greatest modern sailor), he blessed them together. 'Maria was profoundly disturbed afterwards,' Meneghini continued.

> I could see an unusually glowing intensity in her eyes. When we returned to the yacht that evening, for the first time in all the years we were married she refused to come to bed.
> 'You can do what you like,' she told me, 'I am staying right here.'

I believe that my wife's affair with Onassis, sparked by the Patriarch's blessing, began in practice that evening. . . . Before that fated day I never thought even remotely that she would involve herself with another man. Be that as it may, from that day the rest of our time on the *Christina* became for me a living hell while Maria was gayer and appeared to be having a wonderful time, dancing continuously, and always with Onassis. I tried to convince myself that as Maria was, after all, still a young woman, it was not such a bad thing if she once in a while let her hair down and enjoyed herself. Having persuaded her to take the cruise in the first place, her renewed vitality was the best confirmation that the sea air her doctor had prescribed suited her.

However, three days later all my hopes that the whole thing was a storm in a teacup were dashed. When we returned from a party on shore to the *Christina* at 4 a.m., I went to bed immediately but Maria stayed behind to continue her dancing with Onassis. She never came to bed that night and in the morning assumed, at the slightest provocation, a rather offensive attitude towards me. 'You never leave me alone, trying to control my every move as if you are my jailer or some loathsome guardian. Can't you see you are suffocating me. I cannot be kept hemmed in all my life.' Maria then picked on my appearance, that I was never dressed elegantly and that I lacked all spirit of adventure.

Meneghini spent the day wondering at his wife's overwhelming change of heart. It did cross his mind that perhaps a dangerous relationship was developing between Onassis and Maria but he thought of reasons to dismiss such ideas at least for the moment: Maria had recently been asked

Callas with Sir Winston Churchill on board the Christina.

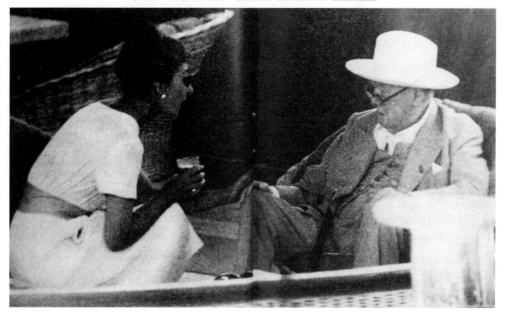

to appear in a major film and she might well be seeking advice of a business nature from Onassis who was, indisputably, highly astute and experienced in such matters.

Contrary to Meneghini's illusions, not only did Maria's attitude towards her husband not mellow but if anything it became harsher. When, on the following night around midnight Meneghini said that he was tired and going to bed, Maria responded indifferently: 'You just do that, I'm staying here.' Unable to sleep, Meneghini related what followed that night:

It was around 2 a.m. when I suddenly heard the door of our cabin open. In the darkness I faintly saw the figure of a woman almost completely naked. She entered the cabin and threw herself on the bed. Taking it for granted that Maria had at last come to bed, I embraced her, whereupon I realised immediately that she was not my wife. The woman was sobbing. It was Tina Onassis. 'Battista,' she said, 'it is so miserable for both of us. Your Maria is downstairs in the lounge in my husband's arms, and there is nothing we can do about it. He has taken her away from you.'

At first I naturally found Tina's confidences perplexing but soon I began to understand her. 'I have already decided to leave my husband,' she went on, 'and his present infidelity will get me my divorce. But you two were so much in love. When I first met you I envied the love and affection you had for one another. I feel especially sorry for you Battista and for poor Maria who will soon discover what kind of man he is.' Tina later revealed to me that her life with Onassis had never been happy and that he was a brutal drunk.

For obvious reasons it is difficult to know how much truth there is in Meneghini's story, which he made known twenty years later when the other three principal characters were dead. In his effort to convince the world that his wife, a happily married woman, would not have left him had Onassis, a debauched and unscrupulous seducer, not enticed her, Meneghini's feelings played havoc with his imagination. For instance, why was Tina almost naked when she walked into his cabin in the middle of the night and stayed there for some time? What if Maria had suddenly returned, or Onassis could not find his wife at two in the morning on a relatively small ship? Furthermore, since Tina had decided to part from her husband and was glad to have such excellent grounds for divorce, she could have done worse than, together with Meneghini, surprise the clandestine lovers. A plausible explanation is that Meneghini, lying sleepless alone while his wife was somewhere on the boat with Onassis, allowed his justifiable worry and suspicion to drag Tina, the hitherto absent protagonist, into his calamity.

The figments of Meneghini's imagination are exposed more conclusively in another of his stories. Writing in 1981, he alleged immorality on the *Christina* during the fated cruise. He first invented quite a number of extra guests:

On board were important people – Winston Churchill with his wife, his daughter Diana, his doctor Lord Moran, his secretary Anthony Montague Browne and his nurse. Churchill had also brought along his beloved little dog, Toby [Meneghini seems to have mistaken Toby for a *canis* when in fact it was a canary]. There were also Fiat's Gianni Agnelli with his wife Marella and many other Greek, American and English personalities. . . . For most of these people, life on board was frivolous and carefree. Their way of life was very different from that to which Maria and I were accustomed and to us these people appeared to be a little crazy. Several of the couples changed partners. The women, and also the men, often sunbathed nude and played with each other quite openly and in front of everyone. To put it bluntly I had the impression of finding myself in the middle of a pigpen.

By the time Meneghini wrote this most of the people concerned were dead. However, when his book was published in England in January 1983, Montague Browne, very much alive, put the record straight in a letter to *The Times* (23 January 1983) and demolished Meneghini's *mise-en-scène* on board the *Christina*, writing:

This is of course a total fabrication. Those present on this cruise, in the summer of 1959, were Sir Winston Churchill and Lady Churchill, Lord and Lady Moran, Mrs Diana Sandys (Sir Winston's eldest daughter) and her young daughter, Celia, and my wife and myself. Our hosts were Mr and Mrs Onassis. Professor and Mrs Garofalides (Mr Onassis's sister and brother-in-law) and Signor Meneghini and his wife were also of the party. . . . Neither Signor Agnelli nor his wife were ever present on any of the cruises on which Sir Winston sailed. Moreover there were no other 'Greek, American or English personalities'. Even on a yacht the size of *Christina* there would not have been room for anyone else. . . . He [Meneghini] suggests that episodes of gross impropriety took place. . . . It is unimaginable that Sir Winston and Lady Churchill or any of those associated with them would have tolerated anything of the nature described by Signor Meneghini. Moreover, the late Mr and Mrs Onassis were scrupulous in the care they took of Sir Winston on these cruises.'

Considering the dignity of the people present on this cruise one must be allowed to ponder for a moment on Churchill's amusement had he been aware of Meneghini's silly little fable.

But to return to the events, as related by Meneghini in 1981, that followed the end of the cruise. Within three hours the Meneghinis were in Milan, having flown from Nice in one of Onassis's private planes. There was no conversation between them except for Maria's statement that contrary to their earlier arrangement to go straight to Sirmione she was staying, alone, in Milan. Battista, she added, would be much better off at Sirmione, where he would be closer to his sick mother. Meneghini protested, saying that he had business to finish in Milan. In the end Maria agreed that he could work at night in Milan but spend the day at Sirmione. Two days later, Meneghini professed, Maria summoned him at noon to Milan and told him bluntly that their marriage was finished. She had decided to stay with Onassis. The shock was too much for Meneghini. He remained speechless as Maria continued: 'Ari and I have been caught in this twist of destiny and we cannot fight it. Its force is beyond us. We have done absolutely nothing wrong and have so far behaved strictly according to the accepted rules of morality and honesty, but neither of us can be apart from each other any longer.'

Maria then said that Onassis was in fact in Milan and anxious to talk to Meneghini, who readily agreed. Onassis arrived at ten that evening. Their meeting, which lasted a good five hours, was very civilized, both sides attempting to outdo one another in their courtesy and agreeing to try and keep the scandal to a minimum. According to Meneghini he told Onassis and Maria, both of whom were apparently behaving like two twenty-year-olds in love: 'As there is no other way out of this situation I will be helpful in expediting your plans.'

This does not sound very convincing, but as financial considerations had not yet been discussed Meneghini was playing his condescending part, while Onassis, no less hypocritically, was trying to evade moral issues. Neither Maria nor Onassis, who was of course still a very much married man, wanted to be denounced as an adulterer, for though they swore they had not broken any rules, they knew that many would not believe them.

Eventually Onassis departed, and Maria and her husband slept in their matrimonial bed for the remaining few hours of the night. It was the last time they shared it. Two days later, at Meneghini's instigation, Onassis and Maria travelled to Sirmione for another *vis-à-vis* confrontation. The civility that had characterized their previous meeting now vanished into thin air.

When they arrived Onassis was in high spirits. He had apparently been drinking whisky all the way from Milan. As soon as they began to talk, which was after they had dined, both men became quarrelsome, trading recriminations and almost coming to blows. At one point Onassis accused Meneghini of cruelty towards Maria, saying that although he knew he had lost her, he was making difficulties so as to deny her any happiness. Meneghini retaliated by calling Onassis all the abusive epithets he knew. 'Yes.' replied Onassis, 'you may well be right, but I am also a powerful millionaire and the sooner you get it into your head, the better it will be for everybody: I will never give up Maria for anyone or anything — people, contracts and conventions can all go to hell. . . . Battista, how many millions do you want to let Maria free? Five, ten?'

'You are a disgusting drunk,' Meneghini shouted back at him, 'and you make me want to vomit. I would have knocked your block off if you were at all able to stand up.' It was Maria's screaming and compulsive sobbing that stopped them from fighting. Apart from accusing Maria of ingratitude, Meneghini refused to discuss the matter any further. When Onassis offered his hand as a conciliatory gesture Meneghini told him, 'I do not shake hands with scum. You invited me on your accursed yacht and then you stabbed me in the back. I now cast a curse on you that you never find peace as long as you live.' They never saw or spoke to one another again. Meneghini then went to bed, leaving Maria with Onassis.

On the following day Maria asked Meneghini by telephone for her passport and the little painting of the Madonna that she always had with her in the theatre. She also requested Meneghini to continue to handle her business affairs for the remainder of her engagements, which only extended till the following November. He refused. Maria then agreed to have a legal separation forthwith; she wanted her complete freedom and Meneghini was not to annoy her with any further discussions. The lawyers would see to everything. More recriminations followed on the telephone between Maria and her husband, especially when property matters came to be discussed. On 28 August Meneghini, in a moment of anger, decided to denounce his wife and Onassis as adulterers, but his lawyer promptly informed him that as Maria was an American citizen she could not be incriminated in Italy on that count.

Undoubtedly Meneghini's version of events after the cruise was generally, though not wholly, true; he knowingly distorted some and avoided disclosing other crucial issues of his confrontation with Onassis, or more precisely with his wife, which led to the break-up of his marriage. A truer account was to come much later, though not from Meneghini.

Apart from a vague hint in the papers on 30 August that there might be some dissension between Callas and her husband the press, which in the past had often reported even the most trivial of details concerning the famous singer, now seemed oblivious to what was going on behind the scenes. Nor was anything so much as suspected by their friends and acquaintances, which might perhaps go some way to corroborate Maria's declaration to her husband that she and Onassis had not done anything wrong during the cruise. Not that any of their fellow guests would have gossiped about it had anything scandalous happened, but the sixty-strong crew probably would have done and the press would have been alerted in no time. After the Callas–Onassis liaison became common knowledge, some of them suddenly 'knew' everything and, with considerable embroidery, contributed to the transformation of a likely story into fact.

The press first got wise to the affair on 3 September, three weeks after the termination of the cruise, when Callas and Onassis were discovered dining tête-à-tête in an exclusive restaurant in Milan and afterwards were photographed arm in arm outside the Hotel Principe e Savoia. The next day Callas's house in Milan was besieged by reporters and photographers. Eventually she made a statement which was printed on the 6th:

I confirm that my separation from my husband is complete and final. It has been in the air for some time and the fact that it has actually happened during the cruise on the *Christina*

Callas with Onassis in Milan, 1960.

is purely coincidental. The lawyers are now working on the case and will make an announcement in due course. . . . I am now my own manager. I ask for understanding in this painful personal situation. Only a genuine friendship exists between myself and Mr Onassis. I also have business connections with him; I have received offers from Monte Carlo Opera,[2] and there is also a prospect for a film. . . . It is not important who is to blame. The breaking of my marriage is my greatest admission of failure.

Onassis, who was on his yacht in Venice at the time, merely echoed Maria's words: 'We are simply good friends.'

In the meantime Callas began recording *La Gioconda* at La Scala. Apart from a great number of reporters, many friends and colleagues, such as Visconti, Nicola Zaccaria and others, and most of the theatre's personnel were there to greet her. The first to welcome her at the entrance of the theatre was none other than Ghiringhelli, the man who had driven her out of La Scala eighteen months before. Now he dropped his aloofness and was absolutely delighted to see Maria back in the 'home' where she belonged, even though she was there only for a recording.

With his usual hypocrisy, Ghiringhelli further insinuated – unfairly – that Meneghini had been the cause of their past disagreements and, as he was now out of the way, the gates of La Scala would always be open for Maria Callas. In due course Ghiringhelli asked her formally to return in any role of her choice and entirely on her own terms.

The day she completed the recording Maria left with Onassis for a cruise on the *Christina*. Insisting that he had only been acting as a go-between in the Meneghini break-up, Onassis told the press that he was taking her (his sister Artemis and her husband would also be on board) because she had had a difficult time and needed a rest. In the end he all but exploded to the repetitive question about his personal feelings: 'Of course I would be flattered', he finally declared, 'if a woman with the class of Maria Callas fell in love with someone like me! Who wouldn't?' What Onassis failed to say was that his wife would not be joining them this time.

With both Maria and Onassis well out of reach, the press concentrated on Meneghini, who now took the centre of the stage with a vengeance. Once his last glimmer of hope of keeping his wife was extinguished, his side of the story centred almost entirely on Onassis and hardly less on the financial considerations that his separation from his wife would unavoidably entail. His state-

Callas with Onassis at Monte Carlo, 1963.

Callas with Onassis somewhere in Africa.

ments, which far outnumbered and even outwitted those of Callas and Onassis put together, included such comments as: 'It is very true that the separation which means the end of our marriage is irrevocable. I do hope that we can reach a mutual agreement amicably. The causes are very well known: the association between Maria Callas and Aristotle Onassis. I bear no bitterness towards Maria, who has been honest and truthful, but I cannot forgive Onassis. The laws of hospitality were sacred for the ancient Greeks.' At another time Meneghini criticized Onassis with even more bitterness calling him, 'The man with an ambition like Hitler, who wants to own everything with his accursed millions and his accursed cruise and his accursed yacht. ... He wants to add varnish to his tankers with the name of a great artist.' Then, in a more introspective though contradictory mood, he exclaimed 'They love each other like children.' It was only when Meneghini at a critical point concentrated his strategy on the financial settlement that he brought himself directly to denigrate Maria, but again on materialistic rather than moral grounds. 'We are, the three of us, like characters in a drama,' he said, describing Maria as a Medea, Onassis as merely a multi-millionaire (inferring that he had nothing else to offer) and himself as a tough nut to crack when it came to the point. This preamble was followed by his main thrust to thwart any analogy between him and a contemporary merchant of Venice: 'It was I who made Callas what she is,' he declared, 'and she showed her appreciation by stabbing me in the back. She was fat and drably dressed, more like a penniless gypsy refugee without career prospects, when she came into my life. Not only did I pay her hotel bill but I also became her guarantor so that she could remain in Italy. This can hardly be described as exploitation on my part, of which, apparently, I am now accused! Make no mistake that when it comes to the point of splitting everything down to our poodle, Maria will get the head part and I will end up with the tail.'

On 16 September Callas left the *Christina* in Athens to fulfil a concert engagement at Bilbao. In the first half of the concert, which included excerpts from *Don Carlos* and *Hamlet*, she was in such poor form both vocally and dramatically – never before had she been so detached – that she got a very chilly reception. This induced her to pull herself together in the second half, and particularly in the final item, the mad scene from *Il pirata*, she rose to the occasion and saved her reputation.

As soon as the concert was over Maria rejoined the *Christina* until 22 September, when she

Visconti greets Callas on her arrival at La Scala to record
La Gioconda *in 1959.*

flew to London for a concert at the Festival Hall. The programme consisted of one long scene each from *Don Carlos*, *Hamlet*, *Macbeth* and *Il pirata*. Unlike at Bilbao six days earlier, Callas in London was in excellent form, her voice expressing a new mellowness. It was a memorable night and she surpassed herself in the sleep-walking scene from *Macbeth* and in the mad scene from *Il pirata*. Everybody was filled with curiosity as to whether she would give London her enthralling characterization of Lady Macbeth in the new production of the opera due at Covent Garden during the forthcoming season. She would not commit herself.

While in London, she learned of Meneghini's statements to the press, which had been circulated everywhere, and telephoned him in a rage. Insults were hurled, culminating in Maria threatening to go to Sirmione one of these days to shoot Meneghini. 'And I will be waiting to machine-gun you down,' he shouted back. After this confrontation they never spoke to each other again.

Immediately after her concert was over Callas returned to Milan for an urgent conference with her lawyers over the settlement of joint property with her husband. This necessitated the postponement for a week of her appearance on British television. On her return her conductor, Nicola Rescigno, was suddenly taken ill with a virus. After a hectic last-minute search for a suitable substitute, Sir Malcolm Sargent was thrilled to be chosen. Callas sang superbly in two highly contrasting arias: 'Sì, mi chiamano Mimì' (*La bohème*) and 'L'altra notte' (*Mefistofele*). Another concert in Berlin completed her engagements in Europe.

In the last week of October, in the midst of a great furore, Callas crossed the Atlantic to give a concert in Kansas City and to appear at the Dallas Civic Opera, the last of her contracted engagements. The publicity this time revolved almost entirely around her private life, as Meneghini had filed suit for legal separation for which the hearing was set for 14 November at Brescia. Because of the unavailability and silence of the principal characters, save for Meneghini, it was becoming rather difficult to keep the Callas–Onassis affair constantly in the news. The press, however, succeeded in tracking down Maria's mother, who was working in Jolie Gabor's jewellery shop in New York.

Jolie, mother of film stars Zsa Zsa and Eva, had met Evangelia when they both appeared in a television programme featuring the mothers of famous daughters. At the end Mme Gabor, who quickly sensed the importance of having Maria Callas's mother working for her, offered Evangelia a job. Evangelia knew nothing about her daughter's friendship with Onassis but that did not prevent her from snatching as much of the limelight as she could. Here was, after all, an excellent opportunity to denigrate her 'heartless' daughter: 'Meneghini was a father and mother to Maria,' she announced. 'Now she no longer needs him. Women like Maria can never know real love. . . . I was her first victim. Now it is Meneghini. Maria will marry Onassis to further her boundless ambition; he will be her third victim.'

Although a bomb hoax interrupted Callas's concert in Kansas City for almost an hour she did not lose her nerve and gave a very creditable performance. At Dallas, however, her first Lucia found her below standard. She was too exhausted mentally to concentrate and had several vocal mishaps, in particular missing the high E flats in the mad scene. 'I had the note. What happened?' she kept telling herself backstage (Lucia does not appear again in the opera). She then sang several consecutive E flats with perfect pitch but even though she was in very much better form for her second and last Lucia two days later, she did not risk these particular notes.

After the performance she flew to Italy for the hearing of her separation suit. The crowd gathered outside the court at Brescia was clearly on Meneghini's side. To them he appeared the wronged husband who should have known better than to marry a foreigner. 'You will be much better off with a nice Italian girl, next time,' they shouted. Maria was greeted with stony silence. Although Meneghini's writ accused her of behaving with her lover in a manner incompatible with elementary decency, by the end of the six-hour hearing a separation was granted by mutual consent on the grounds of discord and conflicting business interests. Their estate was divided between them: Maria kept the house in Milan and most of her jewellery, Meneghini the villa at Sirmione and the rest of their real estate. Everything else, paintings and other objects of value, was divided equally.

The next morning Maria rushed back to the United States, arriving in Dallas on the day of the dress rehearsal for *Medea*. The strain and fatigue of the hearing and the hurried transatlantic journeys do not seem to have affected her for her performance engendered superlative reviews. 'Again she gave us a Medea of tenderness, fury and impassioned singing, and she was rewarded with standing ovations,' *Musical America* reported.

Nicola Zaccaria, who was singing Creon in these *Medeas*, told me that especially in his big scene with Callas he felt a new heart-rending quality in her voice when Medea pleads to be allowed to stay one more day with her children: 'I did not have to act my part because I was genuinely moved. For me it became a living emotion.'

The two *Medeas* in Dallas were Callas's last contracted engagement. Even before they were over she was flooded with offers from agents to represent her, as well as from theatres to sing anything she wanted on any terms. Maria did not even consider them. She returned to Milan and then joined Onassis on the *Christina* at Monte Carlo.

A few days later the newspapers announced what Tina Onassis intended to do with her life. Ever since the fateful cruise, she had maintained a dignified silence, at least in public; she watched, it seemed, from a distance the development of her husband's association with Callas. Neither his persistent denial that he and Maria were planning marriage, nor Callas's press comments – 'There is no romance. Mr Onassis and his wife are my very dear friends. I hope you will not wreck our friendship' – had impressed Tina. It is almost certain that her final decision to divorce her husband was taken on the day Onassis left with Callas from Venice for a second cruise. On 25 November (eleven days after Callas was legally separated from Meneghini) Tina filed divorce proceedings in the New York State Supreme Court, charging her husband with adultery. On the same day she also issued a statement to the press: 'It is almost thirteen years since Mr Onassis and I were married in New York City. Since then he has become one of the world's richest men, but his great wealth has not brought me happiness with him nor, as the world knows, has it brought him happiness with me. . . . Mr Onassis knows positively that I want none of his wealth and that I am solely concerned with the welfare of our children. I deeply regret that Mr Onassis leaves me with no alternative other than a New York suit for divorce.'

Much to the surprise and disappointment of the media, the arbitrators of famous people's matrimonial problems, Tina did not cite Maria Callas as co-respondent but another woman merely named J.R. These initials clearly referred to Mrs Jeanne Rhinelander, an old school friend of Tina's, with whom she had caught Onassis *in flagrante delicto* at her home in Grasse five years previously. When officially named as co-respondent, Mrs Rhinelander merely expressed her astonishment that 'after so many years of friendship of which everybody knew, here and in the United States, Mrs Onassis should use this as a pretext to gain her freedom'.

Many others, however, volunteered their own interpretation of Tina's curious magnanimity towards Callas. Had Onassis bargained with his wife to refrain from exposing Maria, in return for his silence regarding her own misdemeanours? It was an open secret that during the previous couple of years the Onassis marriage had been less than harmonious. Because of her husband's repeated adultery, the very young Tina (in 1959 she was twenty-eight, he fifty-four and they had been married for over twelve years) had herself committed a few indiscretions. There was no question of bribing Tina in any other way, as she had made clear in her divorce suit that she wanted none of Onassis's wealth (her father was still a very rich man) and that her sole concern would be for the welfare of their children. There was another motive, perhaps the strongest, in Tina's generosity: she would not give Callas the satisfaction of considering herself a victorious rival. Moreover, Mrs Rhinelander would serve two purposes simultaneously: to provide Tina with the divorce and to demonstrate conclusively to Callas that in Onassis's life there had been other women before and there would undoubtedly be more after her.

The evening Tina's statement was published a greatly relieved Maria thought it prudent to move from the *Christina* to the Hotel Hermitage, where in fact she was nominally booked, and Onassis dined alone with Prince Rainier and Princess Grace. Onassis's statement followed the next day and was cleverly constructed to leave the press none the wiser: 'I have just heard that my wife has begun divorce proceedings. I am not surprised, the situation has been moving rapidly. But I was not warned. Obviously I shall have to do what she wants and make suitable arrangements.'

It is difficult to know how Onassis really felt about his pending divorce. He did not contest his wife's actions; indeed, he wanted the world to think he was trying for a reconciliation. Was he, in fact, protecting Maria's name from further scandal? It must also be stressed that in the late 1950s divorce, for whatever reasons, was still, particularly for Greeks, considered a public disgrace for both the rich and the poor, especially if they had children. Hence Onassis was prepared to agree to all his wife's wishes. The case took its normal course and eventually Tina got her divorce and the custody of her two children. In the meantime Maria spent December alone in Milan, while Onassis was rushing around the world on business and trying to settle his marital problems.

The 1959–60 season at La Scala celebrated the return of Renata Tebaldi. She sang in *Tosca* and later in *Andrea Chénier* with considerable success. In vain did the press try to rekindle the old rivalry between her and Callas. When asked whether she would be attending Tebaldi's opening night, Callas replied, 'Now that Renata is returning to La Scala it will be much more constructive if public attention is focused on this important event with absolutely no interferences of any kind. . . . I have closed many chapters this year and as far as I am concerned, it is my sincere wish to close this chapter as well.'

Later, commenting on her return to La Scala, Tebaldi changed completely the reason she had given *Time* magazine in 1956 for her departure from this theatre during the previous season. At that time she had put the blame entirely on the uncongenial climate that existed at La Scala and had said that she left of her own accord, allowing nobody to influence her decision. In her second version Tebaldi primarily blamed Callas and only to some extent the theatre management. 'I decided to leave La Scala', she explained, 'because Callas had monopolized this theatre and, worse still, the attention that was paid to her was too much to take. . . . It was very hard for me but unfortunately I had no alternative. Callas was given the choice of the best operas in the repertoire. It was unfair to the other artists and it was unfair to me. . . . Afterwards La Scala often asked me to change my mind but I was stubborn and refused to return so long as Maria Callas reigned there.'

There were no more comments from either of them, nor did they meet in public until 1969, when Callas was in the audience at one of Tebaldi's performances of *Adriana Lecouvreur* at the Metropolitan. Even then, Callas was accused of coming to the theatre to cast an 'evil eye' on Tebaldi. At the end of the performance she applauded warmly and Rudolf Bing, who had escorted her to the theatre on that evening, promptly asked her if she would like to go backstage. Smiling, Callas nodded eagerly. Bing knocked at the door of Tebaldi's dressing-room and called, 'Renata, I have an old friend here to see you.' Tebaldi opened the door and the two singers for an instant found themselves face to face. Without a word they fell into each other's arms, moved to tears. The hatchet was well and truly buried.

The burial of the hatchet: Tebaldi and Callas held together by Bing.

Important though Tebaldi was (and a great deal of attention was focused on her return to La Scala), her performances as Maddalena, perhaps her best role, fell just short of generating the frenzy of excitement the Milanese craved since Callas's departure eighteen months before. During Tebaldi's four-year absence Callas had given them several outstanding portrayals, which drew to the theatre a new audience from a much wider section of the public, including a greater percentage of the younger generation than ever before.

Following Callas's reconciliation with Ghiringhelli the Milanese felt confident that, notwithstanding the recent upheavals in her private life, she would soon be back at La Scala, for they remembered Emilio Radius's wise words in 1954 that there was room at the same time for both these most important artists. But it was not to be, for Callas found herself unable for the moment to accept any engagement. She had been under tremendous strain for over two years and her recurrent vocal problems (she had, as we have seen, narrowly escaped disaster in her first Lucia at Dallas) now culminated in a crisis which, contrary to popular belief, had very little directly to do with her separation from her husband, or the new man in her life. Her remarks in Dallas that all she cared for was to be with Onassis were misconstrued, perhaps deliberately, by those who, many years later, claimed to have heard them.

336

Determined to solve her problems Maria Callas retired, temporarily anyway, from the operatic stage while the world wondered and speculated about her 'deafening' silence.

---

1   Meneghini means the Patriarch of Constantinople Athenagoras I.
2   Onassis was at the time the main shareholder of the Société des Bains de Mer, Monaco, which controlled the Monte Carlo Opera House.

CHAPTER FIFTEEN

DIVORCE AND RETURN TO THE STAGE

SO FAR, ALL through her adult life Callas had managed to maintain a reasonable balance between the artist and the human being. 'There are two people in me,' she remarked. 'Maria and Callas. I like to think that they go together because in my work Maria is always present. Their difference is only that Callas is a celebrity.' The success of this collaboration, however, was because Maria had been the passive partner and always ready to serve Callas with total dedication and without compromise. With the break-up of her marriage and her relationship with Onassis, which now became much closer than either of them would admit publicly, the woman was for the first time allowed to dominate the artist, or so it seemed. The truth of the matter was that Callas was facing the first stages of her vocal decline and wisely would not accept any engagements for the foreseeable future.

During the turbulent days of her confrontation with her husband after the cruise on the *Christina*, Meneghini found out from Maria's heart specialist, who had examined her on 27 August, that her heart had returned to normal and her blood pressure, which had always been dangerously low, had climbed to 110. Ironically, the doctor also told Meneghini that he should thank the Lord for the beneficial effects of the holiday.

Callas's second cruise with Onassis also did her good and indeed, helped her to carry out her few contracted engagements. However, before long her health was again showing signs of deterioration; her blood pressure was prone to drop suddenly to a dangerously low level and her periodic painful sinus ailment took a turn for the worse, so much so that it affected her singing considerably. These physical illnesses were in turn the basic cause of her ragged nerves, further aggravated by the uncertainty of her relationship with Onassis. But it must be stressed that it was because of her vocal difficulties, which undermined her self-confidence, that she sought refuge in her relationship with Onassis and not the other way round, allowing her personal affairs to take priority over her art. 'I want to live just like a normal woman,' she said. This is not meant to refute the fact that Callas fell in love with Onassis but to discredit the popular belief that she sacrificed everything for this love, thereby bringing on the deterioration of her vocal resources and the subsequent curtailment of her career. To her dying day Callas never sacrificed even a minute fraction of her art for anybody or anything.

When the first months of 1960 went by without even an announcement of future engagements the world, led by the media, concentrated on her affair with Onassis, speculating on a possible marriage and wondering whether she was really finished as the supreme singer. In fact, during this period Callas was more often than not alone at her home in Milan. Onassis had not yet been officially divorced and some thought that he was still trying, or at least pretending to try, for a reconciliation with his wife. His children – Alexander was twelve, Christina nine – understandably did not like Maria, whom they held responsible for the break-up of their family. They would have felt the same about any woman, or man, who came between their parents, although they had never really taken the Rhinelander episode seriously. It was therefore imperative and prudent for Onassis not to appear, whatever the motive, as the instigator of the divorce, so that he would maintain his children's love and respect. Furthermore, he would not be demolishing what little had been achieved in protecting Callas's name when his wife named Mrs Rhinelander as co-respondent. Moreover, in order not to offend against Italian law of that period, when divorce was impossible, Maria could not be seen too often in public alone with another man, for Meneghini could easily have brought charges of immorality against her. In these circumstances, whenever Maria was on the *Christina* Onassis made sure that his sister and brother-in-law were also on board.

While the press were all but writing off Callas as a singer and impatiently trying to probe into her rather mysterious relationship with Onassis, her mother seized the opportunity to jump on the bandwagon. Following her appearance on television with Jolie Gabor (when they had spoken about their famous daughters) Evangelia now exploded on the literary world with *My Daughter Maria Callas* (1960). The book (ghosted by Lawrence Blochman) presented formally, as it were, the abandoned mother who had made every sacrifice for the good of her ungrateful and heartless daughter. Full of serious inaccuracies and twisted, if not altogether invented, episodes in Maria's childhood and later life, it could not have been more denigrating. Evangelia proceeded to give interviews to anybody who would listen, with the result that some magazines wrote scathing articles about Callas's ingratitude towards her mother, while others, it is true, dismissed the book outright. Nevertheless, it was extremely hurtful for Maria, especially at a time when she had so many problems both with her voice and her personal life, and was virtually alone. All the same, she kept her composure, responding neither to her mother nor to the book and Evangelia soon realized that she had misfired again; she did not become a best-selling author, nor did she succeed with her blackmailing tactics to get any closer to her daughter. As far as Maria was concerned, her mother blew any chance there might have been of a reconciliation. (The aftermath of Callas's relationship with her family is dealt with later in this book).

By June, things began to look up for Maria. Tina Onassis decided to drop the adultery charge involving Mrs Rhinelander (in New York State adultery was essential for divorce) and quickly got her uncontested divorce and custody of her children in Alabama. Maria was now able to spend much more time with Onassis and henceforth on the *Christina* she acquired the status of *patronne*, becoming very popular with the crew. Even more important for her was the improvement in her health, as the crippling sinus trouble had at last subsided, her blood pressure was stable and she was able to practice singing without tears. She was delighted, therefore, to accept an invitation to sing in Greece.

Authorized by the Festival of Athens's council, Mme Ralli[1] had initially approached Callas while she was singing Medea in London during the previous June. I went with her to see Callas at the end of the dress rehearsal. For some reason Mme Ralli sounded untypically dictatorial on this occasion, telling Callas, 'You must sing Medea in Greece, your country, too.' Maria took exception to this rather offhand remark thrown at her only a few minutes after her gruelling performance. 'What do you expect me to do? Go down on my knees and beg to sing in Greece? Why doesn't the Festival of Athens engage me in the proper way? Everybody else does,' Maria replied curtly. She then chatted with me about irrelevant matters. Later on I found the opportunity of telling Maria that Mme Ralli had meant only to be friendly and informal, believing this was what was expected of her. 'Maybe I was a little on edge and came on a bit too strong,' Maria commented. This was not all that surprising when one remembers how Callas was treated at her concert for the Festival of Athens two years previously and, with good reason, had declared, 'Never again.'

However, the second meeting of the two women went very well and Callas was favourably disposed to the idea of singing in Greece and awaited a formal invitation. The contract did arrive and once she got over her ailments she whole-heartedly agreed, especially as the current director of the Athens Festival was an old and respected friend, Costis Bastias, whom Maria knew from the days when she had sung with the Athens Opera. Above all, however, her greatest incentive in accepting this engagement, when she was fully aware of the enormous amount that was expected of her, was her renewed confidence in her vocal capabilities and no less the fact that her old master, surrogate father and friend, Tullio Serafin, would be her conductor.

The plan was that under the auspices of the Athens Festival the Athens Opera would be staging performances with Callas in the vast ancient theatre at Epidaurus. Previously only ancient Greek drama had been given in this unique open-air arena with its amazing acoustics, which Callas had had the opportunity to try out on her excursion during the cruise on the *Christina* the previous August. Initially *Medea* was suggested, but Maria felt that her compatriots wanted to hear her in *Norma* so the opera was changed; she would sing Medea in the following year. Minotis and Tsarouchis would be staging *Norma* and Antonis Fokas, Greece's most famous costume designer, was also engaged. The proposed cast at first included Mirto Picchi as Pollione, Adriana Lazzarini as Adalgisa and Nicola Zaccaria as Oroveso. Zaccaria was not free because of a previous engagement at the Salzburg Festival and Feruccio Mazzoli replaced him. Lazzarini also fell ill and had to withdraw. The management was faced with a problem as Adalgisas are not easy to find. The very promising young Greek mezzo-soprano, Kiki Morfoniou, was suggested to Callas who immediately referred the matter to Serafin. After an audition Morfoniou was engaged.

Prior to the performances at Epidaurus Callas had agreed to make a recording of Rossini and Verdi arias in London and give a concert at Ostend, both engagements also serving as a warm-up, as she had not sung in public for nine months. She was not satisfied with the recording and did not give permission for its release. In the circumstances, the concert appeared an even greater challenge which she was willing to meet until struck down with acute laryngitis about twelve hours before the performance. It was cancelled: a disappointing start, to say the least, for a come-back but as the cancellation was not due to cold feet but to a genuine case of laryngitis Maria did not lose her courage.

When, towards the end of July, she arrived in Greece to prepare for *Norma* she was, in some ways, a new Maria: a very calm and patient woman who appeared to have achieved an emotional balance. An apartment was built for her next to the Museum of Aesculapius, opposite the theatre, as Epidaurus was then almost a five-hour journey by road from Athens. It was three years since the concert at the Herodes Atticus Theatre in Athens and this time there were no crises, artistic or political; the country of her ancestors received Callas with open arms and the Greeks had never before fought so hard for tickets. Georges Kalogeropoulos, who had arranged to spend his summer holidays in Greece, was the only member of Maria's family present. Onassis, too, was there to admire her in her most famous role and met Kalogeropoulos for the first time. The men's direct manner of calling a spade a spade endeared them to one another. The *Christina*, in celebratory illumination, was anchored in the sea inlet of the nearby village, Old Epidaurus, pre-pared for a party after the performance.

Everything was planned carefully to make this performance, the first of its kind in Greece, a memorable one, with the exception of one thing: the usually reliable Greek weather suddenly became most capricious. The gala first performance of *Norma* had to be cancelled practically at the last minute, as rain, unheard of during August, poured down continuously for the entire evening, and a mass of disappointed people trekked back to Athens. Shortly afterwards the festival authorities announced that the first performance would replace the second, which was can-celled. There was no mishap of any kind on the night of the rescheduled gala and they came in their thousands to fill the vast theatre to capacity: it was estimated that 18,000 people saw the performance, which they could hear perfectly. All the singers of the Athens Opera who were not taking part, including some who had resented Maria Kalogeropoulou's rise to fame in her early days in Greece and conspired to block the renewal of her contract, were now in the audience to admire their famous compatriot.

On her entrance Callas, as the Druid Priestess, looked so regal that the audience gasped, then released their tension by giving her an ovation. At the same time two white doves (ancient Greek symbols of love and happiness) were released by somebody in the audience and momentarily landed by the footlights, before disappearing in the nearby forest. Maria had not yet sung a note. She was deeply moved. The feelings evoked in her by her compatriots were for a precious moment greater than the strength of her art, so much so that her first phrases in the opening recitative were uneven, but at the same time imbued with a strange mysticism which seemed to blend with this environment, sacred to the Greeks and indeed to any visitor. She was in good voice and dispelled any fears that she was finished. Callas went on to give a most poignant interpretation which brought tears to all eyes. In the second act, when she and Morfoniou sang the celebrated duet 'Mira o Norma', which marks the reconciliation of the two women, the enthusiasm of the audience knew no bounds. One might say this also symbolized the complete re-acceptance of Maria Callas by her fellow countrymen. There were no flowers at the end. Instead, a wreath of laurel from the Greek earth was placed at the feet of Greece's famous daughter.

The gods, however, put Maria through one more trial. By the next and final performance she had fallen ill. In spite of her high temperature she defied her doctor's advice not to sing and went ahead without mishap. These were Callas's first opera performances in Greece since the early days. She donated her fee of about $10,000 – a great departure from her 1500 drachmas per month during the war – to a scholarship fund ('Callas Scholarships') for poor but able young singers. The Greek government thought this the right moment to express its appreciation for Maria Callas's art by decorating her with the Medal for Merit.

For the first time in her life Maria knew that her compatriots loved and appreciated her and she had never before felt so Greek. When I ran into her during this period on the island of Tinos in the Aegean, where Onassis had taken her to make a pilgrimage to the church with the miraculous icon of the Virgin Mary she appeared to be in the highest of spirits. Dressed simply in black and with a black chiffon scarf decorated with a few sequins over her head, Maria looked much younger than her years and the personification of Greek beauty. She was exuberant and smiling. 'It is wonderful to be happy and know it right at the time you are,' she said as she was returning to the *Christina*.

Summer was practically over when Callas sailed away from Greece. She would be returning to sing Medea at Epidaurus in the following August. As her Norma was such a success and she had brought to this role a new tenderness and deeper meaning, EMI decided to re-record the opera with her. The cast included Corelli (Pollione), Christa Ludwig (Adalgisa), Zaccaria (Oroveso) with Serafin as conductor, and the recording was made in Milan.

Callas, Ludwig and Serafin at a piano rehearsal for the recording of Norma *in 1960.*

Callas and Ludwig having a break during the recording of Norma.

Maria then began work on a new role for an old theatre. After an absence of two and half years (since she had sung Imogene in *Il pirata*) Callas was returning to her beloved La Scala, in the role of Paolina in Donizetti's *Poliuto*. The part was carefully chosen and, though not easy, does not on the whole expose the voice to any great problems, nor does it require unusual dramatic outbursts. Corelli, Bastianini and Zaccaria completed the excellent cast and Votto was the conductor.

Initially the production of *Poliuto* was planned meticulously by Visconti and Benois, but the former withdrew from the project in mid-November for reasons that had nothing to do with La Scala but were in protest against the Italian government: the censor had insisted on cuts in his film *Rocco e i suoi fratelli*, alleging that it was libellous to southern Italian emigrants. Moreover, Visconti had trouble with his production of Testori's play *L'Arialda* which had opened in Rome and been banned for obscenity. (It was also banned in Milan in the following February.) Consequently he vowed never again to work for any Italian state-subsidized theatre. To Maria he apologized profusely by telegram, explaining how painful it was for him to have no alternative but to withdraw from *Poliuto*. It was indeed painful, 'above all because I shall be deprived of the greatest gratification that I find in working with you ... nevertheless I am sure you will understand my predicament and approve of my decision.' Maria answered Visconti promptly and warmly, expressing her solidarity and distress about the unjust situation in which he found himself 'that is so preposterous and so contradictory to common sense'. The opera was eventually directed by Herbert Graf, who took over three weeks before the première.

On St Ambrose's Day 1960 La Scala opened its season with *Poliuto*. It was an unusually glittering gala, with the auditorium decorated with thousands of carnations for the occasion. The theatre was packed to capacity, many tickets having changed hands at exorbitant prices on the black market. Among Onassis's guests were the Rainiers, the Begum Aga Khan and an appreciable proportion of the 1960s international Jet Set. Also present were a large number of theatre, film and opera stars, who had come to welcome back the ex-queen of La Scala. Interestingly, Callas's adversaries seemed to have vanished, despite the fact that during her exile from La Scala Tebaldi had returned there to considerable acclaim.

The *Poliuto* performances found Callas in variable form, though the Italian critics seem to have paid more attention to the unusually glittering audience at the première than to the artistry presented on-stage. The most constructive reviews were by the British. Harold Rosenthal (*Opera*, February 1961) reported that 'Callas was far from being in good voice at the third performance, and although at the fifth the voice was under firmer control, on both occasions her first act was vocally poor . . . a lot of the time the tone sounded empty and hollow, and she seemed to produce more of those strident top notes than usual. Then suddenly would come a few minutes of sure and exquisite singing, of phrases so full of significance that little thrills would run down the spine. . . .'

Andrew Porter (*Musical Times*, February 1961) heard a different Callas:

No one will believe me when I say I heard the only performance, of the five she gave, at which Maria Callas found her peak form (a matinée on December 18, for the record). But so it was. She was spellbinding, secure, confident and inspiring confidence. To every role Callas brings something new. To Paolina it was not only beauty of presence, phrase, gesture and inflexion, but an almost physical enactment of the workings of grace, from the first stirrings when this pagan heroine listens to the Christians' hymn, to the supernatural radiance which floods her in the final scene as she resolves to join the Christians in martyrdom. Callas bewitches me, I confess it; I thought *Poliuto* a fine opera.

Callas's feelings about her return to La Scala are interesting (although she did not reveal them to me until some time in the 1970s, when she considered recording a recital with di Stefano). I suggested that she might include Paolina's entrance and duet with Poliuto. 'After all,' I commented, 'Paolina was your last triumph at La Scala.'

Although she said nothing about recording it, she reminisced about her return to La Scala in 1960:

It was a very emotional time for me and in some ways difficult. After my absence from the stage for over a year, I had only sung Norma twice at Epidaurus three months before *Poliuto*. But this wouldn't have mattered had it not been at La Scala. You see, spiritually I never left La Scala but, physically, I was returning there as an estranged artist. Would the public accept me on these terms? I was very nervous about this as it had really nothing to do with my artistic capabilities. But people are influenced. Also my voice had undergone rather significant changes since I had last sung at La Scala. Nevertheless, I was happy during that period, and the relative tranquillity I had found gave me the strength to return 'home', And then there were my colleagues in *Poliuto* who were not only excellent artists but genuine friends, always ready to stand by me through thick and thin. Above all, however, I would not have sung in this opera had not Paolina captured my imagination; her conversion to Christianity (from the moment the first seeds are sown right at the beginning of the opera), that eventually elevates her to her sublime sacrifice, proceeds convincingly. She does not merely follow her husband to her death. Her love for her husband had been instrumental, indirectly, in her finding her faith. And I could convey her feelings vocally. At least I hope I have.

The subscribers to La Scala celebrated Callas's return by offering her a gold medal, a gesture never before made to any artist in the long history of the theatre.

As it happened Paolina was Callas's last new role. *Poliuto* did bring her back to La Scala successfully but henceforth her performances were to be very few and far between. She might have got over her mental exhaustion, if not her blood-pressure problem, but she also knew that her vocal resources were not as reliable as once they had been and in these circumstances it was inevitable that her confidence would have suffered also. Wisely, she decided to undertake the minimum that her physical and vocal capabilities would allow, which is why she continued to seek an emotional outlet in the social life revolving around her relationship with Onassis. She kept her house in Milan, but more often than not she was in Monte Carlo or on the *Christina*; the compensations of this life-style offered her a way to relax, enjoy leisure and live for herself. Social life, which had by her choice been absent in her youth and hardly filled the years of marriage to Meneghini, was now thrust upon her and she accepted it willingly but only as a temporary substitute. Her dedication to her art had in no way waned, but because of her vocal decline the occasions on which this dedication was demanded of her were becoming fewer and fewer.

Her next appearance after *Poliuto* was in the spring of 1961, when she took part in a benefit concert at St James's Palace in London in aid of the Edwina Mountbatten Trust. On this occasion she sang arias from *Norma*, Massenet's *Le Cid*, *Don Carlos* and *Mefistofele*, to the piano accompaniment of Sir Malcolm Sargent.

It was the start of summer and after a holiday at Monte Carlo and a Mediterranean cruise she began preparations for her return to Greece to sing Medea at Epidaurus. The action of the opera, like the classical Greek play on which it is based, takes place in Corinth, which is in the Epidaurus region. No theatre could be more appropriate for the re-enactment of the tragedy of Medea and Callas, with great pride, prepared her role meticulously. Minotis and Tsarouchis were again staging the opera, Vickers sang Jason, Giuseppe Modesti Creon, Morfoniou Neris and Rescigno conducted.

Medea was scheduled earlier in July in order to avoid a recurrence of the mishap when the first *Norma* had had to be postponed the previous year because of rain. It was all the more amazing when again, two hours before the performance, it suddenly began to pour. But it proved a false alarm as the downpour lasted for only a few minutes and the sun reappeared. The opening performance found Callas on top form. She sang and acted Medea with total conviction and with a new refinement which brought a better balance between the character's moments of extreme fury and tenderness, and completely captivated the huge audience. In its seamless cohesion the performance was nothing short of a theatrical miracle and Maria Callas was hailed with the reverence befitting a Greek goddess. The following day the mayor of Athens bestowed on her their Gold Medal, giving her the freedom of the city, and Callas again donated her fee to the scholarship fund she had founded the previous year. There were, as ever, some critics who voiced a few rather pedantic unfavourable remarks about her singing but the general consensus was that she was still the greatest singer in the world and her Medea at Epidaurus fully deserved the acclaim it was given.

Georges Kalogeropoulos again made the trip to Greece to be near his daughter. This time he also brought his other daughter, Iakinthy, who had not seen Maria since 1950. It was a happy meeting and the only occasion since the early days in Athens when Maria had two members of her family together at one of her performances, but no development followed in the relationship of the two sisters. The suggestion that her mother might attend the second *Medea* did not materialize; for reasons of her own Evangelia stayed away. There was another important absentee from the first *Medea*; business affairs made it possible for Onassis to arrive only in time for the second and last performance.

Callas's artistic success at Epidaurus was witnessed by Wally Toscanini who, feeling confident that her vocal resources were substantially restored, persuaded Ghiringhelli to mount a new production of *Medea* at La Scala. The 1961–2 season was inaugurated with Verdi's *La battaglia di Legnano* in which Corelli and Antonietta Stella were the leading singers. It was an interesting rather than a stimulating performance. Four evenings later Maria Callas in *Medea* generated all the excitement that is traditionally associated with the opening of the season at La Scala. The same team which had staged the work at Epidaurus was engaged and Jon Vickers was again Jason, but Creon was sung by Nicolai Ghiaurov and Neris by Simionato. The conductor was Thomas Schippers, new to Cherubini's opera.

Callas began her entrance recitative with her usual dramatic intensity. She followed it with the aria 'Dei tuoi figli', singing with a beautiful legato line. When, however, about half-way through a slight but noticeable insecurity crept once or twice into her voice the 'hissing snakes', who had been in hibernation for some time, suddenly awoke. What followed is best told in Schippers's words:

> I did not agree that there was anything wrong with Callas's singing but from the top of the gallery came an awful hissing sound. Maria continued but when she came to the words '*Ho dato tutto a te*' ('I have given up all for you'), shaking her fist at the gallery instead of at Jason, she sang the word '*Crudel*' ('Cruel man') and then stopped completely, creating a suspense-filled pause. She glared up at the gallery and then sang the second '*Crudel*' directly at the public, forcing it into a deathly silence. There was no more hissing, nor was there any vocal insecurity in Maria's singing. She was very successful and the audience responded favourably, appreciating all the new refinements which she brought to this great role of hers.

Meanwhile La Scala was planning a grand revival of Meyerbeer's star-studded opera *Les Huguenots*, to be staged in the spring during the Milan Fair. Although no definite plans were made it was hoped that Callas would participate in this production with the Australian soprano Joan Sutherland – the Clotilde to Callas's Norma of her London début – as one of the other stars. Callas would sing Valentine, Sutherland the Queen.

After her *Medea* performances Maria spent the next two months mainly at Monte Carlo in continued semi-retirement from the operatic stage. On 27 February she appeared on the concert platform at the Festival Hall in London, to face a cheering crowd. It had been a long time since her last appearance on this stage, but she was not forgotten. The concert was a success, though not without some unfavourable comments from the critics, who thought her voice had lost some of its volume and security. Others, in the minority, found that although there was a certain deterioration, especially in the high notes, in other ways her voice had much improved, with its newly acquired suppleness and greater refinement of expression. Nevertheless, the impression remaining with the public was that, despite its outstanding virtues, it was showing marked signs of decline. A large section of her programme consisted of music which is within the mezzo-soprano range, such as 'O don fatale' (*Don Carlos*) and 'Pleurez mes yeux' (*Le Cid*), and which she sang in the original French. Callas's recording of French arias had appeared a few months earlier and with her wonderful rendering of the Massenet air on the concert platform it was evident that a new repertoire was now available to her.

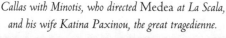

Callas with Minotis, who directed Medea *at La Scala,
and his wife Katina Paxinou, the great tragedienne.*

Following the concert Callas recorded a Donizetti–Rossini recital in London and then began a short concert tour in Germany. She sang, with fair success, in Munich, Hamburg, Essen and Bonn, where a painful eye irritation (due to contact lenses) forced her into hospital until only a short time before the concert which, surprisingly, turned out to be the most successful of the tour.

Back in Milan, La Scala staged *Les Huguenots* as planned but with Simionato as Valentine, the role Callas might have sung. She did, however, repeat her *Medea* in two performances a little later. Even though it was the end of the season, when usually the Milanese begin to disappear for the summer, the theatre was full to capacity. But alas, it would have been better if the second *Medea* had not taken place, for it came as close to disaster as any Callas performance ever could. She tried to play the role in her usual convincing way, and as far as style and good taste were concerned she was, as always, perfection. In fact, she more or less scored in everything except in the most important requisite: her vocalization. On this occasion all her other virtues could not compensate for the alarming deterioration which so suddenly afflicted her voice.

The next eighteen months were virtually inactive, but once Maria had got over her sinus ailment, which was probably the primary cause of her recent vocal difficulties, she began to work hard on her instrument. Elvira de Hidalgo was summoned and the most famous singer in the world became a student again, trying to overcome new technical obstacles.

There were no performances at Epidaurus in the summer of 1962. After her Medea there, Callas was offered *Poliuto* in the following year and declined – the summer heat in Greece was proving too tiring – but she promised to consider returning in 1963. The press, however, ignored her vocal problems and accused her of putting her social life and her affair with Onassis before her duty to art; her every move was reported and when the media ran out of social news, they would occasionally mention possible stage appearances – rumours which never materialized.

None the less, on 4 November Callas made a surprise appearance on the British television programme *Golden Hour from Covent Garden*. She sang 'Tu che le vanità' (*Don Carlos*) and the 'Habanera' and 'Seguidilla' from *Carmen*, giving London the first indication of the formidable eponymous heroine she might make in that opera. Immediately after her television appearance Covent Garden, as well as opera houses elsewhere, offered her the role but she would not consider it. On this occasion, the first since *Medea* at La Scala, the public might have liked what they saw and heard, but she knew that she was still some way from vocal recovery. To sing three arias on television is one thing; to appear in a complete opera quite another. She continued to work hard on her voice, while the musical public, who can be as heartless as they can be loving, were because of her 'silence' digging the grave of Maria Callas the singer.

Even so, by the end of the year rumours were rife about Callas's return to the stage. Although nothing materialized there was some basis for these reports inasmuch as she had been approached by La Scala for two new productions for the 1963–4 season. One was the role of the

Countess in *Le nozze di Figaro*, the other either the title role or that of Ottavia in Monteverdi's *L'incoronazione di Poppea*. Covent Garden, too, was planning *Il trovatore* for her with Corelli as Manrico, to be conducted by Georg Solti and directed by Visconti. Furthermore, arrangements were being made for her to appear in Paris. For a long time there had been talk about *Medea*, then *Norma* was scheduled. But with the change of management at the Opéra it was decided that in the spring of 1963 Callas would sing Violetta in *La traviata*, the performances to be directed by Visconti. Moreover, there was La Scala's plan to visit Russia and it was understood that the contract stipulated that Callas be in the company. None of these engagements came to pass. During the whole of 1963 she sang only six concerts in Berlin, Düsseldorf, Stuttgart, London, Paris and Copenhagen. With the exception of the Paris concert, in which arias from Massenet's *Werther* and *Manon* were included, the programme for all of them was the same: arias from *Norma*, *Nabucco*, Puccini's *Gianni Schicchi*, Musetta's 'Waltz' from *La bohème* and the death scene from *Madama Butterfly*. She was enthusiastically received everywhere and everyone was delighted to see her back, even if only on the concert platform. Vocally, however, Callas was not secure. Trouble with high notes in some numbers was too noticeable to be ignored. Yet in others she had no problems and brought back much of the excitement of old times.

Still no operas were undertaken, while rumours continued to circulate and the international press often published announcements of Callas's imminent return to the stage: Gluck's *Orfeo ed Euridice* in Dallas, *Medea* in New York, *La traviata* and *Anna Bolena* (*Il trovatore* was postponed for later) at Covent Garden and so forth. The truth was that the offers were made, but Callas did not accept any of them. She loved the roles and if she had had the required vocal resources she would unhesitatingly have agreed to sing them. But she had not and for a time she thought that perhaps she might never recover them and began to see life from a different point of view. After twenty-five years of endless hard work, self-sacrifice and putting duty to her art above all else, she looked for a relaxing, normal life, free from the incessant burden of responsibility that her career had constantly demanded. At the same time deep down she cherished the hope that this carefree life would provide the key to the restoration of her health and confidence.

The day after her concert in London Sir David Webster, then general administrator of Covent Garden and a great friend of Callas, offered her a new production of *Tosca*. The cast included Tito Gobbi, indisputably the greatest Scarpia of the generation and Renato Cioni as Cavaradossi. Carlo Felice Cillario would conduct and the director would be Franco Zeffirelli. Callas did not commit herself immediately but promised to give the proposition serious consideration.

Although *Tosca* was not really one of Callas's favourite operas the title role is easy for a singer who has been trained in the *bel canto* method. Therefore at that period of her career, and as her health had improved considerably, she believed that with Tosca she would not be taking too great a risk for her return to the stage. As she also had time on her hands she thought a great deal about the work and was able to justify in her own mind the heroine's motivation, thus liking the role better than she had done before. Furthermore, Maria had always been happy with everybody at Covent Garden and now felt she would have all the support and encouragement necessary from Gobbi, the great singing-actor and exemplary colleague, and from Zeffirelli, with whom she had worked so successfully before. Notwithstanding this seductive climate, it was, in all probability the support she had recently found from Michel Glotz, a producer for EMI in Paris, that finally decided her to take on the role. It was his encouragement that led to a new spate of Callas on disc. She had already recorded for him with success two recitals of French arias and was later to follow with a third, as well as with *Carmen* and a new *Tosca*. Glotz may have used Callas to fulfil his own ambitions but the fact that he was able to inspire her with confidence at a time when she needed it to carry out her own artistic ambitions is in itself an achievement: the Covent Garden *Tosca* might have taken place had Glotz not existed but he was undoubtedly a crucial factor. Zeffirelli, who had refused several offers to direct *Tosca* in the past, said that this was 'because I needed in the soprano a personality who could comprehend my approach. My conception of Tosca was that of an exuberant, warm-hearted, casual woman, and not the grand diva who arrives at the church with four dozen roses, a walking stick, wearing a large hat with feathers, etc. Tosca was never like this. It was amazing how fast Maria brought her to life in the way only she could.'

When Callas sang *Tosca* in London her voice was in much better shape than at the previous year's concert. There was still a fair amount of instability on some notes but as this happened only occasionally it did not lessen the audience's involvement with the drama. Due to her unique vocal and dramatic subtlety, further stimulated by Gobbi's extraordinary artistry, Tosca's tragedy had never seemed more vivid and compelling. Public and critics agreed that this was the greatest Tosca within living memory. They also found several new revelations in this most popular work, yet on closer examination of Puccini's score everything was already there: Callas merely brought out the composer's intentions, which she understood to the full.

Harold Rosenthal (*Opera*, March 1964) wrote that 'this Tosca was warm and feminine, deeply in love with Cavaradossi. ... She was impulsive and deeply religious ... the voice is so much part of the whole of a Callas performance that one cannot really separate it from the acting. She colours her voice such as a painter does his canvas, and if it is not as large and sumptuous as it once was, it still is an amazing instrument, and its timbre highly individual.'

The most perceptive review came from Philip Hope-Wallace (*Guardian*) who wrote: 'True, there were times when the lamp of her art burned low, but it was always bright. You want more power and support behind those shrieks of anguish in Act Two. But how superb the whole delivery in the first act: what detail, what caressing and isolating of key words. All the detail was lovely; some of it unforgettably striking. I have not known Callas so magnificently in control of the situation (if not of the top of the voice) for a long time ...'

With the London triumphs over, Maria returned to Monte Carlo and Paris, where by now she had established a permanent residence in the elegant avenue Foch. Her visits to Milan, where she still had a home, were becoming less frequent after her separation from Meneghini and in March 1964 she decided to sell it. This was the house that had been her castle in the most triumphant years of her career. Now another strong bond with the city of Milan was broken.

In the meantime La Scala's visit to Russia was arranged for the autumn of 1964 and Callas was asked to sing in *Anna Bolena*, but she declined. Although the success of *Tosca* in London had encouraged her to undertake eight performances of *Norma* at the Paris Opéra during the forthcoming May–June, she wanted to wait for the outcome of this rather difficult venture before she could commit herself to anything else, for in spite of the fact that she was now living in Paris only a relatively small French audience had any first-hand knowledge of her art. Of course the world-famous prima donna was widely known from reports and recordings, but she had sung in

Maria Callas, Paris, 1963.

the French capital on only two isolated occasions and never in a complete opera: one the Gala for President Coty, the other the concert in 1963.

The advent of *Norma* with Callas generated enormous interest, the French press considering the occasion an historic one for the Opéra. As 24 May, the day of the first performance, approached their anticipation reached dizzy heights. Callas had not sung in *Norma* since the summer of 1960 at Epidaurus (having also recorded the opera) and, apart from her recent Tosca at Covent Garden, had done no opera for two years. Music lovers arrived from far and wide to hear her in one of her greatest roles, though feelings were divided. Some were confident that she could still cast a spell with her singing, others feared that she might not.

The gala première was a glittering event for the Parisians who crowded the theatre. Although everything in the auditorium was perfect it was by no means the same on the other side of the footlights. Vocally Callas was on far from top form. It was her exceptional dramatic powers and the way she coloured every phrase that confirmed her supremacy in this extremely difficult role. Those who went to hear primarily a voice were disappointed, and rightly so, for she sang with the minimum possible vocal resources. But people who were there to witness an incomparable characterization left the theatre satisfied. Difficulty on some high notes and a lowering in volume were most evident in this performance, which became a combination of torment and triumph for her. The promise she had shown in *Tosca* only a few months before had hardly materialized, though one cannot really compare the two operas which brought Callas back to the stage: *Tosca* is by far less demanding in every respect, whereas the exacting music of *Norma*, with its abundantly flowing phrases, requires the singer to provide a variety of different vocal colours, in addition to exemplary technique.

It must, however, be said that Callas did, on occasion, surmount her vocal difficulties. The third *Norma* found her almost on top form. She dared everything – the high notes and the cadenzas – and consequently her performance was fully rounded. Not so on the fourth which was saved from disaster only by her dramatic mastery. But she found her form again, albeit only intermittently, for those that followed.

Except for Fiorenza Cossotto (Adalgisa), all Callas's colleagues in this production were very helpful to her. Corelli was most co-operative, as were Prêtre (the conductor) and Zeffirelli, all appreciating the privilege of working with this Norma. Cossotto, who obviously had forgotten Callas's generosity when she had helped her during a performance of *Medea* in London in 1959, now took advantage of Callas's occasional vocal insecurity; she would hold on to notes unnecessarily in her duets with Norma, thus impressing those who revel in this kind of endurance test. But Cossotto, like all egocentric singers, went too far. Knowing that the volume of Callas's voice was somewhat limited in these performances, she would sing as loudly as she could at every opportunity. In contrast Maria, facing such inartistic competition, gave some of the quietest singing imaginable; the louder Cossotto sang, the softer the notes which Maria produced. Inadvertently Cossotto helped Maria – but with what lack of generosity. Thus ended the Paris performances of *Norma* which, in spite of everything, were of considerable consequence. Zeffirelli, summing up Callas's portrayal, gets to the root of the matter. He said: 'I had known her Norma from her early days in Rome and at La Scala. But in Paris she was immensely more refined and subtle, infinitely more mature, more real, more human, more profound. Everything was reduced to the essence. She had found what it takes to hit the heart of an audience in a way she had never before achieved. If the voice was not all it had been, what did it matter in the light of what she expressed in every other respect?'

These *Normas* also indicated that Callas, notwithstanding her sporadic vocal shortcomings, might be on the way to recovery. Her serious sinus affliction had passed its crisis and she was looking stronger. This was also confirmed to a degree when not long after her final performance she recorded a complete *Carmen*. Callas found that the role lay for the most part comfortably in her middle register, with few high notes, and her vocalization displayed much of its best quality and former technique. When the recording was released her highly individual interpretation of this heroine, so difficult to cast successfully, was enthusiastically received. Could this be the first step towards a stage performance? Regrettably it was not. She had no such plans.

In July Maria was again sailing with Onassis to Greece. He had bought a small uninhabited island named Skorpios, near Lefkas in the Ionian Sea. His intention was to build a splendid country house and turn the island into his private estate. Construction had started already when the *Christina* anchored in Skorpios's natural harbour. The days were peaceful and Maria began to relax and enjoy being away from crowded cities. During their stay they often visited Lefkas, where in August a festival of folk-dancing and singing takes place. One day Maria quite spontaneously participated in the festival, singing 'Voi lo sapete, o mamma' from *Cavalleria rusticana* and a few traditional Greek songs. It was a very happy occasion for everybody. The inhabitants of Lefkas were excited and honoured beyond description to have with them Maria Callas, a Greek and the greatest singer in the world. She too was delighted to communicate so directly with her compatriots and was moved to tears when all ten thousand islanders saw her off as she sailed away.

Invigorated and feeling all the better for her holiday, Maria returned to her apartment on the avenue Foch in Paris. In November she bought a much bigger and more beautiful flat on the avenue Georges Mandel, a short distance away. She hoped to move into it the following spring and this confirmed that she intended to make Paris her permanent home.

It had been an eventful year, if not completely successful none the less promising. Callas had returned to opera and, more important, she seemed to have overcome the bigger problems of her vocal crisis. With renewed confidence she made a new recording of *Tosca* in December. Even though her previous version, made in 1953 with di Stefano and Gobbi, and conducted by Victor

Maria Callas, Paris, 1964.

De Sabata, had been universally acclaimed, the new one (with Carlo Bergonzi and Gobbi, conducted by Prêtre) was a revelation. Despite her diminished vocal resources Callas, with incomparably deepened artistry, surpassed herself as the definitive Tosca.

The success of the recording further convinced her that *Tosca* was the least risky opera for her at that stage in her career. She agreed to sing it during February 1965 at the Paris Opéra and also to repeat *Norma* there in the following May. In an exchange scheme between Covent Garden and Paris, the London production of *Tosca* was to be taken to Paris, while the Paris *Norma* (both operas staged by Zeffirelli) would be seen in London. The plan was for Callas to repeat *Tosca* in London in March and possibly to sing in *Norma* later in the season. Meanwhile another important announcement was made regarding her appearances. After six years, since her falling out with Rudolf Bing, she was returning to the Metropolitan. Significantly, their quarrel was resolved soon after she had broken with her husband and to reconcile them it sufficed for Michel Glotz to ask them to lunch at a restaurant in the Bois de Boulogne in October 1959. At first Bing offered her *La traviata* but at the time she did not feel confident of doing her best in this work. Eventually *Tosca* was chosen, and only two performances were arranged for March 1965, following her Paris appearances.

The same year also promised some very interesting recordings. A complete *Macbeth* with Callas as Lady Macbeth had been long overdue and a new *Traviata* was very much on the cards. Although a recording with her as Violetta already existed, it was rather an old one and besides, her interpretation of this loveliest of heroines had deepened greatly since the early days of her career.

In February Callas began a series of eight performances of *Tosca* at the Paris Opéra. As in London during the previous year, Cioni and Gobbi were the other principals and Prêtre conducted. Everything started most auspiciously. Apart from some lowering in volume, which was not crucial, Callas was vocally in much better condition than she had been in the last five years; her voice was steadier, the high notes mellower and the timbre had slightly more body to it. She also looked stronger, was more agile and gave the Parisians and the numerous visitors from all over the world a most rewarding portrayal, further refined since her London appearances in this role. Clarendon, the eminent music critic, described the performance as an unforgettable theatrical experience. 'I have seen *Tosca* many times – hundreds, but last night I was convinced it was really the first time,' he wrote. So great was the demand for tickets that an extra performance was announced (with Corelli as Cavaradossi) and sold out immediately.

Hardly had the applause died down in Paris when Maria left for New York, to prepare for her appearances at the Metropolitan in the same role, Tosca, which she had sung on her last appearance there seven years before. New York had always been rather a controversial city for her. In a place where publicity seems to be all-important, it was inevitable that fervent support as well as hostility would be created. As far as the Metropolitan was concerned Maria found that hardly anything had changed. She could not help being sharply, though justly, critical about the shabbiness of the staging and, as had been the case when she had rehearsed *Traviata* on a terrace with chalk marks, once more, incredibly, she was not give a stage rehearsal. Fortunately she had sung the opera many times with Gobbi as Scarpia, Corelli sang Cavaradossi in the first performance and Richard Tucker in the second, and Cleva conducted.

Meanwhile the crowds, hoping for standing-room tickets, formed outside the theatre days before the box-office opened and touchingly they hung a banner reading 'Welcome Home, Maria' across the front of the house. It was indeed a welcome home. On her first entrance she was greeted with six whole minutes of applause, an experience unparalleled even for her. From then on the evening turned into a personal triumph, as Callas quite clearly reclaimed the throne at the Metropolitan. Not that she was vocally as sure as she had been when she was last heard there. Her voice was now noticeably smaller and occasionally a slight insecurity crept in on some sustained notes. But the artistry with which she used her vocal resources, notwithstanding the flaws, was a stunning revelation of what the human voice can achieve. The next morning the reviews, full of encomiums for Callas's performance, appeared on front pages, which happens in New York normally only for the Met's seasonal opening.

Harold Schonberg (*New York Times*, March 1965) declared: 'Her conception of the role was electrical. Everything at her command was put into striking use. She was a woman in love, a tiger cat, a woman possessed by jealousy. . . . This was supreme acting, unforgettable acting.'

Alan Rich (*Herald Tribune*) was even more enthusiastic: 'The voice I heard last night . . . had a creamy lightness to it which summoned up memories of her earliest recordings. She has somehow achieved this without losing her astounding ability to make the voice the servant of the drama. . . . It was – simply as singing – one of the most remarkable vocal achievements in my memory. . . . The whole [second] act, in fact, was a stunning study in humanity.' There was now none of the hostility shown towards her in previous years, and it made her happy to be back in her home town and to be friends with the world – for at moments of such complete acknowledgement and acceptance it seems to be the 'whole world'.

Six days later she left for Paris to prepare for *Norma* at the Opéra. She was happy rehearsing her great role as the Druid Priestess who renounces everything for love and the musical world looked forward to her performance with equal enthusiasm. The diva had recently been singing much better than for some time and possibly in no other role could she be heard to greater advantage. In the meantime she recorded for French television a half-hour programme in which, apart from the interview – mainly about her views on singing in opera – Callas sang arias from *Manon*, *Gianni Schicchi* and *La sonnambula*. The concert was to be televised on 18 May, during the period of her *Norma* performances. Everything was progressing agreeably until three days before the first *Norma*, scheduled for 14 May, when Maria suddenly became unwell. There was an abrupt lowering of her blood pressure and the unseasonable heatwave with an extremely dry atmosphere afflicted her with pharyngitis. Probably her low blood pressure was to some extent psychological. Meneghini had recently been stirring up trouble. He had, since their separation in 1959, always watched Maria; now he filed for a new hearing, hoping that the court would decree that only she was to blame for the break-up of their marriage. Apart from the moral issue, such a decision would also have benefited Meneghini financially as he would then, according to Italian law, be entitled to a bigger share of their common properties. Under these conditions Callas, bowing to the public conception that prima donnas are invulnerable, proceeded to fulfil her engagement. At the dress rehearsal she hardly sang, but saved her voice and physical strength, a departure from her usual procedure of singing full out. For the first two performances Simionato, Maria's old friend and great colleague, was cast as Adalgisa. Though still quite formidable (she had been one of the finest artists on the operatic stage), Simionato was now at the end of her long career and wanted to sing again with Maria before retiring. Cossotto returned for the other performances and Gianfranco Cecchele was the Pollione.

On the night of 14 May the Paris Opéra was packed with the usual elegant first night audience. A few seconds before the curtain the house manager announced Maria's state of health: 'Nevertheless, Callas will sing, but she begs for your indulgence.' Her singing varied from adequate to good and although much of the fire in her voice was missing she nevertheless managed to produce several memorable moments.

With medical care Maria soon felt reasonably well and happily looked forward to the next performance. At 4 p.m. on the day of the second *Norma*, however, her blood pressure dropped dramatically and indeed alarmingly. After having coramine injections, she insisted on going on-stage. It was a most courageous effort, for due to the after-effects the injection can sometimes induce – nausea and some loss of balance – she could hardly walk straight. The first two acts were barely passable, but in the third and fourth acts (the opera was given in four acts), after a slight vocal mishap, she gathered her strength and with a superhuman effort saved her reputation. Almost certainly the abrupt fall of her blood pressure was by and large psychological. For when I saw her in her dressing-room at the end of this performance she told me that she had heard that Meneghini and two of his Italian friends were in the audience. Upset that he might come to see her, Maria asked me to go to the stage door, keep watch and run back to inform her the moment he arrived. But he did not; only the other two came to see her and she gave them no opportunity to mention Meneghini.

Alas, Maria's apparent recovery in the second half of the opera was only temporary but as there was no understudy – the theatre management would only present *Norma* with Callas – she agreed to carry out the remaining three performances. After further medication and rest, she managed these without serious mishap, if with great effort. But in the last performance, though she was singing fairly well, albeit with noticeably diminished volume and her stage movements confined to the bare minimum, she found it impossible to appear in the last scene. In fact she had begun to run out of steam earlier, when she was too exhausted to change her costume after the second act.

Surprisingly there was no scandal this time, as there had been in Rome in 1958, when Callas abandoned *Norma* after the first act. In Paris, when it was announced that she had been able to get so far only with great effort, but now had to abandon the opera, the audience showed their sympathy by leaving the theatre in dead silence. Later many, including the Shah of Persia and Empress Farah Diba, touchingly expressed their solidarity by sending her flowers. She only said sadly, 'I beg Paris to forgive me but I shall return.' The reality was that Maria had had a nervous breakdown and a complete rest was ordered by her doctor. Embarking on the *Christina* in Monte Carlo the following day for a cruise to the Greek islands, Maria, still very conscious of what had happened, had this to say: 'It was not I who was singing. I could not hear myself but I thought I was hearing somebody else, a stranger to my ears.'

A little later, while she was cruising in Greek waters, a Milan court, announcing its decision on Meneghini's claim, through the public prosecutor, that Callas alone was responsible for the break-up of their marriage, blamed them both, finding Meneghini guilty of having caused considerable 'losses' to Maria's career and adding that at the time of their separation and afterwards he had seriously damaged her personal reputation with his statements to the press. On the other hand her association with Onassis was found by the court to be far beyond what was customary in social life and ordinary friendship.

Meanwhile rest and the hot Mediterranean sun showed how beneficial they could be and Maria, looking well and relaxed, returned to Paris two weeks before her next engagement; four performances of *Tosca* at Covent Garden — one to be given before the British royal family as a charity gala in aid of the Royal Opera House Benevolent Fund.

In London, as always, Callas was eagerly expected. Reports of her Paris breakdown only a month before did not discourage keen opera-goers — thousands of whom had queued, many of them for five days, for tickets at prices never before paid at Covent Garden. They were touchingly optimistic that she would rise to the occasion. A recent photograph of her looking radiant at a ball in Paris, given by the Rothschilds, further confirmed her well-being to wishful thinkers. Everything seemed in order until Monday, 28 June, when she was expected to arrive in London a week in advance for rehearsals. Throughout the day friends and well-wishers sent flowers to the Savoy Hotel where she would be staying, but Maria did not appear. In Paris it was merely stated that she would not leave her flat at present. By Wednesday it was known that she had had a sudden relapse. She was again suffering from low blood pressure and was forced to cancel. No matter how hard she tried her doctors decided that nobody under such conditions should or could undertake four performances of any opera. In the end, after Maria's staunch insistence, the doctors agreed that she could undertake just one at her own risk.

Undeniably the public would be greatly disappointed, but the artist's distress must not be overlooked. Above all, Callas wanted to sing and if she did not she would be the greater loser. A statement from Covent Garden said: 'Miss Callas sends her deepest regrets to her many admirers in London and begs them to realize that she would never cancel these performances without real necessity.' Concurrently the house announced that Marie Collier, the Australian soprano, would appear in place of the indisposed Callas. Then came the awful dilemma as to which performance Callas would sing. Quite naturally, the Royal Gala was chosen. It was in a good cause and people had paid unprecedently large sums of money for tickets, to a very great extent in order to hear Callas. Furthermore, the royal family would be present. Nevertheless, this decision was at first received controversially but presently the press were very understanding. Only one London news-paper did try with some success to make a scandal of it: they remembered Callas's past upsets and disagreements with other opera houses and also protested strongly at her decision to sing only at one (and that the royal) performance.

A silent Maria eventually arrived in London only two days before the event. She could not even participate in any rehearsals and her only statement was, 'I am deeply grateful for the inter-est that the press and my admirers have shown. I have come against my doctor's wishes to do one performance. I had to choose one performance out of the four and I felt I was doing what the English people would have wanted when I chose to sing before their queen. I hope I have not chosen badly. I hope I have not upset too many people.'

On 5 July, before Queen Elizabeth, the Duke of Edinburgh, the Queen Mother and a capac-ity audience, Callas sang in *Tosca*. Not surprisingly, there was not much volume in her voice, but she managed to use her diminished vocal resource most artistically, achieving a *tour de force* entirely by means of inflexion and colour. At the end Sir David Webster remarked: 'She sang some things as beautifully as I have ever heard. But it is right – from the physical point of view – that she should sing only one performance.' The critics generally were of the same opinion as Harold Rosenthal (*Opera*, August 1965) describing Callas's portrayal as 'still unique in our day and . . . all of a piece. . . . I had the feeling that we might well be witnessing her last London stage perfor-mance. I hope I am wrong, for she still has the power to illuminate the part she is singing as no other singer can.'

The following day Maria went to Greece, where the climate is so beneficial. For the months that lay ahead there was going to be no work, no singing – only the rest that would, with medical attention, restore her health. In the autumn she returned to her home in Paris. Even though she did not know it, her retirement from the operatic stage had already begun.

I   Maritsa Ralli was on the board of the Athens Opera. She had executive powers in contracting singers.

CHAPTER SIXTEEN

DECLINE AND RETIREMENT

EVER SINCE CALLAS'S separation from her husband and the beginning of her close association with Onassis at the end of 1959, the international press persistently if not very fruitfully, followed their every move. Once the immediate upheavals of their respective marriages were more less sorted out, neither of them was at all willing to talk about their relationship. What the media managed to get out of them was no more than the cryptic 'We are good friends. ... Unless our friendship is given deeper significance there is no spice.' They were, to be sure, constant companions when their work permitted, but contrary to reports from time to time during the next eight years that their marriage was imminent, no such step was ever taken. As time went on this 'marvellous' friendship between Callas and Onassis became a strange puzzle for the Western world.

Having obtained a divorce as early as June 1960, Onassis was free to marry. Furthermore, in October 1961 Tina, his ex-wife, married the Marquess of Blandford in England. Maria, who was only legally separated from Meneghini, was not so free, as divorce did not then exist in Italy. But as she was born in New York and had retained her American citizenship after her Italian marriage, she would have had no difficulty in obtaining her divorce in America, had she wanted one, and would then have been legally free to marry anywhere except in Italy, where she was still considered a wedded wife and would be liable to the charge of bigamy. Be that as it may, she never took such a step, nor did she publicly say very much about Meneghini except during the time when he tried for a second court hearing (mentioned in the preceding chapter). Her statement then referred to the break-up of her marriage:

> The world has condemned me for leaving my husband – the rift came because I would not let him take care of my business affairs any longer ... that's all he wanted, I believe. He put the screws on all the theatres for more money and it was thought it was I who insisted. Naturally, I wanted to be paid what I felt was my worth, but I never penny-pinched if an important performance or theatre was at stake ...

I had the feeling of being kept in a cage so long that when I met Aristo and his friends, so full of life and glamour, I became a different woman.

Living with a man so much older than myself I had also become prematurely dull and old. . . . Now at last I am a happy, normal woman of my age – even though I have to say that life for me really began at forty, or at nearly forty. I don't know if I would consider marriage again even if I were free to do so. Once you're married, the man takes you for granted, and I do not want to be told what to do. My own instinct and convictions tell me what I should or should not do. These convictions may be right or wrong but they are my own . . .

Later on Maria, who had not applied for a divorce from Meneghini in the six years since their separation, discovered through her lawyers that a Greek law passed in 1946 decreed that all marriages contracted by Greeks outside the Greek Orthodox Church were null and void. Therefore, if the Greek-born Maria, who was married in Catholic Italy in 1949, took up Greek nationality her divorce from Meneghini would automatically follow. When on 18 March 1966 she renounced her American citizenship by handing in her passport at the United States Embassy in Paris, Maria was henceforth free to marry again and go anywhere except to Italy. Immediately this was known, the press again took up the question of her marriage to Onassis, but they both maintained their silence except for Maria's comment, 'freedom is so very nice.'

The press continued to report on them mostly with speculative gossip: if Onassis had guests on the *Christina* without Callas, obviously they must have quarrelled and no doubt he was now interested in some other woman. The gossip went even further, implying that Onassis was ill-treating her, insulting her in public as well as in private and that he had ruined her career. They jumped to this conclusion only because Callas had not sung in public since her single *Tosca* at Covent Garden in July 1965. Then, in April 1967 they turned their attention to a court case that Onassis and Callas were bringing against their Greek friend Panaghis Vergottis of London. Vergottis was also in shipping and, although sixteen years older than Onassis, they had been friends for thirty years. 'He is one of my dearest friends, if not the best I have,' so Onassis described him in 1960.

Callas first met Vergottis at the party Onassis gave at the Dorchester Hotel in London after her Medea at Covent Garden in 1959. Their friendship developed and in 1962 Onassis and Callas spent a happy holiday at Vergottis's house in Cephalonia. 'Vergottis is thirty-four years older than me,' Maria later said, 'and as I had virtually no parents, I had the great joy of considering him more as my father. I was very happy about this and he knew it and he considered me his greatest joy. He was very proud to travel around and participate in my glory.'

By 1967 this apparently wonderful friendship ended in the London law courts in what the judge referred to as a case with elements of Sophoclean tragedy. It all started when Onassis, Vergottis and Callas went into partnership in a company that owned a ship. 'I am a woman who works for a living,' Callas said in court. 'Therefore I was anxious to invest the little money I have gained – a lot to me but little to other people – for the day when I would not be able to work, so that I would have a comfortable income.'

The price of the 27,000-ton cargo ship *Artemision II* was $1.2 million and Callas gave £60,000 as a down payment for twenty-five out of a total of one hundred shares. Vergottis was also to have twenty-five shares and Onassis the rest. Of his fifty shares Onassis said that he would give twenty-six to Callas as a present, so that she would have the majority holding. At the time the deal was decided all three partners were very happy about it, celebrating the occasion with a dinner at Maxim's in Paris.

Presently, however, another project, a film of *Tosca* with Callas in the title role, was indirectly to destroy this seemingly happy partnership. Whereas in the past Callas had always decided, after some thought, against making a movie, the situation was now different. A motion picture would not demand the great strain of a stage performance and Zeffirelli, the brilliant producer of her *Tosca* at Covent Garden, would again be directing her. After a successful screen test at the beginning of September 1965, production of the film was scheduled for a little later in Rome. The sound-track had already been made when Callas recorded *Tosca*, conducted by Prêtre, during the autumn of 1964, and Zeffirelli engaged Renzo Mongiardino and Marcel Escoffier, the team he had used in the stage production of the opera, to design the sets and costumes respectively. However, while preparations were being made a crisis overtook the project: Herbert von Karajan had already acquired the film rights for *Tosca* and was set on conducting as well as producing it himself for his own German company. Initially he tried to engage Callas who refused, because that meant she would be letting Zeffirelli down as he would not have been employed by Karajan's organization. Furthermore, and this was a crucial factor, Callas would have had to make a new sound-track for him, which was of course out of the question, as during that period her voice was at its lowest ebb. Hence Onassis, too, was against the idea that Callas should make the film with Karajan. He wanted her to stick to the original plan but his efforts to buy out the conductor failed; the exorbitant sum demanded by the German company to relinquish the film rights was in reality a rebuff to the offer. *Tosca* with Callas was shelved.

There was, however, a dissenting voice on Callas's refusal to make the film for the Germans: inexplicably, Vergottis tried forcefully to make her change her mind. 'You must make this film under any conditions,' he commanded.

'I must do nothing under any conditions,' Maria replied. 'How can I work with people I do not trust?' She then told Vergottis that he, of all people, should know better. Vergottis was furious. His heart died there and then, he said. More hurt than annoyed and completely unable to fathom Vergottis's stand in this matter, Maria wrote him a charming letter saying that if she had given offence she was truly sorry. But he was adamant and would have nothing to do with her. Moreover, he refused to let her have her twenty-five shares for which she had already paid, claiming now that her investment was merely a loan to the company.

Onassis reacted angrily to this sad and disappointing situation: 'Maybe Mr Vergottis does need to borrow money from Madame Callas. I certainly do not.' When Onassis tried to talk about the matter Vergottis told him that only in court would he discuss anything. 'I want to see you in the witness box, you and her,' he fumed. Onassis was stunned by his friend's blackmailing tactics. Nevertheless, they met at a London restaurant, where Onassis tried again to resolve this incomprehensible dispute. 'Get out of here,' Vergottis shouted, while attempting to throw a bottle at him. There was no alternative for Onassis and Callas but to place an action against Vergottis demanding her twenty-five shares.

In court, Vergottis persistently tried to depart from the case at issue. His counsel took every opportunity to question Callas about her marital status, her relationship with Onassis and so forth. 'These questions must be asked,' he said. Although Callas was willing to answer and did, at one point she raised her hand and her voice and exclaimed: 'These questions do not have to be asked. We are here because of twenty-five shares for which I paid and not because of my relationship with another man!'

The defendant's counsel then cross-examined Onassis, mainly about his relationship with Callas: 'After you got to know Madame Callas did you part from your wife and did Madame Callas part from her husband?'

'Yes,' Onassis replied, 'but the partings were absolutely coincidental.'

'Do you regard Madame Callas as being in a position equivalent to your wife if she were free?'

'No sir, if that were the case we would have no problem in getting married.' Finally Onassis was asked if he felt obligations towards Callas other than those of mere friendship. 'None whatsoever,' he answered firmly.

The court ruled in favour of Callas and Onassis. The judge described Vergottis's behaviour unfavourably: 'I hope', he said, 'that I have made every possible allowance for his age and the fact that he is a sick man; his mind is a tortuous one. Also his whole attitude in the witness box gave me the impression that he had in truth stood on his rights, not only that he might see Madame Callas and Mr Onassis cross-examined at length as to the relationship between them, but that he might use the opportunity of going into the witness box to make such venomous remarks about them as he could slip in before he was stopped by counsel or myself.'

There was no elation on Onassis's part. He merely described the outcome of this sad case as 'the humiliation of an old friend, which I bitterly regret'. Vergottis, however, further contested the court's verdict and appealed, only to lose again in October 1968.

The abortive *Tosca* film also caused the virtual destruction of another friendship. While efforts were being made to buy the film rights from Karajan, so Zeffirelli recounted in his *Autobiography*, Onassis sent him $10,000 for development money: 'One day a rather shady-looking Greek called to see me and handed me a bag containing $10,000 in cash, all very hush-hush, no receipt. We had, of course, already spent it.' Feeling enthusiastic about the project Zeffirelli, on his own initiative and before a licence for the making of the film was secured, engaged designers and a script writer. When presently he told Maria,

> Karajan flatly refused to relinquish the rights of *Tosca*, [she promptly said] so send me my money back.'
>
> 'What money?' Zeffirelli asked. 'You know where it has gone – production petty cash.' $10,000 was nothing and, in any case, it was Onassis's money.
>
> 'It was my money,' she said, her voice rising. 'He made me pay it out of the little I have left.' Then she was screaming, 'Give me my money back.'
>
> It was the other Maria, the woman who hoarded cash with Meneghini; the other Maria who resented paying her father's hospital bills and who loved shopping in Woolworths. I told her that I was out of pocket on the project and could not or would not cough up the ten thousand dollars. She slammed the phone down and that was that. My attempts to help her and save her for her art had ended in acrimony and estrangement. It was a miserable feeling, which clouded a period that should have been full of pleasant anticipation.

Considering only Zeffirelli's version of this matter, it is clear that Onassis (the shrewd businessman) would not be prematurely involved as a financial backer – a claim for damages could be made against him in the event of the project proving abortive. Therefore it was wiser that the $10,000 (not so little in 1965) came from Callas herself and of course on certain conditions. Was it intended to be spent before the film rights were secured? Obviously not. Onassis's thoughtful gesture was made so that Zeffirelli should have some ready money if and when the Germans agreed to relinquish the rights.

Zeffirelli further seriously weakened his case by resorting to unfair and in any case odd assertions. By the time he wrote his autobiography he should have known that it was Meneghini who hoarded cash, not Maria. And she did pay her father's hospital bills and much more. One also wonders just how Zeffirelli intended to save Callas for her art. He conveniently forgot that it was through her that he rose to stardom as a producer in the first place, not the other way round. Be that as it may, the fruitful friendship between two highly talented people ended shabbily.

Ten days before the final verdict on Vergottis's appeal, on 20 October 1968, Onassis's unexpected marriage to Jackie Kennedy, the young widow of the late US President, perplexed both the media and public opinion.

The association between Onassis and the Kennedys had begun a few years earlier. Shortly after his divorce, he became friendly with Prince Radziwill and his wife Lee, Jackie Kennedy's sister. The Radziwills were often seen in the company of Onassis and Callas, on the *Christina* and elsewhere. Nothing much was said about this association until Meneghini took it upon himself, without any evidence, to assure the press that Onassis, tired of Maria, had left her for Princess Radziwill. Ridiculous though Meneghini's fantasies – or wishful thinking – were, they provided the press with sufficient fuel to fill their gossip tank. 'Does the ambitious Greek tycoon hope to become the brother-in-law of the American President?' the *Washington Post* and other newspapers in America and Europe were soon asking. This gossip was, however, overtaken when at the beginning of October Jackie also joined the *Christina* for a cruise. 'We'll go where Mrs Kennedy wishes to go. She is in charge here. She is the captain,' Onassis told the reporters who turned out in droves.

Jackie had in the previous August given birth prematurely to her third child, a son, who died. Through Lee, Onassis suggested that she might well speed her recovery by taking a cruise on the *Christina*. Although Jackie readily accepted the invitation, the President took his time to give his consent; Onassis, together with others during the Eisenhower administration, had been accused of conspiring to defraud the American government by avoiding the paying of taxes due on surplus ships; the conspirators were then banned from the American market. This did not endear him to the American public which now might well take exception to its First Lady enjoying, virtually unaccompanied, Onassis's hospitality. Eventually Jackie was formally escorted by Franklin Roosevelt (son of the former President) and his wife, as well as the Radziwills. The other guests included Princess Irene Galitzine and her husband, and Onassis's sister Artemis and her husband. Anxious to avoid any implications that he would be taking advantage of the inevitable publicity, Onassis decided not to go on this cruise but to leave the *Christina* at the disposal of the First Lady. Because he was not to be on board, Callas also opted to stand down. However, at Jackie's last-minute insistence, Onassis did go – she felt that she could not very well accept such generous hospitality from an absent host. At first he stayed in the background whenever the yacht was in port though before long, again at Jackie's insistence, he was accompanying his guests on their sightseeing excursions.

In the wake of this cruise, particularly when a picture, taken on a Greek archaeological site, of Onassis with Mrs Kennedy and her sister was widely published, a great deal of criticism, mainly based on ignorance and malice, was directed at the 'ambitious Greek tycoon'; he was accused of using Mrs Kennedy to get even with his arch rival, his brother-in-law Stavros Niarchos, who had recently entertained Princess Margaret on his own yacht. Furthermore some reporters, abetted by Meneghini, sought (unsuccessfully) to establish as fact that Onassis had abandoned Callas in favour of Princess Radziwill, and two congressmen in Washington avidly questioned the President's wisdom in letting his wife consort with a foreigner who had been under indictment in the United States. Neither the President nor Onassis paid much attention to this criticism. The press then shifted its interest to 'poor' Callas who was apparently livid with Onassis, that unfaithful rascal – an exposé which also failed to draw any comment from the people concerned.

On 22 November 1963, just over a month after his wife returned from her Greek cruise, President Kennedy was assassinated in Dallas. Onassis went to the funeral in Washington and was a house guest at the White House. For the next four years nothing much was reported about Onassis's association with the Kennedys. He did, however, keep in touch with Jackie by telephone and in the autumn of 1967 he was seen dining with her in New York, though not alone. His daughter Christina, now a young lady of seventeen, was with him and on another occasion Margot Fonteyn and Rudolf Nureyev were also in their company. In the following May Jackie joined the *Christina* on a Caribbean cruise. Callas opted out to forestall the possibility of not being invited.

At that period Robert Kennedy who, after his brother's death, became head of the family, was campaigning for presidential nomination but on 6 June 1968 he, too, was killed.

After his funeral Onassis became a frequent visitor to Newport where Mrs Auchincloss, Jackie's mother, lived. He also visited Hyannis Port where Jackie lived with her children, as did Rose Kennedy, the family matriarch, and Edward her only surviving son. Onassis got on extremely well with them all, especially with Rose Kennedy, whom he had known several years before although not well. In between his trips to America, Onassis continued to spend his time with Maria. He did not tell her anything of his association with Jackie or the Kennedys, though she had some idea of what was going on but could not be certain. The matter came to a head when at the beginning of August Onassis, bluntly and without any explanation, told Maria, who was at the time on the *Christina*, that she should return to Paris where he would see her in September. A row followed and Onassis merely said that he had invited friends for a cruise and wanted to be alone with them. It was not very difficult for Maria to guess who these mysterious friends were and as she was not prepared to be treated in this bizarre fashion she told Onassis that he would not be seeing her in Paris in September, nor anywhere else ever again. She then left the *Christina* with her friend Laurence Kelly, who was also on board at the time. The guests on the *Christina* were of course Jackie and Edward Kennedy, and almost certainly it was during the week-long cruise that Onassis had serious discussions about his marriage contract with the ex-First Lady of the United States. Although the matter was settled, Jackie asked that no announcement be made until she had conferred with Cardinal Cushing (who had married her to Kennedy) about the Vatican's attitude to her marrying a divorcé, and also to prepare her young children for their mother's new marriage.

In the interim Maria went to America with Kelly. The break-up of her relationship with Onassis distressed her and although it was she who had walked out, she felt humiliated at having been driven into this situation. Maria learned officially the identity of the guests who in effect had pushed her out of the *Christina* from an August issue of *Newsweek*, which published a picture of Jackie and Edward Kennedy on their way to join Onassis for a cruise.

Two weeks later Doris Lilly, gossip columnist of the *New York Post*, was the first to say on television that Jackie Kennedy was to marry Aristotle Onassis. The announcement was not believed by the American public, which considered it in bad taste and quite unsuitable for their ex-First Lady to make such a marriage. Nevertheless, on 17 October Mrs Auchincloss made it known through the media that her daughter was planning to wed Aristotle Onassis the following week. The ceremony took place on 20 October in the little chapel on Skorpios according to Greek Orthodox rites. Whatever the motives for this unexpected event, hardly anybody in the know was convinced that the union was based on love.

On the same day Maria, elegantly dressed and with a radiant smile, arrived at the film pre-mière of Feydeau's *A Flea in her Ear* in Paris. She put on a brave face and carried herself magnificently at the party afterwards but in reality she was desolate. I wrote to her at the time not so much to offer my condolences but to reassure her in my own way that she still had friends who thought and cared about her at all times, good and not so good, and that it was useful to remember that 'we are never so happy or unhappy as we imagine'. When, about three weeks later, I was in Paris, *en route* to Italy, a mutual American friend who had been to see her encouraged me to get in touch with her. She was pleased by my visit, but I soon sensed that behind the wide smile and a certain liveliness there was a highly strung and depressed woman. Our conversation mostly centred on life's disappointments and moments of happiness, but as if I had myself just been through such experiences and Maria, an older friend, was advising me how to handle the situation. 'You have a failure,' she said, 'and right then you feel it is the end of the world, and that you will never recover from it. But you must think positively for very often you will discover that it may not even be your failure but a blessing in disguise. One can really benefit as much from failure as from achievement.' It was not very difficult to realize that Maria was talking about the ending of her relationship with Onassis and this was her way of refraining from feeling sorry for herself. She never once mentioned Onassis or anybody directly connected with him. As I was leaving, her attitude became less positive and she made me promise to write to her always.

Although Onassis's marriage was a humiliating blow to Callas her biggest problem was that she had not yet recovered her vocal powers. She never stopped longing to return to the operatic stage. The offers continued to come and in an over-optimistic moment she signed a contract to appear in a new Visconti production of *La traviata* at the Paris Opéra. The hard light of day, however, soon stirred her inborn cautiousness and balanced knowledge of herself and she promptly extricated herself by demanding a month's rehearsal with the orchestra, knowing that the Opéra could not possibly accept such a precondition. She also declined to sing in Menotti's *The Consul.* The root of her refusals was not so much a lack of confidence but her certainty that she would not sing well enough. So when the next best thing came along she allowed her imagination to be captured in order to survive artistically at least until she was ready to sing again.

Her lifeboat appeared in the form of a non-operatic film of *Medea.* She surprised everybody when she agreed to play the title role and it was readily, though superficially, construed that Callas wanted to express her personal drama through the character of Medea: a parallel was drawn between Medea's relationship with Jason, for whom she gave up everything only to be abandoned for another woman, and Onassis's treatment for her. Although such parallels can always be drawn, it can hardly be considered relevant in this case. Callas had been portraying Medea with the utmost conviction since 1953, during a period when she was happily and devotedly married to Meneghini, then unequivocally the only man in her life.

It is of interest to examine the circumstances in which Callas the artist agreed to make the film. They were, to a degree, fortuitous. Franco Rossellini suggested that she would be ideal in the title role of *Medea* to be directed by Pier Paolo Pasolini. The idea was born in 1969, a period when Callas was artistically totally inactive and in fact had neither the voice nor the stamina – and consequently not the confidence – to sing on the operatic stage to a standard comparable with her past achievements. Callas, an opera singer who had never appeared in any other form of theatre and who had previously turned down a number of film offers – both of operatic and of speaking parts – by some of the most talented cinema directors,[1] was persuaded by Pasolini to appear in his non-operatic version of *Medea.*

She had already admired and been moved by Pasolini's *The Gospel According to St Matthew* (1964), a successful screen biography of Christ, and had found *Edipo Re* (1967) impressive, particularly the sober way the director dealt with violence in certain scenes. But these attributes would have meant very little had not his conception of the legend generally, and the character of Medea in particular, been in harmony with her own. So, in an atmosphere of personal frustration and a passionate desire to find a means of expressing herself she saw the venture as an artistic challenge.

'I enjoy a challenge,' Callas told Kenneth Harris (*Observer,* 1970).

Here I have had two challenges. Firstly, to express the passion and turbulence of the ancient legend of *Medea* in a way that makes sense to a modern cinema audience. Secondly, I had to learn to act in front of a camera, and act without singing. I do not sing in this film.

Before I did my screen test for *Medea* I invited Pasolini to dinner. I said: 'If I do this film, and at any time my treatment of the role or my performance in general causes problems for you, do not go to anybody else – come right away and tell me. I shall try to do what you want. You are the director, I am the interpreter, and I shall try to make the role my own only to give it back to the public.'

That there was complete accord between director and interpreter is evident. In an article (*Opera News*, December 1969) Pasolini explained his intentions about the film and acknowledged his appreciation of Callas: 'My problem is to avoid banality while interpreting classical mythology clearly according to modern sensibility. . . . It is from personal qualities in Callas that I realized I could make *Medea*. Here is a woman, in one sense the most modern of women, but there lives in her an ancient woman – mysterious, magical – whose sensibilities create a tremendous inner conflict for her.'

Callas's cinematic portrayal is masterly; Medea emerges as a woman whose culture is sorcery and whose mind is dominated by the Furies. These configurations are made convincing by her telling silences and are also suggested by her black and bristling gem-loaded garments which symbolize the Furies. What validates the interpretation is her ability to embody prehistory and create the belief that Medea lives by her senses alone in a world where nature is governed by obscure and inexplicable forces.

Medea was a controversial film. Whereas it was unanimously praised for its visual excellence Pasolini, contrary to what he had preached, fell rather short in his handling of the actors. Except for Callas, who looked superb in Piero Tosi's pagan costumes and acted with restrained intensity and dignity, the rest of the cast were little more than automata. Nevertheless, the movie had a *succès d'estime*, if no great commercial success except in Paris, where it played for several months in two cinemas. Callas herself liked the film to a degree. When I went with her to see it in New York some time in October 1971 she told me that in her opinion one should really see this sort of motion picture more than once, 'in order to appreciate the long, significant, wonderful silences which eliminate much of the violence by reducing the sound and fury of the tragedy'.

The reviews in general were favourable as far as she was concerned. Janet Flanner (*The New Yorker*, 1971) declared that '*Medea* turned out to contain the greatest acting performance of Callas's career'. Also Jean Gênet's 'Letter from Paris' (*The New Yorker*, 1970) described Callas's portrayal as 'a hypnotic performance endowed with true magnetic power . . . a virtuoso corporeal and psychological triumph. . . . In this new Medea there is contained acting of a supreme dramatic achievement, which will rank the film as a rare work of cinematographic art.'

Nigel Gearing (*Monthly Film Bulletin*, November 1975) thought differently. He summed up *Medea* as a 'work which, like its heroine (an unvaried but charismatic performance by Maria

Callas), can be said to face in two directions at once but draws it major strength from past achievements'.

Subsequently Callas was offered the leading role in a film version of Bertold Brecht's *Mother Courage* but she declined. Even though she enjoyed making *Medea*, she did not really find artistic fulfilment in this medium: her ambition, her priority, was to return to the musical stage and as there seemed to be a marked improvement in her voice she was again hopeful.

However, by the end of 1969 Callas's problem was not only the actual production of her voice but also fear of facing the public after five years of complete silence. It is highly probable that this frame of mind played a crucial part in her acceptance of an invitation by the Curtis Institute of Music in Philadelphia to give a series of opera master classes in February 1971. The classes proved unsuccessful because the students were not sufficiently equipped nor advanced in their studies, as she had originally been assured, and she withdrew after only two days.

Whereas the Curtis failed to benefit from Callas's teaching, the Juilliard School of Music in New York succeeded. Peter Mennin, the director, following the advice of Irving Kolodin, the American music critic and historian, seized the opportunity by guaranteeing Callas that his students would meet her requirements, so she agreed to give twenty-four master classes between 11 October 1971 and 16 March 1972. In the meantime it was arranged for her to hear about three hundred students audition (only half of them from the Juilliard) from a concealed position in the theatre, and from these she chose twenty-six young singers for her classes.

After the first class Callas's feelings were expressed in an interview with John Gruen published in The *New York Times*:

> I feel that opera is really in trouble. Singers accept engagements before they are ready, and once they have experienced being on an operatic stage, it is very difficult for them to come back and study. Humility is not one of our best traits. In my opinion, opera is the most difficult of all the arts. To succeed you must not only be a first-rate musician but a first-rate actor. . . . And so I have accepted these classes at Juilliard in order to help singers start off on the right foot. . . . At any rate, I would like to pass on to the young ones what I myself have learned – from the great conductors I've worked with, from my teachers, and especially from my own research, which has not stopped to this day. We must never forget that we are interpreters, that we are there to serve the composer. This is a great responsibility.

During this period, and after I had attended a master class, she told me, 'one of my most important objectives is to shape my young singers' thinking – at least plant the right seed – into distinguishing between good and bad tradition. Afterwards if they are lucky to have good con-

371

ductors, as I have been, they will get somewhere. You see, good tradition is a blessing as it brings to life subtly and convincingly what is often beneath the surface. Bad tradition, on the other hand, is a curse as it only treats music superficially achieving little more than exhibitionist effects. It is in the same way that irrelevant clichés can ruin a well-written story.'

She then spoke about her studies which took place every morning, including an hour with Alberta Maziello, a coach from the Metropolitan Opera. 'Does your teaching help with your own work?' I asked.

'Not particularly,' she replied. 'Opera singers remain, in a way, students all their lives – at least the good ones. And by the way I do not teach. I advise, I guide, which is different, so that with help and encouragement future singers may discover their own personality, their own individuality.'

At the Juilliard the students were seated in the two front rows of the auditorium with the audience behind them. Punctually at 5.30 p.m. Callas and Peter Mennin appeared on the stage. In his brief introduction Mennin made it quite clear that the master classes were in no way performances and that the audience were expected to be silent observers. Mennin left, the accompanist took his place and Callas, with complete concentration only on her students, commenced the class by asking 'Well, who feels like singing?' A baritone raised his hand and went on to the stage. He chose to sing 'Il balen' (*Il trovatore*). Callas listened to the whole aria without interrupting him. This procedure was followed by all the students. Each first sang an aria of his or her choice, then Callas analysed the performances, helping the singer to understand the character he or she was supposed to portray in all its aspects. Nearly always she also demonstrated herself how it should be sung, thereby explaining points of technique and breathing as well, despite her initial statement that she would primarily concentrate on vocal interpretation. (A few examples of Callas's illuminating remarks to her students are given in the discography.) Throughout the classes she approached her pupils as colleagues and friends, with warmth and even affection. On no occasion did she lose her sense of humour or patronize, or even reproach them, but every piece of advice and explanation was given with authority and with the same dedication and involvement she had always brought to her own singing.

After hearing a few of her students, Callas gave them a brief but enlightening talk:

Future colleagues, you will have to carry on what we singers – I – learned from good composers and good conductors. So you have to become strong enough to fight bad tradition – by proving to a conductor that you know the score faithfully. You must dedicate yourselves. That is why I encourage people to start early. This is your life.

Recitatives are very important because they have to be 'spoken'. Every singer has to find his individual proportions. By this I do not mean that you go crazy doing whatever you want. You have to serve the composer – the style of the composer in each opera. Mozart, or Donizetti, or Verdi, or any other composer, has a different style but also each composer uses a different style in each of his works.

We must never forget that we are musicians. That means we are servants to people who are better than us – the composers, who often died in poverty or misunderstood.

You must make sacrifices such as having the courage to say no to certain contracts and also go on a diet, if you need to – starve yourselves a little bit. (I did quite a bit of that, as you know.) We cannot have our cake and eat it. You must have a direction in life. You see, if you love music enough, you must be a devoted musician. Fame will then come automatically.

The master classes were beneficial to Callas as they paved the way, to a degree, in her return to singing in public. For this step, however, there was another, probably stronger contributing factor. During her latter period at the Juilliard Maria renewed her friendship with Giuseppe di Stefano, her one-time colleague, whom she had first met in Brazil and Mexico City as far back as 1951, but with whom she had last sung in *Un ballo in maschera* at La Scala in December 1957. Di Stefano, who also had been having vocal difficulties, was trying to make a come-back. He had experimented on the concert platform and, because of the warmth of his voice and charming personality, though at this point lacking comparable vocal resources, had met with some success. He urged Maria to join him – not an unreasonable proposition. Having sung together so much in the past, they felt that they could help each other to muster enough confidence. Moreover, seeing that di Stefano was not badly received at his concert in New York, Maria agreed, but so far only to record some Verdi and Donizetti duets with him.

They started work in London at the end of November 1972. In order to avoid publicity the sessions were held in strict secrecy in a church in the City. A few days later, on 4 December, Maria received the sad news of her father's death in Athens – the member of her family who had been closest to her had now gone. She did not record on that day as she developed a hoarseness, but on the following day, the last of the session, returned to the studio where, except for one duet, the recording was completed. However, further sessions proved abortive and no part of this recording was issued.

Some time before this event Callas was asked by the management of the rebuilt Teatro Regio[2] in Turin to direct *I vespri Siciliani*, the opera chosen to inaugurate the theatre on 10 April 1973. She did accept but only on condition that di Stefano would co-direct. *I vespri* was a curious choice for the occasion; not only is it not one of Verdi's best operas, it also has little connection with Turin's (or the Regio's) operatic history. Although it contains a considerable amount of beautiful and expressive music, it is a very difficult opera to produce because it is uneven and has several incongruous situations; for example, the truncated finale portrays inconclusively the thirteenth-century Sicilian uprising and, oddly, the four principal characters are left on-stage with their fate undecided. This production also met with other problems. Inexplicably Gavazzeni turned down the invitation to conduct the opera. The prestigious though elderly Vittorio Gui (he was eighty-eight) accepted but five days before the opening night fell ill and his assistant, Fulvio Vernizzi (the artistic director of the Regio), conducted no more than competently. Furthermore, internal politics played a great part in the appointment of the stage designer, Aligi Sassu, who produced some of the ugliest sets imaginable; she seemed to have drawn inspiration from puppet theatre and with the inappositely colourful costumes and Serge Lifar's rather strange choreography, failed to enhance the dramatic atmosphere of the work and neither Callas nor her co-director could improve the situation. In these circumstances Callas[3] and di Stefano opted for a very static presentation concentrating on the inner dynamism of the music, taking meticulous care in carrying out the composer's intentions. Most successful was Raina Kabaivanska as Elena who responded to Callas's direction and surpassed herself despite her lack of the big and highly flexible voice that Verdi required for this role. Not so Gianni Raimondi as Arrigo. A very good singer, if not a great actor by nature, he appeared, on this occasion tired and perhaps unwell (he was replaced in the fifth and last performance) – only his infectious enthusiasm saved his reputation. The other principals, Licinio Montefusco and Bonaldo Giaiotti, benefited from the direction and gave of their best. Where Callas and di Stefano failed was in their handling of the chorus, whose movements betrayed lack of imagination and experience.

After the *Vespri* performances, Maria again resumed work on her voice. She would practise singing alone and often with di Stefano, who continued to try to persuade her to appear with him in public. There was another man lying in wait for the right moment to give Callas just that little extra assurance which would lead her back to the stage: Sander Gorlinsky, a determined and most experienced impresario, who had managed Callas's affairs in England since 1952 when she made her début as Norma at Covent Garden. In 1959, when Callas separated from her husband, Gorlinsky became her general manager. 'It had been a challenge to me, since that last performance of Tosca she gave at Covent Garden in 1965,' he said. 'I tried for years to persuade her to sing again and she would say: "Well draw up a plan," and nothing would come of it.' The day came, however, when something did materialize. In June 1973, after di Stefano's recital at the Festival Hall which Callas attended, Gorlinsky said over dinner, 'What about it now, Maria?' and she and di Stefano agreed they would tour the world together.

The announcement of Callas's come-back concert with di Stefano in London on 16 September 1973 brought in over thirty thousand applications for under three thousand seats. But it was not to be. Three days before the concert she cancelled on the advice of her ophthalmologist. She had developed a painful glaucoma which required medication; undoubtedly this was a physical complaint, though probably brought to a head by nerves. Callas, who had not sung in public for over eight years, was very apprehensive, but within two months she was fit enough and on 25 October she and di Stefano gave their first recital in Hamburg, accompanied on the piano by Ivor Newton. Their repertoire, consisting of six duets and one aria each, was selected from a printed programme at the time of the concert. They were greeted enthusiastically on their first entrance, particularly Callas, and the audience's excitement and appreciation never waned during the whole evening. The critics, however, described her performance as a mere shadow of her former splendour and referred to the remnants of her once-inexhaustible voice.

On 26 November Callas walked with di Stefano on to the stage of the Festival Hall in London, to face a packed audience which gave them a prolonged ovation before they sang a note. The imminent prospect of hearing her voice again – she looked superb and much younger than her fifty years in a white sheath gown with an ink-blue chiffon cape – filled the public's heart with uncontrollable excitement.

It would be a gross exaggeration and an injustice to both artists to say that their singing generally was anywhere near the standard of their former days. A great deal of the eloquence and resplendence of Callas's voice was missing, particularly in her once-glorious middle register, partly because of fear, which made her overcautious, but mostly on account of her substantially reduced vocal resources: the blazing inner fire was all but extinguished.

Even so there were moments, albeit very few, in the duets from *Don Carlos* and *Cavalleria rusticana* and in 'O mio babbino caro', given as an encore, when she dispensed with caution and produced tones full of magical warmth and vibrancy that brought tears to many eyes. Yes, her voice was almost a wreck compared with what it had been but at those few precious moments it was still the greatest in the world. The generally reserved British forgot themselves and at the end of the recital many climbed on to the stage to greet their idol. Callas was deeply moved by her reception but did not allow herself to be taken in by all this adulation. Later that night, well after the applause had died down, Maria's mood suddenly changed. She became introspective and told me with a touch of melancholy, 'You say that people love me. Yes, it is wonderful that they love me so much in London, even though they love me a little bit more than they should. But they really love me for what I have been and not for what I am now.'

A week later they gave a second concert in London. Both were in slightly better voice and she appeared more confident, if still some way from breaking the ice. 'I do need a year,' she said. 'There is nothing like singing in public to find one's form. It is the only way open to me'

Several other recitals followed in Europe, before they began their extensive North American tour in Philadelphia on 11 February 1974. Callas was in passable form but di Stefano was showing signs of strain. When they reached Boston he felt ill and cancelled. Vasso Devetzi, a Greek pianist, filled in the programme and Callas sang alone. There was more freedom in her voice as her confidence increased. Later in the tour di Stefano was indisposed several times and Callas again performed solo. On 5 March they both sang at Carnegie Hall. They were in rather poor form but the public generally, though not the critics, received them warmly.

Several recitals followed in Korea and Japan, their last appearance being at Sapporo on 11 November 1974. Although offers began to pour in immediately the tour had ended, Callas would not accept any of them. Her come-back was worth the try and even though she was singing better as the tour progressed, inasmuch as the volume and flexibility of her voice grew, in truth she was but a shadow of her former self.

Since her last Tosca in 1965 Callas's strenuous attempts to recommence her opera career had proved unsuccessful. She simply could not restore the power or quality of her voice. As a consequence her great confidence in herself, built on sound foundations both of talent and hard work, which had in the past enabled her to meet many challenges, lost momentum. Her non-singing film, *Medea*, was as far as she was concerned a creditable success and the master classes a distinguished achievement, but her attempt at singing again in public led her into a maze from which she could not see her way out. Apart from some academic interest, her last effort with di Stefano not only failed to add anything to her reputation as a renowned singer but, albeit transiently, to some extent damaged it. She remained fully aware of her true capabilities and although she continued to work on her voice, she never again achieved standards acceptable to her. Nor did she make a tragedy of it.

Although Callas's operatic career effectively came to an end in 1965, her vocal deterioration had really begun to manifest itself as early as 1958; the throbbing vibrato with a suggestion of a wobble on certain top notes was sometimes too pronounced to be ignored. Moreover, occasionally the volume of sound seemed somewhat reduced and the timbre, with less 'body', sounded more lyric than dramatic. At first these periodic problems appeared unimportant, as long as her dramatic talent masterfully covered up for her and thus she continued to give unrivalled performances. She did, however, drastically reduce the number of her appearances, not only because she had fallen out with several opera houses but also because of her vocal problems. In 1959 she would not agree to sing more than five of eight *Medeas* offered at Covent Garden.

After the autumn of that year a ten-month period of silence followed and her return to the stage as Norma, and in the following year as Medea at Epidaurus, seemed to promise full vocal recovery. The promise, however, did not materialize and her opera performances and recitals in the next five years were rather few. Moreover, she was vocally erratic: sometimes she would be in good form, sometimes not. She gave excellent portrayals of Tosca in London, New York and Paris, but in *Norma* at the Paris Opéra in 1965, as we have seen, she broke down and was unable to sing in the final scene, and the end of her stage career came a few months later when she could only manage one of the four scheduled *Toscas* at Covent Garden.

There have been several theories about Callas's decline. Although voices change with the years, in her case the causes were rather complex because they were not all specifically vocal. It will be constructive to consider first the immediate causes which forced her to retire temporarily in 1959.

The flaring up of sinus trouble made her unconsciously force her voice, especially on high notes, as her hearing diminished. In addition, the development of a hernia close to the appendix weakened her considerably. Both afflictions, however, were cured, but time was needed for the damage to be repaired. Recovery was well on the way when her health was threatened with low blood pressure, the roots of which dated from the time of the German occupation of Athens, and which later became partly a psychological problem. Even though this too was overcome, or more precisely checked, she found it too much of an effort to sing in public.

'My biggest mistake', she stated in a moment of desperation, 'was trying to intellectualize my voice. It set me back years. Everyone thought I was finished. I tried to control an animal instinct instead of leaving it as it was – just a God-given gift. On top of that, the press were writing so frequently that I had lost my voice I got to the point of believing it myself. . . . My vocal chords have always been and are perfect, thank God, but I got so many complexes from the continual negative criticism which contributed to what I admit was a vocal crisis. I had a big wobble in my voice . . . and I pushed and opened my mouth too much. The sound just poured out without control.'

What she omitted at the time (but told the present writer seventeen years later in 1977) was that her quarrels with several theatres, each blown up into internationally publicized scandals, and her husband's dishonesty in handling their financial affairs which was crucial in the break-up of her marriage, had a devastating effect on both her emotional and spiritual world. Although these were the primary factors which ultimately hastened her vocal deterioration she did not at the time, at least consciously, attach to them as much importance as she should have done. Instead she saw her situation as a challenge and for a period she even thrived on it: in an effort to prove that she was not the ogre she was made out to be she used her art, the only weapon she had, and often succeeded in rising to great dramatic heights.

Another theory professed that Callas's voice deteriorated because of incorrect training which led her to abuse her vocal chords. This sounds like a plausible reason but all the evidence shows that it could not be further from the truth. Hidalgo had shrewdly discovered Callas's true medium. The fact that she had trained her in the *bel canto* method as a dramatic soprano *d'agilità* dispels any doubt about the correctness of the vocal training. Serafin's expert opinion bears this out. Why else would he, a conservative and very down-to-earth opera conductor, have engaged the twenty-four-year-old Callas to sing the monumental role of Isolde solely on the strength of her Gioconda three months earlier? Furthermore, Callas had only ten weeks to learn the role and a year later Serafin coached her in *Norma* (generally considered the most difficult role in all opera), which she sang with success under his direction in Florence. Brünnhilde in *Die Walküre* and Elvira in *I Puritani*, two totally contrasting roles, followed only a month later, with stupendous success. These extraordinary achievements could not have been accomplished with luck or even courage, but were only possible because of her exceptional and assured vocal technique. The eminent conductor, of all people, knew his singer only too well and he would not have taken an unreasonable risk.

Callas's singing of Wagnerian roles early in her career was in later years considered by some to have brought about the decline of her vocal powers. She herself never accepted this and always maintained that singing Wagner never hurt anyone, provided of course one knows *how* to sing — that is, if you do not push the sound further. As these parts are usually very long and require considerable stamina, an inadequately trained or insufficiently experienced singer will in all probability suffer damage. But before Callas sang Wagner she had had about seven years of stage experience in Athens and several leading roles to her credit.

Serafin, who had offered her the Wagner roles, was of the same opinion. 'I felt', he told me years later, 'that Callas had both the vocal technique and stamina for this music and I was sure that not only would it not be detrimental but highly beneficial in the development of her singing apparatus in general. I was, however, at that time against her singing too many Turandots, though I reservedly gave her my approval, because the theatres wanted her to do this role and she had to establish herself. Her Turandot was very exciting and at that time incomparable.' Incidentally, Callas only sang it in 1948 and 1949 and afterwards, being in a more secure position as a singer, apart from recording it in 1957 with Serafin as conductor, dropped it from her repertoire.

There were those who theorized that she masochistically destroyed herself by her perpetual self-mortifying reverence for the composer — this was in no way self-mortification, but artistic integrity. She declared:

> I will never skim through my music. I have to take chances, even if it means disaster and the end of my career. You see, a musician is a musician. Singers are no different from instrumentalists except that they additionally have words. You don't excuse things in a singer you would not dream of excusing in a violinist or pianist. There is no excuse for not having a trill, in not doing the acciaccatura, in not having good scales. Look at your scores! There are technical things written there to be performed and they must be performed whether you like it or not. How will you get out of a trill? How will you get out of scales when they are written there, staring you in the face?

It was this fierce dedication towards her art that sometimes demanded of her an agonized effort to do what the score required, even at the price of straining her resources and it is this that has been misconstrued as destructive masochism. But people often read into great success or failure, especially of the creative kind, either too much or too little and the most intriguing, out-of-the-ordinary, though not necessarily the most correct, explanation is more readily acceptable.

The prevalent theory that Callas's decline as a singer was the result of her association with Onassis does not stand up to scrutiny either. It was perpetrated by those who, without a grain of proof, determined to turn Callas's life into a 'soap opera' after her death. As already explained, Onassis did not prevent her from seeking advice, thereby undermining her confidence, nor was he jealous of her fame. Callas did seek advice from her teacher, Elvira de Hidalgo, and her by then ageing mentor Tullio Serafin. Hidalgo testified to me that Callas, the uniquely exciting singer of her era, did not hesitate to become a student again.

Dedicated artists do not practice caution in the progress of their mission. On the contrary, they frequently take risks, even if by so doing they precipitate the curtailment of their careers. But if Callas had not given everything she had, if she had not intellectualized her voice sometimes beyond its capability, if she had not sacrificed everything for art's sake, she would never have been the sublime artist that she was, a meteor in musical history.

In the process, quite apart from her quarrels with various theatres and the breakdown of her marriage, she burned herself out; her vocal chords may have been in good condition, but it is only very rarely that they are the crucial cause of voice deterioration. The maintenance of a highly accomplished technique depends more on the mind than on prolonged practice. 'I prepare much more in the mind,' she explained. 'A few minutes' work in the right frame of mind can achieve that which otherwise is gained by grinding away endlessly at exercises.' The reverse also applies. When mental energy is drained and the mind no longer concentrates continually on the inner meaning of the music, a dramatic singer may lose much of his or her technique, if not the volume, with the result that the voice will be deprived of its distinguished quality. This is what happened to Kirsten Flagstad in the early 1950s and what, in the end, also happened to Callas.

With the passing of time it became more difficult for her, although at home she often sang well enough. Her health continued to be a handicap; the low blood pressure would at times manifest itself and drain both her physical and mental energy. Nevertheless, in the summer of 1977 she felt confident enough to undertake to make a recording of Massenet's *Werther* in the following autumn, but she no longer cherished much hope of ever again singing on-stage. She died in September.

That Callas wore herself out, while tragic, was as inevitable as life itself. Great art is excessively demanding and more often than not the soul of the artist acts like the sword that wears out the scabbard. It is also a sophism that the great singers of the past (when there were no aeroplanes to enable them to sing in too many places too often) lasted longer. Some did, but not those of genius who illuminated their roles. The remarkable Giuditta Pasta may have sung for rather a long time but her really extraordinary years numbered only around ten. Malibran died at the age of twenty-eight. Several examples can be given of famous singers (though not great in the real sense) who sang professionally for a very long time. Closer study, however, usually reveals how badly they performed in their later years. Even Nellie Melba, who is always quoted as having had an enormously long career, did not, in fact, quite achieve this. She may have enchanted the world but deep involvement and genius were not her greatest assets. She did sing for many years, but during the latter part of her career she almost confined herself to singing – often badly but, according to some people, remarkably well for her age – in *La bohème*: which presents no great terrors to a singer who has been trained in the *bel canto* method. After a few farewell appearances she retired permanently at the age of sixty-seven.

Whether Callas's twenty-five-year stage career (in 1965, when she retired, she was not yet forty-two but she had been singing professionally since she was sixteen) could have been longer is not of paramount importance. For various reasons the exceptional innovators seldom, if ever, fulfil their mission. 'You set a goal', the great composer Robert Schumann declared, 'which, once attained, is no longer a goal. So you aim higher and higher. Failure is then almost inevitable'.

In the final judgement, neither Callas's technical accomplishment – notwithstanding vocal flaws – nor the amazing range, nor even the singular beauty of her natural gift, is remembered. There is something more mysterious: the expressive melody which echoes in the soul and lingers on. When Callas sang, or more accurately moulded her voice, she shaped a living character – now terrifying, now gentle – and one was carried away. The art of singing would have survived without Maria Callas, but how much poorer the world would have been.

---

1   Michelangelo Antonioni for Shakespeare's *Macbeth*; Zeffirelli for *La traviata*, *Tosca* (see previous chapter) and Tolstoy's *Anna Karenina*; Visconti for *La traviata*, Sara in a theme from the Bible and a role in a film about *Puccini*; Schlesinger for the role of Maria in *The Guns of Navarone*; Joseph Losey for Tennessee Williams's *Boom!* Proposals also for films of opera on stage such as *Anna Bolena* and *Medea* and a role with some singing in Hans Habe's *The Primadonna*.
   Callas made a film (British television) of the second act of *Tosca* at Covent Garden in 1964. Films of some of her concerts and the second act of *Tosca* (Paris Opéra, 1959) have also survived. Some excerpts of her performance of *La traviata* (Lisbon, 1958) also exist. They were secretly filmed with one camera and are dark.
2   The original theatre, built between 1738 and 1740 by Benedetto Alfieri, was destroyed in 1936 by fire.
3   In 1951 Callas triumphed as Elena in *I vespri* at the Maggio Musicale Fiorentino and at her official début at La Scala.

LUCIA DI LAMMERMOOR

Opera in three acts by Donizetti; libretto by Salvatore Cammarano. First performed at the San Carlo, Naples, on 26 September 1835.

Callas first sang Lucia in June 1952 in Mexico City and last in November 1959 at Dallas, a total of forty-three performances.

Left Act 1: *A ruined fountain (haunted by the ghost of a girl killed by her lover) in the grounds of Ravenswood Castle. It is twilight.* Terrified of Enrico, her brother, Lucia (Callas) persuades Edgardo (Raimondi) to keep their love secret. They exchange rings before they part, swearing that in the eyes of heaven they are man and wife: 'Verranno a te sull'aure i miei sospiri ardenti' ('My sigh will come to you on the breeze').

Callas's prodigious insight, that achieved perfect fusion of words and music and her gift of caressing broad melodic phrases, enabled her to express sensual love in Lucia's all too brief hour of happiness (San Carlo, 1956).

Right Act 2: *Enrico's apartments in the castle.* Enrico (Panerai) has discredited Edgardo through a forged letter in the hope that Lucia may be persuaded to marry the rich Arturo and thus save her family from financial ruin. Eventually Lucia submits.

At the sight of the letter, Callas shook as if from an inward tremor. 'Il core mi balzò' ('My heart is breaking') spoke volumes in its hopelessly total submission. In 'Soffriva nel pianto' ('I suffered in tears') all the melancholy, suffering and loneliness of the hypersensitive Lucia was expressed through heart-rendingly private tones: now in a world of her own, she could no longer offer resistance to the madness that was overtaking her.

Right Act 2: Callas as Lucia (La Scala, 1954).

Below *The great hall in the Castle of Lammermoor.* Enrico sees that Lucia signs the marriage contract with Arturo.

Unexpectedly Edgardo appears and angrily claims his avowed bride. As he expresses his conflicting emotions, 'Chi mi frena in tal momento' ('Who can restrain my fury now'), Lucia deplores her misery, Enrico his remorse, Raimondo and Arturo their horror and Alisa her solidarity with Lucia. Their voices combine ingeniously, they separate and reunite in a descending sigh, with Lucia's desperate voice floating above all others. When Lucia ratifies the marriage contract, Edgardo throws his ring back at her, cursing her and the House of Lammermoor (San Carlo, 1956).

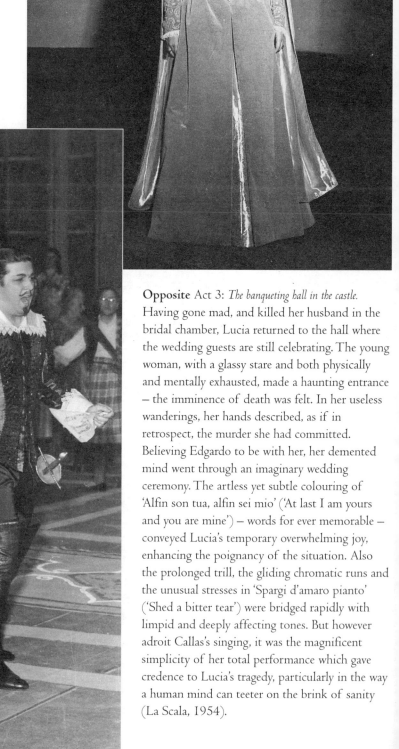

Opposite Act 3: *The banqueting hall in the castle.* Having gone mad, and killed her husband in the bridal chamber, Lucia returned to the hall where the wedding guests are still celebrating. The young woman, with a glassy stare and both physically and mentally exhausted, made a haunting entrance – the imminence of death was felt. In her useless wanderings, her hands described, as if in retrospect, the murder she had committed. Believing Edgardo to be with her, her demented mind went through an imaginary wedding ceremony. The artless yet subtle colouring of 'Alfin son tua, alfin sei mio' ('At last I am yours and you are mine') – words for ever memorable – conveyed Lucia's temporary overwhelming joy, enhancing the poignancy of the situation. Also the prolonged trill, the gliding chromatic runs and the unusual stresses in 'Spargi d'amaro pianto' ('Shed a bitter tear') were bridged rapidly with limpid and deeply affecting tones. But however adroit Callas's singing, it was the magnificent simplicity of her total performance which gave credence to Lucia's tragedy, particularly in the way a human mind can teeter on the brink of sanity (La Scala, 1954).

LA TRAVIATA

Opera in three acts by Verdi; libretto by Piave. First performed at La Fenice, Venice, om 6 March 1853.

Callas first sang Violetta in *La traviata* in Florence in 1951 and last in Dallas in 1958, a total of fifty-eight performances.

Left, below and opposite Act 1: *Violetta's salon in Paris.* Alfredo (di Stefano) passionately pours out his love for Violetta (Callas): 'Un dì felice eterea mi balenaste innante' ('One memorable day you suddenly stood before me').

With feigned superficiality Callas implied that Violetta was only a carefree courtesan but her sighing nervousness betrayed denial of her true feelings. She then gave him a camellia to bring back when it had faded: 'Oh ciel! Domani! – Ebben ... domani ... Addio!' ('What joy, tomorrow! – Well then ... tomorrow ... Farewell') (La Scala, 1955).

Right Violetta muses over Alfredo's declarations of love.

Callas's voice gained in exuberance as she thought more positively: 'Oh gioia ch'io non conobbi, esser amata amando!' ('To love and be loved – a joy I have never known!'). Hesitantly her soul-searching in 'Ah fors' è lui' ('Can he be the right man?') reawakened in her past romantic fantasies as she repeated, with introspective ecstasy, Alfredo's words. It became a yearning to hear them again: 'Di quell' amor ch'è palpito' ('Ah, this is love that palpitates') – until her unhappiness, her loneliness returned. Overtaken by a hectic gaiety, she let her hair down and with a suggestive movement of her pelvis hurled herself on to the table. Then, kicking her slipper off and throwing her head back, she vowed with ironic brilliance to suppress love: 'Sempre libera degg'io folleggiare di gioia in gioia' ('Ever free, I long to hasten from pleasure to pleasure').

Suddenly Alfredo's voice created a conflict within her. She ran to the window to make sure it was him, but panicked when she deemed that the voice was perhaps in her mind; unconsciously Callas cradled her face uttering 'Oh, amore!' – the point of no return.

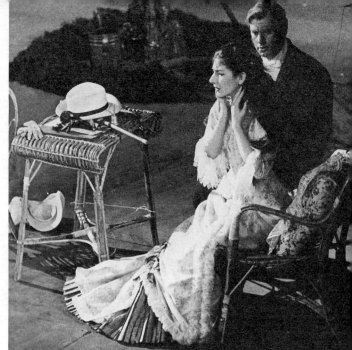

Act 2: *A country house near Paris where Alfredo and Violetta live.* Callas received Germont (Bastianini), Alfredo's father, with timidity and foreboding, but when he accused her of ruining his son's life she checked his brusque manner politely but firmly: 'Donna son'io signore, ed in mia casa' ('I am a woman, Sir, and in my house'). Germont demands Violetta's separation from Alfredo: their scandalous liaison jeopardises his daughter's impending marriage. Callas's initial stillness carried a stark inevitability: 'Ah no! Giammai!' ('Ah no! Never!'), her lyric voice beginning to assume heavier dramatic accents as she protested and pleaded by turn that she would prefer death to separation.

Above With tender resignation and great pathos Callas accepted her supreme sacrifice: 'Se pur benefico le indulga Iddio, l'uomo implacabil' ('Even if God forgives, man remains implacable'). Following a long-sustained B flat on 'Ah!' – as if it were her last cry – she then descended to 'Dite alla giovine sì bella e pura' ('Tell your pure and beautiful daughter'), when Callas's poetic magic performed a miracle of dramatic expression by 'suspending' the long phrase in mid-air so simply, so movingly. All her conflicting emotions were concentrated in this phrase; a little hesitation before the word 'pura' conveyed the embarrassment of Violetta's world – never before had her grief been so concisely and so intimately transfigured. This is the turning point of the opera. She knows that she is lost.

Left Resigned to her fate, Violetta now has to face up to her tragedy.

The full dramatic tone in Callas's voice was heard when before parting she asked Germont: 'Qual figlia m'abbracciata forte così saró' ('Embrace me as you would a daughter. I will then find strength'). He called her a noble woman.

Violetta prepares to leave an unaware
Alfredo for good.

Her face distorted with grief, Callas
forced herself to write a farewell note to
Alfredo, who presently comes in. Anxious
to leave, Callas embraced Alfredo, her face
down so that he will not see her tears:
'Amami Alfredo amami quant'io t'amo . . .
Addio!' ('Love me Alfredo as much as I
love you . . . Addio!') became the
memorable cry of a desperate but dignified
soul. (Later Callas explained that as
women are not very beautiful when they
cry, she wanted Alfredo to remember
Violetta as the most beautiful woman in
his life.)

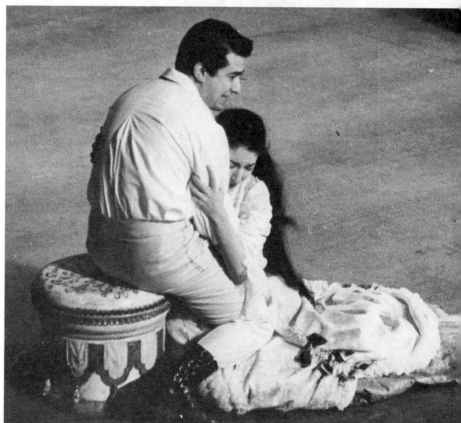

Act 3: *Flora's salon in Paris. A lively party is in progress.* Violetta is a courtesan again. Her admission of having returned to her former lover so infuriates Alfredo that he insults her, throwing his gambling winnings at her: 'Che qui pagata io l'ho' ('I now pay my debt'). After Alfredo has further degraded Violetta by hurling her to the floor, Flora and Gastone support her.

Employing the weakest of tones in 'Alfredo, di questo core' ('Alfredo, what cruel heart'), Callas expressed the feelings of a forsaken woman who has lost her audacity and the desire to live.

Opposite left and centre Callas as Violetta: At Covent Garden, May 1958. **Right** in Lisbon (Kraus as Alfredo) March 1958.

Above left The destitute Violetta, now a living corpse (her tuberculosis is terminal), has dragged herself from her bed to her dressing-table.

Quietly, Callas reread in Germont's letter that Alfredo knows of Violetta's sacrifice and will be returning to her – a glimmer of hope, that vanished as she looked in the mirror; her agonising exclamation 'Oh come son mutata' ('How I have changed') signalled the approach of death. Sadly – her voice weak and heart-rending, but one that spoke volumes – Callas bade her farewell to life, to the happy dreams of the past: 'Addio del passato' – a haunting sigh from the depths of a purified soul.

Above right Alfredo did return but Violetta died as his father came to embrace her as a daughter. Dr Grenvil (Maionica) confirms that she is dead.

LA SONNAMBULA

Opera in two acts by Bellini; libretto by Romani. First performed at the Teatro Carcano, Milan, on 6 March 1831.

Callas first sang Amina at La Scala in March 1955 and last at the Edinburgh Festival (the La Scala production) in August 1957, a total of twenty-two performances.

Right Act I: *The village green.* Amina (Callas) thanks everybody for their good wishes on her betrothal to Elvino.

More ballerina than prima donna in appearance, Callas's *physique du rôle* was a great asset. But it was the disarming simplicity and charm of her singing that primarily established Amina's character. In 'Come per me sereno' ('How wonderful it is for me') the elaborate embellishments (which rise to high E and, at one point, drop two and a half octaves in vocal range) expressed in turn Amina's affectionate side and her passionate sensitivity – the brilliant chromatic semi-quavers her overflowing joy, the high notes at the magic moment when the crest of emotion is reached.

Below At the signing of the marriage contract (the wedding is to take place the following day) Elvino (Monti) places a ring his mother had worn on Amina's finger.

Callas's limpid singing particularly in 'Sposi! Oh, tenera parola' ('Married! Oh, what a sweet word') blended Amina's innocence with the passionate side of her nature.

Rodolfo's room in the inn. It is night. Upset by Elvino's jealousy, Amina sleepwalks her way through the window into Rodolfo's bedroom. Deeply moved by the sincerity of her love for Elvino, Rodolfo leaves, so that she will not be compromised. Amina sinks on to his bed to be, presently, rudely awakened by the villagers and Elvino, who casts her off.

Veiling the tone of her voice, Callas effectively seemed to be singing in her sleep. The timing and vocal colouring in her duet with Rodolfo and the way she suspended her last phrase 'Elvino abbraciami, alfin sei mio!' ('Elvino embrace me! At last you are mine!') were memorably moving. In 'Dun pensiero, e d'un accento' ('Not in the remotest regions of thought'), when Amina awakes in a damning situation, Callas conveyed Amina's cry of sorrow.

The village green with the water-mill in the background.
Elvino, now set on marrying Lisa, the innkeeper,
delays when Amina is seen sleepwalking. As she
crosses a fragile bridge a plank breaks. Still
asleep, she laments the loss of her betrothal
ring, prays for Elvino's happiness and weeps
over some flowers that he once gave her.
Convinced of her innocence, Elvino replaces the
ring on her finger as she awakens in his arms.
They hurry to church for their wedding.

In this scene Callas reached the pinnacle of
her art. Her utterances as in 'L'anello mio' ('My
own ring') were heart-rending, 'Ah, non credea
mirarti, si presto estinto, o fiore' ('Ah, I never
thought this flower would wither so soon')
evoked the sounds of rippling water and sighing
zephyrs. This was exquisite singing, creating a
tender, introspective quality, especially where the
only accompaniment is a viola, while her
fioriture attained the right conclusion of the
built-up emotion. In 'Ah! non giunge uman
pensiero al contento ond' io son piena' ('Ah,
nobody can understand the happiness I feel')
Callas used the cascades of embellishment like a
virtuoso instrumentalist to bring out the essence
of the music, which conveys the bounding
delight of an innocent soul who triumphs over
adversity.

ANNA BOLENA

Opera in two acts by Donizetti; libretto by Romani. First performed at Teatro Carcano, Milan, on 26 December 1830.

Callas sang Anna in 1957 and 1958 at La Scala, a total of twelve performances.

Right Callas as Anna Bolena.

Below Act I: *A hall at Windsor Castle. It is dawn.* While Anna is anxiously awaiting her husband, Henry VIII (who is widely rumoured to have lost interest in his wife) she asks Smeaton, her page, to sing for them, but interrupts his song on the words 'Quel primo amor che. . .' ('That first love which. . .').

A nostalgic calmness but vibrant sound imbued Callas's voice when she thought of her own first love, then a darker colour when her feelings turn to those of regret, even guilt; her grand ambition to become queen made her throw over this love.

Above *The royal hunt is about to commence at Windsor Great Park.* In his plan to divorce his wife Henry (Rossi-Lemeni) has recalled Percy (Raimondi), her youthful love, from exile. Anna is greatly disturbed to see Percy, who presumes that the Queen has brought him back.

Left Encouraged by her brother, Rochefort, Anna agrees, albeit reluctantly and with foreboding, to let Percy see her alone.

Right Henry and his courtiers surprise Anna in what wrongly appear to be compromising circumstances: Percy threatening suicide for the love of Anna, Smeaton (Carturan) accidentally dropping Anna's portrait from his cloak. The King accuses Anna of adultery and orders the arrest of everyone concerned.

Callas maintained the Queen's composure until Henry commanded her to save her explanations and pleas for the judges, whereupon in a unique combination of panic and anger she conveyed eloquently the tragedy and impending humiliation of Anna Bolena: 'Giudici? ad Anna? Giudici. . . . Ah! segnata è la mia sorte, se un accusa chi condanna . . . Ma scolpata dopo morte, e assoluta un dì sarò' ('Judges for Anna? . . . Ah! My fate is decided if my accuser is also my judge . . . But I will find justice after death and will be absolved').

Below Act 2: *Ante-room to Anna's prison in the Tower of London.*

Callas's affectionate tone, when she hoped to find solace in Giovanna Seymour (Simionato), her beloved lady-in-waiting, gradually gathered momentum to culminate in a terrible outburst as she curses her rival, whoever she may be: 'Sia di spine la corona ambita al crine. Sul guancial del regio letto sia la tema ed il sospetto!' ('May the crown for which she has lusted be of thorns, the royal bed be haunted with dread and suspicion').

More bitterness and fury follow when Seymour confesses that she herself is the Queen's rival. Finally Callas's voice assumed the grandeur of forgiveness: 'Ti rimanga in questo addio l'amor mio, la mia pietà' ('In our parting, remember my love and compassion').

Above *A vestibule outside the Council chamber where the peers are conferring.*
Henry calls Anna a shameless woman when she boldly accuses
him of forcing Smeaton into a false confession that he had been
her lover: 'Ella può darmi morte, ma non infamia' ('You may
take my life but not my honour').

Right *The courtyard of the Tower of London.* Anna, sentenced to
death, is lost in illusions which verge on insanity.

Callas sang the deceptively simple melodies with a variety of
subtle colorations; the long phrases, the finest of trills, the
tenderness, were never amiss. 'Ah! dolce guidami castel natio' ('Take
me back to my happy native castle') became the stirring swansong
of an exhausted soul touched by the sweet memory of love. Her
resignation carried a touching melancholy in 'Cielo, a'miei
lunghi spasimi. . .' ('In heaven, where my long suffering. . .') – an
exquisitely embellished version of the traditional song 'Home
Sweet Home'.

When cannons and bells acclaimed Seymour as the new
queen, Callas, in great style – after she had momentarily
searched for her own crown on her brow – soared in trills and
roulades fully employed to express both her rage and forgiveness
of the 'iniquitous couple', in the hope that God might judge her
with clemency.

PART SIX

Finale

• CHAPTER SEVENTEEN •

REMEMBRANCE OF TIMES PAST

CONSIDERING CALLAS'S ARTISTIC eminence, during her lifetime, press reports of the circumstances surrounding the breakdown of her marriage to Meneghini and subsequent liaison with Onassis were relatively sparse. So few hard facts were known about Callas's affair with Onassis and, indeed, of her private life with her husband, that the usually embroidered and occasionally self-contradictory gossip about her was largely kept in check by the danger of expensive litigation. Even Onassis's eccentric marriage to Mrs Kennedy hardly exposed, notwithstanding the extensive publicity surrounding the event, the motivation or feelings of any of the people involved – Callas remained enigmatic.

The truth of the matter was that her personal life, after Onassis's marriage, was not so hapless as some writers later made it out to have been. She never lost touch with Onassis, who came back to her just over a month after his wedding. At first her feelings were divided, oscillating between proud reluctance to have anything to do with him and longing to be with him. It took her a little time to prepare herself emotionally.

'After all,' Onassis teased her at dinner in the house of a mutual friend, 'you have nothing against me except that I, one fine day – no, it was raining cats and dogs if you want the absolute truth – I went and got "hitched". Well here I am and you can't say that I got "hitched" all that much.' Maria, whose sense of humour was sometimes rather slow, was bemused, until their hostess jovially asked Onassis for more of the same and they would drink to it. 'But you, Maria,' Onassis continued in a mock-serious tone, 'were quick to comment that I was as beautiful as Croesus and that I would make an excellent grandfather to my bride's children.' Taken aback, somewhat, to have her own words thrown at her Maria did see at last the lighter side of life and with feigned formality protested that her remarks were not in any sense denigrating. She merely wanted to say that Mrs Kennedy was young and surely that could only be taken as a compliment? As for Croesus, she had always assumed that he was beautiful as well as rich, a fact that had never to her knowledge been disputed. This badinage helped to break the ice, whatever

400

its thickness. The truth about the marriage was not to dawn on Maria until some time later.

Maria and Onassis continued to meet from time to time and their old relationship began to develop into genuine friendship, in which Onassis's rapport – or the lack of it – with his wife played a significant part. There is little doubt that the marriage was based on a contract in which both parties drove a very hard bargain indeed. Nevertheless, it did not take Onassis too long to realize that Jackie and the aura she had brought to his life were leaving a great deal to be desired. Not that he had expected much on the personal level. But what he got was considerably less than he had bargained for. In these circumstances he handled himself, at least in the beginning, with consummate nonchalance. He assumed the role of the great protector rather than that of a normal husband, telling the world that his wife 'is a little bird that needs freedom and security. She gets both from me. . . . She can do exactly as she pleases such as travelling, attending international fashion shows and go out with friends to the theatre or anywhere else. And I, of course, will do exactly as I please. Neither of us questions the other.' Husband and wife continued to live their own lives in perfect harmony. They were only occasionally together, but this arrangement did not create any problems as it would seem it was part of their marriage agreement. Onassis, a man of genuine largess, even managed to stomach Jackie's pathological extravagance; she spent one and a half million dollars on herself in the first year of her marriage alone and other vast sums in redecorating the house at Skorpios.

In February 1970, however, Onassis could no longer ignore the fact that his marriage was rapidly heading for the rocks. His pride was wounded when some letters, written by Jackie to her former companion, Roswell Gilpatric, a married man, appeared in the international press. They had fallen into a dealer's hands and were published, before Gilpatric recovered them by order of the court. Only one letter, which Jackie wrote to Gilpatric a few days after the wedding, was of some concern to Onassis. It ended with the words: '. . . dear Ros – I hope you know all you were and are and will ever be to me.' There was nothing compromising about this, as it did not positively establish infidelity on Jackie's part, but rather a profound friendship. However, the fact that Gilpatric's wife filed divorce proceedings on the day following publication put Onassis on his mettle. It was not so much what the offending letter disclosed that upset him, but his apprehension of becoming a social laughing stock.

Wisely, he took no drastic steps about his wife's ambiguous indiscretion and the press did not make too much of it as far as he was concerned. This in no way deterred him from living up to his dictum, 'And I, of course, will do exactly as I please.' Presently, with more impunity than usual, he sought refuge with Maria, who now became his confidante. He saw a great deal of her on several consecutive days, but when they were photographed together at Maxim's Jackie rushed to Paris to 'reclaim' her husband.

At about this time, speaking to David Frost on American television, Callas said of Onassis that 'he also considers me his finest friend. That is a lot in life. He is charming, very sincere, spontaneous. I am certain that he needs me sometimes because I would tell him the truth. I think he always will come to me with his problems because he knows I would never betray any confidence and above all I would have an objective mind. I too need his friendship.'

After a while Onassis again began to see Callas often. He had many troubles and needed a trustworthy friend: his young daughter, Christina, had made a disastrous marriage with Joseph Bolker, a real-estate agent twenty-eight years her senior, with four daughters from a previous marriage. In his fury, Onassis cut off Christina from her trust and brought so much pressure to bear on the couple that the marriage lasted only seven months. Moreover, three months after Christina's marriage her mother, now divorced from the Marquess of Blandford, had most incredibly married Stavros Niarchos, the husband of her dead sister Eugenia and Onassis's rival and bitter enemy. Eugenia had died on her husband's private Greek island in highly suspicious circumstances (from various physical injuries and a large quantity of barbiturate sleeping pills) eighteen months previously. It was widely believed at the time that Tina's strange marriage was arranged by her mother, so that the family fortunes would be kept together. Three years later, in October 1974, Tina was found dead at the Hôtel de Chanaleilles in Paris. The autopsy gave oedema of the lung as the cause of death but Christina always remained highly suspicious of the circumstances in which her mother died.

The list of disastrous marriages now also included Onassis's own. He could no longer communicate with his wife, as she was unwilling to involve herself in any of his worries or to comfort him. He set about finding a way to end it, once he had managed to reduce to the bare minimum Jackie's legal claim on his estate. Time, however, was to go against him: the death of Alexander, his only son, in an aeroplane accident all but broke him and the serious deterioration of his health robbed him of his extraordinary energy. He died in Paris on 15 March 1975 and was buried on Skorpios.

Onassis's death was a terrible blow to Callas, even though she had been prepared for it for some time. They had always kept in touch. He had been suffering from polymyositis (myasthenia gravis), an incurable though not always a fatal disease, and had already lost the function of some muscles. In the first week of January 1975 Onassis visited Maria at her home in Paris on his way to Athens from America. At the beginning of February he collapsed in Greece and was brought to the American Hospital in Paris for a gall-bladder operation. Maria visited him once, but she was in Florida when he died.

After his death, followed by Callas's two years later, all legal barriers were lifted and some writers and journalists began to misconstrue events in their life together. Lacking any real knowledge of the woman and ignoring the artist, the affair was misguidedly given undue prominence, as if it were the most important event in Callas's life, further implying that in the final analysis her fame, which in this context amounted to notoriety, was acquired because of this association, thereby obscuring the real significance of one of the most influential artists of the century.

The tendency to turn Callas the woman into a 'soap opera' super-queen (an implausible characterization) presented her sometimes as a victim, often suffering from persecution mania, and at others as still an adolescent. Within this contrived scenario Onassis was, of necessity, preposterously cast as principal villain – the jumped-up peasant who became a multi-millionaire but remained a confirmed philistine and male chauvinist pig, and who allegedly ruined Callas's career, before abandoning her to die of a broken heart. In this farrago, hardly worth the trouble of contesting, Meneghini could only be cast in a rather dull secondary role, but that of villain none the less.

The invented Callas–Onassis equation was not only contradictory but could not have been more misconceived. It will suffice to repeat that Callas attained the height of her unique art and was hailed as the greatest singer-actress of her generation long before she met Onassis. In fact, her career was having its final glow when she entered into a relationship with him.

The first exponent of this 'soap opera' scenario was Arianna Stassinopoulos who claimed in her book, *Maria, Beyond the Callas Legend* (1980) – written after Onassis's and Callas's deaths – that at the beginning of her relationship with Onassis Callas declared: '"I'm thirty-six and I want to live – I want a child, but I don't even know if I'm capable of giving birth to another being. . . ." It took the discovery that she was pregnant [in 1967, when Callas was forty-three] to make her see just how much she did want it. . . . Onassis did not. It was painful enough to have the man she adored reject, instead of celebrate, the child of their love, but he went further: he warned her that if she went ahead and kept the child it would be the end of their relationship. . . . Her abortion, at the moment when she longed for a new source of energy and meaning, was her life's greatest might-have-been.'

Though it is possible for a woman to make such a sacrifice, for whatever reason, if the known facts about Callas are examined, such an event and subsequent action on her part would have been most unlikely. Indisputably, Callas yearned to have children. She had often expressed this wish since her marriage at the age of twenty-five. As she did not conceive in the ten years she was married to Meneghini it was wrongly assumed by some that he denied her this happiness because during her pregnancy she would not be earning money.

Stassinopoulos gave this assumption the force of fact by quoting a conversation Meneghini purportedly had with his wife. She wrote: '"One day when she was thirty-four [in 1957]," recalled Meneghini, "Maria confessed to me that, above everything, she wanted a child. She went on saying that again and again. But I told her that having a child would have destroyed the great diva that she had become."'

As Meneghini was alive at the time this was published, he took exception to such 'an absurd fabrication', he wrote in *Maria Callas mia moglie*. 'I lived with Callas for twelve years,[1] day and night, and I knew her better than anybody else. . . . Stassinopoulos never met me nor spoke with me not even on the telephone. She never got in touch with me. Yet in her book not only does she quote conversations about serious matters that I allegedly had with my wife in private, but also my thoughts and even recollections. This alone justifies my indignation.'

Apart from her seemingly unsubstantiated statement about the pregnancy and abortion together with the apparently 'imaginary' conversation Meneghini might have had with his wife, Stassinopoulos offered no other evidence save that some women told her about Callas's pain at recollecting the event later. However, Stassinopoulos revealed how she came to know about the abortion in an interview (*Cosmopolitan*, October 1980) on the occasion of the publication of her book. She says that 'she often dreamed about Callas – she keeps a diary of her dreams – and woke up feeling as if she understood more about Callas's feelings. She felt intuitively certain that Onassis had made her have an abortion – and when she bluffed that she knew about it, she got the confirmation from one of Callas's closest women friends, "How did you know? Only three people knew about it!"'

Even though crucial evidence overwhelmingly undermines such an allegation, the reason I dwell on this subject is because by analyzing it a great deal of light is shed on Callas and also it puts the record straight for Onassis whose ethics were unjustly proclaimed to have been those of a cad.

In one of my meetings with Callas as late as the spring of 1977, she specifically spoke about children: 'I would have been the happiest of women, if I had children[2] and a happy family of course – surely the greatest ideal in life.' It was a period when she was confiding in me especially about her personal life. She never mentioned any pregnancy or abortion and naturally it did not occur to me to ask such a hypothetical question.

Documentary evidence reveals that when Maria married in 1949 she wanted to become pregnant but did not conceive. Her letters to her husband during their early years together when she had to travel alone (shown to me and also later published by Meneghini in 1981) confirm the Meneghinis' unsuccessful attempts at having children. In one letter (Naples, 20 December 1950) she wrote, '"I have to tell you again that I am still without baby. I saw my period on the 18th, right on schedule."' So much for Maria waiting until 1957 to plead, in vain, with her husband for a child.

As Meneghini was then in his mid-fifties and this was his first marriage, he was examined to confirm that he was fertile. After 1952, when Callas's career had taken wing, though still very much in favour of having children she decided in consultation with her husband not to be unduly impatient about not conceiving as she was also often tired and unwell – and she was of course still under thirty years old.

At the end of 1954 she was cured of a tapeworm which was draining her energy. She had also lost her excessive weight and consequently felt better generally but as during the next three years she was involved with some of her greatest portrayals, again she felt that time was still on her side. However, as she had not conceived by 1957, when she was thirty-three, a significant age for first motherhood, she decided to seek medical advice: to her great sorrow it was diagnosed that she could not have children. In actuality Maria was at the time undergoing a series of clinical tests with various specialists that her physician, Dr Arnaldo Semeraro, had advised in order to discover the reason for the fatigue and mental exhaustion she felt before going to the Edinburgh Festival.

After Callas's death and before Stassinopoulos's book was published, I asked Meneghini why they never had children. (I did not mention what Maria had told me about this subject almost a year before.) Unable to conceal his tears Meneghini said, 'From the very beginning of our marriage we both dreamed of having a child. Any man would have been happy and indeed proud to have had children with this wonderful woman!' He then produced the medical report of 1957 (by consultant gynaecologist Carlo Palmieri) which diagnosed malformation of the womb (*malformazione dell'utero*). There was no remedy other than through a dangerous and highly experimental operation which might offer some faint hope but with severely damaging effects on her health and voice. Maria decided against it. The gynaecologist also diagnosed symptoms of early menopause and prescribed a series of injections which delayed it for about a year.

When Meneghini read of the alleged abortion he was overwhelmed with disbelief that Maria, who had the menopause before the age of thirty-five (a year before her separation from her husband), had become pregnant at forty-three and subsequently got rid of the child. He also felt that even Onassis (who was not Meneghini's favourite person) would not have acted in this way – no man would in the event of such a miracle – and that such information was false and published solely as lucrative sensationalism: 'This type of gossip,' Meneghini maintained, 'especially about dead people who cannot answer back, is according to my code of decency and Maria's nothing less than a sacrilegious obscenity. In fact I protested to the London *Times*, but my telegram was published most inconspicuously. It was also given the irrelevant title "Callas on a pedestal" which somewhat dampened my authority.'

In the final analysis the allegation of the abortion is no more than hearsay and based on the criterion that Callas succumbed to the wishes of the man she loved and destroyed the child at a time when she had all but lost him – in reality the child would have been her greatest weapon in keeping Onassis. Even so, he married another but Maria and Onassis maintained and deepened their friendship to his death. We are speaking here of a strong-minded woman with deeply rooted moral and religious values and a man who had, in addition, allegedly ruined her career and insulted her both in public and in private in an appallingly hurtful way. Clearly this strikes one as a gross exaggeration.

Callas's relationship with Onassis, as she described it to me, tallied partly and only in its broad outcome with the existing speculation and not at all with the motives and feelings of the people concerned. 'It was destiny,' she said,

that started my friendship with Ari [she called Onassis either Ari or Aristo. He called her Callas]. Although I was very run down and unhappy at the time, I primarily went on the *Christina* cruise in order to please my husband who was very keen to go. Perhaps in my subconscious I hoped the change and rest in a different environment (my doctor in fact insisted that I needed sea air) would be beneficial both to my health and to the way I felt towards my husband during that period. But everything turned out rather differently.

Almost from the beginning of the cruise I saw in Ari the type of friend I was looking for. Not a lover (a thought that never even crossed my mind in all the years I was married), but somebody powerful and sincere whom I could depend on to help me deal with the problems I had had for some time with my husband. I knew no one else capable or willing to give me this support. Maybe because I always approached my work with utter devotion, there was no time or inclination in me to make close friendships. I believed that my husband would see to all my affairs, other than artistic — that was strictly my department — and comfort and protect me generally, so that I could isolate myself from everyday bothers. This may sound selfish on my part. It probably is, but it was the only possible way if I were to serve art with sincerity and love. In return I gave my husband, from the beginning of our relationship, all the love and consideration that is expected of a devoted wife. This type of relationship was essential to me but only when implicitly honoured on both sides.

A couple of months before the cruise I did in fact try to confide in a friend[3] (who was connected with my work), hoping that he might help me, not to get rid of my husband but take away my financial arrangements from his absolute control. I am not sure whether it was this friend's inability or unwillingness to be involved in other people's affairs, but he evaded my call for help by trivializing my problem and trying to persuade me not to worry too much. You can therefore understand the frame of mind I was in when I began to see Ari's extraordinary qualities. I was rather indifferent to him in our previous meetings, which were four or five. In Monte Carlo, where the cruise began, I was very impressed by his charm but above all by his powerful personality and the way he would hold everybody's attention. Not only was he full of life, he was a source of life. Even before I had the chance to talk to him alone for any length of time (there were about a dozen other people on the yacht and Ari was being very attentive to Sir Winston

Churchill, the man he worshipped), I began to feel strangely relaxed. I had found a friend, the kind that I'd never had before and so urgently needed at the time. As the days went by I felt that Ari was a man who would listen to other people's problems in a positive way. Our friendship had to wait about two weeks to be cemented. Several times on the *Christina* our relatively brief conversations were ended by promising each other that we would talk later.

One night after a lengthy and rather irritating argument with my husband, who went on and on about my future engagements, I got up and went on deck for some air and also to be by myself. That was the first time that I left my husband alone late at night, but I could not take it any longer. Ever since my disagreements with the big theatres which began roughly eighteen months previously, Battista talked of nothing else but engagements – more of the exceptionally high remuneration than their artistic level – and what a fantastic businessman he was.

At the same time I discovered, accidentally, that my husband was secretly making very substantial investments for himself with money from our joint account which was totally sustained by my earnings. When I confronted him with this – not for the money but the reason – he merely shut me up, telling me it was all a figment of my imagination and that financial affairs were his concern. As I had so many other problems I tried, and succeeded to a degree, to ignore my husband's untypical behaviour. But my confidence in him was all but lost. All I needed was somebody to help me handle my situation.

Anyway, to go back to the *Christina*, when I got to the deck on that night, I met Ari standing looking out into the dark sea. He pointed out the island of Mytilene, I think, to me in the distance. For a while we enjoyed our silence. Then – I think I spoke first – we both began philosophizing about life in general. Although he was getting out of life all that he thought he wanted – he was a very hard-working man with amazing drive – he felt that something vital was eluding him. He was at heart a sailor.

I listened, and to a great deal that he said I could find a parallel with my own life. It was daybreak when I returned to my cabin. I am sure our friendship began on that occasion. Suddenly my hopelessness and that terrible irritability, which I had then had for several months, all but vanished. My quarrels with the theatres had given me no elation but disillusioned and distressed me because they could have been avoided. Even though my conscience was clear and I had never acted on whims, Battista should have handled the situations with more diplomacy. That was the beginning of the break-up of my marriage, not Onassis and not the money.

When I told my husband on the *Christina* that I had found in Onassis a great spiritual friend he did not pass any direct comment, though I sensed that he was simply furious;

not so much with me but with the idea that I had found the spiritual support that had been lacking in my life for some time. What happened after that is history.

At this point I remarked that the significance of this history, as she put it, was never revealed. 'What is known about your relationship with Onassis is entirely based on press speculation, with superficial embroidery by other writers. Only during your court case against Vergottis in 1967 did Onassis state that he felt no obligation towards you other than that of friendship. Also the only time you were willing to talk about him was in 1970 [after Onassis had married Mrs Kennedy] when you told David Frost on television in America that Onassis was merely the "finest of friends", that your friendship was mutual, and so forth.'

'You are perfectly right,' she said calmly.

I must say I am rather pleased that you do not also embroider. What Ari said in court was absolutely correct. He was referring to the case and as far as that was concerned he had no other obligations. Let me remind you that the court case was about the shares I had bought with my own money and Ari was far too shrewd a man to let Vergottis's lawyer get the better of him. It was quite clear that Vergottis thought that he would win his case by exposing my relationship with Ari and create a scandal. How misguided! And besides, why should Ari have had any obligations? We were both independent and responsible people. He was not my legal husband. Also what is wrong with what I told David Frost? It was absolutely truthful and I am proud of it.

I then explained that I had never doubted her sincerity, but meant only that nothing constructive had ever been revealed about her liaison with Onassis, not even after his death. No wonder there had been so much speculation and obviously, as is the way of the world, most of it was unfair to both of them. A brief silence followed and I felt that perhaps Maria had had enough of this conversation. However, when I talked about something else she ignored it and said, 'Ari stood by me [at the commencement of their relationship] and I was convinced that at last I had found a man I could trust, for good, unbiased advice. Remember I had all but lost trust in my husband; nobody is happy to be appreciated, even loved, only for their "investment" potential. It became impossible for me to go on in that way. On the other hand I needed the security of a real friend – and, I must repeat, not a lover.' (This part of her explanation provides a reason why Onassis had insulted Meneghini on that night at Sirmione by asking him how many millions he would require to 'release Maria'. Onassis was shrewd enough to realize, from what Maria had told him, that money was of paramount importance to Meneghini. So with tongue in cheek and a little whisky, the exuberant Ari gave a performance, a *tour de force*, at Sirmione that took the wind out of Meneghini's sails.)

'Our friendship', Maria continued,

was further strengthened as the confrontations with my husband were becoming more complicated. (After some beating about the bush, Battista showed his true colours in no uncertain terms: he adamantly demanded complete financial control over me, or nothing.) It subsequently became passionate but only included physical love after I broke with my husband or more correctly after my husband broke with me and Tina Onassis decided to end her marriage.

Following this argument further, Callas maintained that the delay in consummating their love was, at least on her part, due to the fact that her original intention was not to leave her husband but merely to stop having him as her agent. Moreover, it was against her strong religious principles to commit adultery, and in any case she was not emotionally ready for it: 'I have been brought up on Greek moral principles of the 1920s and 1930s and sexual freedom, or the lack of it, had never been one of my problems. Besides, I have always been an old-fashioned romantic.'

Her sincere candour encouraged me to ask further questions which she answered readily:

Yes our love was mutual. Ari was adorable, straight and fearless, and his boyish mischievousness made him irresistible and only occasionally difficult and uncompromising. Unlike some of his friends, he could be generous (and I do not mean only materialistically) to a fault and never petty. Obstinate he was, and quite argumentative like most Greeks, but even then he would eventually come round and see the other person's point of view.

'Mutual love is always wonderful, but what about your quarrels with him, his insulting behaviour towards you?' I asked. 'It had been whispered a few times that not long after your association with him was established he began to insult you in front of other people. I found this difficult to believe.'

Maria's reaction was ambiguous. She did not seem to have taken exception to my matter-of-fact question but her stony silence made me feel a little embarrassed. After a while (which seemed a long time) we both spoke simultaneously. Smiling, and with her head slightly on one side, Maria first talked about something quite irrelevant: 'Do you remember', she said, 'when you gave me the tiny picture of Malibran? I had been looking for one for a long time to put in a locket. When you gave it to me, I thought it dropped from heaven. It was really very sweet of you.'[4]

Afterwards, thinking about her digression, I concluded that she had played for time in order to decide whether to answer my question. She did, and quite eloquently:

It is true that I had quite a few arguments with Ari. For some time I simply couldn't take it and felt angry and unhappy. The situation was getting worse because I became touchy and a little haughty, and probably misconstrued some things as a sign of rejection. The old saying that familiarity breeds contempt was very much at the back of my mind. You see, before I met Ari I had not really experienced lovers' tiffs and being by nature rather shy and introverted (when I am not on the stage), I was losing my sense of humour, not that I have much. When you can't laugh at yourself life becomes dreary. It took time, but once I understood this other side of his character, by and large I accepted it, even though in part I still disapproved of it.

Ari's upbringing had been unusual. His family were well off and cultured and although Greek, quite prominent in Turkish society until the catastrophe of Smyrna.[5] As a young man he had seen and known suffering and used his wits to survive. Whereas he matured as an outstanding businessman, in some other ways, in personal relationships, he did not – relatively speaking. He liked to tease, but if you dared pull his leg in an effort to fish for compliments he would sometimes retaliate like a tiresome schoolboy.

At a dinner party, I think it was at Maxim's, while we were having a pleasant time and everybody seemed to be in a very jovial mood, one of our closest and most likeable friends, a lady, Maggie van Zuylen, passed a teasing remark, saying 'You lovebirds, I am sure you make love often,' or words to this effect. 'We never do,' I commented, smiling and winking at Aristo. His reaction was incredible. Abruptly, but fortunately in Greek, he declared that if that was the case he would make love to any woman except me, even if I were the last woman on earth. I was very upset, not so much over what he had said but the way he said it – particularly when I sensed that other people in the party understood Greek. The worst of it was that the more I tried to silence him the more he went on about it. It took me several days to bring myself to mention this incident. He said that it was he who was embarrassed in the first place. I explained that what I had said was clearly a normal understatement which conveys more effectively the opposite meaning. 'Right,' he answered, 'and mine was a normal overstatement which also conveys, even more effectively than yours, the opposite meaning.'

There were other similar incidents. Although his English was good, especially in business matters, in ordinary conversation when he was arguing, it could sound abrupt, and sometimes brutally so; his English was a literal translation from the Greek, the language he thought in with an Eastern mentality. This also explains his relative lack of sophistication when he was with close friends. He considered this type of social sophistication as affectation, if not sheer hypocrisy, and he expected me to stand up to him and give him as good as I got. This was not because he was a male chauvinist. On the contrary, he liked the company of women very much and really all his life he trusted them more and preferred to confide in them rather than in men. There is possibly a psychological explanation for this. He had lost his beloved mother when he was about six and he was mostly brought up by his marvellous paternal grandmother, apparently quite a philosopher and a formidable woman. With his father it was different. They had a good relationship until they fell out when his father criticized, unfairly, Ari's tremendous and successful efforts in obtaining their release from the Turkish concentration camp. Ari was accused of unnecessarily bribing the Turkish guards with too much money.

Feeling flattered that Maria had told me all this, I ventured to probe further and mentioned an incident I had heard about, from more than one source, which referred to Onassis walking into the room where Callas was discussing a film contract with would-be financiers.[6] He took over by telling Callas that she did not know anything as she was only a 'night-club' singer, whereupon she walked out, leaving him to negotiate. After a chuckle Maria answered,

Of course it is true. Ari wanted to deal with that film contract himself and, with his tongue in his cheek, made that grossly exaggerated remark in order to give me the excuse of walking out and leaving him to handle the situation. We did rehearse it but he surprised me when he mentioned night-clubs. Afterwards we laughed about it, especially when he said that he only tried to imitate me — that is in the way I improvise in my stage movements. Let's face it, in business matters he was second to none. I am rather a naïve businesswoman, always giving primary importance to artistic values. Film business people, including producers, naturally preferred to deal with me. They took it for granted that if I were involved Ari would put up any amount of money. And he would, provided it was a sound investment. It was I who withdrew. He never interfered with my art except in telling me that I should not feel any obligation to continue my singing career. Obviously, he maintained, the stress had come to be too great and as I had more than done my duty (his words, not mine) I was entitled to relax and enjoy my well-earned money. He would have liked me to make films as he believed the strain wouldn't have been excessive. Anyway as far as my artistic career is concerned I always took the decisions. Neither Ari nor anybody else could have influenced me during that stage of my career.

Presently, while we were having a drink, Maria brought up the subject of Onassis again:

I really had only one thing against him. It was impossible for me to come to terms with his insatiable thirst for conquering everything. I appreciate achievement immensely (at one time I considered it the only reason for living but then I was young and unwise) but with him this developed into something else. It was not money — he had plenty and lived like the richest man in the world. I think his trouble was this continuous search, his restlessness to accomplish something new, but more for the bravado than the money. He meant it when he talked about money being very easy to make; 'the difficulty was making the first million, the rest dropped into your lap.'

'This bravado,' I asked, 'did it extend to people? It was widely believed that Onassis always wanted to be seen in the company of famous people and beautiful women. This sort of publicity, which betrays superficiality, not to say immaturity, seems to have attracted him.'

'I would say,' Maria answered,

that this observation was partly true. He certainly liked this kind of thing but only with people that he also genuinely liked or admired. Ari, for example, did not need to be Churchill's nurse. On board the *Christina* Churchill had everything, of course, male nurses as well as his wife and others. He was old and rather feeble but Ari was much more than the perfect host to him. He was the perfect friend, always ready to play cards and amuse him and assist in every way possible. I, too, admired the great old man and once when I remarked to Ari how touching I thought his veneration for Churchill was, I got a marvellous answer: 'We must remember that it was he, the man of our century, who saved the world in 1940. Where would we all be today and in what state without this man!' So you see there was much more to Ari than met the eye.[7] And let me add that he was also friendly and generous to poor and unknown people provided he liked them. He would never forget an old friend, especially if he had come down in the world. There was never any publicity for this side of his character as it does not make interesting news generally. What I cannot comment on with authority is how honest his business transactions were.

When his son died he lost the craving to conquer, which was his lifeblood. This attitude of his was basically the cause of our arguments. Of course I tried to change him but I realized that this was not possible, any more than he could change me. We were two independent people with minds of our own and different outlooks on some basic aspects of life. Unfortunately we were not complementary, but we understood each other sufficiently to make our friendship eventually possible. After his death I felt a widow.

By this stage I had summoned up enough courage to be more personal: 'But why did you not marry him?' I asked, really meaning why did he marry someone else. 'Onassis's strange marriage to Mrs Kennedy makes nonsense of the man you describe, unless he married for love and really fooled us all.'

'Oh, it was partly my own fault,' Maria interposed.

He made me feel liberated, a very feminine woman, and I came to love him very much, but my intuition, or whatever you call it, told me that I would have lost him the moment I married him – he would then have turned his interest to some other younger woman. I also sensed that he too knew I could not change my outlook on life to fit in with his and our marriage would probably have become, before long, a squalid argument. At the time, however, I was not so philosophical about our relationship as I am now – when human emotions simmer down it is easier to see more clearly other points of view and one can put the whole affair (saga is a better word) in a rational perspective. If only one could do this from the beginning! Make no mistake, when he married I felt betrayed, as any woman would, though I was more perplexed than angry, because I could not understand for the life of me why, after so many years together, he married another. My anger was in no way directed against his wife. That would have been unreasonable.

Maria then chuckled and said, 'No he did not marry for love and I do not think that his wife did either. It was more a marriage of business convenience. I have already told you that he was afflicted with a predilection for conquering everything. Once he set his mind on something he was determined to achieve it. I really could never come to terms with this philosophy.'

'Neither can I,' I added. Then realizing that Maria was in a congenial mood, I assumed a more probing manner, testing her by putting forward a theory which I had basically developed partly from published information and hearsay. Above all, however, I wanted to know how much Callas knew about it. 'Is it true, then,' I enquired, 'that this marriage was in fact arranged by the Kennedys, specifically Rose Kennedy, the family matriarch?' Maria's initial response, though silent and a touch aloof but by no means disapproving, encouraged me to continue: 'The remarkably entrepreneurial Onassis offered to finance a future Kennedy campaign for the Presidency. If successful, he hoped for access to the American market which had been denied him since the mid-1940s when he evaded paying taxes on his oil tankers. Anticipating possible Congress opposition as to his trustworthiness, Onassis's next move, with Rose Kennedy's support, was to propose marriage to Jackie. Thus Onassis, husband of the famous widow of President J. F. Kennedy, would become one of the family, as it were, and gain respectability in the United States.'

(The Kennedy women have always been expected to make every sacrifice in serving the all-important interests of the dynasty. The marriage would automatically make Jackie a very rich woman, something that she badly needed at the time, not only for herself but also to safeguard the future of her children. Additionally, Onassis would provide bodyguards for their much-needed protection. Within a few months, however, after Onassis's marriage to Jackie, the Kennedy family virtually lost hope for providing a presidential candidate, at least in the foreseeable future after an unfortunate accident in 1969 when a female friend of Edward Kennedy, the next in line for the presidency, drowned after a party at Chappaquiddick. They had been travelling in separate cars when hers sank, after a small bridge collapsed, and he took ten hours to report it. It is probable she died from asphyxia rather than drowning.)

With a restrained smile, Callas made me feel that she was already familiar with what I had just told her about Onassis's marriage. Her first words were, 'You seem to be well informed, better than I am. Are you in the CIA or something? Well, anyway, I do not regard that as a marriage made in heaven.' Then, shaking her head and pointing a finger at me in feigned remonstrance, she exclaimed, as she often did when wanting to close a topic of conversation 'Let's leave it at that, shall we?'

Nevertheless, I questioned her further regarding Mrs Kennedy. Maria became serious again and answered by saying that Onassis came back to her not long after his wedding, literally in tears over the mistake he had made.

At first I would not let him into the house but, would you believe it, one day he persistently kept on whistling outside my appartment, as young men used to do in Greece fifty years ago – they wooed their sweethearts with song. So I had to let him in before the press realized what was going on in avenue Georges Mandel.

With his return, so soon after his marriage, my confusion changed into a mixture of elation and frustration. Although I never admitted to him that I believed he was going to divorce his wife, I felt that as our friendship at least had survived his marriage, however weak its foundations, his principles regarding human relationships were changing. Anyway, I continued to see him from time to time, and during my concert tours in 1973–4 he always sent me flowers and telephoned occasionally.

'You said that when he died you felt a widow. How do you feel about him now?'

'The word widow is a figure of speech. Naturally I miss him. I have missed other people in my life, as everybody does, for much less. But this is life and we must not make a tragedy of those we have lost. Personally, I prefer to remember the good times, however few these usually are. One of the best things I have learned in life is that people should be assessed by taking into account both their good and bad points. I hope I will be, too. It is the easiest thing in the world to destroy almost anyone by considering merely the flaws in their character.'

'So you feel no bitterness towards him?'

None whatever. I could have, if I were inclined to such feelings. In life everybody can find a reason to be bitter about friends, family, even parents. But there are two kinds of people: those who remain bitter and those who do not. I am happy that I belong to the second category. Most of the bitterness I have experienced had more to do with my career. The so-called Callas scandals, particularly during the time I was singing in *Anna Bolena* at La

Scala, were traumatic experiences. However, even those are now forgotten. Besides, I made my peace with the people concerned and it is of no consequence on whose side the fault was greater. . . . As far as Ari is concerned, of course I miss him but I do try not to become a complete sentimental fool, you know!

At first I was quite taken, touched, by Maria's eloquent simplicity in revealing the emotional side of her character and life. Soon, however, it dawned on me that the crucial factors of her intimate relationship with Onassis, such as their continued friendship after his marriage to another woman, had been only superficially dealt with and indeed, not without contradiction. I responded by whole-heartedly agreeing with her philosophy that one must never become a sentimental old fool. The fact that I only dwelled on this aspect may have betrayed my thoughts. Maria continued to be pleasantly sociable but she was really miles away until, inadvertently, I said, 'A penny for your thoughts.'

She stared at me and then, winking, exclaimed that her thoughts were worth much more.

'I quite agree,' I replied and in a mock-serious tone added, 'but that is all I have. I may sometimes live dangerously but I never bid for anything beyond my means.'

Maria appeared to be enjoying this small talk. She obviously had something on her mind and, as usual when confronted with a personal question, was playing for time. So she kept it going, reminding me a little of Rosina in *Il barbiere di Siviglia* – when at a certain moment Maria boxed my ears lightly, as if to reprimand me for my 'blatant stinginess'. Then, having had enough of this frivolity, she rested her chin on her hand and began:

Everything I have said about Aristo is true, though there was more to it. For some time at the beginning of our relationship we were blissfully happy. I also felt secure and even unperturbed about my vocal problems – well, for the moment. As I have already told you I was learning, for the first time in my life, how to relax and live for myself and even began to question my belief that there was no life beyond art. This frame of mind was relatively short-lived as I discovered that many of Ari's principles, his code of practice, were seriously at variance with mine. I found myself unstuck. How can a man who really loves you at the same time have affairs with other women? He couldn't possibly love them all. For some time it was only a suspicion, which I tried to dismiss, but evidently I could not and it was out of the question to accept it into my moral code in any circumstances. Furthermore, I was too proud to confide such a personal predicament in anybody until I found the ideal friend in Maggie[8] who quickly sensed my problem and, being the genuine person she was, made it easier for me to open up.

Like a mother, sister, friend, she explained to me that there are men who find it impossible to be physically faithful to one woman, especially to their wives: 'Nearly

415

always, a man like that genuinely loves his wife or the woman in his life. To his way of thinking these extra-marital affairs are no more than biological infidelities. He simply, for a thousand Freudian reasons that probably date from puberty, cannot do without them. Sensible wives understand this and thank God that they do, otherwise there would not be any married couples left in France. For a Frenchman, even a happily married one, it is normal to have a mistress. It is a way of life and Frenchwomen, more than others, wisely have learned to accept it. Do not think for a minute that Ari did not have affairs when he was married to Tina and do not think that he did not love his wife, the mother of his children. A man does not, cannot, change some of his ways.'

But I could not then accept this, my reasoning being that I was neither French nor Ari's lawful wife; the role of the betrayed wife was not in my repertoire. I simply missed Maggie's point and though I never brought myself to discuss anything like this with Ari, I am sure he was aware of my inability to come to terms with any infidelity a husband of mine might commit. We were not, therefore, compatible for marriage to each other. You can understand why my philosophy of marriage was wrong in practice but right for me in theory.

Being more practical than I was in such matters, and more experienced, Ari, who did love me but also knew that sooner or later we would have been at daggers drawn had we married (this may sound rather eccentric but I have to accept that it was his way of thinking and therefore not necessarily wrong), married somebody else. But that was an unusual marriage whichever way you look at it. Nevertheless, at the time I was terribly upset and thought him a proper bastard and used other epithets I do not care to repeat. It was later, when he came back and when obviously I began to regain my lost pride, that I was able to put things in a wiser and more realistic perspective. Of course, his immediate explanation was that his marriage was a mistake, his mistake not his wife's, as I bluntly told him; he got exactly what he had bargained for and he had entirely himself to blame. His so-called marriage contract was a bizarre arrangement I could never fathom.

Fortunately for me there was Maggie, who again helped me to rid myself sufficiently of my moral hang-ups, and I took him back. This is how my great friendship with Ari was born. You can call it a passionate friendship.

At this point I realized that Maria was familiar with the real reason for, and conditions of, Onassis's marriage, though not until after he returned to her; undoubtedly it played a great, if not crucial, part in accepting him back into her life. Although this marriage contract was not made public – it was occasionally mentioned in the press after Onassis's death in 1975 – friends of his professed to have known about it and ex-members of the *Christina* crew claimed actually to have seen it. Apparently the marriage was to last seven years, at the end of which Jackie would receive $27 million. It also stipulated that she would not be required to sleep with her husband, nor be obliged to have children by him. Apart from cruises on the *Christina*, where there were always other people with them, Onassis hardly ever lived under the same roof with his wife. Even when he was in New York for considerable periods, once for over two months, he stayed at the Pierre Hotel, not far from his wife's sumptuous fifteen-room apartment. The probing press was always told that Mrs Kennedy Onassis was redecorating – a process that seemed interminable.

Without any prompting from me Maria, half smiling, continued to talk about her relationship with Onassis – as if she wanted to get it out of her system. 'After his marriage we never quarrelled,' she said, her voice gaining strength.

> We discussed things constructively. He stopped being argumentative. There was no longer the need to prove anything either to ourselves or to one another. Furthermore, his business affairs took a turn for the worse; shipping was facing a serious recession and he was also losing Olympic Airlines to the Greek government – a traumatic experience for him because he always considered Olympic to be his special creation. Moreover, his health was declining and the death of his son almost certainly dealt him a final blow. During this difficult period he always came to me with his worries. He was in great need of moral support, which I gave him in the best way I could. I always told him the truth and tried to help him face reality – he appreciated that. Also he was absolutely set on getting a divorce, sooner rather than later, but time proved against him.
>
> I am going to say one last thing which you have, rather tactfully, avoided asking. Yes, my affair with Onassis [the only time she referred to him by his surname] was a failure but my friendship with him was a success.

'Perhaps I may ask a final question on this subject. I do understand perfectly all you say and in many ways I am happy to have heard it from you; fifteen years is a long relationship. But was your attitude towards him, your feelings generally, at the time you were living through this relationship the same as you describe now, almost two years after his death? How much has time healed? You have earlier mentioned your surprise, your disappointment, your anger when he got married.'

For a moment Maria looked hesitant and a little distant, to the point where I almost retracted the question. (I was always careful not to appear bold – a situation that invariably made Callas unresponsive.) 'No,' she suddenly exclaimed,

> my attitude towards him could not have been the same, that is before his marriage. It takes a long time to understand deeply another human being, or yourself for that matter. You

think people are trying to change you, but you do not readily accept that you may be trying even harder to change them. If you are not prepared to accept other people's ways because they do not comply with your own then you can never be objective. My subsequent friendship with Aristo speaks for both of us. It taught me a great deal more. Of course, with the years I became more mature and as, not by choice, I no longer lived so completely for my artistic career I gained more experience in, more understanding of human communication.

When I saw Ari on his deathbed at the hospital he was calm and I think at peace with himself. He was very ill and he knew that the end was near, though he tried to ignore it. We did not speak about old times or much about anything else, but mostly communicated with each other in silence. When I was leaving (I visited him at his request but the doctors asked me not to stay long) he made a special effort to tell me, 'I loved you, not always well, but as much and as best I was capable of. I tried.'

A little moved by her recollection, Maria smiled warmly and quietly said, 'That's how it was.' She then looked at the clock and I realized it was time to leave. I could not bring myself to ask her whether she would have married Onassis had he got his divorce some two years before his death. It was really of no consequence and afterwards I was glad that I had not put the question to her.

Even though Callas did not admit it in so many words, it became clear to me as I got to know her better that her capacity of love for her art had been stronger than for human beings. When, as a young girl, she became aware of her talent she pursued its fulfilment with unmitigated devotion; it was her only weapon of self-preservation. This is not meant to imply that she was incapable of loving. On the contrary, all her life not only did she want to be loved and appreciated as any normal human being instinctively does, but she also needed to give love. At the beginning, she used her talent for singing as the only means at her disposal to secure her mother's love, but for reasons related elsewhere she never succeeded. With her mounting triumph as a professional singer she began to discover that her true, unselfish love was for her art, her mission in life. This applied also to her sexual impulses, which largely found an emotional outlet in her art and made her so convincing in passionate scenes, without resorting to histrionics or vocal exaggeration. This is one explanation why Callas, in real life, was never a promiscuous woman. She was content with what her rather elderly husband had to offer.

The vows she made to art, perhaps at first subconsciously, were absolute, as her actions throughout her life have unequivocally demonstrated; other loves or even affections for human beings, although sincerely felt, were subsidiary and subordinate. Whenever anybody or anything was in any way detrimental to her career, Callas the artist would take full control of the woman and eradicate the obstacle from her life's path. Her affection for Mangliveras, her colleague at the Athens Opera, was closely connected with her artistic ambition; he familiarized her with various aspects of stagecraft and gave her much-needed moral support when, as a novice, she found herself in the highly competitive and hostile environment of the theatre. Likewise, her attachment to Bagarozy. It was genuine enough, but she could only spare it for as long as there was some possibility that he would promote her career.

Her relationship with Meneghini was on a different level. There is no doubt that Maria loved her husband with all the energy, consideration and genuine feelings that she could muster. These qualities came as a package once she realized – and this was second nature to her – that they were ancillary to the fulfilment of her artistic vocation. In addition to her public behaviour towards her husband, which was at all times impeccable, her unwavering devotion to him in private is evident from the numerous letters (quoted earlier) she wrote him when she had to travel alone. Meneghini's own testimony to their mutual love and devotion, also recorded earlier, leaves no doubt that for several years their relationship was harmonious. Most certainly, however, this wonderful harmony was basically dependent for its existence on the progress of her career and in turn to the huge amount of money Meneghini made from it.

The balance of her life began to be upset at the end of 1957 when her career took a downward turn. For the quarrels that resulted in her falling out with several major opera houses she mostly blamed her husband, in whom she thus lost confidence. Furthermore, within the year the first signs of her vocal deterioration also manifested themselves and the fear that she might not be able to work for much longer distressed her. She was broken-hearted at the gynaecologist's report which seemed to confirm her inability to bear children, as well as the premature approach of the menopause. It was a dreadful period of her life and suddenly she realized that she could not fight on alone: 'What do you do', she said later, reflecting on the situation, 'when you cannot trust your mother or husband? I had considered him [Meneghini] something of a screen for me – to protect me from the outside world. ... He did, at first, until my fame went to his head. Battista only cared for money and position. He really helped to create many problems for me ... problems he could not cope with. ... His psychology was misguided and lacked diplomacy. At the end of the day his tactics backfired on me and I paid the consequences.' Inevitably Callas could no longer love or trust a man who was of no use, let alone an obstacle, to her artistic destiny.

It was at this opportune moment that her bond with Onassis began, following her call for help in relieving her husband of his duties as her agent. That was the only change in her life which she wanted. Onassis's renowned business acumen was in fact first sought by Meneghini himself. At that period Callas was most eligible to star in a major film and Meneghini was not slow to appreciate the benefits of such a lucrative project whose materialization could well have been speeded up with Onassis's advice and connections, and above all his possible financial backing, a crucial factor in such enterprises. This explains Meneghini's keenness that they should go on the *Christina* cruise, despite Maria's lack of enthusiasm. Undoubtedly his wife's health at the time was of genuine concern to him and the sea air that her doctor had prescribed was the best medicine for her, but simultaneously he did not in any way underestimate the business possibilities that might arise through their extraordinary host. Without this attractive prospect before him Meneghini would not have been so anxious to persuade his reluctant wife that they should join the cruise – they could easily have found the much-needed sea air elsewhere.

Subsequently the Callas–Onassis relationship developed and in due course they become lovers, though in theory their long liaison put neither of them under any special obligation. At her request he lent his business expertise to protect her interests, not to undermine her confidence or use her eminence primarily for his own ends, as some later accused him of having done – charges which are by and large contradictory and ill-founded. If Callas did not sing he was accused of preventing her because of jealousy. When she did it was alleged that Onassis pushed her into it in order to bask in her glory.

The criticism levelled at him regarding the destruction of Callas's career arose from the fact that she did relatively little at the beginning of her association with him in the summer of 1959 and practically nothing after 1965. But this actually had nothing to do with Onassis, who was also pronounced, gratuitously, a confirmed philistine. His fondness for music in general was average, though it did not extend to opera: 'Even at the age of ten,' he told Willi Frischauer, his biographer, 'when I did not really know what opera was, I formed an aversion against it. The screaming, the yelling! Seeing all these people on stage, I wondered why they did not say right out whatever they had to say. To me it sounded as repetitive as the old Byzantine psalms I had to sing in church, like the Kyrie Eleison. It takes a man half an hour to tell a women, "I love you."' According to Callas, this was so because Onassis could not bring himself to listen to the music and the words as one entity. On the other hand, he had a heartfelt appreciation for music, particularly Greek songs with words that readily made sense to him, which were brought to Greece by his compatriots, the refugees from Asia Minor. Moreover, Onassis apparently could amaze with his playing of Bach fugues on the piano.

Notwithstanding Onassis's dislike of opera, for whatever reason, it would be grossly unfair to disregard his appreciation of Callas the artist, whom he always held in high esteem. In fact, during the years of their liaison he made special efforts to attend several of her performances, not merely first nights. Even more significant was his frank admission that his admiration of Callas was based more on achievement under adverse conditions than on artistic values. His own words to Frischauer speak forcefully:

More than her artistic talent, even more than her success as a great singer, what always impressed me was the story of her early struggles as a poor girl in her teens when she sailed through unusually rough and merciless waters. ... At the age of fourteen this girl earned a scholarship but was so poor that she could only pursue her studies using borrowed music and borrowed books. During the German occupation her family was starving and while studying she not only had to run the house as well but also help to find food, which was very hard to come by. ... For her as a dedicated performer to assert herself in the tough and competitive world of the stage was a great achievement. ...

In actuality neither of the men in Callas's emotional life was any more of a villain than she was, that is if the description is in this case synonymous with human being. They all had significant weaknesses, as well as strengths, and being such diverse characters who believed single-mindedly in their own god they failed to reach a compromise with their lives or with one another.

Ostensibly, Meneghini had several qualifications that constitute a loving and caring husband. His lack of sophistication was compensated for by old-fashioned moral values which were in complete affinity with his wife's. The one serious failing of an otherwise moderate and not unkind man was his blinkered view of life in which there was a fiscal value for everything and everybody, however wonderful and lovable they were to him, had to be a sound investment. He believed in money for its own sake, the making of which seems to have been the kinetic energy of his life.

This weakness throws light on Meneghini's reluctance and dilatory tactics in marrying the young Maria Callas, who was not famous or earning much money in 1949 but had the potential of becoming an opera star. Meneghini was obviously fond of her but his affection, or love, or whatever one might call it, had its source, perhaps unconsciously, in the possibility that one day she would be earning a great deal. But he wanted to make sure first. How else can one explain the obstacles and excuses — such as the difficulty of obtaining a dispensation from the Pope to marry a non-Catholic and other formalities, as well as his family's objections to his marriage — the fifty-three year old bachelor was making for many months in order to delay the wedding? However, when Maria gave him an ultimatum that if they were not married within twenty-four hours she would not go to Argentina with Serafin and the Italian company that was assembled — an important and most lucrative engagement — Meneghini promptly overcame all obstacles and they were married in church a few hours before his wife sailed without him for Argentina.

Later his secret withdrawal of huge sums of money from their joint bank account and his flat refusal to allow Maria to engage another agent, opting for the alternative of losing her, demonstrates vividly Meneghini's idiosyncrasy. That is how he understood the world and therefore he lost his loving wife and ruined his life: to his dying day Meneghini was unable to understand or accept Maria's complete change of heart, which was less sudden than he wished to believe, occurring as it did, over a period of approximately two years.

At one of my meetings with him in 1978 he professed that his wife was seduced by the unscrupulous Onassis and then, as if letting me in on a secret, that Maria's personality had changed totally overnight. Those awful, immoral people whom destiny threw in their path were the culprits. His explanations were so naïve that I believed he was not so much trying to paint himself snow-white to the world as to convince himself that he was blameless and, above all, that Maria really loved him to the end. The eighty-five-year-old man was clinging to his male ego, the only thing left to him. After their separation in 1959 the Meneghinis had never seen or spoken to one another again.

Onassis's case, as far as Callas was concerned, is much simpler. He too, like Meneghini, ruined his personal life and caused, mostly inadvertently, a great deal of unhappiness to people with whom he had been involved. However hard he genuinely tried, he never achieved the ability to love and remained a confirmed philanderer; he abandoned himself to the pursuit of sexual gratification with ephemeral affection and with as many different partners as he fancied. This was the sole reason why his relatively long, and in many ways happy first marriage, which produced two children, failed. The cause of his affliction, other than the hereditary factor, can be traced to his youth in Smyrna, where it was socially expectable to adopt a macho image, the absence of which would inevitably have cast serious doubts on his sexuality. Possessing tremendous energy in his early teens – and obviously a strong libido – he often got into trouble, as when he pinched his female teacher's bottom in public, and by the age of fifteen he had lost his virginity. He grew up to be a very appealing young man, virile by disposition but without physical brutality. His sexual encounters continued with increasing frequency, especially when he emigrated to Argentina, and they never stopped.

Although his association with Callas taught him a great deal emotionally, it was not enough to change him significantly in this respect, much as he might perhaps have wished it. Nevertheless, he benefitted through a deeper understanding of himself, eventually succeeding in establishing a sound friendship, though not real love, with her; he would never have made an acceptable husband but would have brought further unhappiness, albeit not deliberately, to his putative wife and by reflection to himself. His marriage to Mrs Kennedy was no more than a 'business' arrangement – the only kind of marriage he was qualified to contract – and was a dismal failure whichever way one looks at it. A basically generous man without intentional malice in his personal relationships, he was guided by his own hopelessly irreconcilable instincts.

If to Callas the woman Onassis seemed in certain ways more dynamic than her husband it was because by then the artist in her was no longer able to dominate, despite the fact that neither the intent nor the genius had deteriorated – only the vocal resources, her weapons, had declined.

For all that, Onassis was never the paramount event in her life, however much people have tried to depict the liaison as of unqualified importance.

In the final resolution Callas the artist is what matters to the world, and in a superhuman way it also mattered to her exclusively. Consequently Meneghini, despite his misguided ways, was the more important man to her; he was there as a stabilizing force in her personal life during the difficult years when she was striving to build a career. Her own contribution to her husband's well-being was in no way less powerful; apart from her huge earning capacity, she had been a model of the devoted wife to a hitherto lonely older man. And yet the world at large decided to ignore Meneghini and concentrate instead on Onassis, obviously because of the glamorous and exciting life he led. Had Callas left Onassis for Meneghini it is doubtful whether there would have been such international interest, regardless of her eminence.

Still, such observations are merely digressions and without enduring importance, even though some later writers, who never knew the *dramatis personae*, continue to deal with them speculatively. At intervals they pick on other people who had been, in one way or another, associated with Callas's career, such as Pier Paolo Pasolini, the maker of the film *Medea*, suggesting that he might have been one of her lovers. At the end of this bizarre affair, so the story goes, the confirmed homosexual Pasolini abandoned a humiliated Maria. No shred of evidence exists except in the misguided realms of fantasy invented for lucrative sensationalism. There was great rapport between Pasolini and Callas (her only incentive to appear in the film) for as long as the picture was in production – nothing more.

What is of interest is how this basically puritanical woman was motivated in the pursuit of her mission in relation to her personal life. My interpretation of this aspect of her character, by far the most important, derives from my long-standing friendship with Callas and, specifically, from discussions with her at a time when she was sufficiently remote from events and could put her feelings and judgement in objectively balanced perspective.

I once asked her jovially whether, were it possible to relive the past, she would choose her marriage, the period when she reached her artistic peak – say in *Anna Bolena* (1957) – or her saga (as she at one time referred to it) with Onassis.

'This is a hypothetical question,' she responded, her voice betraying a hint of irritation, 'and I cannot be very constructive in giving hypothetical answers.' The matter was dropped but the following day on the telephone she sang a verse from the final scene in *Anna Bolena*: '*Al dolce guidami castel natio. . . .*' ('Take me back to my tranquil native castle'). I listened enthralled and, at the end of it, Maria casually asked, 'I take it you found it satisfactory', but gave me no opportunity to reply. Afterwards, when I thought about it, I considered it her answer to my 'hypothetical' question – the castle in her song was her art.

Having conformed to the maxim that a creator's life is secondary to its creativity, Callas genuinely loved Meneghini as long as he contributed constructively to her artistic mission and Onassis eventually more passionately because that side of her life had come to an end and she no longer found an outlet for her sexual and intellectual impulses in her work.

This rather unethical attitude betrays in one respect a serious flaw in Callas's character as far as human relationships and obligations are concerned – was she as much a villain as Meneghini or Onassis? I think she was. But it was equally true to say of her that a paradoxically superhuman strength in her sincere devotion to art amounted to a personal sacrifice of the kind that enriches the world.

1　Callas and Meneghini also lived together for two years prior to their marriage in 1949.

2　Callas's Greek phraseology can also be taken to mean 'if I could have children'.

3　Callas was referring to an unnamed friend at a recording company.

4　I gave her the miniature of Maria Malibran as a present for her birthday and her opening of the season at La Scala (2 and 7 December respectively) twenty years before this conversation.

5　Aristotelis (Aristotle) Socrates Onassis (1906–75) was born in Smyrna, Turkey. The roots of his Greek-Christian parents were in Kayseri (Caesarea) in the Turkish province of Anatolia. His father, a well-to-do merchant in tobacco, grain and hides, also dabbled in banking. He intended to send his son to Oxford University but with the catastrophe of Smyrna in 1922 the family, together with thousands of other Greeks who lived in Turkey, were taken to Turkish concentration camps. The fortunate who escaped became refugees in Greece and Cyprus, and in Egypt where there was a Greek colony. The Onassis family settled in Athens, but before long Aristotle emigrated to Buenos Aires. After a period of relative poverty during which he did rather humble jobs, his entrepreneurial talent enabled him first to start his own tobacco business and then go into shipping, eventually becoming one of the richest men in the world.

　My father's first cousins, Anna and Paminos Kyrillos, who also lived in Smyrna and were Aristotle's playmates, testified to the standing of the Onassis family; they were cultured and wealthy, and often entertained prominent people, particularly from the embassies, in their beautiful home. Aristotle was a most lovable 'rascal' who could have been as successful on the stage as he was in shipping.

6　This was the contract for *Tosca*, which Callas had agreed to make with Zeffirelli.

7　In 1981 Sarah Churchill, Sir Winston's daughter, told me that Onassis had been a genuine friend of her family. 'My parents' affection for him, and indeed my own, extended beyond his and Tina's impeccable hospitality. Onassis never expected any favours in return or used this friendship in any way for his own ends. Now that he is dead some people run him down. This is no more than groundless gossip and perhaps jealousy.'

8　Maggie van Zuylen, a Syrian born in Alexandria, married Baron Egmont van Zuylen. She became prominent in French society, as well as the Jet Set. Callas met her through Onassis, whose long-standing friend she had been. Very quickly she also became Maria's friend and confidante.

　I first met her in London in 1967 when she was with Callas during the Vergottis–Onassis–Callas court case and once later in Paris. A formidable woman (she was often described as the redoubtable Maggie), she would impress one with her practical worldliness – one would like to count her as a friend. She was about seventy-one years old when she died in 1972.

• CHAPTER EIGHTEEN •

THE MAKING OF THE ARTIST

ALTHOUGH CALLAS SELDOM spoke about her art and career, her description of her ambition and approach was articulate and fascinatingly enlightening as, for example, in her interview with Derek Prouse (*Sunday Times*, 1961) and in her television conversations with Lord Harewood (BBC TV, 1968). Later, after her concert tour of 1974 – the last time she sang in public – I was able to add several important points and elaborate on a few when I discussed with her in greater detail various aspects of her art.

She was adamant that the people who helped her become the artist she was were her teacher Elvira de Hidalgo and the conductor Tullio Serafin. When I mentioned other conductors, De Sabata, Bernstein, Kleiber, Gavazzeni, Karajan, Votto, Giulini, Rescigno and Prêtre, Callas promptly expressed her good fortune at having been able to work with them and said that they had undoubtedly played a major part in any success she had with her performances. 'However,' she added, 'without trying to underrate their ability or artistry, I cannot in all sincerity and humility consider any of them in the same way as Tullio Serafin. This is not a case of comparison but of who has been the greatest influence for me.'

Luchino Visconti, the brilliant producer, belonged to a different category. While Callas felt grateful for her stimulating collaboration with him, she could not put him on the same venerable pedestal as Serafin or Hidalgo. Even so, after Hidalgo and Serafin, Visconti had in all probability been the greatest influence on her artistic development; he refined her physical acting and inspired her to pour out every drop of her talent. She also enjoyed working with other producers such as Franco Zeffirelli, Margherita Wallmann and Alexis Minotis, all of whom contributed to her success.

During her formative years only Hidalgo, and later Serafin, understood her better than she did herself. The apprentice Callas had determination and what is referred to as talent, together with a vague belief that one day she would develop into a great singer. It is this vagueness, together with a degree of humility so necessary in any artist and her teachers' guidance that made Callas possible. 'Like my teacher Elvira de Hidalgo,' she said after she had become a celebrity,

> I began my vocal training at a very early age. As far as I know many great singers, especially women, also started very early. Expert vocal training is essential as it forms what they call your 'spinal cord'. The vocal instrument is like a child. If it is taught correctly how to read and write from the beginning and is well bred generally, it will have a good chance later to succeed. Alternatively, if you do not learn exactly what you are supposed to do, you will always be handicapped.
>
> As I believe a singer's career is largely based on youth, it is necessary for us to begin training as early as possible. Moreover, since this career is relatively short (much shorter than a conductor's) and wisdom is normally attained later, after the training, the earlier this training is accomplished the better. This is even more urgent for Mediterraneans (I am Greek and my teacher is a Spaniard), particularly the girls who, generally speaking, grow up faster or mature faster than those in northern climates.
>
> Anyway, I was lucky to have started very young and especially with Hidalgo, who was, perhaps, the last to have had the real vocal training, the great discipline of *bel canto*. So as a young girl of fifteen I was thrown into her arms, meaning that I learned the secrets, the ways of *bel canto*, a term which literally but grossly misleadingly means 'beautiful song'. *Bel canto* is the most efficient musical training method [the word beautiful here is irrelevant], which prepares a singer to surmount all the complexities of operatic music and, through these complexities, express human emotions with profundity. The method calls for enormous breath control, a firm line and the ability to produce a pure flow of sound, together with the fioritura.
>
> *Bel canto* is a strait-jacket which one must learn to wear whether one likes it or not. It is no different than learning to read and write. In singing, which is also a language, albeit more precise and complex, you have to learn how to form musical sentences, how far your physical strength can go. Furthermore, when you fall you must be able to get back on your feet according to the *bel canto* rules. Flexibility of voice, and consequently coloratura, is vital to all opera singers whether they use it in performance or not. Without this training the singer will remain limited, even lame. It is the same if an athlete, say a runner, trains only the muscles in his legs. A singer must also acquire good taste, which is essential, and a quality which is handed down from one to another. Therefore *bel canto* is the complete schooling without which you cannot sing any opera really well, not even the most modern work.

Responding to my questions about the application of *bel canto*,[1] Callas readily elaborated:

426

It is not correct to refer to some works like those of Rossini, Bellini, Donizetti, as specific *bel canto* operas. In reality there are no such works. This rather superficial differentiation was in all probability invented when, towards the end of the previous century, the *bel canto* method began to be neglected or taught less thoroughly. As the new music, verismo [realism], no longer relied on actual coloratura or other embellishments (which *bel canto* essentially teaches) to express the drama, many singers left the classroom prematurely for the stage in order to become rich and famous quickly. This was ill advised, because these singers still required a full training. Instead, some teachers concocted dangerously abridged singing courses with the inevitable repercussions: in verismo works, for example those by Puccini, singers may survive, albeit to a very limited extent, but in the earlier operas (those inaccurately labelled *bel canto* operas) they cannot – that is if their integrity is to be maintained, and it must be. Make-believe can only be achieved with the utmost sincerity on the performer's part.

Although I started out with a short vocal range (probably with that of a mezzo-soprano), almost immediately, and before any study of consequence, the upper register developed naturally. Therefore I can say that my voice was from the beginning that of a dramatic soprano and very early I sang Santuzza in *Cavalleria rusticana* and the title role in *Suor Angelica* in student performances, then Tosca with the Athens Opera. However, Hidalgo in her coaching continued to keep my voice on the lighter side as this is, of course, one of *bel canto*'s basic rules: however heavy a voice may be it must be kept light (that's not recommendable all the time for everybody, but my voice being a rather odd instrument needed this treatment more) – that is, its flexibility must not only be constantly maintained at all costs but also increased. This is achieved by practising the scales, the trills, the arpeggios and all the *bel canto* embellishments. Pianists use the same approach. I learned all this from the invaluable exercises composed by Concone and Panofka – really marvellous little melodies that make hard work a pleasure. Even though you have to practise these exercises all your life, it is absolutely necessary to learn them before you begin to perform on the stage, otherwise you will meet with disaster.

On the other hand if you are prepared, they help greatly to establish you as a singer. The science and art of *bel canto*, a language of its own, is huge – the more you learn, the less you know you have learned. More problems arise, and more difficulties. You need to give more love to it, more passion, because it is something fascinating and intangible.

I can say that when I left Greece I completed my schooldays and an early preparatory period of performance. By then I had found out, more or less, how far I could go, what I must do. In short I was ready to begin my career, by which I mean I graduated from the workshop. Study with Hidalgo was akin to school and university education, that with

Serafin to postgraduate and finishing school. I learned from Serafin that henceforth my vocal resources should not be confined to the study of *bel canto*, but by means of it to put the note together with the expression and the gesture. 'You have an instrument,' he told me, 'with which you study during rehearsals – just as a pianist does with his piano. But during the performance try to forget you have studied – enjoy your singing, express your soul through it.' I also learned that I must be wary of becoming obsessed with the beauty of a performance; if you relax too much you lose control. You should strive to become the main instrument of the orchestra (which is the meaning of prima donna), and dedicate yourself to the service of music and art, and this is really what it is all about. Art is the ability to express the life of emotion. It is the same in all art – dance, literature, painting. However technically well a painter learns to draw he will have done nothing if he does not produce a picture that is a work of art.

It was Serafin who taught me the meaning of art and who guided me to discover it for myself. A thorough musician and a great conductor, Serafin was also a teacher of the highest subtlety – not of solfeggio but of phrasing and dramatic expression. Without his teaching and guidance, which has always remained with me, I might not have found the meaning of art. He opened my eyes, showing me that there was a reason for everything in music: the fioriture, the trills and all the other embellishments are the composer's expression of the state of mind of the character in the opera – that is the way he feels at that moment, the passing emotions that take hold of him. If, however, these embellishments are used superficially to create a vocal exhibition then they will be counter-productive. They will simply destroy the characterization one should be trying to build.

Nothing escaped Serafin's attention. He was just like a sly fox – every movement, every word, every breath, every little detail was important. One of the first things he told me (which is in fact a basic principle of *bel canto*), was always to prepare a phrase in your soul before you sing it; the audience sees it in your face – then you sing it and without ever attacking a note from underneath or from above. Also, that pauses are often more important than the music, that there is a rhythm, a measure, for the human ear, and that if a note was too long it would cease to have any value after a while. When you speak you do not hang on to words or syllables. The same applies to singing, too. Serafin taught me the proportions of recitative – how it is elastic, the balance altering so slightly that only you can understand it. He further maintained that if you want to find an appropriate gesture and action on the stage you only have to listen to the music – the composer has already seen to that. I act according to the music – to a pause, to a chord, to a crescendo. And so I learned exactly the depth and justification of music. That is why I tried to absorb, like a sponge, all I could from this great man. Although Serafin was a very strict teacher, in performance he would leave you to your own initiative and resourcefulness, but he would always be there to help. If you were not well he would speed up the tempo to help you with your breathing – he was breathing with you, living the music with you, loving it with you. The art of music is so enormous that it can envelop you and keep you in a state of almost perpetual anxiety and torture. But it is not all in vain. It is an honour and great happiness to serve music with humility and love.

The music is also the deciding factor in choosing an operatic role. First I read the music in the same way I would read a book. Then I read the whole score and if I decide to sing the role, I ask: 'Who is she, does the characterization agree with the music?' Frequently it does. For example, the historical Anna Bolena is quite different from Donizetti's. The composer made her a sublime woman, a victim of circumstances, almost a heroine. The music itself justifies the libretto.[2]

Song is the highest, the noblest, manifestation of poetry; therefore good diction is of paramount importance not only because a singer must be intelligible but, more important, because the music should not suffer mutilation. The fact that I always try to find truth in the music does not in any way make the words superfluous. When I auditioned for *Norma* Serafin told me, 'You know the music very well. Now go home and speak it to yourself. Let us see with what proportions and rhythms you come back to me tomorrow. Keep on saying it to yourself, noting the accents, the pauses, the little stresses that create meaning. Singing is speaking in tones. Try to achieve the right balance between the different accents of speech and music, bearing in mind Bellini's style of course. Respect the values but be free to cultivate your own expression.'

Very often the words in opera are naïve, even nonsensical, on their own but acquire tremendous power with the music. Also in a sense opera is today an old-fashioned form of art. Whereas before you could sing 'I love you' or 'I hate you' or words expressing whatever feeling, now you can still sing about it, but if you are going to be convincing it is absolutely necessary to express the corresponding feeling through music rather than through the words and make the audience participate in what you say and feel. Music creates a world on a higher level, but opera needs words to accomplish this. That is why I, an interpreter, a performer, begin with the music. The composer has already found truth in the libretto. 'Music begins where words stop,' as E. T. A. Hoffman said.

But to return to my preparatory stage: you take the music and you learn it as if you were a pupil at the conservatoire – in other words, exactly as it is written, nothing more and nothing less, and at this stage without letting yourself be drawn into the beautiful world of creation. It is what I call 'strait-jacketing'. The conductor gives you his cuts, his possibilities, ideas about what his cadenzas might be – a conscientious conductor should always build his cadenzas according to the style and nature of the composer.

Having broken a score down, you then need a pianist who will not let any mistake in the values of notes slip by you. After about two weeks you need the company and the conductor for piano rehearsals. During my early years I also used to attend, on my own initiative, orchestral rehearsals. I am short-sighted and cannot depend on the cues given me either by the conductor or the prompter. Also I would attend to live into the music. So, when I came to the first rehearsal with the orchestra I was quite prepared, meaning that I was ready to begin the creation of my role.

Naturally, this comes with rehearsal and grows with the performances. Sometimes vocal technique stands in your way. Today a phrase might not come off, but tomorrow, to your delight, it does. Then gradually, familiarity with the music and the character enables you to develop all the tiny nuances which you could only hint at in the beginning. You mould the character: the eyes, the limbs, the whole physical aspect. It becomes a stage of identification at times so complete that I feel I *am* her.

The whole of Italian music is always of flowing movement, however slowly things go rhythmically. When you master this the interpretation will go on growing. Your subconscious will have matured and will always help you out. Everything must be logical, it must add up.

Finally you build the whole thing together – stage, colleagues, orchestra – and eventually you reach the point of performing the opera straight through, which you must do three or four times to measure your strength and learn where you can rest. There is one thing you must do at the orchestral rehearsals: sing in full voice for your colleagues' sake, and above all to test your own possibilities. At this point – it is about twenty days into the production – you have the final dress rehearsal; there is no stopping – it is just like a performance. Then you are practically sick, you are so tired; the following day you unwind and the third day you are ready to go. After the first performance good solid work begins to fill in the blank spots. You have made a sketch – unless, of course, you had plenty of time, but in any case there is nothing like stage performances in front of an audience to fill in the details, the intangible things, that are so beautiful.

The perfection of a role may well take a long time. Eventually I may change hairdos, costumes and so on. Even though my acting springs from the music, instinct does play a part. It must be the Greek in me that speaks as I have done nothing outside the operatic stage. I was quite surprised when once I watched the Greek actor-producer Minotis rehearse the Greek chorus in Cherubini's *Medea* that I was appearing in. (Medea herself is not Greek.) Suddenly I realized they were performing the same movements I did as

Alceste a few years before. I had never seen Greek tragedy performed. When I was in Greece it was mostly during the war and I was studying singing. I did not have much time or money for anything else and yet my movements as the Greek Alceste were similar to those of the Greek chorus in *Medea*. It must be instinct.

I remember that even as a child I never moved much, though I watched a great deal. During my early days at the conservatory in Athens I did not know what to do with my hands. At that time, when I was about fourteen, Renato Mordo, an Italian director of operetta at the conservatory, said two things which have stayed in my mind ever since. One was that you should never move your hand unless you follow it with your mind and soul, a strange way of putting it but it is true. The other was that when your colleague on stage sings his lines to you, you must try at that moment to forget that you know in advance (because this is a role you have rehearsed) what you are supposed to say. Of course you will answer what the libretto demands but make it seem as if all is a first reaction. Naturally it is not enough to know these things but rather how you do them that matters.

It is the same with your gestures. Today you feel like making a gesture which tomorrow may not come naturally; and if it doesn't come naturally to you, you can't hope to convince the public. My gestures are never premeditated. They are linked to one's colleagues, to the music, to the way you've moved before: one gesture is born from another like the remarks in a conversation. They must always be the authentic product of the moment.

Nevertheless, essential though this logical spontaneity is, the most important prerequisite of an actor (opera singers *are* actors) is to identify with the character, as created by the composer and the librettist, otherwise your performance will remain unconvincing and unworthy, however superficially beautiful and impressive you may be. Inarguably you must study every vocal inflexion, every gesture, every glance – instinct is your abstract friend who will keep you on course. However, you will have accomplished nothing if your studies do not, once on the stage, result in a total transfiguration into a new way of feeling, a new way of living. Sometimes it is so difficult you almost despair – like trying to open a safe without knowing the combination. But you must not give up. You must continue to explore all possibilities. This is one of the most fascinating aspects of art – there are always new details, new revelations that further research can yield.

It is our duty to modernize our approach so that we can give opera a breath of fresh air. Cut redundant movements and certain lengthy repetitions (repetition of a melody is seldom really good), because the sooner you come to the point the better – and you must always have a point to come to. As a very general rule, the first time you say something is the only time — try not to risk a second time.

We must always perform faithfully what the composer wrote, but in such a way that the public will listen. This is so because a hundred years ago the public was different — it used to think differently, dress differently. Now we must act accordingly. We make changes in order to make opera a success, while keeping the atmosphere, the poetry, the mysticism that makes theatre work. There is nothing old-fashioned about this — feeling was always real and deep feeling, honest feeling, always will be. Singing is not an act of pride, but an attempt to rise towards those heights where everything is harmony.

From Callas's well-informed comments on vocal art and her own approach it emerges that her artistic integrity was of the highest and, significantly, she pursued her ideals at all times with unrivalled zeal and without compromise. The vital question is, however, to what extent she succeeded. Callas, an artist of infinite variety and resource, evoked different images in different people. These may not always have been universally agreeable but she was never the sort of artist who could be ignored. All great, influential artists often meet with controversy and it is not a crime to disapprove or even dislike them. The crime is rather to ignore them.

Endowed with a two-and-a-half-octave range, enormous by any standards, extending from A natural below middle C to E flat and exceptionally to high F, her low notes had the chesty quality of a true mezzo-soprano or even a contralto, while the middle and upper registers, in addition to being highly dramatic (in fact possessing the characteristics of a tragedienne) could also become appropriately light and playful. Moreover, her ability to change the timbre and colour of her voice to suit the character she was portraying, while still maintaining the high individuality of her singing, made it possible for her to attempt practically any role she chose.

However, the history of singing shows that the unusual, relatively abnormal vocal extension of the dramatic soprano *d'agilità*, precisely what Callas was, cannot be acquired without inevitable weaknesses. These included an occasional unevenness of scale with a guttural quality where the low, middle and high registers merge, and a modest lack of colour homogeneity in the timbre. At times some unruliness generated a raw edge in certain high notes, when sung at full voice, which gave way to a slight stridency and wayward pulse or even, though rarely, a wobble. Callas's periodic vocal flaws, however, were not significant in performance but were noticeable when considered out of context in certain recordings of excerpts (see discography) made late in her career and issued without her approval after her death. Even so her detractors, those who revel in isolated beautiful sounds at all times, superficially all but dismissed her — an absurd criterion in judging an artist, not an apprentice, and damaging to art because it makes nonsense of opera as a whole for the sake of sensational sounds.

What should be asked about Callas's vocal flaws is whether the end justified the means. If one takes into account what opera aims to achieve, in general her faults, when placed in the context of her overall effect and final achievement, can be little more than drops in the ocean. Michelangelo's masterpiece, *David*, in the Galleria dell'Accademia in Florence, is no less a masterpiece because of the technical faults in its fingers or the odd way the body sits on the waist. In fact, the oddity of the upper-body-to-waist relationship enhances its beauty and truth, giving it an almost indefinable lightness – a magical touch that transports it from the workshop to the realm of art.

It must also be said that there can never have been a faultless opera singer, because it is not unusual for one virtue to impair another and transform it into a fault. The process is reversible inasmuch as a fault may be adapted and used as a means of expression. The analogy with Callas is not dissimilar. She was sensitive enough to be aware of her vocal shortcomings and those she could not quite correct she tried to make use of. Indeed, so great was her vocal artistry that she often invested a fault with a subtle significance, making it an integral part of the music and thus turning it to her advantage. How masterfully she could use a slight stridency in the upper register, for instance, to express superbly despair, or loneliness, or defiance.

The dramatic faculties of singers are sometimes so powerful that they demand an appreciable sacrifice of a smooth and even line. Such sacrifice (manipulation is perhaps a better definition) has nothing to do with the standard of technique. Artists of genius are by nature unable always to maintain absolute technique in isolation, nor do they want to. Perfect evenness in a voice at all times will deprive interpreters, at least in part, of dramatic urgency. On the other hand, when liberated from academic restrictions, such artists will often amaze even themselves with their own daring. The unevenness as well as the occasional absence of velvet in Callas's voice could well have been the means by which she acquired the distinctive vocal colours that made her performances so memorable. Of course, her vocal shortcomings were not very pronounced, otherwise she would not have been able to correct them or transform them into virtues. It is also true that there were occasions when the harshness and stridency would not be entirely put to the service of expression. Nor did the 'change of gear', where the vocal registers merge, always create exciting dramatic intensity. Nevertheless, in an overall assessment of her achievement the fact remains that more often than not it did.

Ideally, one would like to believe in the possibility of the perfect singer, but such an artist would, according to nature as we know it, constitute an impressive computer miracle lacking the necessary humanity, or that mysterious and at times almost preposterous quality which can move the human soul. It was Callas's vocal and dramatic skill that enabled her to make use of her inevitable technical faults and thus, at her best, approach (but not achieve) perfection as closely as nature allows. Comparison with Pasta and Malibran, generally considered to have been two of the greatest opera singers that have ever lived, is not inapposite. Their vocal flaws, as recorded by their contemporaries, bore a striking resemblance to those of Callas: 'Even so,' Bellini declared, 'Pasta sang no less like an angel.' Similarly Verdi's pronouncement was, 'In spite of everything Malibran is marvellous – a very great artist indeed.'

Controversies of this kind exist because people have heard on occasion other singers who did not have this or that fault. Callas did not have the vocal evenness and velvety timbre of a Renata Tebaldi and, in the latter part of her career, the volume and steadiness of Birgit Nilsson or the resounding high notes of Joan Sutherland. But that is to pit one singer against three others. More significantly, it must be stressed that whereas Callas could not surpass the individually remarkable attributes of these artists, she possessed a good measure of each of them, in addition to genius and unquestionable artistry – qualities those singers did not have to the degree that she did.

And here we must digress to examine the phenomenon of beautiful voices in general and that of Callas in particular – an aspect of her art which has always been a major factor in the controversy about her as a singer. Callas's own point of view must also be heard: 'It is not enough to have a beautiful voice,' she said with assurance,

> What does it mean? When you interpret a role you have to have a thousand colours to portray happiness, joy, sorrow, anger, fear. How can you do this with only a beautiful voice? Even if you sing harshly sometimes, as I have done, it is a necessity of expression. You have to do it, even if people will not understand. But in the long run they will, because you must persuade them of what you are doing.
>
> It is a fact that there are those who claim that the art of singing is first and last perfect tone, brilliant high notes and little else. Whereas on principle I would be the last person to disapprove of these accomplishments, they are rather superficial if considered in isolation. To my mind this is what every student should be taught until the last, no, the penultimate, year at the conservatoire. Afterwards the student must faithfully employ technique to serve expression (the only reason that technique is acquired). But in the process of transforming himself from a technician to an artist, there will perforce be occasions when the tone cannot and should not be perfect. In any event it is a physical impossibility to maintain perfect tone and always be correct in what you should express. Also, even certain high notes will be strident, sometimes deliberately and sometimes as a price to pay for the sake of expression. This, of course, depends on whether you care more about art itself or about your personal, selfish success – which really is no success. The human voice, when it is serving art with absolute honesty, cannot always physically produce high notes devoid of stridency. Naturally it all depends on how strident these notes are and how imperfect the tone is. You cannot use artistic expression as a pretext for

badly produced intonation and high notes. What we are interested in is whether the credit is on the side of artistic expression, the only goal of all artists.

Referring to the theory that the elemental appeal of high notes is that they evoke the highly charged cries of our primal ancestors' mating calls (and even those of animals and birds), Callas promptly responded, 'High notes are as important as the other notes. They are written by the composer to express the feeling of that moment, when the crest of emotion is reached. Consequently the same high notes should not necessarily be sung in the same way; it is not enough for a high note to be only on pitch and with a healthy ringing tone.'

Inarguably a 'beautiful voice' is one of Nature's marvellous gifts. The sound of a country stream can also be very soothing and the unique voice of the nightingale is a most memorable experience. Whereas the beauty of any sound that pleases cannot be underestimated, the examples given above are not art, nor do they occur by design. A nightingale, always heard for only a few seconds and expressing nothing more than what it instinctively knows, will cease to enchant, let alone hold the attention, if one listens to it for any length of time. One must distinguish between an opera singer, whose purpose is to enhance drama through music, and every other type of sound, however enchanting.

One side of the argument about the beauty of Callas's voice can now be put forward. By beautiful, however, I do not mean that she merely had the ability to sing 'sweetly' – which she usually did when the situation warranted it – rather, it is the fruit of intelligent imagination and study as applied to a given piece of music. However much sweetness a voice may have been endowed with by nature, it will of necessity lose its relevance and appeal when it exists in isolation. The point may be made more strongly when applied to the speaking voice in the theatre, where the musical support is missing. An actor could never be accepted if he delivered his dialogue with only a smooth and agreeable voice, however ravishing this might be to the ear. If vocal inflexions fail to serve dramatic expression they become an irrelevant and even destructive affectation. One should really speak of beautiful singing, not of a beautiful voice. It is similar to comparing an average violinist playing a Stradivarius with, say, Kreisler or Heifetz playing an ordinary violin.

Tullio Serafin was perhaps the first person to put the Callas case in a nutshell. When I asked him directly whether he thought her voice beautiful or ugly his immediate response was, 'Which voice, that of Norma, Violetta, Lucia? Then there was Medea, Isolde, Amina – I can go on. You see, she had different voices for different roles. I have known many of Callas's voices. Do you know, I have never really considered whether her voice was ugly or beautiful. I only know that it was always the right one, and this is more than beautiful.'

His answer – a dictum – is of considerable significance; it confirms to a degree that a great deal in art, both aesthetic and technical, cannot be defined in absolute terms, because most aspects depend more or less on psychology for their validity. Serafin was a musician whose knowledge and experience in operatic singing (his opinion was obviously based on world-wide standards) was accepted generally as having been perhaps the most authoritative of his generation.

All such opinions and judgements, logical and helpful as they are in understanding Callas's artistry, run the danger of giving the impression that her fame and greatness as an opera singer were founded on controversy. This is far from being the case. If I have dealt with the controversial issues first, by presenting her own comments and self-criticism as well as those of others, it is because it may be more constructive to consider the outcome of her achievement in this way, for in the ultimate analysis it is the strength of her virtues that matters most.

As already mentioned, her vocal range was enormous and her voice possessed great virtuosity and agility, and at the beginning of her career, when she was singing dramatic roles that had no coloratura, impressive volume. Later, when she began to sing the operas of the early nineteenth-century composers the volume of her voice diminished somewhat. This was relative and applies only when compared with that of present-day dramatic sopranos who do not attempt coloratura roles. In the nineteenth century when Rossini, Bellini, Donizetti and the young Verdi were producing their operas for precisely the kind of singer Callas was, the vocal demands were applied to the method of composition and exceptional volume could not be expected of a highly flexible voice. For this reason stages then projected considerably into the auditorium, and orchestras were smaller and usually one tone lower than the large, highly pitched modern ones. The singers could thus produce sufficient volume without any undue pressure. Today the different stage structure puts singers (particularly a dramatic soprano *d'agilità*) at a disadvantage as far as volume is concerned.

Another characteristic of the dramatic soprano is the speed with which she executes florid passages. When Callas sang 'Ah! non giunge!', the florid finale from *La sonnambula*, she was initially criticized by some (including the present writer) because, wonderful though it was, it sounded a little laboured since it was rather slow; for at the time this finale was polished off at top speed by light or lyric coloraturas. Although their presentation appeared impressive and superficially exciting, they missed the all-important intention of the nineteenth-century composers who expected florid passages to be slower, so that singers could imbue them with expression, in this case the bounding joy of the character.

The vocal quality that Callas did not in any way lack was that rare gift of colouring appropriately every musical passage with imagination and skill. So highly developed was this gift that she often achieved a miracle of emotional revelation, electrifying the listener. There were other factors which contributed to this achievement: her chest and upper notes were clean and open, and she could alternate them with amazing facility, as well as producing a rapid, pure and sparkling pianissimo. Moreover, unlike the majority of her contemporaries, Callas made words act as a vehicle for the coloration – the consonants helping in articulation and inflexion of notes, the vowels blending the sense of the words with the character of the music.

This tonal colouring was also evident in her coloratura which was without exception an integral part of the dramatic context of the music. There was something fabulous about her fioriture, arpeggios, trills and descending scales, while all the brilliance and sparkle that her roulades and cadenzas possessed never deprived her singing of its dramatic expression. Embellishments were always relevant, supplementing the melodic line and intensifying the emotions – like herbs enhancing rather than smothering the flavour of the dish.

Most of what Callas could do with coloration is concisely contained in her singing of two contrasting pieces from *Norma*; the cabaletta 'Ah bello a me ritorna' where the coloratura introspectively expresses nostalgic thoughts of her lover's return, and the unbridled scales of 'Oh non tremare', revealing terrible anger at her faithless lover. Thus she demonstrated at a stroke, as it were, that true melodic virtuosity is not built upon vocalising. She could also sing so softly and with such apparent lack of effort that tempo and colouring were simultaneously controlled. It was this accomplishment that enabled her to discover the secret of speaking through music; with impeccable intuition she gave the recitatives a strange reality, often delivering them in a mezzo-soprano voice.

Irving Kolodin (*Saturday Review*, November 1955) perceptively opined that 'Callas's kind of voice is what every great artist's means of communication becomes: an extension of her own personality. That personality is dynamic, highly charged, tigerish, and constantly disciplined. So, too, the voice is dynamically dramatic, produced as though it might be torn from the singer's insides, and presided over with an almost visible concern for every word and note she sings. Nothing is thoughtless, left to chance, or without total purpose.'

Callas's physical acting, as distinct from singing – though the two were inseparable – always (except as Rosina in *Il barbiere di Siviglia*) appeared spontaneous and fresh. Some of the greatest directors who had worked with her testified to this. Luchino Visconti's observations and comments (Radiocorriere TV, 1960) on his collaboration with her (he had directed her in *La vestale*, *La sonnambula*, *La traviata*, *Anna Bolena* and *Ifigenia in Tauris*) are most enlightening:

> She had complete freedom to operate within a general framework. Artists of her calibre could never be successfully 'manoeuvred' without allowing their particular idiosyncrasy this type of freedom. My contribution was first to discuss with her all possible aspects of her role and of the work as a whole, and give her certain guide-lines, certain objectives within which to perform; but within these lines she could do what she wanted. I trusted

her implicitly because of her unerring sense of timing, her impeccable musical instinct and talent as a dramatic actress, a tragedienne. . . . We are talking of Callas, and I would defy anyone to direct her differently. I have worked for years with actors, dancers, film stars, singers. Inarguably Callas is the most disciplined and professional artist I have ever had occasion to handle. She always without exception worked at rehearsals with the same intensity and enthusiasm from beginning to end, giving everything she had.

Franco Zeffirelli's appreciation of Callas was equally enthusiastic. Having directed her in *Il Turco in Italia*, *La traviata*, *Tosca*, *Lucia di Lammermoor* and *Norma*, he declared that she was 'the greatest stage talent I have ever known'. Alexis Minotis, who worked with her on *Medea* and *Norma*, commented to me that 'she always asked that I would treat her with the same meticulousness as I would an actress in the straight theatre. Her philosophy was that if her singing were to be any good it should not be at odds with the performance. It never was. Also it was uncanny how she could vary her interpretations and still always make you believe that she was giving the definitive portrayal every time.'

Artists of this calibre are usually inventive; they are capable of improvising when necessary but always at a high artistic level and never for personal effect. Gavazzeni recalled an occasion, when he was conducting *Anna Bolena* at La Scala, on which Callas used her instinct to improvise:

It was actually on the first night when at the end of the final scene Anna was to have been engulfed by a silent chorus of hooded extras who were to conduct her to her death; it was a wonderful effect, a relevant conclusion to the inner drama of the character. Because of an oversight on the part of the stage manager, however, the chorus of extras did not appear and Callas found herself unexpectedly alone. Yet she did not panic. On the spot she improvised a series of movements in perfect harmony with the personality of the character she had evolved and then disappeared upstage. No one in the audience had at all suspected that there was anything amiss – and remember, this was the end of the opera. Subsequently the hooded extras were never used.

Thus when Callas achieved a reasonable compromise between the purely technical and the dramatic demands of her roles, and her accomplishments (accuracy with flexible rhythm, dexterity with dramatic expression, strict discipline with her own and the composer's spontaneity) were concerted with profound musicianship, her interpretations went beyond a complete illumination of the character portrayed. They exalted. Compared with other singers Callas could have been matched on some points and even surpassed on others, but as a complete artist who could convey all the complex facets that make up a living character she was supreme. Moreover, her assured personality (the word is here used advisedly), devoid of vulgarity and expressive of its

Top Callas as Norma with Del Monaco as Pollione at La Scala, 1955.
Left As Lady Macbeth at La Scala, 1952.
Below As Anna Bolena at La Scala, 1956.

Callas as Violetta (with Bastianini as Germont)
in *La traviata* at La Scala, 1955.

Callas at La Scala. **Top** Amina (*La sonnambula*, 1955) and Rosina (*Il barbiere di Siviglia*, 1956). **Below** Ifigenia (*Ifigenia in Tauris*, 1957) and Paolina (*Poliuto*, 1960).

Callas as Tosca with Gobbi as Scarpia at Covent Garden, 1964.

Left Callas as Medea with Ghiaurov as Creon at La Scala, 1962.

Above and below As Medea in Pasolini's non-singing film of *Medea*, 1970.

Right Having recorded *Carmen* in 1964, the nearest Callas got to performing the role on stage was to sit for this portrait of the heroine.

Below and below right Callas and di Stefano on their world concert tour, 1973.

Maria Callas, 1964

Maria Callas, 1968

own period was, with the help of vocal quality, technique and that magical gift instinct, a most significant factor in her ability to give new life to familiar music. It was not by accident that she took a hitherto waltz-sounding Donizetti passage from the 'mad scene' in *Lucia di Lammermoor* and made it into a 'Liebestod'.

Perceptive artists are often hypersensitive and, despite strong artistic resources, paradoxically approach their art with great caution and even fear. In every performance, or so it was with Callas, she felt that she had to prove herself as if she were a débutante.

The ability to transform herself into the characters she portrayed, and her accomplished singing, made it possible to re-introduce in a modern idiom the operas of several neglected Italian composers. Works by Cherubini, Spontini, Rossini, Donizetti, Bellini and early Verdi were triumphantly revived for her. In Callas's hands heroines such as Norma, Violetta, Medea, Rossini's Armida, Imogene (*Pirata*), Elvira (*Puritani*), Anna Bolena and a host of others appeared to be women of flesh and blood, remaining larger than life, even prototypes in some cases. This 'revolution' was similar to the creation of Chekhov's women in the straight theatre at the beginning of the century.

Callas's repertoire ranged from Gluck's *Alceste* (1767) and Haydn's *Orfeo ed Euridice* (1791) to Kalomiris's *Protomastoras* (1915) and Puccini's *Turandot* (1926). She started her career as a typical twentieth-century dramatic soprano, though in the early days in Athens she had made brief excursions into operetta (Suppé's *Boccaccio* and Millöcker's *Bettelstudent*) — always a beneficial experience with its lightness of approach. Other unusual features of her repertoire were the Wagnerian roles of Isolde, Brünnhilde (*Die Walküre*) and Kundry (*Parsifal*) which she only sang during the first years of her international career.

With the advent of *I Puritani* in Venice (1949) Callas's career began to take its true course: the operas of Bellini, Rossini, Donizetti, Cherubini and Verdi were to form the backbone of her stage repertoire. Later she sang more Puccini, such as *Madama Butterfly* (recording *Manon Lescaut* and *La bohéme*) and above all *Tosca*, a role she completely identified herself with, throwing new light on it. She also proved and outstanding interpreter of Gluck's classic music, as Alceste and Ifigenia (*Ifigenia in Tauris*). Her only Mozart role was Constanze in *Die Entführung aus dem Serail*. Listening solely to her last act of *Turandot* it is evident that she would have made a great Salome and Elektra, as well as the Marschallin in *Der Rosenkavalier*. She did not sing in any of Strauss's operas.

Modern opera never attracted Callas. 'A great deal of modern operatic music', she said, some time in the late 1950s, 'bothers, rather than soothes, the nervous system, a fact which stops me from singing these operas. Obviously some modern opera exerts a certain appeal, but I feel it should not be called music. Even the most dramatic music should essentially depend upon simplicity and beauty of line.' She had turned down the offer to create the role of Cressida in

William Walton's *Troilus and Cressida* (1955) and the title role in Samuel Barber's *Vanessa* (1958), though the reason she gave for the latter was that the character of Vanessa had nothing in common with her own spiritual world. If anything, she added, the secondary role of Erika (a mezzo-soprano) would have been more suitable for her.

Practically all Callas's repertoire on stage was sung in Italian. In Greece she always sang in Greek except for a single performance of *Tosca* which was given in Italian, and English songs in English. Later she sang in concerts and recorded 'Ocean! Thou mighty monster' (*Oberon*) in its original English version. She recorded French opera in the vernacular, revealing that a new repertoire was open to her, but she only sang in French on the concert platform.

Her three Wagnerian roles were sung in Italian because at the time this was expected of her. Callas in fact expressed her views on this matter when she went for an audience with Pope Pius V in 1955. The Pope, a known Germanophile, was quite adamant that Wagner in Italy should be sung in German. Although Callas agreed in principle that opera should be sung in the original language, there were special cases that required other considerations. In this case, she felt that for the Italian audience of the early 1950s, which was not accustomed to Wagner's music (in general the Italians have never loved his work passionately), it was imperative to understand the words even though this was to be at the expense of some loss, perhaps considerable, in the music with the different sounds that a translation dictates. Consequently, it would have been a difficult, if not impossible, task to captivate the public if it had had to listen for hours to an incomprehensible language, however marvellous the music. The Pope declined to accept the argument and Callas did not change her views which, she stressed, were only valid for that place, time and particular audience.

It was not so much the number of roles (forty-three leading and one secondary stage roles, and recordings only of *Pagliacci, Manon Lescaut, La bohème* and *Carmen*) that Callas assumed but their type that is important, and the way she performed them. For example, in Donizetti's operas, apart from *Lucia di Lammermoor* only *L'elisir d'amore* and *Don Pasquale* were given with any frequency. Her modern characterization of Lucia, Anna Bolena and Paolina (*Poliuto*) proved decisive in paving the way for other singers to revive most of Donizetti's stage works, particularly his *opere serie*. The same applies to Rossini. The dramatic coloratura of his *Armida* in the hands of Callas persuaded her generation that Rossini's *opere serie* were unjustly neglected. For Bellini she did more: guided by Serafin, she brought about a renaissance of his works. The four — *Norma, La sonnambula, I Puritani* and *Il pirata* — that she sang became part of the established repertoire. Later *I Capuleti e i Montecchi* also entered it. *Beatrice di Tenda* and *La straniera* are gaining ground, having enjoyed several revivals.

Furthermore, had Callas sung more verismo operas she could well have raised this music to the level it deserves. She did sing Santuzza and Turandot at the beginning of her career, but in spite of her success she soon wisely dropped these roles. When later in the 1960s these parts would have been vocally apposite, her career was over. This deduction is not as fanciful as it may sound. Her Maddalena (*Andrea Chénier*), a verismo role, was controversially received almost as much as her Violetta had been at the beginning, but the former role is not as famous. However, closer study of her performance from the 'pirate' recording reveals that her interpretation of Maddalena, as also her Fedora and Tosca, sprang from musical considerations. That which may appear tame or introspective in the absence of superficial and histrionic effects becomes, with deeper understanding, more interesting and exciting.

What made it possible for Callas to augment the operatic repertoire was not only her extraordinary vocal technique and the way she found the *physique du rôle* (only as Rosina in *Il barbiere di Siviglia* on the stage, though not in the later recording, did Callas fail to identify with the character) but also that rarest of gifts, the ability to discover the right style for any music and adapt it to contemporary sensibility. This, though not in isolation but together with all her attributes, was her strongest asset, as it enabled her to bridge the gap between her heroine's age and ours. In opera the process of creativity does not end with the composition of the music but is left to the singers (and the orchestra) to crystallize and manifest. The achievement depends on the success of the performance, otherwise the composer's creation remains unexpressed and possibly misunderstood. Callas's portrayals transcended interpretative art. They became creative art. Only once or twice in a generation is the ideal marriage, the near perfect balance, of musical and dramatic gifts achieved.

Undoubtedly Callas's greatest period, during which she reached the pinnacle of her art, was between 1954 and 1958. An earlier time is not claimed because only by 1954 had she lost her excessive weight and henceforth her portrayals were not only enhanced aesthetically but also, through freer movement, her powers of expression were no longer constrained.

It may be difficult to isolate her greatest roles, but it is no exaggeration to declare her Norma, Violetta, Medea, Leonora (*Il trovatore*), Elvira (*Puritani*), Anna Bolena, Lady Macbeth, Armida, Amina and Tosca to have been the most outstanding within living memory and as yet to remain unsurpassed. Other roles were not significantly less successful, but the ones quoted are more celebrated and generally very demanding artistically. When I asked Callas which role was her best, she hesitated before answering. 'I like all my roles,' she said, smiling. 'There is Violetta, Anna Bolena, Medea. ... Well, at one time I was mad about Fedora. The list is long. You see, I love most the role I am singing.' After a brief pause she added, 'With Norma [the role she sang most often but knew that she could never sing again] it is different.' Not only did Callas consider Norma's musical style as the touchstone of the *bel canto* method but she also felt great affinity with the character:

She is in many ways like me. Norma may appear to be very strong, even ferocious at times, but in actuality she is a lamb who roars like a lion; the grumbling woman who is very proud to show her feelings and proves in the end that she cannot be nasty or unjust in a situation for which she herself is fundamentally to blame. My tears in *Norma* were real.

The evolution of opera gained significantly from Callas's example; several of her contemporaries and successors have, to a greater or lesser extent, been influenced by her. The careers of Renata Scotto, Elena Souliotis, Beverly Sills, Joan Sutherland, Montserrat Caballé, Edita Gruberová, Cecilia Gasdia, June Anderson and others, all very important singers, would otherwise have been restricted as the reformation of the repertoire might not have happened.

In the mid-fifties De Sabata told Walter Legge, the recording director: 'If the public could understand as we do how deeply and utterly musical Callas is, they would be stunned.' Gavazzeni put this in sharper perspective: 'Fifteen years ago in Rome,' he said in 1970, 'when I conducted *Lucia* with Callas, I noticed, during rehearsals, certain unexpectedly expressive qualities in her coloratura passages. I tried to capture these in orchestral echoes of the same phrases. Callas's intuition in this was an invaluable stimulus to me also for the future: certainly from then on, my interpretation of *Lucia* was not the same as before. And if it were so for me, it must have been the same for others.'

Callas's achievement did not depend on the criterion that she was merely the best of her time, but on her ability and talent to reach exceptional artistic heights. Not only does she compare favourably — notwithstanding her vocal flaws — with any operatic artist of the twentieth century, but even when one considers legendary singers of the past, taking into account what we know about them, Callas's musical versatility, it can be argued, was not narrower. Whereas Malibran and Pasta excelled in romantic and classical roles, up to and of their period, Callas could do all this and, in addition, was able to adapt her vocal resources to the later, very different, musical medium of Verdi, Wagner and the verismo composers. There was no Violetta, Isolde, Carmen or Tosca for the earlier singers. Until the advent of Lilli Lehmann in the 1880s there was no singer of sufficient stature able to sing Norma, Violetta, Lucia, Isolde, Carmen. Her repertoire was in fact larger then Callas's, though it did not include Spontini, Puccini or any of the verismo composers.

Several other roles were offered to Callas but they did not reach the stage. In the mid-1950s Ghiringhelli came up with the idea of presenting at La Scala Tebaldi as Maria and Callas as Elisabetta in Donizetti's *Maria Stuarda*. The intention was that the two prima donnas would alternate in the two roles. Tebaldi's flat refusal killed the project.

When in January 1959 Sir Thomas Beecham tried persistently to persuade Callas to sing in Handel's *Atalanta* — he sent her the score as he believed that she was the only singer who could do justice to the work — she promised to consider it seriously. However, within nine months Callas's life changed dramatically, following her separation from her husband, and *Atalanta* was shelved.

Valentine in Meyerbeer's *Les Huguenots*, the Countess in Mozart's *Le nozze di Figaro* and either Ottavia or Poppea in Monteverdi's *L'incoronazione di Poppea* were offered to Callas by La Scala soon after her return there in *Poliuto*. She did not take up the offer, most probably because of her erratic vocal capabilities at that period; Callas was always a very cautious artist. The same applies to *Salome* offered by Karajan, Isolde by Wieland Wagner for Bayreuth, Gluck's *Orfeo ed Euridice* and the soprano part in Verdi's *Requiem* by Dallas Opera, as well as Mimi in *La bohème* (even in concert form). She would at first appear responsive but, without giving any reason, left the projects to die a natural death.

It was somewhat different with Debussy's *Pelléas et Mélisande*, offered by the Paris Opèra. She did consider it and studied the score. 'I wake up at night and think about it,' she told me at the time and went on to sing a few phrases with singular declamation. In all probability she felt it was too risky to undertake so curiously French a role at that stage of her career. She certainly wanted to sing a new part – the spirit was willing, the voice was not. At about this time she studied Bellini's *La straniera* but concluded that the work was rather uneven. Bizet's Carmen was the last new role that Callas considered seriously; she studied it meticulously but she only went as far as recording it and including two arias and the final scene in some of her concerts. Paolina in *Poliuto* remained Callas's last new role.

Several examples of the acute psychology that made up Callas's characterizations are particularly enlightening: 'In Norma's first scene,' Callas told me,

> it is vital to portray the character through Bellini's sublime melody but not with beautiful sounds in isolation. Norma is much more a frantic woman and mother to her Roman lover's sons than the prophetic demigoddess whom only the Druids know. Does she really foresee that the Romans will bring their own destruction? As a philosopher, perhaps yes, as a demigoddess, I think not, even though she is proved right later. She herself does not believe that she is a demigoddess. If she ever did, it is because she had been brought up to believe so, but all that was finished when she fell in love with a Roman, broke her vows of chastity and became a mother. She is merely stalling for time, using her authority and philosophy to pacify the ferocious Druids who demand war against their Roman oppressors. When she finally dominates them, the 'Casta Diva' follows as a consequence – a prayer for peace in which Norma also asks the Chaste Goddess for help and guidance.
>
> In the last act Norma thought that she was in control of the whole situation but lost her head completely when her emotions got the better of her. Nevertheless she remains a noble person to the end and sufficiently so to liberate herself without becoming a traumatic sentimental fool. This is her purification.

443

Unlike Norma, her Medea changed considerably over the years. 'At first,' she told Lord Harewood (BBC TV, 1968), 'I saw Medea as a static and barbaric figure who knows what she wants from the beginning. With time, however, I came to understand her better; Medea was certainly a very nasty character but Jason was even worse than her. She was right in her motives but not in her actions. With a softer hair-do, I tried to give her a softer appearance so that I might portray her more as a living woman.'

Discussing Medea with me, Callas said:

I saw her as fiery, apparently calm but very intense. The happy time with Jason is past; now she is devoured by misery and fury. When I first sang the role it seemed to me that it was important that Medea should have a gaunt jaw-line and a rigidity in the neck. I was considerably stouter then and it was intensely frustrating for me that I couldn't assume that. I did what I could to suggest it by dark shadowing on the neck. Medea is not Greek — let's make that clear. Many people, even critics, made the mistake of saying that my Medea has nothing whatsoever Greek in her, though my blood, may I say, is pure Greek. Medea is the one non-Greek personage in the opera. She is a barbarian Colchian Princess — the civilized Greeks would not accept her on equal terms. A Greek Medea invalidates the drama. The killing of the children is not merely an act of vengeance but more significantly a means of escape from a world that is foreign to her and in which she can no longer live. For Medea and her race, death is not the end but the beginning of a new life. Jason inherits a chaotic world in place of riches and power.

Many consider Violetta (*La traviata*) to be the role in which Callas's artistry was supremely displayed. She first expressed her views about this character to Lord Harewood and later, more elaborately, to me. She said:

I loved Violetta because she acquires great dignity and nobility and is purified in the end without ever becoming a traumatic sentimental fool. She is young and beautiful, but her unhappiness keeps coming back to her all the time in the first act. 'Oh, love, who cares?' she says with irony and laughter even though she does not find it amusing. When the guests leave, she keeps on questioning herself. She had never known love before because she was afraid it would have destroyed her life of egotistic and superficial pleasure. When love forces itself on her, at first she resists but soon she discovers that she too is capable of giving.

In the second act she is not laughing any more, though this is her only hour of true happiness. I always tried to make her look younger and hopeful at the beginning of this act until about one third through her scene with Germont, after which she realizes that she is lost: 'I fought but I should have known better. It cannot work.' She agreed to the sacrifice demanded of her because at that time it was impossible for a demi-mondaine to be accepted, but also because, on account of her illness, she had not the strength to fight.

As the drama progresses, Violetta should move less because of her illness. In this way the music makes a greater impact. Of course, I can afford some movement. In the last act I used a sort of useless gesture such as trying to fetch something from the dressing-table but dropping the hand because I cannot quite manage it. Also because of Violetta's type of illness, and this is of the utmost importance in this role, breathing must be a little shorter, the colour of the voice slightly tired. I tried very hard to convey this state of the character. It is all a question of breath. One really needs a very clear throat to sustain this 'tired' way of singing — very dangerous work, but one has to do it. All true art is dangerously difficult. In this case I feel proud to have succeeded. Some critic [Evan Senior in *Music & Musicians*], I believe in London in 1958, inadvertently paid me the highest compliment when he said that Callas in *Traviata* appeared tired, especially in the last act. I had striven for years to create precisely this essential tired and sick quality in Violetta's voice.

Undoubtedly Aida was Callas's most controversial role. Her detractors did not consider it a vocal 'natural' for her, their criticism directed at Aida's famous aria 'O patria mia', and specifically at the high C which was slightly strident without producing any special dramatic expression, as well as some unsteadiness on the phrase. But these vocal flaws are really only noticeable on Callas's recording of *Aida* (now all but rectified with digital remastering) — where they are isolated and magnified — and were barely noticeable in some of her stage performances. Even so and notwithstanding this isolated scene, which is crucial neither to the development of Aida's character nor to the opera's plot, Callas penetrated more deeply into this role than other singers of her generation. She saw it as a whole and explored Aida's human predicament: the choice between love for a foreign man (an enemy) and love for her country.

The reason why Callas dropped the role rather early in her career (1953) was not because she found it vocally heavy but, as she told me,

For my kind of singer, who has had the *bel canto* schooling, Aida is vocally easy. Of course, you need the necessary stamina. I did like the character, but felt for her up to a point. She is not very imaginative, perhaps too passive, and consequently not stimulating enough. One can make sufficient out of her, but before long the possibilities are exhausted. If a singer produces only a smooth tone, that of course will please, but for a short time, and Aida herself will become insignificant in a drama in which she should be the central character, despite her lack of imagination, and from whom the drama must emanate. This is why so often the emphasis is wrongly shifted to Amneris.

Tosca was one of Callas's most successful portrayals. When Lord Harewood (BBC TV, 1968) asked her how much she liked this heroine, whom she had so vividly brought to life, Callas did not answer directly but discussed the role:

> *Tosca* is too realistic. The second act is what I call 'grand guignol'. The first calls for a woman who is, if not hysterical, very nervous and anxious. She comes out calling 'Mario, Mario!' If you think of her objectively she is a nuisance. Yes, she is very much in love. All she was interested in was to find Cavaradossi. She is basically insecure. That is why with the years I conveyed an impatience in her. Once I found the justification for her behaviour, I saw her in a different light.

Some time in the early 1970s Callas further discussed *Tosca* and Puccini with me. The conversation was sparked off when I asked her whether she really did not like Puccini, as she had been quoted as saying. 'Of course that is not true,' she promptly answered,

> though I must say I cannot love him as much as Bellini, Verdi, Donizetti, Rossini, or Wagner. At one time I was mad about Butterfly and I enjoyed recording Mimi [*La bohème*] and Manon Lescaut. All artists appreciate Puccini's great sense of the theatre though I must say that even now, when I have not sung Tosca for almost ten years, the second act is too much of 'grand guignol' for my liking. But when I am on the stage I like everything that I have agreed to do.
>
> Turandot is another story. People wanted me to sing this role because of my big dramatic soprano voice. At the time the opera was difficult to cast as there were not many sopranos who could do it. It was a challenge and as I was young and totally unknown, a great opportunity to establish myself. I sang the role in several places in Italy and Argentina, but thank God for the advent, or I should say the miracle, of *I Puritani* in Venice. Not long after that I dropped Turandot, as I did other roles. But do not get me wrong. I did not dislike Turandot. Shall we say I did not love her passionately and she just was not doing my vocal chords much good in my early years. Also it is too static a role. Of course, you have to act with your voice, but there again it is restricted. And there were so many other roles open to me that I could identify with musically and psychologically.

Commenting on Mozart's operas, Callas had said that in her opinion 'Mozart must be sung by big dramatic voices. Small voices cannot do justice to his music.' Having been very successful as Constanze (*Die Entführung aus dem Serail*), her only Mozart role, I asked Callas why she did not sing in his other operas and jokingly recalled that at one time there was a rumour in Milan that she was going to sing the title role in *Don Giovanni*, adding that this little story was meant to imply that she could sing anything. 'That might have been a good idea,' Callas promptly replied,

> he is much more interesting than Donna Anna. I am not belittling her music, but really that woman is a crushing bore. Donna Elvira is more interesting – though not much more. She will not take no for an answer. I never considered singing the Queen of Night either, nor the Countess. This does not mean that they are not good roles. An artist must feel for these people if they are to be portrayed with any integrity. Mozart was undoubtedly an extraordinary genius and I cannot imagine the world without him. But generally speaking his operatic music does not really take me out of this world. It is the Mozart of the piano concertos that I love passionately.

The description of Callas's performance by eminent directors and critics as well as by herself is judicious and fascinating. Even so, the secret of it, as it were, the power that generated it or the genius that motivated her, is not in the final analysis revealed. It was, to use her own words, like trying to find the combination of a safe. More often than not she succeeded in opening the safe but without confiding in her audience the combination; nor did she remember it herself, for every time she had to find it anew.

My own observation is that although her performances provided supreme truth by sincerity, intelligence and instinct, indispensable attributes for all artists, these qualities would not have proved productive if they had existed in isolation. Naturally instinct played an important part in her characterizations without, however, ever relying on it in an absolute way. Instead she would make use of it after she had mastered, through tenacious study, the technical side of her art. Early in her career Callas grasped the social, artistic trends of her period, as well as the psychological understanding of her audiences. Determined never to resort to the servility of imitation, she used her whole self, without a trace of sentimentality, to persuade the audience to her own interpretation of a character, warts and all. Above all, what made her performances so uniquely individual and demonstrated conclusively that high art is life itself, was that the characters she portrayed were human beings, full of seductive contradictions: chasteness and eroticism, innocence and guilt, kindness and cruelty, and an exotic ferocity that could change to infinite feminine vulnerability. Callas redefined for her generation the foundations and the contours of acting in opera.

---

1 Previously I had discussed the meaning and aim of *bel canto* with Hidalgo, Serafin, Gavazzeni and the music critic Eugenio Gara. They all seemed to have been in full agreement with Callas.
2 For many years Anne Boleyn was generally considered to have been no less than a nymphomaniac whore who also had an incestuous relationship with her brother. Modern research has found no proof for any of these charges, except that Boleyn's diary contradicts, at certain times, her whereabouts.

CHAPTER NINETEEN

TWILIGHT OF A SACRED MONSTER

T HE MISREPRESENTATION OF the Callas–Onassis affair, which basically alleged that he had ruined her career and then abandoned her, has already been invalidated. Nevertheless, the allegations against Onassis did not end with his death in 1975. His detractors moralized that his behaviour towards her had expedited her death, over two years later, from a broken heart – a romantic conclusion arrived at in order to provide a fitting end to the fabricated 'soap opera' scenario of their liaison. In reality Callas developed a genuine and lasting friendship with Onassis following his marriage to another woman, while also some two years before his death forming a close relationship with Giuseppe di Stefano throughout the duration of their joint concert tour in 1973–1974.

Maria fondly described di Stefano as having been a great support to her: 'Do you know', she remarked, 'what courage and strength Pippo [di Stefano's pet-name] can impart to you by holding your hand on the way to the stage?' And in these words we hear again her inner voice, that of her first love, her art. Di Stefano loved Callas. He wanted to divorce his long-estranged wife and marry her, but Maria would not agree. She felt that it was unfortunate that their relationship had not happened in different circumstances and at an earlier time. Her parting words were 'All or nothing', meaning that there was simply no future for them. After the tour di Stefano went back to his wife, albeit temporarily before getting his divorce, and Maria returned home to Paris.

The last eighteen months or so of her life were spent quietly, though not in seclusion. She had in fact always been happier living this way, even during the years she was married; her home and the theatre in which she was working were her castles. Later, during her association with Onassis when she sang progressively less and less, socializing played a greater role but even so never with much frequency. She had no particular love for lavish parties: one a year – and several smaller supper parties – was ideal for her. However, her life was now different inasmuch as, in addition to living alone, she was without a close relationship. Up to the time of her arrival in Italy in 1947 she had lived with her parents in either America or Greece. There followed twelve

Two of Callas's last portraits, about 1975.

years of association with and marriage to Meneghini, a long liaison with Onassis and a less close relationship with di Stefano. According to her, in May 1977, living alone was not a great calamity and she did not appear to me, as some writers and others professed after her death, to have been a woman with a broken heart. As it happened I saw more of her in the last eighteen months of her life than in the previous ten years. Nevertheless, she was, relatively speaking, lonely; some of her closer friends – such as Maggie van Zuylen – who were not connected with her professionally had died. And she did miss Onassis who had come to be her greatest friend, for although she saw little of him they always kept in touch during the last years of his life.

The people who stopped communicating with her were those whose main interest centred on her willingness and ability to appear again on stage or screen, or to make recordings, or indeed anything that would require their participation. Once such persons, who had formerly claimed to be staunch friends, realized that it was highly unlikely that she would or could make a come-back they turned away from her. Even so, these same people who had not seen or spoken to her during the last eighteen months of her life, if not much longer, after her death readily described her with assumed authority as a sad, pitiful woman with a broken heart, forced to live her last days alone – almost a latter-day Violetta in the last act of *La traviata*. Not only has this description bizarre undertones, but its perpetrators were in no position to know how she really was. Maria was aware of these 'staunch' friends' disappearance, but she was not unduly upset as at the time it suited her. Artistically, it was for her a period of great uncertainty and it was convenient not to have to give reasons or explanations for her virtual retirement from the stage; she continued to work on her voice with some hope of success, though in the late spring of 1977 she gave me to understand that if she were to sing again it would be only to make recordings. She was also pre-pared, in the event of failure, not to make a tragedy of it.

There was, however, a relationship – or rather the absence of it – that saddened her deeply; for many years she had had no personal contact with her mother and sister (Maria had always remained friendly with her father). In 1957 Kalogeropoulos got his divorce and continued to live in New York. Eight years later he married Miss Papajohn, to whom he had been close for several years. At first Maria was furious with her father but none the less she paid his hospital bills fol-lowing an eye operation and continued his monthly cheque. She could not understand why her father had remarried (Maria always thought Miss Papajohn a schemer who took advantage of him), but when he reminded her of his lonely and unhappy life with Evangelia Maria saw his point of view all too clearly. After his marriage, Kalogeropoulos lived for the last six years of his life in Greece with his new wife. Maria saw him only a couple of times before he died, almost blind, in 1972.

She spoke only rarely about her family, for the last time, I remember, in 1977. She began by praising her staff: 'You do not choose your relations but you can choose your adopted family.'

After expressing her gratitude for her maid, Bruna, who though only two years older than herself had been a mother as well as a sister to her, Maria, lowering her voice somewhat to conceal the lump in her throat, said, 'Bruna has also been my devoted nurse. When I was hospitalized she would not let anybody do what she could do herself. She washed me and comforted me like a mother would, really should, do for her child. Although I was not surprised at Bruna's devotion for which I was so grateful, I could not at the same time help feeling that it was really not right. My mother and sister, not Bruna, should have been there. At the hospital, and later at home, I kept asking myself why they were not there with me. Bruna must have read my thoughts because she, in her wise, simple way, would not let me brood over it.'

Our conversation then reverted to my affairs but soon Maria returned unsolicited to the subject of her family:

In spite of my shortcomings, they [her mother and sister] could still have been proud of me; there are a few parents in this world, I dare say, who would have been happy to have a child like me. Instead we have spent most of our adult lives — we still do — miserably alone in different homes, isolated from each other.

A long time ago, when my father was still alive, my sister kept on writing to me that our parents were getting old. Of course I knew this and it also applies to me, to all of us. What really was behind this was that she was asking me for more money. But why have my mother and sister never, never enquired whether I am well or not? Even strangers do! It hurts me very much. Do you know I cannot really get over this, even though, with time, I was able to forget terrible things said to me in moments of anger. I, too, have been harsh when pushed too far.

Realizing that Maria was on the verge of getting too emotional I attempted to change the mood of our conversation with a matter-of-fact question. 'I quite understand you,' I said. 'Parents can be just as ungrateful as their children. It happens both ways — parents usually having the advantage of popular opinion on their side. But have you attempted a reconciliation with your mother, though you may be completely in the right?'

'First, let's not say that I am completely in the right,' Maria promptly commented.

No one is that perfect. Obviously I made mistakes too, even though my intentions were good, especially at the beginning. I always acted correctly and responsibly inasmuch as the main object of my efforts was to keep my parents together. Had I been successful, surely in the long run they would have been appreciative and hopefully my mother would have brought herself to accept that her younger daughter had a little more in her than a big voice with great earning power. However, considering the outcome of my efforts it would have been better had they divorced earlier, though for Greeks, divorce was in those days a shameful scandal, anyway I am not sorry for having tried.

My mother wrote to me that she had regretted my birth and cursed me[1] in a vile way, and all because I refused to give her more money. She even declared me insane, as a result of a minor accident when I was a child.[2] And yet I would have kept her if only she had stopped talking to the press, stopped blackmailing me, and I am talking about a period when I had to devote body and soul to my work and to the battlefield of the theatre. Nevertheless, I should have agreed to see her when some of her friends tried to intervene. Thinking back on it, the situation could not have worsened, really. But I was more hurt than outraged and at the time my wounded pride or whatever you want to call it got the better of my judgement. Consequently for a time I was weak rather than strong enough to believe that I could forget that I ever had a mother. Well, one sooner or later discovers that though the family bond may not be one of man's perfect inventions it is the best available. For some time, then, I found refuge in my husband and in my art, but when my marriage began to break down, I realized that I was alone, as in fact I have always been, ever since I can remember. Then there was Aristo and as you know I also had other things [vocal problems] on my mind.

When, in 1961, my father brought my sister to *Medea* at Epidaurus, suddenly everything seemed to be all right between us. There was no sign of my mother but that would have been too much to expect. No significant development in my relationship with my sister followed. We were really back to square one. Maybe I did not play my part well or perhaps I played it too well. In an effort to be natural and not at all condescending, like we were in our teens, I may have appeared somewhat belligerent. You see, in practice, breaking with my mother meant that I would not be seeing my sister either. The Epidaurus meeting was due to my father's initiative. So you still think I should try. A lot of water has gone under the bridge and what if I am rejected?

'Indeed I do,' I responded. 'But first I would like to hear from you about how eventually, some time in early 1963, you did begin to help your mother financially. How did that come about?'

For a moment Maria was somewhat startled. She then touched my arm and said,

How do you know all these things and remember them after such a long time? Well, I will tell you. A couple of years after my mother wrote that book I was unexpectedly informed by the Welfare Department in New York that she had reached retirement age and was claiming state benefit. However, they also said that I was responsible for providing my poor mother with financial assistance. Immediately I authorized my godfather in New York to settle the matter on my behalf in the way he saw fit.

In the presence of the welfare officer, my godfather offered my mother $200 per month on condition that she stopped approaching the media to provoke publicity against me; the allowance to be increased if after six months she had complied with this proviso. Although she promised faithfully that she would, in a few months she was again up to her old tricks, giving an interview to the Italian magazine *Gente*. Some people never change.

(Such was Evangelia's craving for publicity at any price. On the other hand Maria cannot be fully exonerated. She had ample reason to break with her mother, but she could have been more generous, wiser, in the circumstances. Had she made the effort – the opportunity was there – at the time when she was obliged to give financial support to her mother also to see her, their relationship might well have been rekindled, to their mutual benefit).[3]

Sensing that Maria would rather return to our main topic of conversation, my immediate reaction was,

Even if you are rejected, it will not have been in vain. Give them more money (fortunately you can afford it) and suggest a fresh start with no strings attached. Life may be short but there is still much to be lived for. If they do not reciprocate then they, not you, will have failed. I understand perfectly your grievance against your mother even when you, with reason, were at times adamant. Evidently there was no stopping your mother from doing what she wanted. Perhaps you should have used a different strategy. But I say this disregarding the enormous pressures your career put upon you, let alone the hounding of the press, largely encouraged by your mother. And I also speak a long time after the event. But what about your sister? Had she ever really acted against you? Forgive me for talking like this. Look at it as though it were coming from your younger brother.

'On the contrary,' Maria said with a wink,

I take it as if it is coming from my older brother (and I do not mean in years). There isn't much more I can add about my mother. Perhaps I should have tried harder, but at the time I thought I did everything I could. Because she was my mother I had obviously underestimated how far she would go and how much damage she was capable of causing. As for my sister, it is a different story. At no time in the past did she show any sign of solidarity towards me and she must have known I badly needed it. Admittedly she was busy, as she had always been, with her own life and her own problems. But what about my problems? Instead, my sister appeared to have sided completely with my mother, who undoubtedly poisoned her mind. When my difficulties, specifically with my mother, reached an impasse, following the publication of her incredible book falsely denigrating me (again because I would not give her more money) my sister did not even attempt the role of the impartial mediator. Well, I did give my mother a lot of money at the beginning, as soon as I began to earn it, but she most probably never told my sister; rather, she went on accusing me of being stingy, the heartless daughter who let her mother starve and so forth. She had used the same tactics in Greece before the occupation when she told us that my father never sent any money so that we would turn against him. Anyway, I don't have anything against my sister.

I disagree with nothing you have said and I assure you I took good note. Only I must build my strength, my spiritual strength, first. In real life, you know, I am not Norma or Violetta. It would be nice to have more of their strengths than their weaknesses. I will try.

Many years later, after Maria's death, when I got to know Iakinthy well, I understood her to be a good person (in the real sense of the word) of a mild nature, who usually thinks, perhaps too readily, the best of others unless proved otherwise. She had been completely dominated by her mother whose wishes had always to be obeyed unreservedly. Iakinthy testified that Maria had been phoning her in Athens during the last year or so of her life, albeit irregularly. Always friendly, the sisters talked of routine things and about people they had known in Greece, and once or twice Maria confided that since she no longer sang very few seemed to be interested in her. However, Maria never referred to her mother. It was not until early August 1977 that the sisters' feelings towards one another apparently became warmer and more personal; Maria proposed a meeting when she was next to be in Athens in the autumn,[4] but again, she did not mention her mother. The closest she came in this respect was when she told her sister, 'You are my only family now,' presumably including her mother.

During Maria's early years Evangelia was a great support in her aspiring career. Her motives had, however, always been selfish in the extreme: to acquire fame for herself, as well as the money that usually goes with it, through a gifted daughter. They certainly did not include genuine maternal love for Maria, nor for anyone else for that matter. Even though, before long, Elvira de Hidalgo took over the development of her career and their personal relationship was based on lifelong affection, Maria still craved maternal love.

Afterwards, Evangelia's intransigent demands for money, her refusal to stay with her husband and her more seriously misguided and unjust attempts at the character assassination of her famous daughter pushed Maria into the same all too human but counter-productive trap: she convinced herself that she loathed her mother, whose very existence she tried to ignore.

Nevertheless, after Callas's career was realistically over, when Meneghini hardly existed for her and Onassis and other friends were dead, she did begin to think differently about her mother, despite all that had transpired. Further, there was a stubborn sense of pride – a trait that dies hard at the best of times – that had always afflicted members of the Kalogeropoulos family. At some point in our conversation Maria implied that at a first reconciliatory move her mother might have assumed the role of the great heroine and proclaimed her guilty daughter publicly as the proverbial prodigal child. The real cause of Maria's reluctance to resolve the issue was, however, a fear that her mother would probably reject her, especially as she had been artistically inactive for some time, hence less famous – and she could not cope with that. Consequently, she hoped that breaking the ice with her sister first would stimulate her mother to instigate a reconciliation. She would then take it from there. Whatever the case, Maria once more had unfortunately miscalculated.

On 16 September 1977 Callas died suddenly from possible heart failure at her home in Paris. Her death, as reported by her maid Bruna, who was with her, was quick and only momentarily painful. On that day Bruna woke her at 9.30 a.m. As Callas had been out for several hours on the previous day she was still a little tired but in good spirits. She asked Bruna to invite three Italian friends, who were at the time in Paris, to supper that evening. After having coffee and seeing to her mail, she decided to sleep for a little longer. Eventually she rose at around 1.10 p.m. and, while coming out of the bathroom, became dizzy and felt a piercing pain in her left side; she collapsed without fainting, calling for her maid at the same time. Bruna helped her back to bed and, after giving her some coffee, called the doctor. He was not in and as the telephone of the American Hospital was engaged the doctor of Callas's butler was summoned; but within minutes, at 1.30 p.m. before he arrived, Maria was dead.

Four days later, on 20 September, after a funeral service at the Greek Orthodox Church at rue Georges Bizet in Paris – church services were held at the same time in London, Milan, New York and Athens – the body of Maria Callas was cremated at the cemetery of Père-Lachaise where her ashes were kept temporarily. In June 1979 Karamanlis, the Greek Prime Minister, had Callas's ashes brought to Greece by battleship. On 7 June, after a brief ceremony the ashes were scattered over the Aegean Sea.

Meneghini told me in 1978 that at first he considered Callas's death a misadventure or even manslaughter brought about by irresponsible friends. As a result of insomnia, she had been taking mild tranquillizers and sleeping pills on prescription during the last three years of her life, but he later alleged that Vasso Devetzi, in order to oblige and perhaps make her feel in some way dependent on her, supplied Maria with more potent pills such as Mandrax, an illegal drug in France, which eventually weakened her heart and proved fatal.

Callas first met Devetzi in February 1974. At the time she was on a recital tour with di Stefano, who was taken ill on the day of their concert in Boston. As Callas would not or could not sing for the whole evening on her own and the recital could not be postponed Devetzi, who

The ashes of Maria Callas scattered over the Aegean Sea. 'She gave without taking, enriched mankind and made the Greeks proud.' — Nianias's the culture minister's farewell.

happened to be in Boston, played a few solo piano pieces in place of di Stefano's arias. After the tour was over (November 1974) and Callas had returned home Devetzi, who also lived in Paris, began to befriend her. It was a period when Maria was artistically inactive and relatively lonely. A very shrewd and opportunistic woman, Devetzi took full advantage of the situation, always ready to run errands for Maria in a way which amounted to servility. At the same time she dropped discreet hints that she was Callas's *fidus Achates*. Thus the hitherto obscure pianist, by linking her name with that of a celebrated artist, herself became somewhat better known.

It would seem that Maria, not taken in by this woman's pretended devotion, tolerated her for her usefulness. At the end she became almost indispensable, since apparently she was able to provide the pills Callas needed. When once early in 1977 I commented to Maria without any particular emphasis that it was nice for her to have found a good friend in Madame Devetzi she looked aghast and, with a typical Greek wave of the hand, dismissed the idea of friend, let alone *fidus Achates*. I never again mentioned Devetzi.

To me Maria mentioned her insomnia only casually, even though she was taking sleeping pills rather regularly. When I suggested that she could cure her insomnia by spending some time by the sea or in a mountain village where she could generally live an outdoor life, she thought it an excellent idea. However, she did not follow my advice and as she never mentioned it again it did not occur to me to ask her about it. Much later, after her death, it transpired that it had been more serious than she had led me to believe. Her dependence on pills became a problem in the last six to eight weeks of her life, as was confirmed by Iakinthy, who states in *Sisters* that Maria asked her to send Mandrax pills from Athens.

With Callas dead, Devetzi immediately took control of everything. Using her assumed authority as Maria's confidante, she forced her way into the apartment and within minutes Callas's personal papers had disappeared from the study. By the evening of that day Devetzi, who had appointed herself arbitrator of all proceedings, decreed that according to Maria's wishes (presumably expressed verbally at some time) the body was to be cremated. Using the same argument and without any consultation with Maria's mother or sister, undoubtedly the next of kin, the Greek Archbishop in Paris was persuaded to authorize the cremation. (The Greek Orthodox religion to which Callas belonged does not allow cremation in Greece, nor does it have the facilities. However, if performed abroad, strictly in compliance with the express wishes of the deceased, the Greek Church accedes, albeit reluctantly.)

Devetzi had at least one accomplice. When Meneghini was sufficiently well (he had been recuperating from a heart attack) he travelled to Paris a month after Maria's death and demanded to know why his wife had been cremated. The records at the crematorium showed that a certain Jean Roire acted as Callas's next of kin; he accompanied the coffin after the funeral service and officially asked for cremation, which was carried out within half an hour instead of on the following day as was customary. Meneghini was never able to trace Jean Roire. Eventually he came to the conclusion that perhaps Callas's mother and sister had asked Roire to deal with the formalities of cremation.

Twelve years later Iakinthy, in *Sisters*, threw more light on the aftermath of Callas's death: she arrived in Paris for the funeral (her mother was not well enough to travel), to find that everything had been arranged by Devetzi, who announced that she was merely doing her duty as Callas's closest friend and the only person to know her wishes, and therefore she had the moral right. This *fait accompli* intimidated Iakinthy, who felt a complete stranger in Paris, not having seen her sister for sixteen years, nor having previously heard of Devetzi. Iakinthy was horrified that Maria was to be cremated but could not protest. At the crematorium Devetzi insisted that they should both wait, together with Bruna and Ferruccio, Callas's servants, a Greek cousin of Devetzi and the French M. Roire. Devetzi had already introduced the last as a music critic[5] and close friend, who was assisting her with the funeral arrangements and everything else, and therefore there was nothing for Iakinthy to worry about. Yet the document at the crematorium authorizing the incineration, which Meneghini saw, carried only the name of the mysterious Jean Roire.

On hearing of Maria's death Evangelia, who had never uttered a good word about her when she was alive, at any rate in public, said that it would have been better if she herself had died. Even so, she had recovered sufficiently from her grief when Iakinthy telephoned her from Paris after Maria's funeral to ask which of the famous had rushed to see her dead daughter.

Evangelia Kalogeropoulou, a woman of tremendous drive and resourcefulness, at once inspiring and destructive, lost her way when, very early in life, her lack of wisdom and patience, combined with pathological delusions of grandeur and fame, took over and governed her actions for the rest of her life. She caused enormous problems to all her family, whatever their own shortcomings, with her irrational demands and dictatorial attitude, and all but ruined their lives as well as her own. For years her position as Callas's mother gave her the undeserved benefit of the doubt in her cruel denigration of her daughter, which amounted at times to character assassination. It is very difficult to understand people like Evangelia, so a vicious circle ensues and it is hard to differentiate between perpetrator and victim, though in practice both are part of the tragedy. Following Maria's death, the health of eighty-year-old Evangelia, a diabetic, slowly deteriorated and she died on 20 August 1982.

The immediate cause of Callas's death has never been fully explained. The rumours which circulated, some in the press, included a heart attack, suicide, misadventure and manslaughter. None of these theories, more or less connected to the various pills Callas was taking, will ever be proved; there was no autopsy or inquest. It appears that cremation was the easiest way to achieve a possible cover-up. A body can be exhumed, but it is difficult to obtain and analyze ashes. In this case even the ashes may have been worthless as evidence. Following an incident when Callas's ashes were stolen from the vault of the cemetery but, inexplicably, later returned, Devetzi saw to it that they were kept securely in a bank. The incident may have been staged and the ashes exchanged with others.

The suicide theory is even more difficult to prove, but a contemporary romantic scenario was readily to hand: not only had Callas lost her voice, but the man she loved 'desperately' had abandoned her for another woman. After his death, Callas was left with a broken heart and nothing to live for. Moreover Meneghini, who wrote of his life with Callas a few months before his own death in December 1980, changed his verdict, concluding that she had, in fact, committed suicide.

Meneghini's new evidence rested entirely on a note which he found inside Maria's prayer book. Written by Callas in Italian on writing paper from the Savoy Hotel, it is addressed to T (Callas usually called her husband Titta) and dated summer 1977. It quotes the first lines of Gioconda's famous aria 'Suicidio' ('Suicide') but omits the word itself with which the aria begins: '*In questi fieri momenti, tu sol mi resti. E il cor mi tenti. L'ultima voce del mio destino, ultima croce del mio camin*' ('In these awful moments suicide alone remains to me. Only this occupies my thoughts. Final voice of my destiny. The last cross of my journey'). Although this note is in Callas's handwriting it cannot be said to substantiate Meneghini's rather far-fetched claims. The paper was several years old (before the London telephones were given a new code) and the date, as well as the words 'a T' ('for Titta'), are slightly smaller than the other letters in the note. In other words they could have been forged, and the whole thing might have been another effort on Meneghini's part to convince himself and show the world that Maria's last message was for him.

The most probable explanation for the note is that Callas wrote the words of this aria in order to memorize them. She often used to do this when she was giving concerts because her memory, though excellent for music, was less good for words. These verses may well have been written in 1971 when Callas gave two concerts in London with di Stefano and the piece was in her programme. The last time she stayed at the Savoy was in May 1977. Had she written the message then, as Meneghini claimed, it would have been on paper giving the new telephone code. Besides, it is odd that she then waited until mid-September to take her life.

Other important factors also suggest the unlikelihood of suicide. In the spring of 1977, when I inadvertently mentioned her mother, Callas said that financial support of her family (mother and sister) would continue for the duration of their lives. She had seen to this in her will, which she had written herself. Maria then added that she had taken good care of her servants, Bruna and Ferruccio, had left money for the Callas Scholarship Fund, for another fund for musicians and for the Institute for Cancer Research in Milan. Many of her belongings would go to friends and opera houses. Except for Dr Lantzounis, her godfather, other relations were not included: her uncles, cousins and the rest were willing only to bask in her glory, showing no interest in her before she became famous.

As no will was found after her death either with her lawyer or in her apartment (it was thought that Devetzi might have removed it from Callas's study), Callas was considered to have died intestate; her only beneficiaries being her mother and sister. However, Meneghini promptly put in a claim, producing a will Callas had made in 1954; but both parties concerned, after several months of acrimonious legal dispute, reached a settlement out of court before the legal costs became astronomical. They divided Callas's substantial estate. Meneghini continued to collect her royalties on recordings sold in Italy (at his separation from her in 1959, according to Italian law Meneghini received half of his wife's estate). She was not entitled to his money because he had earned it before they were married. At the time of her death Callas was *only legally separated* from Meneghini in Italy. When divorce became possible in that country – and for Callas to be granted it was a mere formality – she did not attend court on the day for which the case was set.

Discussing Meneghini with me in 1977, she said that it was of no consequence to her whether she was divorced in Italy because she had no plans to remarry. Although I was convinced that at the time her explanation was genuine, I also sensed another motive: she never forgave

Meneghini for 'grabbing' half her money, especially as he had already secretly made huge investments in his own name using her funds from their joint account as we have seen. Furthermore, as things were there was a reasonably strong possibility that she would inherit Meneghini's money – he was, after all, twenty-nine years older than she was. Even if she had lived to file her own will officially she would not have been disqualified from Meneghini's in the event of his death.

Such was the state of Callas's affairs when she died. Had she been contemplating suicide, she would surely have lodged her will safely with a lawyer (she was always an exceedingly meticulous person) in which case her substantial fortune would have been distributed according to her wishes, as was not the case.

In the final analysis the possibility that she died from heart failure is the strongest. The question remains whether this was the result of misadventure or manslaughter due to other people's irresponsible behaviour, or of natural causes. She had a heart condition practically throughout her adult life and Meneghini, despite his suicide verdict, revealed in 1980 that Maria's cardiologist had often been concerned for her health prior to 1959 (the year the couple separated). Maria herself had attributed her sometimes dangerously low blood pressure to the hardships suffered during the German occupation of Athens: 'Even now, when I am well, I feel the effects of the exhaustion that was left to me, like a sad inheritance, by a blood pressure reading 90 at the most.' Moreover, the strong pills Maria was taking for insomnia may eventually have weakened her heart, expediting its failure.

It is of interest to examine Devetzi's subsequent behaviour. After Callas's estate was divided between Meneghini and Iakinthy and her mother Devetzi, with incredible audacity, swindled Callas's sister out of a fortune. Iakinthy, who was dealing with the affairs of Callas's estate, her mother then being a virtual invalid, was completely taken in by this woman, Maria's allegedly devoted friend, and was grateful to her for being so helpful. Before long, Devetzi extorted a cheque for $800,000 in her name from Iakinthy to enable her to form a Callas Foundation for singers, plus a personal gift of $400,000, and as she was the chairman of the foundation she persuaded Iakinthy to name her, not the foundation, as principal beneficiary of her will. Also, from about 190 parcels of Callas's valuable belongings, which were divided between Meneghini and Iakinthy, Devetzi eventually gave her only seven, falsely accusing Meneghini of having stolen the rest. Furthermore, she handled the sale of Callas's Paris apartment but sent Iakinthy only $80,000, fraudulently declaring that the rest of the huge amount of money received merely paid the taxes outstanding on the property for the five years since Callas's death.

Iakinthy remained gullible until 1985, when she married Andreas Stathopoulos, a doctor, and with her husband's counsel the scales at last fell from her eyes. The Callas Foundation, with headquarters at Fribourg, did not exist, no taxes had been due on the apartment, Devetzi had not been Callas's great friend but a mere hanger-on. When Devetzi was confronted she produced, in

460

a desperate effort to save her skin, a photostat of a typewritten letter, with Callas's signature clearly taken from another letter, naming her beneficiary of her estate. This was a childish forgery. Moreover, Iakinthy and her husband presently discovered that she had invested the fortune she had swindled out of them, but had subsequently lost it all. Devetzi, a strange figure, unexpectedly sank into a coma and died in November 1987.

Maria Callas must not be judged in the same way as the sublime artist that she often was. During her last years in retirement, when she could no longer express her feelings and frustrations through her art, she once said: 'I have done some good things in my life but also some not so good. I now pay for my sins.' Almost certainly she was referring to the break-up of her marriage, for she considered it a sin, no matter who the culprit and what the circumstances, such were her deep-rooted religious beliefs. Nevertheless, for her, the supreme tragedies of her life were her failure to gain her mother's love and not having children.

As with most human beings there were the inexorable moments of doubt concerning her identity but these moments were redeemed by the mysterious and irrepressible forces of life that create a yearning for renewal and rebirth. Her declaration to me in 1977, 'I have written memoirs. They are in the music I interpret – the only language I really know!' will ring true for ever. But in the final judgement could she justify her absolute dedication to her art, which she so unhesitatingly and ruthlessly placed above all else? The character of Mary Magdalene attracted her greatly and she lamented the fact that there was no good opera about her. She longed for the opportunity to portray her and perhaps, even to find redemption.

Neither Callas's personal sorrows, nor her happiness, nor her sins, however much we identify with them, matter in themselves. Eventually they will be forgotten. Callas the woman was mortal. The art of the High Priestess, her legacy to the whole world, lives on.

---

1   A Greek woman told me that when in the 1950s she was a seamstress in New York Evangelia, who was working for the same company, was evidently 'disturbed', constantly cursing her famous daughter, wishing her to contract cancer as a punishment for abandoning her mother.
2   Evangelia attributed Maria's alleged incendiary temperament and heartlessness to the concussion she had suffered after

she was hit by a car when she was five years old. In *Sisters*, Iakinthy said that her mother always magnified out of all proportion the seriousness of Maria's slight accident. As we have seen, Evangelia herself had spent a few weeks in 1925 or 1926 at the Belleview psychiatric institution in New York State.

3   Before long Evangelia moved to Athens where her dollars went further and where Iakinthy was living, who would carry out her wishes, in reality her demands.

4   Maria planned to visit Athens on the way back from her holiday in Cyprus during the latter part of September.

5   Years later Iakinthy told me that she thought Jean Roire was a solicitor or accountant.

IFIGENIA IN TAURIS

Opera in four acts by Gluck; libretto in French by Guillard, in Italian by Lorenzo Da Ponte. First performed at the Paris Opéra on 18 May 1779.

Callas sang Ifigenia four times at La Scala in 1957.

Act I: *Before the Temple of Diana in Tauris.* Ifigenia (Callas), daughter of King Agamemnon of Mycenae and Clytemnestra, has long been a priestess of the Goddess Diana on the island of Tauris, where she is virtually a prisoner of the barbarian Scythian King Thoas. After a sudden storm has interrupted Ifigenia's prayers, she relates to her Greek priestesses a recurring dream — her parents' ghosts appear while her brother Orestes is under the threat of the sacrificial knife.

Left With inimitable economy (and sparse orchestration), Callas embodied Ifigenia and her desperate fears, her sorrows, her painful loneliness, her compassion and dignity.

Left Thoas (Colzani) decrees that Ifigenia should sacrifice one of the two Greek strangers who have landed on their shores, so that any impending danger may be averted.

Below Act 2: *Ifigenia's apartment in the temple.* Questioning the strangers, Ifigenia learns that after Clytemnestra murdered Agamemnon she was killed by her son, Orestes, who is also dead. Ifigenia mourns her brother.

In 'O malheureuse Iphigenie' ('Oh, wretched Ifigenia') Callas maintained the composer's classic melodic line but failed to vary the vocal colour, thus allowing some monotony to creep in.

In the Temple of Diana. Moved by the heartfelt plea of one of the strangers to die in place of his companion, Ifigenia concedes. As she raises the knife the victim's cry that his sister died in the same manner in Aulis startles her into the realisation that the captive is Orestes (Dondi). Brother and sister are reunited.

The simplicity of Callas's portrayal – her art that conceals art – was memorably intense and moving. Her exclamation 'fratello' ('brother') at the precise moment of recognition made the Ifigenia of antiquity a living woman.

Ifigenia prays to Diana for help to return with her brother to Greece.

In 'Je t'implore et je tremble' ('I implore you in awe'), Callas achieved extraordinary pathos – the perfect fusion of words and music.

UN BALLO IN MASCHERA

Opera in three acts by Verdi; libretto by Somma. First performed at the Teatro Apollo, Rome, on 17 February 1859.

Callas sang Amelia in *Un ballo* five times at La Scala in 1957.

Act I: *Ulrica's hut.* In a desperate effort to be rid of her illicit love for Riccardo, the Governor, Amelia (Callas) is advised by Ulrica (Simionato), the fortune teller, to gather a magic herb at midnight by the gallows. Riccardo, who has overheard Ulrica, resolves to be there too.

Act 2: *A deserted field by the gallows outside the city walls.* Callas readily established Amelia's predicament – the freezing tone betraying both terror and determination. But it was in 'Che ti resta perduto l'amor!' ('What is left when love is gone') that she conveyed, with introspective pathos, Amelia's very personal drama. The midnight chimes brought back the freezing tone and a suggestion of hysteria, creating an almost hallucinatory effect before 'Deh! mi reggi, m'aita, o Signor' ('Ah, support me, help me, O Lord') reflected a newly found calmness and hope.

In her meeting with Riccardo (di Stefano), their initially hesitant romantic grandeur soon gave way to forthright passionate tenderness, memorably expressing that most elusive feeling of being in love. The ecstasy of 'Eben, sì, t'amo! – M'ami, Amelia!' ('Well then I love you! – You love me, Amelia!') formed the central climax of the opera.

Left Act 3: *Renato's study at home.* Having caught his wife with the Governor in a deserted field, Renato (Bastianini) condemns her to death. Protesting, in vain, her innocence, Amelia begs for a last embrace of her son before she dies.

Callas was rather uneven in 'Morrò, ma prima in grazia' ('I will die but first a final grace') and for some not extrovertly dramatic enough. But as the aria expresses a single sentiment of an upper-class English lady, the drama was appropriately introspective and understated – and within these constraints very moving.

Below *The ballroom at the Governor's residence.* Believing Riccardo to be the culprit for Amelia's supposed adultery, Renato joins the conspirators to assassinate the Governor during a masked ball. While Riccardo is bidding Amelia a sad and passionate farewell, Renato stabs him. The dying Riccardo assures Renato of his wife's innocence and gives him a commission which will take him and Amelia to England. After pardoning all the conspirators, Riccardo falls back dead.

IL PIRATA

Opera in two acts by Bellini; libretto by Romani. First performed at La Scala on 27 October 1827.

Callas sang Imogene in *Il Pirata* five times at La Scala in May 1958 and in January 1959 in a concert version in New York and Washington DC.

Act I: *The sea-shore near Caldora, Sicily.* Imogene (Callas), accompanied by Adele (Angela Vercelli), her lady-in-waiting, offers traditional Caldoran hospitality to shipwrecked sailors. Itulbo (Rumbo), who poses as their leader (Gualtiero, the real captain, is hiding), conceals the fact that they are pirates.

With dignified sweetness Callas established Imogene's romantic character, and in 'Lo sognai ferito esangue' ('I dreamed he was lying in blood') powerfully but introspectively understated her emotional turbulence.

Left *A terrace before the Castle of Caldora. It is night.* Imogene's sympathy is aroused by someone among the shipwrecked. He evades her searching questions but eventually reveals that he is Gualtiero (Corelli), Count of Montalto, who was once her lover. Their joyous reunion is, however, short-lived; Imogene is now the wife of Gualtiero's enemy Ernesto, Duke of Caldora: she married Ernesto to save her aged father's life, but resigned herself to her miserable destiny.

Callas intimated her conflicting feelings passionately but with utmost delicacy: beneath the restraint, the fire was steadfastly blazing. For a brief moment in 'Tu sciagurato! Ah! fuggi' ('Unhappy man! Fly away') the hapless woman rose above her tragedy: she poured out her love, knowing well that all was in vain.

Below *An illuminated part of the castle grounds.* Ernesto (Bastianini) and his knights return in triumph from defeating the pirates, but he is upset at his wife's lack of warmth. He is also suspicious of the shipwrecked men and wants to question their leader.

Left Act 2: *It is almost daybreak.* While Imogene was urging Gualtiero to leave without her, Ernesto surprised them and challenged him to a duel. Ernesto is killed and Gualtiero surrenders himself. During the trial Imogene loses her reason.

Below *A courtyard before the castle.* Slowly leading Imogene's little son by the hand, Callas first conveyed her unbalanced state of mind in most expressive mime. Overcome with grief, in a dimly lit tone she implored her dead husband for forgiveness; the notes fell like 'audible' tears, the effortless pianissimo acquiring a haunting reality. When Gualtiero was sentenced to death, Callas reached Imogene's nadir. Imagining a scaffold for his execution, she entreated the sun to hide her from the horrible sight, 'O Sole, ti vela di tenebre oscure!'; her voice assuming an almost menacing tone but never digressing from the dramatic spirit of the elaborate embellishments: the words 'La vedete! il palco funesto, Ah!' ('Behold! The fated scaffold, Ah!') encompassed Imogene's world – her love, unhappiness, guilt, despair and purification.

POLIUTO

Opera in three acts by Donizetti; libretto by Cammarano. First performed as *Les Martyrs* with libretto in French by Scribe at the Paris Opéra on 10 April 1840. As *Poliuto* (composed 1839), posthumously, at the San Carlo, Naples, on 30 November 1848.

Callas sang Paolina in *Poliuto* five times at La Scala in 1960 and, as it turned out, it was the last role she added to her repertoire.

Act I: *Entrance to a catacomb in Armenia.* Paolina (Callas) is horrified that her husband, Poliuto, has renounced his worship of Jove in favour of Christianity, a religion at the time rigorously condemned. Nevertheless, listening unobserved to Poliuto's baptism she too, in her subconscious, has all but converted to Christianity.

Callas conveyed this supreme feeling through musical means: 'Fin pe'nemici loro! Divino accento' ('They pray for their enemies! What divine generosity!'). Paolina begs Poliuto (Corelli) to keep his new religion a secret, especially from her father, the Roman Governor, and from Severo, the new Proconsul, who is determined to exterminate all Christians.

Above *The great square in Melitene, Armenia.* Severo (Bastianini – right of centre front) and his retinue are greeted by the people of Melitene. He is heart-broken to learn from the Governor, Felice, that his daughter Paolina has married.

Left Act 2: *Atrium in Felice's house.* The High Priest Callistene has fraudulently led Severo to understand that Paolina is still in love with him despite her marriage to Poliuto.

In her meeting with Severo Callas's initial intense agitation gave way to great dignity inspiring her to rise nobly to the occasion: 'Pura, innocente lasciami spirar lontan da te' ('Let me remain pure and innocent away from you').

The Temple of Jove. Callistene (Zaccaria) asks Felice (Pelizzoni) for the death sentence on Nearco who, the previous night, initiated a new follower to Christianity. Nearco refuses to name the neophyte and Poliuto gives himself up. As the guards are about to arrest him, Paolina intervenes, arousing Callistene's fury. In vain she entreats Poliuto to retract his confession and her father to pardon him. When she finally throws herself at Severo's feet, Poliuto curses her as a wanton and shameless woman and angrily overturns the altar. Poliuto and Nearco are led away, while Felice forcibly drags his daughter with him.

Act 3: *The prison of the arena.* Although Paolina fails to persuade Poliuto to revert to his religion and thus escape death she wins his love again. His belief that there can be a better life after death also finally converts her to Christianity: 'Spirarti quei sensi non puote che un Dio! Lo credo. L'adoro' ('You can only be inspired by a God. I too believe in Him. I worship Him'). They both go to die in the arena.

Tosca

Opera in three acts by Puccini; libretto by Giacosa and Illica. First performed at the Teatro Costanzi (Rome Opera) on 14 January 1900.

Callas first sang Tosca (her first professional major role) in Athens on 27 August 1942 and last, which was also her last opera performance, at Covent Garden on 5 July 1965, a total of fifty-five performances.

Act I: *The Church of Sant'Andrea della Valle, Rome.* Mario's (Cioni) delay in opening the door arouses Tosca's (Callas) suspicion that he has another woman with him.

Callas was impulsive, anxious, jealous, passionate. The way she embraced her lover, or stroked his hair, was a lesson in love-making. The sensual beauty of 'Non la sospiri la nostra casetta' ('Do you not long for our little cottage') accounts for her excessive jealousy in recognizing the Marchesa Attavanti's features in Mario's painting. Reassured of Mario's love, Callas, with a blend of coquettishness and *naïveté*, became irresistibly appealing: 'Ma falle gli occhi neri!' ('But do make her eyes black!').

Act 2: *Scarpia's apartment at the Palazzo Farnese.* Scarpia's (Gobbi) brutal torturing of Mario breaks Tosca's resistance; she reveals Angelotti's hiding place.

With dramatic emphasis, Callas alternated pleas with contempt: her cry 'Assassino!' ('Murderer!'), as she dares blast Scarpia, was followed by her almost hushed plea 'Voglio vederlo' ('I want to see him') – as if Tosca was frightened by her earlier boldness. A storm broke out as Mario was dragged back to the torture chamber. Like a wildcat Callas tried to stop him until she ended in a crumpled heap on the floor beseeching Scarpia: 'Salvatello!' ('Save him!')

Above Scarpia's contest with Tosca enters its climax as he hints, with false gallantry, that she can still save Mario.

In a dark, scornful voice Callas flung out the words 'Quanto? Il prezzo!' ('How much? Your price!') The stress on 'prezzo' and the slight movement of her hand implied, naïvely, that she could meet Scarpia on equal grounds.

Right Scarpia demands other recompense: he has vowed to possess Tosca, 'Mia! Sì, t'avrò!' ('Mine!, Yes, I will have you'); Mario is held in pawn! She is free to leave but Mario will be a pardoned corpse.

Above all, Scarpia has rape on his mind; the more Tosca repulses him the more he sadistically lusts after her.

'T'odio, abbietto, vile!' ('I detest you, base villain!') was released with supreme loathing as he chased her maniacally round the room. Crying for help, Callas became momentarily emotionally muted before, in a frenzy, she fell into his arms, hopelessly beating his chest. When he opened her arms, the agony on her face made her look as if she had been crucified.

When Scarpia tells Tosca that Mario has but one hour to live she resorts to prayer. She then humbles herself to Scarpia.

'Vissi d'arte, vissi d'amore' ('I have lived for art and for love') – a lament in which Callas pleaded with God for mercy for her lover by telling Him of her pious actions. Here was a frightened and confused human being who found herself inescapably trapped. Suddenly this apparently imperious woman revealed the vulnerable child in her. The sounds she emitted were like dark honey floating softly. She shaped the penultimate phrase 'Perchè, Signore?' ('Why, oh Lord?') with a ravishing, limpid tone. For a moment one was with her in another world.

Callas's killing of Scarpia was an act of self-preservation. While he was writing the supposed safe conduct for her, she fortified herself with wine, when through the glass she saw the knife, on the table, magnified; her eyes remained riveted on the knife, the glass mechanically finding its way on to the table.

'Tosca finalmente mia' ('Tosca, at last you are mine'), Scarpia declared, whereupon her arm shot up and the knife was plunged into him. After cursing the dying Scarpia, she gradually realised the magnitude of her action: 'E avanti a lui tremava tutta Roma!' ('And before him all Rome trembled!'). Overtaken by hysterical sobs, she placed candles and a crucifix by the corpse before stealing away.

DISCOGRAPHY

As a result of the revolutionary development of recording techniques in the late 1940s that changed the 78 rpm to the long playing (LP) record, first in mono, then in stereo, and high fidelity sound reproduction, Callas's vocal artistry has been captured for posterity. Moreover, the development of digital sound in the 1980s and the reprocessing of Callas's recordings for issue on compact disc (CD) reproduced her voice with more vivid fidelity.

She made her first commercial records in November 1949; following a radio broadcast in Turin (March 1949), Cetra recorded three items from the programme – 'Casta Diva' (*Norma*), 'Liebestod' (*Tristan und Isolde*), 'Qui la voce' (*Puritani*) and issued them as 78-rpm records. Two years later Cetra offered Callas a contract, which provided for three complete operas. However, in July 1952, before she had begun recording, she signed another contract to record exclusively with EMI for seven years, albeit with the understanding that she would carry out her contractual obligations to Cetra. Eventually she recorded only two operas (*La Gioconda* and *La traviata*) with Cetra. Meanwhile she began her outstanding recording career with EMI under the guidance of the enterprising Walter Legge, the artistic director of the company.

Legge first heard Callas's voice from the three 78-rpm records. In his book *On and Off the Record* (1982), published posthumously by his wife, the soprano Elisabeth Schwarzkopf, Legge wrote:

> At the earliest opportunity, 1951, I went to Rome when I knew she was singing... I slipped into the Rome Opera and heard her first act of *Norma*... I telephoned my wife to join me at once for something quite exceptional. She declined: she had just heard the first half of a broadcast of arias by one Maria Callas, and neither wild horses nor the promise of supper at Passetto's could drag her from hearing the second half. At the end of the performance I went to Callas's dressing room and offered her an exclusive contract with the English Columbia [EMI].

What Legge heard that night convinced him that he had found in Callas the ideal soprano for EMI's ambitious and enterprising projected recordings of complete Italian operas. Tullio Serafin, the outstanding Italian conductor and already Callas's mentor, Giuseppe di Stefano, then the most accomplished Italian lyric tenor, and the great operatic artists Tito Gobbi and Boris Christoff had also been engaged. Furthermore, the operatic recordings for EMI would be made with the renowned Orchestra and Chorus of La Scala, Milan, a theatre in which, whenever possible, the operas would be recorded. (Decca, the rival company, had engaged Renata Tebaldi and Mario Del Monaco for a more or less similar operatic repertoire).

Callas's contract with EMI was eventually signed on 21 July 1952 after considerable bargaining over terms and, as Schwarzkopf said in an interview (*Recorded Sound*, January 1981),

> There were terrible difficulties with the firm [EMI] about engaging Callas. I believe Walter went as far as saying that he would hand in his notice... Of course, I was present at many of her recording sessions and rehearsals. She was a meticulous artist, the most prepared artist you can imagine. Nothing was left to chance, but you are not aware of the preparation – it all came out spontaneously. She was such a worker and not ashamed at all of trying again and again.

Legge also wrote that after the contract was signed, 'I decided to make a series of tests of "Non mi dir" (*Don Giovanni*) with Callas, for two purposes – to get the psychological feel of working with her, sensing how receptive she would be to criticism, and to find placings to give at least a decent sound. It was soon clear that she would take suggestions without a murmur. I had found a fellow-perfectionist, as avid to prove and improve herself as any great artist I have ever worked with.'

After Callas's contract with EMI expired in 1959 she continued to record with the same company until February 1969. Her last commercial recording – opera duets with di Stefano – made for Philips during November 1972 and March 1973 has not been released commercially, while the final 'live performance' recording, of her concert with di Stefano at Sapporo, Japan, on 11 November 1974, is also the last time she sang in public (see chronology of performances).

It cannot be said that all Callas's recordings do her full justice; sometimes her good points are minimised and flaws exaggerated. This, however, applies to only a few recordings as, in fact, Callas's singing is ideally suited to the gramophone. Even though half the joy lay in watching her perform on the stage, it is often possible, within the limitations of recorded sound, to feel her presence: her outstanding gift of acting with her voice is never more conspicuously evident than on record. Here there are no stage, no costumes to admire and, above all, Callas cannot be seen. One must rely entirely on the voice or, more precisely, what she does with that voice, and the majority of her recordings (particularly those which have been digitally remastered) capture to a high degree and with remarkable fidelity the tone and art of her singing. I cannot begin to improve on John Steane's definitive summing-up (*Gramophone*, November 1977) written soon after Callas's death in September 1977: 'Most important for us now, she herself learned to act with the voice and to concentrate so much of humanity within that voice that her recordings continue to enrich our experience like the masterpieces of portraiture in our galleries.'

'When performing in a studio in front of a microphone,' Callas interestingly said,

It takes a little more time to get into the role but not very much more. In making a record you don't have the sense of projection over a distance as in an opera house. The microphone magnifies all details of a performance, all exaggerations. In the theatre you can get away with a very large, very grand phrase. For the microphone you have to tone it down. It is the same as making a film; your gestures will be seen in close-up, so they cannot be exaggerated as they would be in a theatre.

During the 1950s, when Callas was making most of her recordings, she told me more than once that she did not really care very much for her records: 'I do not think that many singers do. The timbre of the recorded voice sounds strange and different from the natural voice without microphone and amplification. I would find it unbearable if I had to sing with a microphone at the opera house.'

On one occasion she half jokingly covered her ears with her hands and threatened to leave her house if friends wanted to play her records. However, after the early 1960s, when her performances were few and far between and her vocal resources were diminished, she developed a great interest in the 'pirate' recordings of her 'live' performances. She was particularly happy, and rather proud, that her *Anna Bolena*, *Macbeth* and *Armida* had been preserved, especially as she never recorded these operas complete. They were, in fact, their first ever complete recordings, as were her commercial discs of *I Puritani*, *Il Turco in Italia* and *Medea*.

The discography is complete. Apart from the three 78-rpm records – *La Gioconda* and *La traviata* made for Cetra, *Medea* for Ricordi-Mercury (distributed by EMI) – and a recital (with di Stefano) for Philips, the rest were made for EMI. *Carmen* and two recitals of French arias were sung in the original French, 'Ocean! Thou mighty monster' (*Oberon*) in the original English, all others in Italian.

The dates and locations of recordings have been obtained from EMI, from diaries of other artists who sang with Callas such as Nicola Zaccaria and Giuseppe di Stefano, and some information came from Callas herself.

All her commercial recordings and many 'live' performances have been issued on digital CDs, so far three times, and almost certainly will continue to be reissued. As every reissue is given a different catalogue number, these are omitted from the present survey. All the items of her recital recordings are grouped as originally issued on LPs. They are compiled differently on CDs.

Complete Operas

LA GIOCONDA (Ponchielli): September 1952 – Turin – Cetra

Callas recreates on record Gioconda's demanding and highly complex character with a down-to-earth passion and without ever straying from the melodic line, however supercharged with emotion it may be; her interpretation springs from a musical consideration without compromise. Vocally she is in great form, her opulent singing is tender, passionate and fiery by turns, and appropriately adapted to every situation. Several key phrases, single words, seem to take on new meaning, and vividly create the *mise-en-scène*, the illusion that Callas is physically present.

With highly economical means she establishes the devoted daughter, 'Madre adorata'. The tone and timbre of her voice then change to express her profound sorrow, her loneliness, her unrequited love for Enzo: 'Il mio destino è questo, o morte o amor!' She does more: undertones in her singing hint at the tragedy to come. Different vocal colour is employed for Gioconda's fiery side – her disgust for Barnaba, her hatred of Laura for ensnaring Enzo. In the duet 'E un anatema' with Laura (Barbieri), Callas delivers 'Il mio nome è la Vendetta' as if composed with thunder and lightning; a challenging animal passion guides her, while Barbieri holds her own in a tamer fashion, loving Enzo as the 'light of Creation', in contrast to Callas's electrifying 'Ed io l'amo sic-come il leone ama il sangue'.

Notwithstanding some uneven intonation, where the register changes, Callas's prodigious talent – the infinite variety of relevant inflexions in both words and music that enables her to alternate tender and violent emotions – makes 'Suicidio ... in questi fieri momenti', this 'terrible' monologue, a cathartic experience. It is in her contemplation of suicide that Callas reaches magnificently the climax of the drama. She pours forth vast molten and lyrical sounds, projected from dramatic soprano to opulent contralto as she goes through the gamut of emotion: the introspective fatalism in 'Ultima croce del mio cammin' gives way to almost ethereal beauty (in glorious *mezza-voce*) in 'E un dì leggiadre volavan l'ore', before the complete resignation of 'Or piombo esausta fra le tenebre'. Again, despite some vocal unevenness, it is through Callas's dramatic, florid singing rather than the composer's talent that the ensuing final scene reaches a climatic conclusion – a yardstick for other singers.

Barbieri is excellent. She too rises to the occasion and makes a worthy partner for Callas. Silveri's (Barnaba) musical phrasing is impeccable and full of dramatic impact – his best performance on record. Poggi (Enzo) is rather dull and barely adequate, as are the rest of the supporting cast. The Orchestra and Chorus of RAI, Turin, find in Votto a correct but little inspired conductor.

The digital remastering on CD has made the recording more vibrant and all-round better balanced.

LA GIOCONDA (Ponchielli): September 1959 – Milan – EMI

Technically a better recording, it is further improved in its brilliance and clarity by the digital remastering.

Callas distils her interpretation; a certain simplicity and refining of essentials is evident. Although there is less body to her voice, her intonation is more even, especially in the 'Suicidio', and generally her singing is no less electrifying than in her former recording of the opera. Above all, however, she further perfects her last scene, bringing to it a definitive dramatic uniformity as she goes through the gamut of emotion. In the final choice both recordings remain essential Callas.

Cossotto (Laura) is no Barbieri. Despite her considerable vocal resources she never quite finds her stride in this role. Much the same can be said for Cappuccilli (Barnaba), who is competent in a negative way, mostly lacking Silveri's indefinable quality, which brings excitement and interest in the first recording. All the other singers including Ferraro (Enzo), plod their way through the opera, remaining rather faceless characters. The La Scala Orchestra and Chorus produce more stylistic sounds than those of RAI, Turin, even though Votto is marginally more spirited.

LUCIA DI LAMMERMOOR (Donizetti): February 1953 – Florence – EMI

Callas first sang Lucia in Mexico City (June 1952) with great success. Eight months later and after further performances in Florence she recorded the role. Her interpretation has creative genius sung with a dramatic soprano voice, also capable of crisp, superbly articulated and expressive coloratura. (Before Callas, Lucia was, in the twentieth century, often inadequately sung by light or lyric coloratura sopranos.)

In her first scene Callas establishes Lucia's personality – her extreme anxiety, her fears – as with a portrait that appears on a canvas with a few masterly strokes of the brush, or so it seems. The affectionate, hypersensitive and vulnerable young woman emerges in 'Regnava nel silenzio', where Callas lightens her voice and with perfect legato charges the broad melodic phrases with simple pathos. Her voice then acquires an abandon subtly suggesting Lucia's hour of happiness in 'Quando rapido in estasi' which Callas sings as an embellished melody rather than a melody with superimposed embellishments. She reaches the zenith of her happiness in the duet 'Verranno a te' when in deceptively simple melody, reciprocated by Edgardo (di Stefano), the two lovers achieve a unique fusion of words and music and, caressing the notes, express sensual love affectionately.

With her hour of happiness gone, Callas is again overtaken by anxiety and fear when confronted by her brother Enrico – her melancholy in 'Il core mi balzò', her suffering and loneliness introspectively conveyed in the heart-rending 'Soffriva nel pianto', remain in the listener's inner ear.

Her interpretation of the mad scene has set a standard by which all other performances are measured. She gives the words and music, as well as the wordless passages, profound dramatic significance. Nothing is meaningless, nothing is exaggerated, the coloratura, at all times integrated in the melodic line, acting as an abstract dimension in delineating Lucia's mental state. Phrases such as 'Alfin son tua', tenderly sung and subtly coloured, acquire deeper meaning, becoming for ever memorable. Her performance is a *tour de force* where the magnificent simplicity (her art that conceals art), which conveyed on the stage the sense of Lucia's tragedy, is vividly captured on the recording.

Di Stefano (Edgardo) and Gobbi (Enrico) are excellent, particularly in their scenes with Callas. A little more vocal elegance from di Stefano would not have come amiss. But this would be splitting hairs. The supporting cast, Arie (Raimondo), Natali (Arturo) and Canali (Alisa), make a worthy ensemble, especially in the famous sextet. Under Serafin the Orchestra and Chorus of the Maggio Musicale Fiorentino play and sing with impeccable style and evoke a conducive atmosphere, grave and romantic, for the drama to unfold.

The digital remastering on CD has brought greater clarity and liveliness to the recording.

LUCIA DI LAMMERMOOR (Donizetti): March 1959 – London – EMI

The sound, particularly of the orchestra, is more uniform than in the previous recording and the Philharmonic Orchestra and Chorus under Serafin achieve much eloquence, but Cappuccilli (Enrico), though competent, is inexperienced and unimaginative, and no match for Gobbi on the other set. Also, in spite of Tagliavini's elegant phrasing as Edgardo he is vocally past his prime. It is different with Bernard Ladysz (Raimondo), who is at the top of his powers, but unidiomatic in Italian opera.

Nor is Callas in her best vocal form: her voice sounds thinner, sporadically frayed and occasionally betraying slight insecurity, particularly in the upper register. Nevertheless she compensates for her vocal inequalities by deepening her already unique interpretation; paradoxically, she acquires through vocal means greater profundity by expressing more introspectively, more simply – there is an inward and subtly muted brilliance and delicate suppleness in the tone of her voice – Lucia's fragile and shifting emotions in the mad scene, the focal event of the opera. Her portrayal, notwithstanding some vocal decline and rather inferior colleagues on this occasion, attained a fascinating beauty that lingers on. Her supremacy as a singing actress was to last a little longer.

The digital remastering on CD brings greater clarity and liveliness to the recording and eliminates some of the unsteadiness, particularly Callas's, without introducing any hardness or brittleness to the voices, as sometimes happens in this type of recording.

I PURITANI (Bellini): March 1953 – Milan – EMI

Callas recreates in this first ever complete recording of the opera her incomparable assumption of the role of Elvira. The eloquent significance which she gives to the words, whether in recitative or aria, and her meticulous fulfilment of the composer's intentions have made it possible to hear Bellini's music in the way to which one imagines the composer aspired. Her voice consistently maintains a sensuously limpid tone and gives significant meaning to coloratura passages. It is at its most beautiful in 'A vieni al tempio' (notwithstanding the slight but noticeable unsteadiness of the final phrase), at its most brilliant, but with anxiety and foreboding of her impending mental instability, in 'Son vergin vezzosa' and at its most profoundly moving in the mad scene, 'Qui la voce', particularly in the connecting recitative after the aria – 'Egli piangi forse amò!' encapsulates the art of the singing actress. In the ensuing cabaletta 'Vien diletto' Callas, with highly idiomatic chromatic scales, achieves a uniquely dignified melancholy, punctuated with smiling fleeting brilliance.

Di Stefano somewhat lacks the elegance and style which the part of Arturo ideally requires, but he sings the music for the most part in the original high key, and the warmth and ardour of his voice, and personality generally, are very appealing, particularly in his duet with Elvira, 'Vieni fra queste braccia'. The transposition down a semitone of the duet works better for di Stefano; he is more expressive. Rossi-Lemeni (Gualtiero) can be criticised for poor intonation, but his great style and understanding of Bellini's cantilena, as in 'Cinta di fiori', enable him to portray a credible character. Panerai (Riccardo) uses his vibrant and exciting baritone voice to good effect and provides a relevant contrast to Arturo's character. Serafin, with the La Scala Orchestra and Chorus, gives a lesson in style and good taste.

The digital remastering on CD brings a much needed brilliance to the recording and has all but rectified the distortion at the end of 'A vieni al tempio' with the result that Callas's voice (including the wayward high D) is steadier.

CAVALLERIA RUSTICANA (Mascagni): July 1953 – Milan – EMI

Callas as Santuzza (a role she only sang at the beginning of her career in Athens) gives a passionate performance, expressing realistically the character's feelings and moods within the relative brevity of the role, in a purely musical way – a role technically far more difficult than it appears. She rises to memorable dramatic heights when she vows to continue loving Turiddu even after he has rejected her for another woman, and when she expresses her remorse for having told Alfio that his wife is Turiddu's lover. Callas's ability to scale down her performance to essentials with imaginative musicianship and feeling for the words as in the arias 'Innegiamo' (Easter Hymn) and 'Voi lo sapete o mamma', makes Santuzza a living woman.

Both di Stefano (Turiddu) and Panerai (Alfio) are in excellent voice and completely immersed in their roles, making worthy partners for Callas. Turiddu, one of di Stefano's best roles, is perhaps only second to his Nemorino (*L'elisir d'amore*). Canali (Lola) and Ticozzi (Mamma Lucia) fulfil their supporting roles successfully. Nevertheless, in the final analysis, the greatest honours belong to Serafin, who conducts the La Scala Orchestra and Chorus and keeps all his forces under control with well-considered restraint, enhancing the lyric earthiness of the score.

The recording, however, is rather marred in places by sound distortion. The digital remastering on CD has effected considerable improvement.

TOSCA (Puccini): August 1953 – Milan – EMI

This recording presents Callas's first conception of the role of Tosca based more or less on the old traditional approach: she is in great form, her big, secure voice conveying every shade of expression. Even so, and notwithstanding Callas's imaginative musicianship and refinement of her portrayal which confirmed her as the greatest Tosca both on record and stage, she has not as yet found completely her individual way which was later to revolutionise this most popular role.

Be that as it may, her performance here makes a tremendous impact and many phrases acquire new meaning. Her off-stage call 'Mario!' is electrifying, as is her scene with Mario in the church when she memorably establishes Tosca's religiosity and pathological jealousy – basic character traits without which the plot of the drama cannot proceed. Her suspicion and fury when she recognises another woman in Mario's painting is passionately conveyed, her possessive love of Mario with sensual beauty in 'Non la sospiri la nostra casetta'.

Equally memorable is her dramatic declamation, notably when she alternates pleas with contempt in her terrible fencing battle with Scarpia. 'Vissi d'arte' is most expressively sung, every note is secure with good intonation but, as yet, perhaps with little introspection. One of the most moving moments is in 'Ecco, vedi' when her plea to Scarpia is underlined with the sorrow of one who has to accept fate with resignation.

Gobbi (Scarpia) is vocally secure and dramatically Callas's equal. Although this was the first time they sang together in this opera, there is an incredible interaction between them – perhaps unprecedented in opera within living memory. Di Stefano (Cavaradossi) is in excellent voice, with a warm, lyrical and exciting tone. His phrasing is subtle and, with charm and delicacy, he makes the best of Puccini's hero – unarguably one of his foremost performances on record. The supporting cast, particularly Luise (Sacristan) and Calabrese (Angelotti), give creditable performances. De Sabata conducts the La Scala Orchestra and Chorus with extraordinary musical perception and unerring consideration for his singers. He deserves his share of credit in making this recording a landmark.

The digital remastering on CD has brought clarity, brilliance and better balance to the recording (originally made in mono) to the extent that it sounds new, especially the orchestral playing.

TOSCA (Puccini): December 1964 – Paris – EMI

Following Callas's hugely successful performances in Zeffirelli's production of *Tosca* (Covent Garden, January

1964), the recording was made as a sound-track (the last complete opera Callas recorded) for a film of the opera also to be produced by Zeffirelli. The project, however, proved abortive (see p. 363).

As in the theatre in 1964, Callas portrays on record a substantially different Tosca, one that immediately influenced most of her contemporaries, as well as successive interpreters of this popular role. Though her voice is thinner – its timbre has lost some of its dramatic weight but gained in lyricism – and occasionally unsteady in the upper register, developing a slight pulse in two climactic moments in Act 2, her performance rises to incomparable heights of eloquent expression. Tosca is no longer so much the imperious diva as an insecure, frightened, confused but proud human being who finds herself inescapably trapped. 'Vissi d'arte' is introspectively sung as both lament and protest, with ravishing limpid tone particularly just before the final phrases. For a moment the listener is, with her, out of this world.

Gobbi's Scarpia has followed a similar path. He is vocally a little less secure, but his interpretation has matured to become, like Callas's, definitive. Bergonzi (Cavaradossi) sings with great style and excellent diction and intonation, even though vocally he is somewhat past his peak. He does not have di Stefano's special brand of charm and ardency, highly accomplished though he is. Nor does Prêtre, conducting the Paris Conservatoire Orchestra and the Chorus of the Paris Opéra, have de Sabata's exceptional artistic insight. Nevertheless, Prêtre creates a conducively tense atmosphere in which the characters of the drama feel at home.

The digital remastering on CD has effected some improvement on the unsteadiness of the voices in general.

LA TRAVIATA (Verdi): September 1953 – Turin – Cetra

This was the second and last complete opera recording Callas made for Cetra. EMI's project to record La traviata with Callas as Violetta proved abortive – her contract with Cetra forbade her to re-record the role for ten years. Afterwards, in 1963, Callas herself withdrew from recording La traviata for EMI not only because of a minor accident – when she slightly damaged her ribs – but because of her declining vocal resources.

Notwithstanding the fact that Callas was later to perfect and deepen her interpretation, her recorded Violetta is already highly accomplished, has considerable musical insight and is intensely moving. She is very much at home with the florid music of the first act, the great lyricism of the second and the poignant tragedy of the last. Slight vocal flaws – the occasional tight high note or the lack of a traditionally smooth tone at all times – can be found, to be sure, if her singing is pedantically considered as a mere exercise in solfeggio. These flaws largely only exist when considered outside the context of a total conception of the role. Alan Jefferson's assessment (Opera on Record, 1979) of the recording is most constructive: 'It is a glorious interpretation on her [Callas's] part with the vocal flaws making her singing sound all the more human.'

From the many great moments vividly captured on the recording one can readily single out the introspective analysis of her emotions in 'Ah! fors'è lui'. Here is a young courtesan who first discovers the wonderful, but to her also frightening, feeling of love. Also miraculous is the way she sings the long sustained B flat at the beginning of 'Dite alla giovine', Violetta's most distressing moment. No less memorable is the unbearable intensity in 'Amami Alfredo', the heart-rending calmness that speaks volumes in 'Addio del passato', the infinitely moving and unsentimental 'Ah! gran Dio morir sì giovine' at the beginning of the death scene of the tragedienne who with unerring simplicity gets to the heart of the score, and of the listener. Even so, it would be a disservice to art to declare this portrayal as the ultimate Callas. That was to come later.

Albanese (Alfredo) is more than adequate but Savarese (Germont) monotonously plods his way through his role providing little support for Callas in Act 2, which is central to the drama. Santini conducting the RAI

(Turin) Orchestra and Chorus is competent enough, though he lacks vitality and real understanding of the finer points of the score – he helps little to create the necessary atmosphere.

There is an all-round improvement in the digital remastering on CD.

NORMA (Bellini): April–May 1954 – Milan – EMI

During the period 1948–65 Callas sang Norma on the stage over eighty times and recorded it twice. Unarguably, she established herself as the greatest exponent of the role of her time and all rivals to date (whether on stage or recording) fall short as pretenders to the crown of Norma – a role generally considered to be the most difficult in the operatic repertoire.

Callas succeeded on the stage and to a great extent within the restrictions of a recording, to bring to life Bellini's larger-than-life, near-epic-stature heroine, while remaining a very human woman. Her performance, an eloquent fusion of the words and deceptively easy Bellinian cantilena, achieves almost living emotions: the dramatic declamation of the recitative preceding the lyrical 'Casta Diva'; the biting scorn at Pollione in 'Oh! non tremare'; the nostalgic remembrance of past love ('Oh, remembranza') and eventual reconciliation with Adalgisa, the other woman ('Mira o Norma'); the desperate cry 'O miei figli'; the bitter vengeance in the final confrontation with Pollione in 'In mia man'; Norma's confession ('Son io') and her purification ('Qual cor tradisti') culminating in the infinitely moving finale 'Deh! non volerli vittime'.

Whatever the reason for them, Callas's periodic vocal flaws such as the occasional sharp or strident high note or the less than perfect intonation usually persist in the listener's ear when considered out of context. Taken as a whole, and with the fact that Callas goes a long way towards making them vehicles of dramatic expression, they are well nigh insignificant.

Stignani (Adalgisa) had just passed her peak when she made this recording. Nevertheless, she is still vocally a tower of strength and highly stylistic, though the timbre of her mezzo-soprano, once ideal for this role, occasionally sounds inappropriately rather mature. On the other hand, her voice blends superbly with Callas's – an essential factor in this opera – and their duets are vocal feats. Only in the cabaletta of 'Mira o Norma' does Stignani momentarily lag behind a little.

The two male principals are in a different league. Filippeschi (Pollione) is rather routine, though not dull, and often vocally loud and uncouth. Rossi-Lemeni (Oroveso) may have had the right style and idea of the role, but occasionally he mars his performance singing with a constricted tone and slightly off-pitch. Except for the inexplicable breakneck speed of the chorus 'Guerra! Guerra!', Serafin conducts the La Scala Orchestra and Chorus and guides his principals with great style and finesse.

The original recording (in mono) is only fair, with the Finale much too congested. Although the processed stereo transfer was an improvement, it is the digital remastering on CD that has given it a new lease of life.

NORMA (Bellini): September 1960 – Milan – EMI

Whereas in the first recording Callas as Norma emphasised the warrior, and the ferocity of the betrayed High Priestess, in the second the human side of the tragic heroine is more prominently expressed. Both interpretations are valid within themselves. In the second, Callas's refining of essentials, with an apparent introspective simplicity, makes her portrayal dramatically more telling. On the other hand by 1960 there was a marked decline in her vocal resources, though not in her artistry; her voice was generally less secure, a slight wobble in the upper register is noticeable, though rarely and, perhaps more significantly, her voice had lost some of its dramatic soprano timbre, becoming more lyrical.

The most constructive commentary came from Andrew Porter (*Opera on Record*, 1979). He wrote, 'The two complete recordings are complementary ... an interpretation that was always magnificent has deepened in finesse, flexibility, and dramatic poignancy. True, her voice lets her down ... and yet, how much more moving is it than the simpler, if steadier, messa di voce of the earlier set. ... My reaction is that, on both sets, Callas gives an interpretation of Norma which Sutherland, Caballé and Sills, the heroines of later issues, do not begin to approach.'

Although Ludwig (Adalgisa) is vocally secure and has a smooth and youthful-sounding tone, and her voice blends well enough with Callas's, she is rather unidiomatic and temperamentally not ideally suited to Bellini's *seconda donna*. Both Corelli (Pollione) and Zaccaria (Oroveso) are infinitely better than their predecessors. Corelli uses his big, sensuous voice (perhaps at times rather monotonously too sensuous) with considerable style and dramatic conviction. Zaccaria, in sonorous voice and with great feeling for Bellini's melodic style, portrays a noble Oroveso. Serafin has further refined his reading of the score and, with the La Scala Orchestra and Chorus, brings to it more poetry.

The recording, though much better than the first, was not exceptional until the digital transfer to CD became a revelation. Callas's voice is steadier, the slight wobble has all but disappeared and singers and orchestra have improved significantly, with more clarity and vividness – almost another recording.

PAGLIACCI (Leoncavallo): June 1954 – Milan – EMI

Although one does not readily associate Callas with Nedda, a role she never sang on the stage, the recording confirms that her *bel canto* vocal technique enabled her to sing almost any role. There is much understanding and feeling in her characterisation. In the balatella 'Stridono lassù' Nedda's portrait is vividly drawn in musical colours; her frustrations, anxiety and fear of her husband's brutality, should he discover her lover, are eventually brushed away by the young woman's joy of living. Callas lightens her voice to suit Nedda's personality and in the final scene, in the play within the play, she uses a different voice with theatrical inflexions when she appears as Columbine, the *commedia dell'arte* character.

Di Stefano sounds a younger Canio than the score's requirement, but on the whole he gives an impassioned performance. He is moving in the final scene, though in 'Vesti la giubba', his introspective monologue fundamental to the character and indeed to the opera, his lyrical warmth does not quite compensate for a lack of real dramatic impact. Gobbi gives stature to Tonio both in the prologue and in his encounter with Nedda. Panerai (Silvio) and Monti (Beppe) cannot be bettered in their supporting roles. The La Scala Orchestra and Chorus surpass themselves under Serafin's direction. There is a great deal of thought behind this recording of a very popular opera, revealing freshness of approach with lasting interest.

The digital remastering on CD gives the recording a new vibrancy.

LA FORZA DEL DESTINO (Verdi): August 1954 – Milan – EMI

As with Aida, Leonora's music is best sung by the traditional dramatic or lyric-spinto soprano. But as Callas's dramatic soprano voice also had exceptional agility the role of Leonora was vocally ideal for her – she gives Leonora great stature in an opera where the character is not explicitly the protagonist. Her characterisation is projected with ardour and sincerity and, in moments of desperate vulnerability or redemption, with nobility. A moving melancholy underlines her singing throughout the drama.

Callas reaches the pinnacle of her art in the monastery scene (Act 2), the apex of the opera. Through musical means she expresses tellingly Leonora's mental and physical exhaustion in the recitative 'Son giunta', finding some relief in the prayer 'Madre, pietosa Vergine', appropriately not sung with an even, sweet tone, but with that of an agitated and tormented soul. The increasing intensity of her singing makes a great impact, without distorting the melodic line, reaching and sustaining a dramatic climax in the ensuing duet with Padre Guardiano, 'Più tranquilla l'alma sento', when she begs for refuge. The scene ends with 'La vergine degli angeli' in which Callas's ravishing singing relies not only on beautiful sound but also on fine imaginative musicianship.

There are a few slightly harsh high notes which, if considered in the context, do not mar the delicacy or dampen the excitement of this remarkable performance.

Rossi-Lemeni makes a splendid, totally involved Guardiano, surpassing himself in the duet with Callas. He is in good voice with a minimum of the constricted tone that at times mars his singing. Capecchi (Melitone) has not yet been bettered – at least on record. Nicolai brings vitality to Preziosilla, but occasionally sounds incongruously a little rough. Tagliabue (Carlo), with reduced vocal resources at this stage of his career, gets through the role by his considerable artistry. Tucker (Alvaro) by and large sings with heroic style, if with occasional crude intonation. Serafin and the La Scala Orchestra and Chorus triumph again. He maintains a marvellous balance between the tragic and comic scenes of this inspiring though uneven work.

The digital remastering on CD is an improvement generally and for Callas's timbre which, particularly, is reproduced with greater authenticity.

IL TURCO IN ITALIA (Rossini): September 1954 – Milan – EMI

When in 1950 Callas sang Fiorilla in *Il Turco in Italia* in Rome the opera, first performed in 1814, had not been heard anywhere for a hundred years. With this role she confirmed that she had real seeds of comedy in her.

She is in fine form, her vocal and interpretative resources are consummately fused with flair and gusto. It will be difficult to find, within the bounds of good taste, a more amusing characterisation than Callas's singing of Rossini's deceptively placid vocal line, as in Fiorilla's two duets with the Turk and one with Geronio, her henpecked husband. Her effort to seduce the Turk in 'Siete Turchi' sounds hilarious, as she imbues her singing with guile and provocative vitality. The lightening of her voice is a constant delight, every repeat mischievously just that little bit different. Even more of a comic high point is Fiorilla's moment of reckoning with her husband in 'Per piacere alla signora': Callas achieves a triumph of vocal acting, her singing always remaining accurate and faithful to the score. She is coy and spiteful in turn and then pretends that she is offended and hurt (her disdainful 'Mi lasciate'), shedding a few crocodile tears in 'Senza aver di me pietà'. The husband–wife exchanges reach a climax in 'Per punirvi aver vogl'io' when Fiorilla henpecks him again in no uncertain terms – the final note (top D) with a touch of stridency leaves no doubt of her defiance. In the disguise scene Callas brings a welcome dash of melancholy – Fiorilla's moment of repose, albeit a short-lived one. When finally, out of necessity, she repents and wants to be taken back by her husband Callas, with gross feminine beguilement, still leaves the listener, but not her husband, with the strong suspicion that Fiorilla is really incorrigible.

Even though Stabile as Prosdocimo, the poet, is vocally past his prime, his stylish performance can hardly be bettered. Subtly underplaying his comic part, Calabrese (Geronio) made a sympathetic henpecked husband, while Rossi-Lemeni (Selim, the Turk) gives a masterful portrayal of self-importance. They both enter into the spirit of the work and rise to the occasion, especially in their scenes with Callas. Gedda (Narcisso) and Gardino (Zaida) give creditable performances. After an inexplicably funereal beginning Gavazzeni comes to life and keeps the La Scala Orchestra and Chorus under marvellous control, creating a congenial atmosphere for the characters to manipulate one another.

The digital remastering on CD has corrected some slightly unbalanced passages.

MADAMA BUTTERFLY (Puccini): August 1955 – Milan – EMI

Callas recorded the complete role of Cio-Cio-San (Butterfly) three months before she first sang it on the stage. As in the theatre so in the recording she lightens and modulates her voice, and with a variety of vocal inflexion scales down her personality to identify with Puccini's fragile yet strong-minded fifteen-year-old girl, who acquires maturity within three years and subsequently kills herself.

Notwithstanding some slight insecurity – a raw edge on the high D at the end of 'Ancora un passo' (Butterfly's entrance), Callas is generally in splendid voice, her singing often exerting disarming appeal. Moreover, the 'close-up' effect of the recording brings into sharper focus her subtly introspective feelings – childlike shyness and impulsiveness, vulnerability, a newly found security and love for, and total submissiveness to, Pinkerton. Such is Callas's Butterfly in Act I – initially and for the most part childlike but with a few inter-mittent signs of premature development into a woman – a portrayal of which John Steane (*Gramophone*, March 1987) perceptively wrote that 'the keynote is firmness of mind: a simple factuality which sees right and wrong with the clarity of that miraculous rinsed and lightened voice. Everything here is in place.'

In the second act Callas no longer lightens her voice, except for a moment or two when traces of the little woman are heard as in 'Non mi rammenta più!'. Her performance is so much of a piece that it is difficult to pin-point this or that marvellous moment. But how can one refrain from mentioning 'Tornar a divertir la gente col cantar, oppur, meglio, morire' when Butterfly realises that Pinkerton may never return to her and that only death is her destiny. She dwells on this possibility with a heart-rending shriek, yet is so dignified in 'Morta! Mai più danzar!' Callas sings 'Un bel dì' as if narrating a story. At first in nostalgic pianissimo, her singing becomes totally introspective with childlike tone as she fantasises about those intimate moments when husband and wife are reunited: 'Chi sarà? . . . Chiamerà Butterfly dalla lontana'. With escalating intensity she then betrays her fears, but culminates in a self-reassuring emotional outburst: 'Io con sicura fede l'aspetto'. In the final scene Callas is profoundly moving, her death remaining a dignified and private affair. After her last utterances, 'Addio, piccolo amor! Va, Gioca', one almost feels the dagger plunging into her.

When this recording was first issued, Callas's Butterfly was more unfavourably than controversially received, practically for the same reasons as were her recordings of Aida and to some extent Tosca; she was accused of sacrificing a smooth tone for the sake of expression. It has taken several years for these accusations to be turned into the highest praise. Callas was a modern singer and time was needed to accept that a beautiful sound *per se* is a hollow accomplishment in opera, where singers should be actors, as in the straight theatre.

Gedda was also, at first, misguidedly declared miscast as Pinkerton, mainly because he sounded rather feeble and charming to the extent that Butterfly had the upper hand in Act I. With time, however, and better knowl-edge of the score, Gedda's characterisation was appreciated; Pinkerton, the greatest cad in operatic literature, is also capable of remorse, is intelligent with constructive insight and in line with Callas's conception of her role. The supporting cast, Danieli (Suzuki) Borriello (Sharpless) and Ercolani (Goro), rise to the occasion. Karajan draws some excellent playing and singing from the La Scala Orchestra and Chorus. He interprets the score with penetrating insight and if he performs the composer's climaxes with some professorial reserve, he nevertheless brings all the emotional excitement intended.

The digital remastering on CD has all but smoothed out any sound blemishes, including Butterfly's high D.

AIDA (Verdi): August 1955 – Milan – EMI

When this recording appeared, Callas's Aida was controversially received: she was accused of sacrificing a smooth line and not always producing beautiful sounds, for the sake of dramatic expression. In actuality the criticism that all but superficially dismissed the performance only applied to some unsteady notes at the end of the well-known aria 'O patria mia'. Whereas the criticism was justified as far as it goes, at this distance, today, Callas has won her case, albeit posthumously.

Many critics now declare this recording of *Aida* (digital remastering on CD) the best of several others in which the heroines particularly produce beautiful sounds, often in isolation. There is greater significance in this than a mere change of heart. Our generation is well on course in the realisation – notwithstanding Callas's contribution – that opera must always be music theatre, the singers actors, otherwise this art form will eventually die a natural death. John Steane's words (*Opera on Record*, 1979) come to mind: 'If reduced to just one recording of *Aida* many of us would, I fancy, be found clinging to this one.'

Callas's ability to see the work as a whole sets her apart from all other Aidas within living memory; this is a gripping performance, faithful to the score and repeatedly throwing new light on details of dramatic relevance and interest. She first establishes concisely Aida's situation – the princess–slave who is torn between love and patriotism – in 'Ritorna vincitor', a *tour de force*. But it is the way in which she explores Aida's human predicament in the wonderful series of dramatic duets (with Amneris, Amonasro and Rhadames) that she conquers one's heart.

In 'O patria mia', a lament, Callas surpasses herself in breathing, with pessimistic nostalgia, memories of her fatherland. Her sacrifice of a smooth line – a tonal change of vocal colour – is not a vocal flaw, but a genuine attempt at dramatic expression. Under the circumstances and with this degree of achievement it is foolish to make a big issue over the slight stridency and unsteadiness of the final notes.

Gobbi (Amonasro) exploits the character's emotions – anger, revenge and paternal love – through musical means and rises to Callas's artistic level. Their scene in Act 3 (the Nile Scene) is without equal on record or in the theatre. It generates electricity for maximum dramatic purpose. Almost the same can be said for Barbieri's Amneris, who subtly conveys her unrequited love, unmitigated jealousy and her royal pride. On this occasion the timbre of her voice sounds more distinguished than it really was. Among such a cast Tucker (Rhadames) more than holds his own. Perhaps his singing is not as heroic as is customary, but in the opera we do not see Rhadames on the battlefield, but mostly embroiled in human relationships where passion, not physical strength, is involved.

Zaccaria (King), Modesti (Ramfis), Galassi (Priestess) and Ricciardi (Messenger) are all worthy members of a truly distinguished cast. Serafin conducts the La Scala Orchestra and Chorus with meticulous care and with the kind of consideration that gets the best out of his singers without, however, bringing any special distinction to the big ensembles of the Temple or Triumphal grand scenes.

The digital remastering on CD has brought more vibrancy, more space to the recording and all but rectified Callas's much-publicised unsteadiness in 'O patria mia'.

RIGOLETTO (Verdi): September 1955 – Milan – EMI

Because of Callas's outstanding characterisations of Norma, Medea, Lady Macbeth and other larger-than-life heroines it was assumed that the part of Gilda in *Rigoletto* was not a natural for her. This misguided notion came about since the role, in the present century, was usually sung by light or lyric sopranos (often little more than soubrettes), who could cope with its coloratura passages. In fact, only a dramatic soprano *d'agilità*, the type of singer Callas was, can give that abstract dimension to the music which will illuminate the character in all its facets.

John Ardoin (*The Callas Legacy*, 1977) was the first to note the significance of Callas's portrayal of Gilda. He wrote: 'It is a shame that Gilda did not remain an active part of Callas's repertoire, for she could have forced the musical world to rethink the part as completely as she made it reconsider Lucia.'

Even though Callas sang Gilda only twice on the stage (Mexico City, June 1952), her recording reveals a characterisation of genius. She substantially defied the so-called tradition that Gilda is only a virginally innocent young girl, who always produces sweet sounds and sings coloratura passages with ease. Whereas these requisites are valid, there is a great deal more to Gilda. Callas, in fine, secure form, brings to life the innocent, lonely but passionate girl as she experiences love for the first time: 'Caro nome' is sung with the precision of an instrumentalist and telling dramatic expression. An introspective beauty permeates her singing, with a rapturous moment only at the long-drawn final notes – the aria becomes a memorable study of adolescence.

Callas shows no less insight in the three duets that are central to the drama. Through dramatic differentiation of timbre and variation in the intensity of her singing she expresses romantic love for Gualtier Maldè (the Duke) in 'E il sol dell'anima', and paternal affection for Rigoletto in 'Deh non parlare al misero' and 'Tutte le feste', before and after she has known physical love respectively – after her seduction Gilda quickly reaches maturity and faces with dignity her tragedy when she dies for her worthless seducer.

Having listened to this recording, Teodoro Celli, the Italian critic, remained struck by – among much else – 'one very brief "accent", four notes that Gilda sings in the second scene: The Duke, having furtively entered the garden of Gilda's house, ardently declares his love. Gilda, disturbed, replies to the Duke's "Io t'amo" with "uscitene" . . . I asked Callas why she had given so special an accent to a word of apparently little importance. Callas replied: "Because Gilda says 'Get out' but wants to say 'Stay'!"'

Gobbi, the reigning Rigoletto of his time, projects the character with incomparable musicianship. There is a certain nobility behind his fears and humiliation. If his voice is sometimes a little short in weight, his artistry more than makes up for it. Di Stefano sounds very ardent and insouciant, though somewhat lacking in elegance. With his warmth and charm he makes a more convincing Gualtier Maldè than Duke. Zaccaria is both vocally and dramatically outstanding as a sinister Sparafucile and the supporting cast is worthy of the distinguished company they are in. Serafin conducts the La Scala Orchestra and Chorus with fine musicianship and impeccable taste. With unobtrusive tempi and fine orchestral detail, he provides the impetus for his cast to bring to life the appealing characters of Verdi's and Piave's drama.

The digital remastering on CD has rectified some slight congestion.

IL TROVATORE (Verdi): August 1956 – Milan – EMI

After singing Leonora in *Il trovatore* twenty times in the theatre during 1950–5, Callas recorded the role and, as it happened, never sang it again. At this distance her recording of one of the most vocally difficult roles in all opera has become permanent testimony of the degree to which her art was a major contribution to Italian opera.

Despite the relatively restricted scope of the recording, Callas conveys, with all the formality that is demanded of her as a Spanish aristocrat, Leonora's passionate humanity. She is in excellent form both as lyric and dramatic soprano, the role's absolute requisites. Only the last phrase in 'Tacea la notte' is momentarily squalid. Otherwise, in the aria and ensuing cabaletta, Callas uses the florid passages to heighten the emotions of the character – Leonora's romantic melancholy and her desperate dilemma over the man she really loves, who is an enemy of her aristocratic class. But it is in the last act that she surpasses all known Leonoras and even herself. The trills on the words 'rose' and 'dolente' in 'D'amor sull'ali rosee' take on a new meaning, lyrically and movingly expressing her anxiety and sorrow – they are even more effective, more subtle, than in the theatre.

Then comes the sudden change to the highly dramatic 'Miserere' conveying compellingly Leonora's foreboding – a vocal feat unequalled on any recording or stage. The hitherto omitted – in performance – 'Tu vedrai' (considered to hold up the action) is restored and Callas sings with an almost unbearable though appropriate intensity and without in any way disrupting the melodic line.

Di Stefano does not quite have the vocal weight for Manrico's heroic side, but with lyrical warmth and ardency copes with the role adequately. Practically the same applies to Panerai, who sings with a smooth tone most of the time and fails to express Luna's aggressive character, thereby somewhat upsetting the essential contrast with Manrico. Zaccaria sings Ferrando's music with impeccable clarity and smooth but expressive tone, giving the performance a flying start. Barbieri is correct and fiery, and she uses her less than aristocratic timbre to portray an almost ideal Azucena. Karajan conducts the La Scala Orchestra and Chorus with great insight into detail, at the same time making the music sound interestingly fresh.

The digital remastering on CD and better editing has practically rectified the slight squalliness in 'Tacea la notte' and increased the vibrancy of the recording generally. The recording marked Callas's final collaboration with Karajan – a remarkable association that also produced the recording of *Madama Butterfly* (1954) and stage performances of *Lucia di Lammermoor* (La Scala 1954, Berlin and Vienna 1955).

LA BOHÈME (Puccini): August–September 1956 – Milan – EMI

It is often taken for granted, though not with valid artistic justification, that an acknowledged tragedienne would be miscast in the role of a very young woman where sweet charm or naïve innocence is the basic requisite. By this same token the role of Mimì in *La bohème* (referred to as piccola delicata in the preface to the score) – so far removed from Callas's successful portrayals of highly elevated characters, Norma, Medea, Lady Macbeth to name but a few – could not be imagined by many as a natural for her. But this is not taking into account the music, which gives the character a very powerful abstract dimension: Mimì acquires greater depth of character than the words give her and becomes a tragic figure true to life, as opposed to a woman larger than life. None the less, she is individual in manner, universal in humanity.

La bohème, one of the most popular operas, is almost certainly the most frequently recorded, with over thirty complete versions. Callas never sang Mimì on stage, though she seriously considered it during the early 1960s, by which time, however, her vocal resources had diminished and she would have been taking an unreasonable risk. (Her recording of *La bohème* was first issued in March 1958, twenty months after it was made.)

As it was, Callas dispelled all doubts. Unarguably, she is the most all-round convincing Mimì, establishing the character concisely in vivid colours. Her aria 'Mi chiamano Mimì' and love duet 'O soave fanciulla' with Rodolfo in Act I make such an impact – phrases, even single words, become utterly memorable – that we 'see' before us the shy, fragile, sick little woman who readily wins our sympathy.

In the third and fourth acts Callas is incomparable. Mimì's bottled-up feelings are released in her cry for help (understated, but one that speaks volumes) when she seeks out Marcello, Rodolfo's closest friend: 'O buon Marcello, aiuto'. Her moment of truth follows presently, when she overhears (hiding behind a tree) Rodolfo telling Marcello that his jealousy forces him to leave Mimì, who is ill and dying and whom he cannot help. Callas expresses Mimì's hopelessness and pain in her syncopated utterances 'Ahimè, morire! O mia vita'. No less moving is her poignancy in recollected intimacies at her farewell to Rodolfo: 'Donde lieta uscì al tuo grido d'amore'. The scene carries the conviction of living emotion.

In the death scene Callas is very much like the young woman for whom life was predestined to be short and who had to acquire wisdom in far too brief a time.

On records Callas's noteworthy rivals in this role were Victoria de los Angeles and Renata Tebaldi, who produced sweeter sounds and sang with more even intonation, often ravishing the ear of the listener. But there is much more to the personality and life of Puccini's appealing heroine – the music makes it clear that without the 'pain' (usually absent from the rival recordings) *La bohème* does not make sense. Callas's superiority stemmed from her ability to read between the lines of the score; she then made Mimì a credible human being by appropriately varying the intensity of the character's basically monochromatic vocal line.

Di Stefano as Rodolfo gives one of his best performances on record. Vocally in his prime, his characterisation of the bohemian poet is ardent, impulsive and often inspired. The other bohemians, Panerai (Marcello) and Zaccaria (Colline), surpass themselves, both giving vivid cameo performances fully integrated into the drama. Moffo as Musetta is the weakest member of a distinguished cast; she is vivacious and flighty, but only superficially so – a very promising (she was twenty-one years old at the time) but as yet partially formed characterisation. Votto conducts the La Scala Orchestra and Chorus with considerable *élan* and dramatic impact, if not with inspiration. None the less, he creates the right atmosphere for the actors of the drama.

The digital remastering on CD has made the recording more spacious and clearer, especially the orchestra.

UN BALLO IN MASCHERA (Verdi): September 1956 – Milan – EMI

As in the theatre, on record Callas's assumption of the role of Amelia in *Ballo* is impressive and compelling. She unlocks the secret chambers of Amelia's personality, which is that of a warm and chaste though passionate upper-class English lady. What makes Amelia a very human character is the inbuilt reserve that protects her and gives her strength when torn between an illicit but sincere love and her husband. It is this reserve – suggested in the tone of Callas's voice – which even in the most tempestuous outburst is not completely lost, that enhances the predicament at issue: in her passionate duet with Riccardo (di Stefano), when her reserve all but abandons her, she redresses the balance in 'Ma, tu nobile me difendi dal mio cor' before she responds to his declarations of love. This is exquisite singing, where accomplished technique is put to the service of expression, and maintains the Verdian melodic line in all its splendour. One is only aware of the emotion of falling in love, the most difficult feeling to express with conviction. Callas achieves this through her unique musicianship, which enables her to impregnate words even in the long-span phrases of the love duet with such meaning that they remain memorable.

It is in the appropriately restrained accents that underline 'Morrò, ma prima in grazia', with its single sentiment, that Callas conveys Amelia's personal tragedy. There are some, however, who are not completely won over by her interpretation of this scene. Her detractors maintain that at no point does she lay bare her feelings and consequently her performance remains rather still-born. But then, the upper-class English lady would not so nakedly reveal her feelings and this does not make the situation any the less passionate. In fact, when Amelia's personality is taken into account, it becomes all the more moving.

She is different when she joins in the trio 'Dunque l'onta di tutti sol una' of the conspirators, which include her husband. Her desperate fears are not for herself and she suddenly becomes extrovert.

Di Stefano has a marvellous ring in his voice and his diction is idiomatically clear. Even though the security of his top register is sometimes arguable, the lyric warmth and ardency of his singing and above all his total involvement in his role – he too is inspired in the love duet with Amelia – distinguish his performance. Gobbi (Renato) occasionally fails to maintain a smooth vocal line, but his insight into Renato's personality is so great that one accepts him without reservation. Barbieri's dark timbre is ideal for Ulrica but Ratti as Oscar misfires to a degree; the essential subtle irony eludes her and she is also frequently shrill. The conspirators Maionica and

Zaccaria (Samuel and Tom respectively) could hardly be bettered. The La Scala Orchestra and Chorus perform well under Votto — even though he does not convey any significant subtlety, the cast does it all for him.

With digital remastering on CD, the recording has acquired better balance generally and the singers' slight insecurity, even Ratti's shrillness, is reduced.

IL BARBIERE DI SIVIGLIA (Rossini): February 1957 – London – EMI

It is part of operatic history that Rosina was the only role (out of forty-seven successful portrayals) that defeated Callas when she performed it at La Scala in February 1956. Her problems were not so much vocal, but rather an inability to adapt her personality to that of the character (see p. 195). It is also history that a year later Callas rethought the role for the recording and with a highly accomplished technique and overall sense of style and characterisation sang with gusto, wit and, generally, contagious high-spirited fun. Rosina emerges as mischievously guileful, insinuatingly flirtatious and above all displays the simple charm of the *ingénue* she essentially is, all qualities conspicuously absent from her stage performance.

Callas sings the role in its authentic mezzo-soprano range; the timbre of her voice is subtle and alluring in the middle, the upper register brilliantly agile. Her recitatives are meaningful and delivered with such timing as to give the melodic line and the all-important pauses within the role a unique continuous flow. Furthermore, nothing is sung as merely a show-piece, not even 'Una voce poco fa', in which Callas sinuously but persuasively describes Rosina's contrasting character traits. The devious stress she coyly but firmly puts on the word 'ma' makes one smile even when recollected much later.

She maintains her great *élan* throughout the opera: her brilliantly subtle, playful singing deliciously enlivens the dialogue with Figaro in 'Dunque io son' to achieve the distinction of high comedy. Nevertheless, and notwithstanding Callas's great acumen in all scenes, it is in the Lesson Scene, 'Contro un cor', that she proves her superiority over all Rosinas within living memory, perhaps only matched by Conchita Supervia. Callas sings with a sweet calmness that provides, for once, a moment of repose which the character needs and which also expresses with simplicity and deft sincerity the *ingénue*'s feelings of love.

Gobbi as Figaro may lack some of the freshness, though not the spontaneity, of his earlier recording of 'Largo al factotum', but his performance, especially his scene with Callas, lacks nothing of the great appeal and aplomb that one has come to expect from this unique character of *opera buffa*. Alva as Almaviva is, surprisingly, a little disappointing, due to lack of sufficient vocal colour, and Zaccaria as Basilio, though in excellent vocal form, is evidently not a *basso buffo* and consequently manages to give only an outline, albeit an accomplished one, of Basilio's character. Galliera conducts the Philharmonic Orchestra and Chorus with much insight and exuberance.

Curiously the overture sounded rather dull to the point that it might be assumed not to belong to this recording until the digital remastering on CD gave it more life and greater clarity, as it did to the recording generally.

LA SONNAMBULA (Bellini): March 1957 – Milan – EMI

The recording goes some way to confirm that though much of the joy lay in watching Callas embody Amina in the theatre, it was basically through her singing that she brought the character so vividly to life. Her ability to perform Bellinian cantilena and coloratura dramatically and adapt her vocal timbre accordingly enabled her to reach eloquent heights of poetry: Amina, the charming sleepwalker, became a living creature with a voice of joy as well as of sorrow.

The voice of joy is first heard in her entrance recitative and aria, 'Care compagne. . . . Come per me sereno' when Callas, in fine form, establishes Amina's character: through elaborate embellishments (which rise to high E and, at one point, drop two and a half octaves in vocal range) she expressed in turn Amina's affectionate side and her passionate sensitivity. But it is the chromatic semiquavers together with the high notes that create the magic moment, the overflowing joy, when the crest of emotion is reached.

Callas reaches the pinnacle of her art in the outstanding sleepwalking scene – the summing up of the protagonist in particular and of the work in general. In a most meaningful recitative 'Oh! se una volta sola' she penetrates the depths of Amina's very personal feelings. Her sorrow finds a retrospective heart-rending emotional outlet in 'Ah, non credea mirarti'. The way she begins this aria evokes the sound of rippling water, her singing defying technical description, other than that it is spontaneous and deceptively simple. The long-drawn notes, especially where the only accompaniment is a viola, seem endless and are profoundly moving – Callas's ability through vocal means to create in the listener's imagination the appropriate *mise-en-scène* gives the scene unique poignancy – the masterly use of the veiled tone creating the illusion that she is soliloquising in her sleep, while her fioriture attain the right conclusion of the emotional build-up; a case when the voice alone, without a physical presence, achieves a complete portrayal.

The voice of joy is heard again in 'Ah non giunge', after Amina has awakened. Callas sings the numerous embellishments accurately, but with full dramatic expression (unlike other singers, who wrongly polish off this rondo at top speed, Callas sings it appropriately allegro moderato) and brings out the essence of the situation, that is the bounding delight of an innocent soul who triumphs over adversity.

After Callas's, the most distinguished performance is given by Zaccaria as Rodolfo, who sings with impeccable taste and a great sense of Bellini's melodic line. The timing, the spontaneity, the feeling in his duet with Amina (the first sleepwalking scene) is a vocal feat. Monti as Elvino also sings with considerable taste and apart from a disconcertingly strident high note (which fails to serve dramatic expression) in the last act, encompasses the high tessitura. And yet this Elvino remains a rather faceless character. The supporting cast is first rate. Votto conducts the La Scala Orchestra and Chorus with his usual diligent and sympathetic manner, but without any special insight into this poetic and most appealing score.

The changes from sleepwalking to wakefulness, as well as all the other moods, are expertly captured on the recording, more so in the digital transfer on CD.

TURANDOT (Puccini): July 1957 – Milan – EMI

Despite Callas's great success as Turandot, after twenty-four performances in Italy and Buenos Aires during 1948–9, she abandoned the role – to concentrate on early nineteenth-century Italian opera – only returning to it for the recording in 1957. In the meantime Callas's artistry had reached its peak, but as far as the recording is concerned at the relatively small price of slight insecurity in certain phrases in the uppermost register. Also, and again relatively speaking, her voice in 1957 has become a little less voluminous.

Whereas there have been several other accomplished Turandots, some with steelier and stronger voices, Callas achieves more: she invests the character of the cruel Princess Turandot authoritatively, and with just the right blend of imperiousness and coldness exploits her heavily concealed human vulnerability, her frustrations and complexes, and finally her discovery of love.

Her vocal declamation – an essential quality in this role – both in 'In questa reggia' and the riddle scene, the central episode in the opera, is not only impressive, but masterfully expressive of Turandot's psychological reactions and of the subtle changes in her brutal attitude. When Calaf solves her last riddle she is all but broken, but maintains her arrogance with great difficulty.

In 'Del primo pianto' (Alfano's completion), after Calaf's kiss, she slightly changes the tone of her voice so that the listener discerns not so much the complete melting of the ice in the princess (that had already begun even before Calaf solved her last riddle) but Turandot's mystification in discovering sexual love.

Fernandi sings Calaf's music with a clear, ringing, well-produced voice. His timbre is pleasing and at times exciting, but his characterisation finds little identity. Contrariwise, Schwarzkopf's Liù is meticulously studied and sung with ravishing tone, but in the final analysis she is defeated at her own purpose: her Liù sounds more like a grand duchess than a slave. Zaccaria is in excellent voice and makes a very dignified and moving Timur and Borriello, Ercolani and de Palma as the trio Ping, Pang and Pong give sparkling and well-integrated performances. Serafin's profound understanding of the score and his handling of the singers with constructive consideration also inspires the La Scala Orchestra and Chorus to give a thrilling performance with atmosphere and dramatic point.

The digital CD transfer has improved the recording, especially the choral climaxes, as well as reducing the vibrato in Callas's upper register.

MANON LESCAUT (Puccini): July 1957 – Milan – EMI

Manon Lescaut (1893) established Puccini as the new operatic composer of Italy —more Verdi's heir than any of his rivals.

In their effort to make the libretto different from Massenet's *Manon*, Puccini's librettists all but ruined its dramatic structure; nothing is really shown of Des Grieux's love affair with Manon, who is presented as a naïve *ingénue* and, in a trice, without much justification, a calculating courtesan. Nevertheless, the composer triumphed over these shortcomings, especially in the last act when the drama, totally expressed by the music, achieves great tragic heights.

'Whereas Massenet has felt the drama as a Frenchman, with the powder and the minuet [with refinement and grace],' Puccini declared, 'I feel it as an Italian, with desperate passion.'

On the evidence of this recording it is surprising that Callas never sang Manon on-stage. Apart from a couple of rather pinched high notes, she is in good form, her voice becoming the faithful servant of extraordinary dramatic perception into the heroine's character. There are also beautiful moments when it ravishes the ear and touches the heart with disarming appeal, as she experiences the emotional development of Manon; a naïve and superficial young girl rather than a dangerous coquette, whose acquired sophistication, wantonness and greed eventually destroy her.

Callas sets about her role with natural charm and without calculation when she first meets Des Grieux: 'Manon Lescaut mi chiamo'. Her artless simplicity registers the young girl's regrets for what she is leaving behind, including the young man she has just met. And yet in 'Mi vincete. Quando oscuro l'aere intorn a noi sara', when Manon agrees to see Des Grieux later, Callas subtly betrays her determination to do what she really wants, but did not have the confidence to do before. It is now that she sows the seeds of her inevitable destruction – a downhill journey to the point of no return.

'In quelle trine morbide' is elevated into an introspective monologue when Callas compares the past warmth and love of her humble dwelling with her present loveless luxury where the deathly silence freezes her. The understated 'v'è un silenzio un freddo che m'agghiaccia!' expresses Manon's weakness and strength so convincingly that the listener identifies with her: Manon's tragedy emanates from her inability to choose between love and luxury.

Her death scene beginning with 'Sola, perduta, abbandonata' is a study in hopelessness which, with an absence of any melodramatic sentimentality and expressed solely from a musical consideration, becomes utterly cathartic. The haunting echo of 'Ah, tutto è finito! . . . No non voglio morir! Amore aita!' remains in one's inner ear. Callas has the desperate passion that Puccini gave to his music, but she conveys it with a restraint that makes it all the more powerful.

Notwithstanding the pinched notes mentioned, once Callas's special brand of youthfulness, controlled but desperate passion, and melancholic and painful loneliness have captured the listener's imagination they never let go.

Happily, the same can be said for di Stefano's deeply felt portrayal of Des Grieux. He too has the desperate passion, the ardency, the warmth – this is one of the most exciting performances on record. The supporting cast – Fioravanti (Lescaut), Calabrese (Gerone) – are worthy of the outstanding protagonists. Serafin conducts the La Scala Orchestra and Chorus with subtlety, insight into Puccini's changing moods, all in tremendous style and appears to 'sing' with his singers in full harmony.

The transfer to CD has given the recording extra clarity of sound. Callas's vocal timbre sounds truer, the squalliness of the above-mentioned notes has all but disappeared. This is not meant to imply that the recording has been doctored, but better editing, digital remastering and, in this case, the better pressing of the discs accounts for the improvement.

MEDEA (Cherubini): September 1957 – Milan – (Ricordi), EMI

It is entirely because of Callas's presence that *Medea* was revived in 1953 after many years of neglect due to the enormous difficulty in casting the title role. At the time of the recording she was suffering from exhaustion (in addition to her numerous stage performances, she had recorded several operas including *Turandot* in the preceding months and had just left the Edinburgh Festival feeling unable to give an extra performance in *La sonnambula*, see p. 258).

Although her voice is in only fairly good condition, Callas rises to the occasion and repeats her outstanding portrayal of Medea, the legendary woman who became synonymous with a living curse to humanity: she expresses the most brutal as well as tenderest human emotions with profound insight and musical invention of infinite variety. Her characterisation, which comprises desperate love, scorn and hatred, leads to a most fearful revenge on the husband who so basely betrayed her and the conflicting but fatal feelings for her children are conveyed almost as living emotions to make her portrayal complete and reach inexorably its appalling conclusion.

Callas immediately penetrates into the personality of the grandiose Medea: 'Io Medea' has the impact of a thunderbolt. Presently the tone of her voice changes to feminine tenderness, when the notes flow, in her effort to win back her husband: 'Ricordi il giorno tu, la prima volta quando m'hai veduta?' Rebuffed, Callas is at her most moving: she sings the word 'crudel', which occurs several times, an abrupt cry of grief from the depths of her heart, before her tone becomes totally submissive in 'Pietà! Torna a me'. She then abandons all traces of softness to become a menacing and wounded tigress in her electrifying confrontation with Jason: 'Nemici senza cor'.

In the last act Medea the sorceress is heard. With devastating effect she rages and grovels by turns, when she summons the infernal gods in 'Numi, venite a me, inferni Dei'. The effect is shuddering at the terrible moment when she decides to slay her children, but suddenly becomes tender and loving in 'O miei tesor' as if shaken by an earthquake of remorse. Callas concludes her characterisation, when all the inbuilt tensions are released, with unbearable calmness. 'Eran figli tuoi', after she has killed her children, is sung with the resignation of a murderess who is already a living ghost. Her final phrase to Jason, 'A sacro fiume io vo' colà t'aspetta l'ombra mia' encapsulates Medea's world.

Notwithstanding Callas's extraordinary vocal technique (Medea is fiendishly difficult – almost an impossible role), musicianship and all her other attributes, it is her ability, the mysterious quality, through vocal means to create in the listener's imagination the appropriate *mise-en-scéne* that carries one away. Apparently there is an unsteady B flat in 'Dei tuoi figli' and I would agree, but the impact of Callas's performance has quickly persuaded me to forget it as in the same way I have come to regard her occasional slight vocal insecurities as mere drops in an ocean.

Despite limited vocal resources Picchi sings Jason's music with good intonation and intelligence. Modesti (Creon) simply lacks stature, though vocally he is quite reliable. Surprisingly, Scotto makes heavy weather of Glauce's role, particularly of the words, which she appears not to have digested, and somewhat mars the vocal line of her otherwise accomplished singing. Pirazzini (Neris) is vocally and dramatically in top form. Serafin conducts the La Scala Orchestra and Chorus with a blazing intensity devoid of any ostentation or overstatement and, despite several cuts or because of them, maintains an overall balance of the score with great style and constant interest.

The recording was made by Mercury under the auspices of Casa Ricordi, Milan. It was distributed by EMI. When first issued on LP the quality of sound was only fair and occasional choral passages were not well-balanced. The digital remastering for CD and adept editing brings an all-round clarity and improved balance to the recording with the unsteady B flat that I would not hear all but rectified.

CARMEN (Bizet): July 1964 – Paris – EMI

Although Callas never sang Carmen on-stage, her characterisation in the recording is very individual and honest. For the most part she sings the 'Habanera' as a soliloquy of Carmen's philosophy of life, rather than flaunting herself in the manner of a cabaret *danse excentrique*. In the card scene her foreboding is audible as much in the tone of her voice as in the words, providing the clue to Carmen's impending tragedy. Similarly, the fatalism in the final scene, expressed through musical means, becomes inexorably the natural conclusion of the drama. What Callas lacks to some extent (despite her idiomatic use of the French language) is Carmen's mischievous humour, a constituent of the extraordinary fascination and sex appeal she so readily exerts on men.

Nevertheless, this is a committed and convincing interpretation within its conception, even though it owes, wrongly, more to Mérimée's ruthless, wild and ill-humoured Carmen than to Bizet's (and his librettists Meilhac and Halévy) independent, brutally honest and fatally charming heroine. Callas's greatest achievement, which sets her apart from other exponents of this role, is her ability to express the Spanish gipsy's violent and passionate temperament through elegant French music – the opera's contradictory requisite.

Gedda (José) cannot be faulted vocally and his singing is subtle to a degree, but fails to make sufficient dramatic impact in the last two acts. Andrea Guíot is a dramatically convincing Micaëla – the best on record – but Massard is no more than adequate as Escamillo. Prêtre conducts the Paris Opéra Orchestra and Chorus with vitality, if not with any special individuality.

The digital CD has marginally brought more vibrancy to the recording.

For a long time Callas refrained from discussing the role, but simply and unfussily dismissed suggestions and indeed persistent offers for performing Carmen on-stage. When Visconti offered to produce the opera for her she said that she could not do it because she was not able to dance like a gipsy. Besides, she did not want to show her ankles which were not very elegant. To me, who dared suggest this role – when in the early 1970s

Callas was seriously considering a return to the stage – she first sweetly said that it was not a bad idea, but then pirouetted coyly and, with tongue in cheek, declared, 'You see, I do not really have the *physique du rôle.*'

However, it is evident from what she said to Lord Harewood (BBC TV, 1968) and to me after her initial light-hearted but evasive jokes, that she had analysed the role meticulously, but finally decided not to perform it on-stage:

> I find the character of Carmen better drawn, more efficient, in Mérimée's novel than in Bizet's opera. Firstly, the vocal colour mezzo-soprano Bizet gave to her is, to my mind, too dark for a Spaniard or a gipsy; usually they are tense and nervous, and speak very quickly. A high-pitched voice is more appropriate for such a character. Secondly I see the drama more suitable for a film. Carmen herself is very virile, a very strong character and more of a man than a woman. She behaves towards men like a man feels about a woman. I think she should be very static on the stage. From the first moment, she sees José like an animal sees its prey and tries with an intensity to hypnotise it. Carmen knows exactly from the beginning how José feels about her. She does not care about his feelings, only about her own. I, personally, am not sure whether, with the necessary stillness, one can convey this on the stage. It is the same at the end of the opera. Carmen should not move an inch. She is bored to destruction with José and wants to get it over and done with. I see very little action on her part. But the whole affair is still against my principles. I am by nature more idealistic, more romantic.

Notwithstanding Callas's valid comments, there could also be, in my opinion, an element of truth that she would not bring herself to portray a slut. Rightly, she obviously did not consider Donna Fiorilla (*Il Turco in Italia*) to be in any way sluttish.

Be that as it may, it is my strong belief that Callas would have solved all the problems of the role and would have met the challenge, had she, at the time Carmen came into her life (a stage performance requires a much greater effort than a recording), been vocally secure. Her vocal resources were fast declining and in July 1965 (the recording was made during the previous July) she gave her last stage performance (*Tosca* at Covent Garden). Afterwards she only went as far as including the 'Habanera', the 'Seguidilla' and the final scene in some of her concerts.

Recitals

(a) I PURITANI (Bellini): 'Qui la voce . . . Vien diletto'
(b) NORMA (Bellini): 'Casta Diva . . . Ah bello a me ritorna'
(c) TRISTAN UND ISOLDE (Wagner): 'Liebestod'
November 1949 – Turin – Cetra

(a)   It introduced the voice of Maria Callas outside Italy and proved even then, to an unsuspecting world, what a consummate singing actress she was. Here at last was someone who could sing Bellini's cantilena, and who had the agility and expression for the equally difficult coloratura. In the aria and cabaletta (the connecting recitative is omitted) Callas captures all the melancholy and dreamy fragility of Elvira's character. No other recording demonstrates so well the voice of Callas at its freshest yet mature and in its most glorious state; it is a hauntingly memorable sound, so personal, whose magnificence and beauty is not in isolation but fully adapted and dramatically integrated into her singing.

There may well be truth in the rumour that Arturo Toscanini considered this recording to be the best of his favourite single piece of music.

(b) The opening and connecting recitatives and choral interjections are omitted. Although Callas was later to bring more subtlety to the cavatina and make it more of a prayer, this is already a marvellous performance, with finely delicate phrasing and perfect intonation. The cabaletta is not as refined – though it is meticulously executed – somewhat lacking the all-important introspection that was later to be achieved. There is also some distortion of sound in this section. Three months after the recording was issued Callas withdrew it, feeling she could do much better, particularly singing this outstanding operatic scene complete with choral support.

(c) It is sensuously and movingly sung, at once intimate yet universal. Callas is vulnerable, pleading, both lovelorn maiden and eternal woman, with no suggestion of the masculinity that often creeps into the voice of many an Isolde. The only drawback of this recording for some is that it is not sung in the original German but in Italian – a rather superficial criticism for Callas whose voice, in full bloom, captures most profoundly the essence of this sublime musical transfiguration that is the reconciliation of love and death.

The three recordings are conducted by Arturo Basile with the RAI, Turin, Orchestra. They were first issued on 78 rpm.

The digital remastering on CD ('Casta Diva' was reissued after Callas's death) is an all-round improvement.

PUCCINI ARIAS: September 1954 – London – EMI

Callas is in excellent vocal form, notwithstanding isolated unsteady top notes (not unsteady singing) and, with her extraordinary insight, musicianship and that almost undefinable ability to read between the notes, brings her own individuality to Puccini's music, making it sound fresher than ever.

She obviously saw the slave Liù in *Turandot* as not merely sweet and vulnerable, but as a determined, fatalistic and sympathetic young woman. She sings the arias 'Signore ascolta' and 'Tu che dí gel sei cinta' in a masculine way that interestingly brings out the masochistic tendencies of the character – an individualistic and valid characterisation. Perhaps Callas puts too much weight into 'O mio babbino caro' (*Gianni Schicchi*) and one might almost believe that young Lauretta is playing her 'tragic' plight for real, until Callas, with charm (a quality almost absent until then), underlines the last 'pietà' with a disarmingly subtle melodramatic touch. 'Senza mamma' (*Suor Angelica*) is most expressively sung, with Callas vividly establishing the little heroine Angelica (a role she only performed while a student at the Athens Conservatory in 1940), but her excellent legato singing is somewhat marred by an unsteady note (top A) at its close. The CD transfer has minimised this defect.

The other items are: 'In quelle trine morbide' and 'Sola, perduta, abbandonata' (*Manon Lescaut*), 'Mi chiamano Mimì' and 'Donde lieta uscì' (*La Bohème*), 'Un bel dì vedremo' and 'Tu? tu? piccolo Iddio!' (*Madama Butterfly*) and 'In questa reggia' (*Turandot*). Serafin with the Philharmonia Orchestra complements the artistic individuality of the singer.

OPERATIC ARIAS: September 1954 – London – EMI

Although this recital mostly contains excerpts from operas which Callas did not sing on-stage – *Adriana Lecouvreur, La Wally, Lakmé, Dinorah* – her extraordinary vocal technique as a dramatic soprano *d'agilità* and versatile artistry, enable the listener, even from these excerpts, to picture her in the corresponding roles.

In 'Io son l'umile ancella' and 'Poveri fiori' (*Adriana Lecouvreur*), 'Ebben? Ne andrò lontana' (*La Wally*) and 'La mamma morta' (*Andrea Chénier*) Callas, with impeccable taste and devoid of any melodramatic sentimentality, conjures up more credible living characters than the respective composers achieved on paper. She rises to great dramatic heights in 'L'altra notte' (*Mefistofele*), a performance which Rodney Milnes (*Opera*, July 1980) described as 'another *locus classicus* of the conjunction of technique, intelligence and worthwhile words and notes'.

The same applies to the florid items which are sung dramatically with a faultless sense of rhythm, and not as vehicles of meaningless vocalistic exhibition: Callas is the only singer who invokes the sound of bells with her voice – the required essence of the music in the Bell Song 'Dov'è l'Indiana bruna?' (*Lakmé*). She also makes the Shadow Song 'Ombra leggiera' (*Dinorah*) unusually interesting. Even more successful is the Bolero 'Mercè, dilette amiche' (*I vespri Siciliani*) in which Callas, in stunning voice, rapturously expresses Elena's happiness. Some have noticed a flatness on a top E – this cannot be disputed, but in context must surely be ignored as of no serious consequence. 'Una voce poco fa' (*Il barbiere di Siviglia*) is surprisingly highly embellished, but Callas uses every note to portray the *ingénue* Rosina who, as she brags, can, if need be, turn into a viper at a stroke. Serafin conducts the Philharmonia Orchestra with his usual artistry, particularly in the dramatic music. A little more *élan* in the florid music would not have come amiss. The CD transfer has added more vibrancy and even improved considerably on the flatness of the top E.

CALLAS AT LA SCALA: June 1955 – Milan – EMI

'Tu che invoco; o Nume tutelar' and 'Caro oggetto' are the only excerpts Callas recorded from *La vestale*, an opera she sang with great success a few times at La Scala in 1954. Callas may not always employ the velvety voice that Rosa Ponselle, her only formidable predecessor on record, had in this music, but she brings Giulia, the vestal virgin, compellingly to life with dramatic urgency (which Ponselle often lacked), impeccable musical style and unusually telling feeling for the words.

There is a noticeable lack of atmosphere in 'Dei tuoi figli' (*Medea*), mainly because its recitative is not included and Callas simply does not enter fully into the mood of the aria – surprisingly when compared with what she achieved two years later in the complete recording of *Medea*.

'Come per me sereno' (*La sonnambula*) and 'Qui la voce' (*I Puritani*), both from the corresponding complete recordings, are included in the present recital. Serafin conducts the La Scala Orchestra.

VERDI HEROINES: September 1958 – London – EMI

The three excerpts 'Vieni! t'affretta!', 'La luce langue' and the Sleep-walking Scene 'Una macchia' from *Macbeth*, confirm Callas's absolute supremacy as Lady Macbeth, a role that she only sang a few times at La Scala in 1952, but never recorded complete. Her interpretation, an overwhelming testimony that opera is drama expressed in music, has not been surpassed either in the theatre or on record. It is difficult to single out particular words or phrases which Callas especially illuminates – the whole being utterly memorable and of a piece, the impact of her vocal inflexions affecting the listeners in different ways.

In 'Ben io t'invenni ... Anch'io dischiuso (*Nabucco*) Callas as Abigaille achieves almost as much, even though she is not in as secure and fine vocal form as in *Macbeth*. The final note (top C) in the *Nabucco* excerpt is very strident and poor recording further makes it sound off-pitch. Nevertheless, her declamation in the recitative is authoritatively expressive and the aria (with its Bellini-like cantilena), is sung in fine legato.

'Tu che le vanità' (*Don Carlos*), delivered in the grand manner, establishes vividly the character of Elisabetta di Valois.

In 'Ernani! involami' (*Ernani*), Callas lightens and even sweetens her voice. Her Elvira (the only role in this recital that she never sang on-stage) is ardent yet introspective. Rescigno conducts the Philharmonia Orchestra with vitality and considerable insight, creating a congenial atmosphere, particularly in the Sleepwalking Scene in *Macbeth*.

The CD transfer has brought more clarity and better balance between orchestra and singers – and has all but corrected the pitch and reduced considerably the stridency of the final note in *Nabucco*.

MAD SCENES: September 1958 – London – EMI

This is an outstanding recital in which Callas confirms her artistic superiority over her contemporaries. Forty years later she still remains unsurpassed.

In each of the three scenes included Callas brings to life the heroine of the corresponding opera in the way that only a dramatic soprano *d'agilità* is capable of. Both as Anna in 'Piangete voi? . . . Al dolce guidami' (*Anna Bolena*) and Imogene in 'Oh! s'io potessi. . . Col sorisso d'innocenza' (*Il pirata*), Callas sings the deceptively simple melodies with an infinite variety of vocal colorations that are never amiss; they transcend art. As Ophelia (*Hamlet*), a completely different role and the only one in this recital that she never portrayed in the theatre, Callas lightens her voice in 'A vos jeux, mes amis' and, with touching innocence and melancholy, is lost in a reverie oblivious to her approaching death. Callas sings this scene in the original French and shows how idiomatically and meaningfully she uses the language to enhance her interpretation. Rescigno conducting the Philharmonia Orchestra is most considerate and provides every support for his soloist to express a wide variety of feeling.

The recording is fine, except for some loud notes in *Il pirata*, which have been corrected substantially in the digitally remastered CD transfer.

FRENCH OPERAS: March–April 1961 – Paris – EMI
CALLAS À PARIS: May 1963 – Paris – EMI

By the time Callas recorded these recitals, which reveal that a new repertoire was open to her, a decline in her vocal resources, though not her artistry, was evident. The tone of her voice is occasionally raw and somewhat thin. On the positive side her passionately perceptive insight into the words and music, which she cogently unites, succeeds in distilling the whole drama with creative individuality.

The range of her repertoire recorded here is enormous. It spans Gluck's *Orphée et Euridice* (1762) to Charpentier's *Louise* (1900) and includes soprano and mezzo-soprano roles. Whereas other sopranos have also attempted this repertoire, Dalila in Saint-Saëns's *Samson et Dalila* had always been the property of the mezzo-soprano or contralto.

FRENCH OPERAS includes 'J'ai perdu mon Eurydice' (*Orphée et Euridice*), 'Divinités du Styx' (*Alceste*), 'L'Amour est un oiseau rebelle' (Habanera) and 'Près des ramparts de Séville' (Seguedilla) from *Carmen*, 'Printemps qui commence', 'Amour! Viens aider ma faiblesse!' and 'Mon coeur s'ouvre a ta voix' (*Samson et Dalila*), 'Je veux vivre' (*Roméo et Juliette*), 'Je suis Titania' (*Mignon*), 'Pleurez, mes yeux' (*Le Cid*) and 'Depuis le jour' (*Louise*).

CALLAS À PARIS includes 'O malheureuse Iphigénie!' (*Iphigénie en Tauride*), 'D'amour l'ardente flamme' (*La Damnation de Faust*), 'Comme autrefois' (*Les Pêcheurs de Perles*), 'Je ne suis . . . Adieu, notre petite table' and 'Suis-je gentille . . . Je marche' from *Manon*, 'Werther! Qui m'aurait dit . . . Des cris joyeux' (*Werther*) and 'Il était un Roi de Thulé . . . O Dieu! que de bijoux . . . Ah! je ris' (*Faust*). Prêtre conducts the first recital with the French National Radio Orchestra, the second with the Paris Conservatoire Orchestra.

MOZART, BEETHOVEN, WEBER ARIAS: December 1963–January 1964 – Paris – EMI

Callas is in variable vocal form. She is at her best in 'Ah, perfido' (Beethoven) and 'Ocean! Thou mighty monster' (*Oberon*), where her artistry, vocal technique and determination triumph over her declining vocal resources. In Beethoven's concert aria she exploits masterfully the most expressive inflexions in her voice to portray compellingly the betrayed proud woman, whose anger and recriminations conceal a loving heart. Callas's singing has the same vitality and fire in 'Ocean!' where, with a skilful mixture of declamatory recitative and arioso, she expresses Rezia's thoughts and emotions. Through sheer determination Callas does not allow herself to be let down by her voice. Unexpectedly, however, the Greek-American Callas pronounces the English words with a slightly foreign accent.

In 'Or sai chi l'onore', 'Crudele? … Non mi dir', 'In quali eccessi … Mi tradì' (*Don Giovanni*) and 'Porgi amor' (*Le nozze di Figaro*) Callas's voice does, more or less, let her down. There are several moments of interesting insight into Donna Anna's or Donna Elvira's predicaments, but on the whole, and notwithstanding Callas's unfailingly perceptive intentions, her vocalisation is, by and large, rather too laboured for comfort. Rescigno conducts the Orchestre de la Société des Concerts du Conservatoire.

The CD transfer is an improvement inasmuch as Callas's vocalisation is steadier with fewer raw edges.

VERDI ARIAS: December 1963–February 1964 – Paris – EMI

Although Callas is in variable vocal form, her singing here is much more controlled than in the previous recital, which she also recorded in December 1963.

Of the four roles included on this disc Callas only portrayed Elisabetta (*Don Carlos*) on-stage and included Eboli's (*Don Carlos*) 'O don fatale' in concerts.

The long scene from *Otello* 'Mia madre … Piangea cantando (Willow Song) … Ave Maria' is a unique performance. No other Desdemona, at least on record, has shown so much poignant dramatic awareness. There is, however, a limit to the extent that art can triumph over physical disability. Callas's singing may be, relatively speaking, under control and the high notes are managed well enough, but there is no way, especially in this type of music and in the 'close-up' of a recording, to disguise the fact that the voice has not only lost much of its body but, more significantly, that its tone is occasionally a little hollow. Had Callas recorded this music five years earlier it would undoubtedly have become the definitive performance.

In Elisabetta's short 'Non pianger' (without chorus) Callas's vocal insecurity is even more exposed, though again, by artistic means, the listener is moved to a degree. It is a different story with 'O don fatale', a dramatic aria usually sung by a mezzo-soprano in the theatre. Apart from some lack of body on a high C, Callas's vocal tone is more secure and enhances rather than detracts from the dramatic impact of the declamatory first section or the cantilena of the middle. All in all, this highly dramatic monologue becomes a revelation. The same can be said for 'Salvami' and 'O, cielo! … Ah, dagli scanni eterei' (*Aroldo*) in which Callas's voice finds its best form in this recital. It would appear that these items and Eboli's aria were recorded in February 1964 about three weeks after Callas successfully made a stage come-back as Tosca at Covent Garden. Rescigno conducts the Orchestra de la Société des Concerts du Conservatoire.

ROSSINI AND DONIZETTI ARIAS: December 1963–April 1964 – Paris – EMI

This recital of excerpts from roles which Callas never performed on-stage, considered in isolation, is not representative of the outstanding opera singer she was. In her singing here there are only flashes of genius and few of those who hear her for the first time will be convinced of her reputed legendary artistry. The truth of the matter is that this recording was made more or less at the end of her singing career, a period when her vocal resources not only had declined considerably but also were unreliable. Whereas the glory of Callas's singing had been her effortless ability to get through the technical part of the music and have unlimited reserves to make her voice the servant of dramatic expression, she now needed her energy, physical and mental, to get through the musical notes and had very little left for vocal coloration and inflexion. Nevertheless, there are still moments when the ineffable grandeur of her singing, her genius, the illumination of a word, a phrase, becomes a memorable experience, though this is more readily appreciated by listeners familiar with her past artistic achievement. She is at her most consistently successful in 'S'allontanano alfine! . . . Selva opaca' (*Guglielmo Tell*) and 'Tranquillo ei posa! . . . Com'è bello' (*Lucrezia Borgia*). The other excerpts are 'Nacqui all'affanno' (*Cenerentola*), 'Convien partir' (*La figlia del reggimento*), 'Bel raggio lusinghier' (*Semiramide*) and 'Prendi; per me sei libero' (*L'elisir d'amore*). Rescigno conducts the Paris Conservatoire Orchestra.

MARIA CALLAS IN BELLINI AND VERDI – EMI

The excerpt from *Il pirata* was recorded in November 1961 in London and conducted by Antonio Tonini with the Philharmonia Orchestra. The others from *Attila* in February 1964 and from *I vespri siciliani*, *I Lombardi*, *Un ballo in maschera* and *Aida* were recorded in April 1964 in Paris and conducted by Rescigno with the Paris Conservatoire Orchestra. (Except for *Attila* and *I Lombardi*, Callas sang the other operas in the theatre.) However, Callas would not agree to this recording being issued (in fact at the time she had also recorded other excerpts from *I Lombardi*, *Un ballo in maschera* and *Il trovatore*) and in 1969 she re-recorded the Verdi excerpts, but again felt dissatisfied with her effort.

In 1972 Peter Andry of EMI and Walter Legge listened to these recordings again. 'At once we were both much impressed', Andry wrote, 'by the powerful characterisations Callas gave to the various heroines here assembled. Who could sing like this? Who indeed could keep one's attention riveted on every inflexion and breath – none but Callas. And this is why, almost ten years after these performances were recorded in Paris and London, we decided that these arias, which bear the inimitable stamp of Maria Callas, should be issued to take their place among the many treasures she has given us.'

For the present recording, parts from the 1969 tapes were spliced into those of 1964.

Notwithstanding Andry's valid reasons for making this recording available, it would be misleading and in some ways unfair, both to the artist herself and particularly to those who may be hearing her for the first time, to consider this recital as representative testimony of Callas's unique artistry. As with the *ROSSINI AND DONIZETTI* recital, the present one was made at the end of Callas's singing career – when her once incomparable vocal resources and technique became, at best, unreliable. And yet, listening carefully to this recording, someone who has already experienced and been moved by Callas's singing, either in the theatre or in earlier recordings, will find it possible to discover in the embers of a once-blazing fire treasures whose value is beyond that of a sentimental souvenir.

Callas, to be sure, is vocally ill at ease. She is careful, at times over-careful, but her genius frequently overshadows everything and the result is a triumph of artistry over physical disability; in the final analysis (how true Andry's words are) one is confronted with the belief that no one else can sing like this, no one else can invest a characterisation so powerfully.

In 'Sorgete . . . Lo sognai ferito, esangue' (*Il pirata*) Callas reveals Bellini's dramatic recitative and great ability in interpreting words through music. Among the Verdi items the most successful is 'Liberamente . . . Oh! nel fuggente nuvolo' (*Attila*), where Callas's voice is relatively secure and her singing acquires a vitality and a vividness that is very moving. This balance of vocal security and dramatic expression is not quite maintained in 'Arrigo! ah parli a un core' (*I vespri Siciliani*) or in 'Ritorna vincitor' (*Aida*); on the positive side there is the grandeur of her phrasing, which is both exciting and moving, but she is uncomfortable in passages that require agility.

One is not sure whether the editing (particularly the combination of the 1964 and 1969 tapes) has done more harm than good. 'O madre dal cielo soccorri' (*I Lombardi*) suffers worst and almost the same can be said for 'Ecco l'orrido campo . . . Ma dall'arido stelo' (*Un ballo in maschera*). Both Tonini and Rescigno give the fullest support and consideration to their singer.

MARIA CALLAS – THE LEGEND

Callas recorded 'Come per me sereno' and 'Oh, se una volta sola. . . . Ah, non credea . . . Ah, non giunge' from *La sonnambula* in September 1955, four months after she had sung her first performances in this opera (conducted by Bernstein) at La Scala. The present recording was not planned. On the day she finished making *Rigoletto* in Milan, with studio time left, Serafin persuaded her, without much difficulty, that it would be fun to record some excerpts from *La sonnambula*, her latest success. As there was no chorus available the recitative, as well as other verses of 'Sovra il sen' in the first item, were omitted. For the same reason the cadenza that links the two verses of 'Ah, non giunge' was also left out, as were practically all embellishments from both excerpts.

Callas never gave permission for the release of this recording, primarily because of the aforementioned limitations rather than the inadequacy of her singing. In any case, eighteen months later she recorded a complete *Sonnambula* with Votto conducting. However, in the late sixties these excerpts were issued on 'pirated' records in America. The present official recording was first issued by EMI in 1978, about six months after Callas's death.

Callas is in top form: her voice is fresh and secure, and the beauty of her effortless, expressive and quite moving singing is of the kind that lingers on. However, if Callas's art is judged on exalted standards – and it must be – there is in her singing of these excerpts a lack of spontaneity, due not so much to the singer's shortcoming, but to the curtailing of the libretto and the absence of the important participation of the chorus. Nevertheless, this is a recording that one cannot be without.

Four other excerpts from Verdi operas, also recorded many years before, are posthumously issued for the first time. Both Medora's Romanza 'Egli non riede ancor . . . Non so le terre' and Gulnara's cavatina 'Ne sulla terra . . . Vola talor' from *Il corsaro*, were recorded in February 1969, by which time Callas's career was finished. Even though she was working hard on her voice (she had been studying again with her old teacher Elvira de Hidalgo) to maintain her technique, her vocal resources were so diminished that her singing was little more than a shadow of its former self. What she accomplished was with a 'reconstructed' voice and as such she was no longer a dramatic soprano but a fragile instrument, at best capable occasionally of producing lyrically expressive passages. Rescigno conducts the Orchestre du Théâtre National de l'Opéra, Paris.

'Tacea la notte placida . . . Di tale amor' (*Il trovatore*) and 'Morrò, ma prima in grazia' (*Un ballo in maschera*) were recorded in April 1964, with Recigno conducting the Orchestre de la Société des Concerts du Conservatoire de Paris. Callas's voice is in marginally better condition than in the previous two excerpts, but it cannot begin to compare with her earlier recordings of this music, though she has somewhat deepened her characterisation, particularly in the second excerpt, by bringing to it a certain touching melancholy. But none of these Verdi excerpts adds anything to Callas's reputation as one of the greatest singing actresses of all time.

CALLAS – THE UNKNOWN RECORDINGS

In the 'Liebestod' (*Tristan und Isolde*) recorded 'live' in recital (Herodes Atticus, Athens, 5 August 1957) and conducted by Votto with the Athens Festival Orchestra, Callas repeats her individual interpretation with greater vividness and spontaneity than in her studio recording of the aria also sung in Italian (Cetra 78 rpm). The same can be said for 'Tu che le vanità' (*Don Carlos*) and 'Oh, s'io potessi ... Col sorriso d'innocenza' (*Il pirata*), also recorded 'live' at a recital in Amsterdam on 11 July 1959 and conducted by Rescigno with the Concertgebouw Orchestra.

The Rossini items, 'Nacqui all'affano ... Non più mesta' (*Cenerentola*), 'S'allontanaro alfine! ... Selva opaca' (*Guglielmo Tell*) and 'Bel raggio lusinghier' (*Semiramide*), were recorded in 1961–2, 1961 and 1960 respectively and conducted by Tonini with the Philharmonia Orchestra. They are markedly superior to the versions recorded in 1963–4 conducted by Rescigno with the Paris Conservatoire Orchestra inasmuch as Callas was vocally more secure, her voice having greater body to it.

The Verdi items, recorded in 1969 and conducted by Resigno with the Paris Opéra Orchestra, are different takes from those issued previously where, in fact, parts of some of the 1969 tapes were spliced into those of 1964.

These 1969 Verdi items, including Gizelda's prayer 'Te Vergin santa' (*I Lombardi*), 'Arrigo! ah parli' (*I vespri Siciliani*) and 'Liberamente or piangi' (*Attila*), demonstrate Callas's great effort to make the best of what amounted to a mere shadow of her once phenomenal vocal resources. She succeeds, relatively speaking, in producing a 'reconstructed' voice of sorts, interestingly and occasionally movingly used (for that matter, anything sung by Callas, even with a thread of a voice, had its moments), but it is a negative victory of art and almost superhuman determination over physical and perhaps psychological disability. The result not only has not added to the singer's reputation but has, to a certain extent, served to increase the number of her detractors, albeit those hearing her for the first time.

Even though a minute percentage of Callas's outstanding and manifold recorded legacy demonstrates the frailty of her vocal resources at the end of her career, it has misguidedly and disproportionately deterred a number of people from becoming acquainted with the artistry of the oustanding singing actress of the century.

Both the Rossini and Verdi items (studio recorded) of the present recording were not approved by Callas. They were issued posthumously in 1987 (the tenth anniversary of her death) fortunately and considerately for the artist on the same record with the three earlier, more representative 'live' performance items.

MASTER CLASSES: October–November 1971 and March–April 1972 – Juilliard School of Music, New York – EMI.

The twenty-three (forty-six hours) master classes were recorded and are preserved in music schools and libraries. The present commercial recording contains excerpts on 3 CDs.

Callas listened to her students' singing. She then discussed with them, as well as demonstrating by singing herself, various aspects of interpretation and technique.

Those items which Callas had recorded commercially (all except *Fidelio*, *Don Carlos* and *Rigoletto*) are included in full after each corresponding lesson. Additionally, it is of special interest to hear Callas, for the first time, during the lessons, in Leonore's aria in *Fidelio*, the baritone aria from *Rigoletto* and Eboli's (and Tebaldo's) music from *Don Carlos*.

Items included are:

'Crudele? ... Non mi dir' (*Don Giovanni*)

'Abscheulicher' (*Fidelio*)

'Dei tuoi figli' (*Medea*)

'Casta Diva' (*Norma*)

'Una voce poco fa' (*Il barbiere di Siviglia*)

'Cortigiani, vil razza dannata' (*Rigoletto*)

'Nel giardin del bello' (*Don Carlos*)

'Qui m'aurait dit ... Des cris joyeux' – Air des lettres (*Werther*)

'Sì, mi chiamano Mimì' (*La bohème*)

'Che tua madre' (*Madama Butterfly*)

Callas's farewell speech to her students.

Callas also recorded other various items which have also been posthumously released. These are: 'Non mi dir' (*Don Giovanni*), recorded as a test in Florence in August 1952 and conducted by Serafin with the Orchestra of the Maggio Musicale Fiorentino; 'D'amore al dolce impero' (*Armida*) and 'Arrigo! ah parli' (*I vespri Siciliani*) in July 1960, 'Com'è bello' (*Lucrezia Borgia*) and 'Come innocente giovane ... Leger potessi in me!' (*Anna Bolena*) in November 1961 and 'Nacqui all'affanno' (*Cenerentola*) and 'Ocean! Thou mighty monster' (*Oberon*) in April 1962, all conducted by Tonini with the Philharmonia Orchestra in London; 'D'amor sull'ali rosee' (*Il trovatore*) recorded in Paris in April 1964 and conducted by Rescigno with l'Orchestre de la Société des Concerts du Conservatoire Paris; a record (for Philips) of duets with di Stefano in London during November and December 1973 and conducted by Antonio de Almeida with the London Symphony Orchestra. This included 'Io vengo a domandar' (*Don Carlos*), 'Ah, per sempre, o mio bell'angiol' (*La forza del destino*), 'Gia nella notte densa' (*Otello*), 'Quale, o prode' (*I vespri Siciliani*), 'Una parola o Adina' (*L'elisir d'amore*) and an incomplete 'Pur ti riveggo' (*Aida*). Although Philips, respecting Callas's wishes, never issued the record, a 'pirated' version appeared.

A great number of 'pirate' recordings of Callas's 'live' performances have been issued first on tape then on LP and eventually on CD by various private companies often identified by no more than a few initials. Cetra, EMI, BJR and VERONA have also issued several of these recordings. The quality of sound varies, with those issued by EMI and BJR generally the most satisfactory. For fuller details of the recordings listed see chronology of performances.

Operas

AIDA: Bellas Artes, Mexico City, 8 June 1950 and 3 July 1951; Covent Garden, London, 4 June 1953.

ALCESTE: La Scala, Milan, 4 April 1954 (poor sound).

ANDREA CHENIER: La Scala, Milan, 8 January 1955.

ANNA BOLENA: La Scala, Milan, 14 April 1957, EMI.

ARMIDA: Comunale, Florence, 26 April 1952 (last act soprano–tenor duet missing).

UN BALLO IN MASCHERA: La Scala, Milan, 7 December 1957.

IL BARBIERE DI SIVIGLIA: La Scala, Milan, 16 February 1956.

IFIGENIA IN TAURIS: La Scala, Milan, 1 June 1957, EMI.

LUCIA DI LAMMERMOOR: Bellas Artes, Mexico City, 10 June 1952; La Scala, Milan, 18 January 1954; Stadtische Oper, Berlin, 29 September 1955, EMI; San Carlo, Naples, 22 March 1955; Metropolitan, New York, 8 December 1956; RAI, Rome, 26 June 1957.

MACBETH: La Scala, Milan, 7 December 1952, EMI.

MEDEA: La Scala, Milan, 10 December 1953; Civic Opera, Dallas, 6 November 1958; Covent Garden, London, 30 June 1959; La Scala, Milan, 11 December 1961.

NABUCCO: San Carlo, Naples, 20 December 1949.

NORMA: Bellas Artes, Mexico City, 23 May 1950; Covent Garden, London, 8 November 1952; Teatro Giuseppe Verdi, Trieste, 19 November 1953; RAI, Rome, 29 June 1955; La Scala, Milan, 7 December 1955; Opera, Rome, 2 January 1958 (Act I only); Paris Opéra, 25 June 1964, 14 and 17 May 1965 (Act 2 only), 21 May 1965 and 29 May 1965.

PARSIFAL: RAI, Rome, 20 and 21 (Parts I and II) November 1950.

IL PIRATA: Carnegie Hall, New York, 27 January 1959, EMI.

POLIUTO: La Scala, Milan, 7 December 1960, EMI.

I PURITANI: Bellas Artes, Mexico City, 29 May 1951.

RIGOLETTO: Bellas Artes, Mexico City, 17 June 1952.

LA SONNAMBULA: La Scala, Milan, 5 and 13 March 1955 (excerpts); Grosseshaus, Cologne, 4 July 1957; King's Theatre, Edinburgh, 21 and 26 August 1957.

TOSCA: Bellas Artes, Mexico City, 8 June 1950; Municipal, Rio de Janeiro, 24 September 1951 (incomplete); Bellas Artes, Mexico City, 1 July 1952; Covent Garden, London, 21 and 24 January 1964; Paris Opéra, 22 February 1, 3 and 13 March 1965 (mostly poor and uneven sound); Metropolitan, New York, 19 and 25 March 1965; Covent Gardens, London, 5 July 1965.

LA TRAVIATA: Bellas Artes, Mexico City, 17 July 1951 and 3 June 1952; La Scala, Milan, 28 May 1955, EMI and 19 January 1956; São Carlos, Lisbon, 27 March 1958, EMI; Covent Garden, London, 20 June 1958.

IL TROVATORE: Bellas Artes, Mexico City, 20 and 27 June 1950 (excerpts); San Carlo, Naples, 27 January 1951; La Scala, Milan, 23 February 1953.

TURANDOT: Colón, Buenos Aires, 20 May 1949 (Riddle Scene only).

LA VESTALE: La Scala, Milan, 7 December 1954.

I VESPRI SICILIANI: Communale, Florence, 26 May 1951, EMI.

A few other performances are known to have been preserved, but as yet have not been made available. These are: *Tristan und Isolde* (La Fenice, Venice, 1948 and Grattacielo, Genoa, 1948); *Die Walküre* (La Fenice, Venice, 1949); *I Puritani* (Communale, Florence, 1952); *Don Carlos* (La Scala, Milan, 1954) and *Fedora* (La Scala, Milan, 1956, very poor sound).

Concerts

RAI, Turin, 12 March 1951 (incomplete) and 18 February 1952.

RAI, San Remo, 27 December 1954.

RAI, Milan, 27 September 1956.

TV CBS, New York, 25 November 1956.

Herodes Atticus, Athens, 5 August 1957.

State Fair Music Hall, Dallas, 20 November 1957 (rehearsal for 21 November).

TV BBC, London, 7 June 1958 and 23 September 1958.

Paris Opéra, 19 December 1958.

Liederhalle, Stuttgart, 19 May 1959 and 23 May 1963.

Festival Hall, London, 23 September 1959 (poor sound and incomplete), 31 May 1963, 26 November 1973 and 2 December 1973.

ITV, London, 3 October 1959.

St James's Palace, London, 30 May 1961.

Musikhalle, Hamburg, 16 March 1962.

Madison Square Garden, New York, 19 May 1962 (poor sound).

ITV Covent Garden, London, 4 November 1962.

Deutsche Oper, Berlin, 17 May 1963.

Théatre des Champs-Elysées, Paris, 5 June 1963.

RTF-TV, Paris, 18 May 1965.

Congress Zentrum, Hamburg, 25 October 1973.

Philharmonie, Berlin, 29 October 1973.

Rheinhalle, Düsseldorf, 2 November 1973.

Deutsches Museum, Munich, 6 November 1973.

Jahrhundert Halle Höchst, Frankfurt, 9 November 1973.

NHK, Tokyo, 12 October 1974.

Fukuoka, Japan, 24 October 1974.

Sapporo, Japan, 11 November 1974.

Video Recordings

DÉBUTS À PARIS – 19 December 1958 – Live, Paris Opéra – EMI

Arrival at the Opéra

La forza del destino (Verdi): Overture.

Norma (Bellini): Act 1: 'Sediziose voci ... Casta Diva ... Fine al rito ... Ah! bello a me ritorna' with Mars (Oroveso).

Il trovatore (Verdi): Act 4: 'Vanne lasciami ... D'amor sull'ali rosee ... Miserere' with Lance (Manrico).

Il barbiere di Siviglia (Rossini): Overture. Act 1: 'Una voce poco fa'.

Tosca (Puccini): Act 2. With Gobbi (Scarpia), Rialland (Angelotti), Lance (Cavaradossi), Hurteau (Sciarrone). Sebastian conducting the Paris Opéra Orchestra and Chorus.

MARIA CALLAS IN CONCERT – 18 May 1959 – Live, Musikhalle, Hamburg – EMI

La vestale (Spontini): Act 2: 'Tu che invoco'.

Macbeth (Verdi): Act 1: 'Nel di della vittoria . . . Vieni, t'affretta'.

Il barbiere di Siviglia (Rossini): Act 1: 'Una voce poco fa'.

Don Carlos (Verdi): Act 4: 'Tu che le vanità'.

Il pirata (Bellini): Act 2: 'Oh! s'io potessi dissipar le nubi'.

Rescigno conducting the Symphonicorchester des NDR.

MARIA CALLAS IN CONCERT – 16 March 1962 – Live, Musikhalle, Hamburg – EMI

Le Cid (Massenet): Act 3: 'De cet affreux combat . . . Pleurez, mes yeux'.

Mireille (Gounod): Overture.

Carmen (Bizet): Prelude; Act 1: 'Habanera'; Act 3: Entr'acte; Act 1: 'Seguidilla'.

La forza del destino (Verdi): Overture.

Ernani (Verdi): Act 1: 'Surta è la notte . . . Ernani involami'.

La cenerentola (Rossini): Act 2: 'Nacqui all'affanno . . . Non più mesta'.

Don Carlos (Verdi): Act 3: 'O don fatale'.

Prêtre conducting the Symphonicorchester des NDR.

MARIA CALLAS AT COVENT GARDEN – Live, Covent Garden – EMI

Don Carlos (Verdi): Act 4: 'Tu che le vanità'.

Carmen (Bizet): Prelude; Act 1: 'Habanera'; Act 3: Entr'acte; Act 1: 'Seguidilla'.

Prêtre conducting the Orchestra and Chorus of the Royal Opera House, Covent Garden. *Golden Hour* – 4 September 1962.

Tosca (Puccini): Act 2. With Gobbi (Scarpia), Cioni (Cavaradossi), Bowman (Spoletta), Wicks (Sciarrone).

Cillario conducting the Orchestra and Chorus of the Royal Opera House, Covent Garden – filmed 9 February 1964.

CHRONOLOGY OF PERFORMANCES

Basically the annals of Maria Callas's performances have been assembled from the various theatres she appeared at, newspapers and magazines (*Opera* and *Discoteca*). However, in various instances even the annals of the theatres proved wrong because sometimes, especially in Italy, the announced dates are not met and the records not always amended accordingly (e.g. Callas's Italian début at the Arena di Verona). In such cases actual programmes of performances were the most reliable sources of information. These were usually kept by some theatres, fellow singers (neither Callas nor Meneghini kept any) who had appeared in the same performances, such as Silvio Maionica, Nicola Rossi-Lemeni, Mario Del Monaco, Tito Gobbi, Nicola Zaccaria and others, and members of the audience.

A certain amount of checking was done through some incomplete diaries which Meneghini kept after 1947. Callas herself was very helpful about the actual operas and even the other principals and conductors she sang with, but as her diary was even less complete than Meneghini's, she had no idea of exact dates.

The same applied to her performances in Greece. She could remember everything except actual dates and she had no diary. However, the discovery of programmes, the diaries of other Greek singers such as Antonis Dhellentas, the tenor of most of Callas's Greek performances, Nicola Zaccaria, who was then singing in the chorus of the Athens Opera, Elvira de Hidalgo and reviews in Greek newspapers and the German-language periodicals *Deutsche Nachrichten in Griechenland* and *Wiener Illustrierte* provided the information. But even programmes were sometimes misleading. For Callas's professional début (*Boccaccio*) I was previously misled in accepting 27 November 1940, as the programme of the performance owned by a member of the audience who had been present at Callas's appearance in *Boccaccio* carried this date in ink. This we now know to be definitely wrong. *Boccaccio* was first performed in Athens in January 1941.

For her student performances, Callas was again very vague about dates, but drew my attention to the existence of George Karakantas of Athens, a teacher of hers at the National Conservatory and opera producer, who in fact was most helpful, as were Elvira de Hidalgo and music critic Athena Spanoudi of Athens, whose mother had been one of the leading music critics in Greece during the 1940s. Moreover, Polyvios Marsan of Athens also researched Callas's chronology of performances in Greece.

In addition to what is documented, Hidalgo (and Callas herself) told me that Callas sang during her early years in Greece the soprano parts in Handel's *Messiah*, Pizzetti's *I tre canti Greci*, Bach's *St Matthew Passion*, Mozart's *Requiem* and Haydn's *Requiem*, but could not remember where or when and I have been unsuccessful in my research. It is also known that during these years Callas sang on the radio in Athens, but again nothing more has been discovered except that she sang duets with Arda Mandikian.

Callas's role is given after the title of the opera and an asterisk (*) indicates her first appearance in the role. First names of other members of the cast can be found in the index. c. denotes conductor, p. producer, d. designer. If two designers are given (d. & di.) the first refers to the stage sets and the second to the costumes. Producer and designer are given for new productions and in revivals when known to have existed.

A cross (†) after the date indicates that the performance exists on 'pirate' recording; a double cross (‡) that part of the performance has survived. A triangle (Δ) indicates that the quality of sound is very poor.

Student Performances

1938
Concert
'Leise, leise' (*Der Freischütz*)
'Plus grand, dans son obscurité' (*La Reine de Saba*
– Gounod)
'Two nights' – Greek song (Psaroudas)
'O dolci mani' (*Tosca*) with Cambanis.
Piano: Valtetsiotis.
National Conservatory (Ethnicon Odeon) at
Parnassus Hall, Athens.
April 11.

1939
* *Cavalleria rusticana*: (Santuzza)
Simiriotis (Turiddu), Kopanou (Mamma Lucia),
Athenaios (Alfio), Efthymiadou (Lola).
c. Vourtsis, p. Karakantas, d. Papadopoulou.
National Conservatory at Olympia Theatre,
Athens.
April 2, 9, 16.

Concert
'Belle nuit' – Barcarolle (*Les Contes d'Hoffmann*)
with Bourdakou.
'Ritorna vincitor' (*Aida*)
'I will not forget' – Greek song (Psaroudas)
'O terra addio' (*Aida*) with Cambanis
Piano: Valtetsiotis.
National Conservatory at Parnassus Hall,
Athens.
May 22.

Concert
'Ocean! Thou mighty monster' (*Oberon*)
'Ah! je suis seule' – air de mirroire (*Thaïs*)
Piano: Valtetsiotis.
National Conservatory at Parnassus Hall,
Athens.
May 23.

Concert
Un ballo in maschera: (Amelia) Act 3, Scene 1
Athenaios (Renato), Hoidas (Sam), Alimbrantis
(Tom)
Piano: Nicolaidi, p. Kiparissi.
Cavalleria rusticana: (Santuzza) Scene including
'Voi lo sapete' and Turiddu–Santuzza duet
Koronis (Turiddu), Sakellariou (Lola), Kopanou
(Mamma Lucia)
Piano: Nicolaidi, p. Karakantas.
National Conservatory at Olympia Theatre,
Athens.
June 25.

1940
Concert
'Mira o Norma' (*Norma*) with Mandikian
Piano: Koundouris.
Athens Conservatory (Odeon Athenon), Athens.
February 23.

Concert
Duets, possibly from *Norma*, *Aida* and *La Gioconda*
with Mandikian.
'Nacqui all'affanno' (*Cenerentola*)
Athens Radio.
April 3.

* *Suor Angelica*: (Angelica)
Efstratiadou (La zia principessa), Stroilain (La
Badessa), Constantinou (La Zelatrice),
Mandikian (La maestra delle novizie),
Zographou (Suor Genovieffa), Spavera (La suora
infermiera)
Piano: Koundouris, p. & d. Hidalgo.
Athens Conservatory, Athens.
June 16.

Professional Performances

1940

The Merchant of Venice (Shakespeare)
Minotis (Shylock), Papadaki (Portia),
Dendramis (Bassanio).

As the play was given with Humperdinck's incidental music and songs, Callas said, many years later, to Minotis (and once to me) that she had sung in the wings, dubbing Portia's song. Some have disputed this, merely on the strength that Papadaki had a good and well-trained singing voice and usually sang her songs herself in the plays in which she appeared. Though this was true, there are occasions when actors would not sing their own songs, however accomplished they are, because the production of the speaking voice is so different from that of singing and they may sometimes find the sudden change disconcerting, especially in Shakespearean verse.

It is also rather unlikely that Callas sang Jessica's song. If that were the case, she had no reason to say that she dubbed Portia's. She may, of course, not have sung it in all performances. Even so, memory is not always infallible.
Greek National Theatre, Athens.
October 21, 22, 23, 24, 27.

1941

* *Boccaccio*: (Beatrice)
Glynos (Boccaccio), Remoundou (Fiametta),
Horn (Prince Pedro), Ksirellis (Lotterighi)
c. Zoras, p. Mordo, d. Clonis, di. Fokas.
Athens Opera at Pallas Hall, Athens.

Callas did not sing in the first performance on 21 January, which was given in concert. Stage performances continued until 9 March. Most probably Callas, who shared the role with Ghalanou, sang in February and March.

Boccaccio: (Beatrice)
Glynos (Boccaccio), Remoundou (Fiametta),
Malliagros (Prince Pedro), Ksirellis (Lotterighi)
c. Zoras, p. Mordo, d. Clonis, di. Fokas.
Athens Opera at Park Theatre (open air),
Athens.
July 3, 4, 5 (two perfs), 6 (two perfs), 8, 9, 10,
11, 12 (two perfs), 13 (two perfs), 15.

1942

* *Tosca*: (Tosca)
Dhellentas/Kourousopoulos (Cavaradossi),
Ksirellis/Calogeras/Vasilakis (Scarpia)
c. Vassiliades, p. Yannopoulos, d. Clonis, di.
Fokas (Tosca's costumes by Zographos).
Athens Opera at Teatro Klathmonos Square.
August 27, 28, 30, September 2 & 4 & 6
(Calogeras), 8 (in Italian) & 10 & 12 & 13 & 16
& 18 & 20 & 22 & 24 & 26 & 27 & 30
(Kourousopoulos, Vasilakis).

Concert

Rossini arias, duets and songs with Epitropakis,
Papanastassiou, Flery, Calogeras
Pianist/conductor: Parides.

Concert given for 150th anniversary of Rossini's birth organised by the Italian military authorities of occupation at Cinema Pallas, Salonika.
October.

1943

Ho Protomastoras
Callas sang in the intermezzo between the first and second act of the opera with Nikita, Damashioti, Zographou, Kokkori, Kolassi, Kourahani
c. Zoras.
Athens Opera at National Theatre, Athens.

February 19, 21, 23, 26, 27, March 2, 5, 6, 11, 13, 16, 20.

Concert
with Epitropakis, Angelopoulos and others
Music unknown.
  Benefit concert in aid of students' soup-kitchen in Nea Smirni, Athens.
Sporting cinema in Nea Smirni, Athens.
February 28.

* *Stabat Mater* (Oratorio by Pergolesi): (Soprano)
Mandikian (contralto)
c. Lykoudis.
Italian Institute of Culture for Greece (Casa d'Italia), Athens. The performance was broadcast live.
April 22.

Tosca: (Tosca)
Dhellentas (Cavaradossi), Ksirellis (Scarpia)
c. Vassiliades, p. Yannopoulos, d. Clonis, di. Fokas (Tosca's costumes by Zographos).
Athens Opera at Teatro Klathmonos Square.
July 17, 21, 25.

Concert
'Care Selve' (*Atalanta* – Handel)
'Nacqui all'affanno' (*Cenerentola*)
'Poveri fiori' (*Adriana Lecouvreur*)
'D'amor sull'ali rosee' (*Trovatore*)
'They are marrying my love' – Greek song (Lavda)
Piano: Parides.
Teatro Costa Mousouri (open air), Athens.
July 21.

Concert
Arias by Rossini including
Desdemona's 'Assisa a piè d'un salice' (*Otello*)
Othello's 'Ah! si, per voi già sento' (*Otello*)
'Inflammatus et Accensus' (*Stabat Mater*).
Teatro White Tower, Salonika.
August 2.

Concert
Lieder by Schubert and Brahms.
Teatro White Tower, Salonika.
August 3.

Concert
'Abscheulicher!' (*Fidelio*)
'Ah! je suis seule' – air de mirroire (*Thaïs*)
'Ritorna vincitor' (*Aida*)
'Et incarnatus est' (Mozart)
'Canciones español' (Turina)
'They are marrying my love' – Greek song (Lavda)
Piano: Ghythoniatis.
  In aid of Greek Egyptian students in Athens.
Olympia Theatre, Athens.
September 26.

Concert
'Abscheulicher!' (*Fidelio*)
'Bel raggio' (*Semiramide*)
'D'amor sull'ali rosee' (*Trovatore*)
'Canciones español' (Turina)
Pianist/conductor: Androutsopoulos.
  In aid of tuberculous employees.
Teatro Kotopoulli-Rex.
December 12.

1944
* *Tiefland*: (Marta)
Dhellentas (Pedro), Mangliveras (Sebastiano), Vlachopoulos/Papadopoulou (Nuri), Remoundou (Pepa), Moulas (Tommaso)
c. Zoras, p. Mordo, d. Zographos.
Athens Opera at Olympia Theatre, Athens.
April 22, 23, 25, 27, 30, May 4 & 7 & 10 (Papadopoulou).

Cavalleria rusticana: (Santuzza)
Dhellentas (Turiddu), Tsoumbris (Alfio), Bourdakou (Mamma Lucia), Kourahani (Lola)
c. Karalivanos, p. Mordo, d. Zographos.

Athens Opera at Olympia Theatre, Athens.
May 6, 19?, 28?.

Concert
'Casta Diva' (*Norma*)
c. Zoras.
    In aid of poor artists.
Athens Opera at Olympia Theatre, Athens. Also broadcast German Radio Station, Athens.
May 21.

* *Ho Protomastoras*: (Smaragda)
Dhellentas (Protomastoras),
Mangliveras/Athenaios (Rich Man), Ghalanou (The Singer), Bourdakou (The Old Woman)
c. Kalomiris, p. Karantinos, d. Clonis, di. Zographos.
Athens Opera at Herodes Atticus Theatre, Athens.
July 30, August 5 (Athenaios).

* *Fidelio*: (Leonore)
Dhellentas (Florestan), Vlachopoulos (Marzelline), Mangliveras (Pizarro), Generalis (Don Fernando), Moulas (Rocco), Kokolios (Jacquino)
c. Hörner, p. Walleck, d. Clonis.
Athens Opera at Herodes Atticus Theatre, Athens.
August 14, 15, 17, 22, 25, 31, September 1, 3, 6, 7, 9, 10.

Concert
    Concert for troops.
Music unknown.
Salonika.
October.

1945
Tiefland: (Marta)
Dhellentas (Pedro), Mangliveras (Sebastiano), Vlachopoulos (Nuri), Remoundou (Pepa),

Moulas (Tommaso)
c. Zoras, p. Mordo, d. Zographos.
Athens Opera at Olympia Theatre, Athens.
March 14, 15, 24.

Concert
English songs:
'Willow-willow' – Desdemona's song (Anon)
'Love, I have won you' (Ronald)
Song cycle *On Wenlock Edge* (Vaughan Williams)
    1. On Wenlock Edge
    2. From far, from eve and morning
    3. Is my team ploughing
    4. Oh, when I was in love with you
    5. Bredon Hill
    6. Clun
with quintet accompaniment.
c. Karalivanos.
    English Musical Afternoon for British troops.
Athens Opera at Olympia Theatre, Athens.
March 20.

Concert
'Batti, batti, o bel Masetto' (*Don Giovanni*)
'Bel raggio' (*Semiramide*)
'Ritorna vincitor' (*Aida*)
'D'amor sull'ali rosee' (*Trovatore*)
'Ocean! Thou mighty monster' (*Oberon*)
'Spanish Popular Songs' (Granados)
Greek Folk Songs (Kariotaki and Poniridi)
Piano: Aliki Lykoudi.
Teatro Kotopoulli-Rex, Athens.
August 3.

* *Der Bettelstudent*: (Laura)
Koronis (Simon), Damashioti (Palmatica), Papadopoulou (Bronislava), Epitropakis (Ollendorf), Kazantzis (Casimir)
c. Evangelatos, p. Mordo, d. Anemoyiannis.
Athens Opera at Teatro Alexandras Avenue, Athens.
September 5, 6, 7, 8, 9, 11, 12, 13.

1947
* *La Gioconda*: (Gioconda)
Nicolai (Laura), Canali (Cieca), Tucker (Enzo),
Tagliabue (Barnaba), Rossi-Lemeni (Alvise)
c. Serafin, p. Cardi, d. Cardi, di. Grappelli e
Calisti.
Arena di Verona.
August 3, 5, 10, 14, 17.

* *Tristan und Isolde*: (Isolde)
Barbieri (Brangaene), Tasso (Tristan), Torres
(Kurwenal), Christoff (King Marke)
c. Serafin, p. Frigerio.
La Fenice, Venice.
December 30, January (1948) 3, 8, 11.

1948
* *Turandot*: (Turandot)
Soler (Calaf), Rizzieri (Liù), Carmassi (Timur)
c. Sanzogno, p. Frigerio.
La Fenice, Venice.
January 29, 31, February 3, 8, 10.

Turandot: (Turandot)
Soler (Calaf), Ottani (Liù), Maionica (Timur)
c. de Fabritiis, p. Cardi.
Teatro Puccini, Udine.
March 12, 14.

* *La forza del destino*: (Leonora)
Vertecchi (Don Alvaro), Franci (Don Carlo),
Siepi (Padre Guardiano), Canali (Preziosilla),
Serpo (Fra Melitone)
c. Parenti.
Politeama Rossetti, Trieste.
April 17, 20, 21, 25.

Tristan und Isolde: (Isolde)
Lorenz (Tristan), Nicolai (Brangaene), Torres
(Kurwenal), Rossi-Lemeni (King Marke)
c. Serafin, p. Cardi.
Teatro Grattacielo, Genoa.
May 12, 14, 16.

Turandot: (Turandot)
Masini (Calaf), Montanari (Liù), Flamini
(Timur)
c. de Fabritiis, p. Frigerio, d. Benois.
Terme di Caracalla, Rome.
July 4, 6, 11

Turandot: (Turandot)
Salvarezza (Calaf), Rizzieri/Tognoli/de Cecco
(Liù), Rossi-Lemeni (Timur)
c. Votto, p. Salvini, d. Casarini.
Arena di Verona.
July 27, August 1 (Tognoli), August 5 & 9 (de
Cecco).

Turandot: (Turandot)
Del Monaco (Calaf), Montanari (Liù),
Maionica (Timur)
c. Questa.
Carlo Felice, Genoa.
August 11, 14.

* *Aida*: (Aida)
Turrini (Radames), Nicolai/Colasanti
(Amneris), de Falchi (Amonasro)
c. Serafin.
Teatro Lirico, Turin.
September 18, 19 (Colasanti), 23, 25
(Colasanti).

Aida: (Aida)
Turrini (Radames), Pirazzini (Amneris), Viaro
(Amonasro)
c. Berrettoni, p. Cardi, d. Sormani, di. Chiappa.
Teatro Sociale, Rovigo.
October 19, 21, 24.

* *Norma*: (Norma)
Picchi (Pollione), Barbieri (Adalgisa), Siepi
(Oroveso), Danieli (Clotilde)
c. Serafin, p. Bassi, d. Benois.
Comunale, Florence.
November 30, December 5.

1949

* Die Walküre: (Brünnhilde)
Voyer (Sigmund), Torres (Wotan), Magnoni (Sieglinde), Pini (Fricka), Dominici (Hunding)
c. Serafin, p. Cardi.
La Fenice, Venice.
January 8, 12, 14, 16.

* I Puritani: (Elvira)
Pirino (Arturo), Savarese (Riccardo), Christoff (Giorgio), Masini (Enrichetta), Maionica (Gualtiero)
c. Serafin, p. Cardi.
La Fenice, Venice.
January 19, 22, 23.

Die Walküre: (Brünnhilde)
Voyer (Sigmund), Neri (Wotan), Magnoni (Sieglinde), Cabrera (Fricka), Carmassi (Hunding)
c. Molinari-Pradelli.
Massimo, Palermo.
January 29, February 10.

Turandot: (Turandot)
Laczò (Calaf), Montanari (Liù), Petri (Timur)
c. Perlea, p. Scafa, d. Cristini.
San Carlo, Naples.
February 12, 16, 18, 20.

* Parsifal: (Kundry)
Beirer (Parsifal), Siepi (Guernemanz), Cortis (Amfortas), Dadò (Klingsor)
c. Serafin, p. Duhan, d. Mancini.
Opera, Rome.
February 26, March 2, 5, 8.

Concert
'Liebestod' (*Tristan*)
'Casta Diva' (*Norma*)
'Qui la voce' (*Puritani*)
'O patria mia' (*Aida*)

c. Molinari-Pradelli.
RAI, Turin.
March 7.

Turandot: (Turandot)
Del Monaco (Calaf), Arizmendi (Liù), Zanin/Rossi-Lemeni (Timur)
c. Serafin, p. Erhardt, d. Chini, di. Magnoni.
Colón, Buenos Aires.
May 20‡, 29 (Rossi-Lemeni), June 11, 22.

Norma: (Norma)
Vela (Pollione), Barbieri (Adalgisa), Rossi-Lemeni (Oroveso)
c. Serafin, p. Piccinato, d. Ortolani.
Colón, Buenos Aires.
June 17‡, 19, 25, 29.

Aida: (Aida)
Vela (Radames), Barbieri (Amneris), Damiani (Amonasro), Rossi-Lemeni (Ramphis)
c. Serafin, p. Basaldúa, d. Ortolani.
Colón, Buenos Aires.
July 2.

Concert (*Norma* and *Turandot*):
'Casta Diva' with Rossi-Lemeni (Oroveso)
Act 3 *Turandot* with Del Monaco (Calaf), Arizmendi (Liù), Rossi-Lemeni (Timur)
c. Serafin.
Colón, Buenos Aires.
July 9.

San Giovanni Battista (Oratorio by Stradella): (Herod's daughter)
Pirazzini (St John the Baptist), Siepi (Herod), Berdini (The Councillor), Corsi (Herod's mother)
c. Santini.
Chiesa di San Pietro, Perugia.
September 18.

* Nabucco: (Abigaille)
Bechi (Nabucco), Sinimbergi (Ismaele), Neroni
(Zaccaria), Pini (Fenena)
c. Gui, p. Brissoni, d. Sormani.
San Carlo, Naples.
December 20†, 22, 27.

1950
Norma: (Norma)
Penno (Pollione), Nicolai (Adalgisa), Pasero
(Oroveso)
c. Votto, p. Cardi.
La Fenice, Venice.
January 13, 15, 19.

Aida: (Aida)
Del Monaco (Radames), Pini (Amneris), Protti
(Amonasro), Feliciati (Ramphis)
c. Erede.
Teatro Grande, Brescia.
February 2, 7.

Tristan und Isolde: (Isolde)
Seider (Tristan), Nicolai (Brangaene), Franci
(Kurwenal), Neri/Neroni (King Marke)
c. Serafin, p. Frigerio, d. Preetorius.
Opera, Rome.
February 6, 9, 19, 25, 28 (Neroni).

Norma: (Norma)
Masini (Pollione), Stignani (Adalgisa),
Neri/Cassinelli (Oroveso)
c. Serafin, p. Sanine, d. Benois.
Opera, Rome.
February 23, 26, March 2, 4, 7 (Cassinelli).

Concert
'Ocean! Thou mighty monster' (*Oberon*)
'Ah! fors'è lui' and 'Sempre libera' (*Traviata*)
'D'amor sull'ali rosee' (*Trovatore*)
'Ombra leggiera' (*Dinorah*)
c. Simonetto.

RAI, Turin.
March 13.

Norma: (Norma)
Picchi (Pollione), Gardino (Adalgisa), Stefanoni
(Oroveso)
c. Berrettoni.
Massimo Bellini, Catania.
March 16, 19, 22, 25.

Aida: (Aida)
Del Monaco (Radames), Barbieri (Amneris), de
Falchi/Protti (Amonasro)
c. Capuana.
La Scala, Milan.
April 12, 15, 18 (Protti).

Aida: (Aida)
Picchi (Radames), Stignani (Amneris), Savarese
(Amonasro)
c. Serafin, p. Scafa, d. Cristini.
San Carlo, Naples.
April 27, 30, May 2, 4.

Norma: (Norma)
Baum (Pollione), Simionato (Adalgisa),
Moscona (Oroveso)
c. Picco.
Bellas Artes, Mexico City.
May 23†, 27.

Aida: (Aida)
Baum/Filippeschi (Radames), Simionato
(Amneris), Weede (Amonasro)
c. Mugnai.
Bellas Artes, Mexico City.
May 30†, June 3, 15 (Filippeschi).

Tosca: (Tosca)
Filippeschi (Cavaradossi), Weede (Scarpia)
c. Mugnai.
Bellas Artes, Mexico City.
June 8†, 10.

522

Il trovatore: (Leonora)
Baum (Manrico), Simionato (Azucena),
Warren/Petroff (di Luna), Moscona (Ferrando)
c. Picco.
Bellas Artes, Mexico City.
June 20†, 24, 27‡ (Petroff).

Tosca: (Tosca)
Inghilleri (Cavaradossi), Pelizzoni (Scarpia)
c. Questa.
Salsomaggiore.
September 22.

Tosca: (Tosca)
Turrini (Cavaradossi), Azzolini (Scarpia)
c. Questa.
Teatro Duse, Bologna.
September 24.

Aida: (Aida)
Picchi (Radames), Stignani (Amneris), de Falchi
(Amonasro)
c. Bellezza, p. Azzolini, d. Benois.
Opera, Rome.
October 2.

Tosca: (Tosca)
Masini (Cavaradossi), Poli (Scarpia)
c. Santarelli.
Teatro Verdi, Pisa.
October 7, 8.

Il Turco in Italia: (Fiorilla)
Bruscantini (Selim), Calabrese (Geronio), Valletti
(Narciso), Canali (Zaida), Stabile (Prosdocimo)
c. Gavazzeni, p. Guerrieri.
Teatro Eliseo, Rome.
October 19, 22, 25, 29.

Parsifal: (Kundry)
Baldelli (Parsifal), Christoff (Gurnemanz),
Panerai (Amfortas), Modesti (Klingsor)

c. Gui.
RAI, Rome.
November 20† (Act 1), 21† (Acts 2 and 3).

1951
La traviata: (Violetta)
Albanese (Alfredo), Mascherini (Germont)
c. Serafin, p. Bassi, d. Vagnetti.
Comunale, Florence.
January 14, 16, 20.

Il trovatore: (Leonora)
Lauri-Volpi/Vertecchi (Manrico), Elmo
(Azucena), Silveri (di Luna), Tajo (Ferrando)
c. Serafin.
San Carlo, Naples.
January 27†, 30, February 1 (Vertecchi).

Norma: (Norma)
Gavarini (Pollione), Nicolai (Adalgisa), Neri
(Oroveso)
c. Ghione.
Massimo, Palermo.
February 15, 20.

Aida: (Aida)
Soler (Radames), Pirazzini (Amneris), Manca-
Serra (Amonasro)
c. Del Cupolo.
Comunale, Reggio, Calabria.
February 28.

Concert
'Ma dall'arido' (*Ballo*)‡
'Io son Titania' (*Mignon*)‡
Variations by Proch on 'Deh torna mio ben'†
'Leise, leise' (*Freischütz*)
c. Wolf-Ferrari.,
RAI, Turin.
March 12.

La traviata: (Violetta)
Campora (Alfredo), Poli (Germont)

c. Molinari-Pradelli.
Massimo, Cagliari.
March 14, 18.

Concert
'Casta Diva' (*Norma*)
'Qui la voce' (*Puritani*)
'O patria mia' (*Aida*)
'Ah! fors'è lui' and 'Sempre libera' (*Traviata*)
c. La Rosa Parodi.
Teatro Giuseppe Verdi, Trieste.
April 21.

* *I vespri Siciliani*: (Elena)
Bardi-Kokolios (Arrigo), Mascherini
(Monforte), Christoff (Procida)
c. Kleiber, p. Graf, d. Vagnetti.
Comunale, Florence.
May 26†, 30, June 2, 5.

* *Orfeo ed Euridice*, Haydn: (Euridice)
Tygesen (Orfeo), Christoff (Creonte)
c. Kleiber, p. Salvini, d. Coltelacci.
Pergola, Florence (world stage première).
June 9, 10.

Concert
'Casta Diva' (*Norma*)
'Ombra leggiera' (*Dinorah*)
'O patria mia' (*Aida*)
Variations by Proch on 'Deh torna mio ben'
'Je suis Titania' (*Mignon*)
'Ah! fors'è lui' and 'Sempre libera' (*Traviata*)
Piano: Bartoletti.
Grand Hotel, Florence.
June 11.

Aida: (Aida)
Del Monaco (Radames), Dominguez (Amneris),
Taddei (Amonasro)
c. de Fabritiis.
Bellas Artes, Mexico City.
July 3†, 7, 10.

Concert
'Pace, pace mio Dio' (*Forza*)
'Morrò, ma prima in grazia' (*Ballo*)
c. de Fabritiis.
Radio, Mexico City.
July 15.

La traviata: (Violetta)
Valletti (Alfredo), Taddei/Morelli (Germont)
c. de Fabritiis.
Palacio de las Bellas Artes, Mexico City.
July 17†, 19, 21, 22 (Morelli).

Norma: (Norma)
Picchi (Pollione), Barbieri (Adalgisa), Rossi-
Lemeni (Oroveso)
c. Votto.
Municipal, São Paulo, Brazil.
September 7.

La traviata: (Violetta)
di Stefano (Alfredo), Gobbi (Germont)
c. Serafin.
Municipal, São Paulo, Brazil.
September 9.

Norma: (Norma)
Picchi (Pollione), Nicolai (Adalgisa), Christoff
(Oroveso)
c. Votto.
Municipal, Rio de Janeiro.
September 12, 16.

Concert
'Sempre libera' (*Traviata*).
c. Votto.
    Red Cross Benefit.
Municipal, Rio de Janeiro.
September 14.

Tosca: (Tosca)
Poggi (Cavaradossi), Silveri (Scarpia)

c. Votto.
Municipal, Rio de Janeiro.
September 24.

La traviata: (Violetta)
Poggi (Alfredo), Salsedo (Germont)
c. Gaioni.
Municipal, Rio de Janeiro.
September 28, 30.

La traviata: (Violetta)
Prandelli (Alfredo), Fabbri (Germont)
c. Giulini
Teatro Donizetti, Bergamo.
October 20, 23.

Norma: (Norma)
Penno (Pollione), Simionato (Adalgisa),
Christoff/Wolowski (Oroveso)
c. Ghione.
Massimo Bellini, Catania.
November 3, 6, 17, 20 (Wolowski).

I Puritani: (Elvira)
Wenkow (Arturo), Tagliabue (Riccardo),
Christoff (Giorgio)
c. Wolf-Ferrari.
Massimo Bellini, Catania.
November 8, 11, 13, 16.

I vespri Siciliani: (Elena)
Conley (Arrigo), Mascherini (Monforte),
Christoff (Procida)
c. De Sabata/Quadri, p. Graf, d. Benois.
La Scala, Milan.
December 7, 9, 12, 16, 19, 27 (Quadri), January
3 (1952).

La traviata: (Violetta)
Pola (Alfredo), Savarese (Germont)
c. de Fabritiis.
Teatro Regio, Parma.
December 29.

1952
I Puritani: (Elvira)
Conley (Arturo), Tagliabue (Riccardo), Rossi-
Lemeni (Giorgio)
c. Serafin, p. Frigerio, d. Benois.
Comunale, Florence.
January 9, 11.

Norma: (Norma)
Penno (Pollione), Stignani (Adalgisa), Rossi-
Lemeni (Oroveso)
c. Ghione, p. Frigerio, d. Marchioro.
La Scala, Milan.
January 16, 19, 23, 27, 29, February 2, 7, 10.

Concert
'Vieni! t'affretta!' (*Macbeth*)
'Ardon gli incensi' Mad scene (*Lucia*)
'Anch'io dischiuso' (*Nabucco*)
'Dov'è l'Indiana bruna' – Bell Song (*Lakmé*)
c. de Fabritiis.
RAI, Rome.
February 18†.

La traviata: (Violetta)
Filacuridi (Alfredo), Mascherini (Germont)
c. Molinari-Pradelli, p. Moresco.
Massimo Bellini, Catania.
March 8, 12, 14, 16.

* *Die Entführung aus dem Serail*: (Constanze)
Menotti/Duval (Bionda), Munteanu (Pedrillo),
Prandelli (Belmonte), Baccaloni (Osmin),
Bernardi (Selim)
c. Perlea, p. Giannini, d. Fini.
La Scala, Milan.
April 2, 5, 7 & 9 (Duval).

* *Armida*: (Armida)
Albanese (Rinaldo), Ziliani (Goffredo),
Salvarezza (Eustazio), Filippeschi (Germando
and Ubaldo), Raimondi (Carlo)

c. Serafin, p. & d. Savigno.
Comunale, Florence.
April 26‡, 29, May 4.

I Puritani: (Elvira)
Lauri-Volpi/Pirino (Arturo), Silveri (Riccardo),
Neri (Giorgio)
c. Santini, p. Frigerio, d. Benois.
Opera, Rome.
May 2, 6, 11 (Pirino).

I Puritani: (Elvira)
di Stefano (Arturo), Campolonghi (Riccardo),
Silva (Giorgio)
c. Picco.
Bellas Artes, Mexico City.
May 29†, 31.

La traviata: (Violetta)
di Stefano (Alfredo), Campolonghi (Germont)
c. Mugnai
Bellas Artes, Mexico City.
June 3†, 7.

* *Lucia di Lammermoor*: (Lucia)
di Stefano (Edgardo), Campolonghi (Enrico),
Silva (Raimondo)
c. Picco.
Bellas Artes, Mexico City.
June 10†, 14, 26.

* *Rigoletto*: (Gilda)
di Stefano (Duke), Campolonghi (Rigoletto),
Garcia (Maddalena), Ruffino (Sparafucile)
c. Mugnai.
Bellas Artes, Mexico City.
June 17†, 21.

Tosca: (Tosca)
di Stefano (Cavaradossi), Campolonghi
(Scarpia)
c. Picco.

Bellas Artes, Mexico City.
June 28†, July 1.

La Gioconda: (Gioconda)
Poggi (Enzo), Nicolai (Laura), Inghilleri
(Barnaba), Tajo (Alvise), Canali (Ciecca)
c. Votto, p. Moresco, d. Filippini.
Arena di Verona.
July 19, 23.

La traviata: (Violetta)
Campora (Alfredo), Mascherini (Germont)
c. Molinari-Pradelli, p. Cardi, d. Filippini.
Arena di Verona.
August 2, 5, 10, 14.

Norma: (Norma)
Picchi (Pollione), Stignani (Adalgisa), Vaghi
(Oroveso), Sutherland (Clotilde)
c. Gui/Pritchard, p. Enriquez, d. Barlowe.
Covent Garden, London.
November 8, 10, 13 (Pritchard), 18†, 20.

* *Macbeth*: (Lady Macbeth)
Mascherini (Macbeth), Penno (Macduff),
Tajo/Modesti (Banquo)
c. De Sabata, p. Ebert, d. Benois.
La Scala, Milan.
December 7†, 9, 11 (Modesti), 14, 17
(Modesti).

La Gioconda: (Gioconda)
di Stefano (Enzo), Stignani (Laura), Tagliabue
(Barnaba), Tajo/Modesti (Alvise)
c. Votto, p. Frigerio, d. Benois.
La Scala, Milan.
December 26, 28, 30, January 1, 3 (1953),
February 19 (Modesti).

1953
La traviata: (Violetta)
Albanese (Alfredo), Mascherini/Tagliabue

(Germont)
c. Questa, p. Marchioro, d. Benois.
La Fenice, Venice.
January 8, 10 (Tagliabue).

Lucia di Lammermoor: (Lucia)
Lauri-Volpi/di Stefano (Edgardo), Bastianini (Enrico), Arie (Raimondo)
c. Ghione, p. Marchioro, d. Benois.
Comunale, Florence.
January 25, 28, February 5, 8 (di Stefano).

Il trovatore: (Leonora)
Penno (Manrico), Stignani (Azucena), Tagliabue (di Luna), Modesti (Ferrando)
c. Votto, p. Frigerio, d. Benois.
La Scala, Milan.
February 23†, 26, 28, March 24, 29.

Norma: (Norma)
Corelli (Pollione), Barbieri (Adalgisa), Neri (Oroveso)
c. Santini, p. Piccinato, d. Benois.
Opera, Rome.
April 9, 12, 15, 18.

Lucia di Lammermoor: (Lucia)
Turrini (Edgardo), Taddei (Enrico), Arie (Raimondo)
c. de Fabritiis.
Massimo Bellini, Catania.
April 21, 23.

* *Medea:* (Medea)
Guichandut (Jason), Barbieri (Neris), Petri (Creon), Tucci (Glauce)
c. Gui, p. Barsacq, d. Coutaud.
Comunale, Florence.
May 7, 10, 12.

Lucia di Lammermoor: (Lucia)
Poggi (Edgardo), Guelfi (Enrico), Cassinelli

(Raimondo)
c. Gavazzeni.
Opera, Rome.
May 19, 21, 24.

Aida: (Aida)
Baum (Radames), Simionato (Amneris), Walters (Amonasro)
c. Barbirolli, p. Benthall, d. Cruddas.
Covent Garden, London.
June 4‡, 6, 10†.

Norma: (Norma)
Picchi (Pollione), Simionato (Adalgisa), Neri (Oroveso)
c. Pritchard.
Covent Garden, London.
June 15, 17, 20, 23.

Il trovatore: (Leonora)
Johnston (Manrico), Simionato (Azucena), Walters (di Luna), Langdon (Ferrando)
c. Erede, p. Gellner, d. Hill.
Covent Garden, London.
June 26, 29, July 1.

Aida: (Aida)
Del Monaco/Filippeschi/Zambruno (Radames), Nicolai/Pirazzini (Amneris), Protti/Malaspina (Amonasro)
c. Serafin/Ghione, p. Pabst, d. Lolli.
Arena di Verona.
July 23, 25, 27 (Filippeschi), 30, August 8 (Zambruno, Pirazzini, Malaspina, Ghione).

Il trovatore: (Leonora)
Zambruno (Manrico), Danieli (Azucena), Protti (di Luna), Maionica (Ferrando)
c. Molinari-Pradelli.
Arena di Verona.
August 15.

Norma: (Norma)
Corelli (Pollione), Nicolai (Adalgisa), Christoff (Oroveso)
c. Votto.
Teatro Giuseppe Verdi, Trieste.
November 19†, 22, 23, 29.

Medea: (Medea)
Penno (Jason), Modesti (Creon), Barbieri (Neris), Nache (Glauce)
c. Bernstein, p. Wallmann, d. Fiume.
La Scala, Milan.
December 10†, 12, 29, January (1954) 2, 6.

Il trovatore: (Leonora)
Lauri-Volpi (Manrico), Pirazzini (Azucena), Silveri (di Luna), Neri (Ferrando)
c. Santini, p. Frigerio, d. Furiga.
Opera, Rome.
December 16, 19, 23.

1954
Lucia di Lammermoor: (Lucia)
di Stefano/Poggi (Edgardo), Panerai (Enrico), Modesti (Raimondo)
c. & p. Karajan, d. Ratto.
La Scala, Milan.
January 18†, 21, 24, 27, 31, February 5, 7 (Poggi).

Lucia di Lammermoor: (Lucia)
Infantino (Edgardo), Bastianini/Maero (Enrico), Tozzi (Raimondo)
c. Questa, p. Cardi, d. Scaioli.
La Fenice, Venice.
February 13, 16, 21 (Maero).

Medea: (Medea)
Gavarini (Jason), Tozzi (Creon), Pirazzini (Neris), Tucci (Glauce)
c. Gui, p. Maestrini, d. Coutaud.
La Fenice, Venice.
March 2, 4, 7.

Tosca: (Tosca)
Ortica (Cavaradossi), Guelfi (Scarpia)
c. Ghione.
Carlo Felice, Genoa.
March 10, 15, 17.

* *Alceste*: (Alceste)
Gavarini (Admeto), Silveri (High Priest), Panerai (Apollo), Zaccaria (Oracle)
c. Giulini, p. Wallmann, d. Zuffi.
La Scala, Milan.
April 4†Δ, 6, 15, 20.

* *Don Carlos*: (Elisabetta)
Ortica (Don Carlos), Rossi-Lemeni (King Philip), Stignani (Eboli), Mascherini/Silveri (Rodrigo)
c. Votto, d. Benois.
La Scala, Milan.
April 12, 17, 23, 25 & 27 (Silveri).

La forza del destino: (Leonora)
Del Monaco (Don Alvaro), Protti (Don Carlos), Modesti (Padre Guardiano), Gardino (Preziosilla)
c. Ghione.
Teatro Alighieri, Ravenna.
May 23, 26.

* *Mefistofele*: (Margherita)
Tagliavini/di Stefano (Faust), Rossi-Lemeni (Mefistofele), de Cecco/Cavalieri (Elena)
c. Votto, p. Graf, d. Cristini.
Arena di Verona.
July 15, 20 (di Stefano, Cavalieri), 25 (Cavalieri).

Lucia di Lammermoor: (Lucia)
Tagliavini (Edgardo), Savarese (Enrico), Maionica (Raimondo)
c. Molinari-Pradelli.
Teatro Donizetti, Bergamo.
October 6, 9.

Norma: (Norma)
Picchi (Pollione), Simionato (Adalgisa), Rossi-Lemeni (Oroveso)
c. Rescigno.
Lyric Theater, Chicago.
November 1, 5.

La traviata: (Violetta)
Simoneau (Alfredo), Gobbi (Germont)
c. Rescigno.
Lyric Theater, Chicago.
November 8, 12.

Lucia di Lammermoor: (Lucia)
di Stefano (Edgardo), Guelfi (Enrico), Stewart (Raimondo)
c. Rescigno.
Lyric Theater, Chicago.
November 15, 17.

* *La Vestale*: (Giulia)
Corelli (Licinio), Stignani (High Priestess), Rossi-Lemeni (High Priest), Sordello (Cinna), Zaccaria (Aruspice)
c. Votto, p. Visconti, d. Zuffi.
La Scala, Milan.
December 7†, 9, 12, 16, 18.

Concert
'Martern aller Arten' – 'Tutte le torture' (*Entführung*)
'Ombra leggera' (*Dinorah*)
'Depuis le jour' (*Louise*)
'D'amor al dolce impero' (*Armida*)
c. Simonetto.
RAI, San Remo.
December 27†.

1955
* *Andrea Chénier*: (Maddalena)
Del Monaco/Ortica (Chenier), Protti/Taddei (Gerard)

c. Votto, p. Frigerio, d. Benois.
La Scala, Milan.
January 8†, 10, 13, 16, February 3, & 6 (Ortica, Taddei).

Medea: (Medea)
Albanese (Jason), Christoff (Creon), Barbieri (Neris), Tucci (Glauce)
c. Santini, p. Wallmann, d. Fiume.
Opera, Rome.
January 22, 27, 30.

* *La sonnambula*: (Amina)
Valletti (Elvino), Modesti/Zaccaria (Rodolfo), Ratti (Lisa)
c. Bernstein, p. Visconti, d. Tosi.
La Scala, Milan.
March 5†, 8, 13‡, 16, 18, 24 & 30 (Zaccaria), April 12, 24, 27.

Il Turco in Italia: (Fiorilla)
Rossi-Lemeni (Selim), Calabrese (Geronio), Valletti (Narciso), Gardino (Zaida), Stabile (Prosdocimo)
c. Gavazzeni, p. & d. Zeffirelli.
La Scala, Milan.
April 15, 18, 21, 23, May 4.

La traviata: (Violetta)
di Stefano/Prandelli (Alfredo), Bastianini (Germont)
c. Giulini, p. Visconti, d. de Nobili.
La Scala, Milan.
May 28†, 31 & June 5 & 7 (Prandelli).

Norma: (Norma)
Del Monaco (Pollione), Stignani (Adalgisa), Modesti (Oroveso)
c. Serafin.
RAI, Rome.
June 29†.

Lucia di Lammermoor: (Lucia)
di Stefano/Zampieri (Edgardo), Panerai
(Enrico), Zaccaria (Raimondo)
c. & p. Karajan, d. Ratto.
Stadtische Oper, Berlin (La Scala Company and
production).
September 29†, October 2 (Zampieri in final
scene).

I Puritani: (Elvira)
di Stefano (Arturo), Bastianini (Riccardo),
Rossi-Lemeni (Giorgio)
c. Rescigno.
Lyric Theater, Chicago.
October 31, November 2.

Il trovatore: (Leonora)
Björling (Manrico), Stignani/Turner (Azucena),
Bastianini/Weede (di Luna), Wildermann
(Raimondo)
c. Rescigno.
Lyric Theater, Chicago.
November 5, 8 (Turner, Weede).

* *Madama Butterfly:* (Cio-Cio-San)
di Stefano (Pinkerton), Alberts (Suzuki), Weede
(Sharpless)
c. Rescigno, p. Koyke.
Lyric Theater, Chicago.
November 11, 14, 17.

Norma: (Norma)
Del Monaco (Pollione), Simionato/Nicolai
(Adalgisa), Zaccaria (Oroveso)
c. Votto, p. Wallmann, d. Benois and Fiume.
La Scala, Milan.
December 7†, 11, 14, 17, 21, 29 (Nicolai),
January (1956) 1, 5, 8 (Nicolai).

1956
La traviata: (Violetta)
Raimondi (Alfredo), Bastianini/Protti/Colzani

(Germont)
c. Giulini/Tonini, p. Visconti, d. de Nobili.
La Scala, Milan.
January 19†, 23 (Protti), 26, 29, February 2, 5,
18, 26, March 9, April 5, 14, 18 (Colzani), 21,
25, 27, 29 & May 6 (Tonini).

* *Il barbiere di Siviglia:* (Rosina)
Alva/Monti (Almaviva), Gobbi (Figaro), Rossi-
Lemeni (Basilio), Luise/Badioli (Bartolo)
c. Giulini, p. Piccinato, d. Benois, di. Vellani
Marchi.
La Scala, Milan.
February 16†, 21, March 3, 6 & 15 (Monti,
Badioli).

Lucia di Lammermoor: (Lucia)
Raimondi (Edgardo), Panerai (Enrico), Zerbini
(Raimondo)
c. Molinari-Pradelli, p. Brissoni, d. Cristini.
San Carlo, Naples.
March 22†, 24, 27.

* *Fedora:* (Fedora)
Corelli (Loris), Colzani (De Siriex), Zanolli
(Olga)
c. Gavazzeni, p. Pavlova, d. Benois.
La Scala, Milan.
May 21†∆, 23, 27, 30, June 1, 3.

Lucia di Lammermoor: (Lucia)
di Stefano (Edgardo), Panerai (Enrico), Zaccaria
(Raimondo)
c. & p. Karajan, d. Ratto.
Staatsoper, Vienna (La Scala Company and production).
June 12, 14, 16.

Concert
'Tu che invoco' (*Vestale*)
'Bel raggio' (*Semiramide*)
'A vos jeux, mes amis' (*Hamlet*)

'Vieni al tempio' (*Puritani*)
c. Simonetto.
RAI, Milan.
September 27†, broadcast first on December 8.

Norma: (Norma)
Del Monaco/Baum (Pollione), Barbieri
(Adalgisa), Siepi/Moscona (Oroveso)
c. Cleva, p. Yannopoulos, reset by Elson.
Metropolitan, New York.
October 29, November 3, 7, 10, 22 (Baum,
Moscona).

Tosca: (Tosca)
Campora (Cavaradossi), London (Scarpia)
c. Mitropoulos.
Metropolitan, New York.
November 15, 19.

Television
Tosca (excerpts from Act 2)
London (Scarpia)
c. Mitropoulos.
CBS, New York.
November 25†.

Norma: (Norma)
Baum (Pollione), Barbieri (Adalgisa), Moscona
(Oroveso)
c. Cleva.
Academy of Music, Philadelphia (Metropolitan
Company).
November 27.

Lucia di Lammermoor: (Lucia)
Campora/Tucker (Edgardo),
Sordello/Valentino (Enrico), Moscona
(Raimondo)
c. Cleva.
Metropolitan, New York.
December 3, 8†, 14 (Valentino), 19 (Tucker,
Valentino).

Concert
'Casta Diva' (*Norma*)
'D'amor sull'ali rosee' (*Trovatore*)
'Ah, fors'è lui' and 'Sempre libera' (*Traviata*).
'Regnava nel silenzio' (*Lucia*)
'Vissi d'arte' (*Tosca*)
Piano: Schaefer.
Italian Embassy, Washington, DC.
December 17.

1957
Concert
'Ah! non credea' (*Sonnambula*)
'Ombra leggera' (*Dinorah*)
'In questa reggia' (*Turandot*)
'Casta Diva' (*Norma*)
'D'amor sull'ali rosee' (*Trovatore*)
'Il dolce suono' Mad Scene (*Lucia*)
c. Cleva.
Civic Opera House, Chicago.
January 15.

Norma: (Norma)
Vertecchi (Pollione), Stignani (Adalgisa),
Zaccaria (Oroveso), Collier (Clotilde)
c. Pritchard, p. Barlowe, d. Enriquez.
Covent Garden, London.
February 2, 6.

La sonnambula: (Amina)
Monti/Spina (Elvino), Zaccaria (Rodolfo),
Ratti (Lisa)
c. Votto, p. Visconti, d. Tosi.
La Scala, Milan.
March 2, 7, 10, 12, 17, 20 (Spina).

* *Anna Bolena*: (Anna)
Rossi-Lemeni (Enrico VIII), Simionato
(Seymour), Raimondi (Percy), Carturan
(Smeton)
c. Gavazzeni, p. Visconti, d. Benois.
La Scala, Milan.
April 14†, 17, 20, 24, 27, 30, May 5.

Ifigenia in Tauris: (Ifigenia)
Albanese (Pilade), Colzani (Thoas), Dondi
(Oreste)
c. Sanzogno, p. Visconti, d. Benois.
La Scala, Milan.
June 1†, 3, 5, 10.

Concert
'Ah! fors' è lui' and 'Sempre libera' (*Traviata*)
'Il dolce suono' Mad Scene (*Lucia*)
c. Moralt.
Tonhalle, Zurich.
June 19.

Lucia di Lammermoor: (Lucia)
Fernandi (Edgardo), Panerai (Enrico), Modesti
(Raimondo)
c. Serafin.
RAI, Rome.
June 26†.

La sonnambula: (Amina)
Monti (Elvino), Zaccaria (Rodolfo), Angioletti
(Lisa)
c. Votto, p. Visconti, d. Tosi.
Grosseshaus, Cologne (La Scala Company and
production).
July 4†, 6.

Concert
'Pace, pace mio Dio' (*Forza*)
'D'amor sull'ali rosee' (*Trovatore*)
'Regnava nell silencio' (*Lucia*)
'Liebestod' – in Italian (*Tristan*)
'A vos jeux, mes amis' (*Hamlet*)
c. Votto.
Herodes Atticus Theatre, Athens.
August 5†.

La sonnambula: (Amina)
Monti (Elvino), Zaccaria (Rodolfo), Martelli
(Lisa)

c. Votto, p. Visconti, d. Tosi.
King's Theatre, Edinburgh (La Scala Company
and production).
August 19, 21†, 26†, 29.

Concert
'Tutte le torture' (*Entführung*)
'Qui la voce' (*Puritani*)
'Vieni t'affretta' (*Macbeth*)
'Ah! fors'è lui' and 'Sempre libera' (*Traviata*)
'A dolce guidami' Mad Scene (*Anna Bolena*)
c. Rescigno.
Civic Opera, State Fair Music Hall, Dallas.
November 21.

* *Un ballo in maschera*: (Amelia)
di Stefano (Riccardo), Bastianini/Roma
(Renato), Simionato (Ulrica), Ratti (Oscar)
c. Gavazzeni, p. Wallmann, d. Benois.
La Scala, Milan.
December 7†, 10, 16, 19, 22 (Roma in final
act).

1958
Norma: (Norma)
Act 1: Corelli (Pollione), Pirazzini (Adalgisa),
Neri (Oroveso)
c. Santini
Opera, Rome.
January 2†.

Concert
'Non mi dir' (*Don Giovanni*)
'Vieni! t'affretta!' (*Macbeth*)
'Una voce poco fa' (*Barbiere*)
'L'altra notte' (*Mefistofele*)
'Anch' io dischiuso' (*Nabucco*)
'A vos jeux, mes amis' (*Hamlet*)
c. Rescigno.
Civic Opera House, Chicago.
January 22.

La traviata: (Violetta)
Barioni/Campora (Alfredo), Zanasi (Germont)
c. Cleva.
Metropolitan, New York.
February 6, 10 (Campora).

Lucia di Lammermoor: (Lucia)
Bergonzi/Fernandi (Edgardo), Sereni (Enrico),
Moscona/Scott/Tozzi (Raimondo)
c. Cleva.
Metropolitan, New York.
February 13†, 20 (Scott), 25 (Fernandi, Tozzi).

Tosca: (Tosca)
Tucker (Cavaradossi), Cassel/London (Scarpia)
c. Mitropoulos.
Metropolitan, New York.
February 28, March 5 (London).

Concert
'Casta Diva' (*Norma*)
'D'amor sull'ali rosee' (*Trovatore*)
'L'altra notte' (*Mefistofele*)
'A vos jeux, mes amis' (*Hamlet*)
c. Morelli.
Cinema Monumental, Madrid.
March 24.

La traviata: (Violetta)
Kraus (Alfredo), Sereni (Germont)
c. Ghione.
São Carlos, Lisbon.
March 27†, 30.

Anna Bolena: (Anna)
Siepi (Enrico VIII), Simionato (Seymour),
Raimondi (Percy), Carturan (Smeaton)
c. Gavazzeni, p. Visconti, d. Benois.
La Scala, Milan.
April 9, 13, 16, 19, 23.

* *Il pirata*: (Imogene)
Corelli (Gualtiero), Bastianini (Ernesto)

c. Votto, p. Enriquez, d. Zuffi.
La Scala, Milan.
May 19, 22, 25, 28, 31.

I Puritani: (Elvira)
'Qui la voce' Mad Scene:
Robinson (Giorgio), Shaw (Ricardo)
c. Pritchard.
Centenary Gala, Covent Garden, London.
June 10.

Television
'Vissi d'arte' (*Tosca*)
'Una voce poco fa' (*Barbiere*)
c. Pritchard.
Empire Theatre, Chelsea, London.
June 17†.

La traviata: (Violetta)
Valletti (Alfredo), Zanasi (Germont)
c. Rescigno, p. Guthrie, d. Fedorovitch.
Covent Garden, London.
June 20†, 23, 26, 28, 30.

Television
'Casta Diva' (*Norma*)
'Un bel dì' (*Butterfly*)
c. Pritchard.
Empire Theatre, Chelsea, London.
September 23†.

Concerts
'Tu che invoco' (*Vestale*)
'Vieni! t'affretta! (*Macbeth*)
'Una voce poco fa' (*Barbiere*)
'L'altra notte' (*Mefistofele*)
'Quando me'n vo' (*Bohème*)
'A vos jeux, mes amis' (*Hamlet*)
c. Rescigno.
Municipal Auditorium, Birmingham, October
11
Municipal Auditorium, Atlanta, October 14

Forum, Montreal, October 17
Maple Leaf Gardens, Toronto, October 21
Public Music House, Cleveland, November 15
Masonic Auditorium, Detroit, November 18
Constitution Hall, Washington DC, November 22
War Memorial, San Francisco, November 26
Shrine Auditorium, Los Angeles, November 29
Kiel Auditorium, St Louis, January 11 (1959).

La traviata: (Violetta)
Filacuridi (Alfredo), Taddei (Germont)
c. Rescigno, p. Zeffirelli.
Civic Opera, State Fair Music Hall, Dallas.
October 31, November 2.

Medea: (Medea)
Vickers (Jason), Zaccaria (Creon), Berganza (Neris), Carron (Glauce)
c. Rescigno, p. Minotis, d. Tsarouchis.
Civic Opera State Fair Music Hall, Dallas.
November 6†, 8.

Concert
'Casta Diva' (*Norma*) with Mars (Oroveso)
'D'amor sull'ali rosee' and 'Miserere' (*Trovatore*) with Lance (Manrico)
'Una voce poco fa' (*Barbiere*)
Act 2 (*Tosca*) with Lance (Cavaradossi), Gobbi (Scarpia)
c. Sebastian.
Opèra, Paris. December 19†.

1959
Concert
'L'altra notte' (*Mefistofele*)
'Una voce poco fa' (*Barbiere*)
'A vos jeux, mes amis' (*Hamlet*)
c. Ormandy.
Academy of Music, Philadelphia.
January 24.

Il pirata (Imogene)
Ferraro (Gualtiero), Ego (Ernesto)
c. Rescigno.
Concert performance by the American Opera Society, Carnegie Hall, New York, January 27†;
Constitution Hall, Washington, DC, January 29.

Concert
'Non mi dir' (*Don Giovanni*)
'Vieni! t'affretta!' (*Macbeth*)
'Bel raggio' (*Semiramide*)
'Suicidio' (*Gioconda*)
'Col sorriso' (*Pirata*)
c. Rescigno.
Teatro del Zarzuela, Madrid.
May 2.

Concert
'Tu che le vanità' (*Don Carlos*)
'L'altra notte' (*Mefistofele*)
'Una voce poco fa' (*Barbiere*)
'Vissi d'arte' (*Tosca*)
'Quando me'n vo' (*Bohème*)
'Col sorriso' Final Scene (*Pirata*)
c. Rescigno.
Liceo, Barcelona.
May 5.

Concerts
'Tu che invoco' (*Vestale*)
'Vieni! t'affretta!' (*Macbeth*)
'Una voce poco fa' (*Barbiere*)
'Tu che le vanità' (*Don Carlos*)
'Col sorriso' Final Scene (*Pirata*)
c. Rescigno.
Musikhalle, Hamburg, May 15
Liederhalle, Stuttgart, May 19†
Deutsches Museum, Munich, May 21
Kursaal, Wiesbaden, May 24.

Medea: (Medea)
Vickers (Jason), Zaccaria (Creon), Cossotto

(Neris), Carlyle (Glauce)
c. Rescigno, p. Minotis, d. Tsarouchis.
Covent Garden, London (Dallas Civic Opera production).
June 17, 22, 24, 27, 30†.

Concert
'Tu che invoco' (*Vestale*)
'Ernani, involami' (*Ernani*)
'Tu che le vanità' (*Don Carlos*)
'Col sorriso' Final scene (*Pirata*)
c. Rescigno.
Concertgebouw, Amsterdam, July 11†
Théâtre de la Monnaie, Brussels, July 14.

Concert
'Tu che le vanità' (*Don Carlos*)
'A vos jeux, mes amis' (*Hamlet*)
'Ernani, involami' (*Ernani*)
'Col sorriso' Final scene (*Pirata*)
c. Rescigno.
Coliseo Albia, Bilbao.
September 17.

Concert
'Tu che le vanità' (*Don Carlos*)
'A vox jeux, mes amis' (*Hamlet*)
'Una macchia' Sleep-walking scene (*Macbeth*)
'Col sorriso' Final Scene (*Pirata*)
c. Rescigno.
Royal Festival Hall, London.
September 23‡.

Television
'Sì, mi chiamano Mimì' (*Bohème*)
'L'altra notte (*Mefistofele*)
c. Sargent.
Taped on October 3† at Wood Green Theatre, London.
Televised on October 7.

Concert
'Non mi dir' (*Don Giovanni*)

'Ernani, involami' (*Ernani*)
'Tu che le vanità' (*Don Carlos*)
'A vos jeux, mes amis' (*Hamlet*)
c. Rescigno.
Titania Palast, Berlin.
October 23.

Concert
'Non mi dir' (*Don Giovanni*)
'Regnava nel silenzio' (*Lucia*)
'Ernani, involami' (*Ernani*)
'Col sorriso' Final scene (*Pirata*)
c. Rescigno.
Loew's Midland Theatre, Kansas City.
October 28.

Lucia di Lammermoor: (Lucia)
Raimondi (Edgardo), Bastianini (Enrico), Zaccaria (Raimondo)
c. Rescigno, p. & d. Zeffirelli.
Civic Opera, State Fair Music Hall, Dallas (Covent Garden production).
November 6, 8.

Medea: (Medea)
Vickers (Jason), Zaccaria (Creon), Merriman (Neris), Williams (Glauce)
c. Rescigno, p. Minotis, d. Tsarouchis.
Civic Opera, State Fair Music Hall, Dallas.
November 19, 21.

1960
Norma: (Norma)
Picchi (Pollione), Morfoniou (Adalgisa), Mazzoli (Oroveso)
c. Serafin, p. Minotis, d. Tsarouchis, di. Fokas.
Greek National Opera, Epidaurus, Greece.
August 24, 28.

* *Poliuto*: (Paolina)
Corelli (Poliuto), Bastianini (Severo), Zaccaria (Callistene)

c. Votto/Tonini, p. Graf, d. Benois.
La Scala, Milan.
December 7†, 10, 14, 18, 21 (Tonini).

1961
Concert
'Casta Diva' (*Norma*)
'Pleurez, mes yeux' (*Le Cid*)
'L'altra notte' (*Mefistofele*)
'Tu che le vanità' (*Don Carlos*)
Piano: Sargent.
St James's Palace, London.
May 30†.

Medea: (Medea)
Vickers (Jason), Modesti (Creon), Morfoniou
(Neris), Glantzi (Glauce)
c. Rescigno, p. Minotis, d. Tsarouchis.
Greek National Opera, Epidaurus, Greece.
August 6, 13.

Medea: (Medea)
Vickers (Jason), Ghiaurov (Creon), Simionato
(Neris), Tosini/Rizzoli (Glauce)
c. Schippers, p. Minotis, d. Tsarouchis.
La Scala, Milan.
December 11†, 14, 20 (Rizzoli).

1962
Concert
'O don fatale' (*Don Carlos*)
'Pleurez, mes yeux' (*Le Cid*)
'Nacqui all'affanno' (*Cenerentola*)
'Al dolce guidami' Final scene (*Anna Bolena*)
'La luce langue' (*Macbeth*)
'Ocean! Thou mighty monster' (*Oberon*)
c. Prêtre.
Royal Festival Hall, London.
February 27‡Δ.

Concert
'O don fatale' (*Don Carlos*)

'Pleurez, mes yeux' (*Le Cid*)
'Nacqui all'affanno' (*Cenerentola*)
'Habanera' and 'Seguidilla' (*Carmen*)
'Ernani, involami' (*Ernani*)
c. Prêtre.
Deutsches Museum, Munich, March 12
Musikhalle, Hamburg, March 16†
Städtischer Saalbau, Essen, March 19
Beethovenhalle, Bonn, March 23.

Concert
'Habanera' and 'Seguidilla' (*Carmen*)
Piano: Wilson.
    President Kennedy's forty-fourth birthday
celebration.
Madison Square Garden, New York.
May 19.

Medea: (Medea)
Vickers (Jason), Ghiaurov (Creon), Simionato
(Neris), Rizzoli (Glauce)
c. Schippers, p. Minotis, d. Tsarouchis.
La Scala, Milan.
May 29, June 3.

Television
'Tu che le vanità' (*Don Carlos*)
'Habanera' and 'Seguidilla' (*Carmen*)
c. Prêtre.
Covent Garden, London ('Golden Hour' concert).
November 4†.

1963
Concert
'Casta Diva' (*Norma*)
'Anch'io dischiuso' (*Nabucco*)
'Quando me'n vo' (*Bohème*)
'Tu! tu! piccolo iddio' (*Butterfly*)
'O mio babbino caro' (*Gianni Schicchi*)
c. Prêtre.
Deutsche Oper, Berlin, May 17†

Rheinhalle, Düsseldorf, May 20
Liederhalle, Stuttgart, May 23†
Royal Festival Hall, London, May 31
Falkoner Centret, Copenhagen, July 9.

Concert
'Bel raggio' (*Semiramide*)
'Nacqui all'affanno' (*Cenerentola*)
'Air des lettres' (*Werther*)
'Adieu, notre petite table' (*Manon*)
'Anch'io dischiuso' (*Nabucco*)
'Quando me'n vo' (*Bohème*)
'Tu! tu! piccolo iddio' (*Butterfly*)
'O mio babbino caro' (*Gianni Schicchi*)
c. Prêtre.
Théâtre des Champs-Elysées, Paris.
June 5†.

1964
Tosca: (Tosca)
Cioni (Cavaradossi), Gobbi (Scarpia)
c. Cillario, p. Zeffirelli, d. Mongiardino, di.
Escoffier.
Covent Garden, London.
January 21†, 24†, 27, 30, February 1, 5.

Television
Act 2 (*Tosca*)
Cioni (Cavaradossi), Gobbi (Scarpia)
c. Cillario.
Covent Garden, London ('Golden Hour' concert).
February 9†.

Norma: (Norma)
Craig/Corelli (Pollione), Cossotto (Adalgisa),
Vinco (Oroveso)
c. Prêtre, p. & d. Zeffirelli, di. Escoffier.
Opéra, Paris.
May 22, 25†, 31, June 6, 10 (Corelli), 14, 19,
24.

1965
Tosca: (Tosca)
Cioni/Corelli (Cavaradossi), Gobbi (Scarpia)
c. Prêtre/Rescigno, p. Zeffirelli, d. Mongiardino,
di. Escoffier.
Opéra, Paris (Covent Garden production).
February 19, 22, 26 (Corelli), March 1† & 3† &
5 & 8 & 10 & 13 (Rescigno).

Tosca: (Tosca)
Corelli/Tucker (Cavaradossi), Gobbi (Scarpia)
c. Cleva.
Metropolitan Opera, New York.
March 19†, 25† (Tucker).

Norma: (Norma)
Cecchele (Pollione), Simionato/Cossotto
(Adalgisa), Vinco (Oroveso)
c. Prêtre, p. & d. Zeffirelli, di. Escoffier.
Opéra, Paris.
May 14†, 17†, 21† & 24 & 29† (Cossotto). Last
scene cancelled on May 29 because of Callas's
indisposition.

Television
'Adieu, notre petite table' (*Manon*)
'Ah! non credea' (*Sonnambula*)
'O mio babbino caro' (*Gianni Schicchi*)
c. Prêtre.
Recorded on May 2† at RTF, Paris.
Televised on May 18.

Tosca: (Tosca)
Cioni (Cavaradossi), Gobbi (Scarpia)
c. Prêtre, p. Zeffirelli, d. Mongiardino, di.
Escoffier.
Covent Garden, London.
July 5†.

1969
Medea film: (Medea)
Gentile (Jason), Girotti (Creon), Clementi
(Glauce), Terzieff (The Centaur).

A non-singing version filmed at Goremme (Turkey), Aleppo (Syria) and Italy, June–July. Director: Pasolini, p. Rossellini, d. Tosi. World première in Rome, June 9 (1970)†.

1971
Master Classes
Philadelphia Curtis Institute of Music.
January, two classes.
Juilliard School of Music, New York.
October 11, 15, 18, 21, 25, 28, November 1, 4, 8, 11, 15, 19, February (1972) 7, 10, 13, 17, 21, 24, 28, March 2, 9, 14, 16.

1973
I vespri Siciliani
Callas acted as producer in collaboration with di Stefano. Kabaivanska (Elena), Raimondi (Arrigo), Montefusco (Monforte), Giaiotti (Procida)
c. Vernizzi, d. Sassu.
Reopening of Teatro Regio, Turin.
April 10.

Master Class
With the participation of di Stefano.
Festival Hall, Osaka, Japan.
May 20.

Concerts: (Callas and di Stefano)
Callas selected numbers from the arias and duets (with di Stefano) listed; the selection varied from concert to concert.
Piano: Newton/Sutherland.
Arias:
'Pleurez, mes yeux' (*Le Cid*)
'Habanera' (*Carmen*)
'Suicidio' (*Gioconda*)
'L'altra notte' (*Mefistofele*)
'Non pianger, mia compagna' (*Don Carlos*)
'Tu che le vanità' (*Don Carlos*)
'O mio babbino caro' (*Gianni Schicchi*)

'Quando me'n vo' (*Bohème*)
Duets:
'Laisse-moi' (*Faust*)
'C'est toi, c'est moi' (*Carmen*)
'Una parola, o Adina' (*Elisir*)
'Ah! per sempre' (*Forza*)
'Io vengo a domandar' (*Don Carlos*)
'Tu qui Santuzza?' (*Cavalleria*)
'Quale, o prode' (*Vespri*).
Congress Centrum, Hamburg, October 25
Philharmonie, Berlin, October 29
Rheinhalle, Düsseldorf, November 2
Deutsches Museum, Munich, November 6
Jahrhundert Halle Höchst, Frankfurt, November 9
Nationaltheater, Mannheim, November 12
Palacio Nacional de Congresos y Exposiciones, Madrid, November 20 (Sutherland)
Royal Festival Hall, London, November 26†, December 2
Théâtre des Champs-Elysées, Paris, December 7 (Sutherland)
Concertgebouw, Amsterdam, December 11 (Sutherland)

1974
Concerts: (Callas and di Stefano)
The following were added to the 1973 concert programme:
'Voi lo sapete' (*Cavalleria*)
'Sola perduta abbandonata' (*Manon Lescaut*)
'Air des lettres' (*Werther*)
'Vissi d'arte' (*Tosca*)
'Adieu, notre petite table' (*Manon*)
'Mì chiamano Mimi' (*Bohème*)
Piano: Sutherland.
Istituto Nazionale per lo Studie alla Cura dei Tumeri (Institute of Tumour Research), Milan (given privately for the patients), January 20
Liederhalle, Stuttgart, January 23 (cancelled because of di Stefano's sudden indisposition, but Callas sang 'O mio babbino caro').

Academy of Music, Philadelphia, February 11
Massey Hall, Toronto, February 21
Constitution Hall, Washington DC, February 24
Symphony Hall, Boston (Callas sang alone
because of di Stefano's indisposition. Pianist
Vasso Devetzi filled in the programme),
February 27
Civic Opera House, Chicago, March 2
Carnegie Hall, New York, March 5
Masonic Auditorium, Detroit (Callas sang alone
because of di Stefano's indisposition. Pianist
Ralph Votapek filled in the programme), March
9
State Fair Music Hall, Dallas (Callas sang alone
because of di Stefano's indisposition. Pianist
Earl Wild filled in the programme), March 12
Miami Beach Auditorium, March 21
Ohio Theatre, Columbus, April 4
C.W. Post Center Auditorium, Brookville, L.I.,
New York, April 9
Carnegie Hall, New York, April 15
Music Hall, Cincinnati, April 18
Opera House, Seattle, April 24
Civic Auditorium, Portland, April 27
Queen Elizabeth Theatre, Vancouver, May 1
Shrine Auditorium, Los Angeles, May 5
War Memorial Opera House, San Francisco,
May 9
Place des Arts, Montreal, May 13
Women's University, Seoul, Korea, October 5, 6
NHK, Tokyo, October 12†, 19
Fukuoka, Japan, October 24†
Bunke Kaikan, Tokyo, October 27
Osaka, Japan, November 2
Hiroshima, Japan, November 7
Sapporo, Japan, November 11†

SELECT BIBLIOGRAPHY

Ardoin, John: *Callas at Juilliard – Masterclasses* (Robson, London, 1988)

Ardoin, John: *The Callas Legacy* (Duckworth, London, 1977)

Ardoin, John and Fitzgerald, Gerald: *Callas* (Holt, Rinehart and Winston, New York, 1974)

Bing, Sir Rudolf: *5000 Nights at the Opera* (Doubleday, New York, 1972)

Bragaglia, Leonardo: *L'arte dello stupore* (Bulzoni Editore, Rome, 1977)

Callas, Evangelia: *My Daughter Maria Callas* (Fleet, New York, 1960 and Frewin, London, 1967)

Callas, Jackie: *Sisters* (Macmillan, London, 1989)

Cederna, Camilla: *Chi è Maria Callas?* (Longanesi, Milan, 1968)

Frischauer, Willi: *Onassis* (Bodley Head, London, 1968)

Galatopoulos, Stelios: *Callas La Divina* (Dent, London, 1966)

Galatopoulos, Stelios: *Callas, Prima Donna Assoluta* (W. H. Allen, London, 1976)

Gambetti, Giacomo (ed.): *Medea, un film di Pier Paolo Pasolini* (Garzanti, Milan, 1970)

Gara, Eugenio: *I grandi interpreti: Maria Callas* (Kister, Geneva, 1957)

Gavoty, Bernard: *Vingt grands interprètes* (Editions Rencontre, Lausanne, 1960)

Gobbi, Tito: *My Life* (Macdonald and Jane's, London, 1979)

Gobbi, Tito: *On his world of Italian Opera* (Hamish Hamilton, London, 1984)

Herzfeld, Friedrich: *La Callas* (Rembrandt Verlag, Berlin, 1959)

Jellinek, George: *Callas, Portrait of a Prima Donna* (Ziff-Davis, New York, 1960)

Lorcey, Jacques: *Maria Callas* (PAC Editions, Paris, 1977)

Marsan, Polyvios: *Maria Callas: Her Greek Career* (a chronology) (Gnosis, Athens, 1983)

Meneghini, Gian Battista: *Maria Callas mia moglie* (Rusconi, Milan, 1981)

Merlin, Olivier: *Le Bel Canto* (René Julliard, Paris, 1961)

Rémy, Pierre-Jean: *Callas: une vie* (Editions Ramsay, Paris, 1978)

Riemens, Leo: *Maria Callas* (Brunn & Zoon, Utrecht, 1960)

Scifano, Laurence: *Luchino Visconti: The Flames of Passion* (Collins, London, 1990)

Segalini, Sergio: *Callas: Les images d'une voix* (Editions Francis van de Velde, Paris, 1979)

Stassinopoulos, Arianna: *Maria: Beyond the Callas Legend* (Weidenfeld & Nicolson, London, 1980)

Wisneski, Henry: *Maria Callas: The Art Behind the Legend* (Doubleday, New York, 1975)

Zeffirelli, Franco: *Autobiography* (Weidenfeld & Nicolson, London, 1986)

Articles

Buckley, Jack: 'An Ancient Woman' (film *Medea*) (*Opera News*, New York, 13 December 1969)

Celli, Teodoro: 'A Song from Another Century' (*Saturday Review*, 31 January 1959)

Du-Pond, Carlos Diaz: 'Callas in Mexico' (*Opera*, April 1973)

Galatopoulos, Stelios: 'The Divine Callas' (*Records & Recordings*, March 1972)

Kelly, Lawrence V: 'Callas' (*Gentry*, Spring 1957)

Kolodin, Irving: 'What Makes Maria Sing' (*Saturday Review*, 2 February 1974)

Leibowitz, Rene: 'Le secret de la Callas' (*Les Temps modernes*, July 1959)

Radiocorriere TV: 'Processo alla Callas' (November 1969)

Soria, Dorle: 'Artist Life' (Callas as stage director) (*Musical America*, August 1973)

PICTURE ACKNOWLEDGEMENTS

All photographs are from the author's collection. The author thanks the following original sources for their assistance:

Associated Press: 328, 329
courtesy of Bellas Artes, Mexico: 169, 170
Biffi, Milan: 244
Callas archives: 15, 18, 20, 25, 27, 33, 38, 57, 77, 322 (photographer: Megalokonomou), 323; *Medea* (film) between pages 432 and 433
courtesy of Colón, Buenos Aires: 154 (top)
courtesy of Comunale, Florence/Locchi: 121, 160 (bottom), 166
courtesy of Decca: 336
Dhellentas archives: 42, 43, 59, 62, 63
courtesy of EMI, Angel/Pattelani: 223, 224
courtesy of EMI, Angel/Christian Steiner: 449
courtesy of EMI, London/Clark: 352, 355
courtesy of EMI, London/Christian Steiner: concert and portraits betwen pages 432 and 433
courtesy of EMI, Pathé Marconi/Claude Poirler: 275
Giacomelli, Venice: 66–9, 154 (bottom)
Hidalgo archives: 29, 30, 258 (photographer: Megalokonomou)
Locchi, Florence: 71, 72, 164, 165, 167, 168
Mangliveras archives: 61 (bottom)
Meneghini archives: 188, 192
courtesy of Metropolitan Opera archives: 276
Pic, Paris: 218 (bottom)
Houston Rogers: 391 (bottom left & centre), 478 (top), 479 (top), 480
Rome Opera/Savio: 70
courtesy of San Carlo, Naples/Enzo Aita: 151, 153
courtesy of São Carlos, Lisbon: 391 (bottom right)
Sim, London: 220, 308, 310
Donald Southern: 477, 478 (bottom), 479 (bottom), 481
Spettacoli Lirici, Arena di Verona: 64 (left), 91, 95, 136, 190, 285
Theatrical Museum, Athens: 58
Troncone, Naples: 73, 74, 152, 156 (left), 157 (bottom), 381, 382 (bottom)
Wiener Illustrierte: 40, 61 (top)
Zaccaria archives: 60
original sources unknown: 39, 51, 54, 55, 78, 222, 330

All other photographs by Erio Piccagliani

INDEX

Arena di Verona

La Scala, Milan

Covent Garden, London

Herodes Atticus, Athens

Metropolitan, New York